Aggregates

Sand, gravel and crushed rock aggregates
for construction purposes

Geological Society Engineering Geology Special Publications
Series Editor J. C. CRIPPS

GEOLOGICAL SOCIETY ENGINEERING GEOLOGY SPECIAL PUBLICATION NO 9

Aggregates

Sand, gravel and crushed rock aggregates for construction purposes

(second edition)

EDITED BY

M. R. SMITH

Imperial College of Science, Technology & Medicine, London

L. COLLIS

Sandberg, London

1993
Published by
The Geological Society
London

THE GEOLOGICAL SOCIETY

The Society was founded in 1807 as The Geological Society of London and is the oldest geological society in the world. It received its Royal Charter in 1825 for the purpose of 'investigating the mineral structure of the Earth'. The Society is Britain's national learned society for geology with a membership of 7374 (1992). It has countrywide coverage and approximately 1000 members reside overseas. The Society is responsible for all aspects of the geological sciences including professional matters. The Society has its own publishing house which produces the Society's international journals, books and maps, and which acts as the European distributor for publications of the American Association of Petroleum Geologists and the Geological Society of America.

Fellowship is open to those holding a recognized honours degree in geology or a cognate subject and who have at least two years relevant postgraduate experience, or have not less than six years relevant experience in geology or a cognate subject. A Fellow who has not less than five years relevant postgraduate experience in the practice of geology may apply for validation and, subject to approval, will be able to use the designatory letters C. Geol (Chartered Geologist).

Further information about the Society is available from the Membership Manager, The Geological Society, Burlington House, Piccadilly, London W1V 0JU, UK.

Published by The Geological Society from:
The Geological Society Publishing House
Unit 7
Brassmill Enterprise Centre
Brassmill Lane
Bath
Avon BA1 3JN
UK

(*Orders:* Tel. 0225 445046
  Fax 0225 442836)

First edition published 1985
Second edition published 1993

British Library Cataloguing in Publication Data
A catalogue record for this book is available from the British
Library

ISBN 0-903317-89-3

Cover photo: courtesy of Redland Aggregates Ltd

Filmset by Bath Typesetting Limited
Printed in Great Britain at the Alden Press, Oxford

Distributors
USA
  AAPG Bookstore
  PO Box 979
  Tulsa
  Oklahoma 74101-0979
  USA
  (*Orders*: Tel. (918) 584-2555
    Fax (918) 584-0469)

Australia
  Australian Mineral Foundation
  63 Conyngham St
  Glenside
  South Australia 5065
  Australia
  (*Orders*: Tel. (08) 379-0444
    Fax (08) 379-4634)

India
  Affiliated East–West Press PVT Ltd
  G-1/16 Ansari Road
  New Delhi 110 002
  India
  (*Orders*: Tel. (11) 327-9113
    Fax (11) 331-2830)

Japan
  Kanda Book Trading Co.
  Tanikawa Building
  3-2 Kand Surugadai
  Chiyoda-Ku
  Tokyo 101
  Japan
  (*Orders*: Tel. (03) 3255-3497
    Fax (03) 3255-3495)

Contents

Foreword xv
Preface xvii
Working Party Members xix
Acknowledgements xx

1. **Introduction** 1
   1.1. Background 1
   1.2. Objectives 2
       1.2.1. First edition 1985 2
       1.2.2. Second edition 1993 3
   1.3. Geographical factors 4
Reference 4

2. **Occurrences and associations of sources** 5
   2.1. Introduction 5
       2.1.1. Rock and rock categories 5
       2.1.2. Geological time scale and the rock sequence 5
   2.2. Aggregates from the igneous and metamorphic rocks 7
       2.2.1. Igneous rock 7
       2.2.2. Metamorphic rock 10
   2.3. Aggregates from the sedimentary rocks 11
       2.3.1. Limestone 12
       2.3.2. Sandstone 13
       2.3.3. Other sedimentary rocks and natural waste materials 14
   2.4. Occurrence of sand and gravel, and of conglomerates 14
       2.4.1. Factors influencing the distribution of sand and gravel in Britain 15
       2.4.2. Fluvial deposits 16
           2.4.2.1. River channel or alluvial deposits 16
           2.4.2.2. River terrace deposits 17
           2.4.2.3. Alluvial fans 19
       2.4.3. Glacial deposits 19
           2.4.3.1. Moundy glaciofluvial deposits: eskers, kames and kame-terraces . . . 20
           2.4.3.2. Terraced glaciofluvial deposits: outwash (sandar) and fans 21
           2.4.3.3. Periglacial phenomena and deposits 24
           2.4.3.4. Screes, block-fields and head deposits 24
       2.4.4. Coastal deposits 24
       2.4.5. Marine deposits 26
       2.4.6. Gravels in the solid formations 27
   2.5. Aggregate materials in desert regions 28
   2.6. Aggregate materials in tropical regions 30
   2.7. The effects of alteration and weathering 31
       2.7.1. Alteration 32
       2.7.2. Weathering 32
   2.8. The influence of geological structure 33
       2.8.1. Rock structures and geological structures (primary and secondary structures) . . . 34
           2.8.1.1. Depositional structures and rock textures (primary structures) in
                    sedimentary rocks 34

2.8.1.2. Primary structures in igneous rocks 34
2.8.2. Secondary geological structures 36
2.8.2.1. Dip and strike 36
2.8.2.2. Folds 36
2.8.2.3. Faults and joints 36
References 38

3. Field investigation of deposits **41**
3.1. Introduction 41
3.2. Desk study 41
3.2.1. Topographic maps 41
3.2.2. Geological maps 41
3.2.3. Aggregate resource maps 42
3.2.4. Derivative resource maps 44
3.2.5. Reports and small-scale maps 46
3.2.6. Geological, geophysical and aggregates maps covering UK offshore areas . . . 46
3.2.6.1. Sand and gravel resource appraisals 47
3.2.7. Geoscience libraries in Britain 47
3.3. Field investigation 47
3.3.1. Satellite imagery 47
3.3.2. Aircraft remote sensing 49
3.3.3. Geophysics: airborne and ground geophysics 49
3.3.3.1. Airborne methods 49
3.3.3.2. Ground methods 49
3.3.3.3. Marine geophysical methods 53
3.4. Geological appraisal for aggregate assessment 53
3.4.1. Geological classification and stratigraphical position 53
3.4.2. Field relations 54
3.4.3. Thickness of the deposit 54
3.4.4. Structure of the deposit 54
3.4.5. Bulk composition 55
3.4.6. State of weathering and alteration of the rock mass 55
3.5. Sample collection 55
3.5.1. Drilling for sampling, hard rock 55
3.5.2. Shallow pits and trenches 56
3.5.3. Drilling for sampling, sand and gravel 56
3.5.3.1. Hand auger boring 56
3.5.3.2. Power auger machines 56
3.5.3.3. Hollow-stem augers 56
3.5.3.4. Light cable-percussion boring 58
3.5.3.5. Reversed circulation drills 58
3.6. Marine exploration 58
3.6.1. Echo sounder 60
3.6.2. Side-scan sonar 60
3.6.3. Sampling 60
3.6.4. Seismic and acoustic prospecting techniques 60
3.7. Presentation of field and test results 61
3.7.1. Cross sections and maps 61
3.7.2. Estimation of aggregate reserves and resources; definitions of terms 61
3.7.3. Basic resource categories 61

3.7.4. Methods for estimating amounts   62
3.7.5. Reliability of the estimates   62
3.7.6. Some factors affecting the yield of a prospect   64
3.8. Exploration and development of aggregate prospects   64
References   64

4. **Extraction** **73**
4.1. Introduction   73
4.2. Hard rock quarries   74
    4.2.1. Introduction   74
    4.2.2. Overburden removal and disposal   74
    4.2.3. Primary fragmentation   79
        4.2.3.1. Introduction   79
        4.2.3.2. Drilling   79
        4.2.3.3. Blasting   81
        4.2.3.4. Explosives   82
        4.2.3.5. Detonators   82
        4.2.3.6. Regulations   82
        4.2.3.7. Blast specification   83
        4.2.3.8. Ripping   84
    4.2.4. Secondary breaking   85
    4.2.5. Loading   85
        4.2.5.1. Rope operated face shovels   85
        4.2.5.2. Hydraulic excavators   86
        4.2.5.3. Hydraulic backhoes   86
        4.2.5.4. Wheeled loaders   86
    4.2.6. Hauling   88
4.3. Sand and gravel operations   89
    4.3.1. Introduction   89
    4.3.2. Overburden removal   89
    4.3.3. Excavating techniques and equipment   89
        4.3.3.1. Wet working   90
        4.3.3.2. Dry pit working   91
    4.3.4. Loading and conveying   91
4.4. Marine aggregates   91
    4.4.1. Introduction   91
    4.4.2. Recovery of marine aggregates   91
4.5. Extraction, planning and scheduling   92
    4.5.1. Introduction   92
    4.5.2. Quarry plans   93
    4.5.3. Overburden payrock ratios   93
    4.5.4. Overburden removal   93
    4.5.5. Haul roads and conveyor routes   93
    4.5.6. Equipment selection   94
        4.5.6.1. Introduction   94
        4.5.6.2. Drilling equipment   94
        4.5.6.3. Loading equipment   94
        4.5.6.4. Hauling equipment   94
4.6. Environmental issues   95
    4.6.1. Introduction   95

		4.6.2.	Noise	95
		4.6.3.	Dust	95
		4.6.4.	Blasting	96
			4.6.4.1. Ground vibration	96
			4.6.4.2. Air blast	96
		4.6.5.	Nuisance	96
			4.6.5.1. Noise nuisance	96
			4.6.5.2. Dust nuisance	97
		4.6.6.	Visual impact	97
		4.6.7.	Restoration	97
	4.7.	Future trends	98
		4.7.1.	Super quarries	98
		4.7.2.	In-pit crushers	98
		4.7.3.	Underground quarrying	99
References			100
Appendix A4.1.		Diagrams of extraction equipment in use in 1992	101

5. Processing **107**
	5.1.	Introduction	107
	5.2.	Comminution	108
		5.2.1.	Introduction	108
		5.2.2.	Primary crusher selection	109
		5.2.3.	Jaw crushers	110
		5.2.4.	Gyratory crushers	111
		5.2.5.	Impactors	111
		5.2.6.	Vertical shaft impactors	113
		5.2.7.	Cone crushers	113
		5.2.8.	Gyratory disc crushers	114
		5.2.9.	Rolls crushers	115
		5.2.10.	Grinding	115
	5.3.	Sizing	116
		5.3.1.	Introduction	116
		5.3.2.	Objectives of sizing	117
		5.3.3.	Screening	117
			5.3.3.1. Principles	117
			5.3.3.2. Inclined vibrating screens	118
			5.3.3.3. Horizontal vibrating screens	120
			5.3.3.4. Arrangement of vibrating screens	120
			5.3.3.5. Trommel screens	120
			5.3.3.6. Grizzly screens	121
			5.3.3.7. Miscellaneous screening devices	121
		5.3.4.	Classification	122
			5.3.4.1. Principles of classification	122
			5.3.4.2. Gravitational hydraulic classifiers	122
			5.3.4.3. Centrifugal (cyclonic) hydraulic classifiers	123
			5.3.4.4. Air cyclones	124
	5.4.	Beneficiation	124
		5.4.1.	Introduction	124
		5.4.2.	Scalping and sizing	125
		5.4.3.	Washing and scrubbing	125

5.4.3.1.	Marine dredged aggregates	126
5.4.3.2.	Rinsing	127
5.4.4.	Density separation	127
5.4.5.	Shape sorting	127
5.4.6.	Magnetic separation	129
5.4.7.	Sorting	129
5.4.8.	Other separation processes	129
5.5.	Solid–liquid separation: dewatering	130
5.5.1.	Drainage	130
5.5.2.	Use of screens	130
5.5.3.	Use of classifiers	131
5.5.4.	Thickeners	131
5.5.5.	Filtration	133
5.6.	Storage and distribution	133
5.6.1.	Storage	133
5.6.2.	Outloading	134
5.7.	Environmental considerations	136
5.7.1.	Noise	136
5.7.2.	Dust	136
5.7.3.	Nuisance	136
5.8.	Process and quality control	137
5.9.	Plant flowsheets	137
5.9.1.	Sand and gravel processing plant	137
5.9.2.	Hard rock (roadstone) process plant	139
5.10.	Future	141
References		143

6. Description and classification of aggregates — **145**

6.1.	Introduction	145
6.2.	Descriptive and classification schemes in general	145
6.2.1.	Classical geological schemes	145
6.2.2.	Descriptive and classification schemes for engineering purposes	145
6.2.3.	The description and classification of rock weathering	146
6.2.4.	Classification schemes based on specific properties	149
6.2.5.	The use of local and traditional names	149
6.3.	Basic considerations on the description and classification of aggregates	150
6.3.1.	The purpose and requirements of a classification scheme for aggregates	150
6.3.2.	Aggregate type	150
6.3.3.	Description of physical characteristics	150
6.3.4.	Petrological classification	151
6.3.5.	Test data	151
6.4.	Classification schemes for aggregates	151
6.4.1.	Historical development within the United Kingdom	151
6.4.2.	Current British Standards	153
6.4.3.	American Standards	155
6.4.4.	Europe	156
6.4.5.	Southern Africa	156
6.4.6.	Recommended approach	156
6.5.	The petrographic description of aggregates	159
6.5.1.	General	159

6.5.2. ASTM C295 159
6.5.3. Draft BS 812: Part 104 160
6.5.4. Rock samples 160
6.5.5. Precision of quantitative methods 162
6.5.6. Site inspection of aggregates sources 162
References 162
Appendix A6.1. Extract from BS 812: Part 102: 1989. Petrological description of natural
aggregates 164

7. Sampling and testing **167**
7.1. Introduction 167
7.2. Sampling 167
7.2.1. General considerations 167
7.2.2. Sampling procedures 168
7.2.2.1. Quarry face rock 168
7.2.2.2. Sand and gravel deposits 168
7.2.2.3. Aggregate products, sand and gravel 168
7.2.2.4. Aggregate products, crushed-rock quarries 169
7.2.3. Sample size 169
7.3. Statistical considerations 169
7.4. Repeatability and reproducibility 170
7.4.1. Repeatability (r) 170
7.4.2. Reproducibility (R) 171
7.4.3. Sampling considerations 171
7.5. Testing 171
7.5.1. Physical tests 172
7.5.1.1. (a) Aggregate grading 172
(b) Sand equivalent value 173
7.5.1.2. (a) Aggregate shape 173
(b) Flakiness index, I_F (BS 812: 1989) 173
(c) Elongation index I_E (BS 812: 1990) 173
(d) Discussion 173
(e) Angularity 175
(f) Sphericity and roundness 176
(g) Surface texture 176
7.5.1.3. Relative density, bulk density and water absorption 176
7.5.1.4. Bulk density (unit weight) 176
7.5.1.5. Aggregate shrinkage 177
7.5.2. Petrographic examination of aggregates 177
7.5.3. Mechanical tests 177
7.5.3.1. Strength 177
7.5.3.2. Aggregate impact value (AIV) 177
7.5.3.3. Aggregate crushing value (ACV) 178
7.5.3.4. Discussion 178
7.5.3.5. Ten per cent fines value 180
7.5.3.6. Modified aggregate impact test 181
7.5.3.7. Other non-standard values 181
7.5.3.8. Tests on ledge or lump rock 181
7.5.4. Durability and frost susceptibility 183
7.5.4.1. Mechanical tests 183
7.5.4.2. Physico-chemical tests 186

            7.5.5.   Chemical tests   189
                     7.5.5.1.   Organic content   189
                     7.5.5.2.   Chloride content   189
                     7.5.5.3.   Sulphate content   190
                     7.5.5.4.   Potential alkali reactivity   190
                     7.5.5.5.   Draft British Standard procedures   191
            7.5.6.   Adhesion tests   192
                     7.5.6.1.   Static immersion tests   192
                     7.5.6.2.   Chemical immersion tests   192
                     7.5.6.3.   Dynamic immersion tests   193
                     7.5.6.4.   Immersion mechanical tests   193
                     7.5.6.5.   Immersion trafficking test   193
                     7.5.6.6.   Coating tests   193
                     7.5.6.7.   Discussion   193
     7.6.   Quality assurance   193
     7.7.   European Standards   194
References   195

8. Aggregates for concrete **199**
     8.1.   Introduction   199
     8.2.   Specification   200
     8.3.   Classification and composition   200
     8.4.   Aggregate properties: introduction   201
     8.5.   Maximum size and grading   202
     8.6.   Particle shape   204
     8.7.   Particle surface texture   205
     8.8.   Bulk density   205
     8.9.   Particle density   205
     8.10. Water absorption   206
     8.11. Mechanical properties   206
     8.12. Durability   208
            8.12.1.   Soundness   208
            8.12.2.   Alkali reactivity   209
            8.12.3.   Frost susceptibility   211
     8.13. Impurities   212
            8.13.1.   Clay, silt and dust   212
            8.13.2.   Chlorides   213
            8.13.3.   Shell   214
            8.13.4.   Organic matter   215
            8.13.5.   Alkalis   216
            8.13.6.   Sulphates   216
            8.13.7.   Chalk   217
            8.13.8.   Mica   217
            8.13.9.   Pyrites and other metallic impurities   217
     8.14. Aggregate drying shrinkage   218
     8.15. Thermal movement   218
     8.16. Fire resistance   220
References   220

9. Aggregates for mortar **225**

9.1. Introduction 225
9.2. Types of mortars 227
    9.2.1. Masonry (brickwork or general purpose) mortars 227
    9.2.2. Rendering and plastering 227
    9.2.3. Floor screeds 228
9.3. Description, classification and testing of mortar sands and fillers 229
    9.3.1. Description and classification 229
    9.3.2. Sampling and testing of fine aggregates 229
    9.3.3. Grading of sands 229
    9.3.4. Impurities 231
    9.3.5. Testing for fines 233
9.4. Influence of sand and fines characteristics on mortar properties 234
    9.4.1. Workability 234
    9.4.2. Water retentivity 234
    9.4.3. Strength 235
    9.4.4. Durability 235
9.5. UK specifications and practice 235
    9.5.1. Masonry mortars 235
    9.5.2. External renderings 237
    9.5.3. Internal plastering 237
    9.5.4. Floor screeds 238
9.6. Specifications and practice outside the UK 239
9.7. Occurrence of mortar sands in the UK 241
9.8. Engineering performance and problems of mortars with particular reference to UK
    case histories 243
    9.8.1. Effect of grading 243
    9.8.2. Current experience 245
    9.8.3. Future trends in the use of sands 246
    9.8.4. Artificial aggregates used in mortars 246
9.9. Discussion 246
References 247

10. Aggregates in unbound pavement construction 249
    10.1. Introduction 249
    10.2. Primary aggregates 250
        10.2.1. Igneous rocks 250
        10.2.2. Sedimentary and unconsolidated sediments 251
        10.2.3. Metamorphic rocks 251
    10.3. Secondary aggregates 251
        10.3.1. Overview 251
        10.3.2. Colliery spoil 251
        10.3.3. Spent oil shale 251
        10.3.4. Power station ashes 252
        10.3.5. Waste from quarries 252
        10.3.6. Incinerated refuse 252
        10.3.7. Demolition wastes 252
        10.3.8. Metallurgical slags 252
    10.4. Resistance to wear 252
        10.4.1. The degradation process 252
        10.4.2. Types of degradation 252

10.4.3. Influence of particle shape and size 253
10.4.4. Influence of moisture content 253
10.4.5. Influence of grading on aggregate degradation 253
10.4.6. Engineering effects of degradation 254
10.4.7. Correlation between tests and service behaviour 255
10.5. Resistance to decay 255
10.5.1. Mechanisms and assessment 255
10.5.2. Discussion 257
10.6. Effects of water migration 257
10.6.1. Permeability 257
10.6.2. Frost heave and thaw weakening 257
10.6.3. Moisture movements and salt damage in road foundations 257
10.7. Specifications 259
10.7.1. Department of Transport (United Kingdom) 260
10.7.2. Discussion of the DTp specification 260
10.7.3. European specifications 260
10.7.4. Non-European specifications 261
References 261
Appendix A10.1. Horizontal permeability of drainage layers 263
A10.1.1. Direct measurement 263
A10.1.2. Empirical estimates 263

11. Aggregates in bituminous bound construction materials 265
11.1. Introduction 265
11.2. Petrological types of aggregate used in bituminous compositions 265
11.3. Desirable properties of aggregates for bituminous mixes 265
11.4. Influence of aggregate petrography on engineering properties 266
11.4.1. Crushing strength 266
11.4.1.1. Igneous rock 266
11.4.1.2. Sedimentary rocks 266
11.4.1.3. Metamorphic rocks 266
11.4.1.4. Artificial aggregates 266
11.4.2. Resistance to abrasion 267
11.4.2.1. Igneous rock 267
11.4.2.2. Sedimentary rocks 267
11.4.2.3. Metamorphic rocks 267
11.4.2.4. Artificial aggregates 267
11.4.3. Resistance to polishing 267
11.4.3.1. Igneous and metamorphic rocks 267
11.4.3.2. Sedimentary rocks 268
11.4.3.3. Artificial aggregates 269
11.4.4. Resistance to stripping 269
11.4.4.1. Influence of aggregate petrography 270
11.4.4.2. Influence of binder and adhesion agents 272
11.4.5. Resistance to weathering effects in service 273
11.4.6. Ability to contribute to strength and stiffness of total mix 273
11.5. Detailed requirements and conflicting requirements for aggregates for bituminous
pavement materials 273
11.5.1. Detailed requirements: strength 274

11.5.2. Detailed requirements—polishing resistance and abrasion resistance: Department of Transport (UK) 277
11.5.3. General comments 280
11.5.4. Detailed requirements—Property Services Agency UK (Airfields Branch) . 280
11.5.5. Relationship between mix composition and desirable aggregate properties 280
11.6. Conclusions 282
References 282
Appendix A11.1. Adhesion tests 284

12. Railway track ballast 285
12.1. Introduction 285
12.2. Rock types suitable for track ballast in Great Britain 286
12.3. British practice 286
12.4. European practice 287
12.4.1. Germany 287
12.4.2. France 287
12.4.3. Italy 288
12.4.4. Spain 288
12.5. US practice 288
References 289

13. Aggregates for use in filter media 291
13.1. Introduction 291
13.2. Key properties of filter aggregates 292
13.2.1. General 292
13.2.2. Grading 292
13.2.3. Aggregate strength 292
13.2.4. Particle durability 292
13.2.5. Particle shape 292
13.2.6. Particle texture 292
13.2.7. Surface coatings 292
13.2.8. Particle porosity 293
13.2.9. Chemical reactivity 293
13.3. Testing of aggregates 293
13.4. Water treatment; filtration through sand 293
13.4.1. General 293
13.4.2. Filter bed sand 294
13.4.3. Filter gravel 295
13.5. Aggregates for biological percolating filters 295
13.6. Filters for civil engineering structures 295
13.6.1. General 295
13.6.2. Specification of aggregates 297
13.7. Concluding remarks 297
References 298

Appendix: Aggregate properties 299

Glossary 307

Index 331

Foreword

Aggregates are fundamental to our built environment and will be into the foreseeable future. We are fortunate to have an abundance of construction raw materials in Great Britain. However, we must ensure that they are utilized in a sustainable and efficient manner. Knowledge of the sources, methods of working and processing and selection of aggregate materials of adequate quality is essential to ensure the construction of serviceable, safe, durable and cost-effective structures.

The Government is committed to reducing the environmental impact of aggregates extraction and to encouraging more efficient working, processing and prudent use of raw materials such as aggregates. The formulation of relevant specifications and their appropriate implementation by well trained and informed engineers has environmental benefits in reducing waste and maximizing the beneficial use of natural resources. This book brings together information on all aspects of aggregates provision from exploration to end use drawn from a wide variety of expert sources. It builds upon and updates the extensive knowledge base of the first edition.

I am sure that this second edition will be used as widely as the first edition and will be helpful to planners, civil engineers, the aggregates industry and educationalists.

Tony Baldry MP
Parliamentary Under Secretary of State
Department of the Environment

Preface

"The growth in demand for aggregates in Great Britain seems unending". This comment, at the beginning of the report by the Government's far-sighted Verney Advisory Committee on Aggregates in 1976 seems as applicable now as it was then, as were their comments on the growing public consciousness of the adverse environmental impact caused by mineral extraction.

The current demand in Britain per capita is some 5.2 tonnes per year, a level just below Western Europe's average but sufficient to require some 300 million tonnes of extraction per year. For such a major industry, three times as large as coal, Britain now has in place a strong framework of legislation for planning and control of extraction, processing and distribution, as well as health and safety. This has important implications upon the design and practice of extraction and processing operations.

Improved specifications and the understanding of the performance of construction materials continue to evolve by research and, especially at the present time, by harmonization of standards throughout the European Community. The concept of quality assurance, introduced to improve the efficiency and competitiveness of British Industry, also demands that employees are informed of all aspects of the industry of which they form a part.

This Working Party Report, however, is primarily concerned with the technology of aggregates from winning through to their processing, testing and use and is the work of the Geological Society's Engineering Group. It was some four years in the making and is more or less a completely rewritten edition of its widely acclaimed predecessor. Nevertheless, the foreword to the first edition is still, in the main, most appropriate for the second edition.

The Report remains one of several important Working Party Reports and other documents published by the Geological Society in the past two decades, which focus the geological viewpoint and the help that applied geology can provide to related industries. The Membership of the Working Party, like so many of our national committees and other bodies, continues to be drawn from professional representatives of all facets of the industry, including government, who give freely of their or their employers' time.

The work has again been long and for the most part very enjoyable. All the committee and, indeed, everybody who has helped in so many ways, including understanding spouses and neglected families, deserve thanks and praise. The brunt of the early work was borne by the secretary to the committee, Dr I. Sims, and the latter work by two editors, Mick Smith, from a University, and Laurence Collis, from a Materials Consulting Practice, to all of whom special thanks.

I hope you agree again that it has been worthwhile.

P. G. Fookes
Chairman of the Working Party
Winchester, November 1992

Principal corresponding members and members of first working party

Professor A. D. Burnett* (1978–1981) Department of Geology, Florida Atlantic University, Boca Raton, USA

Professor D. M. Ramsay* (1978–1984) Department of Geology, University of Glasgow, Glasgow

Dr A. Hartley† (1978–1983) Director of Civil Engineering Studies, Leeds Polytechnic, Leeds

Mr C. Loveday (1989–1990) Tarmac Quarry Products Ltd, Ettingshall, Wolverhampton

Dr R. H. Jones (1992) Department of Civil Engineering, University of Nottingham, Nottingham

Members of the second working party

L. Collis* (1989–1992) Consultant, Sandberg, Consulting, Inspecting and Testing Engineers, London.

Professor P. G. Fookes* (Chairman) (1989–1992) Consultant Engineering Geologist, Winchester, Hants.

R. A. Fox* (1989–1992) Manager, Land Search and Exploration Department, Ready Mixed Concrete (United Kingdom) Ltd, Feltham, Middx.

G. P. Hammersley (1989–1992) Manager, Technical Services, Laing Technology Group Ltd, Mill Hill, London.

P. M. Harris* (1989–1992) Principal Scientific Officer, British Geological Survey, Keyworth, Notts.

I. E. Higginbottom* (1989–1992) Consultant, Wimpey Environment Ltd, Hayes, Middx.

Dr G. Lees* (1989–1992) Retired; formerly Head of Department, Department of Transportation and Highway Engineering, University of Birmingham, Birmingham.

D. I. Roberts (1989–1992) Partner, Land and Mineral Resource Consultants Ltd, Yate, Avon.

A. R. Roeder (1989–1992) Principal Concrete Technologist, British Cement Association, Wexham Springs, Slough, Bucks.

Dr I. Sims* (Secretary) (1989–1992) Associate, Sandberg, Consulting, Inspecting and Testing Engineers, London.

Dr M. R. Smith (1989–1992) Senior Lecturer in Quarry Engineering, Imperial College, London.

Dr R. G. Thurrell* (1989–1992) Retired; formerly Regional Geologist, Eastern England Land Survey, British Geological Survey, Keyworth, Notts.

Dr G. West (1989–1992) Head of Aggregates Section, Transport Research Laboratory, Crowthorne, Berks.

Dates in parentheses refer to time served on Committee.
* Member of first working party 1978–1984.
† Dr A. Hartley was Secretary to the first Working Party until his untimely death in December 1983 after which time the duty was performed by R. A. Fox.

Acknowledgements

The Working Party has received considerable help from individuals, organizations and companies too numerous to mention who have contributed in some way to this second edition of the report by providing advice, information and illustrations or by acting as reviewers and referees for particular chapters. To all of these the Working Party is most grateful.

Inherent in this edition are the contributions made to the first edition by members of the first working party, separately listed, and by other individuals acknowledged at the time as follows; R.B. Adamson, D.J. Ayres, W.H. Baxter Ltd, N.E. Beningfield, K.M. Brook, W.R. Dearman, M.S. Eglinton, W.J. French, D.J. Harrison, Holmpress Ltd, J.R. Hosking, J.P.R. Jordan, M.F. Maggs, J.M. Morrison, J. Newbery, D.J. Pain, R.D. Pass, K.R. Peattie, D.C. Pike, A.B. Poole, G.F. Salt, A.C.E. Sandberg, J.M.P. Soper, F.S. Strongman and P. Vaughan. To this list must now be added the names of A.M. Aitken, C.A. Auton, W. Barratt, E. Cash, R.E.T. Hall, P. Horswill, J.L. Knill, T. King, J. Laxton, T. Lees, J.W. Merritt, R. Ryle, D.C. Shutes, J.F. Troy and M.J. Walker.

The very significant contribution made by Companies whose staff were afforded the time and permission to accomplish the task of the Working Parties cannot be overstated. Particular mention should be made of:

British Cement Association	Ready Mixed Concrete (UK) Ltd
British Geological Survey	Sandberg
Laing Technology Group	Transport Research Laboratory
Land and Mineral Resource Consultants Ltd	Wimpey Environmental Ltd

Grateful appreciation is also recorded for drawing, clerical and word processing assistance provided to the editors by the Department of Mineral Resources Engineering, Imperial College and especially to Mr T. Allen, Ms S. Curley and Mrs K. Clarke.

Dr M. Smith (editor) also expresses his gratitude for the support of a lectureship at Imperial College by the sponsors of Quarry Engineering namely:

Allis Mineral Systems (UK) Ltd	Pioneer Aggregates (UK) Ltd
ARC Ltd	R. J. B. Mining Ltd
Blue Circle Industries Plc	Redland Aggregates Ltd
Burlington Slate Ltd	RMC Roadstone Ltd
Cleanaway Ltd	Rugby Cement
Evered Bardon Plc	Steetley Quarry Products Ltd
Hepworth Minerals and Chemicals Ltd	Tarmac Quarry Products Ltd
ICI Explosives	Tilcon Ltd
Nordberg (UK) Ltd	Wimpey Asphalt Ltd
Orenstein and Koppel Ltd	

This edition has been produced with support from the Sand and Gravel Association

The Sand and Gravel Association represents the planning, legislative, technical and other interests of 90 of Britain's sand and gravel producers. It is a leader in encouraging ever higher environmental standards and its widely acclaimed Restoration Awards Scheme has recognized exceptional achievement for over 20 years.

Sand and Gravel Association, 1 Bramber Court, Bramber Road, London W14 9PB, UK.

1. Introduction

1.1. Background

Aggregates are defined here as particles of rock which, when brought together in a bound or unbound condition, form part or the whole of an engineering or building structure.

Natural sand, gravel and crushed rock aggregates are fundamental to the man-made environment and represent a large proportion of the materials used in the construction industry. Re-use of aggregates is now becoming a more common practice and the substitution of natural aggregates by artificial aggregates made from waste products of other industries is a small part of the industry.

Production of aggregates for civil engineering and building construction is one of the world's major industries. Quarrying is the largest industry in terms of volume in the United Kingdom with production in 1989 three times greater than that of coal. It has trebled over 30 years from 100 million tonnes in 1959 to 300 million tonnes in 1989 (see Fig. 1.1). Sand and gravel production in 1959 was 67% of the total. Crushed rock provided the balance of 33%. By 1989 this had altered considerably, with rock production 169 million tonnes (58%) and sand and gravel 131 million tonnes (44%). Growth in demand continues strongly and there is good evidence to support a growth rate of 3.0% per year over the next 20 years and a total production of around 400 million tonnes has been forecast for the year 2000.

Approximately comparable figures for aggregate production in 1988 were, for example, USA 1719 million tonnes and France 374. Per capita production for USA was 7.0 tonnes and France 6.8; West Germany 6.7, Italy 5.0, Switzerland 8.2 and Belgium 3.9. The current demand in UK per capita is 5.2 tonnes/year, a level below the western European average. For further production statistics see §4.1.

Despite the importance of geological materials in civil engineering design and construction, the discipline of engineering geology has traditionally been concerned more with interaction between the engineering structure and its geological environment than with the performance of rock aggregates in the structure itself. This imbalance is being recognized and adjusted in the fields of teaching, practice and research, but an inhibiting factor is the profuse but highly dispersed nature of the literature on aggregate materials. There is a lack of reference manuals and textbooks, or even broadly based review publications, giving a comprehensive coverage of the subject, though this is beginning to change. The available information is scattered through innumerable Standards, specifications, research reports, professional papers and articles in the commercial press. Consequently, those who are concerned with construction, but are not materials specialists, often find difficulty in identifying the literature to guide them in defining and implementing specification requirements.

Therefore in 1978, the Engineering Group of the Geological Society established a Working Party whose aim was to create a reasonably comprehensive document to overcome this difficulty. The members of that Working Party were drawn from persons known by the Engineering Group to have been particularly concerned with construction materials, as producers, specifiers, users or researchers, in order to provide a broad range of expertise. Besides a wide general experience, each member had special knowledge reflected in the subject matter of the sections to which he contributed and, in most cases, in his previous publications.

The first Working Party convened in 1978 and its Report was published in 1985. It proved to be very popular, as indicated by sales and press comments. In 1986 it won for its editors the SAGA Brewis Trophy for the best publication of that year for the aggregates industry.

By 1989 only a few copies of the Report were still available for sale. Numerous developments in the industry had taken place and considerable changes had been made in national and international specifications. With the coming of the European Single Market in 1992, the Engineering Group, therefore, decided to reconvene the Working Party with a brief to prepare an updated second edition for publication at that time.

The second edition Working Party contains many of the original working party, strengthened by additional members drawn mainly from industry. A small number were not available to become working party members again because of changes in their available time but, fortunately, were able to become principal corresponding members. One of the original editors had to relinquish this office, also because of his constrained avail-

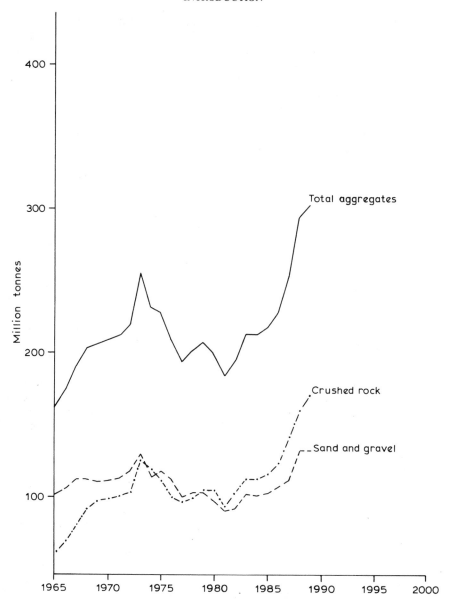

FIG. 1.1 UK production for natural aggregates 1965–1989 (source: BGS).

ability but, fortunately again, could continue to serve as a full member.

This report, comprising a substantially revised and amended second edition, is the result of the reconvened Working Party.

1.2. Objectives

1.2.1. First edition 1985

The following is reproduced from the first edition. Most of it remains true for the second edition and it is also an historical statement for the background of the Report.

At the first meeting of the Working Party in 1978 the objectives were defined. They remained little changed during the course of the work and are outlined below.

'To review the influence of the occurrence, mineral composition and geological history on the engineering properties of aggregate materials. These would include both coarse and fine natural or crushed rock aggregates, whether for use in a bound or unbound condition, the main fields of use being in concrete and mortar, road pavements, railway track ballast and biological or drainage filter media. No account would be taken of artificial aggregate materials, such as slag, expanded clay, calcined bauxite or sintered flyash, or of completely synthetic products, such as expanded polystyrene beads or additives. Aggregates used for protective purposes (e.g. for rockfill breakwaters, rip-rap or gabions), or as general fill materials would also be excluded, except for purposes of comparison or explanation. Soils bound by cement or bitumen would not be considered as aggregates for the purposes of this publication.

To identify the main factors influencing aggregate behaviour in various operational and environmental conditions.

To identify relevant standards and other specifications and codes of practice and, where appropriate, to summarize and discuss some of the currently accepted limits.

To explore some of the problems commonly encountered in applying specifications and codes. For example: limits for different properties might be incompatible with each other; properties might be specified which would tend to be mutually exclusive for geological or other reasons; or particular specifications might not be appropriate to the available materials or to the local environment. It would not be the intention to propose alternative specifications so much as to assist the reader in the interpretation and implementation of selected portions of the existing standards and codes of practice and in the development of specifications where these are not already available.

To identify areas in which present knowledge is deficient.

To concentrate primarily on aggregates produced in the United Kingdom but to refer, whenever possible, to aggregates in some other countries where British specifications, design and construction practices are, or are likely to be, followed.

To consider aggregates essentially in terms of their intrinsic properties as engineering and geological materials. To some extent their engineering performance may be a function of design, but the latter has been seen as a mainly extrinsic factor to which only limited consideration has been given.

To review the different geological situations in which sources of aggregate materials can occur. However, no attempt would be made to quantify UK national resources, or to forecast trends in supply and demand, already considered at length elsewhere (Verney 1976). It was decided that it would be beyond the scope of this publication to deal in any detail with the many commercial and environmental factors which influence the practical usefulness of a source and contribute to a proper evaluation of its reserves.

To achieve the maximum possible breadth and balance by inviting advice and criticism from a range of individual specialists, professional institutions, learned societies, industrial associations and research bodies.'

Although the objectives focus on specific areas within a wide and ill-defined field, it is recognized that difficulties remain. For example, Standards and Codes of Practice are under more-or-less continuous revision throughout the world, with the rapid progress of experience and research in this subject making it virtually impossible for a review such as this to be up-to-date and wholly comprehensive in all aspects. An example is the Trade Group Classification in BS 812: 1975 which was under active revision during the period in which this report was being prepared. This classification has for decades been a source of much academic discussion and practical difficulty, which has led to a view that it is unsatisfactory in various respects. Chapter 6 reviews various classification schemes, including the current British Standard scheme, together, with the Working Party's proposals for an alternative system, designed to overcome some of the more misleading features of the current methods.

Moreover, it should be clear that the concepts and investigative techniques involved are drawn from a wide scientific spectrum, in which geologists, chemists, materials scientists and engineers, physicists and statisticians, to name the more obvious disciplines, all collaborate with professional construction engineers and production staff. Any document which links such diverse fields to a common theme will inevitably be considered by persons of widely differing vocational backgrounds. Consequently, basic material is included which an expert in a particular field might consider over-simplified. However, it was believed that this approach was justified in order to serve a wide readership and, moreover, the Working Party hoped that many elementary facts might assume a new significance when presented in relation to the central theme.

The first complete draft of the Report was submitted for open discussion in September 1981 during the 17th Annual Regional Meeting of the Engineering Group, held at the University College of North Wales, Bangor. The suggestions and criticisms made then and subsequently received from delegates have been considered in the preparation of this publication, together with those invited from particular individuals and organizations. However, the views expressed in the Report are those of the Working Party members.

1.2.2. Second edition 1993

In the early meetings of the reconvened Working Party during 1989, the objectives were again defined. These remained similar in principle to those of the first edition reported in §1.2.1 but with changes made in emphasis or to take into account developments and trends, as follows.

'To update the Report to be compatible with current working practices and principles.

To update relevant Standards and other specifications and Codes of Practice, with increased emphasis on the harmonization of European Standards.

To take into account the increasing emphasis being placed on planning of mineral extraction, quality assurance and control, and protection for the environment, but recognizing that the Report would not have the intention nor enough space to permit extended treatment of these subjects.'

The Working Party decided specifically that three changes in content would be made in the second edition.

The chapter on aggregate description and classification would be completely revised and the proposed CADAM classification of the first edition would not be pursued.

Some account would be taken of artificial aggregate materials such as slag, expanded clay, calcined bauxite or sintered flyash, where appropriate in the context of individual chapters, although discussion on their production would not be included.

Test result data on the properties of aggregates would be included.

It is most strongly emphasized by the Working Party that the test result data should only be used with considerable caution. Rocks of identical or similar name and petrological descriptions do vary widely in their properties due to fabric and textural differences, state of weathering and/or alteration, small mineralogical differences, differences in induration, cementation, cohesion and grain boundary conditions, microfracturing, stress history and method of working in the quarry, processing and subsequent history. It must not be assumed that similar aggregates from different locations will have closely similar properties: they may or may not. Reliance should be placed on comprehensive sampling and testing and quality control of the individual aggregate sources.

The warning given in the first edition on the rapid progress and changes being made in the world's Standards and Codes, which are under more-or-less continuous revision, still remains, as do the suggestions that the current rapid progress of experience and research made it virtually impossible for the Report to be completely up-to-date or wholly comprehensive.

The constraints emphasized in the first edition on the catholic nature of the subject matter of the Report and background interest, training and experience of its readers remain such that an expert in any particular field might consider the basic material included in that field as over-simplified.

As a result of the Working Party's deliberations, there are substantial changes in the text. The chapter headings and layout are broadly similar to the first edition. However, the text of most chapters has been selectively changed and substantially lengthened with inclusion of new and updated references, tables and figures. Changes amounting to complete rewrites have been made to chapters 2, 3, 4, 5, 6, 9 and 13. The remaining chapters are all changed significantly in many ways with new and additional text, data, tables and figures. The glossary remains largely similar but is updated with new material and, in addition, an appendix on aggregate properties has been added.

Again, the Report, in an early draft stage, was presented for open discussion on 16th January 1990 at a Geological Society Engineering Group meeting in London. The suggestions made then and also subsequently received, have been considered in the final revision of the Report, together with those from invited corresponding individuals and organizations. However, the views expressed in this Report are again those of the Working Party members.

1.3. Geographical factors

Although mainly concentrating on British practice, it is hoped that this edition will still have a wide geographical application, subject to due consideration of the effects of local climate and geological history. For example, weathering can be of much greater importance in wet tropical or hot desert conditions, and some of the generalizations relating to the performance of certain rock types in Britain could be misleading if applied in very different climatic regimes. Igneous or metamorphic rocks may be impaired by deep weathering in wet tropical regions and, as a result, provide aggregates which could deteriorate rapidly in service: another example is when inherently weak limestones may be transmuted locally at the ground surface into strong calcretes under semi-arid conditions. Local geological history will have an equally important influence. For instance, the Mesozoic and Cenozoic sedimentary formations in Britain are almost devoid of rocks capable of yielding hard coarse aggregate, but strata of the same age in the Alps, which have recrystallized under conditions of high temperature and stress, are generally strong and durable. Geological age of itself, therefore, will have only a local significance as an element in the description of an aggregate and should always be considered in conjunction with the topographical and climatic location of the material.

Reference

VERNEY, Sir R. B. (Chairman) 1976. 'Aggregates: The Way Ahead'. Report of the Advisory Committee on Aggregates. HMSO, for Department of the Environment, London.

2. Occurrences and associations of sources

2.1. Introduction

This section is intended primarily as an introduction and guide for non-geologists engaged in the aggregates industry. It is intended to be useful in understanding the more straightforward day-to-day geological situations that arise in the development and management of workings. It provides a basis for recognizing the more complex and intractable problems for which specialist geological advice is likely to be needed.

A main contribution of geologists to the study of aggregates is the recognition that rock material owes its properties to its origin, its mineral composition and to the geological processes that have affected it through time. Knowledge of the qualities that determine the suitability of a rock (or concentration of rock fragments) for use as aggregate enables the prospecting geologist to make an informed search for new deposits, recognizing and defining the clear, though not always simple, relationships that exist between the composition, texture, grain-size, fabric and state of weathering of a rock and its likely performance as an aggregate in an engineering structure or other application.

2.1.1. Rock and rock categories

Rock is natural material that forms the crust of the earth. Some rocks are relatively soft, that is to say, weak and easily deformable. Others are hard, strong and durable. Rock so defined includes the 'soil' of engineers (that is, all unconsolidated deposits overlying bedrock). However, it does not cover the soils of pedologists (the earthy materials forming the ground in which land plants can grow). Rocks may be examined in cliffs and quarries at the surface and in mines and boreholes. Three broad categories of rock are distinguished here according to their origins (rather than their composition or strength).

Igneous rocks derive from molten material that originated below the earth's surface and solidified at or near the ground surface (for example, basalt and granite; see §2.2.1 and Table 2.2).

Sedimentary rocks result from the consolidation into layers of loose sediment derived from the breakdown of older rocks, the fragments having been transported and deposited by water, ice or wind (for example, mudrock,

sandstone and conglomerate). Some rocks in this category have formed by chemical or organic processes (for example, some limestones) whereas others, the pyroclastic rocks, include debris from volcanic eruptions (lumps of lava, rock and fine dust) which falls to earth to form bedded deposits (§§2.3 and 2.4; Table 2.4). In their unconsolidated or loosely aggregated condition, accumulations of rock materials (whether derived from the weathering of igneous, sedimentary or metamorphic rock masses) are known as *superficial deposits*. They are commonly Quaternary, mainly Recent in age (Table 2.1) and include glacial, fluvial, lacustrine, wind-blown, coastal and marine deposits, as well as residual materials. New rock debris may be added by weathering and the deposit subjected to erosion, degradation and relocation by natural processes.

Metamorphic rocks derive from pre-existing igneous and sedimentary rocks but have been changed from their original state by heat and pressure at depth in the Earth's crust to acquire conspicuous new characteristics (for example, schist, gneiss, hornfels; §2.2.2. and Table 2.3).

2.1.2. Geological time scale and the rock sequence

It should be noted that the relationship between the rock masses of which the Earth is made, whether on the global, continental, national, local or microscopic scales, resulted from complex sequences of interactive geological events which may have begun when the planet took on tangible form (perhaps 4.6 billion years ago) and have continued over geological time.

Geological time is too long to be readily comprehended but an outline of the geological time scale is essential in placing events and the major time divisions, names and terminology into the established chronological context (Table 2.1).

All geological maps, which show the location, chronological sequence ('age order') and detailed inter-relations of rock units in the map area, are accompanied by a stratigraphic column, usually on the map margin. It acts as an index and explanation to the colours and notations used on the map and schematically represents, in a generalized vertical section, the relative ages of the rocks shown, with the oldest rocks conventionally placed at the base of the column just as they would normally be when originally deposited.

TABLE 2.1 *The stratigraphical column showing the divisions of geological time and their age (after Harland et al. 1990)*

Age (Ma BP)	Geological age			
	Epoch	Period	Era	Eon
0.01	Holocene (Recent)	Quaternary	Cenozoic ('recent life')	Phanerozoic ('evident' life, i.e. many fossils)
	Pleistocene			
1.6				
5.2	Pliocene	Tertiary		
	Miocene			
23				
	Oligocene			
35				
	Eocene			
56				
	Palaeocene			
65				
146	(Numerous epochs recognizable throughout the world)	Cretaceous	Mesozoic ('middle life')	
		Jurassic		
208				
		Triassic		
245				
		Permian	Palaeozoic ('ancient life')	
290				
		Carboniferous		
363				
		Devonian		
409				
		Silurian		
439				
		Ordovician		
510				
		Cambrian		
570				
		Precambrian	Proterozoic ('early life')	
			Archaean < Origin of the Earth	
4600				

Apart from a relatively small quantity of manufactured lightweight aggregate used mainly in special applications, the vast bulk of construction aggregates is produced directly from strong rock formations by crushing or from naturally occurring particulate deposits such as sand and gravel.

There are two principal sources of aggregate materials: the unconsolidated deposits of rock fragments that constitute part of the superficial ('surficial' or 'drift') deposits, and the hard ('solid') rocks, which must be quarried and prepared by machinery or, where labour is plentiful in developing countries, by hand. The most sought-after aggregate materials are commonly derived from the older, more compact sedimentary formations, particularly limestones and sandstones, from igneous and metamorphic rock masses and from naturally occurring concentrations of particulate deposits, such as sand and gravel and conglomerate (Prentice 1990).

Most hard rocks can be used for coarse aggregate because experience shows that they are likely to perform adequately in a wide range of less demanding applications. Very substantial quantities of 'good quality' sound material are required for structural concrete and road pavement construction, the major uses of aggregate, for which stringent specifications apply. Bearing in mind that the suitability of new aggregate sources for demanding applications can only be determined by empirical laboratory tests, the estimation of rock properties can often be achieved quite accurately with experience and is a very important skill for the practising geomaterials engineer or geologist (Fookes 1991). There are many good aids to estimation in the published literature:

TABLE 2.2 *A classification of igneous rocks on silica percentage and grain size*

Acid	Intermediate	Basic
Coarse-grained (plutonic) rocks (grain size larger than about 5 mm; liable to be brittle from presence of large crystals)		
Granite	Syenite	Gabbro
Granodiorite	Diorite	Norite
Medium-grained (hypabyssal) rocks (grain size between 5 and 1 mm; crystals commonly intergrown—good roadstones)		
Microgranite	Porphyry	Dolerite
Granophyre	Porphyrite	
Fine-grained (volcanic) rocks (grain size less than 1 mm, i.e. below the range of the unaided eye; some rocks liable to be brittle and splintery—otherwise good aggregate material)		
Rhyolite, pumice	Trachyte	Basalt
Felsite	Andesite	

←——————— Continuous variation in properties and composition ———————→

Light colour	Dark colour
Low relative density (2.6)	High relative density (2.9)
High silica percentage (66% +)	High ferro-magnesian (mafic)
orthoclase feldspar	minerals and plagioclase feldspar

(after Fookes 1975)

British Standard 5930 (1981), the International Society of Rock Mechanics Rock Characterization Testing and Monitoring (Brown 1980) and the Geomorphological Field Manual (Gardiner & Dackombe 1983). Nevertheless, it is generally accepted that there is an approximate correlation between aggregate quality and rock porosity; it may often be taken as a very rough working rule that an otherwise suitable rock with a water absorption value of less than about 2% will usually produce a good quality aggregate and that rocks with values exceeding about 4% may not. A study of correlations between certian physical and mechanical test data derived from the 10–14 mm fraction of borehole samples from glacio-fluvial gravels in the Kelvin Valley, east of Glasgow (Gribble 1990) has shown that gravel with a water absorption value of 3% or less yielded aggregate test values that would satisfy a wide range of British Standard specifications. The study also showed that the proportions of different rock types in the gravel influenced the water absorption value less than the degree of weathering. The wide-scale effects of alteration and weathering processes on aggregate materials in the ground are discussed in §2.7.

2.2. Aggregates from the igneous and metamorphic rocks

2.2.1. Igneous rock

Although igneous rocks (that is, rocks which have solidified from a fluid rock-melt or magma) exhibit a very wide range of chemical compositions, as reflected in the intricacies of their nomenclature and classification (Table 2.2), their suitability for aggregate depends also on their mineral constituents, their crystalline fabric and texture and the degree of chemical alteration and of weathering (if any); these in turn relate to their modes of occurrence (Figs 2.1 & 2.2). A full discussion of the petrological and other characteristics relevant to the description and classification of aggregate materials will be found in Chapter 6. The plutonic rocks formed at depth in large masses (granite, diorite) are typically coarsely crystalline, whereas smaller bodies which may have been intruded as dykes, sills and bosses into country rocks have a medium to finely crystalline texture (microgranite, dolerite) perhaps, in some examples, with a scattering of larger crystals (porphyry). Extrusive igneous rocks have solidified rapidly as lava flows on the surface or under the sea and they may be of glassy or micro-crystalline texture (basalt, andesite). Lava flows may be of little use for aggregate if they include flow-banded strongly jointed, vesiculate (slaggy) or brecciated members. Fragmental (pyroclastic) materials such as dust, ash, tuff and rock debris ejected from volcanoes also may not be useful unless they have become indurated into hard rock by heating (welded tuff) or compacted by burial or cementation (agglomerate). Ancient volcanic and volcaniclastic rocks, for example, in South Africa (Anon 1991) can yield high-quality aggregate.

On the other hand, pumice, a highly vesicular sometimes froth-like lava resulting from the expansion of gases during solidification, is a naturally occurring light-weight aggregate much favoured by the construction industry for making low density concrete blocks for inner leaf and cavity insulation.

From a chemical point of view, the vast majority of igneous rocks are made up by combinations of only eight elements. Of these, oxygen is dominant, next is

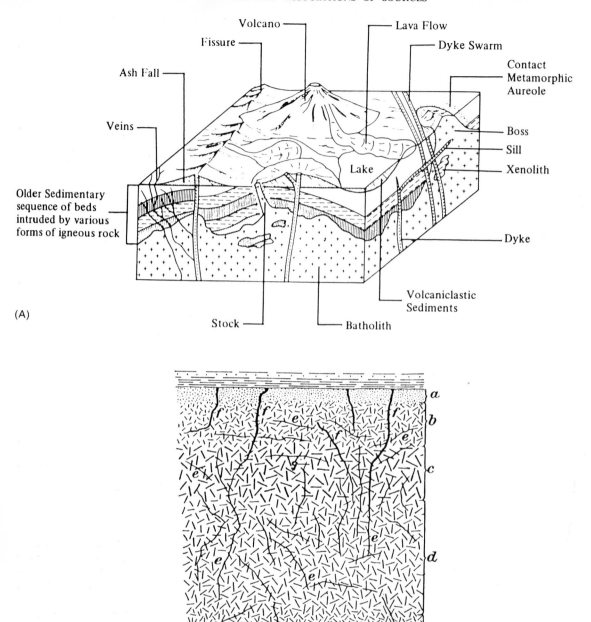

FIG. 2.1 Igneous rock bodies. (A) Typical shapes and associations of large and small igneous rock bodies and their relation to the country rocks. (B) Diagrammatic section through a thick (±35 m) quartz-dolerite sill (after Robertson & Haldane 1937). *Notes.* (*a*) Rock very fine grained or glassy at the chilled top and bottom contacts; country rock is seldom brecciated and fragments rarely ingested except where sill is strongly transgressive. (*b*) 3–5 m of fine grained dolerite, possibly but rarely containing calcite or quartz filled bubbles ranged parallel with sill contacts. (*c*) Coarse grained dark rock with irregular patchwork of lighter minerals occupying perhaps 25% of the sill thickness. (*d*) Medium grained vaguely patchy rock mass constituting 50% of the sill volume. (*e*) Ramifying fine grained quartzo-feldspathic veins, up to a few centimetres in width, most common near top of sill, sometimes parallel to contact. (*f*) Quartz-calcite veins with pyrite common at top of sill but rarely extend deeper than zone C. (*g*) Rectilinear jointing of sill, typically distinct from the veining, is accentuated by weathering near the surface and leads to much poorer, broken stone.

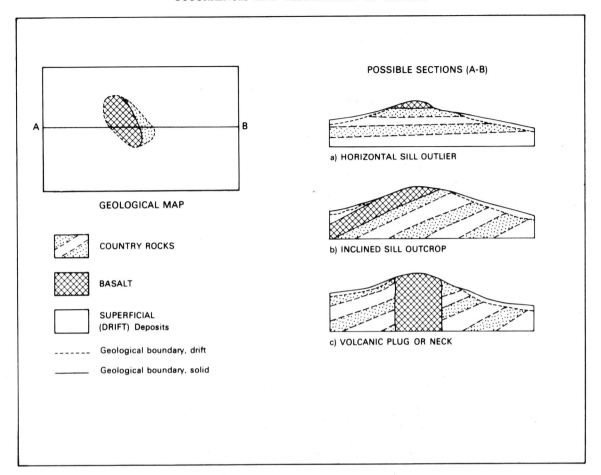

POSSIBLE SECTIONS (A-B)

a) HORIZONTAL SILL OUTLIER

b) INCLINED SILL OUTCROP

c) VOLCANIC PLUG OR NECK

GEOLOGICAL MAP

COUNTRY ROCKS

BASALT

SUPERFICIAL
(DRIFT) Deposits

------- Geological boundary, drift

——— Geological boundary, solid

FIG. 2.2. Geological map of an occurrence of igneous rock with possible subsurface extensions of the rock body shown in geological sections (after Tomkeieff 1964).

silicon and then aluminium, iron, calcium, sodium, potassium and magnesium. In terms of oxides, silica (SiO_2) is by far the most abundant, ranging from 40% to 75% of the total, and the silica percentage forms the basis of a threefold classification into acid, intermediate and basic categories.

In general, silica-rich (acid) igneous rocks, which typically contain free silica in the form of clear, colourless quartz crystals and opaque but pale-coloured feldspars, are generally paler and lighter in weight than the intermediate and basic rocks which have increasing amounts of dark-coloured ferromagnesian minerals of higher density and only very rarely any free quartz. An outline classification of igneous rocks according to these features is shown in Table 2.2.

Much of the crushed igneous rock aggregates in Britain is produced from fine- to medium-grained basic rocks (dolerite and basalt) and, to a lesser extent, from fine-grained acidic rocks (felsite, porphyry and microgranite); increasing amounts come from certain of the coarse-grained rocks (granite and diorite) worked in large quarries. Many quarries are, however, located in small intrusions of dolerite and basalt, for example in Wales and the Welsh Borders, in Devon, and in the Carboniferous Limestone of the Pennines in Derbyshire. The Whin Sill and related intrusions are sources in Northern England and the Midland Valley quartz-dolerite sill-complex in Scotland (see, for example, Figure 2.1B). There is a large production from the Antrim Basalts in Ulster and the Old Red Sandstone basalts and andesites in Fife and Tayside, in Scotland (Quarry Management and Products 1977a; Merritt & Elliot 1984). Volcanic necks and dykes tend to be more attractive to quarrying than other minor intrusions (Fig. 2.1) because they combine a relatively restricted land-take with long life and scope for making processing plant unobtrusive. Although workings in sills may provide a wider range of aggregate products due to variations in grain-size and rock fabric, they are more extensive and extraction strategies are often seriously constrained by down-dip increases in overburden thickness. Lavas, which tend to vary greatly in thickness, composition and depth of weathering, must be regarded as 'discontinuous' resources, so that only thicker occurrences, such as the Lower Old Red Sandstone lavas in the Ochil and Sidlaw hills northeast of Glasgow, are likely to be viable (Harris 1978).

Some coarse-grained rocks may be less attractive for aggregate in some applications because of their relatively low crushing strength which arises from fracturing along the cleavages of the coarse crystalline constituents.

Igneous rocks are unevenly distributed in Britain. In southeast England, where the demand for aggregate is greatest, such rocks do not crop out. There are only small outcrops of igneous rocks in the Midlands but outcrops are extensive in southwest England, west and northwest Wales, parts of northern England and in Scotland (Harris 1978). In Northern Ireland, igneous rocks are the source of more than half the aggregate produced (British Geological Survey 1990).

Though many granites yield good aggregate, the quality is not uniform. For example, the fine-grained core of the Land's End granite in Cornwall is exploited, rather than the coarse-grained material which comprises the greater part of the intrusion. The feldspars in many, such as the nearby St Austell granite and some parts of the Arran granites in Scotland, may be deeply weathered or changed to china clay (kaolinization); they are prone to considerable attrition during normal handling and transport. However, in some applications, faint alteration may enhance the effectiveness of an aggregate in service. For example, dolerites in the Central Scotland sill-complex provide high-PSV roadstone because of the mix of exposed hard and soft mineral grains. The igneous rocks of Leicestershire include granodiorite at Mount Sorrel and several other major intrusions of diorite have assumed considerable economic importance because of the rarity of hard rock in southern England (Quarry Management and Products 1974). Production of crushed rock for roadstone from the Leicestershire quarries amounts to 25% of total igneous rock output in Great Britain.

Several Ordovician porphyritic felsites and microgranites in North Wales, the Threlkeld microgranite (Cumbria) and the Newer Granites of the Scottish Highlands (Smith & Floyd 1989) are examples of sources of good quality aggregates (although many of the last-named may be highly decomposed in places); a few are distinctively coloured and therefore useful for decorative finishes and road surface dressings. The Strontian Granite, a coastal batholith on Loch Linnhe, at Glensanda in Scotland, has been developed as a major source of crushed rock aggregate for distribution exclusively by sea to southern Britain as well as distant markets. When fully operational in the mid-1990s, the Glensanda superquarry is scheduled to produce 7.5 million tonnes per annum of pale pink, medium-grained, porphyritic bio-tite-granite which, on the evidence of test results, will yield low-shrinkage concreting aggregate suitable for most construction uses. Most of the aggregate used for all applications in Hong Kong is granitic (Earle 1991). A wider range of rock types, like felsites and andesites, will satisfy less demanding applications for coloured aggregate in footpaths, tennis courts, hard shoulders and in decorative dressings for buildings.

2.2.2. Metamorphic rock

Since metamorphic rocks result from the alteration of existing igneous, metamorphic and sedimentary rocks by heat, pressure and chemical activity, they comprise a very complex range of rock types (McLean & Gribble 1979; Blyth & de Freitas 1984). Thermal or contact metamorphism takes place when rocks are heated by the intrusion of a mass of molten igneous rock. Clayey rocks, such as shales and mudstones, may recrystallize into hard, dense, flint-like rock, termed hornfels, whilst quartz-rich rocks, the greywackes and sandstones, fuse or recrystallize into quartzites and psammites which can provide high-quality aggregates (Table 2.3).

The first effect of progressive regional or dynamic metamorphism (that is, the wide-scale alteration induced by extreme pressure and heat through the deep burial of rocks in the crust) is to impart foliations; the foliation may not always be visible to the naked eye, though individual mineral grains may exhibit strain lines when seen under the microscope. Where local pressure-induced movement occurs, the rocks become sheared. Platy or foliated structures in metamorphic rocks indicate that high shearing stresses have been a principal agency in their formation and the aggregate potential of such rocks is reduced since aligned elongate rock fragments may induce anisotropic weaknesses in concrete and platiness reduces the abrasion resistance of road surfacing.

More intense metamorphism gives rise to widespread recrystallization of minerals and, in extreme conditions, many rock constituents melt and may be intruded as an igneous body. In these conditions clay-rich sediments first form slates, which are characterized by closely spaced cleavage planes perpendicular to the direction of greatest pressure, then phyllites (foliated rocks containing much white mica) and finally schists and pelitic gneisses, in which the constituent minerals tend to be irregularly aligned imparting an uneven, wavy, 'schistose' texture. Gneisses are formed from igneous, metamorphic and sedimentary rocks in more extreme conditions. They are typically coarse-grained and banded in structure, reflecting differences in original composition accentuated by segregation of the constituents during recrystallization and flow under great pressure deep in the crust. Striped or injection gneisses may result from the injection of thin sheets of molten material (com-

TABLE 2.3 *Generalized chart showing the origin and classification of common metamorphic rocks*

Original rock	Metamorphic environment—temperature and pressure conditions	
	Low grade—shallow burial	Medium and high grade—deep burial
clay, shale and volcanic tuff	Foliated platy rocks (effects of pressure paramount) slate	phyllite, schist, gneiss*
clayey sandstone	greywacke-sandstone*†	quartz-mica schist, fine-grained gneiss
clayey limestone	slaty marble*†	calcareous schist
granite*, quartzitic tuff	sheared granite, slate	granite-gneiss*, quartz-mica schist
basalt*, basic volcanic tuff	green (chlorite) schist	amphibolite (amphibole schist) hornblende gneiss*
any parent rock	Non-foliated, massive rocks (effects of increased temperature paramount)	hornfels* (some recrystallization but often original features still present)
quartzose sandstone*	quartzitic sandstone*	quartzite* (includes mica if impure) = psammite*, granulite* (essentially quartz, feldspar + some mica)
limestone* and dolostone*	marble* (if impure, contains a wide range of calcium and magnesium silicates with increasing metamorphic grade)	

* Rocks most likely to be useful for aggregate.
† Some rocks containing clay minerals may not perform satisfactorily in some applications.

monly rich in quartz and feldspar) along parallel planes in a variety of country rocks; migmatites generally form by partial melting (and recrystallization) of the host rock. Such rocks are commonly massive and granular and can yield good quality aggregate. The main metamorphic rocks derived from common rock materials are classified in Table 2.3.

The wide diversity of metamorphic rocks arises from the variety of metamorphic processes and pre-existing rocks that are available for metamorphism and their usefulness for aggregate is equally variable. It is probably generally true to say that the originally clayey, foliated or platy rocks must have been subjected to extreme or high grade metamorphism and to have undergone recrystallization to render them potentially useful as aggregate; the massive quartzitic metamorphic rocks probably provide the best prospective aggregate sources, although some may be too hard to be worked economically for undemanding applications.

Few metamorphic rocks are of more than local importance as aggregates in the UK as they are commonly remote from the main centres of population. However, some thermally metamorphosed rocks such as the hornfels adjacent to the Shap granite in Cumbria are of value because of their high crushing strength and in Cornwall and Anglesey metamorphic rocks contribute very significantly to local aggregate production. The aggregate potential of igneous and metamorphic rocks, which together contribute 85% of Scottish crushed rock aggregate production, has been reviewed comprehensively by Merritt & Elliot (1984) and Smith & Floyd (1989). Worldwide, vast tracts of the major continents consist of exposed regional metamorphic and associated igneous

rocks, which represent the worn-down roots of ancient, largely Precambrian (older than about 590 million years, see Table 2.1) mountain ranges. The shield areas of Canada, northern Europe, eastern South America, Africa and eastern Asia, in contrast with geologically more recent mountain belts, are generally strongly denuded terrains of relatively subdued relief but with highly metamorphosed rock units giving a choice of aggregate sources. The prospector must bear in mind, however, that long exposure to earth processes and different climatic regimes may have reduced the value of such rocks in terms of aggregate potential.

The younger, steep-sided, high-relief terrains of the European Alps, the Andes and the Himalayas represent some of the most challenging environments for discovery and effective use of aggregate materials: the metamorphic rocks are commonly of varying metamorphic grade, are subject to continuing geological processes (contemporary uplift, compression and seismicity) and geomorphological activity, such as vigorous erosion and mass movement, particularly in tropical, sub-tropical, periglacial and glacial climatic zones (e.g. Fookes & Marsh 1981).

2.3. Aggregates from the sedimentary rocks

As the result of the denudation of the rocks of the land surface through processes of weathering (mechanical and chemical, see §2.7.2) and of erosion during transport by moving water and ice, and by wind, large amounts of detrital and chemical, including biochemical, materials

TABLE 2.4 *Outline classification of sedimentary rocks*

Main character	Constituent material (unconsolidated)	Equivalent rock (consolidated)
Detrital (mechanically sorted) including volcanic		
Diamictic	Till (boulder clay)	Tillite
Pebbly	Pebbles, gravel (over 5 mm)	Conglomerate*, agglomerate* (volcanic)
	Scree (talus), volcanic ejecta	Breccia*, volcanic breccia*
Sandy	Sand (0.06–5.0 mm)	Sandstone*, with varieties according to cement (siliceous, calcareous, clayey, ferruginous) or admixture of minerals other than quartz (feldspar, lithic fragments = arkose*, greywacke*, tuff*)
	Silt (0.002–0.06 mm), loess	Ganister, brickearth
Muddy	Clay (less than 0.002 mm)	Shale, mudstone
Chemical and biochemical (organic)		
Calcareous	Shells, corals, crinoids	Limestones* (shelly, coral crinoidal)
	$CaCO_3$ precipitated	Oolitic limestone, stalactite, tufa
	$CaMg(CO_3)_2$ precipitated or replacement	Dolostone* or dolomitic limestone*
Siliceous	Silica gel, siliceous fossils	Flint*, chert*, diatomite
Saline	Salt (lake) precipitates	Evaporites, duricrusts*
Carbonaceous	Peat, liquid hydrocarbons	Coals, oil-shale
Ferruginous	Iron carbonate, iron silicate	Siderite, chamosite ores

* Rocks most likely to be useful for aggregate
(after Blyth & de Freitas 1984).

become available to form new sedimentary deposits. In addition, some sediments originate as ash, dust and rock debris from volcanism (volcaniclastic deposits) and others, like peat and coal, are principally organic residues and are not derived from pre-existing rocks.

Sedimentary rocks are generally divided into clastic (or detrital) rocks on the basis of a convenient grain-size classification (giving pebbly, sandy and muddy categories) and chemical and bio-chemical (organic) rocks, on the basis of the predominant raw material (Table 2.4). Sources of aggregates in the unconsolidated sediments (the drift deposits) are described in §2.4; some materials suitable for aggregate in the compacted, indurated and cemented deposits will be reviewed in §2.4.6, but the limestones and sandstones described here are of wider occurrence.

2.3.1. Limestone

This term is applied to the large and petrographically diverse group of sedimentary rocks in which the carbonate fraction (very commonly as calcium carbonate) exceeds the non-carbonate. Thus, if more than 50% of sand-sized quartz, silt or clay is present, the rock is calcareous sandstone or calcareous mudstone, rather than limestone. Similarly, the progressive admixture of magnesium carbonate as dolomite ($CaMg(CO_3)_2$) gives rise to magnesian limestone (up to 10% dolomite), dolomitic limestone and finally dolostone, in which more

than 50% of dolomite is present. As limestones and dolostones are commonly the most indurated members within the younger sedimentary sequences, they may yield good aggregate provided they have a dense crystalline or cemented fabric and are not weakened by the existence of cavities or high porosity.

The limestones and dolostones, which are the main carbonate rocks of importance for aggregates, form a diverse, polygenetic group; some are detrital (particulate) sediments, others are of chemical or biochemical origin. They tend to be soluble in rainwater and easily re-deposited, so that their original characteristics may be considerably changed after deposition and burial.

The detailed petrographical description and classification of limestones (e.g. Dunham 1962; Folk 1962) are complex and simpler schemes more appropriate for use in engineering contexts have been proposed, for example, by Fookes & Higginbottom (1975) and Burnett & Epps (1979), to which the reader is referred. For a comprehensive review of the availability, exploitation and use of limestone and dolostone, including their occurrence and applications in the aggregates field, refer to Mineral Dossier No 23 (Harris 1982).

Limestones, which commonly range in colour from dark grey to white and may be tinted by small amounts of ferruginous or other components, are characteristically bedded rocks often containing many fossils; they are readily scratched with a steel blade and, with the exception of dolostone, they effervesce in cold dilute hydrochloric acid. Many limestones may be described as 'shelly', that is they contain the debris and more rarely well preserved examples of fossil shells, such as bivalves, corals and crinoids ('sea-lilies'), which may constitute a large part of the rock: algal, coral, brachiopod and crinoidal limestones take their names from prominent fossil constituents. The reef limestones form mounds or 'build-ups' (reef-knolls and bioherms) or largely unbedded rock of more limited occurrence and the oolitic limestones, which may also contain much shelly and clayey material, are characterized by the predominance of concentrically layered grains of sand-size calcium carbonate resembling in appearance the hard roe of a fish. All of these rocks are more durable and useful for aggregate when they are indurated, crystalline, fine-grained in texture and particularly when the matrix which holds the grains together is itself crystalline.

In the UK, Carboniferous Limestone currently provides about 60% of national crushed rock aggregate production (British Geological Survey 1990) and it probably represents the largest resource of good-quality aggregate in British sediments. These limestones, which are commonly thickly bedded and structurally simple, give rise to fairly extensive well drained uplands in which large quarrying operations can be established economically. The main occurrences and centres of extraction (Ashworth 1975) are in the Mendip Hills (Quarry Management and Products 1975; Al-Jassar & Hawkins 1991), around the northern rim of the Bristol coalfield, in the uplands at the periphery of the South Wales coalfield and in North Wales, in the Derbyshire Dome (Harrison & Adlam 1984), on the borders of the Lake District, in North Yorkshire and Lancashire and to a minor extent in Scotland. In the north Pennines, several thin limestone beds are interbedded with soft sandstone and shale (Yoredale facies). One of the more prominent of these, the Great or Main Limestone, extends into Durham and Northumberland.

Other major limestones being worked for aggregates include the Devonian limestones between Torquay and Plymouth and to a lesser extent the Silurian limestones in the Welsh Borderlands. Many Permian magnesian limestones are acceptable for 'good-quality' aggregate and are quarried widely in Nottinghamshire, Derbyshire, Yorkshire and Durham (Collins 1991). Although the weaker more porous post-Triassic limestones in southern and eastern England will not generally satisfy the specifications for good-quality aggregate, samples of Middle Jurassic crushed limestone aggregate with water absorption values up to 9% have yielded ten per cent fines values above 50 kN in laboratory tests (Collins 1983, 1986b) and might be utilized in appropriate applications. Certain of the more indurated Jurassic and Cretaceous limestones are quarried locally for building and ornamental dimension stone but mainly for 'fill' and low-strength mass concrete applications. In southern and eastern England, however, some potentially useful, good quality pre-Triassic limestones and other aggregate materials lie at no great depth beneath the Mesozoic cover. For example, Carboniferous Limestone occurs beneath Cambridge and it underlies the Coal Measures on the northern limb of the now-abandoned Kent coalfield. In the future, such concealed resources might become economically exploitable by mining (Verney 1976, chapter 9), as they are in Kansas, USA (Harris 1976).

2.3.2. Sandstone

Sandstone (or arenite) is a lithified accumulation of sand grains which are acknowledged by most authorities to range in size (or grade) from about 0.06 to 2 mm in diameter, though exceptionally particles up to 5 mm in size may be included (Chapter 6). The grains, which are predominantly of quartz, were produced by weathering and attrition of pre-existing rocks and were sorted, abraded and transported by moving ice, air and water from sources outside the basin of deposition, where they became consolidated (commonly by cementation) into a coherent rock. Coarse-grained sandstones with angular or subangular particles are termed gritstones and the admixture of other materials, in addition to quartz, gives rise to a range of arenaceous rocks. For example, a feldspathic sandstone is termed arkose and the presence of lithic (rock) fragments and clay minerals produces the so-called 'dirty' sandstones or greywackes.

The use of sandstones, arkoses, greywackes and their low-graded metamorphic derivatives as aggregate requires that they should have high strength, low porosity and, for pavement wearing course applications, that they should be resistant to polishing (Harris 1977). To be useful, the quarried material should not contain excessive amounts of weathered constituents and mica or exhibit small-scale bedding laminations or jointing discontinuities, as they may result in the crushed product becoming unacceptably flaky and weakened by the alignment of the constituent grains. Interbeds of mudstone and shale may be troublesome in the extraction and processing of otherwise attractive greywackes.

A review of the suitability of some British arenaceous rocks for roadstone (Hawkes & Hosking 1973) relates the petrography to the results of physical and mechanical tests on 86 samples specially collected from a range of pre-Permian formations, exposed mainly in disused and working quarries. It demonstrates that high-quality road surfacing materials exist widely in the Carboniferous sandstones of the West Country and South Wales. They are also extensively represented in the Lower Palaeozoic sediments of Wales, Cumbria, North Yorkshire (Sloan et al. 1989) and the southern uplands of Scotland.

A study of the geomechanical properties of six British sandstones ranging in age from Lower Old Red Sandstone to Triassic, has demonstrated the wide variation in their physical and mechanical character and hence their usefulness as construction materials (Hawkins & McConnell 1991). Test results show the potential suitability of the sandstones for use as building stone, armourstone, rip-rap, aggregate sub-base, aggregate dressing and concrete (Hawkins & McConnell 1991, table 7).

Although quartzites occur fairly widely, their outcrops are not extensive either laterally or vertically. Examples which are exploited for aggregate include the Cambrian quartzites of Hartshill, near Nuneaton, and the Precambrian Holyhead Quartzite in Anglesey. The Dalradian and Caledonian quartzites and Torridonian sandstones of the Highlands and Islands of Scotland, though remote from markets, are potential sources of strong, abrasion-resistant aggregates (Smith & Floyd 1989).

The Carboniferous sandstones and gritstones of the Millstone Grit and Lower Coal Measures of Northern England, quarried traditionally for dimension stone, now commonly provide aggregate for relatively undemanding applications but they tend to be porous and weak (Collins 1986a, 1989). On the other hand, the Pennant Sandstones in the Upper Coal Measures of South Wales and the Carboniferous and adjacent Devonian rocks of North Devon are strong and have very good polish-resistant properties, but, like the greywackes, they often have to be worked selectively from amongst substandard interbedded materials (Cox et al. 1986).

In southeastern England, an area virtually without indigenous hard rock aggregate resources, a minor source of hard calcareous sandstone and sandy limestone, the Kentish Ragstone, forms part of the Hythe Beds of the Lower Greensand. A similarly hard fine-grained sandstone in the top of the Jurassic Portland Beds has been worked as a by-product from gypsum mining in southern Sussex (Quarry Management and Products 1979). Both have been used for roadstone.

In addition to these granular quartz rocks, cryptocrystalline chert and flint are important aggregate materials. They commonly exist as discrete nodules, lenticles, seams and cavity infillings in a range of rock formations and, because of their resistance to degradation and attrition, they contribute large quantities of gravel grade material to sediments and they may be recycled many times. Chert is essentially, though not exclusively, siliceous material of sedimentary, often organic origin (such as sponge spicules, diatoms) lithified by a cement of redistributed, minutely crystalline silica, to form nodules and beds in rock formations of almost every geological age. The term flint is applied exclusively to often high purity silica concentrations which form bands and nodules on bedding planes and joints in the White Chalk of the Upper Cretaceous of western Europe and elsewhere. The flints are typically hard, compact and durable and they are the predominant constituent of the

much sought-after glacial and fluvial gravels of eastern and southern England. Certain forms of amorphous silica, for example, opaline silica as well as certain other natural materials, may be chemically reactive with strongly alkaline cement pastes and must be avoided in mass and structural concrete applications (French 1991; see also Chapter 8).

2.3.3. Other sedimentary rocks and natural waste materials

Although the fine-grained (muddy) sediments, which comprise possibly widely varying mixtures of clay, quartz (silt-grade) and carbonate, are not useful for aggregate, their indurated derivatives such as claystone, siltstone, argillite and slate (Fookes & Higginbottom 1975), may be acceptable in applications for which specifications are relatively undemanding and such factors as frost susceptibility can be ruled out. Except where good-quality aggregates are unavailable, it is unlikely that workings for the supply of such materials would be specially commissioned. Waste materials from collieries, oil-shale workings, slate quarrying and metal mining are more usual sources of these so-called secondary aggregates. Colliery shale is amongst the most widely available in Great Britain and has been used as sub-base and base material in the construction of lightly trafficked roads (Gutt et al. 1974) particularly as a cement-bound granular material. Pulverized fuel-ash (pfa) or fly-ash, a fine alumino-silicate dust derived from coal-fired electricity generating stations, is a constituent in the production of light-weight ('breeze') building blocks. Boulders of slate waste from slate quarrying have been used for armourstones in sea defence works on the North Wales coast (Fookes & Poole 1981; Dibb et al. 1983a, b).

2.4. Occurrence of sand and gravel, and of conglomerates

Sand and gravel deposits are accumulations of the more durable rock fragments and mineral grains which have been released from their parent rocks by physical weathering processes or abraded by the action of ice (glaciers) and then worn and sorted by water (rivers and waves) and the wind. Deposits consisting of boulders, cobbles, pebbles and granules when cemented or lithified are known as conglomerate; the spaces between the pebbles are often largely filled with sand (Fig. 2.3). The properties of gravel and, to a lesser extent, of sand largely depend on the rocks from which they are derived, although during their transport prior to deposition weathered or otherwise weaker fragments tend to be selectively worn away so that the resulting aggregate material is usually stronger than the crushed parent rock

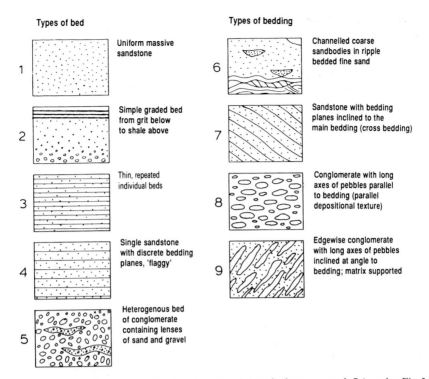

Types of bed

1 — Uniform massive sandstone

2 — Simple graded bed from grit below to shale above

3 — Thin, repeated individual beds

4 — Single sandstone with discrete bedding planes, 'flaggy'

5 — Heterogenous bed of conglomerate containing lenses of sand and gravel

Types of bedding

6 — Channelled coarse sandbodies in ripple bedded fine sand

7 — Sandstone with bedding planes inclined to the main bedding (cross bedding)

8 — Conglomerate with long axes of pebbles parallel to bedding (parallel depositional texture)

9 — Edgewise conglomerate with long axes of pebbles inclined at angle to bedding; matrix supported

FIG. 2.3. Sedimentary structures in detrital deposits. Structures 2 and 6, and when truncated, 7 (see also Fig. 2.21), can indicate 'way-up' (see text). After Sherbon Hills (1975).

(Harris *et al.* 1974, p. 336). On the other hand, where transport distances are short, for example in glacio-fluvial environments and alluvial fans, deleterious constituents, such as mudflakes and fragments of coal and chalk, may remain and reduce the attractiveness of a prospective deposit for aggregate.

The principal sources of sand and gravel are relatively young and unconsolidated superficial deposits (called Drift in the UK) which have accumulated in the recent geological past usually, in the northern hemisphere at least, since the onset of the Pleistocene Ice Age. In North America, these deposits are termed surficial deposits or regolith. All older (pre-Quaternary) geological deposits, which form the bedrock, country rock, formation or rock head upon which the weaker Drift materials rest, are grouped together as the Solid formations. Drift deposits include marine, beach and lacustrine deposits, alluvial deposits, hill and mountain slope solifluction wastes largely of periglacial origin, as well as glacio-fluvial deposits resulting from the Pleistocene ice-sheets. Older deposits in the bedded sequence of strata at many levels in the geological column may not be sufficiently unconsolidated to be regarded as sand and gravel. They exist as pebble beds, conglomerates or pebbly sand-stones which may have to be processed by blasting and crushing.

Much useful information, in addition to that given below, on the nature and occurrence of these aggregate-bearing deposits (amongst others) including guidance on their identification and description, will be found in the British Standard Code of Practice for Site Investigations, particularly Section 8 and Appendix G (BS 5930: 1981).

2.4.1. Factors influencing the distribution of sand and gravel in Britain

The far-reaching influence of water in the fluvial and glacial environments on the formation of sand and gravel deposits and associated distinctive landforms is relatively well known in Britain. Merritt (1992) has used these associations to describe British onshore occurrences and their potential as sources of aggregate by reference to three characteristic depositional provinces or terrains.

The terrains, which have contrasting landforms (geomorphology) and Quaternary geology, can be defined by the limits of ice advances at different stages during the Ice Age (Fig. 2.4). The upland terrain (Terrain I) is characterized by fresh, relatively unmodified erosional and depositional landforms and the sand and gravel deposits, part of the so-called 'Newer Drift', tend to have a clear surface expression. They have been exposed to weathering and erosion for only a few thousand years since the ice associated with the Devensian glaciation (the last extensive ice advance) began to retreat from northern England, Wales and Scotland. In northern Britain, ice accumulated again during very cold later periods mainly as isolated corrie and valley glaciers which have left particularly fresh deposits.

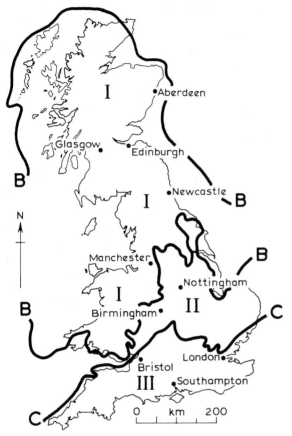

FIG. 2.4. The limits of the three geomorphological terrains (I to III) described in the text. Ice limits (conjectural) after Bowen *et al.* (1986); B–B: Devensian (last major) glaciation (maximum *c.* 18 000 years ago, in Britain. C–C: maximum of the Anglian ('Great Ice Age') glaciation (about 0.5 Ma BP).

The sand and gravel of Terrain II, to the south, covering the English Midlands and East Anglia, has accumulated over a period of up to half a million years, since the climax of the Anglian glaciation which marked the maximum advance of the ice fronts into southern Britain. The geology of the drift deposits in this terrain is complicated. They have been affected by one or more glaciations, several prolonged periods of arctic, periglacial climate and at least two phases of relatively warm and humid interglacial climate. Extensive river deposits came into being, including major terrace spreads both in this terrain and beyond it, in the unglaciated parts of southern Britain, which constitute Terrain III.

There is no direct evidence that southern England was ever covered by ice-sheets although glacial meltwaters certainly flooded in from the north, particularly during the Anglian and later stages, bringing extensive spreads of fluvial gravels and sands which now remain as important resources in the terrace gravels of the Lower Thames Valley and southern Essex. Long exposure of the landscape of southern Britain to periods of periglacial climate interspersed with phases of humid temperate weathering and erosion means that existing high-level superficial spreads of sand and gravel up to several million years old, have been affected by the periodic growth of ground ice in the active layer and redistributed down-slope by processes of mass movement (gelifluction). Many of the older deposits in Terrain III have become deeply weathered and clay-enriched in their upper part, making them generally unattractive for extraction, though concentration of durable rock types such as flint, vein-quartz and quartzite by the removal of degradable lithologies has taken place.

2.4.2. Fluvial deposits

Of all the aggregate-bearing superficial Quaternary deposits in Britain the alluvial deposits (including the river terrace gravels) which have been naturally processed by running water, are the most important, especially in southeast England and the Midlands. They generally carry little overburden and, depending on their location in a valley, they may have a high water-table and can be extracted using wet working techniques. Their particle size distribution and thickness are more consistent and they usually contain a lower proportion of fines—that is silt and clay grades—than the glacial and fluvio-glacial outwash gravels.

2.4.2.1. River channel or alluvial deposits. In the normal course of events, the finest grained products of weathering and erosion (clay and silt) are carried farther afield than the sand and gravel, which may come to rest in stream channels to form a significant resource that may be continuously or seasonally replenished, particularly in large river channels and near mountainous tracts. Many rivers in northern Britain and Wales have gravelly beds and they have been traditionally dredged for aggregate, for example the River Clyde in Lanarkshire and the Ystwyth in west Wales. Problems arising from the lowering of water tables, the pollution of habitats through accelerating siltation and other environmental considerations are increasingly limiting these operations. The middle and lower reaches of many major rivers worldwide are the source of often large volumes of dredged sand suitable for many applications, especially land reclamation and sea defence schemes.

In California and elsewhere, the dredging of aggregate from active river channels ('in-stream mining') contributes significantly to production, although the practice may change the dynamic equilibrium of a river: it may improve land drainage but increase scouring and erosion of the channel, as well as cause damage to bridge abutments, riverside buildings and fishery interests (Sandecki 1989). Predictive modelling and monitoring of stream flow, sediment supply, channel gradient and meandering processes have assisted in the management and control of dredging operations (Schumm 1981; Edgar 1984).

During flooding, sand and gravel as well as the fines may be spread extensively over the flood-plain. Commonly, wide spreads of potentially useful aggregate exist beneath a cover of silty alluvium, particularly in areas where, during the recent geological past, the streams were more vigorous and transported greater volumes of coarser material than they do today.

Meandering and splitting of sediment-choked streams may produce braided flood-plain deposits of gravel and sand, such as those of the River Spey in Scotland. The Kesgrave Sands and Gravels formation, in southern East Anglia, is probably the largest body of sorted fluvial braided sediments in the British Isles (Merritt 1992); it represents the flood-plain deposits of the pre-glacial (that is pre-Anglian) River Thames, which took a much more northerly course than that of the present river (Rose 1983).

2.4.2.2. River terrace deposits. River terraces represent the dissected remains of former flood-plain de-posits. As a river progressively erodes its valley, it cuts down its channel to lower levels and stepped terraces remain on bedrock benches that are characteristically present on both flanks of a valley (Figs 2.5 and 2.6). The terrace deposits, like those of the flood-plain, commonly coarsen upward and are capped by clayey and silty material. However, the higher, older terraces having been subjected to processes of weathering and erosion for longer, characteristically carry less residual overbur-den (though possibly some later spreads of wind-blown sand or silt). This may contain significantly reduced thicknesses of sand and gravel and the particles may be contaminated by weathering products, such as clay and iron oxides by leaching. The material in the oldest terraces may be useful only as low-quality aggregate, particularly where the gravel itself includes rock types that are susceptible to weathering.

Although flood-plain and terrace gravels are particu-larly favoured sources of aggregate, they are nevertheless subject to unpredictable discontinuities and variations in quality. The persistent changes in the location of the river channel after flooding and the meandering and braiding of the streams, result in clay, silt, sand and even gravel-filled channels, scour-hollows (Berry 1979) and washouts, often of wide extent (Fig. 2.7). Indeed, where a river catchment contains easily degraded rocks, such as mudstone, weak siltstone, sandstone and coarse-grained feldspathic rocks, potentially useful aggregate-bearing deposits may be generally lacking, as for example, in the terraces of the central Wealden rivers of Sussex and

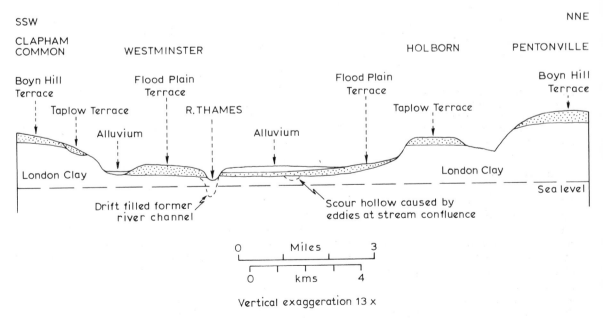

FIG. 2.5. Idealized cross section of the Thames Valley in central London showing the relationship between the major river terrace deposits and the alluvium of the present river.

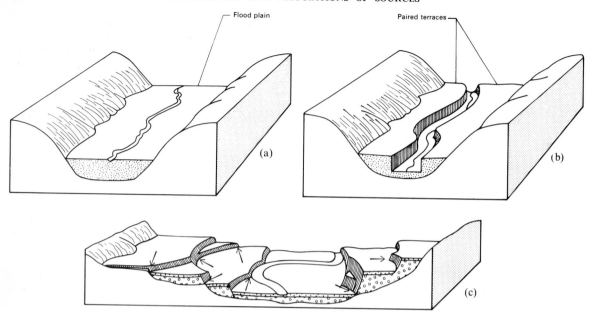

FIG. 2.6. The formation of river terraces. (a) Deposition of valley-floor deposits. (b) Erosion of deposits leaving remnants of old flood plain as paired terraces. (c) Unpaired terraces may result from the effects of downward and lateral erosion; the lateral migration of the stream may be arrested when it intercepts resistant bedrock. After Leet *et al.* (1978).

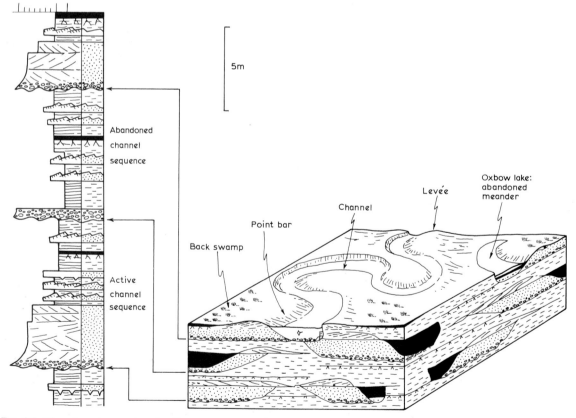

FIG. 2.7. The sub-environments and sedimentary sequence of an alluvial flood plain cut by a meandering river channel (from Selley 1982).

Kent. In general, the composition of the sand and gravel in the upper parts of a river basin reflects that of the rocks in the uplands drained by its tributaries. The extensively worked gravels of the Thames in the vicinity of Oxford are largely derived from the Jurassic oolitic and shelly limestones of the Cotswolds (Cullimore *et al.* 1976; Hopson 1982) with only small fractions of quartzite and other rock types. Thus, they have provided somewhat less attractive concreting aggregates than the predominantly flint gravels of the middle and lower reaches of that river and of many others in southeast England, which drain the chalk uplands or the predominantly flinty drifts that mask them (Squirrell 1976, p. 4; 1978, p. 6). In terms of national importance, the terraces of the River Trent and its tributaries are second only to those of the Thames valley as sources of good-quality aggregate; they contain a high proportion of moderately well sorted pebbles mainly of durable quartzite derived from the Triassic 'Bunter' Pebble Beds of the north Midlands. Contamination of the gravels by weaker rock material derived from tributary catchments and other drift deposits is low.

2.4.2.3. Alluvial fans. An alluvial fan or alluvial cone is formed when a stream carrying large volumes of sand and gravel, often from a glacial upland, enters an adjacent valley or plain and, although the surface of the fan-shaped body characteristically slopes gently, the deposit of sand and gravel at the proximal end (upper fan, Fig. 2.8) may be thick. Because of frequent shifting of the distributary streams, fan deposits ordinarily contain lenticular beds and tongues of poorly sorted sand and gravel interbedded with varying, though usually small, proportions of silt and clay. The rock particles (clasts)

are generally subangular to subrounded and in large fans, much of the fine material may have been washed far afield (Fig. 2.8). Whereas fluvial fan deposits are characteristically of limited extent and have clast-supported and dense fabrics, fans found in more hilly upland terrains, for example in northern Britain, are likely to contain more heterogeneous, largely matrix-supported, silty and clay-contaminated deposits derived from sheet floods and debris flows.

2.4.3. Glacial deposits

Glacial deposits are commonly much less predictable than alluvial deposits in almost every respect. The shape of the aggregate-bearing bodies associated with glacial till (boulder clay) and glaciofluvial outwash, their particle-size distribution, particle shape and composition, thickness and extent, vary widely. Equally, the landforms associated with the accumulation of these deposits and from erosion by glacial ice, are distinctive (Figs 2.9, 2.10 and 2.11). The part that water has played in the deposition of the sediments (and hence, their usefulness as a source of natural aggregate) is the most important criterion in their grain size classification.

Thus, till, which has been formed directly from the ice without the intervention of water in quantity, is unstratified and unsorted material embodying all size grades from clay to boulders. Because of this mode of origin, till is unlikely to provide a potential source of aggregate, unless the matrix is predominantly sandy rather than clayey (Aitken *et al.* 1979). Morainic drift or hummocky moraine, which occupy extensive 'moundy' tracts in

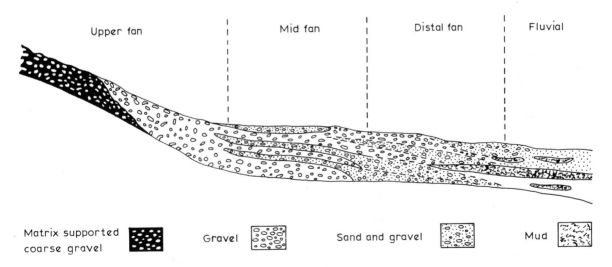

Fig. 2.8. Alluvial fan spread on a plain by a river carrying debris from an upland. Upper fan, depending on the climate, may have clast-supported, though most typically matrix-supported sediments; sheet-like gravelly and sandy deposits characterize the mid-fan; finer grades are typical of the distal fan and fluvial extremity. After Reineck & Singh (1980).

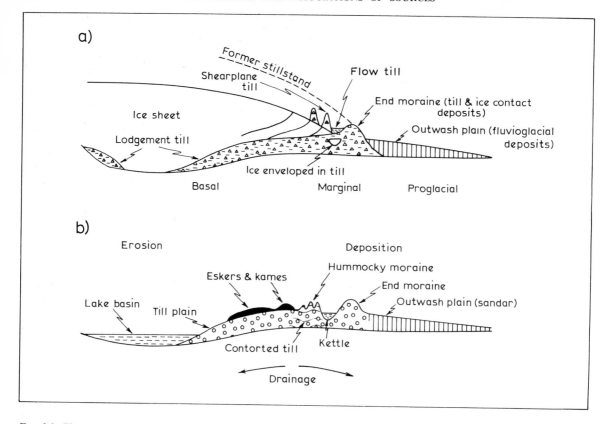

FIG. 2.9. The relationship between the various glacial materials and landforms associated with ice standstill and retreat (see Fig. 2.11 also). After West (1977). (a) The location of basal, marginal and proglacial deposition near the maximum extension of an ice sheet. (b) After retreat of the ice, till and ice-contact deposits remain.

northern Scotland and North Wales, are characteristically disordered, heterogeneous mixtures of particulate, vaguely stratified and cohesive, clay-bound deposits, also of low aggregate potential. Similar, but smooth, oval-shaped mounds of till or englacial debris, known as drumlins, may rise as much as 30 m above the general terrain: they may be moulded over an upstanding core of solid rock (a roche moutonnée when exposed), their long axes being characteristically aligned with the direction of ice movement.

On the other hand, sediments of former glacial outwash plains (sandar), which have been carried from the ice front by melt-water and then laid down in fairly well sorted, stratified deposits, provide relatively good prospects (Fig. 2.12). Between these two types of deposits, roughly stratified ice-contact deposits (such as kames and eskers) constructed near or within the ice and washed to some extent by melt-water, also provide potential sources of aggregate.

2.4.3.1. Moundy (mound-like) glaciofluvial deposits: eskers, kames and kame-terraces.
Isolated, sinuous eskers (linear or beaded, steep-sided ridges) occur in upland terrains, but they are commonly less than 10 m high and typically of poorly sorted, coarse to very coarse debris emplaced by streams under or within glacier ice. Eskers with a better commercial potential tend to have formed relatively late in the decay of an ice-sheet in valleys or on lower-lying ground where they may form laterally extensive complexes of eskers and kames. Many systems mark the conjunction of distinct ice streams or of former ice-sheets, for example, at Carstairs in Lanarkshire (Laxton & Nickless 1979) and the Brampton Esker/Kame Complex in Cumbria (Jackson 1979). A kame is an irregularly shaped, rounded mound of sand and gravel formed mainly of water-sorted sediments within or immediately adjacent to a cavity in an ice body.

The sediments forming the larger esker and kame systems were partly laid down in ice-walled channels, cavities and tunnels, and partly as deltas in temporary ice-walled or ice-marginal lakes. Rapid changes in depositional environment during their formation have resulted in particularly heterogeneous deposits that contain clasts of a wide range of particle size. This heterogeneity, coupled with the great thickness (>40 m) of some of these deposits, can make this type of resource very attractive to the industry because a broad range of

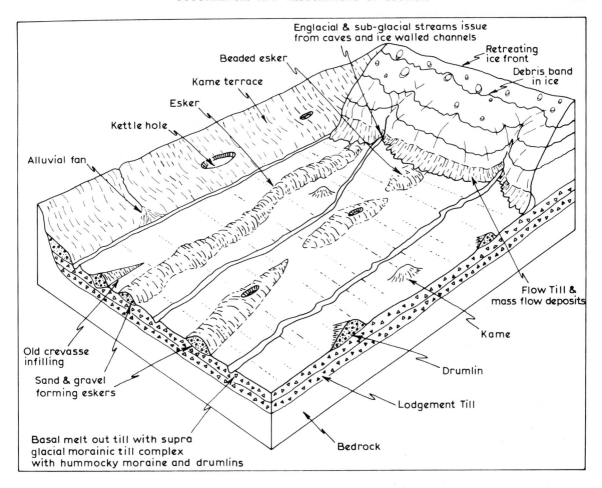

FIG. 2.10. Formation of kames and eskers. After Fookes *et al.* (1975).

end-use specifications can be met. The Carstairs complex of ridges, for example, has central, linear cores of clast-supported, often matrix-rich, cobble gravel flanked and partially overlapped by much better-sorted, cleaner, more sandy material.

Many moundy deposits of sand and gravel identified on geological maps as glaciofluvial in origin seem to have accumulated largely as deltas in ice-marginal lakes. They coarsen upward from clayey silt through sands to coarse clean gravel, and form flat-topped mounds (kame-plateaux), sometimes with organic silts and sands occupying kettle-holes in their surface. Such glacio-deltaic deposits are reported in the upper valley of the River Irvine in Ayrshire (Nickless *et al.* 1978) at Brack-letter, near Fort William (Peacock & Cornish 1989) and many other localities throughout the Scottish Highlands.

2.4.3.2. Terraced glaciofluvial deposits: outwash (sandar) and fans. In general, outwash debris decreases in particle size with the distance it has been carried from the ice-

front and varies in lithological composition according to the provenance of the ice-sheet and the range of rock types it has incorporated. In upland terrains, glacio-fluvial terraces may have been formed in contact with glacier ice (as kame terraces), and tend to be coarse, poorly sorted and heterogeneous deposits often inter-stratified with beds of cohesive till-like mass-flow ma-terial. Unlike fluvial terraces, they may also be pitted with kettle-holes which cause considerable thinning of the sand and gravel locally. Nevertheless, terraced glaciofluvial deposits are much sought after as sources of coarse aggregate: the outwash fan-delta at Wrexham, Clwyd (Wilson *et al.* 1982; Thomas 1985) extends to more than 40 km². The deposits become finer eastward from the Welsh upland and they coarsen upward, suggesting that the fan grew out into shallow water (Dunkley 1981).

In the glacial terrain of the Midlands and East Anglia, the extent of the outwash deposits, the degree of sorting and their thickness depend on the scale and duration of

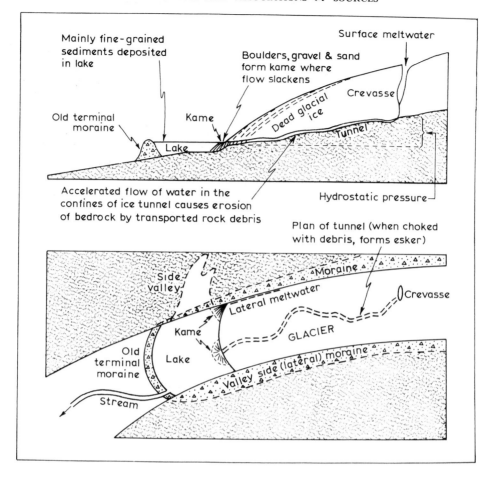

FIG. 2.11. Idealized glaciofluvial and ice contact landforms. After Fookes *et al.* (1975).

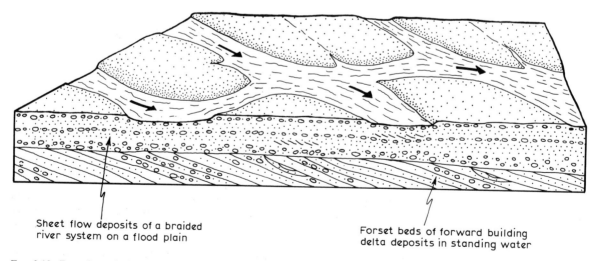

FIG. 2.12. Deposits typical of a glaciofluvial delta (infilling a proglacial lake) which has been buried by continued influx of gravel and sand carried by a braided river system. After Clemmensen & Honmark-Nielsen (1981).

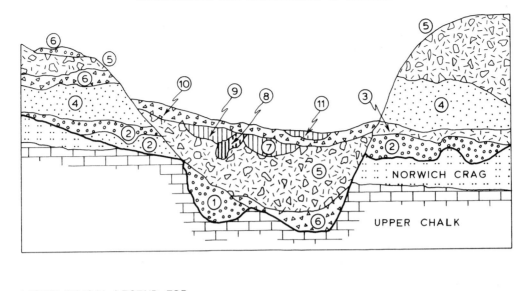

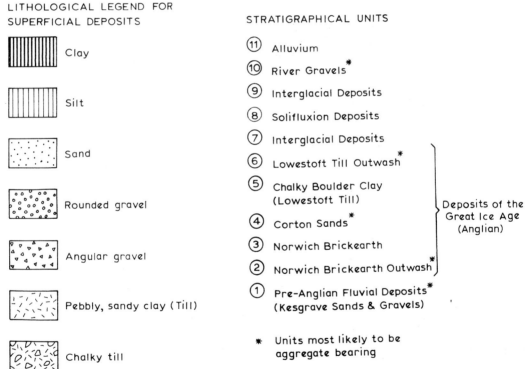

LITHOLOGICAL LEGEND FOR
SUPERFICIAL DEPOSITS

Clay

Silt

Sand

Rounded gravel

Angular gravel

Pebbly, sandy clay (Till)

Chalky till

STRATIGRAPHICAL UNITS

⑪ Alluvium

⑩ River Gravels*

⑨ Interglacial Deposits

⑧ Solifluxion Deposits

⑦ Interglacial Deposits

⑥ Lowestoft Till Outwash*

⑤ Chalky Boulder Clay
(Lowestoft Till)

④ Corton Sands*

③ Norwich Brickearth

② Norwich Brickearth Outwash*

① Pre-Anglian Fluvial Deposits*
(Kesgrave Sands & Gravels)

} Deposits of the
Great Ice Age
(Anglian)

* Units most likely to be
aggregate bearing

FIG. 2.13. Schematic section illustrating relationships within the superficial (drift) deposits of east central Norfolk, England.

glacial and glaciofluvial activity, the waxing and waning of the glaciers and ice-fields and the consequent advances and retreats of the glacial and periglacial climatic zones and their associated depositional environments. Gravels may, therefore, pass laterally into tills of the same glacial episode over several kilometres, they may be sandwiched between materials from earlier and later ice advances, or intermixed and contorted by the effects of readvancing ice or of deep freezing of the ground (cryoturbation). In East Anglia and Essex, spreads of chalky till in the form of basal melt-out and lodgement till are generally, though not invariably, underlain by outwash sheets or otherwise associated with irregular masses of *glacial sand and gravel* (Nickless 1971; Clarke

1975). An impression of the complexity of depositional associations in glacial deposits in northern East Anglia is shown in Fig. 2.13. In southern East Anglia, the deposition of sands and gravels of the Kesgrave Formation (Rose & Allen 1979), probably by a braided river, the proto-Thames, preceded the ice-advance of the Anglian glaciation, and so the resource is largely concealed beneath till. The Kesgrave deposits are generally moderately well sorted, free from silt and clay and of good concreting quality, comprising mainly flint, quartzite and vein-quartz pebbles in pale, micaceous quartzose sand. It constitutes a major resource and is probably the largest body of sorted sediment of Quaternary age in Britain.

In central southern England, there are extensive spreads of sand and gravel of uncertain age or origin called Plateau Gravel on Geological Survey maps, a term which probably includes gravels of glacial, fluvioglacial and fluvial provenances.

2.4.3.3. Periglacial phenomena and deposits. The term 'periglacial' denotes climatic and ground conditions peripheral to active glaciation, under which frost action is the predominant weathering process. Frost shattering of rocks and deep freezing of the ground result in the downslope movement of the weathering products, some of which may be useful as a source of aggregate. Periglacial processes are associated with very cold climatic conditions such as those near the margins of glacial ice in the polar regions. Approximately one-fifth of the Earth's surface is currently underlain by permanently frozen ground (permafrost) and there is evidence in the glacial deposits of the northern hemisphere that during the Pleistocene the area affected by cold climates was much greater.

Most periglacial effects from the Pleistocene glaciations are well preserved in southern and eastern England between the limits of the last (Devensian) glaciation and the wind-blown silt (loess, brickearth) and sand (cover-sand, dunes) belts of northern and central Europe, but they are not restricted to this area: periglacial phenomena can be found over the whole of Britain because the periglacial environment moved progressively northward as the ice front retreated. Periglacial phenomena are, however, more commonly preserved and more evident in the south in Terrains II and III (see §2.4.1). In the unglaciated terrains of southern Britain (and elsewhere) the highest (oldest) river terraces merge with widespread deposits of Plateau-, Hill- or Pebble-Gravel, and like those described variously on Geological Survey maps as Taele Gravel, Downwash Gravels, Combe Deposits and Head are commonly too clayey to be worked for other than common fill or 'hoggin'.

2.4.3.4. Screes, block-fields and head deposits. Repeated freezing and thawing breaks off flakes and fragments from exposed rock surfaces by 'ice-wedging' in fractures and joints and by inducing differential movements in the rock mass. The mechanical disintegration of rocks in upland areas may produce large amounts of predominantly angular rock debris or talus. In the absence of running water and where slopes are steep, large-scale accumulations of debris near to the angle of rest (*screes*) may provide a ready source of coarse aggregate material, though it must be remembered that it may have been adversely affected by long exposure to weathering and any disturbance by working may render the loose material unstable and therefore hazardous. Where the ground is flatter, frost-shattering may give rise to *block-fields* of angular stones which may migrate only slowly downslope in response to gravity, if at all, as the result of heaving by ice crystals, thawing, spalling and the alignment of the fragments into patterned ground.

In soft-rock terrains, when climatic conditions are or have been such that little or no running water is available and the ground is subjected to alternate freezing and thawing, surface and near-surface materials may creep down-slope (solifluct), and form a structureless, commonly crudely stratified, deposit termed *head*. Such debris from local formations may be partly weathered and contain useful material where it is derived from high-level terrace or plateau gravels, for example, the so-called Downwash Gravels in the Aldershot district (Dines & Edmunds 1929; Clarke *et al.* 1979, 1980). In the vicinity of Chelmsford, Essex, gravelly head of late Pleistocene age is widespread but so heavily contaminated by clay as to be of little use as aggregate and this is commonly so in present-day periglacial environments.

The effects of periglacial freeze–thaw phenomena on the distribution of potentially useful aggregate materials may be far reaching. They may generally disrupt and redistribute existing deposits through the development of patterned ground by ice-wedging, mix deposits by frost heaving and sub-surface contortions, form deep pockets of gravel and sand in clay formations mobilized by the growth of ice crystals (cryoturbation), and deposits may be spread out on slopes as the result of downhill solifluction and thinning of hill cappings by soil creep. Although evidence of small-scale and post-depositional disturbances of incoherent deposits by frost-heaving is fairly common-place, large-scale diapiric phenomena, affecting the distribution of sand and gravel deposits are much less so. On Danbury Hill near Chelmsford, Essex, however, a fluvio-glacial outwash sheet overlying soft bedrock (London Clay) has been thrown into large-scale compressional folds of some 30 m amplitude as the result of frost heaving in periglacial conditions (Fig. 2.14).

2.4.4. Coastal deposits

Coastal deposits, as distinct from the 'terrestrial' gravels

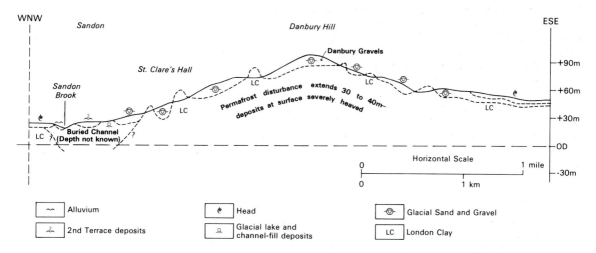

FIG. 2.14. Geological sketch section across the area of Danbury Hill, east of Chelmsford, Essex, showing the effect of large-scale frost heaving on the distribution of superficial deposits (Clarke 1975).

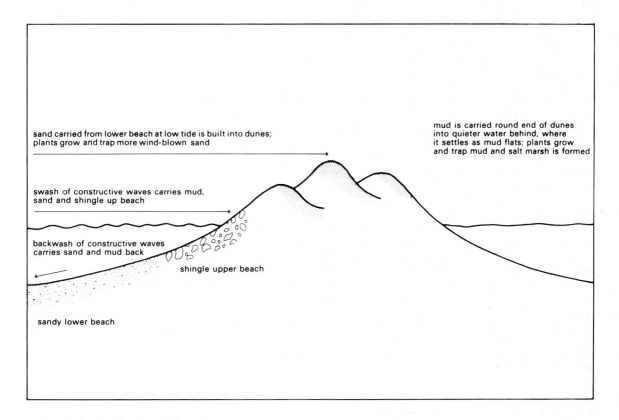

FIG. 2.15. Shoreline depositional features.

described above, accumulate near the margins of permanent water bodies, between the lowest low tide mark and the top of the storm beach, as the result of wave action on the rocky or debris-strewn shores of large lakes, estuaries and the sea. Some material derived by denudation from land areas may be deposited near a coast, the coarse fraction contributing to beach shingle, where the energy of breaking waves will tend to build a storm beach above normal high water level (Fig. 2.15). The deposits may be augmented by ice-rafted dropstones and by rock ballast formerly jettisoned by sea-going boats in shallow water prior to taking on cargoes. Because of the erosive and winnowing action of waves and currents, cobbles and pebbles tend to be swept high onto the coast (back-shore) and the sands and finer particles out to sea. Beach gravels are, therefore, commonly strongly localized vertically but laterally extensive along the shore and they are characteristically well rounded and well sorted both in terms of particle size distribution and shape (discoid pebbles characterize beaches fed by flaggy or lath-shaped rock debris); beach gravels also reduce in grain-size from the top of the beach into deep water so that on exposed shores, a stable beach will rarely contain material finer than medium sand (about 0.2 mm). Movement of materials also takes place along the shore by the process of long-shore drifting and deposits accumulate in ridges and bars, which in particular circumstances may coalesce to form extensive shingle ridge deposits (such as that at Aldeburgh, Suffolk, and the complex at Dungeness, Kent) or influenced by long-shore drifting and winnowing, they may demonstrate a progressive gradation from coarse to fine-grained deposits along a beach. For example, Chesil Beach extends 24 km from the Isle of Portland to Burton Bradstock, Dorset, grading from boulders to fine gravel and sand westward.

The extraction of aggregate from present-day beach and near-shore deposits must be approached with care; there may exist a very delicate balance between erosion and accretion which might be upset if the supply of material is changed whether by the construction of sea defences (such as a sea wall, or the emplacement of groynes) or by the removal of aggregate by digging from beaches, foreshore or off-shore zones.

Fluctuations in sea level relative to the land have caused beach deposits to be drowned (see below) or raised. Raised beaches are common in Scotland because the upward movements of the land in response to the removal by melting of the late glacial ice-sheets has been greater than the consequential rises in sea level. The late-glacial beaches were the first to emerge. They are associated with spreads of glaciofluvial outwash so that they are generally more heterogeneous, rest at a higher level and hence are more commonly exploited than the predominantly more cobbly post-glacial beaches. Parts of the Ayrshire coastal plain and the firths of Tay and Forth have late-glacial beaches but the largest resources occur where glacial meltwaters entered the sea to form

deltas, as for example, at Beauly, Inverness-shire and at Kyleakin, on Skye, where cross-stratified pebbly sands are overlain by clast-supported gravels (Mykura *et al.* 1978). In the English Fens, raised beach deposits of the Wash, together with extensive spreads of river terrace gravel, constitute a significant resource at Market Deeping in Lincolnshire, around March, Cambridgeshire, and elsewhere beneath the fenland.

2.4.5. Marine deposits

It is likely that many gravels found beneath the shallow seas well away from the present coastlines were originally laid as beach, fluvial or fluvio-glacial deposits which have been drowned by the general post-glacial (Flandrian) rise in sea level. The approximate limits of the maximum ice cover on land as well as offshore around the coasts of the British Isles during the major glacial phases of the Ice Age (Quaternary), indicate that the Western Approaches, the English Channel and Thames Estuary have not been glaciated and so do not contain the glacial deposits, such as boulder clay (till) or morainic deposits, which are widespread around the Northeast Coast, Scotland, Northern and Southern Irish Sea areas. However, glaciofluvial sands, gravels and cobbly deposits were laid by meltwaters around the wasting margins of ice fields onto the present-day onshore and offshore areas alike (the latter having been drained as the result of the worldwide drop in sea levels arising from the growth of the polar ice caps). Although potential coarse aggregate deposits are commonly restricted in size (eskers, fans) some more extensive spreads remain, such as the outwash sands of the Dogger Bank (Oele 1971) and the gravelly sands of East Anglia (Harrison 1988) and around Japan (Narumi 1989).

Fluctuations in the level of the sea at different times during the Quaternary mean that cycles of fluvial erosion and deposition in response to changes in base level will have given rise at times to the cutting of deep channels and valleys on the sea floor and at other times to extensive spreads of gravels, sands and muds. The definition of the distribution and stratigraphy of the resulting terrace remnants, now below sea level, and the tracing of buried channels offshore and their relations to the glaciofluvial spreads, is rendered more difficult by the present-day movement of sand and gravel by wave and tidal current action in the nearshore and offshore zones. The older deposits have also undergone many cycles of reworking brought about by fluctuations in sea level since they were laid down. Whilst sand may migrate as sand-waves on the shallow sea floor (to depths of 180 m or so) under the influence of currents with velocities in excess of about 27 km/h, it seems unlikely that pebbles will do so on a large scale in currents of less than 75 km/h though it is thought that concentrations of

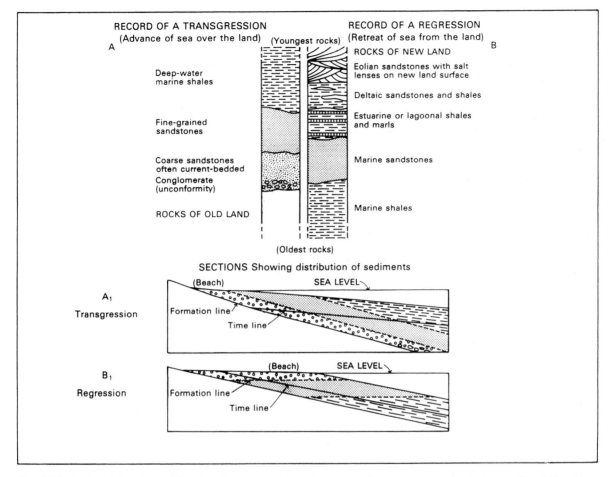

FIG. 2.16. Sea-board deposits resulting from the transgression and regression of the sea, as seen in borehole cores (A and B) and in idealized horizontal sections (A$_1$ and B$_1$). Note that in the sections lines parallel to the sea-bed are time lines as they join sediments deposited contemporaneously; lines essentially parallel to gravel, sand and clay deposits are formation lines and are those commonly shown on geological survey maps.

gravel result from submarine erosion of till or other gravelly deposits and the winnowing of fine sediment. Offshore deposits may be replenished, often seasonally, by debris from the marine erosion of coastal deposits and from subaerial and glacial erosion of near-shore land areas of high relief. The material may be transported and distributed over considerable distances by fluvial and tidal currents (Nunny & Chillingworth 1986).

2.4.6. Gravels in the solid formations

Although modern shoreline gravels account for only a small proportion of available resources because they are confined to relatively narrow linear tracts, many of the sand and gravel deposits in the 'solid' rock sequence take the form of basal pebble beds. Their origin has been traditionally attributed to the transgression of shoreline gravels with a rise in sea level, resulting in the deposition

of a relatively thin sheet of basal gravel, which may be indurated or cemented to form a conglomerate. The Tertiary Blackheath Beds in north Surrey and the Bovey Beds near Newton Abbot, Devon, which have been worked on a small scale, are examples. North of Glasgow, two lenticular pebbly beds belonging to the Carboniferous Douglas Muir Quartz-conglomerate (Paterson & Hall 1986) have been quarried as premium grade low-shrinkage aggregate.

Conversely, when deposits are laid down on a slowly rising sea-floor, successive layers are related such that coarser grades come to rest on the finer parts of older layers as the sea regresses from the land. The Westleton Beds of Suffolk (Hey 1967; Hey & Auton 1988) are beach-plain gravels, containing abundant near-spherical pebbles of black flint derived from Tertiary strata, formed during the regression of the sea in which the Pliocene Crags of East Anglia were laid down. The Crags constitute a large resource of marine and estuarine

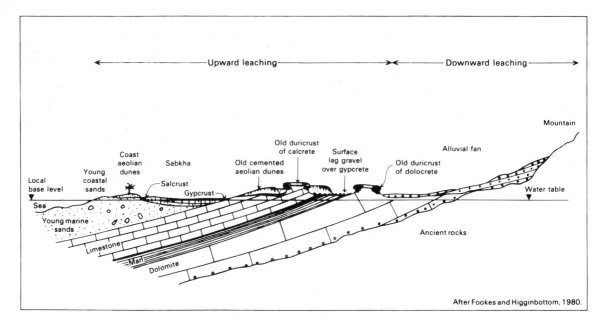

Fig. 2.17. Idealized section from desert coast to mountain interior showing typical associations of landforms and superficial deposits. After Fookes & Higginbottom (1980).

sand extending westward into Hertfordshire but partially concealed beneath glaciofluvial sand and gravel, till and deposits of the Kesgrave Formation (Gibbard & Zalasiewicz 1988). Sand predominates over gravel in the Crags (Hollyer & Allender 1982) and much of the resource is contaminated by shell debris and iron-staining. The record of marine transgression and regression as demonstrated in a borehole core is shown in Fig. 2.16.

Perhaps the largest volumes of gravelly sediments have been formed as alluvial fans or deltas under arid or semi-arid conditions, particularly where gravel-carrying torrents debouched into an intermontane tract. The Triassic 'Bunter' Pebble Beds of the Sherwood Sandstone Group of the north Midlands and the Budleigh Salterton Beds of approximately the same age in east Devon are the main source of gravel from pre-Quaternary formations in Britain. The proportion of conglomeratic material relative to largely pebble-free sandstone varies widely and the workings tend to exploit only the most pebbly developments, sand being generally regarded as a secondary product. The predominant pebbles are very hard, well rounded, buff to liver-coloured quartzite held in a loosely cemented sandy matrix (Thompson 1970; Piper 1982). They are processed by light crushing and washing to remove the fines, which occur mainly as green mudstone seams and sand. More strongly indurated conglomerates may be potentially workable when weathered or affected by periglacial conditions. Weathered Devonian conglomerates are worked on a small scale in Strathmore, Scotland.

2.5. Aggregate materials in desert regions

The effects of climate and groundwater conditions on the geological materials in an arid region, such as the Middle East where much experience on the use of indigenous aggregates has accumulated (Fookes & Higginbottom 1980), are mechanical (thermal fracturing, wind erosion) and chemical. The widespread excess of evaporation over rainfall induces persistent upward leaching of salts, particularly carbonates, sulphates and chlorides, causing the mechanical disintegration of porous rocks through the growth of crystals in the pores.

Where a high saline water table is present as in the coastal sabkhas and salinas of the desert interior, 'duricrusts', composed of substances transported by solution in the pore fluids, may be developed. The most widespread crusts consist of calcium and calcium-magnesium carbonates ('calcrete' and 'dolocrete'), calcium sulphate ('gypcrete', or 'gypcrust' where weakly cemented) and sodium chloride ('salcrust').

Although the development of a duricrust may effectively strengthen the uppermost few metres of an originally weak material, such as the porous Eocene limestones on the western and southern shores of The Gulf, the immediately underlying leached layer may be rendered weaker and more porous than the unaltered parent material. More commonly in cement-bound materials the build-up of salts is deleterious in aggregates

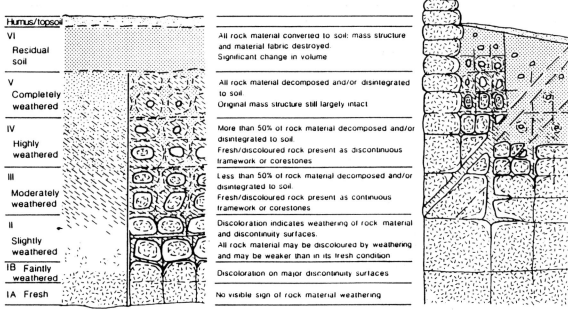

Humus/topsoil	
VI Residual soil	All rock material converted to soil: mass structure and material fabric destroyed. Significant change in volume.
V Completely weathered	All rock material decomposed and/or disintegrated to soil. Original mass structure still largely intact.
IV Highly weathered	More than 50% of rock material decomposed and/or disintegrated to soil. Fresh/discoloured rock present as discontinuous framework or corestones.
III Moderately weathered	Less than 50% of rock material decomposed and/or disintegrated to soil. Fresh/discoloured rock present as continuous framework or corestones.
II Slightly weathered	Discoloration indicates weathering of rock material and discontinuity surfaces. All rock material may be discoloured by weathering and may be weaker than in its fresh condition.
IB Faintly weathered	Discoloration on major discontinuity surfaces
IA Fresh	No visible sign of rock material weathering

A. Idealised weathering profiles – without corestones (left) and with corestones (right)

Rock decomposed to soil
Weathered / disintegrated rock
Rock discoloured by weathering
Fresh rock

B. Example of a complex profile with corestones

Fig. 2.18. Diagrammatic weathering profiles of jointed and faulted (igneous) rock bodies. The weathering grade is indicated at left (see Table 2.5). After Geological Society Engineering Group Working Party Report (1990).

for use in concrete, although they may be usable in unbound applications and in bituminous mixes. The typical distribution of some common duricrusts is illustrated in the idealized section shown in Fig. 2.17 which also shows the distinction between areas of upward and downward leaching.

Downward leaching commonly takes place where periodic flooding in the mountains and foothills and associated wadis effectively prevents the accumulation of sulphates and chlorides, though cementation by the less soluble carbonates may still occur in these zones of modern deposition, particularly in the coarse deposits which are not moved by the periodic floods. Thus, the active wadis in the mountains and parts of their alluvial fans where they open out on to the piedmont are the main sources of well graded, relatively clean sand and gravel. The deposits are generally poorly sorted, occurring as torrent-bedded localized spreads, but they can yield the most acceptable 'all-in' natural aggregate in a desert region. The wind-blown dune sands of the deep interior of deserts, consisting predominantly of silica and silicate lithic grains, are commonly too fine-grained, rounded and dusty to be attractive for aggregate uses.

The carbonate sands of coastal origin, which comprise the water-worn debris of modern marine organisms, are

more acceptable, despite the frequency of porous, sometimes hollow shells contaminated by evaporite salts. In some areas, the carbonate sands of the coastal dunes have contributed, through the action of onshore winds, to the aeolian dunes farther inland, where, with increasing distance from the sea-board sabkhas, contamination by sulphates and particularly by chlorides tends to decrease. Selective working of the lower, more coarse-grained parts of dunes and blending dune sand with other material, such as crushed-rock sand, can yield commercially acceptable fine aggregate, provided that the crushed component possesses reasonably good particle shape, does not increase the concentration of chemical contaminants and does not contain excessive amounts of fines.

Of the hard rock sources in deserts, many of the calcretes suffer from the variable and random nature of the hardening process as well as potentially serious chemical problems; dense crystalline nodules may be surrounded by weak absorptive stone or contain veins of clay with pronounced selling properties, which must be removed from the aggregate. In semi-arid areas, red clay soils ('terra rossa') may cover the hardened ground and invade solution-widened joints in limestone terrains. Generally speaking, the most promising hard rock

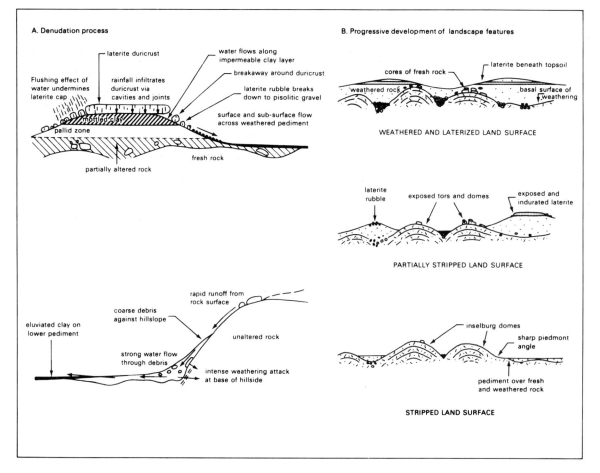

FIG. 2.19. Possible aggregate sources in a landscape subject to a seasonal tropical climate (Savanna type, between the afforested humid tropics and the deserts). After Thomas (1971).

sources in arid regions are the igneous and metamorphic rocks, which have good soundness, aggregate crushing and absorption characteristics, when unweathered.

2.6. Aggregate materials in tropical regions

In hot, wet areas the decomposition of rocks through chemical weathering is intense, penetrates to greater depths than in other climatic conditions and generally exceeds the effects of physical disintegration. In the inter-tropical zone weathering of rock produces clay-rich weathering mantles generally up to 100 metres deep and exceptionally very much more (Fookes *et al.* 1971), and fresh, unweathered and unaltered bedrock which might be expected to yield aggregate is commonly not readily accessible (but see below).

The distinction between soil and the weathering mantle is hard to draw (Geological Society Engineering Group Report 1990). The weathered rock that is still in place tends to retain features of the unweathered rock and is separated from the overlying loose mantle of more or less transported material by stone lines of varied composition and controversial origin. In strictly residual soils, weathering attacks the rock by progressively permeating joint-bounded blocks, leaving kernels of fresh material (corestones) within envelopes of decomposed rock. Further attack reduces the kernels by spheroidal wasting until total decomposition results in the formation of red earth residual soils (Fig. 2.18). In areas with heavy rainfall, dissolved chemicals are leached out and bases such as calcium and magnesium (and even silica) may be removed, leading to higher concentrations of alumina, iron oxides and hydroxides and the formation of clay minerals, such as kaolinite. Layered lateritic soils may have an iron-rich layer which may harden to iron-stone gravel (ferricrete) (West & Dumbleton 1970).

Bauxitic soils may harden to alucrete and soluble silica may be redeposited as silcrete (Summerfield 1983),

TABLE 2.5 *Weathering and alteration grades*

Term	Grade*	Description	Materials characteristics†
Fresh	IA	No visible sign of rock weathering	Aggregate properties not influenced by weathering. Mineral constituents of rock are fresh and sound.
Faintly weathered	IB	Discoloration on major discontinuity (e.g. joint) surfaces	Aggregate properties not significantly influenced by weathering. Mineral constituents sound.
Slightly weathered (this grade is capable of further sub-division)	II	Discoloration indicates weathering of rock material and discontinuity surfaces. All the rock material may be discoloured by weathering and may be somewhat weaker than in its fresh condition.	Aggregate properties may be significantly influenced by weathering. Strength and abrasion characteristics show some weakening. Some alteration of mineral constituents with micro-cracking.
Moderately weathered	III	Less than half of the rock material is decomposed and/or disintegrated to a soil. Fresh or discoloured rock is present either as a continuous framework or as coretones.	Aggregate properties will be significantly influenced by weathering. Soundness characteristics markedly affected. Alternation of mineral constituents common and much micro-cracking.
Highly weathered	IV	More than half of the rock material is decomposed and/or disintegrated to a soil. Fresh or discoloured rock is present either as a discontinuous framework or as corestones.	Not generally suitable for aggregate but may be suitable for lower parts of road pavement and hardcore
Completely weathered	V	All rock material is decomposed and/or disintegrated to soil. The original mass structure is still largely intact.	Not suitable for aggregate, or pavement but may be suitable for select fill
Residual soil	VI	All rock material is converted to soil. The mass structure and material fabric are destroyed. There is a large change in volume, but the soil still has not been significantly transported.	May be suitable for random fill

* After Geological Society (1977).
† After Fookes *et al.* (1971).

especially in well drained situations where the parent material is siliceous and carries little alumina. Reprecipitation of silica may take place also in porous strata below the weathered zone in warm humid conditions, especially where periodic drying out can occur, for example, on the borders of tropical forests. Such hardened layers are commonly exhumed by erosion so that they may form flat-topped relict hills capped by duricrust masses that typically range between 2 m and 10 m in thickness (Fig. 2.19). Most silcretes contain more than 60% SiO_2 and calcretes ('caliche') up to 97% $CaCO_3$ (Goudie 1973) and both are potentially valuable sources of aggregates. However, they are not likely to provide such good quality aggregate material as crushed rock, but an understanding of their formation, variability and distribution may help in the search for the most durable developments (Geological Society Engineering Group Report 1990). It is unlikely that ferricretes and calcretes will be suitable for other than moderately demanding applications in construction and road building: silcretes may be more durable and versatile, however.

Rain forest is developed on a variety of rock types and in a wide range of topographic situations. High plateaux and gently sloping uplands of Africa, the East Indies,

Malaysia, Brazil and other parts of South America (Sanders & Fookes 1970) may be deeply though irregularly weathered, both in depth and laterally. Occasional hills of fresh rock (inselbergs) may rise sharply from a surrounding plain to a height of tens or even hundreds of metres; limestones in particular, in tropical forests, may also give rise to a distinctive landform—the so-called 'haystack hills', and may contain much potentially useful aggregate.

2.7. The effects of alteration and weathering

In some parts of the world, particularly in the tropics and desert regions, local aggregate materials are affected by widely different geological and climatic conditions. They may contain impurities, such as leached and evaporite salts, which would not be expected in unacceptably large concentrations in temperate countries. The physical and chemical stability of rock materials in the ground (and in use) can vary widely: for example, joints and fractures in a source of aggregate in temperate conditions may not raise serious doubts about its poten-

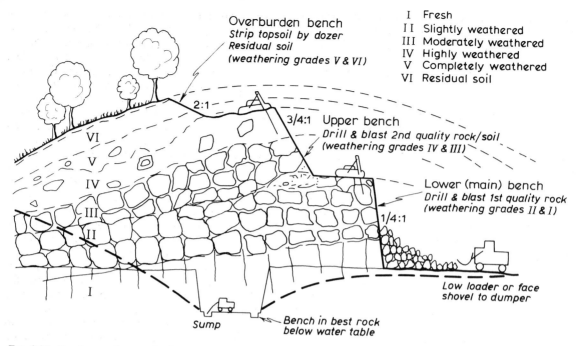

FIG. 2.20. Good quarrying practice in a weathered rock overlain by residual soil (Fookes 1991).

tial suitability (indeed they may assist quarrying and processing) but in tropical conditions they may greatly accelerate the effects of already rapid weathering processes and in a hot arid environment may allow deleterious substances to penetrate into the rock mass. Thus, the recognition of familiar rock types or geological formations is no guarantee that usable aggregates will be obtainable from them. Ideally, only fresh or faintly weathered rock material should be used for aggregate (Table 2.5).

2.7.1. Alteration

Destructive alteration of rocks, as distinct from weathering, arises from internal deep-seated and often wide-scale geochemical processes. For example, at a late stage in the solidification of an igneous rock release of accumulated volatile substances or mineralizing fluids may extensively alter the rock, as a whole by affecting the chemical and hence physical stability of widely distributed minerals, or selectively by invading previously-formed discontinuities in the mass. There may be a gradation from fresh granite to completely kaolinized granite in which the feldspars have been altered to the clay-mineral kaolinite.

Alteration is not necessarily deleterious: the in situ recrystallization of existing rocks due to thermal and regional metamorphism gives rise to a wide variety of rocks, many of which may yield higher-grade aggregate than the unaltered parent material. For example, shales and slates may be recrystallized to become hornfels and, similarly, sandstone may be converted to metamorphic quartzite (§2.2.2).

2.7.2. Weathering

Weathering is brought about by the exposure of rock materials, commonly during long periods of geological time, to the varying climatic conditions at the Earth's surface and various definitions and discussions of the engineering effects of weathering have been published (Weinert 1964; Sanders & Fookes 1970; Dearman 1974; Ollier 1975; Fookes 1980; Fookes et al. 1988; Fookes 1991).

There are two main types of weathering: one dominated by mechanical disintegration, including removal by solifluction, the other by chemical decomposition. Generally, both effects act together but, depending on the climate, either process may be dominant. Mechanical weathering, found particularly in arid or cold climates, results in the widening of discontinuities and the formation of new breaks by rock fracture arising from differential expansion and contraction, wetting and drying and from the effects of repeated freezing and thawing; mineral grains are loosened and often fractured. The crystallization of mineral salts brought near to the surface of rock masses by evaporation and capillarity has similar effects, which must be recognized and such zones avoided, particularly in potential aggregates for use in concrete in desert environments.

Chemical weathering may be much accelerated in humid hot climates and penetrate to depths in excess of 300 m, perhaps as much as 1500 m (Fookes *et al.* 1971). It eventually leads to the decomposition of certain of the silicate minerals to clay minerals: the feldspars and ferro-magnesian minerals in igneous and metamorphic rocks are particularly susceptible, though some minerals, notably quartz, are resistant to attack and may survive unaltered. Dissolution of silica and carbonate cements in sandstones and limestones, in common with chemical weathering generally, commonly results in the progressive discoloration of the rock and the degree of weathering can often be described and assessed subjectively from the change in rock colour. Of the various published engineering classifications of weathering grade (see reviews by Little (1969) and Sanders & Fookes (1970)), those proposed by Weinert (1964), for the field determination of the state of weathering of igneous rocks for use as roadstone in South Africa, and by Fookes *et al.* (1971) for rocks in the Dartmoor area, appear to have general validity. The aggregate classification of Fookes (1980) is recommended and reproduced here (Table 2.5).

Weathering tends to become less with depth but may locally extend along discontinuities deep into otherwise fresh rock and some rock types may be more susceptible to weathering processes than others. The great variability in the depth of weathering in wet tropical regimes imparts a highly irregular profile to the upper surface of the fresh rock and makes the definition of possible quarry sites very uncertain unless a substantial outcrop is actually visible at the surface. Otherwise, extensive drilling and geophysical investigations may be required before accessible, potentially useful rock is located. A representation of good quarrying practice in a weathered rock overlain by residual soil is shown in Fig. 2.20.

Weathering profiles may also be of great antiquity. They may be repeated in a rock sequence and they may not reflect the response of the rocks to the present climate but to previous environments: the contemporaneous weathering of the upper surfaces of successive lava flows to lateritic residual soils or 'boles' provides an example, only the relatively unweathered lavas being quarried for aggregate, as with the Antrim Basalts in Northern Ireland. On the other hand, the breakdown of the matrix by weathering in some sources of aggregate, such as breccia, conglomerate or clay-bound sand, may enhance their value by reducing the costs of extraction, processing or beneficiation. Inland of Peterhead, in Scotland, for example, degraded granite has been worked as a source of fine aggregate in which to bed pipelines and in Strathmore, Old Red Sandstone conglomerates, which were deeply weathered during the Tertiary period, yield gravel.

The record of rock weathering on Dartmoor, in southwest England (Fookes *et al.* 1971) has involved long-term sub-tropical or wet, warm-temperate climatic conditions inherent from their exposure during Tertiary times, as well as moderate to strong mechanical weathering in periglacial conditions during the Quaternary (Table 2.1). In some localities, the rock type (chert, limestone, dolerite, granite) and in others the effects of geological structure and consequential exposure to alteration and weathering, are major factors in the disintegration and decomposition ('rotting') of the rocks. Deep weathering patterns may also be related to the longevity of the topography; for example, high-level erosion surfaces (Fookes *et al.* 1971). However, the deep weathering of granite bedrock at Jos, Nigeria (Ollier 1975), typical of many weathering situations in tropical and southern Africa, is attributed to variations in the bedrock geology rather than to topographic situation.

Although discoloration may be an indication of weathering and alteration in rocks, the extent of the deterioration may not be easily distinguished except by means of a full petrographic analysis of a thin section of the rock. Such an examination should be undertaken to help assess the suitability of the rock for particular aggregate uses as indicated in Chapter 6.

2.8. The influence of geological structure

Structural geology, including rock-structure, embraces the recognition and interpretation of the form, arrangement and internal structure of rock bodies (whether igneous, sedimentary or metamorphic). The influence of geological structure on the character and distribution of aggregate materials forms a very important element in their discovery and appraisal and for the working of quarries.

An understanding of geological structures, whether through field investigations, the use of maps, cross sections, block diagrams or photographs (see Chapter 3) is essential for appraising aggregate-bearing rock units and relating them to the regional geology. More detailed studies of rock structure (or fabric) involving the arrangement of linear, planar or textural elements (represented by such features as bedding planes, platy partings, slaty cleavage, foliation and flow banding in different categories of rock) are likely to provide useful guidance on the potential and quality of rock material for aggregate, as well as indicate potentially unsuitable rock. The definition of weaknesses that may arise from the preferred directions of cleavages or fractures in individual mineral grains and crystals and the recognition of alteration and weathering effects, through the microscopic examination of specially prepared rock slices, may form an important part of the appraisal of aggregate material (French 1991).

2.8.1. Rock structures and geological structures (primary and secondary structures)

Any geological cross section showing sedimentary rocks in various attitudes: flat-lying or inclined, folded or faulted—perhaps in places intruded by igenous rocks, covered by lava flows and contact metamorphosed, represents the geological structure of the rock units (Figs 2.1 and 2.2). Their shapes and attitudes are the result firstly of processes connected with their original formation when their *primary stuctures* (e.g. bedding, rock texture) were developed, and secondly, of all later processes that have affected them, such as mechanical deformation (folding, faulting, rock-cleavage) or chemical reconstitution (some metamorphic rocks), which are regarded as *secondary structures*.

The description of the various structures and discontinuities that might affect a rock mass is the first step in the appraisal of a rock material for any application (whether for the design of a new quarry or to better predict the likely characteristics of an aggregate produced from it, for example) and the data should be assembled in a form amenable to subsequent processing and analysis. A recommended system is that outlined in the description of rock masses for engineering purposes (Geological Society Engineering Group Working Party Report 1977).

2.8.1.1. Depositional structures and rock textures (primary structures) in sedimentary rocks. The most striking feature of most sedimentary rocks is their *bedding or stratification*. An individual *bed* or *stratum* may be distinguished by some over-riding characteristic, such as composition (limestone, sandstone etc.), texture or grade (siltstone, sandstone or conglomerate), hardness, colour or by variations in these features, such as *graded bedding* (Fig. 2.3–2); grains of different sizes have settled at different rates, coarse grains being at the bottom of the bed, finer grains at the top. Where the bedding planes within a bed are inclined fairly regularly to the separation planes between the beds, the structure is known as *cross-bedding* or cross-stratification (Fig. 2.3–7). In large-scale examples, such as the foreset beds in a delta, cross-bedding may be confused with true bedding and lead to the over-estimation of deposit thickness unless the true nature of the 'false-bedding' is recognized (Fig. 2.21). Current-bedding or ripple-bedding is small-scale undulose bedding typical of rapidly deposited sand, giving often interfering ripples. The splitting of slabs of ripple-bedded sandstone characteristically reveals ripple marks. The downstream migration of ripples may produce a succession of miniature foreset beds truncated at the top, after the manner of eroded cross beds (Fig. 2.21) or delta-foresets.

Whilst it is clear in undisturbed horizontal strata that the individual beds rest in a chronological succession of decreasing age one upon the other (the concept of superposition), the original or natural 'way-up' of a sequence of beds that has been folded, faulted or over-turned can also be determined by reference to sedimentary structal features such as those mentioned above. This may be very important in unravelling the geological structure of a tract of country or aggregate prospect.

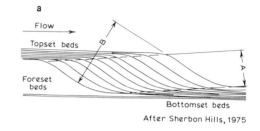

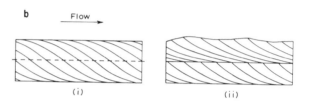

FIG. 2.21. Bedding typical of a delta. (a) The true thickness of the foreset beds is A, not B, which is the sum of apparent bed thicknesses, that might be collected from scattered measurements made without references to the delta structure. (b) Cross-stratified deposit truncated by erosion (to broken line in (i)) and covered by a new cross-bedded unit, producing a composite false-bedded sedimentary structure (ii), which can also be a useful indicator of 'way-up'.

2.8.1.2. Primary structures in igneous rocks. These are mainly recognizable as the features of progressive crystallization of the molten rock: crystals form a meshwork with liquid between the grains and flow structures may be imprinted at any time before final solidification of the melt. Most flow structures are represented by some form of texture, composition or colour banding or layering, or in sub-aqueous lava flows by pillow structure—formed progressively as lava, extruded from cracks in existing pillow-shaped masses, solidified rapidly, building into a closely-knit pile of rock-pillows. In most igneous rock bodies there is commonly a gradation in crystal distribution, resembling graded bedding in sediments, the heavier minerals being concentrated horizontally into the darker bands, often near the base. Layering and other structures may be used in mapping and interpreting the regional structure of large igneous complexes. Similarly, studies of the shape and order of emplacement

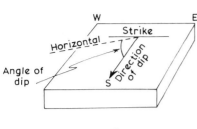

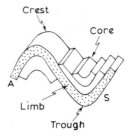

Dip and strike

Antiform (A) and synform (S) nomenclature

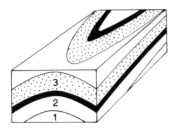

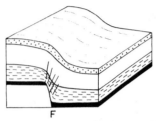

Anticline, gently plunging to lower left showing effect on outcrop pattern

Monocline in surface stratum passing downward into a fault (F)

FIG. 2.22. Dip, strike and common folds.

of pillow lavas can elucidate the chronological succession in laval fields and lead to the identification of particular rock bodies over considerable distances.

Textures and structures due to flow are revealed by the parallel orientation of tabular or platy constituents, such as large crystals (phenocrysts) or fragments of country rock (xenoliths) caught up in the magma or the parallel alignment of elongated crystals, giving flow structure or flow layering. Very commonly such layering is parallel with the contacts of igneous masses with the confining country rocks and so may be used to elucidate the wide-scale structure of large igneous rock bodies.

Quarry engineers should be aware also that layered rocks may have preferred directions of breaking or weakness which may be transferred to any aggregate produced from them. Undesirable platy or elongate fragments may result from the crushing of laminated, closely bedded or strongly layered sedimentary rocks (e.g. siltstone, flaggy limestone), flow-banded fine-grained igneous rocks (rhyolite, basalt) and many of the foliated metamorphic rocks (gneiss, schist) as well as some examples of hornfels and quartzite, which may exhibit aligned joints and fractures even after recrystallization during metamorphism.

The development of fractures during the solidification of igneous rocks is commonplace. Jointing in large intrusions may be widely spaced (1–2 m), but it is typically more frequent in lava flows, dykes and sills (Geological Society Engineering Group Report 1977). *Colum-nar jointing* divides the rock-mass into columns that are ideally hexagonal in cross section (though they may vary from three-sided to eight-sided depending on the distribution of cooling centres) and range from about 1 cm to a few metres in cross section. The long axes of columns are generally at right-angles to cooling surfaces, that is, to the top and bottom of flows and sills and to the walls of dykes. Spheroidal cracking and *cup and ball jointing* (contiguous concave–convex joints) result from lengthwise contraction after the columns have formed. Columnar jointing gives rise to distinctive quarry face and well known natural features like The Giants Causeway in Northern Ireland, the Colonnaded escarpment at The Palisades on the Hudson River in New York State and the sea-cliffs of the Island of Staffa in the Western Isles of Scotland.

In addition to columnar jointing, sub-horizontal *platy jointing* may be developed during cooling in minor igneous intrusions producing slabs a few centimetres thick. However, in major bodies (like granite plutons or batholiths—Fig. 2.1A) flat-lying or gently inclined joints, commonly accompanied by two further sets of vertical or steeply dipping rectangular joints, break the rock-mass into large cuboidal blocks, typically with sides of between 1 and 3 m. Jointing of this kind may be particularly well developed near the roof of a magma chamber; unroofing of such a coarsely jointed rock-mass by weathering and erosion may lead to the formation of block-fields and tors, which may form upstanding features in the landscape. Such primary discontinuities offer pathways for weathering processes and they facilitate quarrying. They are, however, difficult to distinguish from similar (but secondary) jointing arising from later earth movements.

2.8.2. Secondary geological structures

These have affected rocks after, often long after, their formation, commonly as the result of earth movements or tectonic activity. Uplift, tilting, compression, faulting and folding of rocks give rise to typical structures which have a direct influence of the distribution of rock-materials (and of aggregates) at and near the surface of the Earth's crust. The following outline of the more commonplace geological structures may be augmented by reference to appropriate text books and for that reason the complexities of nomenclature and theory will be avoided.

2.8.2.1. Dip and strike. Two fundamental concepts in structural geology are *dip* and *strike*. The maximum slope of a tilted rock-bed is the dip and the compass bearing and angle of declination (measured from the horizontal by means of a clinometer) are the direction and angle of dip respectively. The strike is the bearing of a horizontal line drawn on the bed at right angles to the dip (Fig. 2.22).

2.8.2.2. Folds. Compression of strata, arising from earth movements (or even, near the surface, from the effects of gravity) may induce bending or buckling into *folds*. An arched fold, in which the two sides (limbs) dip away from each other, is an *anticline* (or antiform) and the rocks that form its centre (or *core*) are older than the outer strata. A *syncline* (or synform) has inward-dipping limbs and the strata in the core are younger than those below them. A flexure joining areas of approximately flat-lying beds but at different levels relative to each other is a *monocline* (Fig. 2.22).

Continued and more intense compression accompanied by burial in the Earth's crust may produce more tightly packed structures (such as chevron folds, isoclinal folds). The weaker, more yielding, ductile beds (*incompetent beds*) may accommodate to the shape of the harder, stronger and possibly more brittle beds (the *competent beds*) and as a result distinctive structures may be imprinted onto the rocks. *Fracture cleavage* comprises parallel fracturing in mechanically deformed, incompetent rock, such as a shale folded between stronger beds. The deformation of brittle rock may give rise to *tension gashes* which may be filled by minerals such as quartz or calcite. The relative movement of adjacent beds during folding (bed-over-bed movement) may result in the shearing of weak layers, grooving or polishing of bedding planes or other cracks, together with recrys-

tallization of minerals along them oriented in the direction of movement. Such smoothed or lineated rock surfaces are known as *slickensides*. All of these effects tend to reduce the usefulness of the rocks for aggregate.

Deformation by extension may result in the breaking or pinching of competent beds into rod-like, sausage-shaped pieces (*boudins*) parallel with the strike, the adjacent less competent material having been squeezed into the gaps. This structure is common in strongly deformed sedimentary and metamorphic rocks which can nevertheless yield useful aggregate materials, worked selectively if necessary.

All of these structures can arise from the application of forces mainly (though not exclusively) tangential to the Earth's surface, subjecting rocks to compression, tension and shear stresses in the folding processes at different levels in the crust. Folds vary from small, simple and a few metres in extent to very large, complicated, compound and many kilometres across; they may include folded mountain chains made of many folds (like the Andes, Himalayas and the Alps) or large, open flexures like the Paris and London basins or the Wealden dome of southeast England.

2.8.2.3. Faults and joints. The development of fractures, including faults and joints in the rocks of the Earth's crust may be associated with folding and buckling, or with other tectonic events. *Faults* are fractures along which there has been displacement of the two sides of the break; *joints* are those where no perceptible displacement has taken place. Groups of faults and sets of joints may both form patterns from which the stresses that caused them (and may have affected the strength of the rocks locally) may be deduced.

Three main kinds of faults may be recognized: namely, normal faults, reverse (or thrust) faults and strike-slip (tear, transcurrent or wrench) faults. Their effects can best be appreciated by reference to diagrams (Fig. 2.23). A fault in which the displacement of strata lying above an inclined fault is downward relative to adjacent strata, is a *normal fault* (Fig. 2.23a) and a *reverse fault* is one in which the displacement is upward (Fig. 2.23b). The movement is essentially horizontal in a *strike-slip fault*, that is, along the strike of the fault (Fig. 2.23c), and such movement may be (regarding the near side as fixed) to the right (dextral) or left (sinistral) or a combination of movements at different times: the San Andreas Fault in California is dextral, but the net shift of 65 miles on the Great Glen Fault in Scotland comprises a sinistral shift of 83 miles in the Devonian and dextral shift of 18 miles during the Cenozoic (Holgate 1969).

Consideration of the principles outlined here will show that the effects of faulting and folding may seriously influence the accessibility of rock material for extraction at a particular locality. In block diagrams 2.23a, b and c, the prospective yield of useful material (stippled ornament) from workings situated on the near and far sides of the faults, and the importance of careful planning of quarry development, will be apparent.

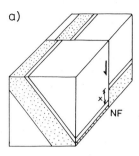

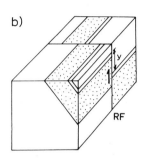

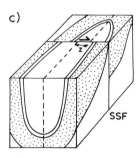

FIG. 2.23. (a) Effect of normal fault NF on dipping strata. The throw of the fault is x. (b) Effect of reverse dip fault on dipping strata. The throw of the fault is y. (c) Effect of an E–W strike slip fault (SSF) on a southward plunging syncline. The amount of the dislocation is shown by the horizontal shift z.

Joints are partings or fractures showing no discernible movement or displacement: they are a common feature of almost all rocks. Groups of parallel joints are joint sets and the term joint system applies to two or more intersecting sets. Statistical analysis of the frequency, orientation and continuity of jointing is useful in structural geology studies (Sloan *et al.* 1989). Apart from joints that arise mainly from the crystallization of

igneous rocks (see §2.8.1.2) (and are regarded as primary rock structures), most joints develop later from the relief in situ of tensional or shearing stresses acting on the rock mass. They may result from shrinkage or contraction, compression and crumpling of a rock body (in which jointing is directly related to folding and faulting), unloading by erosion and large-scale earth movements involving flexuring, rifting, subsidence and uplift of crustal tracts.

Shrinkage joints may develop from freezing or drying of sediments and the expulsion of gases or groundwater from burial by later deposits. Joints in folded sediments commonly intersect at right angles and perpendicular to bedding planes. In dipping and folded beds, the direction of joints frequently coincides with their dip and strike (*dip-joints* and *strike-joints* respectively). Others from where tension is greatest at the crest of a fold (*tension joints*) and two sets of *oblique shear joints* may coincide with planes of maximum shear stress (Fig. 2.24). In extreme examples, the incidence of jointing may be such that the usefulness of the rock material for aggregate is prejudiced by mechanical weakness and weathering.

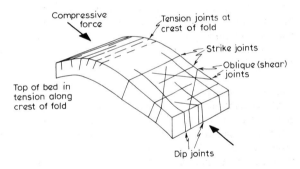

FIG. 2.24. Joint directions in a folded stratum (Blyth & de Freitas 1984).

Contraction joints, columnar jointing and intersecting sets of *rectangular joints* are characteristic of igneous rocks, originating as the molten rock cools and contracts (§2.8.1.2). On the other hand, *flat-lying joints*, known as *sheet joints*, are thought to be developed during denudation and unloading, particularly of the upper parts of large granite masses. They are characteristically accompanied by other joints, also commonly in granites, in steeply inclined or vertical sets intersecting at right angles; diagonal sets may also be present.

In faulted ground, the rock mass is commonly traversed by joints parallel to the plane of faulting suggesting that they formed at the same time in the same stress field. Typically, the joints become more frequent near a fault, where they may begin to exhibit signs of movement (slicken sides); where pressures were great, the rock may be completely broken up and pulverized to form fault-gouge.

The spacing of major and minor joint sets varies widely according to the rock types and geological history of an area. The ease of quarrying in hard rocks largely depends on the regular (or irregular) nature of the joints, their continuity, direction and spacing. Joints are natural pathways for groundwater movement and they are a major factor in promoting rock weathering. The description and consistent recording of discontinuities in rock masses are consequently of the greatest importance in the appraisal and development of aggregate sources (Geological Society Engineering Group Report 1977).

References

AITKEN, A. M., MERRITT, J. W. & SHAW, A. J. 1979. *The Sand and Gravel Resources of the Country around Garmouth, Grampian Region.* Mineral Assessment Report, Institute of Geological Sciences, No. 41.

AL-JASSAR, S. & HAWKINS, A. B. 1991. The Carboniferous Limestone of the Bristol area: a review of the influence of the lithology and chemistry of its use as a geomaterial. *Quarterly Journal of Engineering Geology*, **24**, 143–158.

ANON 1991. A major hard-rock quarry in South Africa— Anglo-Alpha's 1M tonnes/year Eikenhof Quarry. *Quarry Management and Products*, **18**, pt 1, 13–15.

ASHWORTH, K. A. 1975. Limestones in the UK. *Industrial Minerals*, **90**, 15–28.

BERRY, F. G. 1979. Late Quaternary scour-hollows and related features in central London. *Quarterly Journal of Engineering Geology*, **12**, 9–29.

BLYTH, F. G. H. & DE FREITAS, M. A. 1984. *A Geology for Engineers*, 7th Edn. Edward Arnold, London.

BOWEN, D. Q., ROSE, J., McCABE, A. M. & SUTHERLAND, D. G. 1986. Correlation of Quaternary glaciations in England, Ireland, Scotland and Wales. *Quaternary Science Reviews*, **5**, 299–340.

BRITISH GEOLOGICAL SURVEY. 1990. *United Kingdom Minerals Yearbook 1989.* British Geological Survey, Keyworth, Nottingham.

BRITISH STANDARDS INSTITUTION, BS 5930 : 1981 *Code of Practice for Site Investigations* (formerly CP 2001).

BROWN, E. T. (ed.) 1980. *Rock Characterisation Testing and Monitoring, ISRM Suggested Methods.* Pergamon, Oxford.

BURNETT, A. D. & EPPS, R. J. 1979. The engineering geological description of carbonate suite rocks and soils. *Ground Engineering*, 41–48.

CLARKE, M. R. 1975. *The Sand and Gravel Resources of the Country East of Chelmsford, Essex.* Mineral Assessment Report, Institute of Geological Sciences No. 13. HMSO, London.

——, DIXON, A. J. & KUBALA, M. 1979. *The Sand and Gravel Resources of the Blackwater Valley (Aldershot) Area.* Mineral Assessment Report, Institute of Geological Sciences No. 39.

——, RAYNOR, E. J. & SOBEY, R. A. 1980. *The Sand and Gravel Resources of the Loddon Valley Area.* Mineral Assessment Report, Institute of Geological Sciences No. 48.

CLEMMENSON, L. B. & HONMARK-NIELSEN, M. 1981. Sedimentary features of a Welchselian glaciolacustrine delta. *Boreas*, **10**, 229–245.

COLLINS, R. J. 1983. Concrete from crushed Jurassic limestone. *Quarry Management and Products*, **10**, 3 (March 1983), 127–138.

—— 1986a. Concrete using porous sandstone aggregate. *Quarry Management and Products*, March 1986, 33–42.

—— 1986b. *Porous Aggregates in Concrete: Jurassic Limestones.* Building Research Establishment Information Paper 2/86.

—— 1989. *Porous Aggregates in Concrete: Sandstones from NW England.* Building Research Establishment Information Paper 16/89.

—— 1991. *Magnesian Limestone Aggregate in Concrete*, Building Reserach Establishment Information Paper 2/91.

COX, F. C., DAVIES, J. R. & SCRIVENOR, R. C. 1986. The distribution of high-grade sandstone for aggregate usage in parts of south-west England and South Wales. Report for Department of the Environment (Keyworth, Nottinghamshire: British Geological Survey).

CULLIMORE, R. N., PIKE, D. C. & JORDAN, J. P. R. 1976. *Jurassic Rock Gravels as Concrete Aggregates.* Technical Paper 9, Sand and Gravel Association, London.

DEARMAN, W. R. 1974. Weathering classification in the characterisation of rocks for engineering purposes in British practice. *Bulletin of the International Association of Engineering Geologists*, **9**, 33–42.

DIBB, T. E., HUGHS, D. W. & POOLE, A. B. 1983a. Controls of size and shape of natural armourstone. *Quarterly Journal of Engineering Geology*, **16**, 31–42.

——, —— & —— 1983b. The identification of critical factors affecting rock durability in marine environments. *Quarterly Journal of Engineering Geology*, **16**, 149–161.

DINES, H. G. & EDMUNDS, F. H. 1929. *The Geology of the Country around Aldershot and Guildford.* Memoir of the Geological Survey of Great Britain.

DUNHAM, R. J. 1962. Classification of carbonate rocks according to depositional texture. *In*: HAM, W. E. (ed.) *Classification of Carbonate Rocks.* Memoir of the American Association of Petroleum Geologists, Tulsa, Oklahoma, **1**, 108–121.

DUNKLEY, P. N. 1981. *The Sand and Gravel Resources of the Country North of Wrexham, Clwyd.* Mineral Assessment Report, Institute of Geological Sciences, No. 61. HMSO, London.

EARLE, Q. 1991. The quarrying industry in Hong Kong. *Quarry Managment*, **18**, pt 2, 19–24.

EDGAR, D. E. 1984. The role of geomorphic thresholds in determining alluvial channel morphology *In*: ELLIOTT, C. M. (ed.) *River Meandering.* American Society of Civil Engineers, 44–54.

FOLK, R. L. 1962. Spectral subdivision of limestone types. *In*: HAM, W. E. (ed.) *Classification of Carbonate Rocks: a Symposium.* American Association of Petroleum Geologists, Tulsa, Oklahoma, 62–84.

FOOKES, P. G. 1980. An introduction to the influence of natural aggregates on the performance and durability of concrete. *Quarterly Journal of Engineering Geology*, **13**, 207–229.

—— 1989. Civil engineering practice. *In*: BLAKE (ed.) *Geology for Engineers*, 4th edn. Chapter 7.

—— 1991. Geomaterials. *Quarterly Journal of Engineering Geology*, **24**, 3–15.

——, DEARMAN, W. R. & FRANKLIN, J. A. 1971. Some engineering aspects of rock weathering with field examples from Dartmoor and elsewhere. *Quarterly Journal of Engineering Geology*, **4**, 139–185.

——, GORDON, D. L. & HIGGINBOTTOM, I. E. 1975. Glacial landforms, their deposits and engineering characteristics in the engineering behaviour of glacial materials. *Proceedings of a Symposium of Midland Soil Mechanics and Foundation Engineering Society* reprinted by *Geo-Abstracts*, Norwich, 1978.

——, GOURLEY, C. S. & OHIKERE, C. 1988. Rock weathering in engineering time. *Quarterly Journal of Engineering Geology*, **21**, 33–58.

—— & HAWKINS, A. B. 1988. Limestone weathering: its engineering significance and a proposed classification scheme. *Quarterly Journal of Engineering Geology*, **21** 7–32.

—— & HIGGINBOTTOM, I. E. 1975. The classification and description of near-shore carbonate sediments for engineering purposes. *Géotechnique*, **25** (2) 406–411.

—— & ——. 1980. Some problems of construction aggregates in desert areas, with particular reference to the Arabian peninsula. I – Occurrence and special charateristics II – Investigation, production and quality control. *Proceedings of the Institution of Civil Engineers*, Part 1, **68**, February 1980, 39–90.

—— & MARSH, A. H. 1981. Some characteristics of construction materials in the low to moderate metamorphic grade rocks of the Lower Himalayas of East Nepal. 1 Occurrence and geological features; 2 Engineering characteristics. *Proceedings of the Institution of Civil Engineers*, Part 1, **70**, 123–162.

—— & POOLE, A. B. 1981. Some preliminary considerations on the selection and durability of rock and concrete materials for breakwaters and coastal protection works. *Quarterly Journal of Engineering Geology*, **14**, 97–128.

FRENCH, W. J. 1991. Concrete petrography: a review. *Quarterly Journal of Engineering Geology*, **24**, 17–48.

GARDINIER, V. & DACKOMBE, R. 1983. *Geomorphological Field Manual*. Allen & Unwin, London.

GEOLOGICAL SOCIETY ENGINEERING GROUP WORKING PARTY REPORT. 1977. The description of rock masses for engineering purposes. *Quarterly Journal of Engineering Geology*, **10**, 355–388.

—— 1990. Tropical Residual Soils. *Quarterly Journal of Engineering Geology*, **23**, 1–101.

GIBBARD, P. & ZALASIEWICZ, J. A. 1988 (eds). *Pliocene–Middle Pleistocene of East Anglia—Field Guide*. Quaternary Research Association, Cambridge.

GOUDIE, A. S. 1973. *Duricrusts in Tropical and Sub-tropical Landscapes*. Clarendon, Oxford.

GRESSWELL, R. K. & LAWRENCE, G. R. P. 1978. *The Work of the Sea, Rivers and Ice*. Hulton Educ. Pub.

GRIBBLE, C. 1990. The sand and gravel deposits of the Strathkelvin valley. *Quarry Management and Products*, Vol. (July) 29–31.

GUTT, W., TEYCHENNÉ, D. C. & HARRISON, W. H. 1974. The use of lighter-weight blast furnace slag as dense coarse aggregate in concrete. *Magazine of Concrete Research*, **26**, 123–143.

HARLAND, W. B., COX, A. V., LLEWELLYN, P. G., PICTON, C. A. G., SMITH, A. G. & WALTERS, R. 1990. *A Geological Time Scale*. Cambridge University Press.

HARRIS, P. M. 1976. Underground limestone mining in the U.S.A. *Transactions of the Institution of Mining and Metallurgy*, A., **85**, 75–84.

—— 1977. Sandstone. Mineral Dossier No. 17, *Mineral Resources Consultative Committee*, H.M.S.O., London.

—— 1978. Igneous and metamorphic rock. Mineral Dossier No. 19, *Mineral Resources Consultative Committee*, H.M.S.O., London.

—— 1982. Limestone and Dolomite. Mineral Dossier No. 23, *Mineral Resources Consultative Committee*, H.M.S.O., London.

——, THURRELL, R. G., HEALING, R. A. & ARCHER, A. A. 1974. Aggregates in Britain. *Proceedings of the Royal Society, London*, **A339**, 329–353.

HARRISON, D. J. 1988. *The Marine Sand and Gravel Resources of Great Yarmouth and Southwold, East Anglia*. British Geological Survey, Technical Report WB/88/9.

—— & ADLAM, K. A. McL. 1984. *The Limestone and Dolomite resources of the Peak District of Derbyshire and Staffordshire*. Mineral Assessment Report, British Geological Survey, No. 144.

HATCH, F. H., WELLS, A. K. & WELLS, M. K. 1972. *Petrology of the Igneous Rocks*. Thomas Murby, London.

HAWKES, J. R. & HOSKING, J. R. 1973. British arenaceous rocks for skid-resistant road surfacings. *Quarry Managers Journal, London*, **57**, 39–47.

HAWKINS, A. B. & McCONNELL, B. J. 1991. Sandstones as geomaterials. *Quarterly Journal of Engineering Geology*, **24**, 135–142.

HEY, R. W. 1967. The Westleton Beds reconsidered. *Proceedings of the Geologists' Association*, **78**, 422–445.

—— & AUTON, C. A. 1988. Composition of pebble-beds in the Neogene and pre-Anglian Pleistocene of East Anglia, pp 35–41 *In*: GIBBARD, P. L. & ZALASIEWICZ, J. A. (eds) *Pliocene-Middle Pleistocene of E. Anglia—Field Guide*. Quaternary Research Association, Cambridge.

HOLGATE, N. 1969. Palaeozoic and Tertiary transcurrent movements on the Great Glen Fault. *Scottish Journal of Geology*, **5**, 97–139.

HOLLYER, S. E. & ALLENDER, R. 1982. *The Sand and Gravel Resources of the Country Around Hollesley, Suffolk*. Mineral Assessment Report of the Institute of Geological Sciences, No. 83, HMSO, London.

HOPSON, P. M. 1982. *Summary Regional Assessment of the Sand and Gravel Resources of the Middle and Upper Thames and its Tributaries*. Open File Report 82/5 Industrial Minerals Assessment Unit, Institute of Geological Sciences, Keyworth, Nottingham.

JACKSON, I. 1979. *The Sand and Gravel Resources of the Country Around Brampton, Cumbria*. Mineral Assessment Report of the Institute of Geological Sciences No 45. HMSO, London.

LAHEE, F. H. 1961. *Field geology*. 6th edn. McGraw-Hill.

LAXTON, J. L. & NICKLESS, E. F. P. 1979. *The Sand and Gravel Resources of the Country around Lanark, Strathclyde Region*. Mineral Assessment Report of the Institute of Geological Sciences No. 49.

LEET, L. D., JUDSON, S. & KAUFMAN, M. E. 1978. *Physical Geology*, 5th edn. Prentice-Hill, New Jersey.

LITTLE, A. L. 1969. *The Engineering Classification of Residual Tropical Soils*. Proceedings of the 7th International Conference on Soil Mechanics and Foundation Engineering, Mexico **1**, 1–10.

McLEAN, A. C. & GRIBBLE, C. D. 1979. *Geology for Civil Engineers*. Allen & Unwin, London.

MERRITT, J. W. 1992. A summary of British onshore sand and gravel resources and a critical review of methods used in their appraisal. *Engineering Geology*, **32**, 1–9.

—— & ELLIOTT, R. W. 1984. *Hard-rock Aggregate Resources: Central Scotland Mineral Portfolio*. British Geological Survey Technical Report.

MYKURA, W., ROSS, D. L. & MAY, F. 1978. *Sand and Gravel Resources of the Highland Region, Scotland*. Report No. 78/8, Institute of Geological Sciences. HMSO, London.

NARUMI, Y. 1989. Offshore mining in Japan. *Rock Products* 64–68.

NICKLESS, E. F. P. 1971. *The Sand and Gravel Resources of the Country South-east of Norwich, Norfolk. Description of 1 : 25 000 resource sheet TG 20.* Report of the Institute of Geological Sciences, London 71/20.

——, AITKEN, A. M. & McMILLAN, A. A. 1978. *The Sand and Gravel Resources of the Country around Darvel, Strathclyde.* Mineral Assessment Report, Institute of Geological Sciences, No. 35, HMSO, London (pp 153 and resource map).

NUNNY, R. S. & CHILLINGWORTH, P. C. H. 1986. *Marine Dredging for Sand and Gravel.* HMSO, London (Department of the Environment Minerals Planning Research Project Report).

OELE, E. 1971. The Quaternary geology of the southern area of the Dutch part of the North Sea. *Geologie en Mijnbouw,* **50,** 461–575.

OLLIER, C. D. 1975. *Weathering.* Longman, Edinburgh.

PATERSON, I. B. & HALL, I. H. S. 1986. *Lithostratigraphy of the Late Devonian and Early Carboniferous rocks in the Midland Valley of Scotland.* Report of the British Geological Survey, **18,** No. 3.

PEACOCK, J. D. & CORNISH, R. 1989. *Field guide: Glen Roy area, Scotland.* Quaternary Research Association, Cambridge.

PIPER, D. P. 1982. *The Conglomerate Resources of the Sherwood Sandstone Group: Stoke-on-Trent.* Mineral Assessment Report, Institute of Geological Sciences, No. 91. HMSO, London.

PRENTICE, J. E. 1990. *Geology of Construction Materials.* Chapman and Hall, London.

QUARRY MANAGEMENT AND PRODUCTS 1974. Buddon Wood Quarry. A major new development in Leicestershire by Redland Roadstone. *Quarry Management and Products, London,* **1,** 161–176.

—— 1975. Developing and operating a mammoth quarry. *Quarry Management and Products, London,* **2,** 12.

—— 1977. New processing plant at Scottish basalt quarry. *Quarry Management and Products, London,* **4,** 117–121.

—— 1979. Road materials from Underground. *Quarry Management and Products, London,* **6,** 246–248.

REINECK, H. E. & SINGH, I. B. 1980. *Depositional Sedimentary Environments,* 2nd edn. Springer, New York.

ROBERTSON, T. & HALDANE, D. 1937. *The Economic Geology of the Central Coalfield, Area I: Kilsyth and Kirkintilloch.* Memoir of the Geological Survey of Scotland.

ROSE, J. (ed.) 1983. *Diversion of the Thames—Field Guide.* Quaternary Research Association, Cambridge.

—— & ALLEN, P. 1977. Middle Pleistocene stratigraphy in south-east Suffolk. *Journal of the Geological Society, London,* **133,** 83–102.

SANDECKI, M. 1989. Aggregate Mining in River Systems. *California Geology* (Report of Division of Mines and Geology April 1989).

SANDERS, M. K. & FOOKES, P. G. 1970. A review of the relationship of rock weathering and climate and its significance to foundation engineering. *Quarterly Journal of Engineering Geology,* **4,** 289–325.

SCHUMM, S. A. 1981. Evolution and response of the fluvial system, sedimentologic interpretations. Society of Economic Palaeontologists and Mineralogists, Special Publication 31, 19–29.

SELLEY, R. C. 1982. *Ancient Sedimentary Environments.* Chapman and Hall, London.

SHERBON HILLS, E. 1975. *Elements of Structural Geology,* 2nd edn. Chapman & Hall, London.

SIMPSON, B. 1966. *Rocks and Minerals.* Pergamon, London.

SLOAN, A., LUMSDEN, A. C., HENCHER, S. R. & ONIONS, R. I. 1989. Geological and geotechnical controls on operational planning at Ingleton Quarry (W. Yorkshire) *In* GASKARTH, J. W. & LUMSDEN, A. C. (eds), *Proceedings of the 6th Extractive Industry Geology Conference, University of Birmingham, UK.* Institution of Geologists, London.

SMITH, C. G. & FLOYD, J. D. 1989. *Hard-rock Aggregate Resources: Scottish Highlands and Southern Uplands Mineral Portfolio.* British Geological Survey Technical Report WF/89/4.

SQUIRRELL, H. C. 1976. *The Sand and Gravel Resources of the Thames and Kennet Valleys, the Country around Pangbourne, Berkshire.* Mineral Assessment Report of the Institute of Geological Sciences, No. 21.

—— 1978. *The Sand and Gravel Resources of the Country around Sonning and Henley, Berkshire, Oxfordshire and Buckinghamshire.* Mineral Assessment Report of the Institute of Geological Sciences, No. 32.

SUMMERFIELD, M. A. 1983. Silcrete. *In:* GOUDIE, A. S. & PYE, K. (eds) *Chemical Sediments and Geomorphology.* Academic, London, 59–91.

THOMAS, G. S. P. 1985. The Late Devensian glaciation along the border of north-east Wales. *Geological Journal,* **20,** 319–340.

THOMAS, M. 1971. Savanna lands between desert and forest. *Geographical Magazine* **44,** 185–189.

THOMPSON, D. B. 1970. Sedimentation of the Triassic (Scythian) Red Pebbly Sandstones in the Cheshire Plain and its margins. *Geological Journal,* **7,** 183–216.

TOMKEIEFF, S. I. 1964. The economic geology of quarried materials—2 Igneous and metamorphic rocks. *Quarry Managers Journal, London,* **48,** 85–94.

VERNEY, Sir R. B. (Chairman) 1976. *Aggregates: The Way Ahead.* Report of the Advisory Committee on Aggregates. H.M.S.O., for Dept. of the Environment.

WEINERT, H. H. 1964. Basic igneous rocks in road foundations. South African Council of Science Industrial Research, Report No. 218, *National Institute of Road Research Bulletin,* **2,** 1–47.

WEST, G. & DUMBLETON, M. J. 1970. The mineralogy of tropical weathering illustrated by some west Malaysian soils. *Quarterly Journal of Engineering Geology,* **3,** 25–40.

WEST, R. G. 1977. *Pleistocene Geology and Biology,* 2nd edn. Longmans, London.

WILSON, A. C., MATHERS, S. J. & CANNELL, B. 1982. *The Middle Sands, a Prograding Sandar Succession; its Significance in the Glacial Evolution of the Wrexham–Shrewsbury region. In* IGS short communications. Report of the Institute of Geological Sciences, No. 82/1. H.M.S.O., London, 30–35.

3. Field investigation of deposits

3.1. Introduction

The location of aggregate materials through the appraisal of geological and geotechnical information and the eventual selection of sites from which to extract them, requires the collation of data from many sources through desk studies, followed by field reconnaissances and the evaluation of prospects to the necessary level of geological assurance. After the identification of a possibly useful deposit, further, more specific investigations of its physical and mechanical characteristics may confirm that it is potentially useful as aggregate, i.e. it is a *resource* (McKelvey 1972), and that certain parts of it may be capable of being worked at a profit in prevailing market conditions and so may be regarded as a *reserve* (§3.7.2).

Whilst the main objective of this section is to outline methods for investigating and reporting on possible sources of aggregate, some attention is also given to operational, commercial, environmental and planning matters which, along with the geological factors, have to be considered by the engineer or geologist during the assessment of reserves for a quarrying prospect.

3.2. Desk study

Although the assembly of published and unpublished data will draw primarily on the collation of available previous geological and geotechnical work, particularly geological maps and records, and site investigation reports, many other sources may give a lead to the presence of aggregate (Dumbleton & West 1976; Rose 1976; Eastaff *et al.* 1978). Thus, previously unreleased records of mining and quarrying operations, former aggregate workings or of investigations for them or for civil engineering works such as major road schemes, may be relevant, along with land use or soil surveys for agricultural purposes, old topographic maps and even local oral tradition from well sinkers, farmers and the local population (Chaplow 1975).

3.2.1. Topographic maps

The prime value of contoured or even hill-shaded topographic maps, lies in their portrayal of physiographic features (land forms) which may give an indication of the possible presence of aggregates and their accessibility (e.g. §§2.4.1, 2.4.3). Even the most rudimentary maps and sketches showing the courses of streams and the positions of hill ranges can be helpful for exploring virgin country and planning further work (3.3). If topographic maps and air photographs do not exist, the prospector should prepare a sketch-map using any means at his disposal: he should walk over the ground, record the location of the main physiographic features and of possible aggregate materials and fix them by estimation or by using dead-reckoning techniques, and if the opportunity arises, he should construct a scale plan by plane-table, compass traverses, the use of a surveyor's aneroid and also establish a photographic record. Such an initial effort may prove to be invaluable for planning, locating and interpreting subsequent air photographs and satellite imagery.

The interpretation of landforms from aerial photography and satellite imagery is a major aid in delineating superficial and bedrock geology, unravelling the geomorphology and geological structure, and the resource boundaries over extensive tracts of country and locally, depending on the scale and resolution of the imagery. From the point of view of restraints on establishing aggregate extraction operations, remote sensing can provide considerable guidance on old workings, existing workings, present land-use, accessibility and areas already sterilized by other developments of land.

At the reconnaissance stage, small-scale maps at 1 : 250 000 to 1:50 000 scales with contouring at 10 m intervals or more may be adequate but, at later stages in an investigation, large-scale maps for plotting the locations of all relevant information will be needed for prospect evaluation. Working maps down to 1 : 500 scale demonstrating such details as property boundaries, drainage lines and directions, the location of specimen trees, visual intrusion studies and intervisibility information in support of submissions for planning approvals for site development, quarry management and the eventual restoration of the workings, will be indispensable (McCall 1989).

3.2.2. Geological maps

The essential prerequisite when prospecting for aggregates is a geological map. If none exists, geological mapping specifically for mineral aggregate deposits should be undertaken using appropriate supporting investigative techniques. First and foremost, a thorough walk-over survey, including the examination of natural exposures, hand augering, pitting and geomorphological mapping (Doornkamp *et al.* 1979; Doornkamp 1989) will provide invaluable initial guidance; the use of ground geophysics (Zalasiewicz *et al.* 1985; Auton 1992) in conjunction with small-scale drilling and sampling by man-portable equipments may help to refine the geological interpretation in some circumstances. In addition, particularly in little-known terrains and in developing countries, remote geophysical and optical sensing from aircraft (or even from spacecraft) may be useful.

There is no doubt that, at the site investigation stage, the evidence of good geological mapping can be used to reduce the frequency and cost of drilling and sampling by tying point data into an interpretative pattern, which is the crux of the mapping exercise (Himus & Sweeting 1968; Anon 1972; Barnes 1981). Conversely the geological mapping is constantly refined to accommodate new evidence on the variability of deposit thickness and quality until the interpretation is judged to be good enough for aggregate assessment at whatever degree of sophistication, whether for measurement of regional resources or proof of reserves for extraction. The exercise of this judgement is the particular expertise of the geologist concerned with aggregates (Fox 1979; Merritt 1992).

In the United Kingdom, the New Series 1 : 50 000 geological maps together with the detailed descriptive memoirs of the British Geological Survey (BGS) (established as the Geological Survey of Great Britain in 1835 and known as the Institute of Geological Sciences (IGS) from 1965 until 1983) are interpretations and summaries derived from the national archive of subsurface records and 1 : 10 000 scale, formerly 6-inch to 1 mile, field survey maps (which have formed the basis of geological surveys in Britain since well before the turn of the century). These detailed maps, published for most coalfields and some other areas, are available for consultation in manuscript or can be purchased as photocopies or prints from dyeline masters. Approximately 80% of the UK is mapped on this scale and, although the quality of the interpretation embodied in some older maps varies considerably (Gordon *et al.* 1982), they provide invaluable guidance on the occurrence and distribution of formations that are potentially useful for aggregate. The main scale of publication, however, is now 1 : 50 000 and the sheet boundaries and availability of these maps (and of the one-inch to the mile maps, which they are replacing) are given in Appendix A3, Fig. A3.1. Over 400 sheets are in print: updated index maps and lists are published in the annual printed maps catalogue and in the Annual Reports of the BGS.

Other specialist publications of the Survey may also be useful in the search for sources of aggregates, for example, engineering geology maps such as those for

Belfast and Milton Keynes, geophysical maps, both gravity and aeromagnetic, hydrogeological maps and aggregate resource maps. Soil survey maps, such as those produced at 1 : 25 000 and 1 : 50 000 scales by the Soil Survey and Land Research Centre (formerly the Soil Survey of Great Britain) provide systematic inventories of the soils in an area and embody information that can be interpreted for a range of unforeseen purposes (Avery 1987). Increasingly such data is being used for locating well drained sandy and gravelly horizons in the upper 2 m that may give a clue to thicker resources (McCormack & Fohs 1979), and in such matters as land restoration schemes as part of land-use planning following mineral extraction. In the English fenland, geological maps have been compiled largely from soil survey data (Gallois 1988) with field reconnaissance, and indications of the occurrence of sand and gravel deposits confirmed.

Geological profile or sequence maps, first developed in the Quaternary terrains of Holland and Germany (de Mulder 1987) from hand auger, shallow drilling and ground geophysics data, show the succession and relationships of distinct beds of unconsolidated sediments, including aggregate materials at particular localities. This system has been applied elsewhere (McMillan & Browne 1987).

3.2.3. Aggregate resource maps

Maps showing the occurrence of aggregate resources are being produced increasingly by geological surveys and similar bodies in many parts of the world (Moldan *et al.* 1982; Wolff 1987) for use by minerals and land-use planners, the extractive industry and their advisors, the environmental concerns and many others. Most aggregate resource maps are directly based on geological mapping and may form an 'element' or part of a 'thematic set' or 'portfolio' of applied geology maps portraying information on soils, geochemistry, engineering geology, hydrogeology and so on. The range of subjects of environmental concern dealt with may be very large and, by combining information from two or more elements, perhaps by means of computerized data sets, maps showing potential conflicts between different possible uses of land can be derived. In some instances, such conflicts may be further addressed through overview studies based on the collation and integration of information collected largely from existing data holdings, as, for example, the effects of sub-watertable extraction of construction materials from a developed aquifer (Harrison *et al.* 1992).

The appraisal of sand and gravel deposits has been approached in different ways by investigators, depending on the objectives of the work and the funds available. Most national, centrally funded surveys are inventorial and take the form of computerized, relational

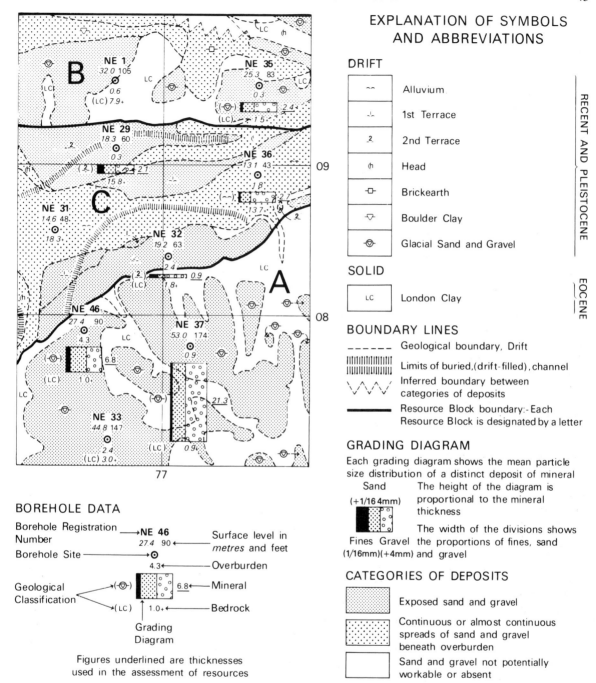

EXPLANATION OF SYMBOLS AND ABBREVIATIONS

DRIFT

~~	Alluvium	RECENT AND PLEISTOCENE
⌐	1st Terrace	
2	2nd Terrace	
⌂	Head	
⌐□	Brickearth	
▽	Boulder Clay	
⊘	Glacial Sand and Gravel	

SOLID

LC	London Clay	EOCENE

BOUNDARY LINES

‒ ‒ ‒ ‒ ‒ Geological boundary, Drift

⊪⊪⊪⊪⊪ Limits of buried,(drift-filled), channel

\/\/\/ Inferred boundary between categories of deposits

▬▬▬ Resource Block boundary:- Each Resource Block is designated by a letter

GRADING DIAGRAM

Each grading diagram shows the mean particle size distribution of a distinct deposit of mineral

Sand (+1/16 4mm)   The height of the diagram is proportional to the mineral thickness

Fines Gravel (1/16mm)(+4mm)   The width of the divisions shows the proportions of fines, sand and gravel

CATEGORIES OF DEPOSITS

Exposed sand and gravel

Continuous or almost continuous spreads of sand and gravel beneath overburden

Sand and gravel not potentially workable or absent

BOREHOLE DATA

Borehole Registration Number → NE 46

Borehole Site → ⊘

Surface level in metres and feet ← 27.4 90

Overburden ← 4.3

Geological Classification → (⊘) → (LC)

Mineral ← 6.8

Bedrock ← 1.0+

Grading Diagram

Figures underlined are thicknesses used in the assessment of resources

FIG. 3.1. Extract from a sand and gravel resource map, showing the distribution of potentially workable deposits in part of the Chelmsford area, Essex, England. The map is divided by 1 km squares of the National Grid (Thurrell 1981).

databases, so that the required output of minerals, maps and reports can be produced rapidly and updated periodically (Neeb 1986). Advances towards digital map production are being made.

Desk syntheses of existing information on the nature and occurrence of possible aggregate sources are an

economical way of approaching resource assessment. Data from geological survey borehole and map archives, from the records of civil engineering contractors and their clients, well sinkers, museums and local planning and public service authorities can be assembled as deposit maps, often of extensive areas. Provided an appropriate distribution of relevant data points is available, an outline appraisal of possible resources may be feasible often with only minimal checking of natural and quarry exposures on the ground (Clarke *et al.* 1982; Cox *et al.* 1986; Sumbler & Samuel 1990: Stevens *et al.* 1991). Most methods of resource appraisal, however, rely on field investigations designed to yield the maximum of useful information at modest cost.

In recent years, up to the mid-1980s, drilling and sampling surveys designed specifically to appraise the amount and main physical characteristics of the major occurrences of sand and gravel in England, Wales and Scotland were commissioned by the Minerals Planning Division of the Department of the Environment, and the results, in the form of 1 : 25 000-scale resource maps with reports, are published in the Mineral Assessment Reports of the Geological Survey. More than 140 reports have been published (Appendix A3, Fig. A3.2). The objective of these surveys (which included the identification of chemical-grade limestone resources, as well as those used primarily as aggregate, conglomerate and sandstone) is to provide information at the 'indicated' level (Bureau of Mines and Geological Survey, 1948, 1976) primarily for land use and mineral planning purposes by local and central authorities and by the extractive industry. The standardized procedures (Thurrell 1971, 1981; Auton 1985) allow comparison of the quality and quantity of resources from widely scattered localities and over extensive tracts of country throughout the gravel fields of Britain. Users can readily relate the findings to their own map and records holdings.

The investigations add very significantly to the national geological archive, particularly in regard to glacial and fluvial deposition, Quaternary stratigraphy and the refinement of the mapping of the drift deposits and hydrogeology. For the purposes of these regional sand and gravel assessments, the BGS has adopted a metric grain-size classification (Archer 1970) based on that of Willman (1942) and after consulting widely, fixed arbitrary physical criteria in order to define on the resource maps and in the borehole logs, the occurrence of 'potentially workable' sand and gravel, that is, 'mineral' (Dunkley 1979; Fig. 3.1).

In contrast to the well-tried procedures for assessing extensive spreads of glaciofluvial sand and gravel in lowland Britain, the appraisal of discontinuous, more scattered deposits typical of more recently deglaciated, upland regions required a more flexible, cost-effective approach: much greater use of air photographs, forming the basis of geomorphological mapping but with little field control (McLellan 1967, 1969; McLellan & Bryant 1975; Fookes *et al.* 1991) has provided the basis for some surveys in Scotland (Chester 1980). Given an adequate pre-existing borehole database and well documented geology, acceptable indications of the potential resource can be adduced (Chester *et al.* 1974; Morey *et al.* 1991). However, the integration of this method with geological mapping, drilling, pitting and geophysical investigations, as appropriate, though more costly and time-consuming, is likely to give more reliable and practically useful results on deposit quality and thickness (Merritt 1981; Anon 1985; Crimes 1985; Auton & Crofts 1986; Auton *et al.* 1988). Many such studies have been undertaken in Great Britain in recent years by private sector and university contractors supported by public funds; it is regrettable that the majority of these results, though publicly available, remain unpublished and the scattered data sets have not so far been collected into a national inventory.

Resource assessments based on predictive modelling of depositional environments (Martin & Lovell *in* Martin 1981), require detailed analyses of the sediments exposed in sections and trial pits or interpreted from borehole records. Despite their dependence on frequent exposures, such studies may lead the investigator to the most attractive prospects through improved understanding of fluvial and glaciofluvial sedimentary regimes. A similar, more extensive approach has been applied in County Durham in northeast England (Stevens *et al.* 1989): a comprehensive model of local glacial recession and glaciofluvial deposition, based mainly on pre-existing borehole and site investigation records and geological maps, has been used to predict the distribution and main physical characters of the aggregate-bearing deposits, and resource maps produced (Morey *et al.* 1991).

3.2.4. Derivative resource maps

Summaries and collations of earlier resource assessments often provide illuminating overviews of more extended areas and it may be expedient to re-examine data holdings in order to clarify or emphasize particular characteristics of the resources. A summary of the limestone resources of the Peak District of central England (Harrison & Adlam 1985) draws on the assessments of industrial and aggregate grade resources outlined in six component 1:25 000-scale surveys. The main summary product is a 1:50 000-scale coloured resource map showing the distribution of the limestones over 540 km^2 of country, classified on their $CaCO_3$ content: the criterion most closely related to end use. Contamination by chert, clay wayboards, dolomitization and significant chemical contaminants are charted on smaller marginal maps and text-figures, which also include the results of index testing for aggregate potential: 55% of this resource is useful for aggregate.

A summary report on the river gravels of the Middle and Upper Thames Valley (Hopson 1982) combines and extends the findings of 14 previously published aggregate surveys into a single map compilation at 1:100 000 scale. Another review of the predominantly glaciofluvial

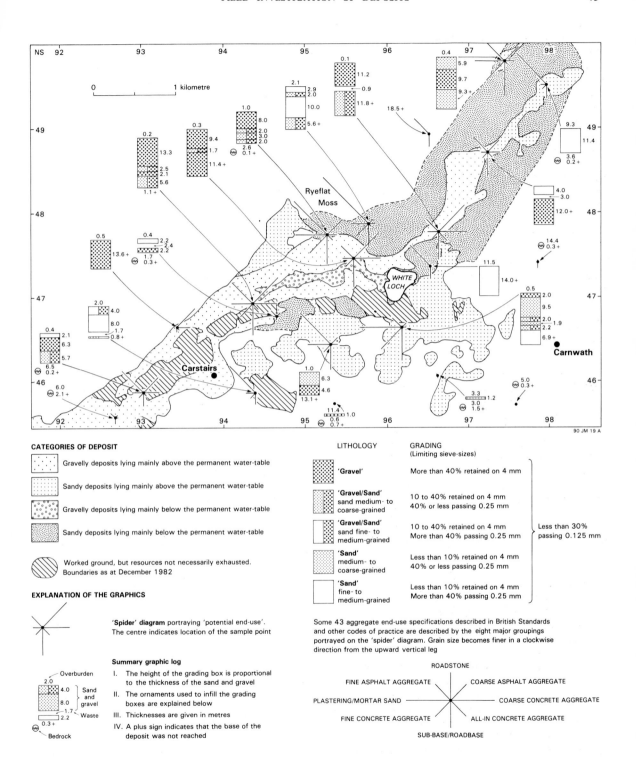

FIG. 3.2. Extract from a sand and gravel resource map of the Carstairs–Carnwath area, Strathclyde, Scotland, showing the suitability of the aggregate for any of eight classes of end-use by grade (see §3.2.4) (After Merritt *et al.* 1983).

outwash gravels in Essex and South Suffolk (McKeown & Samuel 1985) incorporates a 27-map portfolio of computer-generated plots from very large data sets and compares particle-size distribution figures and aggregate and waste thicknesses against different arbitrary limiting criteria.

In the regional collation studies in Scotland (also undertaken by BGS for the DoE), information on particle-size distribution published in the mineral assessment reports was further analysed in terms of the end-use potential of the sand and gravel deposits (Merritt *et al.* 1983; Laxton 1992). The gradings data were analysed by computer using two complementary approaches. They represent a development of work undertaken by the Manitoba Department of Energy and Mines. The first classifies the deposits proved in boreholes into waste *or* one of five classes of potentially workable sand and gravel. The classification assists in correlating deposits identified in boreholes with those mapped at the surface and the results are plotted as a graphic log for each bore site.

The second method analyses samples in terms of 43 end-use specifications. The results for all samples in a borehole are combined and plotted as 'spider' diagrams, each leg representing, by its length, the suitability and abundance of the aggregate for one of eight classes of end-use by grade (Fig. 3.2). Considered together, these graphics assist in understanding the three-dimensional distribution of sand and gravel and link them to possible end-uses. Knowledge of the distribution, volume and potential economic usefulness of deposits on a regional scale can form the basis for ranking deposits in terms of their commercial attractiveness.

3.2.5.   Reports and small-scale maps

Examples of maps showing the general distribution of natural aggregate and hard rocks suitable for crushing in Great Britain accompanied the Survey's contribution on national resources to the Report of the Advisory Committee on Aggregates (Verney 1976). In Scotland, outline studies of sand and gravel occurrences in each of the Regions were published (for example, Peacock *et al.* 1977). The Ministry of Housing and Local Government published 1:625 000-scale maps showing occurrences of gravel and limestones in Britain in 1965, and the official Quaternary map of the United Kingdom is also available at this scale (Institute of Geological Sciences 1977).

Outline studies of aggregate resources based largely on geological archive material supported by limited reconnaissance field checking have become commonplace for rapidly and economically constructing resource maps, often covering very extended tracts or even whole administrative areas, in a form suitable for physical planning (McCall & Marker 1989). These maps consti-

tute an independent, geologically based input to structure and local (zoning) plans. They assist in the development of coherent mineral policies in which issues such as the need to avoid sterilization of resources have to be balanced; they are of value also to landowners and the extractive industry because they give general guidance on the location of prospective deposits which might warrant site-specific resource potential studies. Examples of available outline studies include that on the sand and gravel resources of northeast Illinois, USA (Masters 1978), which incorporates a 1:125 000 resource map and classifies deposits by means of their expression in the landscape (outwash plain, kame, valley train, beach ridge, etc.) and the thickness, grade and extent of the potential aggregate (range from the coarsest cobbly glaciofluvial gravels to fine sands in dunes).

In Scotland, appraisals of hard rocks as sources of crushed rock aggregate (Merritt & Elliott 1984; Smith 1989) which outline 'more or less continuous' and 'discontinuous' resources, on either 1:100 000 or 1:250 000-scale maps. The maps further identify rock masses that may be expected to yield aggregate potentially suitable for 'low-shrinkage' concrete, 'skid-resistant' surfacing and 'general purpose' applications, among others.

3.2.6.   Geological, geophysical and aggregates maps covering UK offshore areas

The British Geological Survey (BGS) began the systematic survey of the UK continental shelf in 1966 and by 1986 had completed the reconnaissance data acquisition. During this survey over 225 000 km of seismic traverses have been run, seabed samples and shallow cores obtained from more than 30 000 sites and over 500 boreholes drilled. Data have also been assimilated from commercial exploration and site investigations and from hydrographic and academic sources. Offshore geological data are held by BGS in a comprehensive computerized database.

This survey has been directed towards the production of geological maps at a scale of 1:250 000 based on sheet areas measuring 1° latitude by 2° longitude (Fig. A3.3). Separate maps illustrating Aeromagnetic Anomalies, Gravity Anomalies, Solid Geology, Quaternary Geology and Sea Bed Sediments are available for all sheet areas. The first of a series of descriptive handbooks (United Kingdom Offshore Regional Report: Andrews *et al.* 1990) on the regional geology offshore, companion to the British Regional Geology series, was published in 1990 and maps at 1:1 000 000 scale are also being published.

The regional mapping programme offshore does not provide sufficient detail to allow an adequate assessment of marine sand and gravel resources because sample sites and seismic lines are commonly too widely spaced. Despite these constraints, interpretation of available data can provide the necessary geological framework for the investigation of marine aggregate resources.

3.2.6.1. Sand and gravel resource appraisals. In 1986 the BGS undertook a programme of marine aggregate resources appraisal based on a two-tier approach. The first stage of this commissioned programme is a series of desk studies covering the main offshore gravel fields of the British Isles. The first such study (Balson & Harrison 1986), drew together all information on the geology, distribution of seabed sediments, bathymetry and the local hydraulic regime for the southern North Sea, in order to identify potential resource areas which merited additional surveys to quantify in broad terms the available resource. These resource assessment surveys form the second stage of the approach.

Subsequently, desk studies have covered the South Coast of England (Hamblin & Harrison 1988), the Bristol Channel (Evans 1988) and the East Coast (Humber area) (Harrison 1992). Resource surveys have investigated areas off Great Yarmouth, East Anglia (Harrison 1988; Harrison & Ardus 1989) and off the South Coast around the Isle of Wight and Beachy Head (Hamblin & Harrison 1989).

The survey reports describe the distribution of resources and the geological controls which determine their quality and quantity: potential resource areas have been identified. The reports are accompanied by maps at the 1:100 000 or 1:250 00 scales showing bathymetry, distribution and thickness of seabed sediments, bedforms and seabed features, solid and Quaternary geology and potential aggregate resources. The reports provide a geological basis for the detailed evaluations undertaken by the marine dredging industry and also give those involved with fisheries interests useful information on bottom conditions, including sediment type, thickness and stability and on the nature of the substrate (bedrock).

3.2.7. Geoscience libraries in Britain

A wide range of geological and specialist maps and publications relating to many parts of the world, including many journals and papers, are available for reference in the main BGS libraries at Keyworth, Nottinghamshire, in South Kensington, London, in Edinburgh and Belfast and in district libraries in Exeter, Aberystwyth and Newcastle offices. They form part of the National Geosciences Information System. The Geological Society, Institution of Mining and Metallurgy and Geologists' Association libraries in London and those in earth science and geography departments in universities and polytechnics may also be consulted, usually by arrangement. Most of their map holdings are at scales smaller than 1:50 000.

3.3. Field investigation

Most small-scale geological maps will provide some basic information on the location of potential aggregates sources but, in unknown terrains and before any fieldwork is contemplated, it may be helpful in identifying possible targets for more detailed investigation to utilize some form of remote sensing, such as satellite imagery, air photographs and possibly airborne geophysical surveys (Beavan 1976; Ritchie *et al.* 1988). In many terrains, for example, recently deglaciated regions, deserts and places where the vegetation cover is thin or broken, the interpretation of aerial photographs is likely to provide immediate indications of the geological structure, the location of major hard rock bodies and the distribution of particular landforms through geomorphological mapping, which may enable the investigator to identify some of the more attractive targets before investigations begin on the ground (Drury 1987). Ground geophysical techniques can usefully augment direct ground exploration since most have to be interpreted against proven ground conditions. Ground geophysics in the aggregates field is a valuable aid in confirming rock associations between sampling points, usually boreholes (Cratchley 1976; Clarke 1983; Cannel & Crofts 1984; Cornwell 1985; Cornwell *et al.* 1989).

3.3.1. Satellite imagery

Data from Landsat satellites either in digital form or as imagery can be enhanced for regional geological studies but the spatial distribution is generally too coarse for mapping aggregates. However, Landsat false colour composite imagery has been used successfully to locate and map areas of indigenous construction material, for example in Botswana. Although detailed studies were limited by Landsat ground resolution, the imagery was effective in the location of calcrete occurrences over large areas at a reconnaissance scale (Beaumont 1979). Multispectral satellite photographs, taken from Skylab, have higher resolution than Landsat and have been used to identify the courses of buried channels on the Plain of Venice in northern Italy. These sand and gravel deposits were delineated by changes in reflectivity caused by variations of soil moisture and vegetation (Cassinis 1977). The use of Skylab photographs was estimated to reduce the need for reconnaissance on the ground by 90%.

Ground resolution has greatly improved in recent

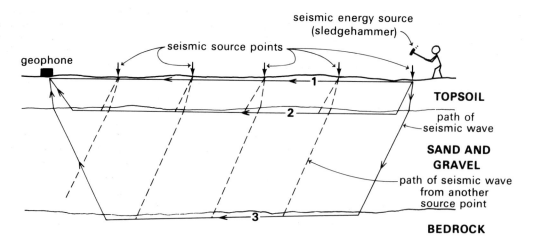

(a) Vertical section through a three-layer sequence showing paths followed by seismic
     waves from hammer-source to geophone.
   1 path from source to geophone through topsoil
   2 refracted path through sand and gravel
   3 refracted path through bedrock

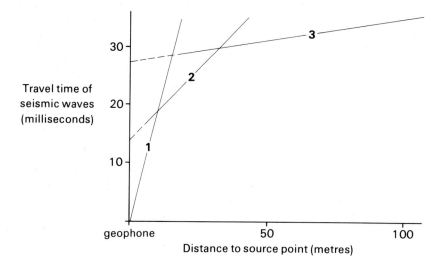

(b) Graph showing time taken for first arrival of seismic energy to reach geophone against
     distance between each source point and the geophone. The three branches on the graph
     represent the three paths in the upper diagram (a). The slope of each element of the graph
     gives information on the rock type and the intercepts on the time axis give an estimate of
     stratum thickness.

[I.F.Smith, BGS]

FIG. 3.3. The principles of hammer seismic surveying with single geophone (I. F. Smith, BGS).

years: the Thematic Mapper, successor to the Multispectral Scanner (MSS) of the earlier Landsats, has a ground resolution of 30 m (compared with 79 m for the MSS). The French SPOT satellite has a resolution of 20 m for multi-band images or 10 m for single-band images and, in addition, can produce stereoscopic images from space.

3.3.2. Aircraft remote sensing

Though much can be done by the non-specialist, photogeological interpretation of stereoscopic photography is a field of expert study (Allum 1966; Dumbleton & West 1970; Drury 1987) which can lead rapidly to the identification of lineaments, soil and rock types and landforms for the production of an outline geological map and to provide a guide to the occurrence of aggregate materials beneath unmodified landforms typical of many recently deglaciated terrains in northern temperate latitudes. Reconnaissance prospecting by aerial photographic interpretation is particulary important and cost-effective in remote terrains, where acceptably accurate topographic maps may not be available, for defining possible access routes for walk-over and site investigations to proceed on the ground. Thermal imagery, obtained from an airborne infra-red linescanner, records emitted radiation from the earth's surface. It is becoming increasingly used to discriminate between superficial materials. Multispectral infra-red remote sensing has been used to differentiate between gravel, sand and silt (Patoureaux 1979).

3.3.3. Geophysics: airborne and ground geophysics

Most geophysical methods of ground investigation locate anomalies or discontinuities between materials with markedly different physical properties and it is always necessary to check the true nature of the anomalies in the light of the known geology and by sinking boreholes. When a correlation has been established, geophysical methods may yield useful results economically and quickly in ground with marked differences in physical properties.

A valuable review of all appropriate geophysical techniques and procedures for particular geological targets (other than measurements from the air) has been published by a Geological Society Working Party and the reader is strongly advised to refer to it (Anon 1988).

3.3.3.1. Airborne methods. Whilst airborne geophysical methods may be used for locating major rock bodies, in other exploration contexts it seems unlikely that useful information specifically about the aggregate potential of solid rocks could be derived. Aerial prospecting for sand and gravel deposits, however, has been successfully undertaken in Canada by utilizing the electrical component in propagated radio waves in the 'E-phase' system (Barringer 1971; Culley 1973). The resistivities of terrains can be continuously computed along survey flight lines, so that a resistivity contoured map can be prepared that is very similar to, but more generalized than, one produced by conventional ground resistivity traversing or conductivity mapping.

Variations in ground resistivity patterns are closely related to the distribution of clay in surface and near-surface drift formations, and occurrences of sand and gravel, for example, are shown as areas of high resistivity in contrast to the more highly conductive non-mineral (waste) deposits containing larger quantities of 'fines'. 'E-phase' maps, like ground resistivity maps, must be interpreted in the light of complementary aerial photographs and topographic and geological data.

3.3.3.2. Ground methods. The three main properties examined by the various geophysical methods are electrical resistivity (or conversely, conductivity), seismic velocity and density. Contrasts in one or more of these properties must exist if geophysical methods are to be successful in differentiating between sand and gravel bodies and other, unwanted, drift deposits and the bedrock. Some of these contrasts are well understood, such as the difference in resistivity between clayey deposits, like most tills, and the associated sand and gravel. The degree of success using geophysical methods in resource appraisal studies has, however, been variable and it is unfortunate, although understandable, that the less successful trials and results are seldom fully documented so that the reasons for dissatisfaction can rarely be re-examined. It is likely that these include the extreme variability of some sand and gravel deposits, their disordered relationships as well as the lack of contrast in physical properties with associated superficial (waste) deposits or the bedrock.

The most commonly used techniques are ground resistivity soundings and conductivity mapping (Auton *et al.* 1988, Appendix E; Hopkins 1989; Auton 1992). Other methods may have successful application in certain situations or for the resolution of specific problems (Cornwell 1985; Cornwell & McCann 1991).

Resistivity soundings. This technique uses expanding electrode (metal pin) arrays to examine the horizontal resistivity layering of the ground, giving interpreted sequences and thicknesses comparable with those obtainable from boreholes. Soundings are well suited to distinctly bedded sequences and the depth of investigation depends on the configuration of the conductors and the spacing of the electrodes. Most commonly used configurations are the Schlumberger and Wenner arrays (Griffiths & King 1981), but for routine deployment by a single operator the technique has been simplified and considerably speeded up by the use of the Offset Wenner

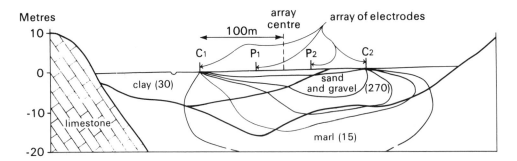

(a) A vertical section through a valley filled with sand and gravel and clay.
The clay and marl have relatively low resistance compared with the sand
and gravel. (Values are ohm-metres). Current paths between the current
electrodes (C_1 and C_2) are shown. The voltage between potential electrodes (P_1 and P_2)
is measured and a resistivity is calculated for a series of separations of electrodes.

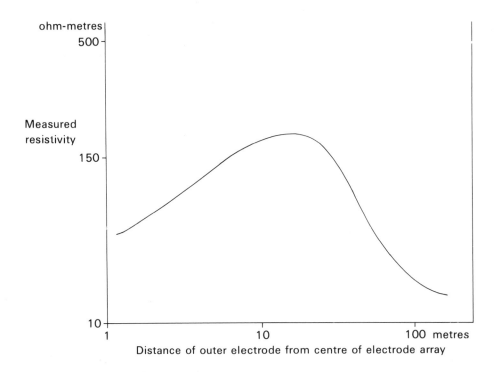

(b) A resistivity sounding curve of measured resistivity plotted against electrode separation.
It is centred as shown on diagram (a) above. Low resistivity is indicated at small
distances, increasing as current is forced to flow through the sand and gravel and
decreasing again at greater distances as more current flows through the marl.

[I.F.Smith, BGS]

FIG. 3.4. The principles of electrical resistivity surveying (I. F. Smith, BGS).

(a)

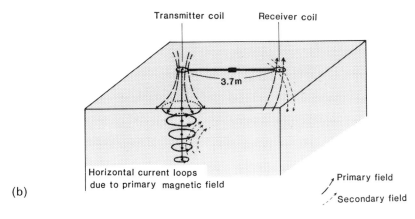

(b)

FIG. 3.5. The elctromagnetic ground terrain conductivity meter (a) (by Geonics Ltd) and the principles of surveying by electromagnetic induction (b) (courtesy C. Auton).

array with a multicore cable and preset electrode connections (Barker 1981).

Resistivity traverses provide a means of determining the lateral extent of deposits by the use of a system of constant electrode separation, the required depth of exploration being fixed by reference to the results of concomitant resistivity soundings. Despite improvements in the speed and efficiency of the technique (Griffiths & Barker 1989), the method has been almost completely superseded by electromagnetic conductivity surveying.

Conductivity mapping has become a standard exploration technique and powerful aid in geological mapping, particularly in drift terrains in lowland Britain (Zalasiewicz *et al.* 1985), during the past decade. The technique involves the detection of secondary magnetic fields that are generated as an induced response to an alternating primary magnetic field (Fig. 3.5(b)). The application of electromagnetic (EM) induction equipments to measure ground conductivity in multilayer deposits (Griffiths & King 1981) permits rapid traversing without the need for ground contacting electrodes. Conductivity meters, such as the Geonics EM31 and EM34

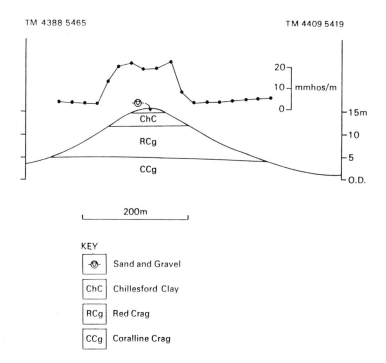

FIG. 3.6. Geological section and conductivity profile (apparent conductivity values are in millimhos per metre—mmhos/m) of a clayey silt stratum (ChC) in a gravelly sand sequence (RCg and Glacial sand and gravel) near Woodbridge, Suffolk, England (Zalasiewicz *et al.* 1985).

(McNeill 1980) produce constant readings of apparent conductivity values (displayed directly on the instrument panel) which can be plotted on to maps and interpreted in the field. The smaller equipment (EM31) is 4 m in length, weighs 9 kg and is designed to be operated at waist height by one person (Fig. 3.5(a)): it is capable of 'exploring' to a depth of approximately 5 m from surface. The larger instrument (EM34) is capable of greater penetration and resolution but is less economical in terms of operator time and progress across the ground.

Conductivity and resistivity methods may be used together. Where conductivity contrasts are obtained, a conductivity contour plan can be produced. The conductivity values are then verified and quantified by taking resistivity soundings along sectors of equal conductivity.

The electrical conductivity of most types of sedimentary rock is mainly affected by their porosity, the composition of pore fluids and the abundance of clay minerals. In drift sequences, dry, sandy, porous materials are characterized by low conductivity values, whereas relatively compact, clay-rich deposits, such as till and alluvium, give higher readings (see Fig. 3.6). The presence of groundwater significantly increases all values, and renders interpretation more difficult.

Seismic surveys. The refraction method, still sometimes used in sand and gravel surveys, is routinely applied when depth and nature of the solid, unweathered bedrock is required; some indication of the composition of the overlying materials may be deduced from their seismic velocities. In some circumstances, for example, when the seismic velocity of the near-surface layer is higher than that of any of the underlying strata (as where sand and gravel overlies clay or contains clay lenticles) the method may fail or not provide a unique solution. However, the method now benefits from the wide choice of seismic energy sources, which also ensures that reflection surveys have much greater resolution, especially through the uppermost few tens of metres (Fig. 3.3). Although applications onshore are limited by high cost, environmental and access problems, at sea continuous seismic profiling is the most widely used method (§3.6).

Ground radar 'images' the near-surface ground in a way similar to seismic reflection surveys, but the method has rather restricted application at present pending the development of technology to achieve greater ground penetration. The penetration of radar energy is limited by the conductivity of near-surface materials and encouraging results have been obtained in dry ground or where fresh water saturates the sediments; little penetration has been achieved in materials with significant clay minerals content and where saline water is present (Glover *et al.* 1989; Unterberger & Thornton 1990).

Gravity methods can demonstrate lateral changes in the density and hence of the thickness of aggregate materials and overburden (Andrew & Lee 1977) but only where site conditions are restricted or unsuitable for conductivity or resistivity surveying would gravity be considered as an option.

3.3.3.3. Marine geophysical methods. Most near-shore sand and gravel surveys incorporate geophysical techniques in conjunction with sea-bed sampling and drilling programmes. Continuous seismic profiling, side-scan sonar and bathymetric surveys are commonly deployed from the same vessel to elucidate the sub-bottom geological structure and the geography of the sea-bed. By combining high-resolution seismic and side-scan sonar records with subsequently collected shallow core and surface samples, the lithology, thickness and classification of the superficial deposits of the sea-bed can be determined reliably. Additional information from sea-bed boreholes, from the use of high-frequency energy sources such as the 'boomer' for greater resolution and of a 'sparker' (or air gun) source for improved penetration, will enable appraisals to be made of the regional geology and the factors influencing the dis-tribution of aggregate materials. A more detailed description of methods is given in §3.6.

3.4. Geological appraisal for aggregate assessment

The geological investigation and succeeding commercial evaluation of a prospective source of aggregate will involve consideration of most if not all of the following geological factors.

3.4.1. Geological classification and stratigraphical position

The correct or even preliminary geological classification of an occurrence of aggregate material in terms of its geological origin (genesis), shape (morphology) and age can convey much information and guidance for the assessment of resource and reserves potential. Terms such as 'glaciofluvial sand and gravel', 'river terrace' or 'raised beach' deposit, or 'dolerite dyke' can provide an

---

TABLE 3.1. *A systematic procedure for the examination and testing of potential aggregate sources*

A. *Reconnaissance of the available materials and establishment of their performance in likely applications*
   1. Establish the geological basis for the investigation by means of a desk study to collate all relevant data and undertake a walk-over field survey (see §§3.2 and 3.4.2), including any special geological investigations (§3.3) to establish existence of potential sources.
   2. Undertake field sampling of likely sources; investigate the characteristics of any existing nearby aggregate sources including the range of end-uses of the products, whether or not they are similar to those for which the present appraisal is being conducted.
   3. Carry out laboratory examinations and tests on samples obtained during phases 1 and 2 above; assess the performance of existing locally available aggregates in use: for example the performance of aggregate *within* concrete as well as of the concrete itself.

B. *Examination of potential aggregate sources—site investigation*
   1. Carry out full-scale trenching, pitting and/or drilling (see §§3.5.2 and 3.5.3) and sampling of the potentially useful occurrences identified from investigations so far, including material from existing local aggregate workings, whether or not it is intended for use.
   2. Carry out laboratory investigations and tests on the samples (see §7) to determine their physical characteristics and potential suitability; relate this information to the known geology of the rock mass(es) under investigation and obtain an indication of the size and distribution of the potential mineral reserve.
   3. In the light of all the new information assess the extent to which selective extraction and special processing techniques may be required to ensure a bulk supply of aggregate of sufficient quality. Review the need for particular processing plant designs.

C. *Aggregate production trials*
   1. Plan and supervise materials extraction and aggregate production trials including representative sampling of end products, selective sampling of both accepted and rejected material.
   2. Carry out further laboratory tests on samples collected from the extraction and production trials, review and finalize extraction methods, production procedures and target qualities for the processed aggregates for approval purposes.

D. *Production control programme*
   1. Establish, approve and implement sampling testing regimes for production control (Producer) and specification compliance (Engineer) purposes.
   2. Devise, approve and maintain data records, reporting proformas and control charts to monitor aggregate quality and variability.

experienced assessor with an invaluable appreciation of the likely physical characteristics of the prospect. An indication of geological age may allow comparison with known deposits elsewhere.

3.4.2. Field relations

These include the three-dimensional shape of the rock mass and the nature of the contacts with overlying and underlying strata, particularly the thickness and type of overburden, and the relationship of the pay beds or bodies to waste (Fig. 2.2). Even when the district under appraisal has already been geologically mapped in detail, at the 1:10 650 or 1:10 000 scales, which is generally the case in much of the UK it is essential that the aggregate assessor should become personally familiar with the main features of the landscape and geology of the prospect by undertaking a 'walk over' survey. Quite often this will be done by the geologist or engineer who

will be co-ordinating the various elements in the investigation of the potential aggregate source (Table 3.1).

3.4.3. Thickness of the deposit

Thickness and variation of thickness of the potentially extractable part of the deposit and the ratio of this thickness to that of the overburden or waste which may have to be removed as spoil are critical factors in resource appraisal. The nature of the waste materials may be such as to require blasting, ripping or simply mechanical excavation, and its potential for use in site restoration schemes following extraction of the resource or as rock-fill in construction projects, should not be overlooked.

3.4.4. Structure of the deposit

This includes the dip and strike of bedding or of other

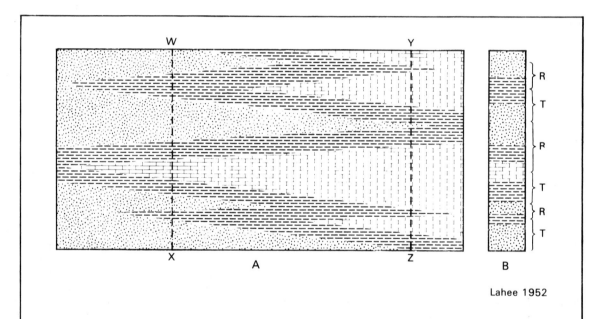

Lahee 1952

Diagrammatic section, A, of deposits laid down during successive transgressions and regressions of the sea, demonstrating that a formation may be characterised by different rock-types in space (laterally) and time (vertically). Land-derived materials have come from the left (sandy deposits grading into clayey deposits in the deeper water) whilst carbonate sedimentation (limestone) predominated out to sea (to the right)

The columnar section, B, taken at WX, shows transgressive (T) and regressive (R) phases of sedimentation; the same phases at YZ produced quite a different lithological succession.

Fig. 3.7. Sediments deposited contemporaneously in different parts of a sedimentary basin may vary widely in lithology (Lahee 1952).

regular plane surfaces, the style and intensity of folding, jointing and faulting, as well as solution effects. Examples of a descriptive terminology for discontinuities and rock structures are given by Fookes & Sweeney (1976), in §2.8 and in Figs 2.1, 2.2 and 2.22–2.24.

3.4.5. Bulk composition

This and variations in it which may arise from rapid lateral and vertical changes in sedimentation (facies variations, Figs 2.3, 3.7 & 3.8) or from differentiation during the crystallization of igneous rocks, should be defined. Such variations may be apparent from observation of exposures or they may require more detailed petrographic studies of the rock fabric and texture. The noting and analysis of sedimentary structures and changes in grade, thickness and composition from exposures, may provide the key to understanding lateral and vertical variations in a deposit and lead to predictive modelling as a spur to further exploration. There may be segregations or inclusions in igneous and other rocks which may be objectionable or deleterious: for example, pyrites in sandstones or reactive constituents in sand and gravel deposits should be noted (West 1991).

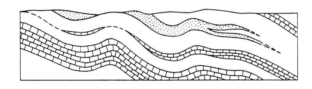

FIG. 3.8. The lensing (or 'pinching') of beds in a gently folded rock succession (Lahee 1952).

3.4.6. State of weathering and alteration of the rock mass

Ideally, only unaltered and unweathered rock material should be used for aggregate, but it is likely that in most near-surface rock bodies some degree of physical and chemical degradation of the originally fresh material will have taken place since its deposition or emplacement. The presence of discontinuities (bedding, shear and fault-planes, cleavages, fissures and joints that are open or openable) and the effects of deep-seated alteration and superficial weathering have a profound influence on the potential suitability of a rock mass for aggregate (see §§2.7, 2.8). In wet humid climates, the effects of tropical weathering may extend to great depths and render most

of the readily accessible rock bodies useless for aggregate, whereas faint physical weathering in some cool temperate conditions, for example, may enhance the potential of a deposit by leaving the aggregate material loosened and more easily extractable. The opening of discontinuities by gentle physical weathering may improve the rippability of some aggregate materials.

3.5. Sample collection

Many of the geological factors in §3.4 can be partly explored, though perhaps somewhat subjectively and interpretatively during the geological mapping and literature study of the prospect. But no matter how skilled the observer, the necessary detailed objective appraisal of the aggregate potential will require specific data on the subsurface extent of the occurrence and of the quality of the rock material obtained from the study of representative samples, which can only be obtained from a programme of drilling, pitting, trenching or excavation, or of sampling from exposures. Advisory literature on the practicalities and pitfalls involved in appraising aggregate sources is widely scattered. The following sections are drawn from British practice (e.g. Eyles 1983). Further advice on drilling and sampling methods will be found in Section 19 of the Code of Practice for Site Investigations (BS 5930: 1981).

3.5.1. Drilling for sampling, hard rock

Drilling for sampling of hard rocks may be undertaken by rotary core drilling machines using diamond-studded crowns and double core barrels with water, mud or air as flushing media. Wireline core drilling and sampling is speedy and economical for prospecting to greater depths. A single outer drill string combines the functions of casing and drill rod and incorporates an outer core barrel and drilling bit. An inner core barrel assembly passes down through the rods and latches into the outer barrel. The complete assembly is drilled down in the normal manner, until the core sample has been taken, whereupon the inner barrel can be retrieved, emptied, and re-inserted without removing the outer string from the borehole. The system can be modified for sampling unconsolidated sediments as well as rock (Focht & Kraft 1977).

The objective in all investigations of hard rocks is to obtain total recovery of the rock cores for description and testing: the core diameter should be large enough to provide sufficient material for the common index testing procedures to be undertaken to British Standard specification (BS 812: 1975) (see §7) and for a vertical slice or slab of the core to be retained for future reference, in such condition that original depth interval markings are preserved (§7). Comprehensive logging should be undertaken according to recommended procedures (Geological Society 1970; BS 5930: 1981). A core diameter of 100 mm, 70 mm (H size or equivalent) or exceptionally 54 mm (NX size or equivalent) may be adequate (BS 4019: 1974—Rotary Core Drilling Equipment). Reconnaissance coring at 32–40 mm diameter may be undertaken for speed and economy by the extractive industry: it is reported that compliance with testing procedures stipulated in BS 812 can be achieved.

The drilling and sampling of compacted, indurated and cemented pebble beds and conglomerates, are notoriously difficult to achieve by rotary methods because detached pebbles tend to foul, jam and seriously abrade the drilling tools. Often strongly-cemented conglomerates can be successfully cored.

By means of down-the-hole reversed-circulation or conventional hammer drilling using a button-bit and air, or air and water as the flushing agents, comminuted samples can be collected in a cyclone with sufficient precision for direct lithological correlations to be made between particle-size analyses of the samples and photographic records of the borehole walls. This method, which follows some of those used by the extractive industry, has been successfully applied in assessing the conglomerate resources of the Sherwood Sandstone Group ('Bunter' Pebble Beds) in Staffordshire (Piper & Rogers 1980; Rogers *et al.* 1982).

3.5.2. Shallow pits and trenches

Trial pits and trenches may be conveniently dug by means of rubber-tyred hydraulic bucket excavators in dry deposits or by low ground-pressure track-laying equipment in adverse conditions and can rapidly provide bulk samples of sand and gravel from depths of 6 m or so. Subject to considerations of safety of men and machines, the diggings, unlike boreholes, permit direct *in situ* examination and logging of deposits in cross section; if necessary, large samples of truly representative material including the fines and large stones, which may be lost from drill-hole samples, can be obtained for trial processing in an existing commercial plant. Hand-dug pits provided with appropriate protective shuttering can be very useful where labour is available.

3.5.3. Drilling for sampling, sand and gravel

3.5.3.1. Hand auger boring. Using lightweight rods and helical, spatulate or bucket samplers up to 200 mm diameter, samples may be taken to 5 to 6 m in suitable ground conditions without the aid of a tripod or casing. The strata must be self-supporting, soft and with only very few pebbles. Sampling of gravelly material and from below the water table is rarely satisfactory. Hand

auger sampling is nevertheless economical and rapid and it provides an ideal first look at a prospect. Hand augering is, of course, a basic tool in geological mapping in 'soft-rock' terrains.

3.5.3.2. Power auger machines. These range from small mobile drills powered by small-capacity petrol engines capable of reaching depths of 10 m or so at 75 mm diameter and operated by one or two men, to large lorry or tractor-mounted rigs which can reach depths exceeding 25 m at 200 mm diameter and more. Sampling may be achieved by means of continuous auger-flights which are attached throughout the whole length of the drilling string or by single flight auger which is mounted only at the leading end of the drill string and must be withdrawn from the borehole for sample retrieval. As only very few auger machines are capable of advancing borehole casing whilst drilling within it, open-hole power auger drills are commonly used but they have numerous disadvantages when precise sampling is required. Unconsolidated material, particularly beneath the level of the water table, tends to collapse into the borehole and renders progress difficult and ultimately impossible; the rotary action of the auger tends to churn the strata, leading to contamination of one layer with another so that accurate sampling is generally very difficult to achieve. The method, nevertheless, can provide good guidance on the thickness of overburden to depths of about 10 m and in dry ground conditions samples of sand and gravel may be brought to the surface though they will have been severely mixed and contaminated with other deposits. However, the auger string may be advanced into the ground by the required sampling interval (commonly between 1 and 3 m) and then withdrawn without rotation. The outer layer of material is struck off the auger-flights so that essentially uncontaminated samples can be taken from around the axis of the auger.

As a reconnaissance tool a power auger has a distinct advantage over other types of drill in that it can quickly penetrate unstable strata without the need for lining tubes. Extra flighted auger lengths can be added at the surface as drilling proceeds but the rate of progress of the drill through the various strata can only be inferred by a skilful operator; the depth from which samples are derived cannot be accurately fixed. Auger machines which can sample from within a casing are much to be preferred both in terms of sampling accuracy and speed (Hill McDonald 1972) though they are not commonly available.

3.5.3.3. Hollow-stem augers. These can penetrate unstable strata without the need for lining tubes and sampling can be done within the hollow stem by rotary coring, augering or by percussive methods to depths of perhaps 50 m in glacial deposits. Although standard power auger rigs may be used, the drilling process absorbs more power and is slower; sample quality,

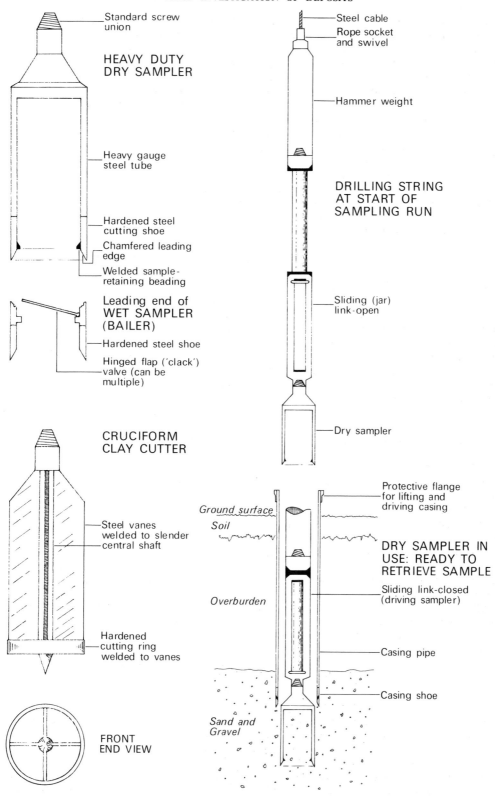

HEAVY DUTY DRY SAMPLER
- Standard screw union
- Heavy gauge steel tube
- Hardened steel cutting shoe
- Chamfered leading edge
- Welded sample-retaining beading

Leading end of WET SAMPLER (BAILER)
- Hardened steel shoe
- Hinged flap ('clack') valve (can be multiple)

CRUCIFORM CLAY CUTTER
- Steel vanes welded to slender central shaft
- Hardened cutting ring welded to vanes

FRONT END VIEW

DRILLING STRING AT START OF SAMPLING RUN
- Steel cable
- Rope socket and swivel
- Hammer weight
- Sliding (jar) link-open
- Dry sampler

DRY SAMPLER IN USE: READY TO RETRIEVE SAMPLE
- Protective flange for lifting and driving casing
- Ground surface
- Soil
- Overburden
- Sliding link-closed (driving sampler)
- Casing pipe
- Casing shoe
- Sand and Gravel

Fig. 3.9. Drilling tools for use with a cable-percussion drilling rig for sampling sand and gravel from unconsolidated (drift) deposits.

however, is likely to be higher than that achieved by open-hole augering.

3.5.3.4. Light cable percussion boring. This is an adaption of standard well-boring methods and commonly utilizes clay cutters, chisels (for breaking up hard rock obstructions) and bailers (for removing water-laden samples from the borehole), working within lining tubes (casing) which enter the ground under gravity as the boring proceeds. To ensure that samples of sand and gravel are truly representative, it is necessary to take samples in dry and if possible undisturbed conditions within the borehole. This can be achieved by driving a sampling tube ahead of the leading edge of the casing by the use of a sinker bar with sliding hammer or jar link; to reduce the length of the equipment (illustrated in Fig. 3.9), the sliding link may be shortened and incorporated with the sampler. In this way, all of the material from within the ideal diameter of the borehole can be sampled dry (Hill McDonald 1972). Slightly clayey and sandy drift deposits containing gravel and even cobble grades (2 to 200 mm) can be sampled from depths to 30 m using a 2-ton percussion rig without seriously breaking the particles, provided tools up to 300 mm diameter are employed and the deposits are not unduly consolidated. A limitation on the depth of drilling is commonly imposed by the capacity of the rig to extract the lining tubes from the ground, though this may be overcome to some extent by the insertion of a reduced diameter tube within the main casing tube (and the substitution of appropriate sampling tools). In waterlogged conditions the tendency for groundwater to rise rapidly up the borehole carrying with it material from beneath the sampling level effectively prevents further sampling unless the casing can be advanced into a watertight stratum. Increasing consolidation of the drift deposits at depths exceeding about 30 m in most terrains, calls for the alternate use of the chisel and sampler. The drilling then proceeds very slowly and the samples are commonly severely broken by the percussive force of the chisel, so that they do not reflect the in situ grading of the deposit.

Other methods of boring are to be preferred in these circumstances. They may include sonic and resonant drill systems (Somerville 1983). Sonic drills (like the vibrocorer, for sea-bed sampling, §3.6.3) employ ultra-high frequency vibrations generated by a motor driven by compressed air, hydraulic power or electricity, to force an open core barrel through sediments, which are fluidized and displaced into the sampler. Resonant drill systems operate by combining the effects of high-frequency vibration with conventional rotary motion and rapid penetration and sampling of sediments and soft rocks can be achieved by using the pull-down force of the winch head. Penetration rates of 30 cm/s in sands and gravels and 7 cm/s in lodgement till have been reported (Dance 1981).

The cable percussion method is nevertheless to be strongly preferred where sampling is the major objective because progress cannot be maintained unless casing is inserted and this ensures that the samples remain uncontaminated (Fig. 3.10). The majority of drillers, who habitually add water to speed the drilling process when unsupervised, should be dissuaded from doing so in the interests of accurate sampling: otherwise much of the fines fraction is likely to be washed out. The machinery is relatively unsophisticated, cheap to buy and simply maintained; its modest size is advantageous in gaining easy access to drilling sites (Thurrell 1981).

3.5.3.5. Reversed circulation drills. These are often of large size, and operate with a double-wall usually non-rotatory drill-pipe system. The flushing medium, which may be air or foam, is forced down the annulus between the outer and inner tubes to a rotating drill bit where it sweeps the sample or rock cuttings back up through the central tube at high velocity, to be collected in a pneumatic separator at the surface. Sampling is uncontaminated and entirely representative; in most conditions the depth of sampling can be accurately located, though the speed of the drilling operation is such that refined sampling and logging may not be achieved unless many hands are available. For economical deployment of such machines, full advantage must be taken of their high output and this can normally be ensured only where extensive prospecting is to be undertaken in relatively open terrains.

3.6. Marine exploration

Resource surveys must be designed to improve knowledge of the regional geology in order to understand better, and thus predict, the occurrence and distribution of marine sands and gravels. Submarine occurrences may represent inundated and reworked fluvial, glacial and shoreline deposits with a variable cover of modern sediments deposited from rivers or derived from erosion of coastal and sea-bed deposits. In certain conditions the fine-grained unconsolidated sediments may migrate as sand waves of considerable amplitude (Veenstra 1969), or may accumulate to form tidal sand banks and periodically cover less mobile coarse aggregate spreads.

Whilst inspection and sampling of sea-bed deposits by divers may provide useful preliminary guidance, more sophisticated follow-up methods of survey and site investigation will normally be deployed. Many of the methods and tools widely used onshore can be adapted to marine applications. For unconsolidated deposits in shallow waters, the cable-percussion ('shell and auger') system of ground investigation is widely used: drilling, sampling and in situ testing are described in BS 5930: 1981. Details of other methods that may be useful for

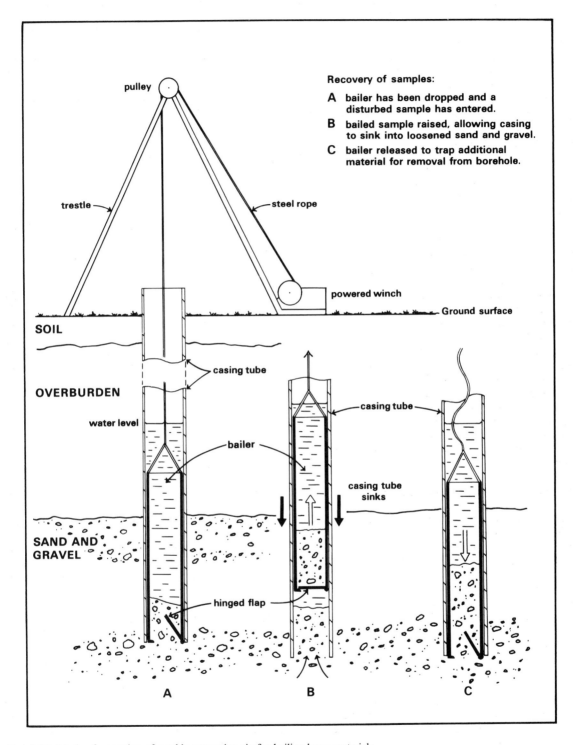

FIG. 3.10. Mode of operation of a cable-percussion rig for bailing loose materials.

marine ground investigations, including the appraisal of geotechnical properties of sea-bed sediments, will be found in BS 6349 (Maritime Structures) Part 1 (1984) and Part 5, Section 2 (1991).

Prospecting should begin with a desk study of available information sources, including Admiralty Charts (published in the UK by the Hydrographer to the Navy) and any more recently collected bathymetric data. Because the charts are prepared for navigation rather than for studies of the materials of the sea bed, suitably detailed surveys designed for resource appraisal of the prospect area as a whole, will be needed. In addition to echo sounding and side-scan sonar traverses for depth measurement, prospecting must cover the distribution, thickness and quality of the potential aggregate materials. The use of shallow seismic reflection profiling based on a closely spaced grid of traverses will help to elucidate the stratigraphic relationships of individual sedimentary units to give a three-dimensional picture, the geometry, of each. Navigational systems for accurate positioning must be used.

3.6.1. Echo sounder

The returning signals can be displayed to give an analogue record of the sea-bed or stored on tape for plotting and contouring. The accuracy of the record can be improved by mounting the transmitter in a towed fish rather than in the hull of the ship but, unless the lines of survey are closely spaced, there is a likelihood that significant variations in sea-bed topography may be missed.

3.6.2. Side-scan sonar

This system involves the transmission of a beam of sound from a towed fish and the collection and display of return signals reflected by irregularities of the sea floor or the texture of deposits, extending over a survey tract up to 1500 metres wide (Simpson 1979). Areas of soft sand, silt and clay give very weak return signals and show as lighter areas on the display, whereas more strongly reflective granular material, such as gravel and boulder clay, gives a stronger return and exposures of bedrock (and the presence of obstructions, such as wrecks) produce the strongest (darkest) reflections.

3.6.3. Sampling

Although these reconnaissance techniques give a general indication of the shape and likely physical constitution of the surface of the sea-bed sediments, positive identification must depend on direct sampling. Samples weighing several kilograms may be collected from the surface of the sea-bed using spring-loaded or mechanically actuated grabs lowered from a ship; larger samples may be dredged. Sampling below the sea-bed can be achieved by dropping a weighted coring tube under gravity. Cores up to 100 mm in diameter and six metres long can be recovered from soft sediments by this method, but in more consolidated materials, like boulder clay, sand and gravel, sampling tubes can be much more effectively advanced by pneumatic or electrically driven hammer drills (vibrocorers). Deeper sampling to depths approaching 20 metres in 100 metres of water can be achieved by means of an air-lift, hydraulic-jetting system combined with a driving hammer. The speed of the sampling operation and the volume of the material collected by this prospecting drill require special arrangements for splitting and storing the samples on board ship; the average daily performance is about ten boreholes of between 6 and 10 m in heavy seas with swells up to 2 or 3 m (Hess 1971).

3.6.4. Seismic and acoustic prospecting techniques

The high cost of prospecting at sea dictates that rather less sampling is likely to be undertaken than on land, and it is normal practice to interpolate between boreholes or sampling stations by means of shallow seismic reflection profiling techniques. The methods require an acoustic source and a receiver to provide a time-scaled acoustic section of the geological structure beneath the sea-bed which is convertible to a true-scale horizontal section of the strata (Dobinson & McCann 1990). For shallow penetration applications, appropriate to aggregate prospecting, the acoustic sources are commonly the pinger, a powerful echo-sounder, which provides good resolution (± 10 cm) in sediments a few metres thick, and the boomer, an electro-mechanical device which generates a shock wave from which reflections to depths exceeding 30 m in drift sequences can be reliably recognized. Fine detail can be discerned in the uppermost 5 m, with differentiation of layers down to 0.5 m in thickness.

Most surveys for sand and gravel include geophysical investigations coupled with grid sampling using a sea-bed drill such as a vibrocorer, but the major shortcoming of sea-bed sampling is the loss of the fine sand, silt and clay fractions from the samples. In these circumstances bulk sampling with a dredger may provide better guidance to the commercial potential of the shallow part of a deposit, but it can give little indication of the quality of the deposits as a whole or of the likely volume of the resource. Shallow coring and surface grab sampling will go far to provide the required ground-truth data to calibrate the geophysical interpretations as well as material for laboratory grading and testing. Marine aggregate resources are commonly classified on the relative proportions of gravel, sand and fines ('mud') in the sediment. Gravel comprises rock particles greater than 5 mm in grade, sand is sediment between 5 mm and 0.063 mm and fines (silt and clay) material less than 0.063 mm grain size.

A valuable illustrated review of techniques applicable to exploration in the shallow seas is given by McQuillin & Ardus (1977).

3.7. Presentation of field and test results

The following procedures, suitably adapted, can apply whether the investigation is wide-scale (regional) or site-specific in approach.

3.7.1. Cross sections and maps

These should show all geolial data needed for estimating the volume and quality of the prospect, and form the basis of an extraction plan, if any. Sections should be drawn to the same scale as the accompanying maps (if possible, without vertical exaggeration) and should cross-refer. (It should be noted that it may not be possible or practical to distinguish the exact detailed stratigraphic relations of folded or thin beds, especially in Quaternary sequences, *at true scale reduction* because of cartographic limitations. Any departure from true scale in sections involves vertical or horizontal exaggeration, so that portrayal, for example, of actual inclination or thickness cannot be maintained.)

In particular, the nature and recorded thickness of overburden and of weathered material should be shown at all data points on both maps and sections: the latter should intersect as many borehole sites as possible, to avoid projecting information onto lines of section.

The results of physical tests on samples should be correlated with the geological interpretation (preferably by plotting them on the maps and sections) so that the incidence of substandard or interbedded waste materials can be readily assessed. For more detailed guidance and for the calculation of volumes of useful and other materials reference must be made to borehole logs and laboratory data sheets.

3.7.2. Estimation of aggregate reserves and resources; definitions of terms

The large literature on the classification of mineral resources is testimony to the complexity of the subject, yet the establishment of limiting physical criteria, which are themselves largely conditioned by economic constraints, is necessary before estimation and comparison of the quality and amount of potentially useful prospects can proceed. American usage has been widely accepted

and a review of terminology (Bureau of Mines and Geological Survey, 1976) defines a mineral *resource* as a concentration of naturally occurring materials in such form that economic extraction is currently or potentially feasible. Material classified as a *reserve* is that part of an identified resource producible at a profit at the time of classification. A diagrammatic presentation of this classification known colloquially as 'the McKelvey diagram' after its originator (McKelvey 1972) is in Fig. 3.11A. It shows how total resources can be categorized in terms of economic feasibility of extraction (economic constraints) and the degree of geological assurance (the level of available knowledge of the physical characteristics).

A simpler system has been proposed for international application by an Experts Group on Definitions and Terminology for Mineral Resources in the United Nations (United Nations 1979), as follows.

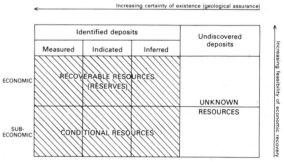

A. A classification of mineral resources after McKelvey.

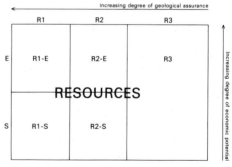

B. A classification of mineral resources, simplified from the United Nations system.

FIG. 3.11. Classification of mineral resources applicable to aggregates: (A) after McKelvey (1972); (B) after United Nations Experts Group (1979).

3.7.3. Basic resource categories

These, categorized as R-1, R-2 and R-3, are distinguished in order of decreasing geological assurance.

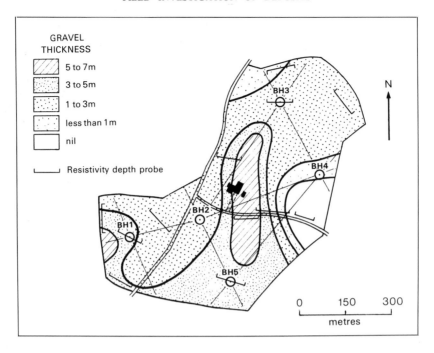

FIG. 3.12. Isopachytes drawn from borehole and intervening resistivity depth probe data for a sand and gravel prospect.

Each of these categories can be further subdivided into those considered to be exploitable under the prevailing socio-economic conditions (sub-category E) and other resources (sub-category S). These categories are set out in Fig. 3.11B. Whilst there may be an inclination to equate the proposed categories with more familiar terms (R-1 = demonstrated, explored; R-2 = inferred, estimated; R-3 = potential, speculative) in the long term, the letter-number combinations should gain acceptance where for reasons of language and established often rather complex usage, the existing subjective descriptive terms will not. It is hoped that increasing acceptance of alpha-numeric terms will encourage clearer understanding of resource evaluations between all users of such data.

3.7.4. Methods for estimating amounts

The investigation of a source of aggregates may be designed as a detailed appraisal, for example, to extend the known reserves for an existing quarrying operation for which the limiting criteria are well established, or it may form part of an inventory of resources on a regional or national scale. In both the requirement is for numerical estimates of the quantity and quality of useful material in the prospect, upon which forward planning can be reliably based. Very commonly, graphical methods have been used in calculating the volume of occurrences, based on geological mapping and drill-hole data. If a

deposit is largely regular in shape, true-scale cross sections may be drawn parallel to each other, at regular intervals and the sectional areas of useful material measured. The volume is given by the product of the means of these areas and the distance between the end sections. Alternatively, the volume of material between adjacent cross sections within the prospect can be calculated and summed. Isopachytes may be drawn on a plan, joining points of equal thickness as demonstrated by borehole or other records (Fig. 3.12). The area between each successive pair of isopachytes is obtained by planimetry and multiplied by the average thickness value represented by them. The sum of the results is the volume of the deposit. Rather more complex calculations based on the construction of triangles with thickness data-points at their corners, or polygons representing the areas of influence of data points may be undertaken by reference to the relevant texts.

3.7.5. Reliability of the estimates

The shortcoming of these largely graphical methods is that the reliability of the estimates cannot be readily demonstrated. The use of simple (or classical) statistical procedures can remedy this (Fig. 3.13), and the calculation of confidence limits using 'Students-t' distribution (Davis 1973; Hull 1981) and variations of it have been used for sand and gravel surveys in the UK. A procedure is set out in each of the Mineral Assessment Reports

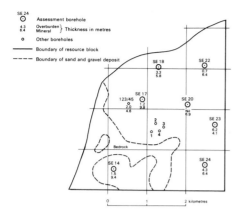

Block calculation

Scale: 1:25 000
Block: Fictitious

Area
Block: 11.08 km^2
Mineral: 8.32 km^2

Mean thickness
Overburden: 2.5 m
Mineral: 6.5 m

Volume
Overburden: 21 million m^3
Mineral: 54 million m^3

Confidence limits of the estimate of mineral volume at the 95 per cent probability level: ± 20 per cent
That is, the volume of mineral (with 95 per cent probability): 54 ± 11 million m^2

Thickness estimate (measurements in metres)
t_b= overburden thickness t_m = mineral thickness

Sample point	Weighting w	Overburden		Mineral		Remarks
		t_b	wt_b	t_m	wt_m	
SE 14	1	1.5	1.5	9.4	9.4	
SE 18	1	3.3	3.3	5.8	5.8	
SE 20	1	nil	–	6.9	6.9	
SE 22	1	0.7	0.7	6.4	6.4	Assessment
SE 23	1	6.2	6.2	4.1	4.1	boreholes
SE 24	1	4.3	4.3	6.4	6.4	
SE 17	½	1.2	} 1.6	9.8	} 7.2	Hydrogeology
123/45	½	2.0		4.6		record
1	¼	2.7		7.3		Close group
2	¼	4.5	} 2.6	3.2	} 5.8	of four
3	¼	0.4		6.8		boreholes
4	¼	2.8		5.9		(commercial)
Totals	Σw= 8		Σwt_b = 20.2		Σwt_m = 52.0	
Means			$\overline{wt_b}$ = 2.5		$\overline{wt_m}$ = 6.5	

Calculation of confidence limits

wt_m	$\lvert(wt_m - \overline{wt_m})\rvert$	$(wt_m - \overline{wt_m})^2$
9.4	2.9	8.41
5.8	0.7	0.49
6.9	0.4	0.16
6.4	0.1	0.01
4.1	2.4	5.76
6.4	0.1	0.01
7.2	0.7	0.49
5.8	0.7	0.49

$$\Sigma(wt_m - \overline{wt_m})^2 = 15.82$$

$n = 8$
$t = 2.365$

L_v is calculated as

$$1.05 \ (t/ \ \overline{wt_m}) \ \sqrt{[\ \Sigma \ wt_m - \overline{wt_m})^2/ \ n(n-1)]} \times 100$$

$$= 1.05 \times (2.365/6.5) \ \sqrt{[15.82/(8 \times 7)]} \times 100$$

$$= 20.3$$

$$\approx 20 \ \text{per cent}.$$

of the British Geological Survey dealing with sand and gravel appraisal, which is generally applicable. The reliability of the estimates of the volume of a source of aggregate is normally a direct reflection of the degree of geological assurance available to the investigator; this in turn enables him to classify a prospect according to the terminology demonstrated in Fig. 3.11.

Geostatistical manipulation of data may provide additional guidance to the prospector, and for the mathematically adept, the procedures may add weight to the professional judgement or 'hunches' of the assessor in evaluating a deposit. Given a set of sample data points (commonly boreholes) and their locations, whatever the parameter under consideration, the method can provide estimates of the value of variables at other, interpolated locations. That is, given a partial finite data set, which represents some phenomenon, geostatistics is designed to provide an estimate of the values at points outside the data set (Royle 1971).

It is claimed that geostatistics provides a better estimate than classical statistics since it takes into account the spatial separations of the samples and their correlation (a function of the geological structure of the deposit) to compute a function called a 'semi-variogram'. This effectively weights values of the relevant parameters according to the distance of the sample points from the point, block or area of interest to calculate the interpolated value.

Geostatistics also offers the advantage of providing an estimate of the error associated with any reserve evaluation or calculated value of a parameter at a point together with a confidence level. For example, calculations might indicate a reserve of X million tonnes at 95% confidence, i.e. there is a 5% chance that the reserve is less than X million. A decision may then be made as to whether such errors or confidence intervals are acceptable and, if not, geostatistics provides a means to calculate the required quantity of additional exploration data that is required to improve the precision of the reserve estimate. It does not replace the need for informed judgement, however, and must be used as an additional tool together with an understanding of the geological structure of the deposit (Clark 1979; Henley 1981).

Geostatistics may be used in prospect valuation to solve two principal problems: to provide an estimate of error and confidence limits. At the reconnaissance or exploration stage, it can provide global estimates, for example, of quality, volume or content of deleterious components, to demonstrate whether or not a prospect is potentially workable (or viable) judged against predetermined criteria. Secondly, it may provide more localized

Fig. 3.13. Calculation of the sand and gravel resources in a hypothetical map area (a resource block) with confidence limits quoted at the two-sided 95% probability level (Source: Mineral Assessment Report series, e.g. Dunkley 1979).

estimates of the quality or value of defined blocks of the resource or reserve that are likely to be economically more attractive for development. The method ideally requires high-quality, regular (non-random) grid sampling in three dimensions for best results, and so has been applied most commonly in high-value metalliferous ore prospecting, where the potential yield might be expected to provide sufficient revenue to justify an expensive sampling programme (Koch & Link 1971; Cheeney 1983). Apart from some experimental work in placer evaluation, it would seem unlikely that geostatistics would find a ready application in high tonnage, low grade operations in the aggregates field. Further discussion may be found in Verly *et al.* (1983).

In practical terms, the approach to the assessment of aggregates adopted by local and central government planners, prospectors for construction materials and trade associations is necessarily generalized and widescale; they are mainly concerned with the appraisal of resources (McLellan & Bryant 1975; Thurrell 1971, 1981). On the other hand, members of the extractive minerals industry must be involved with relatively much more intensive investigations of socio-economic as well as the geological and geotechnical aspects of prospects in order to categorize them as commercially viable. Even when the physical and chemical characteristics of the aggregate source itself have been shown to be acceptable, the influence of operational, marketing, environmental and land-use planning factors, which can be expected to affect each prospect in possibly widely different ways, must be considered before a particular quarrying prospect can be regarded as a reserve (Holroyd *et al.* 1989). Changing economic circumstances may alter the status of a previously classified prospect so that it may become more or less attractive for exploitation.

3.7.6. Some factors affecting the yield of a prospect

It cannot be over-emphasized that the proportion of the potentially suitable aggregate material in a prospect that could be extracted in practice is likely to be much less than the gross estimated volume in the ground. The workable volume may often be limited by a variety of operational and environmental factors (Sloan *et al.* 1989). In normal practice overburden must be dug to clear a quarry face by a distance equal to the depth of overburden, and must be formed to a stable slope, which may be as shallow as 1 in 5 in clay. Within the mineral formation access ramps may sterilize some material, and safety considerations will dictate a stepped profile to the working face. In unconsolidated formations of sand and gravel a safe face height is unlikely to exceed 10 metres and in rock formations, practice in Britain is that benches should not generally exceed 20 metres at 15 degrees inclination, although locally such factors as

geological structure, blasting technique and safety, planning or legal constraints may dictate other limitations. In deep rock excavations the overall sidewall angle will not generally exceed 60° at 65 metre depth, or 40° at 300 metre depth (Roberts *et al.* 1972) (see also §4.5). In developed regions of the world a variety of environmental constraints may prevail and it is the concern of the land-use and development planning interests to resolve conflicting issues (see §4.6).

3.8. Exploration and development of aggregate prospects

A suggested procedure for examining and testing potential aggregate sources is given in Table 3.1. The effective management of a project requires the appointment of a co-ordinating geologist or engineer who will define the objectives of the investigations and provide the field and laboratory personnel with precise terms of reference for each stage through to the production control programme (Morray-Jones 1968; Lovell 1968).

It is advisable to prepare reports at the conclusion of each of the four stages (A, B, C and D of Table 3.1) and a final report should summarize them. The co-ordinator can by then be confident in commencing the concrete mix design or other use for the aggregate and set up trials in situ.

References

ALLUM, J. A. E. 1966. *Photogeology and Regional Mapping.* Pergamon, Oxford.

ANDREW, E. M. & LEE, M. K. 1977. The use of geophysical methods in locating buried valleys in N.E. England. *Geophysical Journal of the Royal Astronomical Society*, **49**, 265.

ANDREWS, I. J., LONG, D., RICHARDS, P. C., THOMSON, A. R., BROWN, S., CHESHER, J. A. & McCORMAC, M. 1990. *United Kingdom Offshore Regional Report: the Geology of the Moray Firth.* HMSO, London for the British Geological Survey).

ANON 1970. Engineering Group Working Party Report on the logging of rock cores for engineering purposes. *Quarterly Journal of Engineering Geology*, **3**, 1–24.

ANON 1972. The preparation of maps and plans in terms of engineering geology. *Quarterly Journal of Engineering Geology*, **5**, 293–382.

ANON 1985. *Research Programme to Assess the Potentially Workable Sand and Gravel Resources in the Wreake Valley, Leicestershire.* Report No. 300/UK/0984, Engineering Geology Ltd/Geomorphological Services Ltd, for the Department of the Environment, London.

ANON 1988. Engineering geophysics. *Quarterly Journal of Engineering Geology*, **21**, 207–271.

ANON 1990. *Sand and Gravel Resources of Lancashire.* Report by Allott and Lomax, Consulting Engineers for Minerals and Land Reclamation Division, Department of the Environment, London.

ARCHER, A. A. 1970. Standardisation of the size classification of naturally occurring aggregates. *Géotechnique*, **20**, 103–107.

AUTON, C. A. 1985. The study of sand and gravel resources in East Anglia: an example of the methods used in bulk mineral assessment. *Modern Geology*, **9**, 117–128.

—— 1992. The utility of conductivity surveying and resistivity sounding in evaluating sand and gravel deposits and mapping drift sequences in north-east Scotland. *Engineering Geology*, **32**, 11–28.

—— & CROFTS, R. G. 1986. *The Sand and Gravel Resources of the Country around Aberdeen, Grampian Region*. Mineral Assessment report, British Geological Survey No 146. BGS, Edinburgh.

——, MERRITT, J. W. & ROSS, D. L. 1988. *The sand and gravel resources of the Country around Inverurie and Dunecht, and between Banchory and Stonehaven, Grampian Region*. British Geological Survey Technical Report, WF/88/1. BGS, Keyworth, Nottingham.

AVERY, B. W. 1987. *Soil Survey Methods*. Soil Survey Technical Monograph, No. 18. Harpenden, England.

BALSON, P. S. & HARRISON, D. J. 1986. *Marine aggregate survey, Phase 1, Southern North Sea*. BGS Marine Report No. 86/38.

BARKER, R. D. 1981. The offset system of electrical resistivity sounding and its use with a multi-core cable. *Geophysical Prospecting*, **29**, 128–143.

BARNES, J. W. 1981. *Basic Geological Mapping*. Geological Society, London, handbook series. Open University Press, Milton Keynes.

BARRINGER, A. R. 1971. Airborne exploration. *Mining Magazine*, **124**, 182–189.

BEAUMONT, T. E. 1979. Remote sensing for the location and mapping of engineering construction materials in developing countries. *Quarterly Journal of Engineering Geology*, **12**, 147–158.

BEAVEN, P. J. 1976. Terrain evaluation. *Manual of Applied Geology for Engineers*. HMSO, London, 171–195.

BRITISH STANDARDS INSTITUTION 1974. *Rotary Core Drilling Equipment*. BS 4019.

—— 1975. *Methods for Sampling and Testing Mineral Aggregates, Sands and Fillers*. BS 812.

—— 1981. *Code of Practice for Site Investigations* (formerly CP 2001). BS 5930.

—— *Code of Practice for Maritime Structures*. BS 6349, Pt 1 (1984) & Pt 5 Sect 2 (1991).

BROWNE, M. A. E. & MCMILLAN, A. A. 1989. *Geology for Land-use Planning: Drift Deposits of the Clyde Valley* (3 Vols.), British Geological Survey Technical Report WA/89/78.

BUREAU OF MINES AND GEOLOGICAL SURVEY. 1948. *Mineral Resources of the United States*. Public Affairs Press, Washington, DC, 14–17.

—— 1976. *Principles of the Mineral Resources Classification System of the US Bureau of Mines and US Geological Survey*. Bulletin No. 1450-A, USGS, 1–5.

CANNELL, B. & CROFTS, R. G. 1984. *The Sand and Gravel Resources of the Country around Henley-in-Arden, Warwickshire*. Mineral Assessment Report, British Geological Survey, No. 142.

CASSINIS, R. 1977. Use of remote sensing from space platforms for regional geological evaluation and for planning ground exploration. *Geophysical Prospecting*, **25**, 636–657.

CHAPLOW, R. C. 1975. Engineering geology and site investigation Pt. 1. Introduction. *Ground Engineering*, **8** (3), 34–38.

CHEENEY, R. F. 1983. *Statistical Methods in Geology for Field and Lab Decisions*. Allen and Unwin, London.

CHESTER, D. K. 1980. The evaluation of Scottish sand and gravel resources. *Scottish Geographical Journal*, **96**, 51–62.

——, CLAPPERTON, C. M., GEMMELL, A. M. D., MURDOCH, W. & SUGDEN, D. E. 1974. The sand and gravel reserves in the Aberdeen and Ellon districts. Internal publication, Department of Geography, University of Aberdeen.

CLARK, I. 1979. *Practical Geostatistics*. Applied Science Publishers, London.

CLARKE, M. R. 1983. Geophysical evaluation of scattered occurrences of sand and gravel in drift deposits. *In*: ATKINSON, K. & BRASSINGTON, R. (eds) *Prospecting and Evaluation of Non-Metallic Rocks and Minerals*. Institution of Geologists, London.

——, ABRAHAM, D. A. & THORNTON, M. H. 1982. *The potential aggregate resources in East Suffolk*. Open File Report, Institute of Geological Sciences, Nottingham.

CORNWELL, J. D. 1985. Applications of geophysical methods to mapping unconsolidated sediments in East Anglia. *Modern Geology*, **9**, 187–205.

——, CANNELL, B. & MCCANN, D. M. 1989. Application of geophysical methods to sand and gravel deposit assessment. *In*: GASKARTH, J. W. & LUMSDEN, A. C. (eds) *Proceedings of 6th Extractive Industry Geology Conference*, University of Birmingham, 255–263.

—— & MCCANN, D. M. 1991. The application of geophysical methods to the geological mapping of Quaternary sediments. *In*: FORSTER, A., CULSHAW, M. G., CRIPPS, J. C. LITTLE, J. A. & MOON, C. F. (eds) *Quaternary Engineering Geology*. Geological Society, London. Engineering Geology Special Publication, 7, 519–526.

COX, F. C., DAVIS, J. R. & SCRIVENOR, R. C. 1986. *The distribution of High-Grade Sandstone for Aggregate Usage in Parts of South-west England and South Wales*. Report for Department of the Environment (Keyworth, Nottinghamshire: British Geological Survey).

CRATCHLEY, C. R. 1976. Geophysical methods. *Manual of Applied Geology for Engineers*. HMSO, London, 110–146.

CRIMES, T. P., MARSHALL, P., HARRIS, A. L., MCCALL, G. J. H., CHESTER, G. K., MUSSETT, A. E., WILSON, C. D. V., BRENCHLEY, P. J., FLINN, D. & HUNT, C. 1985. *Assessment of Sand and Gravel Resources to the South of Shrewsbury, Shropshire*. Department of Geological Sciences, University of Liverpool. Report for the Department of the Environment, London.

CULLEY, R. W. 1973. Use of airborne resistivity surveys for gravel location. *Canadian Mining Metallurgical Bulletin*, **66**, 731, 1–5.

DANCE, D. R. 1981. Resonant vibrational drill systems. *Third Annual Conference, Alaskan Placer Mining Proceedings*, 1–12.

DAVIS, J. C. 1973. *Statistics and Data Analysis in Geology*. Kansas Geological Survey. Wiley, New York.

DE MULDER, E. F. J. 1987. Recent developments in environmental geology in The Netherlands. *In*: ARNT, P. & LÜTTIG, G. W. (eds) *Mineral Resources' Extraction, Environmental Protection and Land-use Planning in the Industrial and Developing Countries*. Schweizerbart'sche, Stuttgart.

DOBINSON, A. & MCCANN, D. M. 1990. Application of marine seismic surveying methods to engineering geological studies in the near-shore environment. *Quarterly Journal of Engineering Geology*, **23**, 109–123.

DOORNKAMP, J. C. 1989. Techniques of map presentation. *In*: MCCALL, G. J. H. & MARKER, B. R. (eds) *Earth Science*

Mapping for Planning, Development and Conservation. Graham & Trotman, London.

——, BRUNSDEN, D., JONES, D. K. C., COOKE, R. U. & BUSH, P. R. 1979. Rapid geomorphological assessments for engineering. *Quarterly Journal of Engineering Geology,* **12,** 189–204.

DRURY, S. A. 1987. *Image Interpretation in Geology.* Allen and Unwin, London.

DUMBLETON, M. J. & WEST, G. 1970. *Air Photograph Interpretation for Road Engineers in Britain.* Department of the Environment, TRRL Report LR 369. Crowthorne.

—— & —— 1976. *Preliminary Sources of Information for Site Investigation in Britain.* Department of the Environment, TRRL Report LR 403 (Revised edition), Crowthorne (Transport and Road Research Laboratory).

DUNKLEY, P. N. 1979. *The Sand and Gravel Resources of the Country Around Maidenhead and Marlow.* Mineral Assessment Report, Institute of Geological Sciences, No. 42.

EASTAFF, D. J., BEGGS, C. J. & McELHINNEY, M. D. 1978. Middle East-geotechnical data collection. *Quarterly Journal of Engineering Geology,* **9,** 37–55.

EVANS, C. D. R. 1988. *The Sand and Gravel Resources of Two Areas in the Bristol Channel and Severn Estuary.* BGS Marine Report No. 88/30.

EYLES, N. (ed.). 1983. *Glacial Geology: an Introduction for Engineers and Earth Scientists.* Pergamon, Oxford.

FOCHT, J. A. & KRAFT, L. M. 1977. Progress in marine geotechnical engineering. *Journal Geotechnical Engineering Division, American Society Civil Engineers,* **103,** 1097–1118.

FOOKES, P. G., DALE, S. G. & LAND, J. M. 1991. Some observations on a comparative aerial photography interpretation of a landslipped area. *Quarterly Journal of Engineering Geology,* **24,** 249–265.

—— & SWEENEY, M. 1976. Stabilisation and control of local rock falls and degrading rock slopes. *Quarterly Journal of Engineering Geology,* **9,** 37–55.

FOX, R. A. 1979. The role of the geologist in quarrying. *Quarry Management and Products,* **6,** 239–245.

GALLOIS, R. W. 1988. *The Geology of the Country around Ely, Cambridgeshire.* Memoir of the British Geological Survey. HMSO, London.

GLOVER, J. M., LEGGO, P. J. & WRIGHT, A. J. 1989. Investigation of mineral deposits using ground-probing radar. *In:* GASKARTH, J. W. & LUMSDEN, A. C. (eds) *Proceedings of the 6th Extractive Industry Geology Conference,* Birmingham University.

GORDON, P., HEYES, A. J., MARKER, B. R. & WOOD, R. J. 1982. Geological basis of land-use planning: a Department of the Environment philosophy for commissioning research. *Transactions of the Institution of Mining Metallurgy (Section B: Applied Earth Science),* **91,** 152–156.

GRIFFITHS, D. H. & BARKER, R. D. 1989. Electrical imaging and examples of its application. *In:* GASKARTH, J. W. & LUMSDEN, A. C. (eds) *Proceedings of the 6th Extractive Industry Geology Conference,* University of Birmingham, England.

—— & KING, R. F. 1981. *Applied Geophysics for Geologists and Engineers.* Pergamon, Oxford.

HAMBLIN, R. J. O. & HARRISON, D. J. 1988. *Marine Aggregate Survey, Phase 2. South Coast.* BGS Marine Report No. 88/31.

—— & —— 1989. *The Marine Sand and Gravel Resources of the Isle of Wight and Beachy Head.* BGS Technical Report WB/89/41C.

HARRISON, D. J. 1988. *The Marine Sand and Gravel Resources of Great Yarmouth and Southwold, East Anglia.* BGS Techni-cal Report WB/88/9C.

—— 1992. *The Marine Sand and Gravel Resources of the Humber.* British Geological Survey Technical Report, WB/92/1.

—— & ADLAM, K. A. McL. 1985. *Limestones of the Peak: a guide to the limestone resources of the Peak District, Derbyshire and Staffordshire.* Mineral Assessment Report, British Geological Survey, No. 144.

—— & ARDUS, D. A. 1989. Geological investigations for marine aggregates offshore East Anglia. *In:* GASKARTH, J. W. & LUMSDEN, A. C. (eds) *Proceedings of 6th Extractive Industry Geology Conference, Birmingham University.*

——, BUCKLEY, D. & MARKS, R. J. 1992. *The limestone resources and hydrogeology of the Mendip Hills.* British Geological Survey Technical Report, WA/92/19.

HENLEY, S. 1981. *Non-parametric Geostatistics.* Applied Science, London.

HESS, H. D. 1971. *Marine Sand and Gravel Mining Industry of the United Kingdom.* NOAA Technical Rept. ERL 213-MMTC 1, US Dept Commerce, Washington, DC.

HILL McDONALD. 1972. *Sand and gravel exploration methods.* Proceedings of Forum in Geology and Minerals, Florida Department of Natural Resources Special Publication, **17.**

HIMUS, G. W. & SWEETING, G. S. 1968. *The Elements of Field Geology.* 2nd ed University Tutorial Press, London.

HOLROYD, P., MULLETT, J. & HALLIDAY, J. S. 1989. A combination of trend, cross-impact, economic and finanacial assessments of sand and gravel extraction in the United Kingdom. Paper 13. *In* GASKARTH, J. W. & LUMSDEN, A. C. (eds) *Proceedings of the 6th Extractive Industry Geology Conference, Birmingham University.*

HOPKINS, D. A. 1989. Limestone quality control using electromagnetic and resistivity surveys. *In:* GASKARTH, J. W. & LUMSDEN, A. C. (eds) *Proceedings of the 6th Extractive Industry Geology Conference, Birmingham University,* paper 27.

HOPSON, P. M. 1982. Summary regional assessment of the sand and gravel resources of the Middle and Upper Thames and its tributaries. (Industrial Minerals Assessment Unit, Institute of Geological Sciences, Keyworth, Nottingham) Internal report 1982/5, for Department of the Environment.

HULL, J. H. 1981. Methods of calculating the volume of resources of sand and gravel. *Appendix* (pp 192–193) to THURRELL, R. G. 1981 *Quarry Management and Products,* **8,** 181–192.

INSTITUTE OF GEOLOGICAL SCIENCES. 1977. *Quaternary Map of the United Kingdom.* (Two 1:625 000-scale sheets, compiled by EDMONDS, E. A., 1977, mainly from work of IGS).

—— 1981. Annual Report for 1980 and 1981. Institute of Geological Sciences, London.

KOCH, G. S. & LINK, R. F. 1971. *Statistical analysis of geological data.* Vols 1 and 2. Wiley, Chichester.

LAHEE, F. H. 1952. *Field geology.* McGraw-Hill, 5th Edn.

LAXTON, J. L. 1992. A particle-size classificaton of sand and gravel deposits as a basis for end-use assessment. *Engineering Geology,* **32,** 29–37.

LOVELL, S. M. 1968. The customer and quarry operator. *Quarry Managers' Journal, London,* **52,** 25–29; discussion 30–36.

MANUAL OF APPLIED GEOLOGY FOR ENGINEERS (Military Engineering, Vol. IV) HMSO. 1976.

McCALL, G. J. H. 1989. Mineral Resources. *In:* McCALL, G. J. H. & MARKER, B. R. (eds), *Earth Science Mapping for Planning, Development and Conservation.* Graham & Trotman, London.

—— & —— 1989. (eds). *Earth Science Mapping for Planning, Development and Conservation.* Graham & Trotman, London.

McCORMACK, D. E. & FOHS, D. G. 1979. Soil Considerations in Siting Highways, Airports and Utility Corridors. *In: Planning the uses and management of land.* Agronomy Monograph No. 21, American Society of Agronomy, Madison, USA, 531–554.

McKELVEY, V. E. 1972. Mineral resource estimates and public policy. *American Science,* **60**, 32–40, Connecticut.

McKEOWN, M. C. & SAMUEL, M. D. A. 1985. *Regional Study of the Sand and Gravel Resources of Essex and South Suffolk.* Report for Department of the Environment, London by British Geological Survey, Keyworth, Nottingham.

McLELLAN, A. G. 1967. *The distribution, origin and use of sand and gravel deposits in Central Lanarkshire.* PhD Thesis, Glasgow University.

—— 1969. Geomorphology and the sand and gravel industry of West Central Scotland. *Scottish Geographical Magazine,* **85**, 162–170.

—— & BRYANT, C. R. 1975. The Methodology of Inventory— A practical technique for assessing provincial aggregate resources. *Canadian Mining and Metallurgical Bulletin,* **68**, 102–108.

McMILLAN, A. A. & BROWNE, M. A. E. 1987. *Dutch and West German Quaternary Profile Mapping Schemes.* British Geological Survey Technical Report, WA/89/63.

McNEILL, J. D. 1980. *Electromagnetic Terrain Conductivity Measurement at Low Induction Numbers.* Technical note TN-6, Geonics Limited, Ontario, Canada.

McQUILLIN, R. & ARDUS, D. A. 1977. Exploring the geology of the shelf seas. Graham & Trotman, London.

MANITOBA DEPARTMENT OF ENERGY AND WORKS, MINERAL RESOURCES DIVISION. 1982. Computer Program No. SG02.

MARTIN, J. H. 1981. *Quaternary : Glaciofluvial Deposits in Central Scotland: Sedimentology and Economic Geology.* PhD thesis, University of Edinburgh.

MASTERS, J. M. 1978. *Sand and Gravel, and Peat Resources in North-east Illinois.* Illinois State Geological Circular No. 503.

MERRITT, J. W. 1981. *The Sand and Gravel Resources of the Country around Ellon, Grampian Region.* Mineral Assessment Report, Institute of Geological Sciences, No. 76, HMSO, Edinburgh.

—— 1992. A critical review of methods used in the appraisal of onshore sand and gravel resources in Britain. *Engineering Geology,* **32**, 1–9.

—— & ELLIOTT, R. W. 1984. *Central Scotland Mineral Portfolio: Hard-rock aggregate resources.* Open file report of the British Geological Survey, Edinburgh.

——, LAXTON, J. L., SMELLIE, J. L. & THOMAS, C. W. 1983. *Summary Assessment of the Sand and Gravel Resources of South-east Strathclyde, Scotland.* Open File Report of the Institute of Geological Sciences, Edinburgh.

MOLDAN, B., CICHA, I., BEDNAR, J., CADEK, J., JETEL, J., KOVANDA, J., OPLETAL, M., POKORNY, J., TOLMASEK, M., VESELY, J., VOLSAN, V., ZEMAN, M. & ZIKMUND, J. 1987. 1: 50 000 Maps of the Environmental Potential of Czechoslovakia (CSSR). *In* ARNDT, P. & LÜTTIG, G. W. (eds), *Mineral Resource' Extraction, Environmental Protection and Land-use Planning in the Industrial and Developing Countries.* Schweizerbart'sche, Stuttgart.

MOREY, A. J., STEVENS, P. F. & SANDERS, M. K. 1991. A new system for the objective interpretation of third-party data in assessments of regional sand and gravel resources *Quarterly Journal of Engineering Geology,* **24**, 77–83.

MORRAY-JONES, R. H. 1968. Specification and quality control of quarry products. *Quarry Managers' Journal, London,* **52**, 15–24; discussion 30–36.

NEEB, P–R. 1986. Establishment of an ADP-based gravel and hard-rock aggregate file at the Geological Survey of Norway. *Fjellsprengningsteknikk, Bergmekamikk/Geotecknikk,* **28**, 1–17. (NGU internal publication).

PATOUREAUX, Y. 1979. An example of the value of infra-red multispectral remote sensing in mapping. *Quarterly Journal of Engineering Geology,* **12**, 181–188.

PEACOCK, J. D. et al. 1977. *Sand and Gravel Resources of the Grampian Region.* Report, Institute of Geological Sciences, No. 77/2.

PIPER, D. P. & ROGERS, P. J. 1980. *Procedure for the assessment of the conglomerate resources of the Sherwood Sandstone Group.* Mineral Assessment Report, Institute of Geological Sciences, No. 56.

RITCHIE, W., WOOD, M., WRIGHT, R. & TAIT, D. 1988. Surveying and mapping for field scientists. Longman, London.

ROBERTS, D., HOEK, E. & FISH, B. G. 1972. The concept of the mammoth quarry. *Quarry Managers' Journal, London,* **57**, No. 7, 229–238.

ROGERS, P. J., PIPER, D. P. & CHARSLEY, T. J. 1982. *The conglomeratic resources of the country around Cheadle, Staffordshire. Description of 1 : 25 000 sheet SK04.* Mineral Assessment Report, Institute of Geological Sciences, No. 57.

ROSE, E. P. F. 1976. Geological maps and other information sources. *Manual of Applied Geology for Engineers.* HMSO, London, Section 7.

ROYLE, A. G. 1971. *A Practical Introduction to Geostatistics.* Report, Department of Mining and Mineral Sciences, University of Leeds.

SIMPSON, P. 1979. Marine geophysical surveys. *Hydrography* (CLS/CMS Autumn 1979), 25–35.

SLOAN, A., LUMSDEN, A. C., HENCHER, S. R. & ONIONS, R. I. 1989. Geological and geotechnical controls on operational planning at Ingleton Quarry. *In:* GASKARTH, J. W. & LUMSDEN, A. C. (eds) *Proceedings of the 6th Extractive Industry Geology Conference.* Birmingham University, Paper 2.

SMITH, C. G. 1989. *Hard rock aggregate resources: Scottish Highlands and Southern Uplands Mineral Portfolio.* British Geological Survey Technical Report, WF/89/4.

SOMERVILLE, S. 1983. Site investigation procedures and engineering testing of glacial sediments. Chapter 11 *in* EYLES, N. (ed.) *Glacial Geology.* Pergamon.

STEVENS, P. F., MOREY, A. J., SANDERS, M. K. & MALLETT, S. H. 1991. Development of a regional model for the Devensian glaciation of County Durham for use in the assessment of sand and gravel resources. *In:* FORSTER, A., CULSHAW, M. G., CRIPPS, J. C., LITTLE, J. A. & MOON, C. F. (eds) *Quaternary Engineering Geology.* Geological Society, London, Engineering Geology Special Publication, **7**, 163–170.

SUMBLER, M. G. & SAMUEL, M. D. A. 1990. *A preliminary study of potential resources of sand and gravel in Buckinghamshire north of the Chilterns.* British Geological Survey Technical Report, WA/90/50.

THURRELL, R. G. 1971. The assessment of mineral resources with particular reference to sand and gravel. *Quarry Managers' Journal, London,* **55**, 19–25.

—— 1981. The identification of bulk mineral resources; the contribution of the Institute of Geological Sciences. *Quarry Management and Products, London,* **8**, 181–193.

UNITED NATIONS. 1979. International classification of mineral resources. *Mining Magazine*, June 1979, 533–536.

UNTERBERGER, R. R. & THORNTON, M. 1990. Radar sees through rocks. *Quarry Management and Products*, **17**, pt 6, 43–44.

VEENSTRA, H. J. 1969. Gravels of the southern North Sea. *Marine Geology*, **7**, 449–464.

VERLEY, G., DAVID, M., JOURNEL, A. G. & MARECHAL, A. (eds) 1983. *Geostatistics for Natural Resources Characterisation, Parts 1 and 2*. NATO ASI series. Reidel, Dordrecht.

VERNEY, Sir R. R. (Chairman). 1976. '*Aggregates: the way ahead*'. Report of the Advisory Committee on Aggregates (HMSO, for Department of the Environment, London).

WEST, G. 1991. *The Field Description of Engineering Soils and Rocks*. Geological Society of London Professional Handbook. Open University Press.

WILLMAN, H. G. 1942. Geology and mineral resources of the Marseilles, Ottawa and Streater quadrangles. *Bulletin of Illinois State Geological Survey*, **66**, 343–344.

WOLFF, F. C. 1987. Development of geological maps for land-use planning in Norway. *In*: ARNDT, P. & LÜTTIG, G. W. (eds) *Mineral Resources' Extraction, Environmental Protection and Land-use Planning in the Industrialised and Developing Countries*. Schweizerbart'sche, Stuttgart.

ZALASIEWICZ, J. A., MATHERS, S. J. & CORNWELL, J. D. 1985. The application of ground conductivity measurements to geological mapping. *Quarterly Journal of Engineering Geology*, **18**, 139–148.

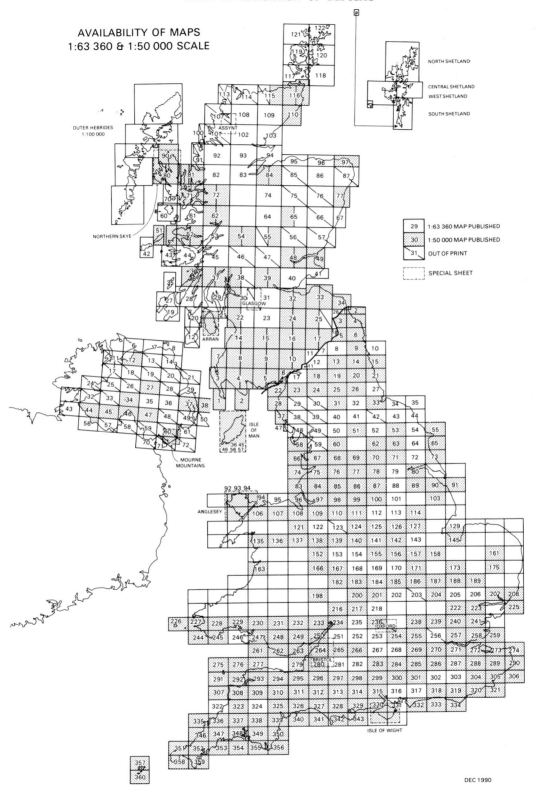

FIG. A3.1 Availability of 1:50 000 and 1:63 360-scale geological maps of Great Britain and Northern Ireland (British Geological Survey). Each map covers an area of 216 square miles (approximately 560 km²); the map sheets conform to the Ordnance Survey Third Series graticule.

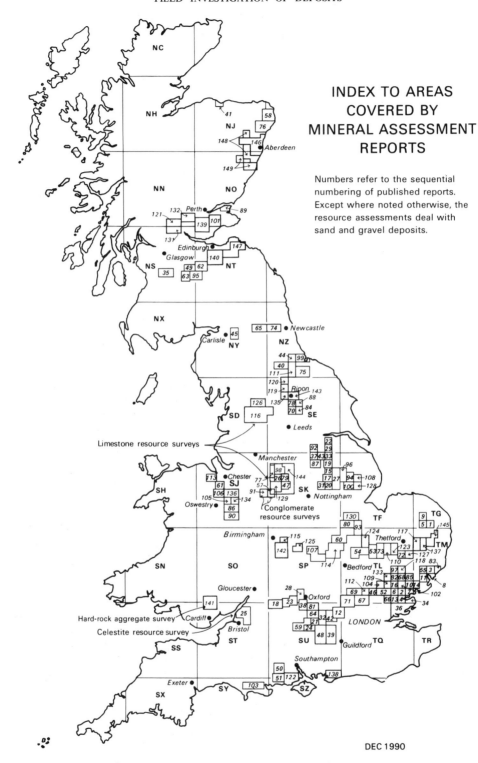

INDEX TO AREAS
COVERED BY
MINERAL ASSESSMENT
REPORTS

Numbers refer to the sequential
numbering of published reports.
Except where noted otherwise, the
resource assessments deal with
sand and gravel deposits.

DEC 1990

Fig. A3.2 Index to the location of bulk mineral resource surveys in Great Britain conducted for the Department of the Environment by British Geological Survey. The majority of the resource maps are published at the scale of 1:25 000 and a few at 1:50 000 scale.

AVAILABILITY OF MAPS
1:250 000 SCALE U.T.M. SERIES

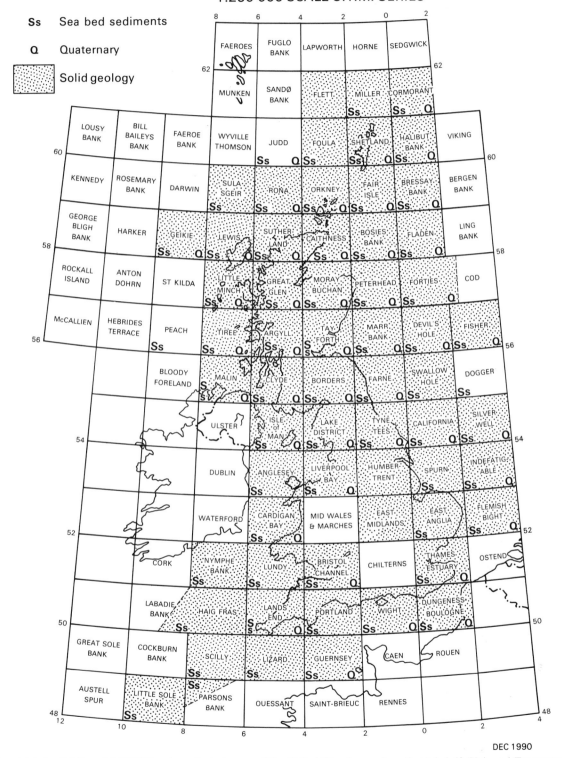

Fig. A3.3 Availability of 1:250 000-scale geological maps of the United Kingdom and continental shelf (Universal Transverse Mercator Series). Each map covers an area of 1° latitude by 2° of longitude. Sheets are indexed by their south-west corner co-ordinates and are also given regional titles for ease of reference. They show three sorts of geological information: Solid geology (S), Quaternary geology (Q) and Sea-bed sediments (Ss) usually on separate sheets. Quaternary geology maps provide information for offshore areas but not for onshore territory (for which see Fig. A3.1).

4. Extraction

4.1. Introduction

The subject of mineral extraction involves a number of highly technical and economically sensitive issues ranging from overburden and waste removal and disposal, through blast design and methods of loading and transporting ore to selection and scheduling of equipment and environmental protection. Many of these issues are more usually associated with the engineering of surface mines for coal and metals and, as such, are the subject of many detailed studies and publications (Martin 1982; IMM 1983; Hartman 1987; Kennedy 1990; Shaw & Pavlovic (in press)).

In the UK, the term 'mine' is defined by law (Mines and Quarries Act 1954) as any mineral extraction operation that takes place underground. Surface extraction is 'quarrying' although metalliferous surface mines are often referred to as 'open-pits' and surface coal mines as 'open-cast'. At the present time, the lower cost of surface mining dictates that almost all aggregates are produced by quarrying. The methods and equipment employed in quarrying rock or excavating sands and gravels are similar to those used in surface mining operations and, in recent times, often approach the scale, capacity and output of large metalliferous mines.

This chapter identifies some of the more important aspects of mineral extraction relevant to aggregate production but is necessarily a simplified and condensed review of the methods and equipment used in the quarrying industry.

The methods and equipment employed to extract aggregates depend primarily on the type of deposit or source rock being worked. The selection of particular techniques and machines requires consideration of a number of factors. Of these, the most basic is the degree of consolidation or induration of the deposit.

Many types of sedimentary rock and most, if not all, igneous and metamorphic rocks require drilling and blasting to reduce the rock mass to a particle size which can be dug from a loose pile. These are often known as 'hard rock' although limestones are technically soft. Sands, gravels and some conglomerates are either unconsolidated or weakly consolidated and may be excavated directly from the ground by suitably powered and formatted machines without the need for any previous disaggregation (Atkinson 1971).

The volume of aggregate produced from all sources has increased dramatically since the 1960s and is set to continue to the end of the century. Table 4.1 shows the trend in output from a variety of sources since 1965 and production statistics are presented graphically in Fig. 1.1.

Although the total annual output of both hard rock and sand and gravel has effectively doubled in the past 25 years, the number of production units has fallen from around 2250 in 1965 to 1550 in 1989. Typically, output from sand and gravel pits in the UK is between 50 000 and 500 000 tonnes per annum with some exceptional outputs in excess of 1 million tonnes. Limestone and hard rock quarry outputs have a wider range from small units producing less than 100 000 tonnes to the so-called 'super quarries' capable of producing 10 million tonnes per annum. A typical limestone or hard rock quarry output is within a range of 500 000 to 1 000 000 tonnes per annum.

The change and rapid growth in the aggregate producing industry in the United Kingdom over the past 25 years has required considerable changes to the equipment being used. Similar changes and growth are to be found throughout most regions of the world. In the United States, it is not uncommon for sand and gravel quarry outputs to exceed 3 million tonnes per annum

TABLE 4.1. *Production of aggregates from various sources within the United Kingdom*

Aggregate source	Aggregate production Millions of tonnes				
	1965	1973	1981	1989	1990
Limestone	58.0	74.9	57.0	106.2	98.2
Sandstone	6.0	14.7	10.0	16.7	14.5
Igneous rock	19.0	38.0	25.0	46.8	48.9
Land sand and gravel	95.0	126.0	90.0	110.5	99.0
Marine sand and gravel	7.0	16.0	11.0	20.0	17.2

and several crushed rock 'super-quarries' producing in excess of five million tonnes are in operation. Similarly, in Continental Europe the trend is towards very high output pits and quarries.

The most significant changes are, however, to be found in the developing countries of the world. Here the largely labour intensive extraction and processing techniques of the past are being replaced by fleets of modern equipment and employment of modern mechanical mining methods to extract aggregate. The pace of these changes is driven by the demand for infrastructures and urban development to be brought to so-called 'Western standards' with the utmost speed.

The marked increases in the output of all aggregate but particularly crushed rock aggregate has led to the quarry industry adopting methods of production scheduling and equipment selection similar to those used in large scale open-pit metalliferous mining. At the same time, although the proportion of land-based sands and gravel production may be less, the total volumes have also increased very significantly and the types of deposit are more varied and often more difficult to work. Accordingly, there is a need to consider, with equal deliberation as for hard rock quarrying, the most suitable methods and machines necessary to excavate sand and gravel.

Factors which will influence the selection of both the equipment and the working method employed include the physical properties of the rock, particularly, density, impact strength and abrasivity. Also of great importance is the required rate of production.

The overriding consideration in the design of the excavation and the selection of equipment for production, the two together effectively constituting the working method, is the operating cost (Shand 1970). Mining engineers and equipment manufacturers have developed computer based mathematical modelling techniques to assist in equipment selection, ensuring the most efficient use of machinery. However, although the trend is towards a mathematical model approach to excavation planning there is no substitute for a thorough basic knowledge of the geology of the deposit and the experience of skilled engineers.

From whichever source aggregates are produced, hard rock quarries, land based sand and gravel or marine sand and gravel there are four basic operations to be considered in the extraction:

(i) overburden removal and face preparation;
(ii) primary fragmentation;
(iii) digging and loading;
(iv) hauling to the processing plant.

With some notable exceptions these operations are very similar for the two main sources of aggregate; hard rock quarries (limestone, sandstone and igneous rock) and land-based sand and gravel pits.

Recovery of aggregate from marine sources of sand and gravel requires quite different scales of operation and equipment from those employed for land based sand and gravel. However, the dredging methods employed are largely developments of those originated for river, estuary or deep sub-water table workings. Modern dredgers are able to work and lift aggregate from increasingly deep water and from deposits which have hitherto been too difficult or uneconomic to work. They are, therefore, in themselves, major and highly sophisticated engineering works.

4.2. Hard rock quarries

4.2.1. Introduction

The hard rock quarries include those working igneous and metamorphic rocks, limestones and dolomites, and the gritstone, quartzite and sandstone group. As discussed in Chapter 2, the modes of origin and deposition vary widely and are reflected in the topographic land forms. The method of excavation and the selection of equipment can be influenced as much by the topographic expression as by the geology of the site.

Basically, however, there are two types of hard rock quarry (i) the hill-side quarry in which the excavated material is hauled down slope to a plant and processing area, see Fig. 4.1 and (ii) the open-pit operation in which the rock has to be hauled up to the plant area, see Fig. 4.2. Hill-side quarries can, and frequently do, become open pit operations once excavation has reached the plant area datum.

4.2.2. Overburden removal and disposal

Thicknesses of overburden material can vary between virtually nil to as much as 100 metres and must be removed or stripped from the payrock formation before extraction commences.

In hard rock quarries the overburden may consist of other indurated rocks or weaker, generally unconsolidated younger formations, for example, sands and marls, or other superficial material such as glacial till or a weathered payrock. The exploration and evelution studies described in Chapter 3 will have determined the thickness and profile of overburden and weathered layers which can be either a simple constant thickness or highly variable and complex (Geological Society 1977). The physical nature, condition and volume of overburden will have considerable influence on the method and type of equipment employed. In some cases, zones of the overburden can satisfy the lower quality demands of another construction use e.g. fill, road-base and becomes a by-product. Fig. 4.3 shows some examples of overburden and weathered rock cover.

FIG. 4.1. A hillside quarry (courtesy of ARC Ltd).

FIG. 4.2. Large limestone quarry showing benches, process plant, rail and road access (courtesy of ARC Ltd).

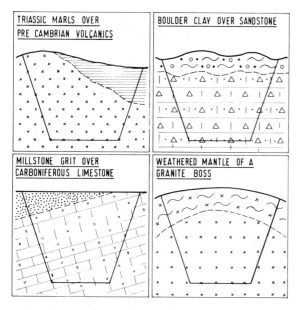

FIG. 4.3. Examples of overburden and weathering cover.

ites of West Africa will almost invariably encounter weathered zones of depth between 15 and 25 metres before acceptable fresh payrock is exposed. The proportion of weathered rock to payrock can be very high. In Hong Kong the ratio is frequently 1:1 so that as much attention needs to be given to the excavation of overburden and waste rock as to the excavation of payrock itself (Earle 1991). An added difficulty is that the weathered profiles are not always a simple function of depth below the surface but can be highly variable and influenced by such factors as joint frequency and continuity. Classification of the weathering grade of overburden cover can be of considerable assistance in assessing the most suitable method of excavation, see Table 4.2.

Assessing the overburden volumes to be removed in relation to the volume of payrock recovered is a very important factor in establishing the basic economics of the extraction operation, see §4.5.

In hard rock quarries, removal of overburden or weathered rock usually involves transporting the waste to remote dumps and this must be regarded as an integral part of the extraction process. There is little opportunity for digging, casting and placing overburden away from the production face directly with a single machine, for example by dragline, which may be common in some sand and gravel operation (Dover 1964).

Unconsolidated or weakly indurated overburden materials can be removed with a variety of excavators often similar to or identical to those used for excavating the payrock. It is, therefore, essential that interchange of duties is carefully considered when selecting equipment. However, the differences in consolidation and attitude may require employment of plant and equipment suited specifically to the particular type of overburden present.

Rope operated face shovels or hydraulically operated shovels and backhoes are the most common digging and loading machines. In suitable conditions the high breakout force of these types of excavator obviates the need for any preliminary loosening of the overburden and they can dig directly into the overburden face.

Overburden can be taken to include soils and sub-soils but soils frequently require careful handling and storage to preserve their fertility (Corker 1987; Samuel 1990). In cases where there is a requirement to restore the site after excavation by use of these soils it is often necessary to conduct a separate specialized survey of soils to identify soil profiles and depths, soil types and volumes. This is most usual for sand and gravel deposits and has a significant effect upon quarry planning, see §4.5.

In Europe and other temperate zones the depth of the weathered layer is generally not a severe problem. In tropical and subtropical climates, however, it is frequently of considerable thickness and it is often necessary to remove large quantities before fresh payrock is uncovered. For example, quarries operating in the gran-

TABLE 4.2. *Classification of weathering grade*

1. **Fresh.** Parent rock showing no discolouration, loss of strength or any other weathering effects.

2. **Slightly weathered.** Rock may be slightly discoloured, particularly adjacent to discontinuities which may be open and will have slightly discoloured surfaces; the intact rock is not noticeably weaker than the fresh rock.

3. **Moderately weathered.** Rock is discoloured; discontinuities may be open and will have discoloured surfaces with alteration starting to penetrate inwards; intact rock is noticeably weaker, as determined in the field than the fresh rock, (The ratio of original rock to weathered rock should be estimated where possible.)

4. **Highly weathered.** Rock is discoloured; discontinuities may be open and have discoloured surfaces, and the original fabric of the rock near to the discontinuities may be altered; alteration penetrates deeply inwards but corestones are still present. (The ratio of original rock to weathered rock should be estimated where possible.)

5. **Completely weathered.** Rock is discoloured and changed to a soil but original fabric is mainly preserved. There may be occasional small corestones. The properties of the soil depend in part on the nature of the parent rock.

6. **Residual soil.** Rock is discoloured and changed completely to a soil in which original rock fabric is completely destroyed. There is a large change in volume. Genesis should be determined where possible.

FIG. 4.4. Hydraulic back-hoe excavator and articulated dump truck used to remove overburden and excavate sand and gravel (courtesy of Redland Aggregates Ltd).

Highly indurated overburden may require drilling and blasting and is excavated as part of the quarry operation. In these circumstances the fragmented overburden rock material will be loaded to dumpers by a suitable excavator and transported to the designated dumping area.

For high volume overburden stripping in weak, unconsolidated materials of considerable thickness, motorized scrapers are commonly employed usually assisted by crawler tractors (bulldozers). This method has the distinct advantage in that the overburden is removed and transported to the dumping area in one operation by one machine, see Fig. 4.5 (Brewster 1987).

In those overburden formations which are weakly cemented thinly bedded or highly jointed, crawler tractors fitted with a rear mounted tooth or tyne are used to rip and loosen the formation, see Fig. 4.6. The overburden materials are pushed by the dozer into piles which can be loaded by an excavator usually of the wheeled type. This ripping and dozing technique can also be used to excavate the payrock in suitable conditions.

Disposal of overburden as part of the extraction phase in aggregate production may take place in areas, remote from the quarry itself, which have been specified within the planning consents and conditions for that purpose. Alternatively, wherever possible, overburden is used as a backfill of worked out areas as part of the restoration programme. All tipping and refuse disposal operations within quarries in the U.K. are subject to the Mines and Quarries (Tips) Act and Regulations, 1969 which call for regular inspection and monitoring and, in the case of 'classified tips', for detailed design and reporting by competent engineers (Walton 1990; Garrard & Walton 1990). Tips must be designed so that they are inherently stable and are adequately drained. Haul roads to the tipping area and point of disposal must be well maintained and suited to the equipment in use. Refuse and waste would usually be delivered to the tip by dump truck or motor-scraper or, in some major and continuous overburden stripping operations, by conveyor. Whichever the method of haul, it is the method of emplacement and compaction which will ensure the permanent security of the tip. Layer tipping as opposed to end tipping (Fig. 4.7) is considered the most preferable technique and requires, in addition to the haulage plant, excavators and dozers to place the material in the correct place and achieve the necessary compaction.

FIG. 4.5. Overburden being removed by scraper with tractor-dozer assistance (courtesy of Caterpillar).

FIG. 4.6. Tractor-dozer fitted with ripper (courtesy of Caterpillar).

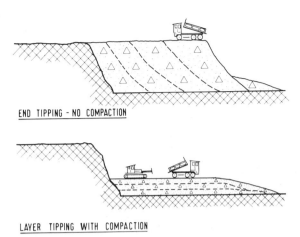

FIG. 4.7. Methods of waste tipping and disposal.

4.2.3. Primary fragmentation

4.2.3.1. Introduction. The major costs in producing rock aggregates are incurred by the crushing plant and the use of mobile plant, particularly loaders. Both of these costs are increased by poor fragmentation. Inefficient loader operation is caused by slow cycle times and machine wear as the machine sorts oversize from the muck-pile. Additional power consumption and wear of crushing equipment is incurred by processing larger pieces and, in the extreme, crushing plant operation is lost whilst blockages of the primary crusher (see Chapter 5) are cleared.

Primary blasting of rock from a quarry face should be designed to obtain the optimum fragmentation and a rock (muck) pile attitude compatible with the plant and equipment used, thus reducing the work effort and the need for secondary breakage. A correctly sized feed to the primary crusher is the key to low cost crushing and screening (Ball 1988).

In hard rock quarries reduction of the rock mass to a lump size that can be handled by the excavating and load out equipment is achieved by drilling and blasting. These activities are complementary and should always be considered together in the context of the prevailing ground conditions (Dalgleish 1989)

4.2.3.2. Drilling. In most quarrying operations there are two principal drilling activities: (a) development drilling; (b) the drilling of production blast holes. Several types of drill are available capable of drilling holes from 50 to 230 mm diameter depending on the purpose of the hole, the rock properties, the size of blast planned and the degree of fragmentation required. Successful blasting depends on accurate and controlled drilling. In the UK, the Quarries (Explosives) Regulations 1988 require that all blast holes are accurately

surveyed and recorded prior to detonation (White 1989; HSC 1989).

The geological structures, rock mass classification and the intact rock properties will determine the drilling and consequently the blasting patterns to be adopted by the quarry engineer. A drilling pattern is shown in Fig. 4.8 which describes the terms used. Of these, spacing and burden are the parameters which will determine the volume of rock produced by each blast. The direction or azimuth of each borehole and the drilling angle are the factors which have considerable influence on the efficiency and the safety of the 'shot'.

Reasonable plans of the drill hole pattern can be produced by simple, traditional survey techniques used carefully by the quarry manager and driller. But where undetected deviations in borehole direction or angle occur overloading or undercharging of the blast can result.

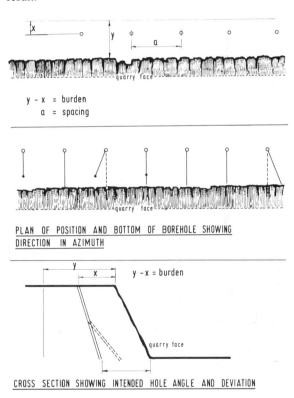

FIG. 4.8. Blast hole patterns and profiles.

A number of highly accurate and computerized in-borehole and quarry face profile survey techniques are now available. These face-profile techniques are laser-based survey systems which rapidly collect basic data which are then downloaded to desktop computers for analysis. The designed burdens, spacings and alignment can be checked against the actual measured values and the blast-hole charges adjusted accordingly (Anon 1988d; Pemberton 1990).

Modern blasting methods tend to favour inclined blast holes. Faces inclined 15° to 25° from vertical are suggested as giving the most satisfactory results in practice (Pass 1970). Some of the benefits of inclined drilling can be listed as follows: (i) safer operation for operatives and machines; (ii) higher benches may be safely blasted; (iii) remnant toes and break-back can be eliminated; (iv) improved fragmentation; (v) higher efficiency and cost reduction in loading, haulage and crushing; (vi) damaging effect of vibration in the surrounding area is decreased.

Essentially, three drilling methods have been employed in quarrying for many years:

(1) rotary drilling for large diameter holes in soft rocks;

(2) down-the-hole, pneumatic drive, rotary percussive methods for medium diameter holes in medium to hard rocks, see Figs 4.9 and 4.11, and

(3) pneumatic, top-hammer, rotary percussive drilling for small diameter holes in hard rock.

FIG. 4.10. Hydraulic top-hammer or drifter blast hole drill (courtesy Tamrock).

FIG. 4.9. Large pneumatic (DTH) blast hole drill (courtesy of ARC Ltd).

In the past few years, however, hydraulic drive has been introduced to both the top hammer drills and large diameter rotaries offering considerable advantages in rates of penetration and power costs, see Fig. 4.10 (Tapaninaho 1987).

Drilling for the development of haul roads, ramps and preparation of new faces usually employs the top hammer, rotary methods using what are termed 'drifter' type drills, see Fig. 4.12. These machines can be set at any angle from horizontal to vertical and can even drill upwards. Being lighter and smaller than the rotary and down-the-hole percussion types, they can be used to reach less accessible parts of a face or quarry development utilizing a zoom facility. Over a long hole, however, there is a tendency for the hole to deviate particularly in broken or highly jointed ground. Drifter type drills are also used very effectively in many hard rock quarries for production blast hole drilling but are limited to shorter holes and the lower production rates.

FIG. 4.11. Crawler mounted DTH drill (courtesy of Halco Ltd).

FIG. 4.12. Small diameter, top hammer (drifter) drill mounted upon articulated arm (courtesy of Boart).

Most quarries employ down-the-hole hammer techniques because of the greater accuracy and range of hole diameters available.

Down-the-hole (DTH) hammer rigs, as the name implies, operate with the pneumatic hammer immediately above the bit at the bottom of the hole. Rotation is effected by a pneumatic motor at the surface rotating the rod string. The method has the great advantage of drilling straight accurately aligned boreholes and at relatively high speeds.

4.2.3.3. Blasting. The theory and mechanics of blasting are the subjects of numerous research studies and publications but, because every quarry is in some way geologically unique, translating that theory into practice is often very difficult.

It is necessary to be aware of the mechanical properties of the rock and the rock mass in order to understand the results achieved and the effects of blasting on particular quarry faces. At the same time the seismic factors involved, which are controlled by the geology and which can become vey important factors because of the need to protect structures both within and without quarry limits, must be thoroughly understood.

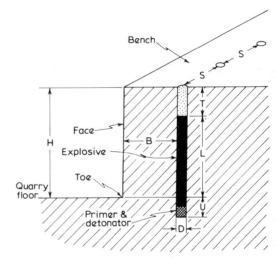

H	Bench height	U	Sub grade drilling
B	Burden	D	Hole diameter
S	Spacing of blast holes	L	Charge length
T	Stemming		

FIG. 4.13. Bench cross section view showing blast terminology.

In order to appreciate why each rock formation or indeed each quarry requires its own unique blasting method and design some knowledge of the theory of blasting should be acquired. A section of a typical blasthole is shown in Fig. 4.13 explaining the terms used (Hemphill 1981).

Following the initial explosion, the shock wave set up

travels at a velocity equivalent to the compressional wave velocity of the rock material. As joints, bedding planes, or the free surface of the quarry face are encountered by the compressional wave, it will be reflected in part or transmitted as a function of the acoustic impedance of the materials either side of the boundary.

Acoustic impedance of a material is a function of its density and its compressional wave velocity. The more closely matched the acoustic impedance of two materials either side of a boundary, the more energy is transmitted in a compressional wave; the less equal, the more energy is reflected. Reflected energy takes the form of tensile or shear waves. When the tensile strength of the rock is exceeded new fractures develop, shattering the rock. New fractures form new reflective surfaces for oncoming compressional waves which are in turn reflected.

At this stage, the expanding gases resulting from the explosion create pressure on the fractured rock, pushing the material in the direction of least resistance and creating the rock pile in front of the quarry face.

Fragmentation is thus determined by a combination of two factors: (i) explosive energy creating new fracture surfaces and (ii) the cleaving of the rock mass along pre-existing planes of weakness such as joints, fissures, bedding planes etc. The latter exercises a large degree of control upon fragmentation, especially when the minimum explosive charge is being used in order to reduce the environmental impact. Thus, the importance of the study of the geological structure of the deposit can be appreciated.

It will also be obvious that some part of the energy will be transmitted through the rock over long distances. This is blasting vibration. Another part is transmitted through the air as a result of the venting of high pressure gases and the movement of the rock face. This is 'air-blast' or 'overpressure'. These aspects are discussed in §4.6.

4.2.3.4. Explosives. Explosive materials used in quarrying are divided into two main groups: high explosives and blasting agents (Atlas 1987; Berta 1990).

High explosives include the nitroglycerine and TNT-based dynamites and gelatines and are used in a wide range of applications. Being both extremely powerful, with a high velocity of detonation, and water resistant, they are used with maximum effect in wet blast holes. They are, however, expensive when used exclusively in primary blasts. Gelignites and other gelatine type explosives can be sensitive to accidental detonation, for example by static electricity or even impact, and require the most rigorous safety precautions.

Blasting agents include ANFO, the mixture of ammonium nitrate and fuel oil, slurries which are mixtures of ANFO, water, and a gel combined with a sensitizer, and emulsions, which are droplets of ammonium nitrate solution in a mixture of oil and wax. These blasting agents, although generally less powerful than high explo-

sives, are less expensive and because they contain raw materials which are not themselves explosives, they can be transported safely and they can be manufactured or mixed on site. (It should be noted, however, that in the UK and most countries a licence is required for the handling, storage and preparation of explosive materials.) They are also less sensitive to accidental detonation. Owing to these advantages ANFO or its derivatives are the most commonly used explosives employed in aggregate producing quarries. They do, however, require a high explosive primer to ensure reliable initiation and complete detonation. A distinct disadvantage of ANFO is that it cannot be used in wet blastholes. In such adverse conditions ANFO has to be pre-packaged or employed in a water resistant slurry form (ICI Explosives Co. Ltd).

4.2.3.5. Detonators. A detonator is essentially a very small quantity of a sensitive explosive compound that can be relatively easily and reliably initiated (fired) by heat or shock and, thereby, initiates the detonation of a larger mass of less sensitive explosive. The most common form of detonator contains a fuse wire and is fired by an electrical current but other types exist initiated by shock. Detonators and the associated firing devices called 'exploders' can be constructed to incorporate time delays, usually measured in intervals of 25 to 30 milliseconds.

Delay detonators and sequences of initiation are extremely useful, if not essential, to the achievement of good fragmentation without unacceptable environmental impacts of blasting, see §4.6.4. The sequence and method of initiation can also determine the profile of the rock-pile and, thus, the efficiency of loading. Three examples are presented in Fig. 4.14 of typical delay sequences that might be employed to:

(a) minimize blast vibration by separating the total blast into a number of individual blast-holes fired in a simple progression;

(b) improve fragmentation by initiating the blast simultaneously from both ends of the face and

(c) a delay pattern for multi-row blasting that is initiated from the centre of the face, thus creating new free faces prior to each subsequent explosion.

The detontion of explosive within an individual blast-hole can also be sequenced if the column is divided vertically by packs of stemming, a procedure called 'decking'.

For reasons of safety, it is advisable to include two detonators for each explosive charge.

4.2.3.6. Regulations. Blasting in British quarries is controlled by The Quarries (Explosives) Regulations 1988. These Regulations, which were issued to promote safe handling and use of explosives and specifically to reduce

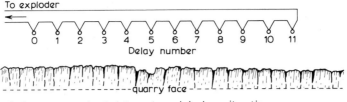

a) Arrangement of delays to minimise vibration

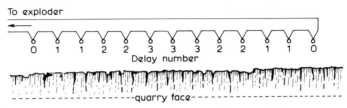

b) Arrangement of delays to improve fragmentation

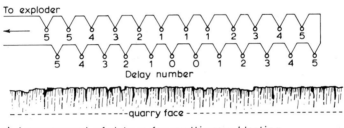

c) Arrangement of delays for multi-row blasting

FIG. 4.14. Blast design and detonating sequences.

the environmental impact of blasting, include three important requirements:

(1) all managers and shot-firers are required to have adequate practical experience and training including successful completion of an accredited course;

(2) the manager must prepare or approve and record a specification for each blast to indicate a profile of the face in front of each blast-hole, the angle, spacing, and burden of each blast-hole, and the type and position of explosives, stemming and system of initiation;

(3) the manager is also required to formulate and publish rules concerning shot-firing procedures (Butler *et al.* 1988; Saunders 1987; HSC 1989).

4.2.3.7. Blast specification. As already discussed, each blast requires determination of a number of factors: (i) hole diameter; (ii) bench height and depth of hole; (iii) burden of holes; (iv) spacing of holes; (v) inclination and alignment; (vi) depth of subgrade; (vii) stemming;

(viii) charge and (ix) choice of explosives and method of initiation. Figure 4.13 shows diagrammatically these various factors.

The choice of hole diameter will be influenced by the geological formation, the bench height, the required fragmentation and the optimum charge weight to achieve fragmentation with lowest environmental effect. Development drilling and blasting will usually employ narrow hole diameters in the range of 65 mm to 105 mm. Production blast holes would be drilled at diameters between 105 mm and 200 mm.

Apart from the general requirement in the Health and Safety at Work Act (1974) for a safe system of work, there is no regulation that specifies a maximum bench height but it is generally agreed that 15 m provides a safe and productive face. In some cases the bench heights and levels will be determined by geological factors. Examples particularly relevant to sedimentary rocks would include: limited strata thickness; vertical variations in quality resulting from changes of sedimentary environment e.g. silica content of limestones; and the presence of intrusions e.g. sills, seams of shale, clay, coal or gypsum etc. that must be excluded from the quarried rock. Geological structure may also be determining through the presence of shallow-dipping faults or major joints resulting from folding that intersect the quarry floor.

In selecting burden and spacing the quarry engineer must consider very carefully the geological composition of the rock and the rock mass condition.

However, the burden, B, is generally considered to be proportional to the hole diameter, D, where $B = nD$. In hard rock formations n will be 30 and in softer formations n equals 40 (Ball 1988). Ideally, the burden should equal the spacing distance, S, but in good blasting conditions a $B:S$ ratio of $1:1.25$ can often be achieved thus reducing the amount of drilling necessary to achieve the desired blast. Common burden/spacing patterns in UK quarries are 3 metres by 3.75 metres or 4 metres by 4 metres, and on occasions 4 metres by 5 metres.

Sub-grade drilling is often necessary to ensure that the rock face is blasted cleanly away from the quarry floor and ensure that 'toes' are not left which would hamper digging and lead to uneven floors. Depending on the rock formation the depth of subgrade is usually 0.3 times the burden distance up to a maximum of 1 metre.

The top of each blast hole is stemmed with drilling fines or sometimes coarse aggregate to ensure that the charge is confined in the blast hole where the rock formation is least disturbed. If the hole were not stemmed, excessive air blast, noise and, in many cases, flyrock would result. As a general rule, stemming length will equal burden.

The amount of explosive used in each hole and in the total blast will depend on the blast hole configuration but mainly on the type of explosive being used. Actual loading densities are usually calculated with the assistance of manufacturers' specifications and recommendations.

The purpose of carefully designed blast hole configurations and the optimum charge weight is to achieve the best possible blasting ratio for the rock being quarried. The blasting ratio gives the amount of rock broken in cubic metres or tonnes per kilogram of explosive used. Typically for fragmentation of strong rocks blast ratios of 4 tonnes per kilogram of explosive are expected ranging up to 12 tonnes per kilogram in weaker rocks.

Blast design can be very time consuming and consequently expensive if each individual blast is to be calculated by the quarry manager. Furthermore, if every new design has to be treated as an experiment, the results may not be cost-effective. The number of variables to be considered is high and, in recent years, more and more use is being made of computer assisted design systems (Cunningham 1989). Mathematical models are now available which compare all the criteria including rock characteristic, explosive type and specification as well as the blast hole configuration and blasting sequences. These can predict the likely fragmentation and rock pile profiles (Adkins 1986) and, in addition, seismic wave generation, vibration and noise levels can be calculated and matched with the requirements of statutory regulations and conditions (Talbot 1988). The larger quarrying companies frequently employ specialist contractors to design and implement blasts although the ultimate responsibility remains with the quarry manager.

4.2.3.8. Ripping. In some circumstances primary fragmentation is not achieved by blasting the rock mass with chemical blasting agents but by mechanical breaking. The technique known as ripping can be applied in formations which are already subject to inherent fracturing through bedding, jointing and cleavage. The technique involves breaking in situ rock by means of a single tooth mounted at the rear of a powerful crawler tractor, see Fig. 4.6 and Appendix A4.1.2. Ripping techniques, although not widely used in established quarries, are particularly useful in short-term construction project quarries, for example, in excavating ferricretes and calcretes in tropical and acid climatic zones.

The major advantages of ripping in some hard rock quarry applications are the considerable economies in ground preparation costs compared with drilling and blasting and the avoidance of the environmental impacts of blasting. The applications where ripping can show the greatest production and economic advantages are (Shand 1970): (a) ripping and dozing into stock piles; (b) ripping and subsequent scraper loading; and (c) ripping and dozer scraping.

Those deposits which are amenable to effective ripping will be determined by:

(i)   the degree of weathering;
(ii) the frequency of fractures, faults, and planes of weakness;
(iii) the crystallinity, nature and grain size of the rock;
(iv) impact strength;
(v)   stratification or lamination of the beds.

A decision to use ripping techniques will depend on a measure of the 'rippability' of the rock, an indication of which can be obtained by seismic wave velocity techniques. These well known geophysical methods make use of the principle that seismic waves travel through sub-surface materials at different speeds, dependent upon the hardness and continuity of the rock together with orientation, openness, surface texture, and infilling of joint planes or other discontinuities. Experience has shown that there are various levels of seismic velocity at which different rock types are likely to be workable (Pass 1970).

Although the seismic wave velocity technique can give a quick and inexpensive assessment of the physical characteristics of the rock, it is not always reliable and confirmation by core drilling and testing is always recommended followed by on-site pilot tets (Shand 1970). Detailed assessment of rock characteristics such as 'fracture spacing' and 'point load strength' made on borehole cores have been demonstrated as a practical means of assessing ease of excavation (Fookes *et al.* 1971).

4.2.4. Secondary breaking

Even a well designed blast will, if geological conditions dictate, produce quantities of rock blocks which require secondary breakage, a problem compounded by the requirement to use the minimum explosive charge to reduce environmental effects. Three methods can be employed to reduce the oversize blocks to manageable size: secondary blasting, drop balling and, increasingly, hydraulic impact breakers (Anon 1988c; Anon 1992b).

Secondary blasting by 'pop shooting' involves drilling a hole in the centre of the boulder which is charged with a gelatine explosive and fired by safety fuse or electric detonators. The method is time consuming, expensive and labour intensive. The alternative plaster shooting requires that the charge of a high-strength gelatine explosive be laid on the boulder and covered by a plastic clay and fired by safety fuse. The method is regarded as less expensive than pop shooting and has less potential for causing damage. Environmentally, the methods are most unpopular because of the high level of noise and air-blast which both pop and plaster blasting produce.

A widely used method for secondary breakage is by means of dropping a steel ball from the height of a dragline boom onto the boulder. The method is slow but highly effective in most rock types. It is, however, generally inconvenient in terms of safety because of the danger of flying rock pieces.

Hydraulic hammers originally designed for breaking hard ground in the construction industry have now been developed for use as highly efficient breakers of large blocks in rock piles, see Fig. 4.15. They have great advantage in situations where noise restrictions preclude the use of secondary blasting. More recently excavation from the rock face by hydraulic hammer has been introduced in Europe particularly in Spain and Italy (Anon 1992a) and on a limited scale in UK.

4.2.5. Loading

Given that an acceptable degree of fragmentation has been achieved, selection of the correct equipment for digging the blasted rock from the face pile and loading for transportation to the process plant depends not least on the required rate of production. Other factors which are taken into account are rock type, height and attitude of quarry faces, the shape of the rock pile, the grading of

rock fragment sizes and the means of transportation (Brundell 1982).

There is no one ideal method or machine type to suit particular rocks or quarry conditions. However, as the quarry engineer seeks to improve efficiency and reduce costs and manufacturers improve and develop various systems, there are trends in favour of particular types. Ultimately, the selection of loading equipment will depend on the particular conditions prevailing in any quarry (Drake 1987; Stevenson 1982).

There are four main types of excavating and loading machines used in hard rock quarries: rope operated shovels; hydraulic shovels; hydraulic backhoes and wheeled front end loaders including articulated versions; and the crawler loaders.

FIG. 4.15. Hydraulic hammer (courtesy of Krupp).

4.2.5.1. Rope operated face shovels. The rope operated shovel has been the most widely used machine for many years, see Appendix A4.1.7. It is suitable for working in all rock types and can handle a variable fragmentation and grading within the capacity of the machine. It is normally powered by a diesel engine but there are electrically driven alternatives. Bucket sizes in quarry use range from as small as $0.5\,m^3$ to $7.0\,m^3$. Loading cycles

FIG. 4.16. Hydraulic shovel excavator loading a dump truck (courtesy of ARC Ltd).

are relatively slow and the bucket filling efficiency is operator dependent.

4.2.5.2. Hydraulic excavators. The use of hydraulic excavators has increased significantly in recent years and is to a large extent replacing the rope shovel. The main advantages are their excavating (digging) power (high break-out force), high bucket filling efficiency, reduced cycle times and lower maintenance costs, see Fig. 4.16 and Appendix A4.1.8 (Oakes 1989; Christoph 1991).

4.2.5.3. Hydraulic backhoes. The hydraulic backhoe's versatility is seen as a distinct advantage in some quarry operations. It can readily be used for both overburden and rock pile duties. When digging and loading from an elevated level into dump trucks, the cycle times are generally fast and the efficiency and accuracy very high,

see Figs 4.4, 4.17 and 4.18 and Appendix A4.1.10 (Tomlinson 1990).

4.2.5.4. Wheeled loaders. Rubber wheeled loaders have been used for quarry floor excavation work to great effect in addition to loading duties in stockyards. The articulated versions are now used in many major high output quarries, see Fig 4.19 and Appendix A4.1.11. Bucket capacities range up to $10 \, m^3$ and cycle times are fast. They are highly manoeuvrable and can be used for load and carry operations over limited distances, thus obviating the need for dumpers. Wheeled loaders do require rock piles to be highly fragmented and are not best suited to selective work. The quarry floor should be dry and firm. Tyre wear is a very important consideration especially when operating on abrasive, hard rock. Protective wheel chains are fitted in most operations.

FIG. 4.17. Hydraulic back-hoe excavator loading a mobile in-pit crusher (courtesy Nordberg).

FIG. 4.18. Hydraulic back-hoe excavator loading a field conveyor system (courtesy Tarmac).

FIG. 4.19. Wheeled loader (F.E.L.) loading a rigid body dump truck (courtesy of ARC Ltd).

4.2.6. Hauling

The final element of the extraction process is to transport the shot rock to the primary crusher of the process plant. In most quarries dump trucks of rigid or articulated construction are used. The former, see Fig. 4.19, are the most widely used although articulated types, see Fig. 4.4, are popular in lower output quarries with limited space for manoeuvre or where difficult ground conditions may exist. Typical capacities range from 15 tonnes up to 75 tonnes with a marked trend towards the open-pit mine giants of 100 and 150 tonne trucks.

Hauling is a major cost factor in the production of construction aggregates and considerable expenditure is incurred on fuel, tyres, and engine wear. All these are reduced by careful attention to haulage road gradients and running surfaces including the running surfaces across quarry floors. Ideally gradients should not be steeper than 1:10 and turns should be as gradual as possible. Tyre wear and damage are considerably reduced when rock fragments are cleared from loading areas and haul routes following each blast.

In many countries there is an increasing move towards in-pit crushing. Where crushers can be operated close to the face they are best fed either directly by the excavator into the hopper from the rock pile, see Fig. 4.17, or by a load and carry operation (Sievert 1973). In these circumstances the need for dumpers is removed and the product is transported to the process plant by conveyors. Conveyors have the great advantage of being able to operate at much steeper gradients than dumpers, typically 1 : 3 as opposed to 1 : 10 (Blower 1990). Conveyor transportation is generally considerably cheaper than the use of dumper truck (Anon 1988b).

4.3. Sand and gravel operations

4.3.1. Introduction

Many of the principles and methods employed in hard rock quarries are equally applicable in sand and gravel extraction. The major differences lie in the higher rate of land use owing to the relatively shallow depths of workings and the need for more immediate environmental control and restoration.

Deposits of sand and gravel are usually unconsolidated and of fluviatile or glacial origin but are sometimes in the form of cemented conglomerates. Often they can be extracted by means of normal earth moving machinery. For convenience they can be divided into dry pits or wet pits, in which the water table is so near the surface that some or all the deposit is under water. In wet pits dewatering or partial dewatering is frequently undertaken to allow the site to be more easily excavated.

The decision to dewater or not will depend on deposit thicknesses, permeability of the sand and gravel, the use of the ground water aquifer and the intended after-use and restoration requirements. The method of dewatering will also depend on deposit thickness, permeability and use of any aquifer. The most commonly used method is simply to install pumps in the initial excavation and pump to draw down the water table and hold the level down during excavation. Construction of single point wells or ring wells may be used in some highly porous formations (Anon 1985). Although some types of equipment and operational methods can be used effectively in both wet and dry workings, different machines and techniques are adopted to suit the particular situation.

4.3.2. Overburden removal

The overburden of fluviatile deposits can be expected to have a fairly regular, relatively thin profile, whereas, in glacial deposits the thicknesses are often greater and can show considerable variation. In either case the overburden removal operations should be designed to minimize the amount of handling and haulage distances in the interests of cost reduction.

Furthermore, owing to restoration commitments it is an essential requirement that topsoils and subsoils are carefully stripped and transferred to storage bunds prior to removal of the remaining overburden cover. Successful agricultural and other afteruse of restored land depends very much on the soil stucture being as little disturbed and damaged as possible during these operations and specially equipped hydraulic backhoes are now commonly used to strip the soils accurately and separately. As has already been mentioned, it is usually necessary or prudent to conduct a separate soil survey to establish the depths and volumes of top-soil and sub-soil. This will enable planning of storage and restoration. It should also be appreciated that soils can be classified into categories of fertility and that each type may require separate storage and to be returned to the area of origin after extraction of minerals.

In fluviatile deposits with very high water tables and which are to be worked wet it is sometimes necessary to lower the water table just sufficiently to clear the overburden level thus allowing the cover to be stripped in dry conditions. Once an initial strip has been completed, water levels can be allowed to recover and the deposit worked by dredge or dragline.

A commonly used removal technique is to employ long reach dragline excavators to dig and cast the overburden into the recently completed excavations in front of the working face. The same machine may be used for excavating the sand and gravel, see Fig. 4.20.

When it is necessary to remove overburden and place in dumps or directly to restoration schemes it is now usual to use back-acting hydraulic excavators working in conjunction with articulated dump trucks, see Fig. 4.4.

Overburden removal is frequently phased as a seasonal activity and motorized scrapers are often used to prepare sufficient ground for a twelve month extraction period working a fast, short contract period, see Fig. 4.5.

Whichever stripping method is used, it is of importance to note that none is 100 per cent efficient and some loss of mineral is to be expected and should be allowed for when calculating reserves.

4.3.3. Excavating techniques and equipment

The excavation technique and equipment employed depends on type of deposit, the general topography of the site, the conditions of planning and restoration, and on the scale of operation. The most influential factor,

FIG. 4.20. Dragline excavator with ADT and field conveyor system (courtesy of RB (Lincoln) Ltd).

however, is again whether the working is to be a wet or dry operation. Some techniques are applicable only to wet or dry working and some can be common to either.

4.3.3.1. Wet working. The most commonly used excavator is the long boom dragline, see Fig. 4.20, which is used equally as much in dry workings and is described later. However, there are some modifications and disadvantages which only apply to wet workings. The bucket fill capacity is rarely better than 50%. In fine sandy deposits there is considerable loss of the fines and the total recovery is at best 75%. Deposits deeper than 10 m cannot be worked and, ideally, working depths should be restricted to 5 m.

Suction dredgers are operated mainly in loosely consolidated deposits although cutting heads and pressure jets can be fitted to the suction pipes allowing harder or more compacted deposits to be broken up and the aggregates recovered. The suction pumps are mounted on barges or on purpose built pontoons. The dredger would normally discharge the recovered aggregate to attendant barges for delivery to the processing plant but floating pipelines are frequently employed to bring the aggregate ashore.

The technique is extensively used for river and estuarine operations in France, Germany, Holland and Bel-

gium with the aggregate sometimes processed on board and pumped ashore via floating pipeline. In the UK suction dredging in river and estuarine operations is comparatively limited but has been very successfully employed to recover sand from deep sub-water workings in the Folkestone beds of the Cretaceous formations.

Grab dredgers have the advantage of being able to work in very deep water and can work deposits containing large cobbles and boulders which the suction dredgers are unable to handle. The grab may be fitted to a crane jib and operated over a wide radius from the deck of a barge or may be constructed to operate through the centre of a dredging pontoon or barge, see Appendix A4.1.14. Recovered aggregate is either discharged to attendant barges or, after partial processing, pumped or conveyed ashore.

Slackline excavators are most applicable to extensive and deep alluvial or glacial deposits which may be systematically worked over wide areas and over a long period. They are also suitable for submerged but free flowing deposits contained in river valleys. Dredged material is stockpiled and can be allowed to drain before recovery by conventional equipment for onward transport and processing, see Appendix A4.1.15. Although a widely used technique on the Continent the method is not used in the UK (Anon 1985).

4.3.3.2. Dry pit working. Excavation of aggregates from dry workings, whether they are naturally dry, i.e. above water table or as a result of dewatering, is usually more efficient in terms of reserve recovery. The methods and equipment employed again depend on the geological conditions, the required rates of production and the constraints imposed by restoration and planning conditions.

Dragline excavators are used extensively as they are in wet workings and are best suited to deposits more than 5 metres thick. In thinner deposits the hydraulic backhoe is currently the preferred machine.

Hydraulic excavators have advantages and disadvantages (Littler 1990). The hydraulic back-hoe excavator can dig harder formations, has a faster cycle time and requires less operator skill to achieve maximum recovery. The dragline, apart from its ability to dig deeper deposits, is more robust and is better suited to feeding adjacent conveyors.

Some deposits which are very loosely consolidated, for example, dune sands and some glacial deposits, can be excavated directly from the face by wheeled front end loaders digging at the toe and allowing the material to rill down towards the machine.

In the USA, particularly in the western states, the extensive deep fluvial fan deposits can be excavated by bulk earth moving equipment. Motorized scrapers with bulldozer assistance are used to excavate load and carry the aggregate deposit over long distances to the process plant. In the United Kingdom there are few deposits for which this method might be considered (Brewster 1987).

4.3.4. Loading and conveying

Wherever possible sand and gravel operations exclude the use of dumpers. Because the maximum particle sizes are generally small enough to be carried by conveyor, long distance transport by conveyor belt is common practice. Using any of the excavator types the as-dug material can be loaded into a hopper fitted with an oversize removal grid and located immediately adjacent to the pit. From the hopper the sands and gravels are fed onto a moveable field conveyor which discharges to a main conveyor, see Fig. 4.18. Conveyor distances of several kilometres are recorded carrying up to 1000 tonne per hour. A popular system layout is a permanent trunk convey which carries the material from a number of field conveyors to the process plant.

4.4. Marine aggregates

4.4.1. Introduction

Since the 1960s, marine dredged sand and gravel has made an increasing contribution to the supply of aggre-

gates in the United Kingdom and in Northern Europe, In 1989, the UK dredging fleet recovered approximately 20 million tonnes of which some 16 million tonnes were landed at UK wharves, the balance going to Germany, Holland, Belgium and France. The contribution to the UK market currently represents approximately 16% of the total demand and is mainly consumed in the south-eastern counties.

The marine dredging industry for the provision of aggregates is expanding rapidly in other parts of the world notably Japan, which is the world leader producing approximately 80 million tonnes annually (Narumi 1989). However, most of this tonnage comprises fine aggregates for ready mix concrete whereas the UK industry produces both coarse and fine aggregates in equal proportions.

Other EC member states do not maintain a marine dredging capacity equal to that of the UK but do have very significant river and estuarine dredging industries not a notable feature in UK.

Marine dredging on the Continental Shelf of the United States has been, until recently, insignificant but recent land use and environmental constraints are causing operators and legislators to reconsider their previously held bias against marine dredging.

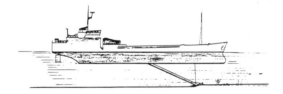

Suction hopper dredger with forward leading pipe (at anchor).

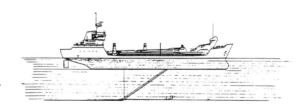

Suction hopper dredger with trailing pipe.

Fig. 4.21. Dredging techniques.

4.4.2. Recovery of marine aggregates

The UK dredging fleet employs two dredging techniques: anchor dredging and trail dredging.

FIG. 4.22. Dredger (courtesy RMC Ltd).

Anchor dredging, as the name implies, requires the dredging vessel to remain stationary whilst operating. A hole or pit is created in the sea bed deposit and production continues while unconsolidated materials fall into the excavation towards the suction head. Periodically the vessel has to be winched forward to maintain a free flow of material or to commence another sub-marine pit. The main advantage of the method is its suitability to working in the deeper deposits. Its principal disadvantage is the poor accuracy of location and a low efficiency of recovery. The method tends to leave a series of pits in the sea bed deposit which, although arguably easier to recolonize by marine life, are disliked by trawler fishermen.

Trail dredging, see Fig. 4.22, is performed while the vessel is underway and excavates the deposit by dragging the dredge head across the surface of the sea bed. Unlike anchor dredging the method cuts smooth trenches in the sea bed deposit and can be more easily controlled to recover only the payable deposit without penetrating the sub-strata. Figure 4.21 shows a schematic description of the two methods. The 'in-board' hydraulic pumps on the ship create suction in a pipe leading from a dredge head on the sea floor and the dredger is able to operate successfully in up to 25 metres of water. The largest dredgers are fitted with 86 cm suction, 76 cm discharge

centrifugal pumps and can load at a rate of 2000 tonnes per hour. With the centrifugal dredge pump mounted overboard within the dredge pipe it is possible to dredge in much deeper waters and the latest vessels will be operating in greater than 45 metres of water. The volume of water lifted in the operation is generally ten times the volume of solid and the cargo hold, which is initially filled with water, gradually becomes filled by the solids as the water is displaced. Some unwanted fine material may be washed overboard during the dredging operation but sea-dredged aggregates must normally be processed ashore, the complexity of the processing depending on the composition of the 'as dredged' material (e.g. the clay and shell content) (Chapman & Roeder 1969). When so designed, it is possible for some dredgers to utilize screens to reject particular materials e.g. clay and shell, but processing at sea in UK waters is not permitted.

Various unloading techniques are used, but the trend is towards self discharging ships since shore based grab cranes have low discharge rates of only 200 to 300 tonnes per hour and are not, therefore, cost effective. They are now largely replaced by drag scrapers which are winched through the cargo to discharge onto conveyors which transfer the materials ashore (Uren 1989).

Some vessels are able to use the suction dredge pump to discharge the cargo but this requires modification of the pump and the cargo hold. The advantage, however, is a high, 2000 tonne per hour discharge rate.

The high capital cost of these specialized dredgers demands maximum utilization for dredging and minimum travel times and idle periods e.g. unloading or waiting for tides. Hence there is a demand for rapid unloading and loading systems. Since many vessels must navigate tidal estuaries to approach the wharf, the design of the dredger, in terms of steaming speed, hold capacity and unloader, may be specifically optimized with respect to a given dredging area and discharge wharf (DoE 1986b).

4.5. Extraction, planning and scheduling

4.5.1. Introduction

The initial planning for excavation of quarries is basically an exercise in economics. The aim of any overall quarry or pit plan is to recover the maximum quantity of the resource available at the required rate of production for the lowest possible cost.

Factors which need to be taken into account include the following.

(1) The definition of that part of the deposit that can be technically and economically worked in relation to property boundaries and surrounding topography; factors which can impose significant constraints.

(2) The quantity of overburden, waste and non-saleable materials which define the basic economics of excavation and, hence, any cut-off limits.

(3) The geological structure and tectonic features of the deposits. Faults, joint sets and interbedded materials can determine the orientation and dimensions of quarry faces, angles of stable slopes which define the limits to the excavation and preferred direction of working.

(4) The hydrogeology of the area determines the need for dewatering systems and the methods and equipment required.

(5) The lithology of rock types and any variations within the total deposit being worked will influence the selection of equipment and costs of production.

4.5.2. Quarry plans

It is common practice for a series of working plans to be drawn up which show the progressive development of the pit or quarry in terms or production rates. These are used to calculate volumes and tonnages and to establish, for example, the position of haul roads, conveyor routes, and stages of restoration. The overall and final design of the excavation will have been determined from the outset by the geological, geotechnical and hydrogeological constraints. Optimum dimensions of faces and direction of working and the safe side wall slopes will be designed by the geotechnical engineer increasingly assisted by computer-aided design systems (Anon 1990; Norton 1991; Denby 1988) but the scheduling of overburden stripping and excavation rates, the methods to be employed and the equipment needed is the province of the quarry engineer and manager.

4.5.3. Overburden payrock ratios

The parameters known as overall and instantaneous stripping ratios, commonly used in open-pit metalliferous mining, are equally applicable in aggregate production, pits and quarries (Plewman 1970). The overall ratio is the total amount of overburden to be removed expressed as a proportion of the total reserve. The instantaneous ratio is the amount of overburden to be removed to uncover the next tonne of payrock at any time in the programme.

Although the overall ratios may be favourable, often better than 1 : 20 in the case of quarries, the instantaneous rate can be very high during some stages in the phased programme and may require deployment of additional equipment. Knowledge of the amount and nature of overburden and waste, as determined by a quarry plan, ensures that adequate provision may be made for its safe disposal in accordance with the statutory regulations (Mines and Quarries (Tips) Regulations) or inclusion in a designed backfill or restoration scheme.

4.5.4. Overburden removal

In quarry operations overburden removal is generally accomplished in one of three ways.

(1) By a continuous stripping operation in step with the advance of the quarry faces providing cleared surfaces immediately ahead of production. This involves minimum initial outlay but requires detailed planning and execution to avoid interruption of quarry operations. In the case that soils and overburden are used immediately, without storage, in a restoration scheme that follows closely behind extraction the term 'progressive restoration' is employed equivalent to 'strip-mining'. This practice is common for sand and gravel quarries.

(2) By a series of stripping phases to give blocks of exposed reserves equivalent to 3, 6 or 12 months of production. Phased stripping may also be programmed to take advantage of climatic conditions. In UK and some parts of Europe overburden stripping is generally considered to be a year round operation. Soils, however, should only be handled when dry which usually restricts operations to the summer months. In other parts of the world, with greater extremes of climate, it is imperative that the correct methods and equipment are selected to suit the conditions. This practice may coincide or be dictated by seasonal variations of climate and is conducive to contracting.

(3) By a one-off stripping operation when all overburden is removed in a single contract to leave the whole reserve exposed. This type of strip would normally be undertaken in large borrow quarries for a civil engineering contract but can be applied to quarries in continuous production. Clearly, it is likely to result in a large, initial visual impact.

As can be appreciated, the detailed planning of overburden and soils removal and the provision of adequate tipping or storage space without interrupting quarry operations, sterilizing reserves or incurring exceptional costs is a very important exercise prior to the development of a quarry.

4.5.5. Haul roads and conveyor routes

As all quarries and pits have differing geological and structural conditions, so the layout of haul and conveyor routes will present a unique problem at each site and frequently change at various stages in the excavation programme. Haul or conveyor routes are frequently planned to take the excavated materials to the crushers or reception hoppers by the shortest possible routes and the most acceptable gradient. However, following this idealized concept throughout the life of a pit or quarry can lead to a multiplicity of haul roads.

Careful staged planning of haulage systems is essential

if loss of reserve through misplaced or redundant routes is to be avoided. Optimum gradient is a controversial subject but in the interests of maximum resource recovery the steepest possible gradient should be sought. Gradients of haul roads in most UK quarries are designed to be as steep as practicable and grades of 1:8 or 1:10 are frequently quoted as being suitable for the modern dump-truck fleet. Road widths and corner radii are determined by the size of the equipment in use and the quarry plan needs to take account of the existing and future dump-truck specifications. Whatever the gradient or width, the essential criterion is that haul routes should be well drained and maintained throughout the life of excavation. The plan must allow for adequate protection of both surface and support, and that all necessary equipment and plant is available at the appropriate time. With the increase in use of in-pit crushers and haulage by conveyor to the processing area, there may be a need to include in the quarry plan modifications to the haulage routes. The use of high-angle conveyors requires considerably less width and support and can lead to additional reserve recovery (Blower 1990).

In most sand and gravel operations, as discussed in §4.3.5, haulage is by conveyor. Wherever possible, the overall plan should ensure that the trunk conveyor is sited on land which will not be excavated and that the number and moves of field conveyors are minimal.

4.5.6. Equipment selection

4.5.6.1. Introduction. Production of aggregate of acceptable quality, at the required rate of production and at economic cost, depends on the selection and utilization of the most suitable equipment to match the conditions. Achieving these objectives is a crucial task of the quarry engineer and also requires careful planning and scheduling of operations. Each phase of the extraction plan will be presented in a series of mine plans and schedules showing the progressive extraction of the payrock minerals and, in most cases, the designed backfill and restoration as well. In the same way the type and numbers of mobile equipment will need to be programmed and scheduled. Planning for equipment replacement is largely a question of the investment policies dependent on the capital depreciation set by the operating company (Shand 1970).

However, during the life of a quarry or pit the rate of output, the ratios of waste to payrock and the dimensions of production faces are all likely to vary and consequently the type, numbers and capacity of all excavation equipment will need to be adjusted to suit the particular requirements.

The optimum number of each machine and their deployment can be determined by consideration of the required rate of production, the geological conditions and performance data for a single unit obtained from comparative experience or the manufacturer.

Just as the quarry profile can be designed by computer so too can the numbers and type of equipment be selected by a variety of software packages now available (Denby 1988).

4.5.6.2. Drilling equipment. Selection of the drilling equipment and method takes into account a number of factors which may vary within a single quarry and will almost certainly vary during the life of a quarry. The rock type and rock mass classification will influence the performance of any drill rig in terms of rates of penetration and wear on rods and bits. Typically a DTH rotary percussion rig will achieve 20 m/h in a soft limestone but only 10–12 m/h in a hard igneous rock or a sandstone. Hydraulic rig penetration rates can vary between 15 and 25 m/h.

The selected drilling pattern of burden × spacing × face height will enable the yield per hole in cubic metres to be calculated. Based on the drill performance, after making allowances for availability and utilization, the yields per blast and the number of drills to achieve the production targets throughout the development can be determined.

4.5.6.3. Loading equipment. The principal factors which need to be considered in selecting the loading equipment and scheduling its deployment throughout the quarry or pit life are: (i) the daily and hourly production rates; (ii) the configuration of quarry faces and the number to be worked; (iii) the expected fragmentation and the maximum lump size; (iv) the capacity and type of haulage trucks; (v) the digging rates, cycle times and efficiencies of each type of excavating machine (Brundell 1982).

As production rates vary throughout the life of a quarry as may the rock conditions, so the number and type of machine need to be scheduled to ensure cost effectiveness of the operation.

4.5.6.4. Hauling equipment. The numbers and capacity of dump trucks will generally be determined by the required production rate, but there are various factors which often influence selection. The type of excavation and ground conditions including manoeuvring space, gradients and running surfaces will decide whether rigid or articulated dumpers are appropriate.

From the mine plan the haulage distances and cycle times can be calculated at any stage and thus indicate the numbers needed. Careful analysis of haulage costs can assist in deciding if alternative methods of moving materials from the excavations to the plant should be adopted. The alternatives might include load-haul-dump using a single machine, a front end wheeled loader in the case of rock quarries, or motorized scrapers in the case of sand and gravel pits.

4.6. Environmental issues

4.6.1. Introduction

The concern for environmental protection can have a profound effect on the operation of quarries and on the methods and type of excavation equipment in use. The quarry operator must, therefore, not only plan for cost effective excavation of overburden and payrock but also plan to achieve an acceptable standard of amenity protection during the excavation phase and the eventual restoration of the site to a beneficial after-use. Equally, the design of excavation and processing operations must take into account the health and safety of operatives within the working environment, hazards of the operation and the impact upon the external environment, often termed nuisance (Waller 1992).

Within England and Wales the safety and health of operatives are legally protected by the Health and Safety at Work Act (1974). More recently, directives have been issued by the European Parliament and new regulations have been published by the Health and Safety Executive (HSE) notably, Control of Substances Hazardous to Health (COSHH) Regulations 1988 (King 1991; Powley 1989).

The principal concerns relevant to the quarrying industry are noise and airborne dusts and the prevention of hearing loss and respiratory diseases respectively. The duty of the employer is to prevent the creation of hazards at source, to provide protective clothing where the hazard cannot be reasonably eliminated, to inform employees of the hazards and to provide health checks and, if appropriate, to monitor exposure.

In terms of impact on the external environment, planning legislation and conditions reinforced by the Environmental Protection Act (1990) cover the major issues which affect the operation of pits and quarries including visual impact, noise, dust and vibration.

4.6.2. Noise

Noise is unwanted sound and can either be a nuisance or a hazard to health. Since noise is energy being transmitted through air it can be measured as energy level or pressure but is normally expressed in terms of a logarithmic scale, the decibel (dB) scale. This scale compares noise level to the threshold of hearing defined as 0 dB or a pressure of 20 µPa. The noise level is also adjusted to take account of the response of the human ear (which is most sensitive to human speech in the frequency range 1 to 10 kHz) to noise of differing frequencies giving the dBA scale. Illustrative sound levels on this scale are: whispering (30 dBA), normal speech (60 dBA), 1 m from a running diesel engine (90 dBA), and the threshold of pain in the ears (120 dBA). Noise is attenuated by distance according to the inverse square law and

measurement of noise generated by equipment must state the distance between source and meter. In terms of potential damage to hearing, both the noise level and duration of exposure must be considered. Regulations within the EC require that the exposure should not exceed 85 dBA during an eight hour working shift and never exceed 130 dBA. Exposure to intermediate noise levels is acceptable provided that the duration is reduced proportionally. In situations where the exposure will exceed 85 dBA(8h), warning notices, training and advice and ear protectors must be provided (Gregory 1987; Moorhouse 1990).

Mobile equipment manufacturers are now required to publish information concerning the noise generated by their products. Most modern equipment is provided with a sound-proofed cabin for the operator. Developments are continuing to assemble quieter machines employing such techniques as silencing, reduced rotation speeds, lower fluid velocities etc.

4.6.3. Dust

Dust is a hazard best prevented at source, for example, by suppression using water sprays or by enclosure of equipment and preventing air entrainment of dust through careful design and selection of operating procedures. The primary objective is to reduce the 'respirable dust', particles sized less than 5 µm, to a very low concentration, e.g. 5 mg/m^3. Particles finer than 5 µm escape the filters of the human body within the respiratory system and may enter and accumulate in the lungs. This is of particular concern if they contain a high free silica content (Tuck 1987).

The Control of Substances Hazardous to Health (COSHH) Regulations (1988) have a significant effect on the type of equipment employed and the methods of operation. The Regulations require that employees and the general public must not be exposed to any hazardous substance. Exposure to hazardous substances must be controlled and any control measures must be regularly monitored and tested. Quarry dusts are considered to be hazardous substances and standards and limitations to exposure, particularly of dusts containing silica and asbestiform minerals, are very stringent, often requiring considerable protective modification to plant and controlled operation and practice (Shenton 1989; Morrison 1991).

Not all dusts are necessarily hazardous if they contain no harmful mineral but airborne dusts, whether hazardous to health or not, are always considered to be a nuisance and the quarry operator must ensure that dust emissions are minimized. The three principal sources of dust within the quarry excavation are: (i) the drilling operation, (ii) the movement of traffic and (iii) the dumping of mineral into hoppers or stockpiles.

In the case of drilling dusts, the remedy is to fit dust

collection and suppression systems to the rigs. These are generally highly efficient and there should be no reason why drilling dust should continue to be a problem.

Suppression of dust arising from roads, traffic or dumping operations is a matter of common sense and good housekeeping. Preparation and maintenance of competent roadways, which can be watered by bowsers during dry weather, and the use of atomizing water sprays as wet dust suppression systems on conveyor transfer points and stockpiles are very effective. The enclosure of stockpiles containing fine materials (<3 mm) has been recommended. Otherwise, it may be possible to schedule or suspend some operations such as tipping to avoid exceedingly dry or windy conditions (DoE 1991).

4.6.4. Blasting

Although blasting operations also generate both noise and dust, ground vibration and 'air-blast' or over-pressure nuisance from blasting probably constitute the major environmental problems faced by quarry operators. These inevitable effects of the detonation of explosives are all controllable provided that the blasting operations are closely monitored and the established rules and practices are followed (McKenzie 1990; Dunn 1989).

4.6.4.1. Ground vibration. The peak particle velocity of a vibration is considered to be the most reliable criterion for assessing the potential for damage or nuisance caused by a quarry explosive. Peak particle velocity (ppv) is a function of the frequency and amplitude of the vibration; ppv $= 2\pi f A$, where f is the frequency in Hz and A the amplitude in mm. Conditions imposed on quarry operators often seek ppv's of 10 mm/s or less at specified distances to ensure no damage to structures nor nuisance to local residents.

One relationship between ppv, distance and the explosive charge weight is given by the following formula:

$$\text{ppv} = K(D/\sqrt{W})^{-n}(\text{mm/s})$$

where K and n are site specific constants of the order of 1000 and 1.0, respectively. W is the explosive charge weight (kg) per detonation, known as the instantaneous charge weight and D is the distance in metres (ICI Explosives Co. Ltd.). Thus, minimizing ppv and vibration is largely achieved by reduction of the instantaneous charge weight. The principal method is the use of delay detonators to separate explosions in each blast. Additionally, the total charge should be reduced to the minimum to achieve satisfactory fragmentation. Modifications of the drilling pattern, e.g. reduction of blast hole diameter will also reduce the charge weight per hole. Geological structure should also be studied in

terms of the propagation of vibration, i.e. the effect of bedding, joint and fault planes must be understood (Borg 1983).

4.6.4.2. Air blast. Air blast or over-pressure is of considerable importance because it is usually accompanied by noise, for example, created by the rattling of windows which is then attributed to ground vibration. Thus, air-blast magnifies the perception of vibrations and incurs increased complaints concerning blast vibration. Air blast is sound energy of a frequency below that detectable by hearing (noise). Since air blast is wave energy propagated through air, it can be influenced by wind speed, temperature, humidity and pressure i.e. local atmospheric conditions (Wilton 1991).

To minimize air blast, the quarry operator should seek to design the blast so that the explosion is contained by the rock. The measures that might be employed include: (i) initiating the blast at or near the bottom of the blast-hole; (ii) reducing or eliminating the use of surface detonating cord or burying the cord; (iii) ensuring that the blast-hole is adequately stemmed; (iv) ensuring that a minimum burden exists in front of each blast-hole and that the face does not contain fissures or other planes of weakness through which gases may vent explosively. The total surface area of the exposed face may need to be reduced by reducing bench height or length or arranging multi-row blasts, since forward movement during blasting can generate over pressure. Finally, blasting may be postponed under adverse meteorological conditions.

4.6.5. Nuisance

If the working environment is satisfactory it is improbable that noise or dust will be a hazard beyond the works perimeter. However, they may constitute a nuisance through disturbance or visual intrusion.

4.6.5.1. Noise nuisance. Noise nuisance is often quantified in terms of noise level above background where an increase of 5 to 10 dBA may constitute a nuisance. Assessment of noise affecting local communities can be made using BS 4142, which assumes that an industrial noise exceeding the background noise constitutes a potential nuisance. Permission to develop a quarry may be granted conditional upon an upper limit of noise level not being exceeded during the day with a different (lower) level specified for night-time. The intrusive effect of noise has been found to be greater, for example, for higher frequencies, irregular and rhythmic sounds and unexpected sounds of short duration. Examination of working practices may be able to eliminate these. The nuisance may be reduced and controlled by restricting the hours of working or even specifying the method and phasing of working. For example, conveyor transport is less intrusive than the use of dump trucks. Bunds, which also usefully store soils or overburden prior to restoration, may be constructed around the perimeter of the operations both as sound barriers and visual screens (Anon 1991).

4.6.5.2. Dust nuisance. The nuisance of dust is difficult to quantify and monitor and tends to be assessed by qualitative or subjective methods (Bate & Coppin 1991).

However, dust nuisance can be mitigated by maintenance and watering of haul roads and sweeping of paved areas and even public approach roads. Road vehicles can be subjected to a wheel-wash and loads either sprayed with water or sheeted. Speed restrictions within the site may reduce dust entrainment. Conveyors and stockpiles containing fine material should be enclosed or provided with wind-boards to prevent dust entrainment and transfer heights should be minimized. The careful siting of stockpiles and tips with respect to the direction of the prevailing wind, proximity of housing, etc. and scheduling or postponing operations to avoid 'dusty conditions' will also be effective in reducing complaints (DoE 1991).

4.6.6. Visual impact

Conditions of planning consent generally require that the visual impact of quarrying operations is minimized and that the excavations are screened from view. Depending on the type of operation and, in particular, the topographic expression of the site, both long distance and near-to views will need to be considered and the expert advice and designs of landscape architects will need to be included as an integral part of the quarry plan.

Screening of workings from near-by views is generally achieved by construction of bunds or mounds of overburden and other waste materials around the periphery of the site. The bunds should be designed and constructed first as engineering structures, often in compliance with the Mines and Quarries Tips Regulations, and then landscaped and planted to provide as natural an appearance as possible. Alternatively, the workings may be screened by an existing or introduced tree and shrub barrier of sufficient density to provide a visual barrier.

Provision of visual barriers often requires that potentially mineral-bearing land is sterilized and the reserves of payrock may need to be adjusted to allow for visual amenity protection. Construction of visual amenity screens may involve a single phase of activity or may be, at larger sites, a semi-continuous operation. In either case the selection and provision of the equipment and scheduling of the task becomes an important part of the excavation planning. Reduction of the visual impact from sensitive, long distance views can often be achieved by orientation of the working faces, adopting a particular face height and length and by selecting a preferred direction of working. The need to design quarry operations to achieve desirable visual protection can again result in some loss of the theoretical geological reserves and should be recognized in the overall costing of the excavation operation. It should be noted, however, that despite the environment desirability of a particular direction of working and face configuration, the geological structure will determine the safest and most effective method of excavation and must, therefore, be taken as the primary criterion.

4.6.7. Restoration

Reclamation of land from which mineral has been excavated is now seen to be not just a requirement of environmental protection and conservation but an essential part of the financial planning and overall viability of aggregate production. Depending on the type of deposit worked, the topography and hydrogeology, pits and quarries are successfully restored to agricultural use, including forestry. Alternatively, particularly in the case of wet working, after-uses might include water sport leisure activities and nature conservation parks. In deep hard rock and limestone sub-water table workings, where restoration to dry conditions may be impossible, a planned after-use as a water resource may be a valuable asset. However, the measures needed to ensure an acceptable water quality would need to be included in the excavation phase (RMC 1986).

The most profitable form of reclamation and restoration is that which can be achieved following filling of the excavation with imported wastes. The practice termed 'Landfill' is nowadays considered as important as the original excavation of mineral. A range of waste materials may be used including domestic, commercial and industrial wastes. The overburden and inherent quarry wastes are utilized as cover and capping materials.

A pit or quarry once back-filled to the original topographic levels or sometimes deliberately contoured to another landform may then be the site of a wide range of after-uses including leisure activities e.g. sports grounds, golf courses and parkland etc., urban development both for domestic housing and commercial use as well as agriculture.

The management of waste disposal into mineral workings requires the most professional and careful attention to technical and legal standards of pollution control. It is fairly common practice for the excavation and backfilling operations to be undertaken simultaneously and frequently directed by a single management and engineering team. In these circumstances the landfill operation will form part of the overall mining plan and will call for detailed design of leachate and methane control, monitoring and dispersal systems (DoE 1986a; DoE 1989a,b).

FIG. 4.23. Load and carry operation with mobile in-pit crusher (courtesy Foster-Yeoman).

4.7. Future trends

Although conventional methods of quarrying hardrock and excavating sand and gravel deposits will continue throughout the 1990s and beyond, the patterns of demand and environmental pressures will lead to major changes in the scale and methods of excavation. The advent of the coastal super quarry, with production rates of 10 million tonnes per annum, is likely to be repeated at a number of locations, and these are likely to be remote from the market areas which they serve (Tidmarsh 1989; Kirk 1990). Consequently the numbers of smaller quarries will continue to decline. It is also likely that in UK and other European countries there will be a marked trend towards underground mining of limestone and igneous rocks, a practice which is already relatively common in some American States notably, Kansas, Ohio and Indiana. As the methods of quarrying and extraction of aggregates are changed and modified so too will the equipment employed.

4.7.1. Super quarries

The most significant factor influencing the extraction programme and equipment selection is obviously the rate of production. At 10 million tonnes per annum a super quarry on a 10-hour shift will be required to deliver rock to the primary crusher at rates up to 4000 tonnes per hour. To produce such tonnages without utilizing large numbers of men and numbers of in-quarry machinery requires a carefully designed mine layout and selection of equipment and operating techniques which are matched to minimize the numbers of operations. Ideally, production of rock for the primary crusher should be kept to two or at most three faces as in the case of conventional lower output units. As quarry faces are likely to be restricted to 15 or 20 metres high the length of faces and travel distances will tend to become very long. This may be offset by increased numbers and capacity of excavating and haulage equipment but can also be achieved by minimizing haulage distance to the primary crusher.

4.7.2. In-pit crushers

Mobile crushers located close to the production face capable of meeting the required outputs are well established and can be operated in a number of ways. They

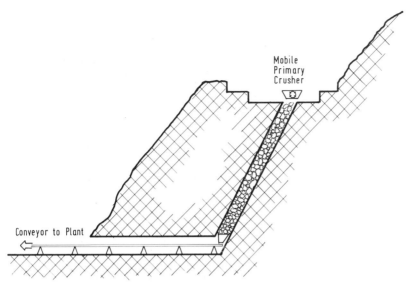

FIG. 4.24. Glory hole–ore pass operation.

can be fed conventionally by dump truck travelling a short distance from face to crusher on one level. Where travel distances can be maintained at less than 100–150 metres, large capacity front end loaders working as 'load-haul-dump' units (LHD) are most effective, see Fig. 4.23. Finally, hydraulic excavators which sit on the shot rock pile can load directly to the crusher feed hoppers with no requirement for dump trucks, see Fig. 4.17. From the quarry face or quarry floor, primary crushed rock is fed to the secondaries and the process plants by conveyor (Collin 1982).

Conveyor systems require considerably less space than haul roads sterilizing less reserves and able to operate at much steeper gradients than dump trucks. The trend towards high-angle, high-capacity conveyor systems will increase the opportunities of introducing mobile crushers located at the production face from deep open pit quarries.

At hillside quarry locations short travel distances and the use of load-haul-dump techniques are possible by feeding the primary crushers via an ore pass or by locating a semi-mobile primary over the ore pass. ARC's Criggion Quarry and Yeoman's Glendsanda Super Quarry (Tidmarsh 1991) have both adopted the technique to considerable effect. Figure 4.24 demonstrates the technique whereby the shot rock is crushed close to the face above the ore pass or glory hole. The travel distances of either dumpers or LHD equipment can be restricted thus reducing numbers. Movement of the primary crusher level by level downwards becomes part of the excavation planning schedules and is included in the mine design programmes.

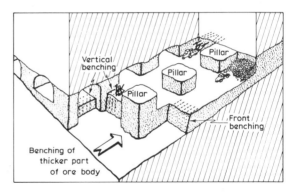

FIG. 4.25. Underground layout.

4.7.3. Underground quarrying

In most instances production of aggregates by underground mining has been achieved by converting conventional quarries. Horizontal drifts or addits are driven into the quarry face to form the mine access or portal. The mining method usually employed is one of room and pillar whereby galleries of specified height and width are mined out parallel to each other separated by rib pillars, see Fig. 4.25. Employing room and pillar techniques 40–70% recovery of a single payrock horizon is usually feasible. In the most favourable circumstance two or three horizons of payrock may eventually be mined out in a concession area. Although the sequence of drilling and blasting, loading and hauling to primary crusher is applicable to underground mining, the equipment used is often significantly different. Drilling of headings or galleries is performed by multi-boom jumbo rigs on which two, three or four drifter type drills are mounted together on one carrier capable of being raised and lowered on hydraulic booms to reach the full height of the heading or room. Some rock formations allow galleries and rooms of such size and condition to be formed that conventional loaders and dumpers are used to lift and transport the shot rock to the primary crusher. Others, particularly where the overall height and room widths are likely to be restrictive, will employ purpose built LHD mine excavators. This equipment is specifically designed for underground operations and clearly has great advantages over conventional quarry methods not least that only one piece of machinery is used.

References

ADKINS, N. 1986. Aids to blast design. *Quarry Management*, October, 35–38.

ANON 1985. Tilcon tee off at Farnham. *Quarry Management*, June, 451–456.

ANON 1988a. A review of impact hammers for quarry applications. *Quarry Management*, February, 23–25.

ANON 1988b. Field conveyor system proves its worth. *Quarry Management*, July, 33–35.

ANON 1988c. Secondary breaking. *Mine & Quarry*, July, 21–28.

ANON 1988d. Laser profiling at Moorcroft quarry. *Mine & Quarry*, February.

ANON 1989. Wellpointing at Berkswell sand and gravel. *Mine & Quarry*, April, 23–24.

ANON 1990. Quarry planning: is there a role for computers? *Mine & Quarry*, May, 19–24.

ANON 1991. Environmental care sways planning decision. *Quarry Management*, April, 15–18.

ANON 1992a. 'Hydraulic breakers work the quarry face'. *Quarry Management*, June, 15–19.

ANON 1992b. Secondary breaking in quarries. *Quarry Management*, June, 21–31.

ATLAS POWDER Co. 1987. *Explosives and rock blasting*, Dallas.

ATKINSON, T. 1971. Selection of open pit excavating and loading equipment. *Transactions of the Institute of Mining and Metallurgy*, **80**, A101–A129.

BALL, M. 1988. A review of blast design considerations in quarrying and opencast mining. *Quarry Management*, June, 35–43 and July, 23–27.

BATE, K. & COPPIN, N. 1991. Dust impacts from mineral workings. *Mine & Quarry*, March, 31–35.

BERTA, G., 1990. *Explosives*. Italesplosivi, Milan.

BLOWER, J. 1990. High-angle conveying in hard rock quarrying operations. *Quarry Management*, October, 35–37.

BORG, D. G. 1983. Some pointers on blasting and blasting techniques. *Rock Products*, February, 27.

BREWSTER, P. 1987. The use of motor graders, dozers and tractors in quarrying applications. *Quarry Management*, September, 27–28.

BRUNDELL, J. 1982. Developments in excavator design and application. *Quarry Management*, February, 19–23.

BUTLER, A., CROOK, R. & SHOVE, G. 1988. Training and the Explosives Regulations. *Quarry Management*, June, 41–43.

CHAPMAN, G. P. & ROEDER, A. R. 1969. Sea-dredged sands and gravel. *Quarry Managers Journal, London*, **53** (7), 251–253.

CHRISTOPH, B. 1991. Improvements on large hydraulic excavators. *Quarry Management*, October, 39–44.

CLARK, G. 1987. *Principles of Rock Fragmentation*. Wiley, New York.

COLLIN, G. 1982. In-quarry crushing. *Quarry Management*, May, 311–317.

CORKER, S. 1987. Bulk soil handling techniques. *M & Q Environment*, **1**, 15–17.

CUNNINGHAM, C. 1989. Computer-aided blast design. *Quarry Management*, September, 33–41.

DALGLEISH, I. 1989. Cost effective drilling and blasting. *Quarry Management*, January, 19–27.

DENBY, B. 1988. Computer aids in quarry design and planning. *Quarry Management*, May, 27–41.

DEPARTMENT OF THE ENVIRONMENT 1972. The Law relating to Safety and Health in mines and quarries, Part 4, QUARRIES, HMSO, London.

—— 1986a *Landfilling Wastes*, Waste management paper No. 26, HMSO, London.

—— 1986b *Marine Dredging for Sand and Gravel*, HMSO, London.

—— 1989a. *Minerals Planning Guidance; The Reclamation of Mineral Workings*, MPG 7, HMSO, London.

—— 1989b. *The Control of Land Fill Gas*, Waste management paper No. 27, HMSO, London.

—— 1991. *Quarry Processes Including Roadstone Plants and the Size Reduction of Bricks, Tiles and Concrete*, Planning Guidance, PG3/8(91), HMSO, London.

DOVER, T. M. 1964. *Stripping of Rock Overburden*. Symposium on Opencast Mining, Quarrying and Alluvial Mining. Institute of Mining & Metallurgy, London, 1–14.

DRAKE, B. 1987. Digging equipment trends in the USA. *Quarry Management*, February, 13–17.

DUNN, P. 1989. Blasting and vibration control in British opencast coal mining. *Mine & Quarry*, February.

EARLE, Q. 1991. The quarrying industry in Hong Kong. *Quarry Management*, February, 19–24.

FOOKES, P. G., DEARMAN, W. R. & FRANKLIN, J. A. 1971. Engineering aspects of rock weathering. *Quarterly Journal of Engineering Geology*, **4**, 139–185.

GARRARD, G. & WALTON, G. 1990. Guidance in the design and inspection of tips and related structures. *Transactions of the Institute of Mining and Metallurgy*, A115–A124.

GEOLOGICAL SOCIETY ENGINEERING GROUP WORKING PARTY REPORT 1977. The description of rock masses for engineering purposes. *Quarterly Journal of Engineering Geology*, **10**, 355–388.

GREGORY, J. 1987. The measurement and control of industrial noise. *Quarry Management*, January, 25–33.

HARTMAN, H. 1987. *Introductory Mining Engineering*. Wiley, New York.

HEMPHILL, G. 1981. *Blasting Operations*. McGraw-Hill, New York.

HSC 1989. *Explosives at Quarries*. Approved Code of Practice, HMSO, London.

ICI EXPLOSIVES Co. *Explosives in Quarrying*. Information leaflet.

IMM 1983. *Surface Mining and Quarrying*, Proceedings of International Symposium, IMM, London.

KENNEDY, B. 1990. *Surface mining*. Seely Mudd series, AIME (Society of Mining Engineers), New York.

KING, J. 1991. *Safety and Legislation*. Institute of Quarrying, Nottingham.

KIRK, M. 1990. Scottish coastal quarries. *Quarry Management*, April, 39–44.

LITTLER, A. 1990. *Sand and Gravel Production*. Institute of Quarrying, Nottingham.

MCKENZIE, C. 1990. Quarry blast monitoring. *Quarry Management*, December, 23–29.

MARTIN, J. 1982. *Surface Mining and Equipment*. Martin Consultants, Golden, Colorado.

MOORHOUSE, A. 1990. Industrial noise in the 1990s. *Quarry Management*, February, 31–36.

MORRISON, J. 1991. Health surveillance in the construction materials industries. *Quarry Management*, December, 37–38.

NARUMI, Y. 1989. Offshore mining in Japan. *Quarry Management*, March, 11–16.

NORTON, J. 1991. Three dimensional surface modelling for mines and quarries. *Quarry Management*, September 37–38.

OAKES, R. 1989. Diesel hydraulic versus electric rope. *Quarry Management*, February, 37–43.

PASS, R. D. 1970. Planning for production. *Quarry Managers Journal, London*, **54** (5), 163–176.

PEMBERTON, J. 1990. Accurate blast hole alignments. *Quarry Management*, May, 15–34.

PLEWMAN, R. P. 1970. Basic economics of open-pit mining. Symposium, Johannesburg, S.A.I.M.M.

POWLEY, D. 1989. The new COSHH Regulations, 1988. *Quarry Management*, October, 32.

RMC 1986. *A Practical Guide to Restoration*. RMC Group plc., Feltham.

SAMUEL, P. 1990. Land restoration to agriculture. *Quarry Management*, October, 25–33.

SAUNDERS, E. 1987. The safe use of explosives in quarries. *Quarry Management*, February, 31–37.

SHAND, A. N. 1970. The basic principles of equipment selection for surface mining. *South African Institute of Mining & Metallurgy, Johannesburg Symposium*, 235–249.

SHAW, C. & PAVLOVIC V. *Surface Mining and Quarrying*, Ellis Horwood (in press).

SHENTON, V. 1989 Control of Substances Hazardous to Health. *Quarry Management*, October, 25–32.

SIEVERT, R. A. 1973. Load and carrying for quarries. *Cement, Limestone & Gravel*, **48** (5), 91–93.

STEVENSON, P. 1982. Loading at the face, *Quarry Management*, March, 175–181.

TALBOT, D. 1988. Recent advances in open pit blasting. *Quarry Management*, March, 31–34.

TAPANINAHO, T. 1987. Development in hydraulic drifter drilling. *Quarry Management*, March, 29–32.

TIDMARSH, D. 1989. Concepts of coastal quarrying. *Quarry Management*, July, 25–29.

—— 1991. The Glensanda experience. *Quarry Management*, November, 17–21.

TOMLINSON, L. 1990. The application of back-acters in the quarry industry. *Quarry Management*, February, 17–23.

TUCK, G. 1987. The control of airborne dust in quarries. *Quarry Management*, April, 23–31.

UREN, M. 1989. Supplying aggregates from the seabed. *Quarry Management*, December, 19–25.

WALLER, R. 1992. *Environmental effects of surface mineral workings*. Department of the Environment, HMSO, London.

WALTON PRACTICE, G. 1990. *Handbook on the design of Tips and related Structures*. Department of the Environment, HMSO, London.

WILTON, T. 1991. The air overpressure problem. *Quarry Management*, July, 25–27.

WHITE, T. 1989. Blasting to specification. *Quarry Management*, December, 27–34.

Appendix A4.1 Diagrams of extraction equipment in use in 1992

A4.1.1. Crawler tractor (bulldozer).

The tractor consists of a power unit fitted with crawler or caterpillar tracks enabling the machine to move over most types of surface. A blade may be attached across the front of the machine (bull dozer), the design of which varies with purpose. A crawler tractor can be employed to draw a scraper-bowl (see A4.1.3) or ripper (see A4.1.2). A dozer can move and spread materials over a short distance, construct stockpiles and tips and assist the loading of scrapers by pushing.

A4.1.2. Ripper.

This equipment is usually attached to the draw-bar of a crawler tractor or a power unit, and consists of a horizontal frame, raised and lowered by hydraulic cylinders in which is commonly mounted a single (sometimes multiple) tine/ripper. The tine breaks the ground through which it is drawn and the equipment is widely applied to fragment unconsolidated, friable and thinly bedded rocks. A recent development is the impact ripper utilizing an hydraulic hammer action to break even more competent rocks such as thinly bedded limestones and weathered overburden.

A4.1.3. Motorized Scraper.

The scraper (box) is usually associated with the rapid, low-cost excavation of earth works or unconsolidated overburden, soils and sands and gravels. It comprises a box or bowl mounted on four wheels fitted with pneumatic tyres which is either towed by a tractor or articulated and motorized. The front of the box is open and the leading edge is fitted with a blade which scrapes the surface of the mineral when the edge is lowered. To facilitate movement of material into the box (and reduce compaction of soils) the box may be equipped with a scraper elevator. It is not suitable for excavation of 'hard' rock, blasted rock or gravels containing boulders. The box is discharged by a ram acting upon a pusher plate.

A4.1.4. Self-contained drill rig.

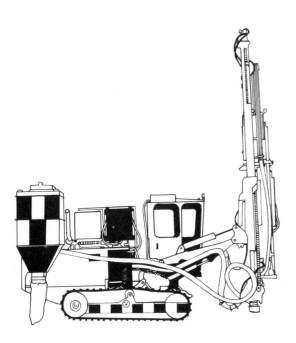

The diagram illustrates a self-contained, crawler mounted hydraulic drill rig complete with operator's cabin and dust collection unit. This drill rig would be suitable for a relatively large, high-output, hard rock quarry. The rig contains a power unit (hydraulic) and a separate compressor to provide air to flush the blast hole. Drilling is 'rotary-percussive', that is the drill stem rotates between percussive blows delivered to the top of the drill rods by a hydraulic 'top hammer'.

In unfaulted solid rock it is claimed that this system results in very high penetration rates and less costly operation. Rod handling is semi-automated and mechanized.

A4.1.5. Crawler drill rig.

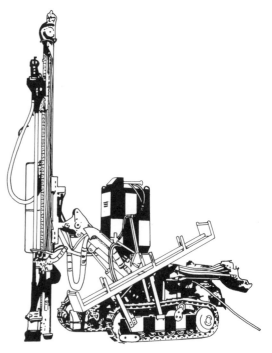

The diagram illustrates a simple, relatively inexpensive crawler-mounted, pneumatic (DTH) drill rig. The crawler, driven by air-motors, tows a separate compressor. This rig would be suitable for a smaller quarry of lower output. The percussion hammer is located within the drill stem immediately above the bit-hence 'down-the-hole' (DTH). It is pneumatically actuated. DTH drilling is claimed to give better directional control of the blast-hole whilst maintaining effective penetration rates even in difficult conditions e.g. faulting, interbedded rocks, jointing etc. Exhaust air from the hammer flushes the blast hole to remove cuttings.

A4.1.6. Drag-line excavator.

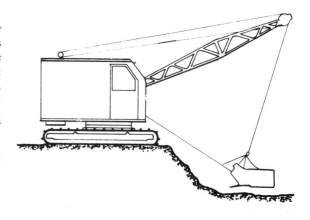

Used mainly for loading directly onto field conveyors or into hauling equipment the dragline is usually mounted on crawler tracks, the long side tracks reducing bearing pressure and increasing stability. The superstructure, comprising power unit, winches, cabin and boom rotate on this base. The machine is usually situated on a bank and is able to excavate material to a considerable depth below the bank depending upon boom length and slope angle. Owing to the length of the boom the machine is capable of extracting mineral over a larger area of ground than any other equipment. A skilled operator may even cast the bucket.

The dragline can be operated 'wet' or 'dry' and can excavate soils, unconsolidated overburden, sand and gravel and well fragmented blasted rock although is not generally suitable for the selective recovery of thinly bedded materials e.g. soils. When excavating sands and gravel from below water level it is usual to create a stockpile to permit drainage before transfer to truck or conveyor.

A4.1.7. Face-shovel rope excavator.

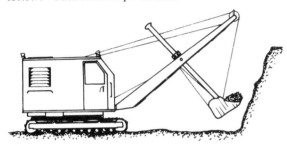

The excavator has a base plate, usually crawler mounted but sometimes wheeled in the smaller machines, upon which rotates the superstructure comprising the power unit (diesel or electric), cable winches, control cabin, boom and bucket arm (stick). The boom has a saddle attachment at about half its length where the bucket arm is attached; the boom and bucket are controlled by cables (ropes) from the cab.

Traditionally, the rope shovel is employed to load dump trucks with blasted rock but it may also dig directly into weakly consolidated materials.

A4.1.8. Hydraulic shovel excavator.

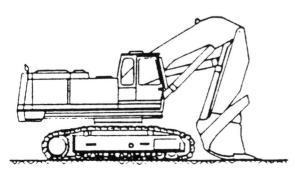

The hydraulic shovel is very similar to the rope shovel which it is steadily replacing in many quarry applications. The rigid, cable operated boom and stick are replaced by a jointed boom actuated by several hydraulic cylinders. The bucket can be precisely positioned and directed normally towards the face/rock-pile rather than constrained to travel in an arc.

The hydraulic shovel is used to dig directly into soils, weak or blasted rock and load into dump trucks. The accuracy of digging and loading, rapid cycle time and high 'break-out' forces create a very versatile and useful machine capable of both high output and selectivity. The excavator is crawler mounted and relatively manoeuvrable and has a bucket capacity between 5 and 35m³.

A4.1.9. Crawler loader.

Although not uncommon in the construction industry these machines, comprising an hydraulically actuated bucket fitted to a crawler tractor, are not ideally suited to most quarrying duties. The bucket sizes are generally small and loading, swinging and dumping require manoeuvring on the tracks.

A4.1.10. Hydraulic back hoe excavator.

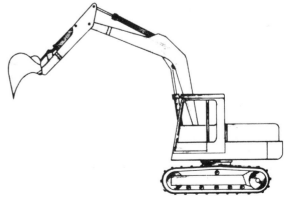

Also known as a 'back acter' this excavator is extremely accurate, rapid and versatile and has become very common both loading blasted rock and digging soils, overburden and sand and gravel. It is usually mounted upon driven crawler tracks, but may be seen on wheels, and can slew through 360°. It is available with a very wide range of bucket sizes and types.

A4.1.11.   Front end wheeled loaders.

Mounted on rubber-tyres and normally with front-wheel steering, greater manoeuvrability has been achieved with these shovels in recent years by use of articulation. Most of the larger models today are of this type.

Whereas smaller units are commonly used to load lorries and rail-wagons and for general yard duties, larger units are becoming common for face-loading of dump trucks and 'load-and-carry' operations. This machine is extremely versatile but is limited by maintenance costs and tyre wear (in abrasive 'hard' rock quarries) and ground conditions (unsuitable for wet, soft conditions).

A4.1.12.   Rigid body dump truck.

On well maintained haul roads the rigid body dump truck can achieve higher speeds and be expected to return lower operating costs than the ADT. The wheel base is short to provide manoeuvrability and a spot target for the excavator/loader. Body height and capacity must be matched to the lift and volume of the loader bucket (usually 4–6 buckets fills the truck) for optimum performance. The number and capacity of the trucks is then determined by considering quarry output and the cycle time of the two-way travel between loader and dumping point. A wide range of truck sizes is available, from 30 to over 150 tonnes capacity, and discharge can be by rear-dump (most common), side or bottom dump.

A4.1.13.   Articulated dump truck.

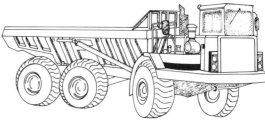

The articulation of the body and the multiple wheel drive create a dump truck that can operate successfully on very poor and constricted haul roads as often found when removing overburden, soils and sand and gravel. However, the increased maintenance requirement and tyre wear can lead to an increase of operating costs. The ADT is generally not suitable for carrying coarsely fragmented, abrasive rock from the face of a 'hard rock' quarry.

A4.1.14.   Floating cranes and floating grab dredgers.

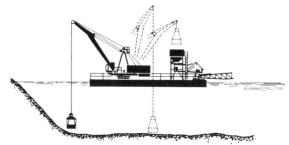

Usually mounted on one end of a rectangular pontoon for loading into barges, floating cranes and grabs are capable of very high speeds of operation. Grabs can deliver to a surge bin with a grid to separate oversize material picked up by the grab, the undersize material being discharged to conveyors and thence to the processing plant.

A4.1.15.   Slack-line excavators.

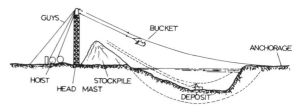

Combining the excavation and transportation of the mineral in one operation, the method is most successful in free-running material.

A4.1.16. Ladder dredgers.

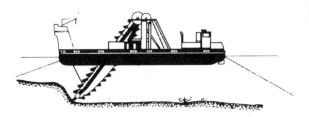

Although considered to have limited use in sand and gravel dredging from below water they do have the advantage of being able to dig hard material.

A4.1.17. Monitors.

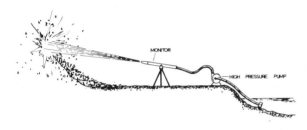

The water nozzles are constructed with a curved inlet and a swivel bearing in such a way that the reaction thrust of the nozzle is taken by the pipe-line anchor. This enables the monitor operator to swivel the jet and aim it at the base of the bank to be undercut. Its use requires a plentiful supply of water, the water jets being used to break up sediments and wash it to a sump and treatment plant.

A4.1.18. Multi-bucket excavators.

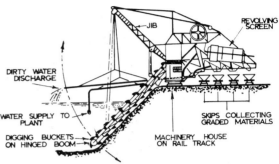

There are two important types of continuous excavator, the bucket-chain and the bucket-wheel. Mounted upon crawler undercarriage or rails the excavator has mobility. The material dug by the buckets is transferred to a conveyor belt which carries the material away. The figure shows a bucket-chain excavator although the bucket-wheel is more common. This type of excavator is not suitable for strong, consolidated rocks but has been applied to unconsolidated soils and overburden, sands, clays, chalk and, especially, brown coal (lignite).

5. Processing

5.1. Introduction

The purpose of the aggregate processing plant is to prepare the rock or mineral in a form suitable for its use as aggregate, commonly defined in terms of particle size and size distribution, particle shape and mechanical properties, e.g. compressive strength. As a result, the process plant usually contains only the unit processes of crushing and grinding (comminution) and sizing together with materials handling and transportation equipment such as conveyors and feeders.

The use of water and wet processing techniques facilitates the sizing of fine particles (classification) and the dispersal and subsequent rejection of finely sized mineral particles, e.g. clays. Consequently, the process plant may frequently also contain pumping and slurry handling equipment and unit processes of solid–liquid separation for final dewatering of the aggregate products and even waste products.

Mineral separation processes are occasionally employed to reject material of undesirable physical or chemical properties. In this respect the process of sizing is commonly used adventitiously or deliberately to separate a particular mineral fraction of the aggregate as will be discussed below.

Comminution is an energy intensive and relatively expensive process whose use must be minimized and the agglomeration of fine particles to create larger sizes is rarely if ever economically justified.

Therefore, as discussed in Chapter 3, in the case of sand and gravel deposits it is important to determine the relative proportions of the 'sand' and 'gravel' sizes. Those deposits in which the proportions most closely match the local demands of the market will obviously be more highly valued than others since significant processing costs may be reduced. In the case of hard rock sources of aggregates it is most important to consider the demands of the market with respect to particle size when selecting comminution equipment and designing the integrated flowsheet of crushing and sizing operations (Mellor 1990).

All plants should be provided with sufficient monitoring instrumentation, e.g. mass flow meters, sampling points and control measures to ensure that the products satisfy the quality requirements of the aggregate use.

In addition, modern plant design must incorporate equipment that ensures a safe and healthy environment within the process plant especially with respect to control of dust and noise. Where the plant is located near habitation this consideration may extend to the environmental impact beyond the works perimeter in terms of noise and dust pollution and even the visual impact of the buildings (Stocks & Down 1977).

In 1989, the production of aggregates within the UK was about 300 million tonnes (BACMI 1989). A few quarries produced in excess of 1 million tonnes and very few in excess of 3 million tonnes. Although plans have been prepared for 'super quarries' producing 10 million tonnes, connected to markets by rail or sea transport (see Chapter 4), it can be appreciated that the bulk of the production is obtained from a multiplicity of small units supplying local markets having capacities between 100,000 and 1 million tonnes per annum, equivalent to a few hundred tonnes per hour (Harris et al. 1988). This situation within the UK is largely brought about by the cost of transport and widespread availability of a relatively low value product such as aggregate which determines that material may only be delivered up to distances of about 50 km by road. The situation is similar in the USA, for example, although there are proportionally more plants processing in excess of 3 million tonnes (Hayes 1990; Rukavina 1987; Tepordei 1987).

Processing plants tend to fall into one of two categories: (i) fixed and (ii) mobile or temporary. Fixed plant constructed upon permanent foundations tends to be associated with relatively larger reserves providing extended life (ideally 30 years or more for hard rocks; ten years or so for sand and gravel) supplying a variety of markets in terms of aggregate type, tonnage and locations (Fig. 5.56). The relatively short life of sand and gravel deposits means that the process plant may be removed and used again on a later development. 'Modular construction' of such plant, that is prior fabrication of units of the structure and installation of appropriate equipment, greatly facilitates both removal and rapid erection. 'Mobile' plants tend to be dedicated to major construction projects, such as airport runways, motorways, dams etc, the life of the operation and volume of the reserve being determined entirely by this single market (Routledge 1962). They may also be employed within a quarry to augment temporarily the capability and the capacity of a 'fixed' plant to satisfy a short-term market or during the development stage (Figs 5.54, 5.55).

In practice, the various requirements of the aggregate market are conveniently met by sizing the material into a number of narrow particle size ranges, for example the 'nominal sizes' within the UK, and supplying these singly or suitably blended as demanded. Furthermore, it is not possible in practice to match exactly the production of various aggregate sizes with the instantaneous demand. Therefore, prominent features of most aggregate processing plants are the bins or bunkers and stockpiles necessary to provide short- and longer-term storage. These represent substantial capital investment and contribute significantly to the visual impact of the plant.

Aggregates are sold by weight and the highway authorities and police often require that loaded vehicles are weighed in order to ensure safety and prevent damage to road surfaces. These factors and the additional requirement for blending sized aggregates necessitate that processing plants are provided with accurate means of weighing materials, e.g. weigh-bridges, weigh-feeders and effective means of proportioning and mixing materials.

5.2. Comminution

5.2.1. Introduction

Natural rocks and minerals, especially those used as aggregates, tend to be strong and brittle, that is they break under applied stress without undergoing significant deformation or strain. They are often also abrasive. These factors are all important in the selection of comminution equipment (Lowrison 1974).

Natural materials have a high compressive strength but are often weak in tension. Unfortunately, outside of the laboratory, it is impossible to subject individual pieces of rock to tensile stress and it is equally impractical to stress each piece just to the point of failure on an individual basis. As a result, many comminution devices employ the simpler technique of applying compressive stress to particles on an indiscriminate basis. Many particles fail since the deformation produced creates internal tensile stresses but others absorb this 'strain-energy' without failure and the energy is subsequently uselessly released as heat. Consequently comminution devices tend to be inefficient in utilization of energy so that techniques and machines are constantly refined and developed to improve their performance.

Impact is an effective method of inducing tensile forces within a particle and is generally a more energy efficient process of comminution. An additional advantage is that impact tends to impart a more regular shape to the broken fragments.

Attrition and abrasion, although effective in producing very finely sized particles when required, are very inefficient processes, causing high wear and maintenance costs and are avoided in aggregate production.

Useful properties of rock when selecting comminution equipment, especially by comparison with other practice, are, for strength: unconfined compressive strength (UCS), aggregate crushing and impact values (ACV, AIV) (see Chapter 7) and even the Bond Work Index (Wi). For abrasivity, useful parameters are; aggregate abrasion value (AAV), free silica content (% SiO_2) and, maybe, the Pennsylvania Abrasion Index (Ai). For common rocks many of these values are well known and tabulated in references (Bond 1960).

Experience has shown that each comminution machine operates most effectively, as measured by capacity, maintenance and power costs, utilization of capital investment etc. within a range of values of the reduction ratio. The reduction ratio (RR) is defined as the ratio of feed size to product size (F/P) where 'size' is defined as the screen aperture that will pass 80% by weight of the material, i.e. retain 20% wt. This reduction ratio varies from 3:1 to 20:1 or even greater but for many crushing devices it is in the range of 4:1 to 8:1. Consequently, comminution proceeds as a series of stages giving rise to the nomenclature of primary, secondary and tertiary crushing for example. At each stage, sizing processes may recover marketable aggregate fractions until the final stage is attained.

Indeed, the essence of good plant design is to consider the comminution and sizing operations as an integrated process although they are discussed separately in this Chapter. In this respect, aggregate crushing differs from the comminution of most mineral ores for which the objective of crushing is to achieve maximum size reduction prior to subsequent grinding to liberate valuable minerals. In aggregate production the crushed rock is separated into size fractions to generate the finished product and the size distribution of the crusher product is of great importance, not just the degree of size reduction.

The particle size distribution of the crusher product will determine the yield of saleable products that can be obtained by sizing alone without recrushing. It also determines the required area of the screens (see §5.3.3). The production of the various sizes should obviously match market demands as closely as possible in order to maximize the economic return although a degree of flexibility in the process plant may also be essential. This factor is important during the selection of the type of crusher and the number of size reduction stages. In the extreme, a simple, inexpensive plant comprising only a single, high reduction stage of crushing may appear attractive from an investment point of view but would permit limited control of the relative proportions of various sizes, see Fig. 5.1. In this respect, the crusher might, for example, produce excessive quantities of aggregates in certain size ranges, especially dust and fine aggregate fractions, and insufficient coarse aggregates. The installation of a larger number of size reduction stages, each of lower reduction radio, combined with screening and recycling of material will provide the control to increase the proportion of material arising within the most desirable size range but at greater cost (see Fig. 5.1).

The deliberate manufacture of fine 'sand-sized' aggregate from hard rock by comminution is seldom justified in the United Kingdom, where large reserves of natural sand are reasonably well distributed geographically, but is practised elsewhere in the world in situations where natural sands are not readily available e.g. Scandinavia and certain states of the USA (Georgia, Missouri, Kentucky, The Carolinas and Virginias). In certain areas, e.g. southwest England, where deposits of natural sand are scarce, the requirement of the local market is met by import from other regions or dredging. Nevertheless, finely sized aggregate derived from hard rock will arise naturally by virtue of the blasting and comminution processes and valuable local markets are likely to exist even for 'dust' fractions e.g. filler for asphalt, agricultural limestone.

§7.5.1). In practice at the final stage of comminution, a crusher may be operated at a low reduction ratio, 2 or even less, to ensure a large proportion of well shaped product.

Crushing may be defined as a comminution process in which the crushing members of the machine, e.g. jaws, may approach closely but will not touch even if no rock is present, i.e. the motion of the members is limited and precisely controlled. Within grinding machines the grinding members are free and do come into contact in the absence of feed rock. The members are commonly referred to as 'media' if in the form of steel rods or balls but may also take the form of steel tyred rollers. The grinding action is most applicable to the production of finely sized particles (< 5 mm).

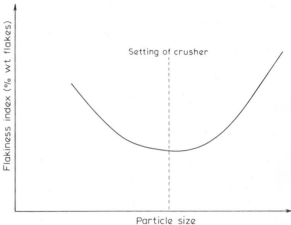

FIG. 5.2. Typical variation of shape with particle size in a crusher product.

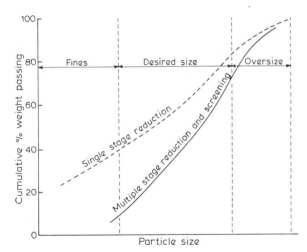

FIG. 5.1. Schematic comparison of particle size distributions produced by single and multiple stage crushing.

Additionally, it should be noted that particle shape of an aggregate can be as important as size for certain purposes, e.g. roadstone and concrete (see §8.6, Table 11.11). It has been observed that the shape of the aggregate particle is determined by a number of factors including rock type, crusher type and reduction ratio. Shape varies depending upon the size of the individual particle relative to both the setting (see §5.2.3) of the crusher and the mean size of the crusher product (Markwick 1936). In general, it has been observed that the particles similar in size to the setting of a cone or jaw crusher exhibit a more regular shape (see Fig. 5.2). Those particles relatively larger and smaller than the setting have a tendency to be more flaky in shape (see

5.2.2. Primary crusher selection

These machines represent the first stage of comminution and are usually of the jaw, gyratory or fixed blow-bar impactor type (McQuiston & Shoemaker 1978). Traditionally, these crushers are fed directly with quarried rock by rear dump trucks (Fig. 5.3) or indirectly by a grizzly type feeder (see §5.3.3.6). The maximum lump size varies but may be as great as 1 or 2 metres.

More recently the high cost of dump-truck haulage has been an incentive to develop in-pit crushing systems. In this system the primary crusher (fixed or mounted in a fully mobile or semi-mobile frame) is located within the quarry (see Figs 4.17 and 4.23). The crusher may then be fed directly by crawler excavators or wheeled front-end loaders obviating the need for dump-trucks (Barlow 1984; Rukavina 1985; Anon (1) 1989, Anon (2) 1988). Systems using dump trucks over short-haul distances and fixed crushers within the pit are also employed (Fig.

5.4). The crushed material is then transported from the quarry to the processing plant by belt conveyor (Robertson 1986; Anon (11) 1988) (see §4.7.2).

FIG. 5.3. Dump truck discharging into a primary gyratory crusher (courtesy Nordberg (UK) Ltd).

FIG. 5.4. Fixed in-pit primary crusher building with conveyors (courtesy ECC Quarries Ltd).

Jaw and gyratory crushers are both capable of handling hard, abrasive rocks and selection is based upon throughput and maximum lump size. Although developments are continuously taking place, impactors are restricted to less abrasive rocks e.g. limestone, but lump sizes in excess of 1 m and capacities up to 1500 tph are attainable.

The selection of the primary crusher is not an isolated decision but must consider the blast design, excavator bucket size and dump truck selection. Larger throughputs usually dictate the handling of larger lump sizes but this is only effective if each piece of equipment is fully utilized. A compromise or optimum design of operations must be achieved comparing costs of drilling and blasting to reduce lump size with capital and operating costs of handling and processing larger lumps. For a given capital investment, the jaw crusher will be able to accept the largest lump size and for throughputs less than 1000 tph a choice exists between the three types. For capacities significantly above 1000 tph it is likely that the gyratory crusher will be selected upon this criterion alone.

5.2.3. Jaw crushers

The jaw crusher compresses the rock between a fixed jaw and a moving jaw to create breakage (Fig. 5.5). The return motion of the moving or 'swinging' jaw permits feed to enter the crushing cavity and sufficiently broken material to discharge by gravity. The maximum dimensions of the feed opening, universally employed to designate the crusher, are termed the 'gape' and the product size is largely determined by the width of the discharge aperture when the moving jaw has retreated fully—the 'open side setting'. The reduction ratio possible is usually in the range 4 : 1 to 6 : 1. The moving jaw may be actuated by one of two principal mechanisms—'single toggle' and 'double toggle' (Fig. 5.6). In the 'double toggle' machine the rotation of an eccentric shaft causes a vertical reciprocating motion of a component called a pitman that is translated by two toggles into swinging action of the moving jaw which is pivoted at its upper edge. The resultant action creates very powerful compressive forces by leverage in the upper zone of the crushing chamber and the almost total absence of abrasive motion (relative vertical motion between jaw plates). Therefore, this machine is most applicable to the

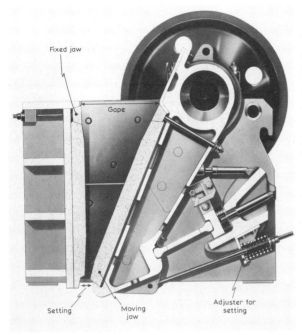

Fixed jaw

Gape

Setting

Moving jaw

Adjuster for setting

FIG. 5.5. Section of a single toggle jaw crusher (courtesy Pegson Ltd).

crushing of very strong, abrasive rocks but is more complex, heavy and expensive than a single toggle crusher. In the single toggle machine the moving jaw is actuated by an eccentric shaft which also acts as the pivot along the upper edge of the jaw. The resultant action includes relative vertical motion between the jaw plates which produces the advantage of greater throughput for less abrasive rocks.

In both cases the jaws are protected by replaceable alloy (manganese steel) liner plates which may be smooth or corrugated to reduce the production of slab shaped particles.

The jaw crusher is suitable for all hard rocks generally used for aggregate.

5.2.4. Gyratory crushers

The gyratory crusher comprises a lined inverted conical crushing chamber within which 'gyrates' an upright conical crushing member, the shaft and cone, protected by a liner called the 'mantle'. The shaft does not rotate but 'gyrates' or 'precesses' compressing material as it moves towards the wall of the chamber and at the same time releasing material at the diametrically opposite point so that crushed rock can descend through the chamber towards the discharge (Fig. 5.7). The frequency of this action is between 100 and 200 cycles per minute and the movement or throw between 20 and 50 mm. The crushers are usually designated by the width of the feed opening and the diameter of the head. The 'gyratory' action can be created in several ways including: (i) a vertical shaft running in upper and lower eccentric bushings supported by thrust bearings or hydraulic means and (ii) the most common, a shaft located by an upper fixed bearing within the spider and supported hydraulically, actuated by an eccentric bushing at the lower point.

The principal advantage of the gyratory crusher is the much greater unit capacity for any given 'gape' or maximum lump size assuming that this capacity can be fully utilized to justify the substantially greater capital cost. The reduction ratio is 4 : 1 to 6 : 1 and the machine is suitable for all hard, abrasive rocks but not for soft, porous material that may compact in the chamber.

Gyratory crushers are sometimes employed at the secondary stage, where cone crushers might be more usual, owing to their ability to accept larger lump sizes.

5.2.5. Impactors

Impactors comprise a lined chamber within which revolves a rotor on a horizontal axis. The rotor is fitted either with swing hammers located by pins or blow-bars of alloy steel located by mechanical or hydraulic clamps (Figs 5.8 & 5.9). The hammers or blow bars impart impact to the rock resulting in comminution that is

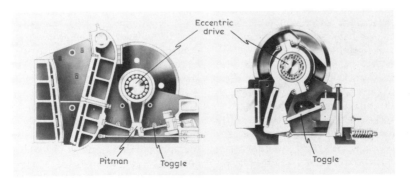

Eccentric drive

Pitman   Toggle

Toggle

FIG. 5.6. Single and double-toggle mechanisms for jaw crushers (courtesy W. H. Baxter Ltd).

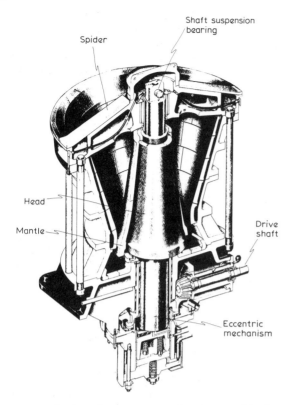

FIG. 5.7. Section of a gyratory crusher (courtesy Nordberg (UK) Ltd).

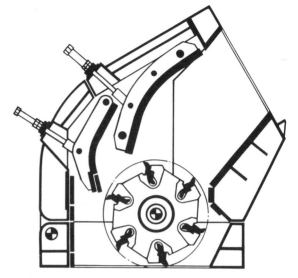

FIG. 5.8. Fixed blow-bar primary impactor (courtesy Holmes-Hazemag).

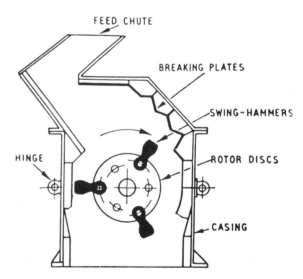

FIG. 5.9. Swing hammer mill (impactor).

energy efficient and a typically cubical product shape. Impact with the rotor, the chamber liners (breaker plates) and interparticulate collision all contribute to comminution. Reduction ratios of 20 : 1 are achievable in a single stage and even 40 : 1 for double rotor impactors. The impactor thus offers several potential advantages of high reduction ratio, low capital and operating cost, ease of installation and low head room requirement and good product shape. Product size can be varied within limits by changing rotor speed and the clearances between rotor and liners.

The major limitation to the application of impactors is abrasive wear. Abrasive wear necessitates the costly replacement of hammers or blow-bars but, more importantly, results in loss of operating time, and low availability. Therefore, impactors tend to be restricted to crushing of non-abrasive rocks e.g. non-siliceous limestones and dolomites and to non-aggregate minerals e.g. coal, gypsum, salt. It has been stated that impactors are not suitable for rocks containing more than 5% free silica. Swing-hammer type impactors are generally applied to the production of the finer sizes of aggregate but impact becomes ineffective at a particle size less than about 3 mm.

The recent developments have mainly concerned the fixed blow-bar type which is now available as a primary crusher that can reduce very large lumps by a combination of impact and 'nibbling' actions. The use of a few large blow-bars forged from special alloys in place of many hammers and the design of the crushing chamber to permit very rapid access for maintenance, e.g. hydraulically actuated mechanisms for opening the casing and clamping wearing items, has overcome to some extent the principal disadvantage of impactors. They are now applied to the crushing of mineral ores, slags and siliceous limestones. Abrasive gritstones, quartzites and even basalt may also be crushed at the final stage by impactors when the value of the cubical shape produced justifies the cost, e.g. surface chippings for roads or decoration.

In most cases the impactor operates in open circuit with no control upon product size other than clearances between rotor and liners, speed of rotation and feed rate. Caged hammer mills are available which include a discharge grating but the problems of wear and blockage can be severe and their use is usually restricted to soft minerals such as clays, coal, etc.

5.2.6. Vertical shaft impactors

These machines represent a recent development to exploit the advantage of cubical product shape whilst overcoming the problem of wear when crushing abrasive rocks (Hill 1985). Particularly popular applications are crushing of oversize flint gravel in situations where an increased yield of sand is desired, 'shaping' of crushed gritstone in the final stage of comminution to produce roadstone surface chippings and the 'manufacture' of sand from hard rock (Robertson 1986).

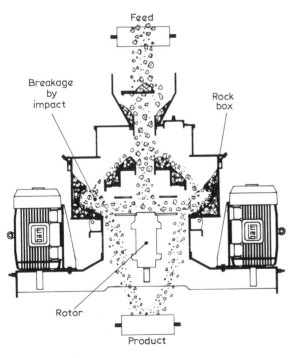

FIG. 5.10. Vertical shaft impactor (courtesy Tidco Ltd).

The machine comprises a horizontal table or rotor that revolves rapidly about the vertical axis of the drive shaft. Crushed rock fed into the centre of the rotor is ejected at high speed by 'centripetal forces' and breaks by impact upon the hardened alloy anvils surrounding the rotor and by inter-particulate collision (Fig. 5.10). The rotor is lined with extremely hard materials such as carbides where appropriate. Wear of the casing may be reduced by the addition of a low ledge or shelf forming a 'rock-box' within which broken rock accumulates thereby obscuring and protecting the internal surface of the casing. Rock particles thus impact upon similar material and not upon the liner plates. These two designs are referred to as 'stone on metal' and 'stone on stone' respectively. The former can produce a greater reduction ratio.

5.2.7. Cone crushers

Although the jaw crusher and gyratory crusher may be adapted to the duty of secondary and tertiary crushing, the greater capacity of the cone crusher results in its almost universal application to crushing of strong, abrasive rocks.

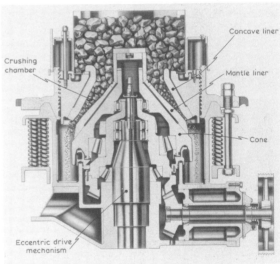

FIG. 5.11. Gyratory CONE crusher (courtesy Pegson Ltd).

Cone crushers are a development of the gyratory crusher patented by Symons in 1930. The crusher comprises a 'gyrating' upright conical crushing member, the head lined with mantle, within a conical crushing chamber lined with wearing metal usually described as 'concaves' (Fig. 5.11). The crushers are usually designated by the diameter, in feet or millimetres, of the head. The significant difference from the gyratory crusher is that the crushing chamber is now also in the form of an upright, truncated cone and the 'gyrating' cone, having an angle of about 45° is supported entirely from beneath by the eccentric bush assembly. A further significant difference is that the eccentric shaft in modern machines rotates very much more rapidly (> 200 rpm) than that of the gyratory crusher. As a result, the crushing action may be considered to fall between compression and impact, resulting in improved energy utilization and product shape. One particular criticism of the cone crusher has been the tendency to produce particles of a flaky shape owing to the geometry of the crushing chamber. This can be counteracted by the use of low reduction ratios and ensuring that the crushing chamber is always full of material, a condition known as 'choke feed'.

The cone crusher is available in several forms to most suit the requirements of the secondary and tertiary stages of comminution (Fig. 5.12). The secondary cone (standard cone) crusher has a steeply inclined, sometimes stepped, crushing chamber formed by the concave and a flatter less steeply inclined conical crushing member. The reduction ratio achieved varies from 4 : 1 to 8 : 1. The tertiary, short-head-cone, crusher has both crushing chamber and cone steeply inclined to promote the gravitational flow of more finely sized material. The reduction ratio varies from 4 : 1 to 6 : 1. A great deal of experience and expert knowledge is now available to optimize the detailed design of the crushing chamber (Zoerb 1953), eccentric throw, etc., in terms of feed size distribution, desired product, power consumption and liner life.

FIG. 5.12. Comparison of secondary, standard (left) and tertiary, short-head (right), cone crushers (courtesy Nordberg (UK) Ltd).

The maximum particle size of the product is largely controlled by the distance between the mantle and concave at the open side of the crusher. Since this clearance cannot be easily measured the closed side setting is usually determined by crushing a piece of malleable lead. As a 'rule-of thumb', the maximum product size is approximately twice the closed side setting. This may be varied within limits by either raising the cone or lowering the concave assembly. Both methods are employed as in (a) the use of hydraulic support of the eccentric shaft and (b) machine threads or hydraulic support of the crushing chamber assembly. Both provide a method for compensating for wear of the liners and providing

overload release in the event that uncrushable material, e.g. tramp metal is contained in the feed. Moreover, hydraulic support provides a means of automatic control upon product size and/or maximum power input without fear of overloading the crusher. This can result in significant improvements in plant productivity (Flavel 1978).

It is common practice to operate secondary and tertiary crushers and grinding mills in closed circuit with a sizing device such as a screen or a classifier as appropriate. The product from the comminution device passes to the sizing unit where oversize particles are removed and then recirculated to the comminution device. With such a circuit it is possible to control the top size strictly, to prevent excessive generation of undesirable fines and to save upon power consumption.

5.2.8. Gyratory disc crushers

These machines are a further development of the cone crusher for the application of crushing strong abrasive rocks to particle sizes of less than 2 or 3 mm to fall within the 'sand' specifications.

The cone crusher is modified such that the crushing chamber and head have a very low angle of inclination (25°) and the crushing faces are almost parallel (Fig. 5.13). Rock passes through the machine slowly as a deep bed of particles transported by the movement of the cone surface. The gyratory action of the head causes this bed rather than individual particles to be repeatedly compressed between the mantle and concave and the production of fine particles by interparticulate breakage. Since the setting no longer directly controls the maximum size of particle in the product, the crusher is always operated in closed circuit with a screen.

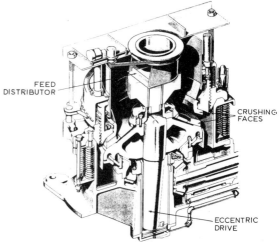

FIG. 5.13. Gyratory disc crusher (courtesy Nordberg (UK) Ltd).

5.2.9. Rolls crushers

A simple rolls crusher comprises two contra-rotating smooth crushing rolls. The shaft of one roll is located by fixed bearings whilst the bearings for the second roll may be moved to alter the 'set' or gap between the rolls. It is usual for the sliding bearing blocks to act against compressed springs thus providing a means of overload release in the event that the feed contains uncrushable material (Fig. 5.14). The reduction ratio of crushing rolls is limited to about 3 : 1. Historically, before the development of cone crushers, their use was common but they suffer from two serious disadvantages: low capacity and wear of the roll surface when crushing abrasive rock. Wear of the roll surface may only be corrected by replacement, expensive surface grinding or metal deposition by welding and they are now largely obsolete in the UK although not uncommon elsewhere.

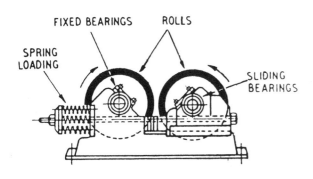

FIG. 5.14. Section of a double rolls crusher.

Nevertheless, the rolls crusher may still find application within small capacity operations, in confined spaces e.g. underground, where the simple construction and low headroom requirement are advantages or processing very soft rocks such as high purity limestones usually quarried for chemical rather than construction industry use (Anon (3) 1987).

Recently, interest has been shown in a form of rolls crusher, the rotary pick. The two rolls rotate at moderate speed and are provided with hardened alloy steel teeth, alloy caps or even carbide tipped spikes—the picks—which break the rock by a combination of compression, tension and shear (Fig. 5.15). These machines are already used in underground mining of soft rocks e.g. coal and gypsum. Similar devices are employed in continuous surface-miners and road surface cold-planers. They are now finding application in surface mining of harder rocks such as limestones where the low headroom requirement and lack of need for substantial foundations are advantages. For example, the device

may be used as an in-pit crusher or introduced at a conveyor transfer point to facilitate materials handling (Anon (3) 1987; Flynn 1988).

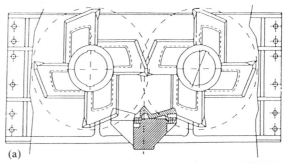

(a)

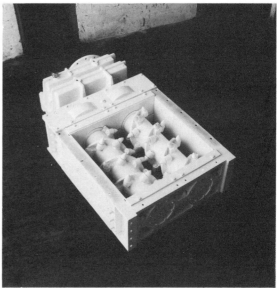

(b)

FIG. 5.15. (a) Rotary pick, 'mineral sizer'. (b) Roll sizer (courtesy MMD Ltd).

5.2.10. Grinding

The grinding device most applicable to the production of aggregate is the rod mill (Fig. 5.16). It may be employed where abrasive rock must be comminuted to sand sized particles. The reduction ratio is typically between 5 : 1 and 20 : 1 with a maximum particle size in the feed of about 20 mm.

The rod mill comprises a cylindrical shell, lined with replaceable liner plates, which rotates upon a horizontal axis. The mill contains a mass of hardened steel rods up to 100 mm in diameter as media which occupies approximately 40% of the volume. The mill is supported at each end by hollow, cylindrical bearings, the trunnions, and driven by a peripheral ring gear. The feed material enters the mill through one or both of the trunnions and is discharged through ports in the shell, either end-peripheral discharge or centre-peripheral discharge if fed through both trunnions. The mill is operated wet in the vast majority of mineral processing plants i.e. a solid to water ratio of about 2 : 1 on a weight basis. Within the aggregate industry, however, the material may be dry or moist.

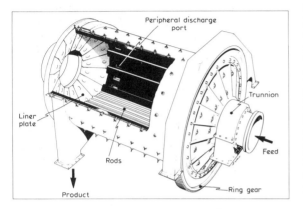

FIG. 5.16. Cutaway diagram of a rod mill (courtesy Trelleborg).

The rotation of the mill causes the rod charge to tumble and cascade producing comminution by a combination of compression and impact. The action of the rods is favourable to the production of 'fine' aggregate since the larger particles holding the rods apart are crushed preferentially and a minimum quantity of very finely sized particles is generated by abrasion and attrition. Nevertheless, the rod mill suffers serious disadvantages when compared to fine crushers; notably lower efficiency of energy utilization and the costly replacement of worn rods.

Other grinding mills have limited application to the production of aggregate from typically strong, abrasive rocks. Finely sized aggregate and dust are generated unavoidably by all forms of comminution device and can be recovered or separated from coarser aggregates by specialized screens, classifiers or cyclones and fabric filters included in dust collection systems. Pulverizers of the edge-runner mill type are extensively employed to produce powders from soft minerals for major end-uses such as agricultural limestone and dolomite, chemicals, fillers for rubber, plastics, paper and paint, fire retardant in coal mines, pulverized coal and raw meal feed to cement kilns. Although none of these uses can be categorized as aggregates, the equipment will be included within the processing plant and similar mineral powders may be incorporated in masonry cements and asphalt. The edge-runner mill comprises alloy steel-tyred rollers bearing upon a rotating horizontal table or fixed cylindrical anvil. The load upon the rollers is created either by the mass of the rollers or springs or centrifugal force (Fig. 5.17). The mill operates dry utilizing air, often preheated to dry moist rock, to transport the ground product to the air classification circuit. Finely ground rock is recovered by cyclones and bag filters whilst oversize particles are recirculated to the mill for further reduction.

5.3. Sizing

5.3.1. Introduction

In the laboratory, particle size analysis is carried out by many methods including sieving (screening) and classification. Sieving of dry material is possible at sizes as fine as 0.05 mm and classification would not be applied to sizes greater than 0.1 mm.

In industrial practice only screening and classification have significant application. Whilst screening of 'bonedry' (<0.5% moisture) material is possible at sizes as fine as 0.1 mm the process is of low capacity. The presence of moisture (typically 3–10% by weight) causes the material to become cohesive and very difficult to screen at sizes less than 6 mm (1/4 in) and impractical at 3 mm. The alternative of drying the material or employ-

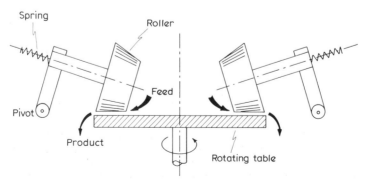

FIG. 5.17. Edge runner mill.

ing heated screens is almost certainly too costly for aggregate preparation. A simpler, less expensive method is to add water to convert the moist feed material into slurry form whereby screens or sieves may be employed for sizing as fine as 0.5 mm: 'wet screening'.

For sizing particles finer than 0.5 mm and often for particles significantly greater in size, the process of classification is employed.

5.3.2. Objectives of sizing

(i) Preparation of finished aggregates in which efficiency and accuracy of sizing are of paramount importance.

(ii) Adjunct to comminution: in which accuracy and efficiency may be of lesser importance than reliability and availability of the process. For example, 'scalping' may be employed to separate fine material to by-pass a stage of comminution set to produce a product of coarser particle size. Screens may be used to protect crushers or even finer screen meshes from damage caused by oversize particles.

5.3.3. Screening

5.3.3.1. Principles. Screening employs apertures, usually square but also round and rectangular, to separate particles into 'oversize' (retained) and 'undersize' (passing) fractions (Partridge 1977; Freebury 1978; Brown 1963). Particles are repeatedly presented to these apertures during the screening process. The separation is strongly dependent upon particle size but is also a function of particle shape and the duration of the screening process. Unlike classification, it is essentially independent of particle density. With respect to shape, only a spherical particle can be defined by a single dimension, d, clearly of little practical import. An irregular particle may be considered to have three orthogonal axes and dimensions measured along these axes, in order of decreasing magnitude, of a, b and c (Fig. 5.18). If the particle is repeatedly presented to the apertures, a screen will define particle size in terms of the two lesser dimensions b and c only. The greatest dimension will not determine the screen 'size'.

With respect to duration of the screening process, the probability of a particle passing through an aperture must be considered. For any aperture shape of area 'A' the probability of the particle described above passing at each presentation can be simply expressed as $(A - bc)/A$. Thus, it can be seen that particles very much smaller than the aperture size have a very high probability, nearly unity, of passing rapidly through the screen. For particles termed 'nearsize', of dimensions greater than 75% of that of the aperture, the probability decreases

significantly. Thus, the duration of the screening process must be extended to ensure that these undersize particles are presented a sufficient number of times to be correctly sized. In laboratory sieving, which is a batch process, the material is retained on the sieve until virtually all undersize has been removed as verified by measurement (see §7.5.1). For continuous screening on an industrial scale this would require screens of impractical length. Thus, in practice, an 'efficiency' of removal of true undersize particles present in the feed of 95% is commonly accepted. The definition of efficiency has been reviewed by Jowett (1963) but a simple measure is the ratio of the mass of undersize recovered to the fine product divided by the mass of undersize contained in the feed (assuming that the screen is undamaged!).

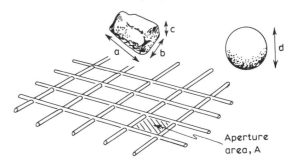

FIG. 5.18. Relationship between particle shape and screen aperture.

Further problems experienced with screening are 'pegging' and 'blinding' (Fig. 5.19). Pegs are particles a little larger than the aperture size (1.0–1.5 × the aperture size) that become lodged in the aperture and reduce the available screening area. 'Blinding' usually results from the moisture in the feed causing fine particles to agglomerate and to adhere to the screen surface ultimately occluding the apertures. Both these problems may be reduced by mechanical vibration of the screen. Selection of flexible and non-wettable screening materials, e.g. rubber or polyurethane reinforced with textile or steel fibre may also be effective.

FIG. 5.19. Problems of screening, pegging and blinding.

Screen capacity is determined by the total screen area, the aperture size and the density of the material. For common materials, values of capacity in terms of tonnes per hour per square metre have been established empirically (Anon (4)). Most of these values are related to the use of woven or welded steel wire mesh, the screen surface, 'deck' or 'mat' comprising square apertures. Woven wire is relatively inexpensive and offers the advantage of greatest 'percentage open area' (ratio of total screen area to area of apertures) and, therefore, capacity per unit area. Disadvantages are poor resistance to wear and corrosion and high noise levels.

Screen mats moulded from rubber and polymers, especially polyurethane, are now common since they are highly resistant to wear and corrosion, reduce the tendency towards blinding and significantly reduce noise levels (Fig. 5.20). The advantage of longer service life and greater availability of the screens compensates for their substantially greater initial cost and the lower value of 'percentage open area' which they exhibit. In this respect, it is necessary to employ a screen of greater total area and cost in any given application to compensate for this loss of open area (Riddell 1985; Goldkuhl 1987). It is also necessary to adjust the aperture size since the greater thickness of the mat reduces the probability of any given size of particle passing through the screen. The aperture may be increased by between 25 and 50% compared to that of a woven wire screen.

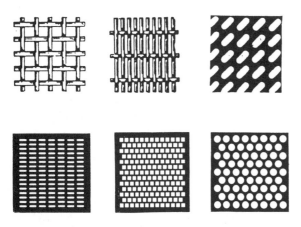

FIG. 5.20. Screening surfaces; upper row; woven wire (square), woven wire (slots), punched plate (slots), lower row; cast polymer, punched rubber mat, punched plate or mat.

Other screening surfaces that may be encountered (Fig. 5.20) are punched steel plate, elongated slots, 'rod decks' and 'piano-wire' screens. Punched plate is very robust but of low open area. It may be applied to horizontal screening of larger sizes and to trommel screens. Elongated slots may be formed of woven wire, punched plate or polymer. The rectangular shape of the aperture reduces the tendency for pegging and blinding and increases the open area. Rod decks employ loosely located, transverse steel rods to create a screening surface. Vibration of the screen causes relative motion of the rods and rotation of the rods both of which oppose

pegging and blinding (Jones 1972). 'Piano-wire' or 'harp' screens employ fine, high tensile carbon steel wires under tension to form elongated 'slot' apertures. The objective is to utilize the vibration of the wires to overcome problems of blinding when screening finely sized moist materials.

Clearly the use of the screen mats described above incurs some loss of precision but this must be off-set against the greater reliability and utilization (availability) of the screens.

5.3.3.2. Inclined vibrating screens. These are the most common type of screen employed in the aggregate industry. The combination of inclined surface (15° to 20°) and vibration produces a continuous screening process during which the fines are rapidly segregated and pass through the screen 'mat' near the feed point (Anon (4)). Retained 'oversize' and 'nearsize' particles are transported across the deck and repeatedly presented to the screen apertures to promote high efficiency of undersize removal (Figs 5.21 & 5.22). The devices are relatively simple, comprising a vibrating frame that may be fitted with a variety of screening surfaces, of modest cost and capable of providing high unit capacity. However, to benefit from these advantages it is most important that the screen is fed correctly, in particular that the entire width of the screen is used and that the feed rate is constant. A disadvantage is that the screen frame itself and the supporting structure must be designed to withstand the vibrational loads but enormous experience is now available. The use of an inclined screen obviously results in a greater headroom requirement and taller structures than horizontal screening equipment. All vibrating screens, by their nature, have a tendency to create noise and dust which may be mitigated by encapsulation and choice of screening surface.

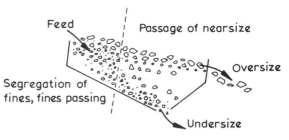

FIG. 5.21. Mechanism of screening by a vibrating screen.

The vibration of the screen can be generated by several means, e.g. eccentric rotation of a shaft, rotation of unbalanced weights or electromagnetic devices. In general, lower frequencies and greater amplitudes are used for the screening of coarser particles. Any element of the screen surface will describe an orbital motion in a plane at right angles to the screen surface (Fig. 5.23).

(a)

(b)

FIG. 5.22. (a) Multiple deck screen (courtesy Parker Plant Ltd). (b) Operating screen (courtesy Nordberg).

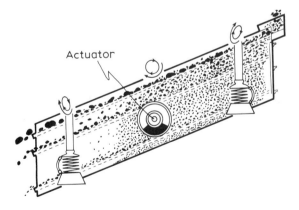

FIG. 5.23. Effect of screen motion upon the sizing process.

The form of the vibration may be modified to suit the particular screening application. At its simplest, the motion is circular. However, it is also possible to design the motion to be elliptical or linear with an axis at an inclination to the screening surface which either favours transport of material (throw) or opposes transport. A positive 'throw' increases oversize transport rate and opposes 'pegging' but may impair screening efficiency by reducing the retention time of nearsize material on the deck. Alternatively, a reverse throw will reduce capacity but improve efficiency by retaining nearsize nad oversize on the deck. For these reasons a great variety of vibrating screens are available, many of which are fitted with means of adjusting frequency, amplitude and direction of the motion. The position of the activator relative to the screen surface is also a variable and screens are available for which the direction of the motion changes as material progresses along the deck. The most benefit is usually obtained by employing a positive throw at the feed end, changing to reverse throw at the discharge end.

It also follows from the above discussion that material may be retained on the deck by reducing the angle of inclination of the screen. This will result in better utilization of the available screening area if applied only to the sizing of the nearsize fraction. Multiple-slope screens, sometimes referred to as 'banana-screens', are now constructed to take advantage of this fact in which the deck is formed of several elements of progressively reducing inclination, see Fig. 5.24.

FIG. 5.24. Banana screen (courtesy of Nordberg).

A further convenience of the vibrating screen is that the frame may be fitted with single, double, triple or even four decks to facilitate the simultaneous production of several particle size ranges. Clearly the screen area will be determined by the capacity of the deck having the smallest aperture size and the decks will usually be arranged in order of decreasing aperture size to minimize wear of the more fragile surfaces. Individual decks may be divided, that is comprise mats of two differing apertures or blank to act as a chute to transfer material within the frame.

The presence of moisture in the feed material to a vibrating screen is especially detrimental to screen performance in that it induces blinding and retards segregation of the fines. Since drying of the feed is usually too costly, a simple remedy is to destroy the cohesion of the particles by further addition of water; a process referred to as 'wet screening'. The water is added through spray bars located above the deck. This practice is most effective when screening in the range 1 to 10 mm and the screen underflow proceeds directly to classifiers.

FIG. 5.25. Horizontal vibrating (resonance) screen (courtesy Nordberg (UK) Ltd).

5.3.3.3. Horizontal vibrating screens. The principal advantage of the horizontal screen (Fig. 5.25) is the saving of headroom and reduced height of required structures. However, since the transport of material must be achieved entirely by vibration the mechanisms and screen frames must be much more massive, robust and expensive. The linear vibrational motion inclined at about 45° is produced by crank-driven connecting rods or contra-rotating eccentric shafts. Since a high level of sliding abrasive wear is to be expected, many horizontal screens are fitted with polymer or punched plate mats. The 'resonance' screen is a design of horizontal screen which exploits the natural frequency of a sprung mass, the screen, to reduce the power input to the screen. Construction is expensive but very long screen frames may be employed.

5.3.3.4. Arrangement of vibrating screens. The most convenient arrangement of screens, screening by selec-

tion, is a cascade series above the storage bins with removal of the finest fraction first (Fig. 5.26). Undersize fractions may then drop directly into bins but the greatest wear is suffered by the most delicate, finest mesh. A vertical array of meshes removing the coarsest fraction first, screening by rejection, can be achieved simply in a multiple deck screen or cascade of screens but provision must now be made for transport of oversize or undersize fractions respectively. A common compromise is to employ a splitter screen to divide the total feed into coarser and finer fractions, often at about 20 to 28 mm in the UK, followed by screening by selection.

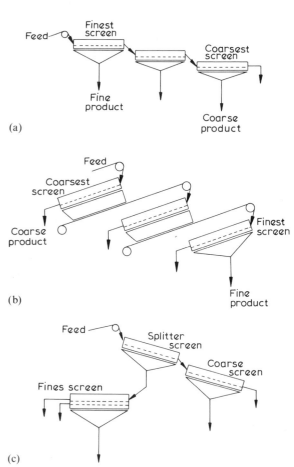

FIG. 5.26. Arrangements of inclined vibrating screens: (a) sizing by selection; (b) sizing by rejection; (c) use of splitter screen.

5.3.3.5. Trommel screens. A trommel screen comprises a cylinder formed from screening media that rotates upon an axis slightly inclined to that of the horizontal (Fig. 5.27). The feed material enters the trommel at the upper elevation and is transported by the rotation of the cylinder until 'oversize' discharges at the lower end.

Undersize is discharged through the walls of the cylinder. The advantages of trommels are; lack of vibration and simple, low-cost structure; ease of multiple sizing by a single unit; rotation promotes dis-aggregation of material and the trommel may fulfil the role of a washer also. Disadvantages are the relatively low capacity and difficulty of maintenance of the screening surface. In most modern installations they have been replaced by the combination of a rotary washing barrel (scrubber) and inclined vibrating screens. However, they remain popular for low-capacity, mobile units.

(a)

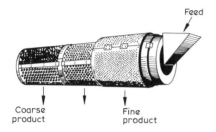

FIG. 5.27. Trommel screen.

5.3.3.6. Grizzly screens. The name grizzly screen is often given to a screen surface for separating particles at a very coarse size e.g. >25 mm and often 200 to 250 mm. As a consequence, the screen surface must be extremely robust and often comprises a series of parallel or slightly divergent alloy steel bars or rails (Fig. 5.28). Indeed, simple fixed or static grizzles may be constructed from rail section or I-section girders. If fixed, the grizzly screen surface must be steeply inclined (40–60°) to promote material flow. It may also be incorporated in a vibrating frame at a lesser inclination to act as both a sizing device and a regulated feeder device. 'Live' grizzly screens are also constructed using a series of rotating cylindrical or elliptical rolls and travelling link assemblies (Fig. 5.28(b)). These devices are less prone to blockage, provide a very positive control upon feed rate to the crusher and can be mounted horizontally to save headroom. The aperture of the grizzly may also be varied if desired. Common applications are described below.

(1) To prevent occasional oversize particles from entering a primary crusher or a materials transport system such as a field conveyor. The oversize may be broken separately by drop-ball machine, hydraulic hammer etc or simply rejected to waste (see Chapter 4).

(2) To remove undersize material from the feed to primary crusher either to by-pass this stage of comminution or to form a distinct quarry product often known as 'scalpings'. This product may be sold or processed separately (see §5.4.2).

(b)

FIG. 5.28. (a) Vibrating bar grizzly screen (courtesy Nordberg). (b) Elliptical roll grizzly screen.

5.3.3.7. Miscellaneous screening devices. The problems common to sizing by screening, pegging and blinding, have been discussed above and, as a result, ingenious techniques are continuously being developed to overcome these problems, some with more successful application than others.

The introduction of polymer and rubber screen mats has been mentioned. Screen mats fabricated from woven and welded stainless steels which resist corrosion may also reduce blinding. Stainless steels have a greater electrical resistance than carbon steels and can be heated by passage of electrical current as a means to reduce blinding. Direct mechanical impact upon the screen mat to dislodge 'pegs' and adherent particles can be provided by 'balls' or by the deliberate inclusion of a few large oversize particles with the feed to any given deck, 'oversize-scouring'. A 'ball-deck' screen comprises the upper sizing mesh and a lower ball-retaining mesh having relatively large apertures. Trapped between the meshes are the elastomer balls which produce the impact upon the underside of the sizing mat.

Other techniques compromise accuracy and efficiency in order to ensure availability. Foremost amongst these are the slot aperture mats, rod decks, piano-wire meshes and the 'probability screens' devised by Mogensen and the N.C.B.

The Mogensen sizer (Fig. 5.29) employs a vertical succession of short decks of progressively increasing inclination contained in a single, compact, lightweight frame to achieve a single size separation. The high angle of inclination of the lower finer decks in particular has the effect that the size cut-point is smaller than the mesh aperture, maybe half the true aperture size. Thus, a difficult size separation at 3 mm, say, may be achieved with a steeply inclined deck having 6 mm apertures with much reduced tendency for blinding. The design of the sizer also employs the principles of probability previously discussed in that each short screen deck is of a length that only passes particles having a size equal to about 70% of the aperture. By suitable selection of the vertical sequence of meshes it can be arranged that no lower deck receives particles in the feed that may act as 'pegs' (Mogensen 1965). Clearly the use of short decks sacrifices some efficiency of undersize removal.

FIG. 5.29. Mogensen probability screen (sizer) (courtesy Mogensen Sizers Ltd).

The N.C.B. (British Coal) 'Ropro' screen employs a radial assembly of stainless steel spokes rotating upon a vertical axis at speeds between 50 and 100 rpm to achieve a size separation. Material is controlled to fall vertically through the spokes as an annular curtain. Smaller particles have a greater chance of passing through the spokes without collision which rejects the larger particles to the oversize stream (Schneiderman 1980; Shaw 1983; O'Brian 1987).

5.3.4. Classification

5.3.4.1. Principles of classification. When a mineral particle suspended in a fluid such as water is acted upon by an external force such as gravity the particle begins to accelerate in the direction of the applied force. As soon as relative motion is established between the particle and the fluid the motion is opposed by a fluid 'drag force'. Rapidly, equilibrium is attained between the two forces and the particle moves with a constant 'terminal velocity'. The magnitude of this terminal velocity is strongly dependent upon the size of the particle but is also determined by particle shape and density and by the viscosity and density of the fluid plus the nature of the flow conditions (Smith & Gochin 1984). However, the discussion can be greatly simplified when considering the classification of aggregate minerals particles of similar shape and density (2600–2800 kg/m^3) by use of water (density 1000 kg/m^3; viscosity approx. 1×10^{-3} Pa s). When acted upon by gravitational forces 'laminar flow' conditions exist and it was shown by Stokes that for particles of size less than about 0.06 mm the terminal velocity is proportional to (size)^2. For larger particles the flow conditions approach the 'turbulent state' under which velocity is directly proportional to size. In either case, separation of particles on the basis of 'terminal velocity' in water offers a sensitive method of sizing.

When particles of more than one density are present those of the same size and shape but higher density than that of the majority attain a greater terminal velocity and behave as 'larger' particles. This will lead to a concentration of denser minerals into the coarser fraction produced by a classifier. Particles of the same size but having a lower density or flaky shape behave as 'finer' particles in that their terminal velocity is lower. This behaviour is useful in that it promotes the removal of undesirable and flaky clay, talc and micaceous mineral particles plus particles of lower density, e.g. porous stone and lignite together with the waste silt fraction.

5.3.4.2. Gravitational hydraulic classifiers. In principle all these devices employ a vertically rising current of water to classify particles in a gravitational force field (Fig. 5.30). The vertical current is established by the incoming feed comprising a slurry of particles causing the overflow of a vessel in the form of a tank or trough or by the injection of water into the base of such a vessel. The size cut-point of the classifier is controlled empirically by adjustment of the feed rate, water injection rate or height of an overflow weir as appropriate. An additional important control which has a large effect on the cut-point is the solid : water ratio in the feed which determines the apparent viscosity of the fluid. Unless this parameter is being deliberately varied to control the cut-point it is important that the ratio is kept constant.

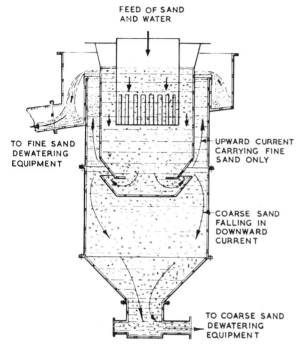

FIG. 5.30. Simple hydraulic classifier (courtesy of Linatex Ltd).

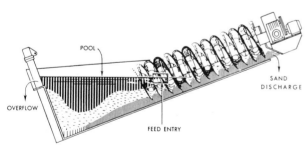

FIG. 5.31. Spiral rake classifier (courtesy of Wemco Ltd).

Many patented types of classifier are available which differ only in the manner of the removal of oversize particles. 'Undersize' particles, with a terminal velocity less than the rise rate of the fluid, are transported with the overflow—a process termed elutriation. 'Oversize' particles settle against the rise rate of fluid to form a sediment often, owing to its consistency, referred to as 'sand'. The sediment is continuously removed from the classifier by one of the following methods: (1) bucket elevators; (2) drag links; (3) helical (spiral) rakes (Fig.

5.31); (4) intermittent discharge via spigot valves. Classifiers equipped with the mechanical methods of sediment removal offer the further advantage of drainage of the 'sand' to produce a readily handleable and saleable product directly. To obtain the sharpest or most efficient size separation a quantity of material is allowed to accumulate in the body of the classifier to form a 'teeter column' (Fig. 5.32). The terminal velocity of these particles is very close to that of the fluid rise rate and they tend to circulate or teeter. Incoming particles are very efficiently sorted by this teeter column which provides an extended retention time and a scouring action useful to eliminate slimes (Raspass 1980).

A limitation of the gravitational classifier is the magnitude of the gravitational force itself. Although the principle is valid for particle sizes less than 75 µm, the terminal velocities, and hence unit capacities, are impractically low. For finer particle sizing it is necessary to generate a greater force to replace gravity.

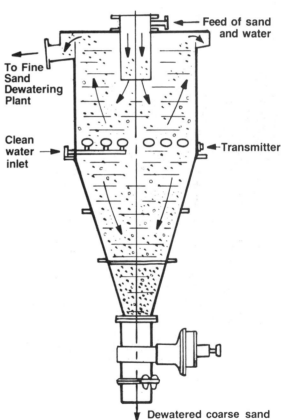

FIG. 5.32. Classifier containing a teeter zone (courtesy Linatex Ltd).

5.3.4.3. *Centrifugal (cyclonic) hydraulic classifiers.* The principal device in this category is the hydrocyclone (Svarovsky 1984). This is simple, compact and employs no moving parts other than the necessary pump. The hydrocyclone comprises a cylindrical vessel often fitted with a tapering conical extension into which the slurry of mineral particles is injected tangentially (Fig. 5.33). The 'cyclone' is provided with two outlets: a smaller outlet or spigot at the apex of the cylindrical portion. This larger axial outlet protrudes into the body of the cyclone to form the vortex finder, the purpose of which is to prevent slurry flowing directly from the tangential inlet to this aperture; the overflow. The cyclone is lined with ceramic or elastomer material to resist erosive wear or may be cast entirely from wear resistance alloy or polyurethane. Injection of slurry into the cyclone creates a vortex and generates 'centripetal' forces many times greater than gravity. Although it is common to mount the cyclone with its axis vertical it will operate at any inclination including inverted.

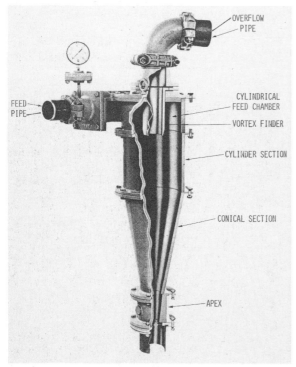

FIG. 5.33. Hydrocyclone (courtesy Krebs).

The classifying processes occurring within the cyclone result in the coarser particles being ejected from the spigot together with a small portion of the water as a 'thickened' slurry in the form of an 'umbrella spray' discharge. The smaller particles, together with the larger portion (60 to 80% by volume) of the water, pass to the vortex finder and overflow. Hydrocyclone classifiers are capable of sizing particles as fine as 0.005 mm (5 µm).

The main control upon the size cut-point, d_{50}, is the diameter of the cylindrical section with lesser control

exercised by the spigot and vortex diameters which may be varied by replacement. Solid: water rate is also critically important as previously discussed.

The flow pattern within a hydrocyclone is complex but may be simply visualized as an outer downwards spiral flow from the inlet towards the spigot and an inner spiral flow around the axis of the cyclone rising from the spigot towards the overflow. The spiral flow pattern 'vortex' is created by the tangential injection and the presence of the vortex finder. The reverse spiral flow is created by ensuring that the spigot aperture is much smaller than the inlet area, thus permitting escape of only 20–40% by volume of the flow. The classifying action takes place radially with respect to the long axis of the cyclone. Overall, within the vortex, there is an inward radial flow of water towards the axis of the cyclone and the overflow. This flow creates a fluid drag force upon the particles, the only source of an inward radial force to provide the 'centripetal' force necessary to cause the particles to rotate in a circular motion within the vortex. For larger, more massive particles, this drag force is insufficient and they are centrifuged to the walls of the cyclone. In this position they are carried to the spigot by the outer spiral flow and discharged. For smaller particles the drag force is greater than the centripetal force and they are carried into the centre of the cyclone to be discharged via the vortex finder. For one particular particle size the 'drag force' and 'centripetal force' will be equal. This is the cut-point size, d_{50}.

5.3.4.4. Air cyclones. Cyclones are available operating upon exactly the same principles but employing air as the viscous fluid medium. They are generally of much larger physical dimensions than hydrocyclones and are commonly employed as dust collectors or classifiers in dry grinding circuits. The pump is replaced by a fan usually connected to the vortex finder and operating as an exhauster.

5.4. Beneficiation

5.4.1. Introduction

Beneficiation or improving the quality of aggregates employs mineral separation processes that exploit the differences between physical or chemical properties of the mineral particles, for example density, magnetic susceptibility, colour, surface chemistry, solubility. When considering any given mineral separation process recognition must also be given to the range of particles sizes that may be treated which is often limited. For aggregate minerals that command a relatively low price it is likely that only simple physical separation processes of high capacity can be applied and then only rarely.

Processes that are only applicable to fine particles or

consume power or chemical reagents are very unlikely to be economically justified.

5.4.2. Scalping and sizing

Sizing processes, when combined with comminution or attrition scrubbing, are useful to reject undesirable clays and weaker portions of the aggregate into the finer size fractions.

A grizzly screen is commonly used for this purpose ahead of the primary crusher to remove friable materials such as clays, shales, gypsum and porous weathered stone from a quarried rock. Igneous rocks often contain weak, weathered or altered minerals in joints, veins and fissures and sedimentary rocks such as limestones are commonly interbedded with bands of shale and clays. In desert environments scalping and sizing may be able to reject deleterious, friable components of the rocks such as concretions containing gypsum and salt. It should be noted that the thin bands of shale, not uncommonly interbedded with limestones and gritstones, pose a particular problem of contamination of concrete and roadstone aggregates. The shale tends to break into particles of slabby shape that are not easily removed by the scalping screening and are, therefore, carried through to the product. Furthermore, the rock will not readily disintegrate when subjected to the washing process. The only solution may be selective extraction in the quarry.

Vibrating screens are employed for scalping at later stages in processing and, ultimately, classifiers are used to remove fine clay particles from sand products.

The 'scalpings' may not always be waste but form a discreet quarry product sold as fill material for example. It may also be useful for the restoration of the quarry or it may be separately processed. The decision as to whether scalpings should be processed by washing depends upon several factors:

(i) the quantity of scalpings generated in order to clean the coarse stone;
(ii) market for scalpings;
(iii) space and permission for disposal without sterilizing reserves;
(iv) supply of water and space for silt lagoons;
(v) market for washed scalpings, especially fine aggregates and sand since the revenue must justify the costs.

However, moist plastic clays tend to adhere strongly to larger pieces of rock and to smear over the surfaces. As a consequence, scalping may be inadequate to clean the stone to meet the specifications for, say, concrete aggregates. In such cases the rock can be washed as described in the following section.

5.4.3. Washing and scrubbing

In the case of sand and gravel deposits, the content of silt and clay may be so high as to cause difficulty in handling, screening or crushing. Consolidated 'hard rocks' such as limestones and gritstones may become intermixed with associated clay bands during the extraction operations. An effective treatment is to disintegrate this material by agitation with water to disperse the clays which may be ultimately removed by classification. Two pieces of equipment are commonly employed for this purpose: the log-washer and the washing barrel or scrubber.

The log-washer (Fig. 5.34) comprises a shallowly inclined trough containing one or two slowly rotating shafts fitted with paddles, flights or tynes. Material and water is fed into the lower part of the trough and powerfully mixed. Dispersed clay and water overflows the trough whilst coarse, cleaned aggregate is transported against the incline of the trough until discharged. The shafts were originally made from logs, hence the name, and the device is generally associated with high clay contents.

FIG. 5.34. Log washer (courtesy Wemco Ltd).

The barrel washer (Fig. 5.35) comprises a cylindrical drum rotating on an axis slightly inclined to the horizontal. The drum is lined with wear resistant material which may also form lifters of linear or spiral form. A depth of aggregate and water is retained in the drum by an annular dam at the discharge end. Rotation of the drum creates vigorous agitation of the feed material with water and transport of the aggregate through the washer. The overflow from the washer usually discharges onto a vibrating screen equipped with water sprays to effect separation of slurried clay and fine aggregate from coarser washed aggregate (Fig. 5.36). In cases where the feed contains a high proportion of sand the washer may be preceded by a wet screen also.

The underflow of these screens passes to a classifier which will separate the clays from the fine aggregate

FIG. 5.35. Sand and gravel processing plant showing wet screens, barrel washer and cyclone tower (courtesy Braham Millar).

which will then often be suitable for direct sale as fine concrete aggregate. Alternatively, a second classifier is employed to divide the sand into coarser and finer fractions often called 'sharp' and 'soft' sand respectively. As already discussed, this classifier achieves a separation between the coarser, denser and more rounded mineral particles directed to the underflow or sand product and the finer, less dense and flaky particles contained in the overflow. Thus, the underflow can be a finished coarse sand product comprising competent mineral particles without impurity. The overflow, however, may comprise a mixed suspension of fine, but competent, sand particles and larger particles of weak, porous and lower density minerals or those exhibiting very flaky shape. This is especially the case where the deposit contains lignite, shale and coal which will tend to contaminate the fine sand in this manner. Fortunately these larger undesirable particles can be relatively easily removed by screening the overflow through sieves of narrow aperture (less than 1 mm) such as sieve bends (Fig. 5.37) to produce a clean fine sand.

5.4.3.1. Marine dredged aggregates. The processing of marine dredged aggregates is no different in principle from the processing of land-won sand and gravel, indeed the materials are almost identical, see Chapter 2. However, the dredged aggregates have a low content of the clay and silt so that there is no need for a log-washer or scrubber barrel. The dredged aggregate does not contain soluble chloride salts but obviously the associated sea-water does. Simple drainage is generally inadequate to reduce the chloride content to a satisfactory level for concrete aggregates.

Therefore, marine dredged aggregates are usually washed with fresh water to reduce the content of the chloride ion to acceptable levels before processing by sizing and crushing as for land-won sand and gravel. This washing is commonly affected by screens supporting polymer screen mats, to resist corrosion, and equipped with water sprays. The chloride content of the fresh water, which is usually recirculated, is closely monitored using specific ion electrodes or conductivity probes to determine the need to replace the water in the circuit (Anon (5) 1989). Silt and clay is removed from the wash water circuit by thickeners (see §5.5.4) and blended with the products as permitted by the relevant specifications. Saline water is discharged to the sea, estuary or sewer although in one case known to the author it is planned to regenerate fresh water by reverse osmosis.

FIG. 5.36. Washer barrel discharging onto wet screens (courtesy Redland Aggregates Ltd).

FIG. 5.37. Sieve bends to remove lignite from classifed sand (courtesy Hepworth M. & C. Ltd).

5.4.3.2. Rinsing. Owing to the strict specification of low dust content for some roadstones, sized aggregates may be washed (rinsed) immediately prior to despatch using wet screens.

5.4.4. Density separation

Much aggregate is won from alluvial deposits laid down by rivers or glaciers. It is possible, although uncommon, that these deposits contain dense minerals of value e.g. ironstone, magnetite, chromite and even precious metals and diamonds—the 'placer deposits' (Rukavina 1986). More usually, the objective is to reject weak porous rock types of typically low density such as chalk and lignite from the gravel. Two density separation processes that treat the relevant range of particle sizes (200–0.5 mm) have been applied: jigging and dense medium separation.

Jigging has widespread application to iron ores and coal processing. The mineral particles are transported by water along a trough which is provided with a perforated base often fabricated from screening media (Fig. 5.38). Repeated vertical pulsations of water cause the mineral particles to stratify according to density almost independently of particle size. The upper layer of low density porous mineral or lower layer of denser valuable mineral may be removed as appropriate. This process has been applied in the UK to beneficiate sand and gravels.

Dense medium separation (Figs 5.39 & 5.40) employs a fluid of density intermediate between those of the two minerals it is required to separate. It is sometimes referred to as 'float–sink' separation. In place of a true liquid a suspension of a finely powdered dense substance, the 'media', is employed. In the popular processes a magnetic substance is used to permit its ready recovery from water used to wash the 'float' and 'sink' products. For suspension densities less than 2700 kg/m^3 the natural mineral magnetite (Fe$_3$O$_4$) is used owing to its low cost. Such suspensions will usually be adequate to remove weak, porous rocks as the float product from siliceous and carbonate aggregates. In order to remove ironstones as the 'sink' product a suspension of higher density containing powdered ferrosilicon alloy (FeSi) is necessary. The use of dense media or heavy media separation (HMS) upon aggregates was first reported in Canada in the 1950s during the period of extensive infrastructure construction and has since been applied in the USA, UK and Denmark (Price 1953; Hanes 1962; Anon 1964). DMS has also been applied in Northamptonshire for the recovery of dense ironstone from gravel.

5.4.5. Shape sorting

Shape sorting is employed to reject flaky particles that are detrimental to many uses of aggregates such as roadstone and concrete. In its truest form, aggregates that have been screened into narrow size ranges such as the 'nominal sizes' by square aperture mats are processed by screens having transverse, elongated or slot apertures. To promote the orientation of the flaky par-

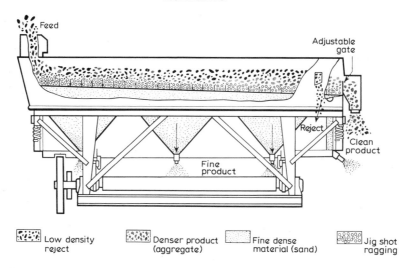

Feed

Adjustable
gate

Reject

Clean
product

Fine
product

Low density   Denser product   Fine dense   Jig shot
reject   (aggregate)   material (sand)   ragging

FIG. 5.38. Diagram of a jig (courtesy Wemco).

FIG. 5.39. Dense medium separator, drum type (courtesy Wemco).

ticles to pass through the slots transverse weirs or baffles can be attached to the mat. The width of the aperture is determined by the definition of a flaky particle e.g. 60% of the nominal screen size in the UK (see §7.5.1). However, some devices referred to as deflaking screens employ conventional apertures and are, in fact, separa-

ting a size fraction from the product of a crusher that has been found to be flaky. It has already been noted that, for example, depending upon rock type, the relatively coarse fraction of the product from a cone crusher may be flaky. This fraction will be crushed to produce an aggregate of smaller size but superior shape.

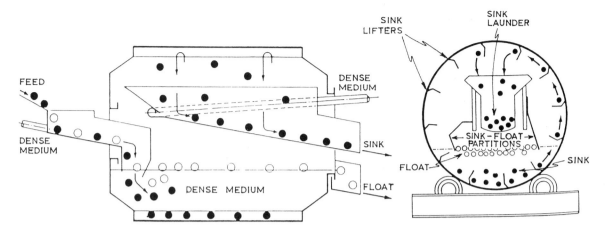

Fig. 5.40. Diagram of a drum type dense medium separator (courtesy Wemco).

5.4.6. **Magnetic separation**

Magnetic separation of typically, hard, dense, magnetic minerals of iron from aggregates is seldom necessary to assure the mechanical competence of the aggregate. Hydrated iron oxide minerals e.g. hematite, geothite are only very weakly magnetic and may be separated, if of economic value or to prevent iron staining of concrete, by density separation. High-intensity magnetic separators employing alloy permanent magnets or superconducting magnets are now available to remove such weakly magnetic mineral particles from more valuable ores such as iron ores, china clays, glass sands and bauxite but have not been applied to aggregates. Pyrite, which occurs in some deposits of sand and gravel, is so weakly magnetic that very little success has been achieved in removing it, even from coal where the incentive is so great, by magnetic separation.

Fig. 5.41. Suspended magnet collecting tramp metal (courtesy Boxmag-Rapid Ltd).

Low intensity magnetic separators containing permanent ceramic (ferrite) magnets or electromagnets are commonly used to remove tramp iron and steel from quarried rocks in order to protect process equipment (Fig 5.41). It should be noted that many modern steel alloys, including stainless steels and manganese steels, are 'non-magnetic'. Therefore, many plants employ detector loops surrounding conveyor belts to initiate alarms or automatically stop the belt in the event that such material is detected in the feed to the process plant.

5.4.7. **Sorting**

Hand sorting of ore to reject deleterious material is undoubtedly still practised around the world and even within the UK for anthracite coal (Anon (9) 1964). It is justified where: (i) separation can be effected at a relatively coarse size; (ii) capital equipment is very costly and labour is cheap; (iii) very obvious visual but no other differences exist; (iv) the removal of a small quantity of impurity is essential to the quality of the product, or (v) the 'impurity' has a significant value, e.g. flints in chalk and limestones sold into the ceramics industries. Mechanized optical sorting based upon colour or reflectivity has been applied to the recovery of such mineral (Rukavina 1986; Anon (10) 1975) and great potential exists for further application.

5.4.8. **Other separation processes**

Mineral processing plants utilize a great variety of physical separation techniques including density separation processes for particle sizes less than 3 mm, e.g. high-intensity wet magnetic separation, electrical separation and photometric and radiometric sorting. To the author's knowledge, none of these has yet been commercially applied to beneficiation of aggregates owing to cost.

Froth flotation is employed for the beneficiation of glass sands and has been used to up-grade raw materials for cement manufacture. Its cost prohibits its use for processing aggregates and the upper particle size limit is of the order of 0.5 mm. Chemical processes such as acid leaching to remove iron minerals have also been applied to the production of glass sands and 'silver sands'. These may be incorporated in special 'white' mortars.

5.5. Solid–liquid separation; dewatering

A slurry of mineral particles capable of being pumped will generally contain less than 40% by volume of mineral equivalent to approximately 65% by weight. As the water content is reduced, several states are recognized: the saturated, capillary, venicular and pendular states. In the saturated state, all the pore spaces are filled with water which, depending upon particle size distribution, will be 5–40% volume. In the capillary state, a meniscus of water forms across the pores between particles. Capillary forces create a negative pressure within the mass of particles which can draw water into the pore spaces. However, the magnitude of this capillary pressure is directly related to the diameter of the pores and, thereby, the size of the particles. It is insignificant for coarse aggregate but incurs moisture retention for finer aggregates as Table 5.1 shows.

TABLE 5.1. *Physical properties of a particulate mass*

Particle size (mm)	Pore diameter (mm)	Capillary pressure (N/m^2)	Surface area (m^2/kg)
10	1.5–4.1	10^2	222
1	0.15–0.41	10^3	2 220
0.1	0.015–0.041	10^4	22 200
0.1	0.001–0.004	10^5	222 000

To remove water mechanically from a particulate mass, the capillary pressure must be overcome by an externally applied force, e.g. gravity, centripetal force (centrifuge) or air pressure. The venicular state describes the progressive removal of water to achieve the final pendular state. In the pendular state, water is present as a film covering the surface of all particles whilst the pores are empty. Further reduction of moisture content is by evaporation and thermal energy input (drying). Mechanical methods are not effective unless the mass may be compressed to expel water. Obviously, the pendular moisture content is a function of particle surface area,

where surface area is inversely proportional to particle size. Pendular moisture content is thus insignificant for coarse aggregates but may attain several percent by weight for fine aggregates.

Dewatering of aggregates is principally concerned with the separation of particles larger than 75 μm from the water and the finer particles. In the form of a slurry it is not economic to recover these finer particles as dry mineral filler and they will usually comprise an unacceptably high proportion of clays and other undesirable minerals. Separation of these finer particles is achieved by prolonged sedimentation in 'settling-ponds', 'lagoons' or 'silt-ponds' to permit recovery of clean water for recycle and re-use within the plant or discharge to surface water courses. Within the UK, limits imposed upon water abstraction and effluent discharge licences, restrictions upon space and concern about the stability of silt lagoons have required the maximum recirculation and re-use of water without the aid of lagoons in order to obtain permissions to develop new quarries. In such cases thickeners must be employed. The sediment or silt is most usually a waste product but it may also be very useful during the restoration of the quarry and, rarely, silty clay may also be sold for tile manufacture. Vacuum or pressure filtration is not justified for dewatering aggregates at present unless it is a necessary part of the disposal method for silt. The high cost of drying prohibits its use other than in the preparation of coated materials.

5.5.1. Drainage

Free drainage of water from heaps of aggregate is a common feature of processing plants, especially those for sand and gravel. The cost is low if adequate space is available. Disadvantages include the visual impact, opportunity for wind-borne dust arising and product intermixing and contamination. Furthermore, an additional stage of handling is incurred for vehicle loading from ground level. Also advantage is often taken of drainage in the storage of aggregates in elevated bunkers.

5.5.2. Use of screens

Screens may be simply adapted to the duty of solid–liquid separation down to a limiting aperture size of about 0.5 mm. The screen surface is usually selected to be robust and corrosion resistant and fabricated from cast polymer, rubber or stainless steel wedge wire (wire rolled in the form of a triangular or trapezoidal cross section). Specialized dewatering screens have now been introduced to treat the 'sand' fractions (Figs 5.42 & 5.43). These vibrating screens are often inclined against the flow of the material to create a deep bed of particles upon the screening surface constructed from closely spaced, vertically orientated strips of elastomer. The screen can accept a feed comprising a thickened slurry of sand-sized particles from which most of the clay and silt have been removed. The particles nearest the screen deck effectively produce a filtration medium which dewaters the slurry although it is also possible to produce a partial vacuum under the deck using a small exhauster fan.

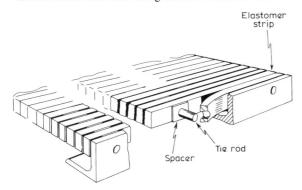

FIG. 5.42. Detail of a dewatering screen (courtesy Linatex Ltd).

FIG. 5.43. Dewatering screen below a hydrocyclone (courtesy Linatex Ltd).

5.5.3. Use of classifiers

Mechanical gravitational classifiers commonly achieve dewatering of the coarser sediment or sand fraction by permitting drainage of this product during its removal. Rake and spiral classifiers are designed to drain the sediment as it is transported up the inclined trough. Other forms of classifier employ perforated buckets mounted upon a wheel or chain system to extract the sediment.

The exception is the hydrocyclone which, despite its advantages of compact size, low cost etc., discharges the coarser underflow product as a slurry containing 50–70% weight solids only. For this reason the cyclone is usually combined with a dewatering screen or a rake classifier or mounted in a tower to create a drainage heap beneath the spigot (Fig. 5.44).

5.5.4. Thickeners

Conventional thickeners are circular tanks of relatively large diameter and shallow depth (Fig. 5.45). The suspension of mineral particles, usually of particle size less than 75 µm, is fed into a central well. Particles settle to the conical base of the tank where slowly rotating rakes assist the compaction of the sediment and also transport the material towards the central discharge point. The discharge is a 'thickened' slurry. Clarified water overflows the periphery of the tank into an annular launder.

The solid–liquid separation (SLS) process is said to take place under 'hindered settling' conditions in which all the particles settle at the same velocity i.e. independently of size, shape and density, owing to collisions and interactions. An interface rapidly develops between the supernatant clear water and the settling mass of particles commonly referred to as the 'mud-line'. Thickener design is based upon the settling rate of this mud-line as determined by experience or testwork and is critically concerned with thickener area (diameter). Capacity is usually expressed in square metres per tonne per hour and typical values are between 20 and 40 m²/t/h. Although providing a simple, continuous means of SLS, the requirement for space and capital investment is often great.

The area required can be considerably reduced by pretreatment of the slurry. Prior thickening using a hydrocyclone is effective and chemical treatment is common.

Coagulation. All mineral particles have a tendency to coagulate to form clusters of larger size that would settle more rapidly. In an aqueous suspension this is often prevented by the mineral surface acquiring an electrical charge through reaction with the ions of water, OH^- and H^+, and ions of dissolved salts. Many silicate and carbonate minerals acquire a negative charge whereas metal oxides may be positively charged under acid con-

FIG. 5.44. Hydrocyclone mounted in a tower (courtesy Linatex Ltd).

ditions. The electrical charge prevents the close approach of two particles and their coagulation under the influence of attractive (dispersion) forces.

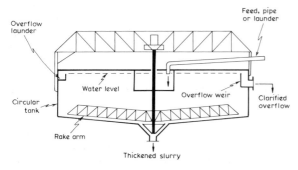

FIG. 5.45. Conventional thickener.

Coagulants are inexpensive, soluble salts added such that the adsorption of the positively charged ion upon the mineral surface neutralizes the negative charge and promotes coagulation e.g. lime (Ca^{2+}), ferrous sulphate (Fe^{2+}), alum (Al^{3+}). Coagules are relatively small groups comprising only a few particles.

Flocculants comprise long polymeric molecules, often based upon polyacrylamide, that absorb onto the mineral surface by hydrogen bonding and other mechanisms. The principal effect of the flocculant is to bind many particles together to form a floc which may be several millimetres in diameter and settles extremely rapidly (Fig. 5.46) (Moss 1978; Lightfoot 1981). Additions (dosage) range from 50 to 500 grams per tonne. The principal objective is to effect rapid recovery of clear water for re-use or discharge. The preparation and mixing conditions are extremely important to the effective use of flocculants and flocculants are relatively expensive. Over-flocculation of the material will lead to waste and the presence of high levels of flocculant in the sand product which may reduce the strength of concrete. A disadvantage of flocculants is that the sediment has a loose, porous structure of high water content. In order to expel water and obtain a handleable material the sediment must be compressed in a roll-press type filter, in a centrifuge or by its own weight in a Deep-Cone thickener (Abbott *et al.* 1973).

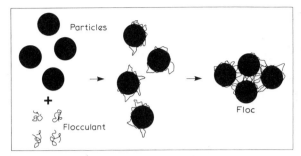

FIG. 5.46. Mechanism of flocculation.

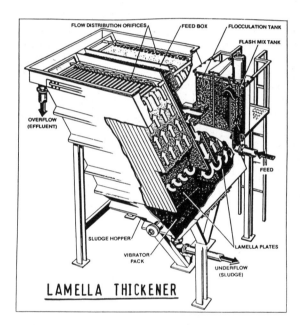

FIG. 5.47. Lamella thickener (courtesy Allis Mineral Systems).

Finally, the space requirement for the thickener can be reduced by installing inclined planar surfaces, plates or lamellae, into the vessel. The solids settle over the short distance onto the plates and then slide down the plate into the conical or hopper section where compression of the sediment occurs under its own weight (Fig. 5.47).

5.5.5. Filtration

The essential feature of a filter is the porous medium in the form of a woven fibre cloth, screen or bed of particles. Fluid is induced to flow through the medium to form filtrate by creation of a pressure difference across the medium. Particles suspended in the fluid are trapped by the medium to form a filter cake. The pressure difference can be created by pressurizing the slurry (pressure filtration) or by evacuating the filtrate side of the medium (vacuum filtration). It is not necessary for the pores in the medium to be smaller than the particles in suspension since interference causes these to bridge over the aperture and filtration proceeds upon a bed of the particles themselves. The high cost of filtration prohibits its use for preparation of aggregates although the principles are exploited in dewatering screens.

5.6. Storage and distribution

5.6.1. Storage

Storage capacity may be created as elevated silos, bunkers or bins or as ground-level stockpiles. Elevated bins are very convenient for loading road vehicles (Fig. 5.48) or rail wagons but too costly to provide more than hourly or daily storage capacity. Longer-term variations in demand are managed using heaps or stockpiles at ground level. The lateral extent of the stockpiles is determined by the natural angle of repose of the material, often less than 30°, and by restrictions imposed upon stockpile and stacker-conveyor heights. The large area required is a significant disadvantage. In smaller operations the stockpiles are reclaimed by mobile shovels which load vehicles directly or through the bunker out-loading system. The cost of 'double-handling' is a further disadvantage of ground stockpiles. In very large operations the stockpiles may be provided with dedicated reclaimers of the 'bucket-wheel' or revolving drum and rake type. More commonly, the stockpile is deposited upon hoppers and feeders installed below ground level and the material is reclaimed onto a conveyor running in a tunnel—a 'ground bunker' (Fig. 5.49). However, the readily recoverable 'live-storage' of aggregate may be only 25% of the volume of the conical pile without the use of mobile equipment to move material towards the hoppers. These stockpiles can be completely covered to exclude rainfall and to prevent dust generation. They are often divided into compartments to accommodate the various gradings and referred to colloquially as 'toast-racks'.

Storage in bunkers is not without problems which include segregation by particle size and blockage, 'hangup'. There is no total solution to segregation except to store aggregates in a number of narrow size ranges. Blockage of bunkers is a more serious problem with finely sized, moist materials. Preventive measures include the lining of bunkers with low-friction materials such as glass and polymers, mechanical rapping devices, air jets, rotating cluster breakers, inflatable diaphragms

FIG. 5.48. Bunkers and truck loading section of a processing plant (courtesy Pioneer Aggregates (UK) Ltd).

and discharge systems such as the table-feeder. Design techniques have been developed for 'mass-flow' bunkers having large discharge apertures and steeply inclined conical sections which avoid segregation and blockage at the expense of much taller structures.

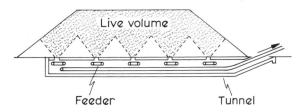

FIG. 5.49. Ground bunker.

5.6.2. Outloading

Aggregates are sold by weight and for the purpose of invoicing and controlling vehicle axle weights a weigh-bridge is required (Fig. 5.50). When loading rail wagons or ships a belt-weigher or system certified as accurate to

0.25% is employed. Within the process plant, belt and bin weighers accurate to 0.5% will be used for process control and for preparing mixes of aggregates to form the feed to coating plants or concrete mixers. Where weigh-feeders beneath bunkers are used to weigh and proportion the components of blended aggregates or weigh single sizes prior to loading road vehicles, it is possible to calibrate these feeders routinely and very regularly against the weights recorded by the weigh-bridge, resulting in high accuracy and little, if any, need to correct loads at the weighbridge (Phillipson 1986; Anon (6) 1989; Anon (7) 1989). To speed the loading and despatch of vehicles the weighbridge can be inte-grated into the ordering and invoicing system. Orders received by the quarry are coded by a name or number system and a datafile is created containing all relevant information, e.g. material type, delivery address, quan-tity, frequency, account, etc. Lorry drivers arriving at the weighbridge are given a magnetic card holding this code at the same time as the driver's identity and vehicle capacity are recorded and the vehicle is tared. Indeed, all this information may also be held as a coded data-file in which the individual vehicles are coded. The driver inserts this card into a reader at the loading point and the lorry is automatically loaded. The driver surrenders

FIG. 5.50. Weighbridge and office (courtesy Pioneer Aggregates (UK) Ltd).

the card as the vehicle is weighed on leaving the quarry and the information is used to prepare the weighbridge ticket and the invoice. In this manner the scope for error by an operator is minimized (see §5.8). The system can be extended to control the delivery fleet by logging truck movements, predicting delivery times and paying truck operators.

The discussion above has assumed delivery by road transport. The greatest advantage of road transport is flexibility in terms of unit size of load, delivery point, frequency of delivery and ability to respond rapidly to increase or fall in demand. The greatest disadvantages are the relatively high cost per tonne-kilometre and environmental intrusion. In the UK and USA, road transport is usually competitive only up to distances of about 50 km, although some special aggregate types, e.g. high PSV gritstone chippings, are transported over much greater distances.

Practical alternatives are rail and waterborne transport and they are much preferred environmentally (Wilson 1988). The concept of remote coastal quarries supplying markets by sea, rivers or estuaries and canals has been mentioned (Rukavina 1990; Yeoman 1987; Tidmarsh 1991). In the UK a conspicuous feature of the geology is that there are no significant sources of hard rock aggregate in the South Eastern counties. Large

tonnages of aggregates are transported by rail from the nearest outcrops in the Mendip Hills (limestone) (Anon (10) 1975) and Leicestershire (granites) (Anon (12) 1990). However, to justify the very large capital expenditure in ship-loading or rail loading facilities required the quarry must produce a large tonnage annually; several million tonnes in the UK. Additionally, the quarry must be either linked to the rail system or adjacent to water. It must also be considered that the customer, either final consumer or distribution centre, will be required to accept large unit loads and invest in expensive terminals. For these reasons the practice is limited to supplying large consumers or distribution depots in large conurbations e.g. London or Birmingham. A recent development in this field has been the self-discharging train (SDT), which does not require sophisticated reception facilities, to increase the feasibility of aggregate distribution by rail (Anon (8) 1989).

Where convenient waterways exist, use is made of ships and barges to carry aggregates, for example the rivers Thames, Trent, Rhine and Seine within Europe, the entire Eastern Coast of North America, the Great Lakes and the Mississippi, Hudson and Illinois rivers (Rukavina 1990). Many quarries in Norway employ sea freight rather than road to export stone to the Northern Coast of Europe, owing to the difficulties posed by numerous ferry crossings. Kirk (1990) has examined the possibility of Scottish quarries doing the same.

5.7. Environmental considerations

The design of the processing plant must (a) provide a safe and healthy environment for the operators and (b) minimize the impact (nuisance) of the plant upon the external environment as discussed in §4.6. For the UK the legal requirements are essentially contained in the Health and Safety at Work etc. Act (1974) and the Environmental Protection Act (1990) plus associated regulations. Equivalent legislation is being introduced throughout the European Community. In addition, quarry operators must consider the requirements of planning consent granted by the Mineral Planning Authority and embodied in the Town and Country Planning Acts. The objective of the E.P.A. is progressively to introduce the concept of 'Best available technology not entailing excessive cost' (BATNEEC) to ensure that affordable measures are adopted such that processes do not release pollutants to the environment or that such emissions are rendered harmless and innocuous, that is, not causing offence or nuisance. Certain processes are defined as 'prescribed' and will need to be licensed before April 1993. These include those processes commonly associated with quarrying, ready-mixed concrete production and coating of roadstone (H.M. Government 1974, 1990; DoE 1988 (1), DoE 1988 (2)).

5.7.1. Noise

The definition of noise levels and legislation are discussed in §4.6 (Gregory 1987; Moorhouse 1990). Noise levels within the process plant may be reduced below the permitted level of 85 dBA by equipment selection, e.g. elastomer screening surfaces and linings to chutes, hoppers and washer barrels. Encapsulation of fixed equipment by flexible curtains or sound adsorbent walls reduces ambient noise and may usefully confine dust. A fully sound-proofed, comfortable control cabin is commonly located in a position commanding a good view over the process plant for the benefit of the plant operators. In view of the impact of noise upon the environment many Mineral Planning Authorities in the UK are specifying maximum noise levels above which plant and machinery may not operate. Sometimes this is expressed as an increase over previous background levels and commonly varies with time of day. Clearly it may be important to conduct noise surveys prior to and after quarry development.

5.7.2. Dust

The hazard posed by respirable dust is discussed in

§4.6.3. In critical areas of the process plant, such as conveyor transfer points, vibrating screens, crushers and dryers, dust laden air can be drawn into ductwork, the dust collection system, by an exhauster-fan. The provision of a dust collection hood over such areas has been replaced in modern plant by enclosure of such equipment. This practice reduces the chance of dust egress and minimizes the volume of air to be treated. The design of seals and enclosures, the calculation of minimum transport velocities and the correct selection of dust collectors and fan is now a specialized engineering skill. The entire system operates at a negative pressure and the ductwork leads the dust-laden air through cyclones and woven fabric bag filters before passing the clean air through the fan to an exhaust stack. The collected dry dust may also form a valuable by-product, mineral filler. Processing plants for sand and gravel that operate entirely wet processes may require no dust collection system (Evans 1975; Tuck 1987).

5.7.3. Nuisance

Noise nuisance may be reduced by the siting of the process plant remotely from the site perimeter or residential properties, sound insulation integral with the cladding of the fixed plant and restricting the hours of working of the plant. A draft document relating to the control of noise at surface mineral workings within the UK was issued by the Department of the Environment in 1992 (DoE 1992(2)).

Dust nuisance can be reduced by the use of scrubbers on exhaust gases, enclosure of process equipment and conveyors, covered stockpiles and wheel-washing and sheeting of lorries leaving the quarry. For the UK, these recommended practices were published by the Secretary of State for the assistance of Planning Authorities (DoE 1991).

The visual impact of the process plant may be controlled by conditions upon maximum height of structures, colour and form of cladding, location of the fixed plant and architectural features. The location of the process plant within the proposed or older workings is often preferred by the planning authorities and prior excavation of a greenfield site to hide a plant has been required. Additional measures are the creation of visual screening banks or bunds around the operation, which also serve to deflect sound, and the establishment of tree screens (see §4.6.6).

A category of nuisance that is of growing concern is that of vehicular traffic, especially lorries, employed to distribute the quarry products. The number of lorry movements may be restricted directly or indirectly by limiting annual production. Lorry routes can also be specified. Clearly a preference exists for quarries served by rail or sea or waterway and remote from urban development but the cost of transport and the location of the major markets within centres of urban development without rail or sea access must also be considered (see §5.6.2).

FIG. 5.51. Quarry process plant control room.

5.8. Process and quality control

The need for process control equipment is self-evident and includes temperature sensors, mass and volume flowmeters, bin-level indicators etc. Such instrumentation provided with remote display and equipment controls grouped together in a central control room (Fig. 5.51), often also the weighbridge office, permits efficient plant performance and a significant reduction in the number of operating personnel. The control room is usually equipped with a mimic display panel depicting the plant flowsheet in diagrammatic form. In the most modern plant control rooms this mimic display is itself created on a VDU screen linked to the central computer control system. This display includes remote instrument displays, e.g. mass flow rates, bunker levels, motor currents and temperatures, and alarms to draw the attention of the operators to faults. Furthermore, condition monitors indicate the status of equipment, e.g. motors and conveyors running or stopped, bin gates open or closed. Automation has been extended on many plants to include the weighing, proportioning and mixing of common products according to coded 'recipes' stored in the computer memory. In addition to saving the repetitive, tedious work of a plant operator this also promotes product quality. Finally, a central computer control system affords a means of logging the performance of the plant in terms of hours, production, raw material consumptions, stock levels, availability, efficiency, etc. and predicting such matters as maintenance and purchasing requirements. The use of closed-circuit television is now common to provide remote viewing of critical components of the process equipment from the control room. Where no central control computer exists,

a programmed logic controller, (PLC), is commonly used to sequence the initiation or de-activation of individual pieces of equipment automatically during the regular requirement for plant start-up or shut-down.

Quality control for the product may be simply effected by regular sampling, analysis and testing (see Chapter 7). However, the introduction of the Quality Assurance (QA) scheme requires that the supplier generates customer confidence that the product will be of adequate quality (BS5750, 1987) see §7.6. Thus, the onus of quality assurance is upon the supplier and the practice of 'acceptance testing' may be obviated. In the UK accreditation under the QA scheme is obtained from an independent authority, e.g. BSI, NAMAS by demonstrating that, in addition to the more usual quality control measures through testing the final product, more rigorous and comprehensive procedures have been implemented with respect to quarrying.

(i) A quality management structure should exist with authority and reporting procedures clearly defined.
(ii) Evaluation of the mineral reserve and testing of raw materials has been carried out to ensure that product quality is attainable.
(iii) Competent design of the process plant and ability to meet performance criteria can be demonstrated.
(iv) Instruments are calibrated and tested on a routine basis.
(v) Operators have undergone appropriate education and training.
(vi) Procedures to proscribe the disposal, re-use or re-manufacture of rejected materials.
(vii) Plant maintenance and inspection procedures are defined.
(viii) Material storage and packing can preserve product quality.
(ix) Procedures for ordering, loading, delivery etc. will avoid errors and cross contamination.

The company is expected to make an explicit statement of Quality Policy and to prepare a Quality Manual for each operation (Grant 1988).

5.9. Plant flowsheets

Descriptions are given of two plant process flowsheets; the first being a plant to produce concrete aggregates from sand and gravel and the second a plant to produce roadstone from a gritstone.

5.9.1. Sand and gravel process plant

Figure 5.52 shows a schematic generalized flowsheet for

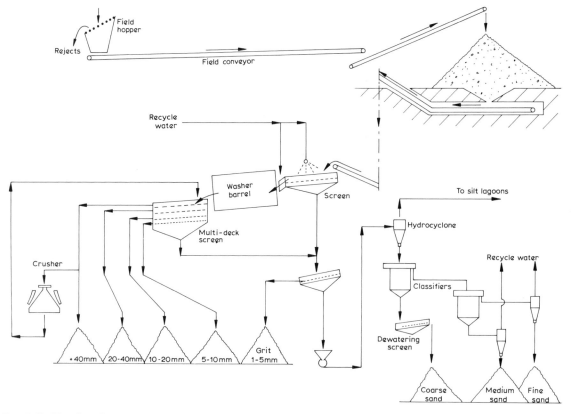

Fig. 5.52. Flowsheet for a typical sand and gravel plant.

a plant processing sand and gravel. The deposit is dug by dragline, front-end loader or back-hoe (see §4.3.3.) and the material loaded through a hopper onto a field conveyor system. At this point a grizzly screen will usually be employed to reject very large particles such as the 'erratics' or boulders encountered in glacial deposits. The conveyor feeds onto a surge or stock pile ahead of the plant. The material is reclaimed by wheeled loaders (small operation) or tunnel conveyor and fed to a screen, often equipped with water sprays, where sand sized particles, probably less than 5 mm, are removed. In cases where the deposit contains large quantities of clays and silt the oversize passes into a washer barrel where any agglomerates are disintegrated. Log washers, monitors or simple mixing tanks or pits may be used to the same effect. The washed gravel, sand and silt and clays in slurry form are discharged onto a multi-deck screen and sized into the saleable product size ranges (Fig. 5.35). In the UK at the present time (1992) the screen apertures are usually 40, 20, 10 and 5 mm. For material containing few agglomerates and very little silt and clays, for example marine dredged aggregates, the washer barrel may be omitted. The water sprays on the screen are, however, much more important and will supply fresh water to reduce the chloride content of the aggregate.

The sized coarse aggregates are stored and drained in bins or heaps.

However, the demand for sand and for gravel in the size range 5 to 20 mm may exceed the natural production of these materials. Therefore, provision is often made for the crushing of coarser fractions, especially plus 40 mm 'rejects', to increase the yield of these products. A cone crusher is depicted as most suitable to crush very coarse rejects into the desirable size range of concrete aggregates. A vertical shaft impactor and even the rod mill may be used to increase the yield of sand.

The minus 5 mm screen undersize, sand fraction, is processed according to the local markets and the particle size analysis of this material. In a simple case the silt is removed by a screw classifier which also partially dewaters the sand product. The sand is finally dewatered on a dewatering screen and drained in heaps. Alternatively, the sand is sized and classified into several saleable fractions. The flowsheet shows a 1 mm screen to remove a grit fraction followed by a hydrocyclone to reject the silt. The intermediate sand fraction is classified to produce a coarse sand and a fine sand. The coarse sand is dewatered by a dewatering screen and the fine sand by a hydrocyclone mounted in a tower above a drainage heap. The various sand fractions can be sold

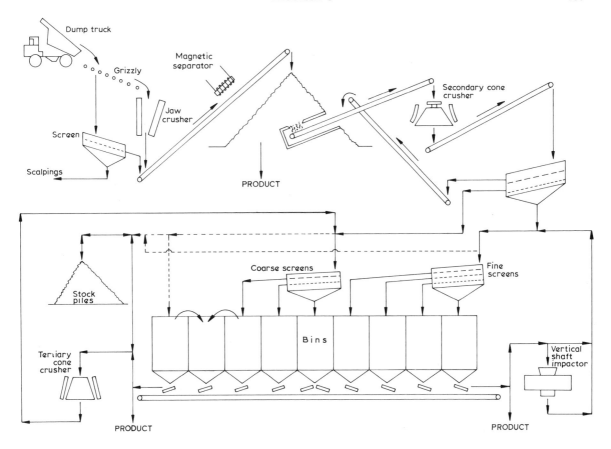

FIG. 5.53. Flowsheet for a typical crushed rock plant.

separately or blended to meet the requirements of, say, concrete sand (see Chapter 8), mortars (see Chapter 9) asphalt sand (see Chapter 11) or filter media (see Chapter 13).

The water containing the silt must be treated before recycle or discharge by settlement in lagoons or addition of coagulants and flocculants and the use of thickeners.

5.9.2. Hard rock (roadstone) process plant

Figure 5.53 depicts the flowsheet for a plant producing various forms of dry (uncoated) roadstone including high PSV (+60) surface chippings. The production of surface chippings would probably require that a gritstone was being quarried. Many igneous rocks, such as granites and basalts, exhibit moderate values of PSV and are suitable for all other types of roadstone (see Chapters 10 & 11) and reference is made to their production. Limestones have a very low PSV but are used extensively in road construction below the wearing course. The operation of a quarry solely for the produc-

tion of high PSV surface chippings cannot be justified so it is likely that any gritstone will also be sold as dry stone, macadams and even concrete aggregate. Since any quarry is likely to contain beds of lower quality and weathered rocks it will also produce fill materials.

The quarried stone is dumped onto a grizzly feeder which removes scalpings and feeds the oversize to the primary double-toggle jaw crusher for breakage. The scalpings are re-screened at a finer size to increase the yield of clean stone.

Where a soft limestone (containing little silica as flint or chert) is being processed the primary crusher may also be a jaw crusher, usually of the single-toggle type, although fixed blow-bar impactors are common. Elsewhere in the flowsheet impactors will be used in place of cone crushers. Where the throughput of the plant exceeds 1000 tph, especially for igneous rocks, the jaw crusher is replaced by a primary gyratory crusher. In this case, the dump trucks usually discharge directly into the crusher and scalping is carried out upon the primary crusher product.

The crushed rock is fed onto a stock-pile ahead of the main process plant from which it is reclaimed by a

FIG. 5.54. Mobile crusher producing DTp type-1 aggregate (courtesy Pegson Ltd).

tunnel conveyor. This arrangement permits the plant to operate outside the hours of the quarry and during interruptions to quarry operations. A market may also exist for this 'crusher-run' material. Reclaimed stone is further crushed by a secondary cone crusher but a secondary gyratory might also be used. In order to increase plant capacity a primary screen can be installed ahead of the secondary crusher to remove material finer than the setting of the crusher which by-passes this stage of comminution. The material is now screened with oversize being recycled to the secondary crusher.

Commonly, the crusher product is divided into coarse and fine fractions prior to sizing as finished products. At this stage it is probable that this simple screening will generate saleable materials having relatively wide size distributions. Type 1 dry stone aggregate for road construction (see Chapter 10) is a good example relevant to the UK which may constitute a substantial proportion of the quarry output. Provision is made for recovery and stocking of this product.

Screening of the crushed aggregate into narrow size

ranges employs multiple deck vibrating screens often mounted directly above the respective storage/outloading bins. However, screening of the secondary crusher product is unlikely to yield sized stone in the proportions demanded by the markets which are usually greater for the finer aggregates. Provision is made for recrushing the coarser fractions through a tertiary cone crusher. Indeed, the bin system can be designed so that once the bins containing coarser sizes are full they overflow automatically to feed the recrushing circuit. Fine aggregates may also be recrushed and recirculated to the fine screens. Machines suitable for this purpose, which may be encountered in various combinations, include fine cone crushers, vertical shaft impactors (illustrated) and gyratory disc crushers for the manufacture of sand. The impactor or cone crusher, operating with a low reduction ratio, may also be used at this stage to impart a cubical shape to the product intended for surface chippings.

The flowsheets for plants, particularly those which have evolved over many years, may appear much more

FIG. 5.55. Modular mobile plant crushing 'granite' (courtesy Pegson Ltd).

complex owing to incremental expansion and equipment replacement. Provision for recovery, recycle and recrushing of stone to meet local (sometimes temporary) market requirements further complicates the flowsheet. Ultimately it is the objective of the quarry manager to maximize the return upon the investment by responding to the demands of the market in terms of quantities and specifications not simply maximizing quarry output of standard materials.

5.10. Future

At the present time (1992) within the UK it seems likely that the demand for construction aggregates will continue, even if the economy stagnates, at a level between 250 and 300 million tonnes. Other countries in Europe, e.g. France and West Germany, and the USA consume even greater quantities per capita than the UK (BACMI 1989). Thus, it can be seen that the quarry industry is not in decline because, despite the opposition to mineral extraction upon environmental grounds, the adequate supply of aggregates at reasonable cost is essential to a developed economy.

General trends, discussed in Chapter 4, including the application for licences to increase the contribution of dredging to the local supply of aggregates and to establish coastal super quarries can be expected to continue. Whether these developments, which would result in the creation of new wharf and quarry process plant, will be permitted against the strong environmental opposition remains to be seen but, in any case, they would not result in the significant modification of processing techniques.

The developments in the immediate future are likely to be concerned with the reduction of the environmental impact of the quarrying industry rather than revolution of the processes. Progressive modification of existing plant to reduce dust and noise nuisance by the techniques discussed above will entail significant additional capital expenditure. In the case of proposals for new plant there have already been examples where the total enclosure of process equipment and storage has been considered in order to eliminate environmental impact. The concern for the conservation and protection of water supplies is already causing process design engineers to consider the treatment and recycle of a large proportion of the process water by techniques such as thickening and filtration.

Further into the future it will become necessary to work deposits of rock, sand and gravel of lower quality, thereby requiring more extensive application of benefi-

Fig. 5.56. Fixed process plant (centre) including covered storage (right), rail link and screening bund (left) (courtesy of Tarmac Q.P. Ltd).

ciation techniques to remove deleterious components. In this repect there may be renewed interest in some of the density separation processes such as jigging and D.M.S. and further development of shape separation and control. Economically, the exploitation of these currently inferior deposits may depend upon joint development of the site with restoration by land-fill or to a commercial leisure amenity. Ultimately it seems inevitable that the economy must accept an increase in the real price of aggregates in order to meet the costs of environmental protection, additional processing and extended transport.

Finally, despite considerable problems, it is probable that the construction industry will be required to increase the use of solid process wastes from other industries, especially the mining industry, and recycled materials such as crushed concrete and asphalt to reduce the demands for quarry development. Evidence is provided

by the fact that an investigation of the potential for the use of recycled materials and 'secondary aggregates' in the UK was recently commissioned from Arup Economics by the Department of the Environment (Arup 1991). Some waste materials are substantially utilized, notably slags and power station ashes. It is reported that recycling of asphalt is common outside the UK and that the practice could be adopted if suitable specifications were developed. Nevertheless, the report identified the large tips of colliery spoil, china clay waste and slate waste that are not utilized because the materials are often of low and variable quality and almost all are remote from the markets. In addition, it is reported that much of the demolition waste generated is also only utilized for low-quality applications such as fill. Thus, there appears to be an incentive for the development of new types of process plant designed to improve the quality of these secondary aggregates. However, it should be noted that 'secondary aggregates' only constitute about 10% of the total at present and a substantial increase in the prices of aggregates will be necessary to justify the expense.

References

ABBOTT, J. *et al.* 1973. 'Coal preparation plant effluent disposal by means of deep cone thickeners'. *Mine and Quarry*, October, 37–50.

ANON (1) 1989. In-pit crushing in Cumbria on track. *Mine and Quarry*, July, 34–35.

ANON (2) 1988. World's largest mobile crusher in Texas. *Quarry Management*, March, 9–16.

ANON (3) 1987. Mobile mineral sizer at Hope quarry, England. *Mining Magazine*, July, 77–78.

ANON (4) undated. Vibrating screen; Theory and Selection, Allis-Chalmers, (Allis Mineral Systems), Wishaw, Lanarkshire.

ANON (5) 1989. Greenwich maritime plant. *Mine and Quarry*, May, 13.

ANON (6) 1989. Process automation at Tyttenhanger quarry. *Mine and Quarry*, March, 13–16.

ANON (7) 1988. Automatic blending and load-out controls at ECC Croft Quarry. *Mine and Quarry*, March, 13–26.

ANON (8) 1989. Redland's SDT. *Mine and Quarry*, May, 21.

ANON (9) 1964. Borough Green quarry. *Mining and Minerals Engineering*, September, 10–18.

ANON (10) 1975. Optical sorting at Swanscombe quarry. *Mine and Quarry*, July, 41–42.

ANON (11) 1988. Major quarry modernisation programme completed. *Quarry Management*, November, 17.

ANON (12) 1990. New Cliffe Hill plant in full production. *Quarry Management*, November, 17–30.

ARUP ECONOMICS & PLANNING, 1991. Occurrence and utilisation of mineral and construction wastes, London.

BACMI 1989. "Statistical year book," British Aggregate Construction Materials Industries, London.

BARLOW, C. 1984. In-pit crushing selected for largest British quarry. *International Mining*, January, 65–67.

BOND, F. C. 1960. Crushing and grinidng calculations, Allis-Chalmers Corp. (reprint from British Chemical Engineering, June 1960).

BRITISH STANDARDS INSTITUTION, B.S. 5750, 1987. Quality Systems, and BSI Handbook 22, Quality Assurance, Milton Keynes.

BROWN, G. J. 1963. Principles and practice of crushing and screening. *Quarry Managers' Journal*, March–September, series of 7 articles.

DEPARTMENT OF THE ENVIRONMENT 1988a. *General considerations and the development Plan System, Mineral Planning Guidance*, MPG1, HMSO, London.

—— 1988b. *Applications, Permissions and Conditions*, Mineral Planning Guidance, MPG2, HMSO, London.

—— 1991. *Quarry processes including roadstone plants and size reduction of bricks, tiles and concrete*, Planning Guidance, PG3/8(91), HMSO, London.

—— 1992. *Control of noise at surface mineral workings*, Draft Mineral Planning Guidance, MPG11.

EVANS, W. L. 1975. Air pollution control in the minerals processing industry. *Mine and Quarry*, December, 18–31.

FLAVEL, M. D. 1978. Control of crushing circuits will reduce capital and operating costs. *Mining Magazine*, March,
207–213.

FLYNN, B. 1988. The concept of primary rock sizing. *Quarry Management*, July, 29–31.

FREEBURY, J. 1978. Practice of screening. *Mine and Quarry*, June, 56–62.

GOLDKUHL, A. 1987. The principles of screening in the range 0.5 to 20 mm. *Mine and Quarry*, November, 39–43.

GRANT, R. M. 1988. Controlling the quality of coated materials. *Quarry Management*, November, 35–46.

GREGORY, J. 1987. The measurement and control of industrial noise. *Quarry Management*, January, 25–33.

HANES, F. E., WYMAN, R. A. 1962. The application of heavy media separation to concrete aggregate. *Bulletin of the Canadian Institute of Mining and Metals*, July, 489–496.

HARRIS, P. M., HIGHLEY, D. E & BENTLEY, K. R. 1988. *Directory of Mines and Quarries*, British Geological Survey, Keyworth.

HAYES, V. 1990. Moving stone; an overview. *Rock Products*, September, 16–21.

HILL, H. E. 1985. Vertical shaft impact crushers. *Quarry Management*, October, 713–722.

H. M. GOVERNMENT, 1974. *Health and Safety at Work etc. Act.* HMSO, London.

—— 1990. *Environmental Protection Act.* HMSO, London.

JONES, O. & SWIFT, R. F. 1972. The application of the loose rod deck in the mining industry. *Mine and Quarry*, July, 25–37.

JOWETT, A. 1963. Assessment of screening efficiency formulae. *Colliery Guardian*, October, 423–427.

KIRK, M. 1990. Scottish coastal quarries. *Quarry Management*, April, 39–44.

LIGHTFOOT, J. 1981. Practical aspects of flocculation. *Mine and Quarry*, February, 51–53.

LOWRISON, G. C. 1974. *Crushing and Grinding.* Butterworths, London.

MARKWICK, A. H. D. 1936. The shape of road aggregate and its measurement, Road Research Bulletin No. 2, HMSO, London.

McQUISTON, F. W. & SHOEMAKER, R. S. 1978. *Primary crushing plant design.* Society of Mining Engineers (AIME), New York.

MELLOR, S. H. 1990. *An Introduction to Crushing and Screening.* Institute of Quarrying, Nottingham.

MOGENSEN, F. 1965. A new method of screening granular materials. *Quarry Manager's Journal*, October, 409–414.

MOORHOUSE, A. 1990. Industrial noise in the 1990s. *Quarry Management*, February, 31–36.

MOSS, N. 1978. Theory of flocculation. *Mine and Quarry*, May, 57–61.

O'BRIAN, R. W. 1987. Coal screening in the fine to medium size range. *Mine and Quarry*, November, 34–38.

PARTRIDGE, A. C., 1977. Principles of screening. *Mine and Quarry*, December, 33–38.

PHILLIPSON, G. R. 1986. Streamlining quarry systems. *Quarry Management*, May, 29–41.

PRICE, W. L. 1953. New HMS plant provides low-cost, high quality gravel. *Engineering and Mining Journal*, April, 86–87.

RASPASS, F. W. 1980. Developments in fine aggregate processing. *Quarry Management*, August, 217–228.

RIDDELL, R. J. 1985. Screening and screen surfaces. *Quarry Management*, September, 649–658.

ROBERTSON, J. 1986. In-pit crusher saves haul costs. *Rock Products*, August, 52–54.

ROUTLEDGE, P. J. 1962. Concrete aggregates for British Columbia construction projects. *Bulletin of Canadian Institute of*

Mining and Metals, July, 484–488.

RUKAVINA, M., 1985. Mobile crusher handles 3000 tph. *Rock Products*, May, 37–40.

—— 1986. Optical sorters aid silica plant. *Rock Products*, September, 39–43.

—— 1987. Top 10 aggregate plants named. *Rock Products*, February, 83–86.

—— 1990. A model plant opens in Canada. *Rock Products*, August, 31–35.

—— 1990. Water shipping gains attention. *Rock Products*, September, 25–34.

SCHNEIDERMAN, S. J. 1980. Rotating probability screen. *World Coal*, August, 29–31.

SHAW, S. R. 1983. The rotating probability screen. *Mine and Quarry*, October, 29–32.

SMITH, M. R. & GOCHIN, R. J. 1984. Classifiers. *Mining Magazine*, July, 27–39.

STOCKS, J. & DOWN, C. 1977. *Environmental Impact of Mining*. Applied Science, London.

SVAROVSKY, L. 1984. *Hydrocyclones*. Holt, Eastbourne.

—— 1981. *Solid–Liquid Separation*. 2nd Edition, Butterworths, London.

TEPORDEI, V. 1987. 1986 aggregate mining data. *Rock Products*, June, 25–31.

TIDMARSH, D. 1991. The Glensanda experience. *Quarry Mangement*, November, 17–31.

TUCK, G. 1987. The control of airborne dust in quarries. *Quarry Management*, April, 23–31.

WILSON, H. 1988. Distribution of quarried materials. *Quarry Management*, 33–35.

YEOMAN, J. 1987. The concept of the mammoth quarry. *Quarry Management*, March, 35–40.

ZOERB, H. M. 1953. Design development of crushing cavities. *Mining Engineering*, June, 603–605.

Processing plant descriptions (not cited in text)

ANON 1974. A major new Derbyshire limestone plant. *Quarry Management*, November.

ANON 1987. Whatley equips for the 21st century. *Quarry Management*, November, 11–30.

ANON 1989. Modular plant at Scottish quarry. *Quarry Management*, December, 11–13.

ANON 1988. Rickney's quarry. *Mine and Quarry*, July, 30–32.

ANON 1988. Woolhampton quarry. *Mine and Quarry*, September, 15–17.

ANON 1989. Greenwich maritime plant. *Mine and Quarry*, May, 13–15.

ANON 1989. Ravelrig quarry: Tarmac Scotland's new site. *Mine and Quarry*, July, 9–10.

ANON 1989. Colnbrook quarry. *Mine and Quarry*, June, 15–17.

ANON 1986. Pioneer boost limestone production in N. Yorkshire with £1.3 million plant investment. *Mine and Quarry*, July, 10.

ANON 1987. Ballidon Quarry. *Mine and Quarry*, April, 9–17.

ANON 1985. ARC's new aggregate factory. *Quarry Management*, September, 629–632.

ANON 1987. Largest hard rock quarry in the Western Cape. *Quarry Management*, March, 19–23.

ANON 1989. Vignats quarry, A Steetley hardrock producer in Normandy. *Mine and Quarry*, December, 13–16.

ANON 1989. NordKalk: Scandinavia's largest limestone producer. *Mine and Quarry*, June, 21–23.

ANON 1987. New 3,500 tons/h primary plant for the US largest stone producer. *Quarry Management*, July, 25–27.

ANON 1986. A giant Belgian limestone quarry. *Mine and Quarry*, February, 13–15.

ANON 1990. New Cliffe Hill plant in full production. *Quarry Management*, November, 17–30.

ANON 1991. Three hard rock quarry sites in New Zealand. *Quarry Management*, June, 47–57.

ARDAENS, A. 1986. A Beaulieu-en-Ferques (Pas-de Calais): un complex de produits naturels, de calcaire dur, le stinkal, et de produits routiers. *Industrie Minerale Mines et Carrieres*, November, 608–612.

BROWN, D. 1989. Chicken grit in Muscovy (USSR). *Mine and Quarry*, February, 16–17.

EARLE, Q. 1991. The quarry industry in Hong Kong. *Quarry Management*, February, 19–24.

FOUCQUIER, J., 1989. Morillon-Corvol: la nouvelle installation de Sandillon (Loiret). *Industrie Minerale-Mines et Carrieres*, April, 51–56.

FOX, P. 1992. Producing rail ballast in Tanzania. *Quarry Management*, March, 17–19.

HAPPY, A. 1992. Production of aggregates in New Zealand. *Quarry Management*, February, 15–19.

HOFFMANN, G. 1992. Quarrying in Antarctica. *Quarry Management*, January, 13–18.

KOG, Y. C. 1990. Processing an inferior sand deposit (Singapore). *Quarry Management*, 33–37.

MATHON, J-P. 1986. Les Carrieres de Pierre Bleue dev Chooz-Givet dans les Ardennes. *Industrie Minerale Mines et Carrieres*, August, 478–484.

ROBERTSON, J. 1981. Conveyor system moves 1 million tons annually (Washington). *Rock Products*, October, 98–102.

—— 1982. Employee's ideas included in design of new 1250 tph plant (Texas). *Rock Products*, July, 35–37.

—— 1983. Computer runs Genstar plant (Maryland). *Rock Products*, September, 41–43.

—— 1983. Vulcan mines tough stone (Virginia). *Rock Products*, September, 47–50.

—— 1985. Old quarry, new plant (Pennsylvania). *Rock Products*, September, 42–45.

—— 1985. Cable conveyor carries 500 tph (Arkansas). *Rock Products*, September, 38–41.

—— 1986. Stone sand meets market demands (N. Carolina). *Rock Products*, June, 36–39.

RUKAVINA, M. 1987. Tandem loading spurs production (Canada). *Rock Products*, February, 75–78.

VIGNAL, A. 1989. Barriaud SA: une evolution exemplaire (France). *Industrie Minerale-Mines et Carrieres*, February, 44–48.

WOODCOCK, J. T., 1980. Industrial Minerals *In*: *Mining and Metallurgical Practices in Australasia*. Australian Institute of Mining and Metallurgy, 677–689.

General references

COULSON, J. M. & RICHARDSON, J. F. 1978. *Chemical Engineering*. 3rd Edition, Volume 2, Pergamon, Oxford.

LITTLER, A. 1990. *Sand and Gravel Production*. Institute of Quarrying, Nottingham.

MULAR, A. & BHAPPU, R. 1980. *Mineral Processing Plant Design*. Society of Mining Engineers (AIME), New York.

PEGSON Ltd., undated. *Aggregate Producers Handbook*, Pegson Ltd., Coalville, Leicestershire.

WILLS, B. A. 1988. *Mineral Processing Technology*. 4th Edition, Pergamon, Oxford.

6. Description and classification of aggregates

6.1. Introduction

The description and, in particular, the classification of aggregates in a manner appropriate to their use in the construction industry has long posed problems, not only of a scientific nature but also from practical and commercial points of view.

Naturally occurring rock materials can be classified in a variety of ways, the method chosen depending on the nature of the rock and the use for which the classification is required. Age, colour, fossil content, grain size, mineralogy, mode of formation and compressive strength are but some of the many approaches that have been used. The most common method is that developed from the classical geological approach, which is based essentially on the mode of formation. Hence natural rock material is divided into three main classes: igneous, sedimentary and metamorphic. These groups are then subdivided, principally on the basis of their mineralogy and texture.

The numerous subdivisions possible in this fundamental geological system inevitably results in a nomenclature which is too cumbersome for general use in the construction industry. As a consequence, various schemes have been developed to simplify the classification of aggregates, some intended for general use, others to meet specific purposes.

Some level of petrographic examination is necessary for virtually all classification schemes and a detailed petrological description can be helpful in assessing the performance of an aggregate and in detecting potentially deleterious substances.

This chapter reviews current classification schemes for natural aggregates and discusses their development. A recommended approach for classification is presented and procedures for the petrographic examination of aggregates are described.

6.2. Descriptive and classification schemes in general

6.2.1. Classical geological schemes

For any aggregate classification scheme which incorporates the petrological composition of the material, it is essential that the rock or deposit has been identified correctly. This identification will be based on a classical geological approach and needs to be undertaken by a suitably experienced geologist/petrologist.

Following the major division of rock material by its mode of formation into igneous, sedimentary and metamorphic groups, it is further classified on the basis of mineralogy and texture. An outline of the classical geological classification schemes is given in Chapter 2 and covered in detail elsewhere for igneous rocks (Hatch *et al.* 1972), sedimentary rocks (Hatch *et al.* 1971; Tucker 1982) and metamorphic rocks (Turner 1968).

A major objective of these classification schemes is to promote uniformity in nomenclature so that all petrologists call the same rock by the same name. In practice this highly desirable objective is not always achieved, a consequence not so much of inconsistency in the petrological description, but rather the lack of a unified approach to classification. This is particularly true in the case of limestones.

This lack of unanimity can lead to contractual problems, particularly if the classification of an aggregate is not accompanied by a detailed petrological description. A good example of this can be seen in many of the sands and gravels in the English Midlands. A major constituent of these deposits is quartz-rich sandstone, which may be variously described as quartzite, orthoquartzite, quartzarenite, pure quartz sandstone and quartzose sandstone, depending on the scheme followed. Current UK specifications for minimizing the risk of alkali–silica reaction in concrete (e.g. Concrete Society Technical Report 30, 1987) describe 'quartzite' as a potentially reactive material, whereas sandstone may be acceptable (depending on the detailed petrology). The implications resulting from the particular term that is used to describe the above rock type are obvious.

For igneous rocks a greater degree of international uniformity in classification exists. However, this positive feature is offset by the greater complexity of the classifications, which far exceed the requirements for aggregates.

6.2.2. Descriptive and classification schemes for engineering purposes

A number of attempts have been made to describe and classify rock materials from both an engineering and a geological point of view. The majority are concerned with material in the 'in situ' condition and these methods of description have generally been associated with the subject field of rock mechanics. The historical development of this work, first documented by Terzaghi (1947), is well expounded in the Geological Society Engineering Group Working Party Report *The Description of Rock Masses for Engineering Purposes* (Geological Society 1977). There have been three main lines of approach: the first based on the petrography of the material, the second on rock parameters as derived from tests (usually related to strength characteristics) and the third on the field condition of the rock mass including details such as discontinuities and degree of weathering. The recommendations contained in the 1977 report, only marginally modified, are incorporated in the revised version of British Standard Code of Practice on Site Investigation (BS 5930: 1981) (formerly BS CP 2001).

The standard requires that rocks in natural outcrops, cores or excavations should generally be described in the following sequence:

   (i) Colour
   (ii) Grain size
   (iii) Texture and structure
   (iv) State of weathering
   (v) Rock name (in capitals)
   (vi) Strength
   (vii) Other characteristics and properties

Appropriate textural and structural terms are defined and, where relevant, these are quantified together with parameters such as strength and state of weathering. The result is a simple description which conveys a considerable amount of precisely defined information about the rock. An example of a description of a rock mass in a quarry face might be:

Dark greenish grey, fine grained, very thinly flow banded, slightly weathered, BASALT, very strong, with large columnar jointing.

This description provides the following information:

   (i) The colour of the rock
   (ii) Its grain size is less than 0.06 mm (the approximate limit of unaided vision).
   (iii) The rock exhibits flow banding, with the width of the bands being between 20 mm and 60 mm.
   (iv) The rock mass is weathered to Grade II (weathering of the rock is indicated by discolouration, but there is no decomposition or disintegration of the rock to a soil).
   (v) The petrological name of the rock.
   (vi) The uniaxial compressive strength of the rock is between 100 and 200 MN/m^2.
   (vii) The rock mass exhibits three-dimensional jointing which is columnar (height greater than cross section) with the cross sectional dimension between

600 mm and 2 m. Further information can be added to the description on the orientation, spacing and condition of the individual joint sets.

While this descriptive scheme is not directly applicable to processed aggregates, it is highly relevant to the descripton of unprocessed rock in existing quarry faces, and in the exploration for new quarries in rock outcrops or drilled cores. BS 5930: 1981 also contains a similar descriptive scheme for soils which is relevant to unprocessed sand and gravel deposits. With this scheme it should be noted that the distinction between sand and gravel is taken at a particle size of 2 mm whereas in aggregate terminology sand and gravel is synonymous with fine and coarse aggregate with a split at 5 mm (BS 882: 1983). Also BS 882: 1983 defines fines (silt, clay, dust) as being material passing a 75 μm sieve, whereas for geotechnical purposes silt is taken as being finer than 63 μm. The difference might be small, but different sieves are used for particle size distribution analysis and this can cause confusion.

Various special descriptive and classification schemes for engineering purposes have been developed, usually in relation to particular rock or soil types. Fookes & Higginbottom (1975) proposed a system of classification and description of near-shore carbonate sediment rocks for engineering design purposes, using grain size and post-depositional induration as the main parameters of engineering significance (Table 6.1). Clark & Walker (1977) have extended the Fookes and Higginbottom system to cover sedimentary materials ranging from total carbonate to total non-carbonate content, also incorporating variations in the particle size and degree of induration together with an approximation of the unconfined compression strength of the material (Table 6.2.). Burnett & Epps (1979) have also developed the original system to cover the carbonate suite rocks and soils.

The terminology used for the description of fine-grained argillaceous sediments is often imprecise and confusing, yet they are an important group of rocks from an engineering point of view. Stow (1981) proposed a classification based on particle size and degree of lithification and fissility (Table 6.3). While these rocks are rarely utilized as aggregate, they are often interbedded with other sedimentary rocks such as limestones which are widely used. Their accurate identification and description both in the field and as a minor constituent in the processed aggregte is, therefore, important.

6.2.3. The description and classification of rock weathering

Knight & Knight (1935) and many other workers have drawn attention to the importance of the degree of weathering and alteration on the potential performance

TABLE 6.1. *Proposed classification of pure carbonate sediments for engineering purposes (after Fookes & Higginbottom 1975)*

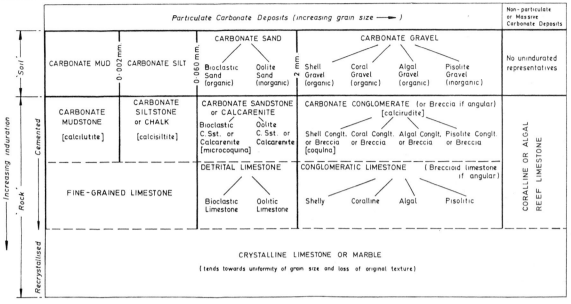

[established alternative names are in square brackets]

TABLE 6.2. *Proposed classification chart for description of Middle Eastern sedimentary rocks (after Clark & Walker 1977)*

NOTES ① Non-carbonate constituents are likely to be siliceous apart from local concentrations of minerals such as felspar and mixed heavy minerals (Emery 1956).

② In description the rough proportions of carbonate and non-carbonate constituents should be quoted and details of both the particle minerals and matrix minerals should be included.

③ The preferred lithological nomenclature has been shown in block capitals; alternatives have been given in brackets and these may be substituted in description if the need arises.

④ Calcareous is suggested as a general term to indicate the presence of unidentified carbonate. Where applicable, when mineral identification is possible calcareous referring to calcite or alternative adjectives such as dolomitic, aragonitic, sideritic etc. should be used.

TABLE 6.3. *Mudrock classification (after Stow 1981)*

Mudrock (>50% silciclastic, >50% less than 63 μm)			
Basic terms			
Unlithified	*Lithified/non-fissile*	*Lithified/fissile*	*Approx. proportions/grain-size*
Silt	Siltstone	Silt-shale	$>\frac{2}{3}$ silt-sized (4–63 μm)
Mud	Mudstone	Mud-shale	silt and clay mixture (<63 μm)
Clay	Claystone	Clay-shale	$>\frac{2}{3}$ clay-sized (<4 μm)

Metamorphic terms		
Argillite	slightly metamorphosed/non-fissile	silt and clay mixture
Slate	metamorphosed/fissile	silt and clay mixture

Textural descriptors	*Approx. proportions*
Silty	>10% silt-size
Muddy	>10% silt- or clay-size (applied to non-mudrock sediments)
Clayey	>10% clay size
Sandy, pebbly, etc	>10% sand-size, pebble-size, etc.

Compositional descriptors	*Approx. proportions*
Calcareous	>10% $CaCO_3$ (foraminiferal, nannofossil, etc)
Siliceous	>10% SiO_2 (diatomaceous, radiolarian, etc)
Carbonaceous	>1% Organic carbon
Pyritiferous Ferruginous Micaceous and others }	Commonly used for contents greater than about 1–5%

TABLE 6.4. *Weathering/alteration grades (after Geological Society 1977)*

Term	Description	Grade
Fresh	No visible sign of rock material weathering.	IA
Faintly weathered	Discoloration on major discontinuity surfaces.	IB
Slightly weathered	Discoloration indicates weathering of rock material and discontinuity surfaces. All the rock material may be discoloured by weathering and may be somewhat weaker than in its fresh condition.	II
Moderately weathered	Less than half of the rock material is decomposed and/or disintegrated to a soil. Fresh or discoloured rock is present either as a continuous framework or as corestones.	III
Highly weathered	More than half of the rock material is decomposed and/or disintegrated to a soil. Fresh or discoloured rock is resent either as a discontinuous framework or as corestones.	IV
Completely weathered	All rock material is decomposed and/or disintegrated to soil. The original mass structure is still largely intact.	V
Residual soil	All rock material is converted to soil. The mass structure and material fabric are destroyed. There is a large change in volume, but the soil has not been significantly transported.	VI

of rock materials. BS 5930: 1981 includes the state of weathering within its rock description scheme based on the classification given in the Geological Society working party report (1977) (Table 6.4). In practice it has been found that materials in grades IA and IB are generally satisfactory as aggregates, while those classed as Grade III or higher are usually unsuitable. Thus Grade II weathering forms the transition zone within which materials may or may not perform satisfactorily when used as aggregates. Within this grade then, it is essential to carry out more thorough testing to assess the soundness, or otherwise, of the material in relation to the proposed use (see Chapter 7). Grade II can be further subdivided, but this can best be done specifically for particular rock types.

The influence of rock weathering on aggregate properties has been described by Fookes *et al.* (1971) and Fookes (1980).

The above weathering classification is most readily applied to igneous and metamorphic rocks, but not always so easily applied to sedimentary rocks. Limestones in particular do not normally undergo a progressive disintegration or decomposition to a soil, but are subject to chemical solution of the carbonate leaving an insoluble residue. Special classification schemes may need to be established to suit particular rock types and also particular climatic and hence weathering regimes.

Weinert (1964, 1974) has studied the performance of basic igneous rocks in southern Africa for road construction. He found performance to be related to the degree of alteration (the secondary mineral content) and climatic environment (for which he developed a climatic index). This classification has been further extended to include mechanical properties of the aggregate and of particular use has been the ratio of the 10% fines value in a dry and saturated condition. This ratio typically shows a good correlation with mass weathering grade and the percentage of secondary minerals.

Weinert's work has relevance to basic igneous rocks in temperate climates as well. In the UK basalts and dolerites are commonly used as crushed rock aggregate, but have a reputation for high drying shrinkage in concrete. This drying shrinkage can be shown to be related to the degree of weathering and alteration of the rock as determined by the visual mass weathering grade and percentage of secondary minerals.

The visual weathering grades described above have been developed primarily for the description of rock masses, but can be applied to drilled core. They are not appropriately applied to processed aggregate, yet it is important that the degree of weathering and alteration of a processed aggregate is determined. This is where Weinert's approach of determining the percentage of secondary minerals by petrographic examination can be used. Work on petrographic weathering indices and their relevance to engineering properties has also been carried out by Irfan & Dearman (1978) in relation to granites.

6.2.4. Classification schemes based on specific properties

Some of the classification schemes previously described have included specific properties such as compressive strength and weathering grade, in addition to the basic petrological characteristics of the rock. Ramsey *et al.* (1974) have prepared a classification of crushed rock aggregate based on mechanical factors which is independent of petrological boundaries. The factors used are those of particle shape and impact strength, which are quantified in the form of the flakiness index and aggregate impact value respectively. The system being based on strength and shape criteria, is limited in that it makes no provision for the assessment of other engineering properties of materials, such as the polishing potential and abrasion resistance which can, in some instances, be critical in relation to their use and performance in-service.

Attention should also be drawn to some important work, developed by Leverett (1970) from Duncan (1969), which investigated the significance of the aggregate index properties of porosity, saturation moisture content and specific gravity, in relation to the engineering characteristics of the aggregate as measured by standard laboratory tests. Although these properties cannot be used to predict particular aggregate characteristics with any great accuracy, there is no doubt that some valuable general assessments can be made and the results obtained appear to justify further work in this area.

The ratio of dry/wet 10% fines value (§7.2.3) has proved successful in evaluating the performance of basic igneous rocks but it must be emphasized that the classification is relevant to a particular type of rock, being used for a specific purpose under defined climatic conditions. This is true of many attempts to use specific physical or mechanical characteristics to classify a rock. It must be recognized that a general classification for suitability based on one or more selected physical or mechanical properties is not feasible and if specific properties are to be used to classify an aggregate they must clearly relate to the purpose for which that aggregate is intended. Also, a particular property measured by a particular test may only be relevant to a particular rock type. Therefore, while such a test may be applied routinely without the need for a petrological description of the rock, the petrological character must have been established in the first instance.

6.2.5. The use of local and traditional terms

Due to the complexity of the normal geological classification systems, local and traditional names were, and often still are, commonly used to describe the materials from which aggregates are commercially produced. In some instances the names are used to describe rocks which are vastly different from those suggested by the more usual scientific meaning of such terms. Thus, the term 'granite' is commonly used to describe a 'hard' rock and even some sedimentary rocks like greywackes and gritstones have been referred to by this name. Similarly, the term 'whinstone' may be used to describe dolerites, greywackes or other compact rocks, while 'marble' is loosely used to describe many compact limestones and other rock types which have not been metamorphosed.

Table 6.5, which shows some typical traditional rock names together with their petrological names or types, illustrates some of these anomalies.

TABLE 6.5. *Some traditional names used to describe rock materials*

Traditional name	Petrological name or type
Clinkstone	Phonolite
Cornstone	Impure limestone
Elvan (Blue elvan)	Quartz porphyry
Flagstone	Micaceous sandstone
Freestone	Sandstone or limestone
Greenstone	General term for quarried materials but often igneous in origin
Hassock	Sand
Hoggin	Sandy, clayey gravel
Hornstone	Chert and silicified tuffs
Pennant	Sandstone sub-greywacke
Rag (stone)	Calcareous sandstone
Thomas ballast	Gravel
Toadstone	Altered dolerite and decomposed tuffs
Trap (rock)	Igneous intrusive or lava
Whin (stone)	Igneous intrusive
Grey Whin	Moine siliceous granulite

6.3. Basic considerations on the description and classification of aggregates

6.3.1. The purpose and requirements of a classification scheme for aggregates

The purpose of any classification is to assign to a class things sharing a similar characteristic. Most classifications contain several levels. In the case of the classical geological classifications described in §6.2.1 the first level is the mode of formation of the rock. This is followed by successive levels based on petrological characteristics of composition and texture. Where the rock material is intended for an engineering purpose it has been shown (§6.2.2) how this basic geological classification can be combined with a classification of specific physical and mechanical characteristics to provide information relating to its performance in use.

In the case of aggregates, the purpose of a classification must be to group together materials which show a characteristic or characteristics relevant to their use as aggregate.

In order to achieve this purpose and be of practical use from a technical, commercial and contractual point of view, the classification must satisfy the following basic requirements:

(i) be simple in concept;
(ii) classify materials on the basis of characteristics that are relevant to their use as aggregates;
(iii) use terms which can be precisely defined and are usable to contract specifications;
(iv) avoid groupings which may unintentionally infer common properties which do not exist in reality;
(v) be applicable to all types of aggregates, including both monomictic and polymictic materials;
(vi) be capable of expansion, as necessary, by the use of supplementary information relating to a particular material or its intended use.

A classification and descriptive scheme for aggregates should contain the following three essential elements:

(i) a description of the aggregate type;
(ii) a description of physical characteristics;
(iii) a petrological classification.

To these can be added further information such as a detailed petrological description and the results of standard tests.

6.3.2. Aggregate type

The aggregate should be described as follows:

(i) whether natural or artificial;
(ii) if natural, whether crushed rock, gravel or sand;
(iii) if a gravel or sand, whether uncrushed, partly crushed or crushed;
(iv) if a gravel or sand, whether land won or marine.

6.3.3. Descripton of physical characteristics

There are certain fundamental physical characteristics of aggregates which are relevant to all uses and which are an important part of any aggregate description. These are:

(i) nominal size
(ii) particle shape
(iii) particle surface texture
(iv) colour
(v) cleanliness: presence of dust, silt or clay.
(vi) presence of surface coatings, encrustations or obviously extraneous material.

The above characteristics should be described using simple, clearly defined terms and the description may be accompanied by relevant quantitative test data as appropriate, for example the particle size distribution, 'fines' content and shape indices.

6.3.4. Petrological classification

It is arguable that to use any natural rock material for an engineering purpose without a knowledge of the rock type is to take the same risk of unforeseen problems which can arise where any unknown material is used in construction. It is equally true, however, that a knowledge of the rock type, or types, within an aggregate cannot in itself be used to judge the suitability of that aggregate for its intended purpose. The inclusion of an accurate petrological name in the description of an aggregate serves two principal functions.

(i) specifications sometimes require or prohibit the use of particular rock types, so that from a contractual position a knowledge of the petrological composition of the aggregate may be essential.

(ii) An accurate petrological classification conveys certain basic information about the characteristics of the aggregate in terms of likely mineralogical composition, grain size and texture. This can be an aid in decision making, such as in selecting the most suitable testing regime to assess the suitability of the aggregate. By way of example, if an aggregate proposed for use in concrete was described as dolerite subsequent testing would be likely to include an assessment of the drying shrinkage of the aggregate, whereas for another aggregate type, say a flint gravel, this may be considered unnecessary.

The amount of information regarding possible aggregate performance which can be safely drawn from a simple petrological name is naturally very limited. However, to be able to provide an accurate petrological classification, a relatively detailed petrographic examination is required by a suitably qualified geologist/petrologist. A detailed petrographic description of the aggregate, prepared by a petrologist experienced in aggregate technology can provide additional very useful information on the likely performance of the aggregate. Particular uses include:

(i) an aid in developing appropriate testing regimes;
(ii) assistance in the interpretation of other test results;
(iii) assessment of aggregate performance where there is no standard or reliable performance test;
(iv) detection of potentially deleterious substances, the more common including:*
    (a) porous and frost susceptible particles;
    (b) weak or soft particles, or coatings;
    (c) rock types susceptible to shrinkage and swelling;
    (d) certain occurrences of salts and other soluble minerals;
    (e) forms of silica or carbonate which may be alkali-reactive in concrete;

* Some of these are only deleterious in certain applications or, under certain conditions or at certain concentrations.

(f) coal, lignite and other organic matter;
(g) iron pyrites and other metallic contaminants;
(h) mica;
(i) shells.

For further details on potentially deleterious substances reference should be made to the respective chapters dealing with particular aggregate uses.

A detailed petrographic examination is particularly important where a new aggregate source is being developed, especially if the materials are of marginal quality. This is recognized by the CIRIA guide to concrete construction in the Gulf region (1984) which states that 'The petrological examination of the constituents of the aggregate particles is an essential preliminary to their use in any region where the quality of the aggregates is unknown.'

It is important to recognize that the petrographic examination should not be used to replace standard tests but as a complement to them. Where relevant, inferences on likely performance drawn from the petrogaphic description should be confirmed by appropriate tests.

6.3.5. Test data

The results of physical, mechanical, chemical or durability tests should be added to the aggregate description as appropriate.

6.4. Classification schemes for aggregates

6.4.1. Historical developments within The United Kingdom

In 1913 the British Standards Institution introduced a list of petrographically named rock types, assembled in groups known as 'Trade Groups', in order to meet the need for a classification of roadstones suitable for engineering purposes. When first published in BS 63, the list was based on the following twelve groups:

Andesite	Gabbro	Limestone
Artificial	Granite	Porphyry
Basalt	Gritstone	Quartzite
Flint	Hornfels	Schist

The number of groups was later reduced to eleven by incorporating Andesite into the Basalt group (BS 812: 1943). Phemister *et al.* (1946) commented that the list 'had been compiled with a view to associating in the same trade group, rocks which may be expected to behave similarly as roadstone'. However, the range of properties of any one group (and even of any one rock type) of aggregate is so large as to make nonsense of any expectation that they will perform in a similar manner either in tests or in service.

Subsequently the British Standards Institution dropped the word 'Trade', firstly suggesting that aggregate materials be given a 'Group Classification' (BS 812: 1967) and then a 'Petrological Group Classification' (BS 812:1975). Apart from very minor variations within the groups, the system remained unchanged. Table 6.8 is an extract from BS 812:1975 and shows the main rock types in common use within the designated groups.

The 'Group Classification' approach illustrates some of the pitfalls of attempting a simplified classification based on petrological terms and these are worthy of consideration by way of example. The main criticisms are as follows.

(i) It is a quasi-petrological classification in that it groups together those rocks which do not necessarily have a clear petrological relationship, yet from these groupings an assumed similarity of engineering characteristics may be and often is inferred; although, as is noted in BS 812:1975, the group names in fact give no reliable guide as to the engineering characteristics of the included rock aggregates.

(ii) The use of precise geological terms as group names is misleading and can lead to unnecessary contractual disputes.

(iii) The mixture of terms within groups as employed in the classification is confusing and thereby open to misinterpretation by supplier and consumer alike. Again, this can lead to contractual problems.

(iv) The system is unnecessarily biased towards igneous and away from carbonate rocks which provide a high proportion of crushed rock output in the United Kingdom. Thus it gives 42 descriptions of igneous and metamorphic rock aggregates which provide about 25% of the UK production of crushed rock aggregate, as compared with three descriptions for limestones and the like which account for about 65%.

(v) The system omits to classify sands and gravels although the consumption of these materials is generally of the same order as that of crushed rock aggregates.

The 'Group Classification' was withdrawn from BS 812 in 1976 and, although no longer included in BS 63 :1987, it persists in BS 594 : Part 1 : 1985 in specifications for coarse aggregate for hot rolled asphalt.

The disadvantages of the 'Group Classification' had been pointed out as long ago as 1935 by Knight and Knight. In relation to roadstones they stated that 'it is not necessary for the road engineer to be familiar with the very large number of rock types recognized by petrologists, but he can decide the suitability of a stone for a particular purpose when he knows its essential features, although he may not be able to give it a specific name. Thus the engineer requires to know what is the approximate class of the stone, what is its mineralogical composition, how fresh it is, whether it is weakened or strengthened by its geological history, and so forth'.

They were of the opinion that a classification based only on mineralogical constitution, structure and geological history was more likely to be appropriate and suggested the general classification of roadstones based on petrology shown in Table 6.6, with the intent that any stone so classified would also be accorded supplementary information of the type noted above.

TABLE 6.6. *Suggested "Classification of Roadstones" according to petrological characters (after Knight & Knight 1935)*

ROCKS		
Igneous	*Sedimentary*	*Metamorphic*
Plutonic	*Calcareous*	
Granite	Limestone	Gneiss
Granodiorite	Domomite	Epidiorite
Diorite	Ironstone	Hornfels
Syenite		Hornstone
Gabbro		Mylonite
Norite		Phyllite
	Arenaceous	Slate
		Schist
	Arkose	Hornblende
	Conglomerate	schist
Hypabyssal	Greywacke	Marble
Aplite	Grit	Quartzite
Granulite	Sandstone	
Pegmatite	Quartzite	
Diabase	Breccia	
Dolerite	Flint	
Lamprophyre	Chert	
Teschenite		
Felsite		
Granophyre		
Keratophyre	*Argillaceous*	
Microgranite		
Porphyry	Shale	
Porphyrite	Mudstone	
Volcanic		
	ARTIFICIAL AGGREGATES	
Basalt		
Spilite		
Rhyolite		
Trachyte	Slag	
Andesite	Clinker	
Dacite		
Greenstone		
Tuff		

Lees (1968) proposed a similar petrological classification system to that of Knight and Knight in which an indication of the mineral grain size is included, as is shown in Table 6.7. Lees also intended that this classifi-

TABLE 6.7. *Suggested "Classification of Roadstones" according to petrological characteristics (after Lees 1968)*

ROCKS

	Igneous		Sedimentary		Metamorphic
Ic	Coarse Granite Syenite Diorite Gabbro	Sc	Coarse Conglomerate Breccia Gravel Scree	Mc	Coarse Gneiss
Im	Medium Microgranite Microsyenite Microdiorite Dolerite	Sm	Medium Sandstone Sand	Mm	Medium Quartzite
If	Fine Rhyolite Trachyte Andesite Basalt	Sf	Fine Shale Mudstone Clay	Mf	Fine Schist Slate Hornfele
		Sca	Calcareous Limestone Dolomite		

ARTIFICIAL MATERIALS

Slag
Calcined bauxite
Calcined flint
Crushed Brick
Pulverized Fuel Ash
Synopal

TABLE 6.8. *Group classification of aggregates from BS 812: Part 1: 1975*

1. *Artificial group*
   crushed brick
   slags
   calcined bauxite
   synthetic aggregates
2. *Basalt group*
   andesite
   basalt
   basic porphyrite
   diabase
   dolerites of all kinds
      including theralite
      and teschenite
   epidiorite
   lamprophyre
   quartz-dolerite
   spilite
3. *Flint group*
   chert
   flint
4. *Gabbro group*
   basic diorite
   basic gneiss
   gabbro
   hornblende-rock
   norite
   peridotite
   picrite
   serpentinite
5. *Granite group*
   gneiss
   granite
   granodiorite
   granulite
   pegmatite
   quartz-diorite
   syenite
6. *Gritstone group*
   (including fragmental
      volcanic rocks)
   arkose
   greywacke
   grit
   sandstone
   tuff
7. *Hornfels group*
   contact-altered
      rocks of all kinds
      except marble
8. *Limestone group*
   dolomite
   limestone
   marble
9. *Porphyry group*
   aplite
   dacite
   felsite
   granophyre
   keratophyre
   microgranite
   porphyry
   quartz-porphyrite
   rhyolite
   trachyte
10. *Quartzite group*
    ganister
    quartzitic sandstones
    recrystallized
       quartzite
11. *Schist group*
    phyllite
    schist
    slate
    all severely sheared
       rocks

cation should be augmented by further information of the type indicated by Knight and Knight. The classifications of Knight & Knight (1935) and Lees (1968) were both based on a classical geological approach. An alternative system using five Classes based on the predominant mineral content of the aggregate was proposed in the first edition of this book (1985). The system referred to as the 'Classification And Description of Aggregate Material' or CADAM attempted to provide a simple classification scheme which was independent of physical properties, except for those which could be inferred from mineral composition. The use of a correct petrological name for the aggregate was encouraged in a supportive role to the Class name. Additional information on the geological age, colour, grain size and fissility of the aggregate could be included. The CADAM scheme is shown on Tables 6.9 and 6.10.

The CADAM system has not been adopted in practice and while this in part reflects a reluctance by the industry to use a scheme which is at variance to current British Standards, it also reflects technical criticisms. The CADAM system set out to avoid the inferred similarity

of properties of the 'Group Classification'. However, it failed in this objective as there was an inevitable assumption that aggregates classified within one of the five simplified Classes would have similar characteristics. The mixture of terms used for the five Classes was also unsatisfactory.

6.4.2. Current British Standards

The 'Group Classification' was withdrawn from BS 812 in 1976. The current version of BS 812: Part 102: 1989 refers to the 'nominal description' of the aggregate which should include the following information.

(a) Type. Use one of the following terms:

   (1) 'crushed rock';
   (2) 'sand' or 'gravel'. In this case record if the aggregate is crushed or partially crushed and,

TABLE 6.9. *The classification and description of aggregate material—CADAM*

		Crushed Rock					Gravel	Sand
				Silicate Class (d)			Natural, Crushed, Mixed	Natural, Crushed Rock, Mixed
1	Form of Aggregate (a)	Carbonate Class (b)	Quartz Class (c)	Igneous	Sediment	Metamorphic		
2	Class			Miscellaneous Materials (e)			Class of major constituents, as for crushed rock aggregates, with petrol. name (if known). Description of minor constituents, e.g. mica, shell fragments, etc. (Mainly applicable to natural sands) (f)	
				Petrological Name (if known)				
3(l)	Geological Ass (g)	Essential for Sedimentary Rock Materials	—	—	Essential	—	Geological Age of deposit, if other than Quaternary (h)	
	Colour (i)	Optional	Optional	Essential	Optional	Essential	Description of major constituent(s) as for crushed rock aggregates	
	Component (j) Grain Size	Optional	Optional	Essential	Optional	Essential		
	Foliation (k)	If applicable	If applicable	—	If applicable	Essential		
4	Other (m) Comment	Any further information likely to be of help in assessing the material e.g. for a Gravel–Glacial deposit.						

Notes:

(a) Indicates the nature of the aggregate material being considered. In the case of Gravel and/or Sand an indication of whether the material is Land-won or Marine-dredged should be included.

(b) Includes ALL materials composed predominantly of Calcium and/or Calcium Magnesium Carbonate, irrespective of origin.

(c) Comprises ALL materials in which Quartz or Free Silica is the dominant mineral, and includes materials such as Flint, Vein Quartz, Quartzites, many Sandstones and Gritstones, some Greywackes and the like.

(d) Comprises ALL materials in which the rock forming silicates are the dominant minerals. These are subdivided according to origin into Igneous, Metamorphic and Sedimentary in order to differentiate between those containing mainly high temperature silicates and those containing a high proportion of clay mineral silicates.

(e) Materials not covered by (a), (b) and (d) above are NOT allocated a Class but the correct scientific name for the material MUST be recorded.

(f) In the case of Gravel and particularly in the case of Sand, the presence of certain materials, even in small quantities, can be important. Note should be made of the occurrence of such materials.

(g) The Geological Age scale to be used in the U.K. is as follows:— Quaternary (to include Pleistocene and Holocene), Tertiary, Cretaceous, Jurassic, Triassic, Permian, Carboniferous, Devonian, Silurian, Cambrian and Precambrian. Where alternative or different age terms are applicable in countries outside the U.K. then these should be used as is appropriate.

(h) The majority of Sand and Gravel deposits worked in the U.K. are of Quaternary age and unconsolidated. The older the deposit the more likely it is to be consolidated.

(i) Colour descriptions should be to a common standard. Reference is made to the Munsell Colour Chart system. (Geological Society of America, 1963), which is useful for both field and laboratory assessments. Should a more accurate colour description be required then this should be carried out under laboratory conditions and it is suggested that the Lovibond–Schofield Tintometer or similar method be used (Hosking and Ritson, 1968). Normally however, such a detailed description would not be included in the CADAM.

(j) A standard Component Grain Size notation should be used. Grain greater than about 2 mm nominal diameter are termed Coarse; those which are less than 2 mm, but which can still be distinguished with the unaided eye, are termed Medium; and those which cannot be distinguished with the unaided eye are termed Fine. The component grain size is applied to the matrix.

(k) Foliation and fissility are particularly important with respect to certain Metamorphic and certain Sedimentary rock materials. Evidence of its occurrence should be recorded as is appropriate.

(l) Entries to be made with respect to Geological Age/Colour/Component Grain Size/Foliation for the different Classes are indicated in the above table as Essential, Optional or Not Applicable.

(m) Additional comments should only be added when that information is likely to be of help in assessing the material and is not to be included in any subsequent more detailed description of the material.

TABLE 6.10. *Suggested form for use of the CADAM system*

AGGREGATE FORM	Crushed Rock		Gravel	Natural / Crushed / Mixed		Sand	Natural / Crushed / Mixed		Land-won / Marine Dredged	
CLASS (or MISCELLANEOUS)	Carbonate Class		Quartz Class		Silicate Class				Miscellaneous Material. (Correct name to be given below).	
				Igneous		Sedimentary		Metamorphic		
Petrological name (if known)										
GEOLOGICAL AGE/ COLOUR/ GRAIN SIZE/ FISSILITY										
Comment (if any)										

Compiled by: _____ Date: _____

CADAM — CLASSIFICATION and DESCRIPTION of AGGREGATE MATERIAL

LOCATION AND SAMPLE DETAILS	Quarry/Pit address: _____ Operator: _____ Sample: Type _____ Size _____ Preparation _____ Supplied by _____	Grid Ref.	Date Rec'd
		Date of sampling	Sampling Cert.No.

when known, if it has been obtained by inland or marine working:

(3) 'artificial'. In this case record if the artificial aggregate is slag, synthetic or broken rubble, etc.

(b) Nominal size
(c) Other. Reference shall be made to the presence of any obvious extraneous pieces in the sample such as clay lumps, organic material, etc.

When it is necessary to describe the aggregate in more detail the Standard requires that an appropriate petrological name is used, preferably taken from the list of terms and definitions given in Table 2 of Appendix A. (Appendix A of BS 812 : Part 102 : 1989 has been reproduced in Appendix A6.1.) In the case of sedimentary rocks the geological age should also be given. In the case of mixed gravels, the aggregate should be described by combining appropriate terms e.g. flint/quartzite.

BS 812: Part 102: 1989 makes two notes. Firstly, that the petrological description 'should be provided by a competent person or authority'. Secondly, that the 'petrological description does not take account of suitability for any particular purpose, which should be determined in accordance with the appropriate British Standards.'

Although the term petrological description is used, the Standard is actually referring to a simple petrological classification and a detailed petrological description is not included. In practice, however, it will frequently be necessary to undertake a reasonably detailed petrological description in order to assign the aggregate an appropriate petrological name. No guidance on undertaking this examination is given, although a draft method is under consideration for publication as BS 812: Part 104.

6.4.3. American Standards

American Standards covering the specification of aggregates for concrete (ASTM C33-86) and roadstone (ASTM D692-88, ASTM D693-84) contain no mandatory requirements regarding the classification of the aggregates. However, ASTM C294-86 provides standard descriptive nomenclature for natural aggregates and ASTM C295-85 describes the standard practice for the petrographic examination of aggregates for concrete.

The American approach is, therefore, broadly similar to that in BS 812: Part 102: 1985 in classifying aggregates by an appropriate petrological name and encouraging the use of a simple standard rock name. A detailed petrographic examination is not mandatory, but is recognized in ASTM C294-86 as being necessary in many cases. Details of the recommended practice for the petrographic examination of aggregates (ASTM C295-85) are described in §6.5.2.

6.4.4. Europe

For most European countries the respective standards for aggregates do not contain a mandatory requirement regarding classification.

France is an exception and French standard NF P18-101(1983) covers the 'vocabulary, definitions and classification' of aggregates. The classification is based on the following.

(i) Particle size
(ii) Density: lightweight < 2 g/cm^3
          normal   2–3 g/cm^3
          heavyweight > 3 g/cm^3
(iii) Origin: natural
          artificial
(iv) Mode of preparation.

French standard NF P18-301 (1983) on natural aggregates for hydraulic concrete makes reference to certain rocks being susceptible to alkali-aggregate reaction. In the absence of a history of use an assessment should be made by a specialist laboratory and reference is made to the petrographic examination of the aggregate in accordance with P18-557 (1980). This document covers the identification of the aggregate on the basis of:

(i) mineralogical composition;
(ii) degree of alteration (methylene blue test—NF P85-592);
(iii) structure;
(iv) relative density and porosity;
(v) index of continuity (NF P18-556).

The standard contains a table of rock families and specific rock names. A rock is classified firstly by its family name and then by its specific name in parentheses, e.g.

    Granite 'granodiorite'
    Sedimentary carbonate 'dolomite'
    Massive metamorphic rock 'gneiss'.

The index of continuity (NF P18-566) is the measured pulse velocity of the rock expressed as a percentage of the theoretical pulse velocity (calculated using the mineralogical composition and standard values of pulse velocity for the minerals).

6.4.5. Southern Africa

Weinert (1980) has proposed a classification of rocks for use in road construction in this region which divides naturally occurring materials into nine groups. The groups are intended to be based essentially on the presence or absence of the mineral quartz, although the mode of formation is also included to some extent. The presence or otherwise of quartz is used to infer the mode of weathering, the durability and the possible suitability of the material for certain road construction purposes. The nine groups employed, together with their best known members, are:

acid crystalline rocks:	granite (but also syenite)
basic crystalline rocks:	dolerite
high-silica rocks:	quartzite (but also hornfels)
arenaceous rocks:	sandstone (but also mica schist)
argillaceous rocks:	shale (but also phyllite)
carbonate rocks:	dolomite
diamictites:	tillite
metalliferous rocks:	ironstone
pedogenic materials:	calcrete and ferricrete

Although the classification proposed by Weinert (1980) is said to be based on the presence or absence of quartz it also introduced the mode of formation into the system in some cases. In consequence mixed terms are used for group names, giving a lack of consistency. For example, some sandstones which would come within the arenaceous group, are likely to contain as much if not more quartz as certain quartzites and hornfels which are grouped as high-silica. Similarly the mineral composition, including the quartz present, of some mica schists is likely to be very similar to that of certain acid crystalline rocks. The group names Diamictites and Pedogenic material are concerned almost exclusively with mode of formation and, in consequence, will cover a wide range of possible mineral content with a wide variety of probable engineering performance characteristics, when embracing materials available world-wide.

6.4.6. Recommended approach

The purpose and requirements of a classification scheme for aggregates have been discussed in §6.3. The three essential elements of a classification are seen as:

(i) a description of the aggregate type;
(ii) a description of physical characteristics;
(iii) a petrological classification.

To this may be added as required a detailed petrological description and the results of standard tests.

TABLE 6.11. *Example of a possible format for reporting the classification and description of an aggregate in accordance with the approach recommended in §6.4.6.*

CLASSIFICATION AND DESCRIPTION OF AGGREGATE					
1.	**AGGREGATE TYPE**				
1.1	Crushed Rock				
1.2	Gravel		Uncrushed		Land Won	
1.3	Sand		Partly Crushed		Marine	
			Crushed			
2.	**PHYSICAL CHARACTERISTICS**				
2.1	Nominal Size				
2.2	Shape				
2.3	Surface Texture				
2.4	Colour (sample condition)				
2.5	Presence of Fines				
2.6	Presence of Coatings				
2.7	Extraneous Material				
3.	**PETROLOGICAL CLASSIFICATION**				
3.1	Monomictic		Polymictic			
3.2	Petrological Name					
			Visual Assessment		Quantitative Analysis	
3.3	Geological Age				
4.	**PETROLOGICAL DESCRIPTION**				
5.	**SAMPLE REF.**		**6.**	**CERTIFICATE OF SAMPLING**	
7.	**SOURCE**				

Attempts at petrological classifications based on simplified groupings such as the BS 812 'Group Classification' and CADAM have not been successful as, whilst not intended, it has been inferred that rock types within the individual groups or classes have similar properties. A preferred solution is to use an accurate petrological name for the constituents of the aggregate, which should be as simple as possible.

The petrological classification should be based on accepted classical geological schemes as appropriate. For sedimentary rocks the geological age should also be given. It is considered desirable that the simple petrological name is accompanied by a detailed petrological description and, within this description, a more detailed classification may be used where appropriate to facilitate petrological comparisons. For example, an igneous rock may be simply classified as *granite*, but the detailed classification could be Adamellite. A sedimentary rock may be given the simple classification Jurassic *limestone*, but the detailed classification could be Biopelsparite.

Where there is not a single accepted petrological classification scheme, for example with Limestone where there are several classical schemes and also modified engineering based schemes (§6.2.3), reference should be made to the scheme used. This is unlikely to affect the simple classification.

Table 6.11 lists the various elements which should be included in the classification and description of an aggregate and serves as an example of a possible format for reporting the information. The proposed scheme attempts to formalize the classification and description of an aggregate while permitting flexibility in the detail of the information depending on the circumstances. As a minimum requirement it is considered that a response should be given to all of the items in Table 6.11. In its most simple form the responses may be based purely on visual assessment, for example the shape may be described by reference to standard terms such as angular and flaky. Where appropriate this could be amplified by the use of a shape index such as the flakiness index. Similarly for petrological composition, in its most basic form this would consist of the simple petrological name with a visual estimate of proportions of the different rock/mineral types, in the case of a polymictic aggregate. Where required this could be supported by a detailed petrographic description with a quantitative analysis of the composition.

When the classification and description is based purely on a visual assessment it is essential that the terms used are consistent. Guidance on this is given below for the specific items in Table 6.11, and reference has generally been made to British Standards where these exist. These can, of course, be changed to CEN standards as they become available or to other national standards as appropriate. It is important that reference is made to the descriptive scheme used.

The proposed classification and descriptive scheme is intended for use with processed aggregates, but with minor modification can be applied to unprocessed gravel, sand or rock samples, as the three essential elements remain the same.

The approach recommended in Table 6.11 complies with the requirements of BS 812: Part 102: 1989, but increases the amount of information which should ideally be presented.

The specific items in the proposed scheme are described below.

(1) *Aggregate type*
The type of the aggregate should be indicated by ticking the appropriate boxes.

(2) *Physical characteristics*
(2.1) Nominal size
The description of nominal size would be based on a visual examination, but this should always be confirmed by a particle size distribution analysis (BS 812: Section 103.1: 1985).

(2.2) Shape
The shape should be described in accordance with BS 812: Part 102: 1989: Appendix C, Table 3) (See Table 6.12). Where relevant this should be quantified by use of a shape index, such as the flakiness index (BS 812: Section 105.1: 1989) and elongation index (BS 812: Section 105.2).

(2.3) Surface texture
The surface texture of the aggregate particles should be

described in accordance with BS 812: Part 102: 1989: Appendix C, Table 4 (See Table 6.13).

TABLE 6.12. *Description of particle shape (from BS 812: Part 102: 1989)*

Classification	Description
Rounded	Fully water-worn or completely shaped by attrition
Irregular	Naturally irregular, or partly shaped by attrition and having rounded edges
Angular	Possessing well defined edges formed at the intersection of roughly planar faces
Flaky	Having one dimension significantly smaller than the other two dimensions
Elongated	Having one dimension significantly larger than the other two dimensions
Flaky and elongated	Having three significantly different dimensions, i.e. length significantly larger than width and width significantly larger than thickness

TABLE 6.13. *Description of surface texture (from BS 812: Part 102: 1989)*

Surface texture	Characteristics
Glassy	Conchoidal (i.e. curved) fracture
Smooth	Water-worn or smooth due to fracture of laminated or very finely grained rock
Granular	Fracture showing more or less uniform size rounded grains
Rough	Fracture of fine or medium grained rock containing no easily visible crystalline constituents
Crystalline	Containing easily visible crystalline constituents
Honeycombed	With visible pores and cavities

(2.4) Colour
The colour of the aggregate can be affected by its moisture content and the quantity of adhering fines. It can vary between an "as-received" sample and a prepared sub-sample especially if the fines have been removed. This may be important for architectural work and the condition of the aggregate should be recorded. For normal purposes it is suggested that the scheme recommended for rock and soil description in BS 5930: 1981 is used e.g. dark greenish grey, light yellowish brown, etc. When it is necessary to quantify the colour it

TABLE 6.14. *Minimum size of sample for despatch to laboratory for petrographic examination (from BS 812: Part 104: Draft)*

Nominal size of aggregate (mm)	Minimum number of sampling increments		Minimum mass to be received in the laboratory (kg)
	Large scoop	Small scoop	
40	80	—	200
20	20	—	50
10	10	—	25
5 or smaller	10 half scoops	10	10

is suggested that the Munsell system is used (Geological Society of America 1963).

(2.5) Presence of fines

Reference should be made to the presence of silt, clay and dust, and whether they appear excessive. It is not possible to distinguish these by visual examination alone and only a very approximate assessment of the proportion can be made. This should always be checked by appropriate testing. (BS 812: Section 103.1:1985 and BS 812: Section 103.2:1989).

(2.6) Presence of coatings

This would include adhering coatings of clay or dust and encrustations of salts, carbonates or marine growth.

(2.7) Extraneous material

This would include obvious contamination, such as clay lumps, organic matter, brick fragments etc.

(3) *Petrological composition*

(3.1) Monomictic or polymictic

Monomictic: Aggregates essentially comprising particles of one rock or mineral type

Polymictic: Aggregates comprising particles of many different rock or mineral types.

(3.2) Petrological name

The most simple accurate petrological name should be used. For polymictic aggregates each rock or mineral type should be listed and the proportion given. It should be stated whether this is based on a visual estimate or quantitative petrographic examination.

(3.3) Geological age

This should be given for sedimentary rocks.

(4) *Petrological description*

It should be indicated whether a detailed petrographic examination has been carried out and where this is the case, the full petrographic report should be provided.

(5) *Sample reference*

This sample reference should be given.

(6) *Certificate of sampling*

A certificate of sampling should be provided in accordance with BS 812: Part 102: 1989.

(7) *Source*

Information on the source of the aggregate should be provided as relevant.

Examples illustrating the use of the proposed scheme are given in Appendix A6.2.

6.5. The petrographic description of aggregates

6.5.1. General

The objectives of the petrographic description of an aggregate have been described in §6.3.2 and are three-fold:

(i) classification;
(ii) an aid in the assessment of aggregate performance;
(iii) detection of potentially deleterious constituents.

The science of petrography, the systematic description of rock, dates back to the mid-19th century. The applications of petrography to the study of aggregates for roadstone and concrete have been described in early work by Knight & Knight (1935), Rhoades & Mielenz (1946) and Mather & Mather (1950). In 1954, ASTM C295 was published on the 'standard practice for petrographic examination of aggregates for concrete'. There has been no British Standard for the petrographic examination of aggregates, although a draft method is under consideration for publication as BS 812: Part 104.

6.5.2. ASTM C295

ASTM C295-85 outlines procedures for the petrographic examination of materials proposed for use as aggregate, including both unprocessed and processed materials. The Standard states that 'the specific procedures employed in the petrographic examination of any sample will depend to a large extent on the purpose of the examination and the nature of the sample'. It therefore permits the petrographer flexibility while providing guidance on procedures for the examination.

The minimum size of the sample for a processed aggregate, irrespective of particle size is specified as 45 kg or 300 pieces, whichever is bigger. The guidance given for processed coarse aggregates is to examine separately the individual sieve fractions of the aggregate and determine the proportion of significant constituent particle types by particle counting. Particles should be discriminated on the basis of petrological composition, condition and presence of coatings. The examination is undertaken visually with more detailed methods such as thin section examination or X-ray diffraction analysis being applied as necessary.

For fine aggregates a quantitative examination is undertaken on each sieve fraction. For fractions over 600 μm the examination is undertaken under a stereoscopic microscope by particle counting. For sizes below 600 μm the reduced sieve fractions are mounted on a glass slide in immersion oil and examined under a petrological microscope. Grain counting is undertaken using a mechanical stage. Where identification is difficult additional methods may be employed. In practice separate examination of all the individual size fractions of the fine aggregate is typically unnecessary. It has also been found that for most aggregates and for most purposes the procedure recommended for the examination of the fine aggregate does not permit adequate identification and thin section examination is invariably required.

6.5.3. Draft BS 812: Part 104

A method for the petrographic examination of aggregates is currently being developed for inclusion in BS 812 as Part 104. The prime use of the method is for the examination of processed aggregates.

The method is under development and subject to precision testing trials. The draft procedures described below may change in the final standard. The minimum size of sample for dispatch to the laboratory is shown on Table 6.14.

All aggregates (coarse, fine and all-in) are subjected to an initial qualitative examination to determine the aggregate type and its general characteristics. The sample is then reduced to a representative test portion for quantitative examination. The minimum mass of this test portion should be as shown in Table 6.15. The quantities given have been calculated to achieve an accuracy of ±10% relative for a constituent present at 20%. A nomograph is given for determining the minimum test portion size required to achieve a ±10% relative error for constituents present at other concentrations (Fig 6.1).

For coarse aggregates the quantitative examination is undertaken on the separate sieve fractions as for ASTM C295, discriminating the particles visually on the basis of significant petrological composition and/or condition; weighing is used rather than particle counting. A more detailed examination may be carried out as necessary; in practice a thin section examination of selected particles of each significant type is normally required.

TABLE 6.15. *Minimum size of test portion for quantitative petrographic examination (from BS 812: Part 104, Draft)*

Nominal maximum particle size (mm)	Minimum mass of test portion
40	50 kg
20	6 kg
10	1 kg
5 or smaller	0.1 kg

For fine aggregate, the draft method requires the reduced test portion is split into two size fractions on a 1.18 m sieve. The coarser fraction retained on the 1.18 mm sieve is further divided into >5 mm, 5 mm to 2.36 mm and 2.36 mm to 1.18 mm fractions. The quantitative analysis of these individual size fractions is determined by visual hand sorting as for the coarse aggregate, a stereoscopic microscope being used to aid the identification of particles. It will generally be necessary to prepare a thin section of selected particles for detailed identification. This is undertaken by embedding the particles in a suitable resin.

For the fraction passing the 1.18 mm sieve the quantitative analysis is undertaken by embedding the material in resin and preparing a thin section for point count analysis under a petrological microscope.

The draft BS 812: Part 104 method can be adapted for the examination of unprocessed sand and gravel samples.

6.5.4. Rock samples

Guidance on the petrographic examination of rock cores and hand specimens is given in ASTM C295-85 and also by the International Society for Rock Mechanics (1981).

The first stage of the examination should consist of a visual description of the macroscopic features of the rock. In the case of rock cores this will entail the preparation of a detailed log and guidance on this is given in BS 5930: 1981 and the Geological Society Engineering Group Working Party Report (1970). Thin sections should be prepared from selected areas within the core or hand specimen giving due consideration to the variability of the rock and the orientation of features such as bedding or foliation. The thin section is examined under a petrological microscope, the detail of the

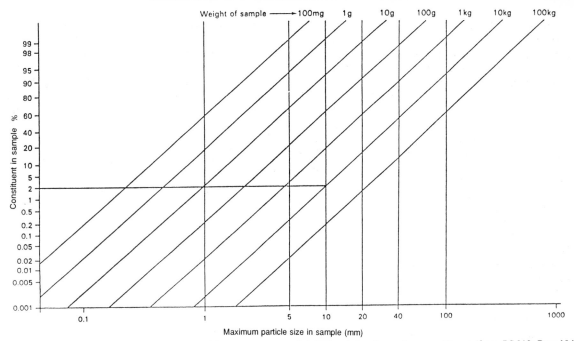

FIG. 6.1. *Mass of test portion necessary to achieve an accuracy of* ± 10% *relative for a given constituent (from BS 812: Part 104 Draft)*

TABLE 6.16. *Form for petrographic report on rock samples suggested by ISRM (1981)*

Project:	GEOLOGICAL DESCRIPTION	
Location:		PHOTO-MICROGRAPH
Co-ordinates:	Rock name.	OF TYPICAL FEATURES
Specimen N°: Collected by:	Petrographic classification:	OF THIN SECTION
Description of sampling point:		
Thin section N°: Date:	Geological formation.	

MACROSCOPIC DESCRIPTION OF SAMPLE

Degree of weathering:

Structure (incl. bedding):

Discontinuities:

RESULTS OF ROCK PROPERTY TESTS

Point load index: Porosity :... ....%

........MPa , wet/dry   Density : ....kg/m³

normal/parallel to foliation   Water absorption:

Any other results:

GENERAL REMARKS

QUALITATIVE   DESCRIPTION

Texture.

Fracturing:

Alteration:

Matrix:

MINERAL COMPOSITION (MODAL ANALYSIS)

MAJOR COMPONENTS	VOL %	MINOR COMPONENTS	VOL %	ACCESSORIES	VOL %

SIGNIFICANCE OF RESULTS FOR ROCK ENGINEERING	GRAIN SIZE & DISTRIBUTION	
	MICRONS	%

description reflecting the purpose of the investigation and the nature of the material.

The International Society for Rock Mechanics (1981) provided a suggested form for a petrographic report (Table 6.16). The suggested headings are helpful in standardizing the petrographic description, although the one-page format is rather restricted where a more detailed description is required.

The thin section examination may be supplemented by instrumental methods such as X-ray diffraction where very fine-grained constituents need to be identified.

6.5.5. Precision of quantitative methods

In undertaking a quantitative petrographic examination, soures of error include:

  (i) initial sampling;
  (ii) sample reduction;
  (iii) counting;
  (iv) misidentification.

The problems associated with the sampling of aggregates are described in §7.2 and are discussed further in relation to petrography in §6.5.6. The errors associated with sample reduction and counting can be calculated and it is intended that guidance will be given in the draft of BS 812: Part 104. The size of the error reflects the estimated proportion of the constituent of interest and the total quantity of particles examined.

These calculations do not, however, take account of any misidentification of constituents. Apparent inconsistencies in the identification of constituents sometimes reflect variations in terminology rather than misidentification, often resulting from use of unnecessarily complex petrological classifications. This indicates the desirability of using the most simple accurate petrological name that is practical.

6.5.6. Site inspectior. of aggregate sources

A single sample of aggregate submitted for a laboratory petrographic examination, or any other tests, cannot be expected to represent the full character and variability of the quarry or pit from which it was taken. Even regular sampling of the aggregate production could fail to detect a localized feature within the quarry which might have a significant effect on the quality or durability of the aggregate. One example of this is localized weathering which could significantly reduce the physical and mechanical properties of the aggregate and its durability. In the case of concrete aggregate there have been instances of undetected veins of opal resulting in damaging alkali–silica reaction in the Val de la Mare Dam in Jersey (Cole

& Horswill 1988) and the Kamburu Dam in Kenya (Sims & Evans 1988).

These problems highlight the importance of a geological inspection of the quarry or pit as part of the routine assessment of aggregate quality. This aspect of aggregate quality cntrol has been seriously neglected, yet a site inspection by a suitably qualified geologist is essential if a reasonable assessment of the variability of an aggregate source is to be made. It will also be of assistance in establishing an appropriate sampling and testing programme for routine quality control.

The Department of Transport Specification for Highway Works (1986) requires a geological site inspection to be made as part of the petrographic appraisal of an aggregate with respect to alkali–silica reactivity.

Procedures for the inspection of existing aggregate sources have been described by Hammersley (1989, 1992).

References

AMERICAN SOCIETY FOR TESTING AND MATERIALS 1975. Standard C294-86 1986. Standard descriptive nomenclature of constituents of natural mineral aggregates. Philadelphia USA.
—— 1984. Standard D693-84. Standard specification for crushed aggregate for macadam pavements.
—— 1985. Standard C295-85. Standard practice for petrographic examination of aggregates for concrete. Philadelphia USA
—— 1986. Standard C33-86. Specification for concrete aggregates. Philadelphia, USA.
L'ASSOCIATION FRANCAISE DE NORMALISATION. 1983. NF p 18–101. Granulates. Vocabulaire-Definitions—Classification.
—— 1983. NF P 18-556. Granulats. Determination de l'indice de continuite.
—— 1983. NF P 18-556. Granulats. Elements pour l'identification des granulats.
BRITISH STANDARDS INSTITUTION 1913. *Specification for sizes of broken stone and chippings*: BS 63.
—— 1943. *Methods for sampling and testing of mineral aggregates, sands and fillers*: BS 812.
—— 1967. *Methods for sampling and testing of mineral aggregates, sands and fillers*: BS 812.
—— 1975. *Methods for sampling and testing of mineral aggregates, sands and fillers. Part 1: Methods for determination of particle size and shape*: BS 812.
—— 1981. *Site investigations*: BS 5930 (Formerly CP2001).
—— 1983. *Specification for aggregates from natural sources for concrete*: BS 812.
—— 1985. *Hot rolled asphalt for roads and other paved areas. Part 1. Specification for constituent materials and asphalt mixtures*: BS 594.
—— 1985. *Testing aggregates. Part 103: Methods for sampling*: BS 812.
—— 1989. *Testing aggregates. Part 103: Methods for determination of particle size distribution, section 103.1 sieve tests*: BS 812.
—— 1989. *Testing aggregates. Part 103: Methods for determination of particle size distribution, Section 103.2: Sedimentation test*: BS 812.

—— 1989. *Testing aggregates. Part 105: Methods for determination of particle shape, Section 105.1 Flakiness Index*: BS 812.

—— 1990. *Testing aggregates. Part 105: Methods for determination of particle shape, section 105.2. Elongation Index for coarse aggregate*: BS 812.

—— *Testing aggregates. Part 104. Procedure for qualitative and quantitative petrographic examination of aggregates*: BS 812 Draft not yet published.

BURNETT, A. D. & EPPS, R. J. 1979. The engineering geological description of carbonate suite rocks and solids. *Ground Engineering*, **12**, 2, 41–48.

CIRIA 1984. *The CIRIA guide to concrete construction in the Gulf region*. Construction Industry Research and Information Association Special Publication 31, London.

CLARK, A. R. & WALKER, B. F. 1977. A proposed scheme for the classification and nomenclature for use in the engineering description of Middle Eastern sedimentaary rocks. *Géotechnique*, **27**, 93–99.

COLE, R. G. & HORSWILL, P. 1988. Alkali–silica reaction: Val de la Mare dam, Jersey, case history. *Proceedings of the Institution of Civil Engineers*, Part 1, **84**, Dec, 1237–1259.

COLLIS, L. & FOX, R. A (eds) 1985. *Aggregates: Sand, Gravel and Crushed Rock Aggregates for Construction purposes*. Geological Society Special Publication No. 1.

CONCRETE SOCIETY 1987. *Alkali–silcia reaction. Minimising the risk of damage to concrete. Guidance notes and model specification clauses*. Concrete Society Technical Report No. 30, 1987.

DUNCAN, N. 1969. *Engineering Geology and Rock Mechanics*, Vol 1 & 2. International Textbook Co.

FOOKES, P. G. 1980. An introduction to the influence of natural aggregates on the performance and durability of concrete. *Quarterly Journal of Engineering Geology*, **13**, 207–229.

——, DEARMAN, W. R. & FRANKLIN, J. A. 1971. Some engineering aspects of rock weathering with field examples from Dartmoor and elsewhere. *Quarterly Journal of Engineering Geology*, **4**, 139–185.

—— & HIGGINBOTTOM, I. E. 1975. The classification and description of near-shore carbonate sediments for engineering purposes. *Géotechnique*, **25**, 406–411.

GEOLOGICAL SOCIETY ENGINEERING GROUP WORKING PARTY REPORT 1970. The logging of rock cores for engineering purposes. *Quarterly Journal of Engineering Geology*, **3**, 1–24.

—— 1977. The description of rock masses for engineering purposes. *Quarterly Journal of Engineering Geology*, **10**, 355–388.

GEOLOGICAL SOCIETY OF AMERICA 1963. *Rock-Colour Chart*.

HAMMERSLEY, G. P. 1989. The use of petrography in the evaluation of aggregrates. *Concrete*, **23** (10).

—— 1992. Procedures for assessing the potential alkali-reactivity of aggregate sources. *9th International Conference on alkali–aggregate reaction in concrete*, London, England, **1**, 411–419.

HATCH, F. H., RASTAL, R. H. & GREENSMITH, J. T. 1971. *Petrology of the Sedimentary Rocks*. Thomas Murby, London.

——, WELLS, A. K. & WELLS M. K. 1972. *Petrology of the Igneous Rocks*. Thomas Murby, London.

INTERNATIONAL SOCIETY FOR ROCK MECHANICS 1981. *Rock characterisation testing and monitoring*. Pergamon, Oxford.

IRFAN, T. Y. & DEARMAN, W. R. 1978. The engineering petrography of a weathered granite in Cornwall, England. *Quarterly Journal of Engineering Geology*, **11**, 233–244.

KNIGHT, B. H. & KNIGHT, R. G. 1935. *Road Aggregates, Their Uses and Testing*. Edward Arnold, London.

LEES, G. 1968. Suggested classification of roadstones, Contribution to discussion. *Proceedings of the 1st Symposium on the Influence of the road surface on skidding*. University of Salford, Paper 2.

LEVERETT, I. J. 1970. Evaluation of rock for use as aggregates and roadstone. *Quarry Managers Journal*.

MATHER, K. & MATHER, B. 1950. Method of petrographic examination of aggregates for concrete. *Proceedings ASTM 30*, 1288–1312.

PHEMISTER, J. *et al.* 1946. Road Research Special Report No. 3 HMSO. London.

RAMSAY, D. M., DHIR, R. K. & SPENCE, I. 1974. The role rock and clast fabric in the physical performance of crushed-rock aggregate. *Engineering Geology*, **8**, 267–285.

RHOADES, R. & MIELENZ, R. C. 1946. Petrography of concrete aggregate. *Proceedings of the American Concrete Institute*, **42**, 581–600.

SIMS, G. P. & EVANS, D. E. 1988. Alkali–silica reaction: Kamburu spillway, Kenya, case history. *Proceedings of the Institution of Civil Engineers*, Part 1, **84**, Dec, 1213–1235.

STOW, D. A. V. 1981. Fine grained sediments: Terminology. *Quarterly Journal of Engineering Geology*, **14**, 243–244.

TERZAGHI, K. 1947. Introduction to tunnel geology. *In: Rock Tunnelling with Steel Supports*. Protor and White, Commercial Shearing and Stampling Co. Youngstown, Ohio.

TUCKER, M. E. 1982. *Sedimentary Petrology: an Introduction*. Blackwell, Oxford.

TURNER, F. J. 1968. *Metamorphic Petrology*. McGraw-Hill, New York.

WEINERT, H. H. 1964. Basic igneous rocks in road foundations. South African Council of Science Industrial Research, Report No. 218, *National Institute of Road Research Bulletin*, **2**, 1–47.

—— 1974. A climatic index of weathering and its application in road construction. *Géotechnique*, **24**, 475–488.

—— 1980. *The natural road construction materials of Southern Africa*. Academica, Cape Town.

Appendix A6.1 Extract from BS 812: Part 102: 1989. Petrological description of natural aggregates

The aggregate should be described by an appropriate petrological name, prefreably selected from the list of terms and definitions given in Table A6.1. which are taken from BS 6100: Section 5.2. In the event that the aggregate cannot be described adequately by the terms in Table A6.1, it should be described by another appropriate petrologically accepted term.

In the case of sedimentary rocks such as limestone or sandstone the geological age of the rock should also be given. The geological age requirement is satisfied by using one of the following terms: Precambrian, Cambrian, Ordovician, Silurian, Devonian, Carboniferous, Permian, Triassic, Jurassic, Cretaceous, Tertiary. For example, different types of limestones are described in terms of their age as follows, Carboniferous limestone, Jurassic limestone, Silurian limestone etc. The age of post-Tertiary materials need not be given.

Where the petrological character of an aggregate is intermediate between any of the terms in Table A6.1, or, where it consists of mixed gravels, the aggregate should be described by combining appropriate terms, e.g. granite/diorite, basalt/dolerite, microgranite/rhyolite, quartzite/granulite, flint/quartzite.

Petrological description does not take account of suitability for any particular purpose, which should be determined in accordance with the appropriate British Standard.

TABLE A6.1. *Rock types commonly used for aggregates*

Petrological term	Description
andesite*	a fine grained, usually volcanic, variety of diorite
arkose	a type of sandstone or gritstone containing over 25% feldspar
basalt	a fine grained basic rock, similar in composition to gabbro, usually volcanic
breccia†	rock consisting of angular, unworn rock fragments, bonded by natural cement
chalk	a very fine grained Cretaceous limestone, usually white
chert	cryptocrystalline‡ silica
conglomerate†	rock consisting of rounded pebbles bonded by natural cement
diorite	an intermediate plutonic rock, consisting mainly of plagioclase, with hornblende, augite or biotite
dolerite	a basic rock, with grain size intermediate between that of gabbro and basalt
dolomite	a rock or mineral composed of calcium magnesium carbonate
flint	cryptocrystalline‡ silica originating as nodules or layers in chalk
gabbro	a course grained, basic, plutonic rock, consisting essentially of calcic plagioclase and pyroxene, sometimes with olivine
gneiss	a banded rock, produced by intense metamorphic conditions
granite	an acidic, plutonic rock, consisting essentially of alkali feldspars and quartz
granulite	a metamorphic rock with granular texture and no preferred orientation of the minerals
greywacke	an impure type of sandstone or gritstone, composed of poorly sorted fragments of quartz, other minerals and rock; the coarser grains are usually strongly cemented in a fine matrix
gritstone	a sandstone, with coarse and usually angular grains
hornfels	a thermally metamorphosed rock containing substantial amounts of rock-forming silicate minerals
limestone	a sedimentary rock, consisting predominantly of calcium carbonate
marble	a metamorphosed limestone
microgranite*	an acidic rock with grain size intermediate between that of granite and rhyolite
quartzite	a metamorphic rock or sedimentary rock, composed almost entirely of quartz grains
rhyolite*	a fine grained or glassy acidic rock, usually volcanic
sandstone	a sedimentary rock, composed of sand grains naturally cemented together
schist	a metamorphic rock in which the minerals are arranged in nearly parallel bands or layers. Platy or elongate minerals such as mica or hornblende cause fissility in the rock which distinguishes it from a gneiss
slate	a rock derived from argillaceous sediments or volcanic ash by metamorphism, characterized by cleavage planes independent of the original stratification
syenite	an intermediate plutonic rock, consisting mainly of alkali feldspar with plagioclase, hornblende, biotite, or augite
trachyte*	a fine grained, usually volcanic, variety of syenite
tuff	consolidated volcanic ash

* The terms microgranite, rhyolite, andesite, or trachyte, as appropriate, are preferred for rocks alternatively described as porphyry or felsite.
† Some terms refer to structure or texture only, e.g. breccia or conglomerate, and these terms cannot be used alone to provide a full description.
‡ Composed of crystals so fine that they can be resolved only with the aid of a high power microscope.

TABLE A6.2. *Examples of completed report forms for classification and description of aggregates*

CLASSIFICATION AND DESCRIPTION OF AGGREGATE

1.	AGGREGATE TYPE					
1.1	Crushed Rock					✓
1.2	Gravel		Uncrushed		Land Won	
1.3	Sand		Partly Crushed		Marine	
			Crushed			

2.	PHYSICAL CHARACTERISTICS	
2.1	Nominal Size	5 mm down
2.2	Shape	Angular
2.3	Surface Texture	Rough
2.4	Colour (sample condition)	Medium grey (sample dry)
2.5	Presence of Fines	High content of dust
2.6	Presence of Coatings	None present
2.7	Extraneous Material	None present

3.	PETROLOGICAL CLASSIFICATION				
3.1	Monomictic	✓	Polymictic		
3.2	Petrological Name	LIMESTONE			
		Visual Assessment		Quantitative Analysis	
3.3	Geological Age	Carboniferous			

4.	PETROLOGICAL DESCRIPTION			Yes
5.	SAMPLE REF.	0001	6. CERTIFICATE OF SAMPLING	Yes
7.	SOURCE	Incline Quarry, Isle of Sodor		

CLASSIFICATION AND DESCRIPTION OF AGGREGATE

1.	AGGREGATE TYPE					
1.1	Crushed Rock					✓
1.2	Gravel		Uncrushed		Land Won	
1.3	Sand		Partly Crushed		Marine	
			Crushed			

2.	PHYSICAL CHARACTERISTICS	
2.1	Nominal Size	10 mm
2.2	Shape	Angular and flaky
2.3	Surface Texture	Rough
2.4	Colour (sample condition)	Black and dark reddish brown (sample dry)
2.5	Presence of Fines	Moderate content of red clay
2.6	Presence of Coatings	None present
2.7	Extraneous Material	None present

3.	PETROLOGICAL CLASSIFICATION				
3.1	Monomictic	✓	Polymictic		
3.2	Petrological Name	BASALT			
		Black fresh to slightly weathered particles		83%	
		Brown moderately to highly weathered particles		17%	
		Visual Assessment		Quantitative Analysis	✓
3.3	Geological Age				

4.	PETROLOGICAL DESCRIPTION			Yes
5.	SAMPLE REF.	0002	6. CERTIFICATE OF SAMPLING	Yes
7.	SOURCE	New Quarry, Pangaea		

CLASSIFICATION AND DESCRIPTION OF AGGREGATE

1.	AGGREGATE TYPE					
1.1	Crushed Rock					✓
1.2	Gravel		Uncrushed		Land Won	
1.3	Sand		Partly Crushed		Marine	
			Crushed			

2.	PHYSICAL CHARACTERISTICS	
2.1	Nominal Size	20mm
2.2	Shape	Angular
2.3	Surface Texture	Rough
2.4	Colour (sample condition)	Light grey (sample dry)
2.5	Presence of Fines	Low content
2.6	Presence of Coatings	None present
2.7	Extraneous Material	Particles of slag

3.	PETROLOGICAL CLASSIFICATION				
3.1	Monomictic		Polymictic		✓
3.2	Petrological Name	GNEISS	68%		
		SCHIST	28%		
		DOLERITE	3%		
		SLAG	1%		
		Visual Assessment		Quantitative Analysis	✓
3.3	Geological Age				

4.	PETROLOGICAL DESCRIPTION			Yes
5.	SAMPLE REF.	0003	6. CERTIFICATE OF SAMPLING	Yes
7.	SOURCE	Underhill Quarry, Bagginshire		

CLASSIFICATION AND DESCRIPTION OF AGGREGATE

1.	AGGREGATE TYPE					
1.1	Crushed Rock					
1.2	Gravel	✓	Uncrushed	✓	Land Won	
1.3	Sand		Partly Crushed		Marine	✓
			Crushed			

2.	PHYSICAL CHARACTERISTICS	
2.1	Nominal Size	20mm
2.2	Shape	Rounded to subangular
2.3	Surface Texture	Smooth
2.4	Colour (sample condition)	Dark greyish brown (sample wet)
2.5	Presence of Fines	Low content
2.6	Presence of Coatings	None present
2.7	Extraneous Material	None present

3.	PETROLOGICAL CLASSIFICATION				
3.1	Monomictic		Polymictic		✓
3.2	Petrological Name	FLINT	82%		
		SANDSTONE	11%		
		QUARTZITE	4%		
		SHELL	3%		
		Visual Assessment		Quantitative Analysis	✓
3.3	Geological Age				

4.	PETROLOGICAL DESCRIPTION			Yes
5.	SAMPLE REF.	0004	6. CERTIFICATE OF SAMPLING	Yes
7.	SOURCE	River Estuary, Borchester		

CLASSIFICATION AND DESCRIPTION OF AGGREGATE (left)

1.	AGGREGATE TYPE					
1.1	Crushed Rock					
1.2	Gravel		Uncrushed	✓	Land Won	✓
1.3	Sand	✓	Partly Crushed		Marine	
			Crushed			

2.	PHYSICAL CHARACTERISTICS	
2.1	Nominal Size	Grading M
2.2	Shape	Rounded to subangular
2.3	Surface Texture	Smooth
2.4	Colour (sample condition)	Light yellowish brown (sample dry)
2.5	Presence of Fines	Low content
2.6	Presence of Coatings	None present
2.7	Extraneous Material	None present

3.	PETROLOGICAL CLASSIFICATION				
3.1	Monomictic		Polymictic		✓
3.2	Petrological Name	QUARTZ 84% CHERT 13% LIMESTONE 2% GLAUCONITE 1%			
		Visual Assessment		Quantitative Analysis	✓
3.3	Geological Age				

4.	PETROLOGICAL DESCRIPTION	Yes
5.	SAMPLE REF. 0005	6. CERTIFICATE OF SAMPLING Yes
7.	SOURCE	Basil Pit, Torquay

CLASSIFICATION AND DESCRIPTION OF AGGREGATE (right)

1.	AGGREGATE TYPE					
1.1	Crushed Rock					
1.2	Gravel	✓	Uncrushed		Land Won	✓
1.3	Sand		Partly Crushed	✓	Marine	
			Crushed			

2.	PHYSICAL CHARACTERISTICS	
2.1	Nominal Size	20 to 5 mm
2.2	Shape	Subrounded to angular
2.3	Surface Texture	Smooth to rough
2.4	Colour (sample condition)	Medium brown (sample wet)
2.5	Presence of Fines	Low content
2.6	Presence of Coatings	Calcareous encrustations
2.7	Extraneous Material	None present

3.	PETROLOGICAL CLASSIFICATION				
3.1	Monomictic		Polymictic		✓
3.2	Petrological Name	QUARTZITE 50% LIMESTONE 30% CHERT 10%			
		Visual Assessment	✓	Quantitative Analysis	
3.3	Geological Age				

4.	PETROLOGICAL DESCRIPTION	No
5.	SAMPLE REF. 0006	6. CERTIFICATE OF SAMPLING Yes
7.	SOURCE	Castle Pit, Nania

7. Sampling and testing

7.1. Introduction

This chapter considers the tests and procedures used to describe or evaluate the physical, mechanical and chemical characteristics of aggregates, for the purposes of (a) prediction of the likely 'in service' behaviour of the material (b) comparison between competing materials (c) specification compliance or (d) quality control. Individual limits are not discussed here but are considered in the appropriate Chapter. Sub-base materials (Chapter 10) sometimes have to use tests in BS 1377, but this section confines itself to BS 812 and the relevant standards from other countries.

7.2. Sampling

7.2.1. General considerations

The first step is the collection of samples. Statistically, a sample can be defined as an individual or group of individuals drawn from a large or infinite population. *Information obtained from samples is only as representative of the material as the samples on which they are performed.* If observations reveal little variation and there has been no bias in collecting, then a small sample or small number of samples may be highly representative of a population. If the variation is large then more and/ or larger samples will be required. Representative sampling, however, is perhaps the most difficult of the control operations to perform satisfactorily. Sampling, as with all types of test, introduces sources of variation and error, so that judgements of materials based on infrequent random tests are fraught with difficulties. In this connection, see also the remarks on sampling in relation to classification given in Chapter 6.

A random sample is one in which each potential observation has an equal chance of being selected. In a geological context there is no particular difficulty if the material is uniformly available, but often this is not the case. For example, rock exposed in natural outcrops is often sampled but frequently it is only the harder parts of a formation which form conspicuous outcrops, while the softer material remains unexposed. In consequence it is often impossible to obtain a random sample.

In reconnaissance investigations, single spot samples provide estimates of the characteristics of the rock. These are only representative, however, if the rock is very uniform. To offset this, a number of spot samples can be combined and split (reduced) to a convenient size, in order to obtain greater representation. *A single sample will yield only a single value for any characteristic, which need not be representative of the whole deposit or rock suite.* The only estimate of variability it provides is the variability which occurs within the sample. If this is less than the variation between samples then it will be a poor approximation to the whole deposit. Variability is inherent in all types of measurement, arising from the raw materials, nature of the plant and the processing, handling practices and methods of sampling and testing. Of these, sampling and testing are commonly a major source of variability. Goodsall & Matthews (1970) demonstrated that sample reduction and the method of splitting lead to variability in respect of the aggregate content, as a large sample is further and further reduced to the amounts used in many laboratory tests (Table 7.1). From this the suggestion is that quartering introduces higher variability in sub-samples than riffling.

TABLE 7.1. *Effect of sample reduction method on standard deviation of aggregate content*

Passing sieve (mm)	6-stage reduction Quartered	riffled	5-stage reduction Quartered	riffled
25.4	5.21	4.45	4.02	2.73
12.7	5.48	3.61	3.88	2.70
3.2	3.1	1.95	2.24	1.55
0.075	0.2	0.15	0.2	0.26

After initial exploration and preliminary sampling has indicated the existence of a body of material suitable for development as an aggregate source, a programme of unbiased primary sampling attempts to prove its dimensions and quality. Primary sampling (a) delimits and establishes the dimensions of the deposit and (b) explores geological variability. Sub-sampling reveals the physical, mechanical and chemical features of the material. Physical properties are intrinsic physical characteristics of a material, e.g. density and porosity. Mechanical properties are a measure of the physical response of the material to external stimuli, e.g. compressive, impact or shear stresses. Further sub-sampling permits investigation of the causes of variation in these features.

Primary sampling in a deposit of large dimensions involves integration of samples from individual points or localities to provide a composite picture of the whole deposit. In quarries or potential quarries, on the other hand, a limited area is sampled to estimate the nature of the final product. In a producing quarry it is a bulk aggregate product which is usually sampled, e.g. stockpiles, etc. The properties or test values obtained from the sub-samples are then attributed to the bulk.

The categories of sample which can be defined are as follows (Fookes *et al.* 1971):

Type sample: composite sample from a groove cut across the complete face, zone or bed.
Typical sample: similar to type samples but not composite.
Single samples: those selected as representative of a zone or bed of homogeneous material of uniform physical character.

7.2.2. Sampling procedures

Samples from existing quarries or pits may be obtained as rock lumps or gravel from the working face, or as finished aggregate products.

7.2.2.1. Quarry face rock. In sampling directly from a quarry face as with a natural outcrop, care must be taken to ensure that the samples reflect the range of variation present. Where there are obvious differences in the nature of the materials, each should be sampled separately. BS 812 specifies the minimum number and dimensions of samples which should be collected.

Another method is to take samples composed of pieces of rock cut out of a small trench or channel, e.g. channel samples, 100×25 mm or 150×12 mm deep and approximately 1 m long. By sampling at regular and close intervals an accurate estimate of quality can be obtained (Northern Mineral Press 1955).

Variation in terms of composition, quality or state is not confined to originally layered or banded rocks, i.e. sedimentary and banded metamorphic rocks. For example, a network of veins, dykes or sheets of totally different composition and degree of alteration may intrude a rock body and demonstrate quite different physical properties from those of the host rock.

Uniform weathering (Chapter 2 and Appendix) may produce a progressive change in rock state inwards from the surface. Non-uniform weathering preferentially controlled by joints, e.g. the common flat-lying joints in granite, can impart a rude form of layering based on variable states of freshness. Hydrothermal alteration may produce similar patterns.

In addition to inhomogeneities resulting from primary sedimentary banding, variability in anisotropic rocks includes:

(a) Igneous rocks: zones of highly vesicular or amygdaloidal texture; flow banding.
(b) Sedimentary rocks: clay layers or films in limestone; micaceous films or aggregates on bedding-planes of sandstones; layer parallel jointing.
(c) Metamorphic rocks: seams of chlorite, mica etc; mica schist bands in gneiss, marble and psammite; schistose horizons in massive amphibolite or granulite.

To obtain material for testing, rock samples may have to be crushed to aggregate in the laboratory. In the controlled and somewhat atypical conditions of the laboratory, however, the available crushing equipment generally produces an aggregate whose character may differ markedly from that in commercial production. Shergold (1963) reports that laboratory-produced aggregates display rougher surfaces, sharper edges and a more cuboidal shape. These differences in turn affect mechanical properties like the polished stone value (PSV) (7.5.4.1) and ten per cent fines value (7.5.3.4), where higher (superior) values were obtained from the laboratory-crushed material. He cautioned, therefore, that such material should only be used in mechanical testing when commercially-produced finished material is not available.

7.2.2.2. Sand and gravel deposits. In sand and gravel pits sampling distinguishes:

(a) Composition, e.g. lithological nature and state of the constituent pebbles.
(b) Grading and shape distribution in the bulk deposit and the size range of the individual components.
(c) Uniformity, e.g. presence of unsuitable material and the possibilities for isolation.
(d) Other physical, mechanical and chemical properties.

Sufficient material is taken to allow mixing and quartering down to a suitable sample size. In the course of sieving the bulk sample the percentage of material retained on 75 mm and 150 mm sieves is an indicator of the crushing which will be required.

7.2.2.3. Aggregate products, sand and gravel. In a working sand and gravel pit the sites for aggregate sample collection are conveyor belts, trucks, hoppers, bins and stockpiles. If stockpiles are sampled the samples should not be taken from the edges or the top, although these are the easiest places from which to do so. In top-loading stockpiles coarser fragments concentrate towards the base of the slope. Samples should be collected from the middle of stockpile faces, points around the pile and at least 200 mm below the surface. The sampling procedure may also need to recognize other forms of segregation and any variations due to drainage.

The principal causes of variability in natural gravel aggregates include pebble lithology, grading, shape and distribution and weathering. In evaluating the quality of an aggregate for concrete, and to some extent for asphaltic concrete, important considerations include the quality of pebbles, shape and cleanness, i.e. presence of coatings (Chapter 2). Grading can be corrected to comply with specifications.

7.2.2.4. Aggregate products, crushed-rock quarries. Crushed rock aggregate should be sampled while in motion, e.g. from conveyor belts or at discharge from bins etc. (Shergold 1963). A minimum of eight increments is collected over a period of a day, the weight depending on the size of the material (Table 7.2).

TABLE 7.2. *Minimum weights for sampling*

Maximum size present in substantial proportion (85% passing) (mm)	Minimum weight of each increment (kg)	Minimum number of increments	Minimum weight despatched (kg)
64	50	16	100
50	50	16	100
38	50	8	50
25	50	8	50
19	25	8	25
13	25	8	25
10	13	8	13
6.5 and less	13	8	13

If collected at a delivery point the samples should be taken from at least eight vehicles arriving at intervals. Collection is made at the time of discharge. Increments are mixed to form a composite sample and then reduced by quartering and/or riffling to the amounts required. In this it should be remembered that such sample reduction is attended by an accumulating variability in aggregate grading analyses (Cox 1973).

If the main sample is taken from a stockpile or other stationary source it should be a composite of at least ten increments drawn from different parts of the bulk. Shergold (1963) stressed the difficulties of sampling stockpiles, stationary vehicles or top surfaces of bins. Stockpiles should be studied at intervals to establish any fluctuation in the product, resulting from plant operation or intrinsic variability. These are major factors which make it difficult to secure representative samples and affect compliance and 'in service' performance.

7.2.3. Sample size

The size of samples which must be collected for physical testing is given in Table 7.3. See also Chapter 6 for the size of sample required for classification.

TABLE 7.3. *Sample sizes compiled from BS 812: 1975 and BGWF INF/9, 1966*

Test	Minimum amount to be available at the laboratory
1. Durability	
i. Nominal maximum size > 12.5 mm	80 pieces
ii. Nominal maximum size < 12.5 mm	3.6–5.4 kg
2. Sieve analysis	
Maximum size up to 63 mm	50 kg
50 mm	35 kg
40 mm	15 kg
20 mm	2 kg
14 mm	1 kg
10 mm	0.5 kg
3. Shape Indices of flakiness and elongation	800 pieces
4. Proportion of impurities	As for sieve analysis

7.3. Statistical considerations

This section presents a brief review of the significant expressions used in analysis of sampling and test data. Further information may be obtained by reference to Grant (1952), Griffiths (1967) and Harr (1977).

The commonest value obtained from a set of observations is the average or Arithmetic Mean, $\bar{X}$, where

$$\bar{X} = \sum_1^\eta \frac{x_i}{\eta} .$$

Here x_i represents the observed value and η the number of observations.

The recording of highest, lowest and average readings fails to give an adequate picture of the property under study. It is important to know the amount by which each value deviates from the average and the measurement of this is given by the variance (σ^2) of the values, or their spread around the mean,

$$\sigma^2 = \sum_1^\eta \frac{(x_i - \bar{X})^2}{\eta - 1} .$$

It is necessary to square the deviations before summing, as the sum of deviations around the mean is always zero, a property of the mean. To reduce the variance to linear units the square root or standard deviation (σ) is used:

$$\sigma = \left(\sum_{1}^{\eta} \frac{(x_i - \bar{X})^2}{\eta - 1} \right)^{1/2}.$$

A relative measure of variation is given by the coefficient of variation (CV), i.e. percentage standard deviation:

$$CV = \frac{\sigma}{\bar{X}} \times 100.$$

In general the average gives the best value of the characteristic being measured, the standard deviation shows the spread in data caused by random variations and by variations in the materials being tested.

When a series of readings is taken, occasional values may have an abnormally large deviation from the mean. These may be suspected of containing an overall error representing a condition very different from that of the remainder of the test. A criterion which determines whether or not this suspect reading may be rejected is based on showing that the reading is not likely to be a random variation. The degree of likelihood of this, however, depends on the distribution of the data. Readings that deviate by more than three times the standard deviation may ordinarily be rejected, and, in the case of a normal (Gaussian) frequency distribution, there is less than one chance in 300 that a reading would fall outside the same range due to random variation.

The averages of samples of size η tend to a normal (Gaussian) distribution as η grows large. In such a distribution, 99.7% of the population will fall within a distance of three standard deviations on either side of the average for the whole population. If random samples of size η are taken it may be expected then, that three means in every 1000 will fall outside these limits, i.e. 99.7% of the means will fall in the range

$$\bar{X} + \frac{3\sigma}{\eta^{1/2}} \text{ to } \bar{X} - \frac{3\sigma}{\eta^{1/2}} \quad \text{(confidence limits).}$$

If the shape of a frequency distribution is not known, an indication of the minimum proportion of a distribution included in a specified range of standard deviations about the mean is given by Tchebycheff's inequality (Woodruff 1966). This theorem states that more than $1 - (1/t^2)$ of any set of observations must fall within the range of $\bar{X} \pm t\sigma$, where $t > 1$. For example, if $t = 3$ this means that more than $1 - (1/3^2)$ or $\frac{8}{9}$ of a set of numbers must fall within the limits $\bar{X} \pm 3\sigma$. The fraction falling outside the limits may well be less than $\frac{1}{9}$; the theorem simply states that it cannot be as much as $\frac{1}{9}$ (Grant 1952). In addition, if all of the observations are to fall in

the range $\bar{X} \pm t\sigma$, then t can be determined from the expression $t = \eta^{1/2}$ (Woodruff 1966), e.g. if $\eta = 2$ all observations must lie between the limits $\bar{X} \pm \sqrt{2}\sigma$. The normal distribution with >99% of its area in the range of 3 standard deviations is well within the limit of inequality.

In the analysis of test results, confidence limits for a probability of 0.1 only become acceptably close with a large number of tests, too high for common practice. In single samples of production aggregate the limits within which test values for strength and durability fall are too high to be represenative of the quarry (Shergold 1963). This indicates that a single sample is not likely to be representative of even a single day's output. He suggested that at least five samples should be tested for the mean results to be representative of the average output at any given time. To offset the large number of samples which would be involved he proposed the combining of samples and mixing to form a composite sample. This could then be reduced to appropriate quantities for testing.

Some tests, like those for aggregate grading and shape, normally apply only to limited consignments and are required for compliance or quality control. In other tests there is a tendency to regard results obtained from one sample as being valid indefinitely. Because of the variability of most aggregates, only recent test values are really valid. In addition, results from one part of a quarry may differ from one another, even when sampled at the same time.

7.4. Repeatability and reproducibility

Important considerations in any tests programme, whatever its aims, are the notions of repeatability and reproducibility (BS 812: 1975). A number of quite different factors can contribute to a spread in test values and to allow for this in comparing results obtained by the same operator or by different operators in different laboratories, some estimate of the distribution of values is necessary.

7.4.1. Repeatability (r)

This is the quantitative expression of the random error associated with a single test operator obtaining successive results on identical material, with the same equipment and constant operating conditions. It is the difference between two single results which would be expected to be exceeded in only one case in twenty, assuming normal and correct operation of the test (BS 812: 1975). This is expressed by

$$r = 1.96\sqrt{2\sigma_1}$$

where σ_1 is the single operator standard deviation within a laboratory.

7.4.2. Reproducibility (R)

This is an expression of the random error associated with test operators working in different laboratories, each obtaining single results on identical test materials when applying the same method. As with r, it is the difference between two single and independent results which would be expected in only one case in twenty. This is expressed by,

$$R = 1.96\sqrt{2}\ \sqrt{\sigma_1{}^2 + \sigma_2{}^2}$$

where σ_2 is the Standard Deviation applicable to all causes of variability other than repeatability, when the results from different laboratories are compared.

In Table 7.4 (BS 812: 1975) values of r and R are given for certain standard physical and mechanical tests. This indicates the greatest differences expected between tests on separate samples.

7.4.3. Sampling considerations

In BS 812: Part 101: 1984 the concepts of repeatability and reproducibility are further refined. In addition to repeatability (r), a repeatability r_1 is defined as the value below which the absolute difference between two single test results obained with the same method using different test portions of the same laboratory sample under the same conditions (same operator, same apparatus, same laboratory, and a short interval of time) may be expected to lie with a probability of 95%.

In addition to reproducibility (R), two reproducibilities R_1 and R_2 are defined. R_1 is the value below which the absolute difference between two single test results obtained with the same method using different test portions of the same laboratory sample under different conditions (different operators, different apparatus,

different laboratories and/or different time) may be expected to lie with a probability of 95%. R_2 is the value below which the absolute difference between two single test results obtained with the same method using different laboratory samples from the same batch under different conditions (different operators, different apparatus, different laboratories and/or different time) may be expected to lie with a probability of 95%.

According to the above definitions, r_1 and R_1 make allowance for sample reduction errors whereas r and R do not. In addition R_2 makes allowances for sampling errors. With many aggregate tests it is not possible to carry out repeat tests on identical material so that r_1, R_1 and R_2 are the measures of variability which will be of use in practice. For example, precision estimates quoting r_1, R_1 and R_2 for the frost-heave test (BS 812: Part 124: 1989) are given below:

Material	Average	r_1	R_1	R_2
Flint gravel	13.5 mm	7.0 mm	8.5 mm	9.0 mm

7.5. Testing

As the several demands on aggregate call for different characteristics, a wide range of tests has been devised to describe the material and assess its potential value. These tests have the principal functions of assisting predictions of 'in service' performance and enabling materials from different sources to be compared. Most assess some physical or mechanical attribute of the material, while a few investigate particular chemical characteristics. The majority are performed on the finished aggregate product, but some can profitably be performed on the ledge rock and are therefore of value in the exploration stage.

The literature is extensive so it has been necessary to abstract considerably and the various standard sources should be consulted for more comprehensive discussion.

TABLE 7.4. *Estimates of repeatability for some standard aggregate tests*

Test	Repeatability (r)	Reproducibility (R)
Relative density:		
i. most aggregates	0.02	0.04
ii. low density porous aggregates	up to 0.4	up to 0.08
Water absorption	5% of value recorded	10% of value recorded
Bulk density	$10\,\mathrm{kg\,m^{-5}}$	$20\,\mathrm{kg\,m^{-3}}$
Aggregate Impact Value	1.0	2.0
Aggregate Crushing Value	0.8	1.5
Ten Percent Fines Value	7 kN	14 kN
Aggregate Abrasion Value	1.5	3.0
Polished-Stone Value	4.9	6.0

The tests described are those which are standard in Britain and USA, but some discussion of non-standard variations has also been included.

Physical tests:

(a) Aggregate grading	BS 882: 1983
	BS 812: Part 103: 1985
	ASTM Designations
	C33 and 136
(b) Aggregate shape, angularity, sphericity, roundness, surface texture	BS 812: Part 105: 1989/90
(c) Relative density, bulk density, unit weight	BS 812: 1975
	ASTM Designations
	C29 and 127
(d) Water absorption	BS 812: 1975
	ASTM Designations
	C127 and 128
(e) Aggregate shrinkage	BRS Digest 35
Petrographic examination	ASTM Designation
	C295

Mechanical tests:

Strength	BS 812: Part 112: 1990
(a) Aggregate Impact Value	
(b) Aggregate Crushing Value	BS 812: Part 110: 1990
(c) Ten Percent Fines Value	BS 812: Part 111: 1990
(d) Franklin Point Load Test	Franklin (1970)
(e) Schmidt Rebound Number	Duncan (1969)
Durability	BS 812: Part 113: 1990
(a) Aggregate Abrasion Value	
(b) Aggregate Attrition Value	BS 812: 1943
(c) Los Angeles Abrasion Value	ASTM Designation C131
(d) Polished Stone Value	BS 812: Part 114: 1989
(e) Slake Durability Value	Franklin 1970
(f) Sulphate Soundness	ASTM Designation C88

Chemical tests:

(a) Chloride content	BS 812: Part 117: 1988
(b) Sulphate content	BS 812: Part 118: 1988
(c) Organic content	BS 1377
(d) Adhesion Tests	Road Research Laboratory 1962

7.5.1. Physical tests

7.5.1.1a. Aggregate grading. Aggregate, both crushed rock and natural, is differentiated at the 5 mm size range into coarse and fine aggregate (BS 882: 1985). In the laboratory a suitably reduced sample is sieved on a standard group of BS sieves and the grading of the sample is obtained (BS 812: 1985). Fine aggregates for concrete are currently classified into three grading classes (Table 7.5) becoming progressively finer from classes C to F (BS 882: 1983).

TABLE 7.5. *Grading of fine aggregates (BS 882: 1983)*

	Percentage by mass passing sieve			
		Additional limits*		
BS Sieve size	Overall limits	C	M	F
10 mm	100	—	—	—
5 mm	89–100	—	—	—
2.36 mm	60–100	60–100	65–100	80–100
1.18 mm	30–100	30–90	45–100	70–100
600 μm	15–100	15–54	25–80	55–100
300 μm	5–70	5–40	5–48	5–70
150 μm	0–15†	—	—	—

* C, coarse; M, medium; F, fine.
† For crushed rock sands the permissible limit is increased to 20 per cent, except when used for heavy duty floors.

In engineering usage the terms describing sediment grading differ from those employed in sedimentology, e.g. a sediment containing a range of sizes from fine to coarse (Table 7.5) would be classified as well-graded in engineering terms but the same term would mean poorly sorted to a sedimentologist.

In sieving an aggregate sample the product is influenced by the shape of the constituents. The intermediate dimension in flaky particles gets larger as they become more flaky and this can affect the shape proportions of a fraction when using sieves with circular as against square holes (Lees 1964).

The volume and size of the particles retained on a particular sieve are conditioned by shape. e.g. elongate fragments in any one size approximate in size to the flaky fragments of the next coarser size (Lees 1964). Sieves, therefore, do not rigorously size the fragments where the shapes are very different. This implies that in an aggregate with a high proportion of elongate grains the particle size would be coarser than in one which is rich in flakes. One consequence of this size variability is that in flaky aggregates there is a higher surface area for a given weight than in elongate or equidimensional samples. These features affect the void-filling characteristics, permeability and strength of concrete and road base aggregates. They are also important considerations in filter design.

Grading data are commonly plotted on semi-logarithmic charts. An alternative method is the employment of parameters which describe the coarseness of each grading and determine whether samples are well-graded, single-sized or gap-graded, e.g. D_{60} the sieve aperture size through which 60% passes. This is a measure of modal size, distinguishing between coarse, medium and fine materials, i.e. $D_{60} > 10$ mm implies coarse grain, $D_{60} > 5$ mm implies medium grain.

An index of grain-size dispersion is the uniformity coefficient, $CU = D_{60}/D_{10}$. When CU is low particles are more or less uniform in size. A well-graded mixture of gravel-sand-silt-clay may exhibit values as high as 1000. Another value, the coefficient of curvature, $CZ = D_{30}^2/(D_{60} \times D_{10})$ together with CU can be used to distinguish well-graded and gap-graded material. Where $CU > 35$ and $CZ < 6$ the material is well-graded: $CU > 15$, $CZ < 6$ is poorly-graded or uniformly graded in engineering terms and $CU > 35$, $CZ > 6$ is gap-graded.

In natural gravels the grading of the material as-dug is an intrinsic characteristic of the deposit, reflecting the environment of formation. In consequence the material may not form a regular graded assemblage conforming to a particular grading class, but rather have deficiencies or excesses in particular size ranges. As the grading required varies with the project there is no unique system of crushing which will satisfy all requirements. Crushed rock or gravel therefore may be screened into a series of 'single size' ranges and subsequently re-mixed in required proportions to satisfy specifications.

The mean grading of a deposit is the average of individual samples. Cox (1973) demonstrated a high repeatability for sieve analyses performed by the repeated sieving of a single sample. On the other hand, careful subsampling of a larger bulk sample, even by the same operator, introduces considerable variability into the grading.

In evaluating the variability induced by sample splitting, Pike (1978) concentrated on particular but significant size levels, e.g. the proportion passing the 5 mm sieve. Successive sample reduction showed a progressive change in the proportion of this size range present. From a bulk sample with 40% passing the 5 mm sieve, successive reduction resulted in a range of values between 34% and 40% by the fifth riffling stage.

The properties of the aggregate which affect the degree of variability induced by the sample reduction include moisture content, absolute grading, particle shape and texture. The variability is lowest in fine-grained aggregates and highest in gap-graded, coarse material.

7.5.1.1.b. Sand equivalent value (ASTM 2419). A rapid field test to ascertain the proportions of clay-like or plastic fines in granular soils and fine aggregate passing ASTM Sieve No. 4 (4.75 mm) is provided by the sand equivalent value. A small quantity of flocculating solution at $22 \pm 3°C$ (solution of calcium chloride, glycerine and formaldehyde) and a measured volume of oven-dried fine aggregate are poured into a graduated plastic cylinder. Agitation loosens the clay-like coatings from the coarser grains. After irrigation with additional solution the clay-like material is forced into suspension above the sand. After a prescribed sedimentation period the heights of accumulated clay and sand are measured and the sand equivalent is expressed as the ratio of the height of sand to clay times 100.

7.5.1.2a. Aggregate shape. In both natural and crushed rock aggregates the constituent particles within a particular size fraction may display a range of shapes. The distribution of shapes reflects intrinsic petrological–petrographic characteristics, together with environmental factors in formation (natural gravels) and production factors (crushed rock aggregate). British Standard BS 812 groups these shapes into six categories: rounded; irregular; angular; flaky; elongated; flaky and elongated (Fig. 7.1a). In the rounded, irregular and angular categories the particles are approximately equidimensional and for many assessments are grouped together as one, termed 'equidimensional' (Lees 1964) or 'cuboidal' (Ramsay 1965).

Several schemes exist for establishing classificatory limits to the proportions of the four shape categories (BS 812; Zingg 1935; Rosslein 1941; Lees 1964) and for the actual measurements of the shape of individual fragments, as illustrated in Fig. 7.1b. In the description of shape, BS 812 emphasizes departure from equidimensional in indices of flakiness and elongation.

7.5.1.2b. Flakiness index, I_F (BS 812: 1989). This is restricted to aggregate coarser than 6.5 mm and is an expression of the weight-percentage of particles, in a minimum sample of 200 pieces, whose least dimension is less than 0.6 times the mean dimension. By mean dimension is meant the arithmetic mean of the side dimensions of the delimiting square-holed sieves. For example, in 14–10 mm aggregate this would be 12 mm. Measurement has been facilitated by the design of the standard shape gauge (Fig. 7.2a).

7.5.1.2c. Elongation Index, I_E (BS 812: 1990). This is the weight-percentage of particles whose long dimension is greater than 1.8 times the mean dimension. Again measurement can be made with a standard gauge (Fig. 7.2b).

7.5.1.2d. Discussion. The most generally desirable aggregates are those with a high proportion of roughly equidimensional (cuboidal) particles. Intrinsic factors such as rock composition and fabric affect the shape of crushed rock aggregate. In the main, strong and hard or brittle rocks produce a higher proportion of flakes than weak types, although the latter generate more fines in

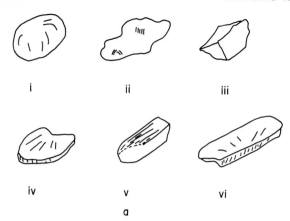

FIG. 7.1a. Particle shape: i, rounded; ii, irregular; iii, angular; iv, flaky; v, elongate; vi, elongate and flaky.

fields, equidimensional, elongate, flakes, flaky-elongate, within which all particles may be classed. Lees indicates a weakness in the BS classification scheme, where simplification of the measurement procedure has led to very broad shape categories. This allows a wide range of shape characters for different populations which have the same values of I_F and I_E. This could affect the behaviour of aggregates in a number of situations and distort comparisons between products of the same rock type. To overcome this deficiency, especially in the more rigorous conditions of a research programme, more precise means of particle measurement have been devised (Rosslein 1941; Lees 1964).

In commercial use, flakes lead to an increase in the specific surface of the aggregate and control the packing pattern and, therefore, porosity and permeability in the unbound conditions. These features, in varying degree, can also affect shear and crushing resistance, tensile and flexural strength in concrete, asphalt and macadam and workability in concrete.

In road surface-dressing, good cuboidal chippings are essential but many desirable rocks are difficult to process for good shape. All rocks do not behave alike under size reduction. Flakiness can be induced in the crushing process and to minimize this, in the more difficult instances, it is important to keep the reduction ratio

$$\frac{\text{mean size of feed}}{\text{mean size of product}}$$

as low as possible, i.e. $3:1$ or $4:1$. Shergold (1959) reviewed the performance of crusher types and listed them in descending order of cuboidal production, i.e. impact, single toggle jaw, gyratory, roll, disc and cone crushers (Shergold & Greysmith 1947).

crushing. It is chiefly at the extremes of strength and fabric anisotropy that grading and shape of the finished product is significantly affected.

In a critical review of aggreate shape and classification, Lees (1964) followed the sedimentological practice of describing particle shape in terms of axial ratios obtained from three orthogonal dimensional axes (longest, intermediate and shortest). Elongation and flatness ratios are

$$\frac{\text{intermediate}}{\text{longest}} \quad \text{and} \quad \frac{\text{shortest}}{\text{intermediate}}$$

respectively (Fig. 7.1b). In this scheme the BS limits for elongation would be 0.55 and flakiness 0.6. These limits divide up a plot of elongation vs flatness ratios into four

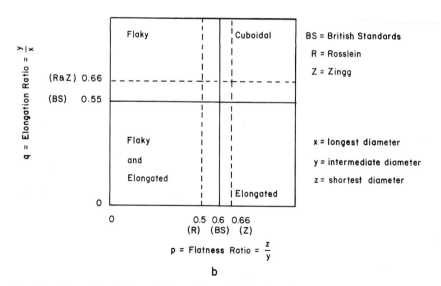

FIG. 7.1b. Three dimension shape categories bounded by arbitrary limits of p and q (Lees 1964).

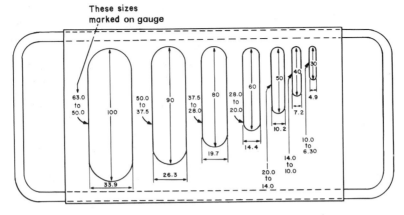

Dimensions in millimetres.   1.5 mm steel sheet rolled over on 8 mm diameter rod.

a

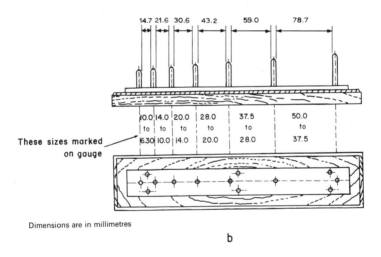

Dimensions are in millimetres

b

FIG. 7.2. Diagrams of British Standard (a) thickness and (b) length gauges (BS 812: 1975).

While the strength of a rock is an intrinsic characteristic, the effective strength of an aggregate particle is modified by its shape and size (§7.5.3). The greater degradation and preferential elimination of flaky particles (Ramsay *et al.* 1974) in a particular size range is related to higher bending moments which can be applied (Lees 1964).

7.5.1.2e. Angularity. This is a measure of the lack of rounding of aggregate particles. This characteristic adversely affects the workability of concrete but can improve the stability of interlocking fragments. As seen in previous sections, the determination of shape characteristics rests heavily on the measurements on individual

particles. As this is time-consuming, several attempts have been made to devise more rapid methods for determining the degree of rounding of gravels through its effect on bulk properties.

One such test, adopted in BS 812: 1975, is based on computation of the percentage of voids in a compacted aggregate. As pebbles in a gravel become less angular, there is a progressive reduction in the proportion of voids (V) as expressed by

$$V = 100 \left(\frac{1 - W}{cG_a} \right)$$

where V is the percentage of voids, W is the weight of a standard volume of aggregate, c is the volume of the cylinder and G_a is the apparent dry relative density of the material.

Since the angularity number (AN) = $V - 33$, where 33 is the percentage of voids in a very well-rounded river gravel, the expression for V can be substituted to express AN:

$$AN = 67 - \frac{100W}{cG_a}$$

AN varies from 0 to 9, the higher number being typical of freshly crushed rock.

Lees (1963) devised a scheme for the determination of the degree of angularity in grains and crushed-rock fragments. This involves either measurement and calculation in accordance with prescribed methods and formula or, more simply, visual comparison with a descriptive chart similar to that proposed by Krumbein (1941) for roundness.

7.5.1.2f. Sphericity and roundness. Wadell (1933) proposed these terms for describing particle shape which varied from spherical to less regular. Sphericity (ψ) is the deviation of a particle from a sphere, i.e. ψ is the ratio of the surface area of a sphere with the same volume as the particle to the surface area of the particle. Because surface area and volume are difficult to measure in small grains he suggested $\psi = d_p/D$ where d_p is the projected diameter and D the diameter of the smallest circle circumscribing that projected area. Alternatively, $\psi_2 = d_e L$ where d_e is the diameter of particles obtained as the diameter of a sphere having the same volume as the particle and L is the length of the particle. The sphericity number ranges between 0 and 1.

Roundness is a measure of the sharpness of corners, i.e. smoothness:

$$p = \sum \frac{r/R}{N}$$

where r is the radius of curvature of a corner of the particle surface, R is the radius of the maximum inscribed circle in the projected plane and N is the number of corners. With wear r approaches R and p approaches l (Harr 1977). In genetic terms roundness is a function of wear while surface texture reflects environmental differences.

The simplest routine estimation of these parameters is facilitated by visual reference to a calibrated set of standards (Krumbein 1941; Lees 1963). Griffiths (1967), however, cautioned that there are psychological deficiencies in the method, owing to the subjective nature of the method and the likelihood of operator error.

7.5.1.2g. Surface texture. This expression of the microtopography of aggregate particles (Krumbein & Petti-

john 1938) reflects petrographic and environmental factors of the original material. This property affects frictional properties and intergranular slip in unbound aggregate and the adhesion of binders or cement. BS 812: 1975 outlines six broad and qualitative categories, e.g. glassy, smooth, granular, rough, crystalline, honeycombed and porous.

A more objective and quantitative scheme was proposed (Wright 1955), but this has not been adopted in the aggregate industry. This method entails analysis of enlargements ($\times 125$) of particle profiles in thin section. This provides

$$\text{Roughness factor} = \frac{100\,Y}{\text{sample length}}$$

where Y is the excess in length of the actual profile (roughness line) over the length of the segmented curve (unevenness line) which represents the general undulations of the roughness line.

7.5.1.3. Relative density, bulk density and water absorption. The relative density of samples of the raw material can be established by one of several conventional techniques using balance or steel-yard and the reader is referred to any textbook of physical mineralogy (e.g. Hurlbut & Klein 1977).

The relative density of aggregate is obtained in a broadly similar fashion (BS 812: 1975) but at the same time a measure of the water absorption can be obtained. For aggregate coarser than 10 mm a thoroughly saturated sample (e.g. 2 kg) is weighed in water (mass B). It is then surface dried and weighed (weight A). Finally it is oven-dried for 24 ± 0.5 hours at 100–110°C, cooled and weighed (weight C).

Relative density (oven-dried)	$= \dfrac{C}{A - B}$
Relative density (saturated and surface dry)	$= \dfrac{A}{A - B}$
Apparent relative density	$= \dfrac{C}{C - B}$
Water absorption (% dry mass)	$= \dfrac{(A - C)}{C} \times 100$

There are variations in the method for finer aggregates using pycnometer, gas jar or specific gravity bottle (BS 812: 1975).

7.5.1.4. Bulk density (unit weight). This is a measure of the weight of material in a unit volume, e.g. lb ft^{-3}, kg m^{-3} etc. This test is described by BS as a rapid means of comparison between different aggregates. In the same test one can obtain the percentage of voids:

$$\% \text{ voids} = \left(\frac{a - (b/1000)}{a}\right) \times 100$$

where a is the relative density of the aggregate on an oven-dry basis and b is the bulk density of an oven-dry aggregate.

7.5.1.5. Aggregate shrinkage. Some rocks exhibit the property of absorbing water with attendant change in dimension. This in turn can have a very significant influence on the shrinkage characteristics of concrete made from this aggregate (Fig. 7.3a) (Edwards 1967). This relationship has been extended to the drying shrinkage of such aggregates and the shrinkage of concrete (Fig. 7.3b) and possibly to bituminous mixes made from it (Edwards 1970b).

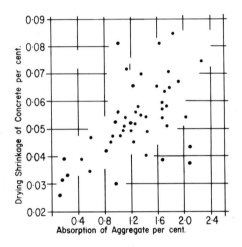

FIG. 7.3a. Relationship between drying shrinkage of concrete and absorption of aggregate.

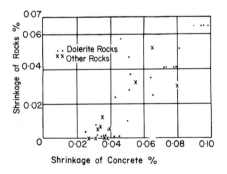

FIG. 7.3b. Relationship between shrinkage of rocks and shrinkage of concrete.

In addition to bulk dimensional change it has been suggested that there may be a connection between the property of shrinkage and unsoundness in concrete (Edwards 1967). This unsoundness is attributed to the internal strains attending cycles of slaking, i.e. wetting and drying.

Higher values of shrinkage, e.g. >0.065%, are frequently associated with dolerite, some basalts, felsites and shales, while lower values are obtained for highly siliceous rocks such as granite, flint, and the calcareous rocks, e.g. limestone. When natural gravels contain significant proportions of high shrinkage rocks then they too may exhibit high shrinkage (Edwards 1970a).

The greatest internal stresses in concrete, with resultant cracking, occur when the differential shrinkage between aggregates and the mortar reaches a maximum, e.g. highly shrinkable sand and non-shrinkable aggregate.

A test for concrete shrinkage has been described by Edwards (1963) in which 28 day old prisms of concrete are immersed in water for four days, then surface dried and measured (l_c). The prisms are then oven-dried at a specified temperature for three weeks, cooled and measured. Drying is continued for a further week followed by measurement of length. This procedure is repeated until a constant length is obtained (l_d)

$$\text{Drying shrinkage (\%)} = \frac{l_c - l_d}{l_d} \times 100$$

7.5.2. Petrographic examination of aggregates

In the first edition of this book the petrographic examination of aggregates was dealt with here. In the present edition this subject is dealt with in Chapter 6.

7.5.3. Mechanical tests

7.5.3.1. Strength. At one time the strength tests for potential aggregates were performed on one-inch cores of intact rock, e.g. uniaxial compressive strength. The correlation between the performance of rock in the intact state and the aggregate form is not consistent, however, in other than general terms (Dhir *et al.* 1971). To simulate the natural conditions more closely a suite of tests was designed which express the various aspects of aggregate strength namely, aggregate impact value, aggregate crushing value and ten percent fines value. These are embodied in British Standard 812: 1990.

7.5.3.2. Aggregate impact value (AIV). In this test a standard sample in the size range 14 mm to 10 mm is subjected to a discontinuous loading in the form of 15 blows from a hammer or piston (13.5 kg to 14.1 kg) falling through 381 ± 6.5 mm (BS 812: 1990) (Fig. 7.4). The sample suffers degradation to a graded assemblage of fines. An arbitrary sieve size, 2.36 mm, is chosen as the diagnostic cut-off level and the percentage of material passing, relative to initial weight, gives the aggregate impact value, and is used as the measure of resistance to granulation. Two tests are performed and the results should be within a numerical value of 1. In this test a lower numerical value indicates a more resistant rock. The reproducibility of results in the test is high (Table 7.2) so that two values per sample are sufficient. The apparatus used in this test is relatively portable and cheap to operate, allowing both laboratory and field testing of aggregate.

of rock types currently exploited in Scotland (Ramsay *et al.* 1974; Edwards 1967) are given in Table 7.6. These values were based on British Standard specifications existing at the time, i.e. direct metric equivalents of previous Imperial dimensions. No study has been made of the effect of changed particle dimensions in the revised Standards.

FIG. 7.5. Aggregate crushing test apparatus.

FIG. 7.4. Aggregate impact test apparatus.

7.5.3.3.   Aggregate crushing value (ACV). In this test a sample of approximately 2 kg is subjected to a continuous load transmitted through a piston, in a compression test machine (Fig. 7.5). A total load of 400 kN is achieved in 10 minutes. As in the AIV the fines passing sieve **BS** 2.36 mm are calculated as a percentage of the initial sample weight. This is the aggregate crushing value. Two values are produced for each test material and values should be within a value of 1. Once again a lower value indicates a more resistant rock.

7.5.3.4.   Discussion. The approximate similarity in numerical values for the ACV and AIV tests was built into the design of the AIV, which was intended to be auxiliary to ACV. Some values of AIV and ACV from a range

TABLE 7.6. *Some values of AIV and ACV for rock types exploited in Scotland*

Rock type	AIV	range	ACV	range
Basalt	11	10–13	16	16–17
Andesite	13	11–16	16	15–17
Dacite	12		13	
Porphyry	13	12–14	12	
Felsite	13	12–15		
Dolerite	13	10–17	19	
Teschenite	22			
Granite	19	17–21	26	23–30
Limestone	17	15–20		
Greywacke	9			
Marble	19	16–21	26	25–28
Psammite	14	14–15		

These tests do not measure strength in the sense of compressive strength in intact rocks, rather they are indices of the resistance to pulverization over a prescribed interval or sequence of loading.

The range of values in Table 7.6 is much smaller than other published accounts, e.g. Shergold (1950), Road Research Laboratory (1959). The difference stems from the use of more rigorously defined rock types rather than the much broader rock associations or trade groups (Chapter 6).

The variation in aggregate impact and crushing values within specific rock type categories, or between broader rock groups, can be attributed to the influence of aggregate particle shape (Ramsay 1965) and geological features such as: bulk composition, e.g. silicate and carbonate rocks etc.; grain size; texture and structure;

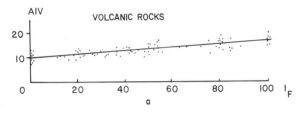

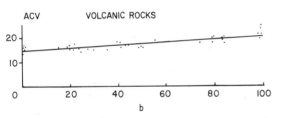

FIG. 7.6. (a) Aggregate impact value (AIV) versus flakiness index (I_F) for a suite of volcanic rocks. (b) Aggregate crushing value (ACV) versus flakiness index (I_F) for a suite of volcanic rocks.

alteration (Dhir *et al.* 1971; Ramsay *et al.* 1974). In addition, methodological factors like apparatus rigidity and the nature of the test substrate can introduce considerable variation into the values obtained for AIV (Ramsay *et al.* 1973).

The shape of the aggregate particles, in particular the index of flakiness, affects both AIV and ACV in a simple rational fashion (Figs 7.6 & 7.7). This is expressed by

$$AIV = C + nI_F$$

$$ACV = C + nI_F$$

where n is the coefficient of flakiness, ranging between 0.04 and 0.1, I_F is the flakiness index and C is a constant reflecting the other geological parameters. Flakiness can introduce differences in AIV and ACV of 30% to 60%, so that comparison of particular values without details of I_F can be misleading. The preferential elimination of flaky particles in the course of testing can be appreciated from Fig. 7.8. This destruction of flakes characterizes both the standard aggregate strength tests and the 'in service' behaviour as surface dressing and open-textured macadam aggregates. In dense bituminous mixes and densely unbound aggregate the mortar or matrix affords particle support, thereby reducing flake failure (Chapters 10 and 11).

Figure 7.6a is a synoptic plot of AIV vs I_F from volcanic rocks in the compositional range basalt to felsite. Values lie within a narrow band indicating similar deformational performance despite the considerable variation in chemistry–mineralogy. This implies that the principal rock-forming silicate minerals of which these rocks are composed have broadly comparable physical properties within the sensitivity of these tests.

The geological parameter C in the above equations is the sum of several characteristics, each of which may have a major or minor influence on the deformational behaviour. The influence of each of these features on

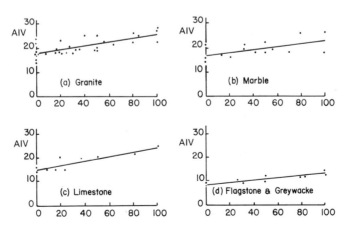

FIG. 7.7. Influence of flakiness index on aggregate impact value (AIV) for (a) granite, (b) marble, (c) limestone, (d) greywacke–flagstone.

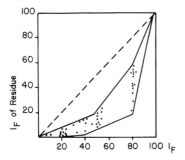

FIG. 7.8. Relationship between post-test flakiness index (I_F) of residue and pre-test flakiness index (I_F).

gross behaviour can be deduced from the intercept on the y-axis (e.g. at $I_F = 0$) in Figs 7.9 to 7.11. For example, if the AIVs for coarse- and fine-grained igneous rocks are compared there is a marked difference. In normal fresh material the variables like structure, bulk petrology and alteration are absent, insignificant or overshadowed so the principal cause of variation in AIV is grain size (Fig. 7.10). The influence of other features can be appreciated from Figs 7.9 and 7.11.

When values of AIV exceed 26 the sensitivity of the test may be impaired, due to the filling of pore spaces between particles with crushed fine material produced in the course of the test. This fine material effectively buffers the remaining fragments from the impact stresses. In the deformation of such material it has been shown (Ramsay *et al.* 1977) that, during the earlier stages of the test, increase in the AIV results from both the granulation of the aggregate and the pulverization of already formed coarser debris (i.e. >2.36 mm). At a certain stage in the test the pattern of behaviour changes and AIV increased dramatically, chiefly at the expense of the broken material in the size range 9.5 mm to 2.40 mm. The insensitivity of AIV in such cases has been countered by modifications to the tests, e.g. ten per cent fines value and modified impact value.

7.5.3.5. Ten per cent fines value. This variation of the aggregate crushing value presents the load required to produce 10% fines rather than the amount of crush for a specific load. A uniform loading rate is applied to cause a total penetration of the plunger of approximately 15 mm (gravels), 20 mm (normal crushed rock) or 24 mm (honeycombed aggregates) in 10 minutes. The fines less

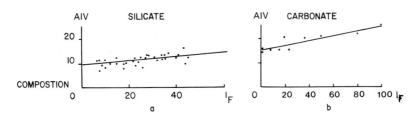

FIG. 7.9. Aggregate impact value (AIV) versus flakiness index (I_F) for (a) silicate (volcanic) rocks, and (b) carbonate rocks.

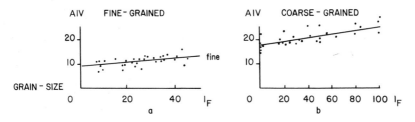

FIG. 7.10. Aggregate impact value (AIV) versus flakiness index (I_F) for (a) fine-grained, and (b) coarse-grained, igneous rocks.

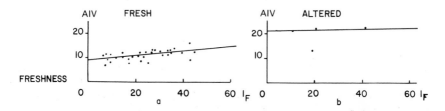

FIG. 7.11. Aggregate impact value (AIV) versus flakiness index (I_F) for (a) fresh, and (b) altered, volcanic rocks.

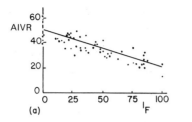
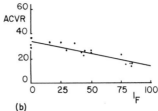

FIG. 7.12. Influence of flakiness index (I_F) on (a) aggregate impact value residue (AIVR), and (b) aggregate crushing value residue (ACVR) for basic volcanic rocks.

than 2.36 mm should fall within 7.5% to 12.5% of the initial weight, the force required to produce ten per cent fines $= 14x/(y + 4)$ where x is the maximum force (kN) and y is the mean percentage fines from two tests at x force (kN).

7.5.3.6. Modified aggregate impact test (Shergold & Hosking 1963; Hosking & Tubey 1969).

For this test the aggregate is saturated, although surface dry. After testing, the sample is oven-dried (12 hours at 100–110°C) before sieving. The test procedure is similar to that of the standard Aggregate Impact test (BS 812) except that the number of hammer blows is limited to that which will yield between 5% and 20% fines. The 'modified AIV' is obtained by multiplying the percentage finer than 2.36 mm by $15/X$ where X is the actual number of blows, e.g. if 5 blows yield 10% fines:

$$\text{modified AIV} = 10 \times \frac{15}{5} = 30.$$

An alternative test for such weak rocks is the ten per cent fines test on water-saturated samples.

7.5.3.7. Other non-standard values.

In both AIV and ACV tests the arbitrary cut-off level of 2.36 mm as the sole index of pulverization gives an imperfect assessment of aggregate response to the rigours of the test (Ramsay *et al.* 1974). Thus an aggregate which gets heavily broken, but not finely pulverized, can apparently compare favourably in AIV and ACV with material less heavily crushed. For example, a basalt with $I_F = 53$ gave an AIV of 16, apparently not much inferior to the average basalt with $I_F = 30$ and AIV of 13 (Ramsay 1965). Sieving the crushed sample to obtain the plus 9.5 mm material established the proportion still remaining within the original size range. In the first basalt this residue was 13.9% as against 35% for the second. These values: aggregate impact value residue (AIVR; Ramsay 1965) and aggregate crushing value residue (ACVR, Dhir *et al.* 1971) have been included as routine values in all subsequent testing by these authors. Both AIVR and ACVR are more sensitive to I_F than the standard values

(Fig. 7.12), although the relationship is a simple linear one:

$$\text{AIVR or ACVR} = C - nI_F$$

where n ranges from 0.11 to 0.33.

When considering the significance of AIV and ACV it should be remembered that an aggregate should exhibit minimal break-up, to particles of any size. The standard tests take no account of the coarser break-down products (i.e. 10 mm to 2.36 mm).

7.5.3.8. Tests on ledge or lump rock.

(a) Franklin point load strength. The Franklin Point Load apparatus is a simple, portable device (Fig. 7.13) for obtaining an indirect measure of the compressive stength of rock cores in the field (Brock & Franklin 1972). It can be used, however, with small irregular lumps as might be obtained from the ledge rock.

A load is applied through round-end conical plattens, the ram being driven by a small hand-operated hydraulic pump. In loading through point contacts the specimens fail in tension at a fraction of the load required in the standard laboratory compression tests. The values obtained in this test correlate well with the laboratory uniaxial compression test so that an estimated value for uniaxial strength can be easily and rapidly obtained. Used in conjunction with an index test like fracture spacing this value forms the basis of a rock quality classification (Fookes *et al.* 1971).

(b) Schmidt rebound number (BS 1881). An experienced geologist can obtain a qualitative impression of the toughness, elasticity and state of freshness of a rock from the impact and sound of his hammer striking the rock. The Schmidt hammer is a simple quantitative extension of this test (Fig. 7.14). Although originally designed as a non-destructive test for concrete it has been applied unmodified to natural rock materials. The results obtained, however, can be strongly influenced by methodological factors such as surface preparation for the plunger and the unsuspected presence of open, face-parallel cracks close behind the rock surface.

The instrument is held tightly against the rock and a

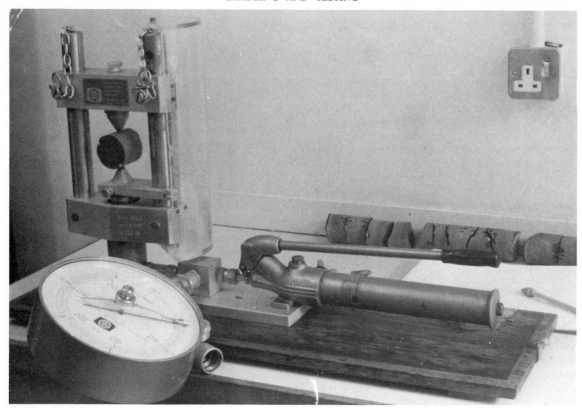

FIG. 7.13. Portable point-load testing machine.

FIG. 7.14. Schmidt concrete test hammer.

spring-loaded hammer or piston, travelling through a fixed distance, applies a known energy input to the rock. The hammer rebounds from the rock, the actual amount being influenced by the elasticity of the rock. This rebound is recorded on a scale as a percentage of the forward travel. Fresh igneous rocks give values of 50 and greater. Where weathering is present and the rock is less elastic and more porous, the Schmidt hammer is sensitive to this change. A number of published studies provide examples of the use of this technique on rocks (Duncan 1969; Geol. Soc. Rep. 1977).

An advantage of this equipment is its probability and ease of operation in the field situation, many readings being obtained in a short time. It is perhaps used to best advantage, however, in combination with other tests of observations such as specific gravity, point load strength, joint spacing etc.

7.5.4. Durability and frost susceptibility

Durability or resistance to wear or decay is a significant requirement of many aggregates. Some aggregates with satisfactory values from the standard strength tests deteriorate with time in the stockpile or 'in service' on roads. The bond between the constituent grains or particles may be intrinsically strong or weak, but frequently is weakened as a result of subaerial processes, past or present, e.g. weathering, frost etc. There are, therefore, two aspects of durability:

(a) Mechanical deterioration or wear
(b) Physico-chemically activated deterioration, e.g. soundness

7.5.4.1. Mechanical tests. (a) Aggregate abrasion value (AAV). This test provides an estimation of surface wear (BS 812: Part 113: 1990) 33 cm^3 of clean 14 mm to 10 mm non-flaky aggregate are set into a polyester resin backing, allowing 6 mm protrusion of the aggregate (Tubey & Szafran 1970). This sample is held against a rotating lap (28 to 30 revs min^{-1}) by a total load of 2 kg, for some 500 revolutions. Leighton Buzzard sand is fed in front of the sample at 0.7 kg to 0.9 kg min^{-1}. The loss in weight during the test is expressed as a percentage of that of the original sample, to give the Aggregate Abrasion Value. The mean of two tests is presented to two significant figures. In this test a lower numerical value indicates a more resistant rock. Values range from 1 for hard flints to over 15 for aggregates which would normally be considered too weak for use in road surfacings (Hawkes & Hosking 1972).

The AAV reflects hardness and brittleness of the constituent minerals, the influence of mineral cleavage and the strength of intergranular bond. Igneous and non-foliate metamorphic rocks yield the highest values within comparable composition ranges. Aggregate abra-

sion value is related in a simple and rational fashion to AIV and PSV for arenaceous rocks (Fig. 7.15) (Hawkes & Hosking 1972).

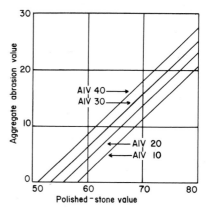

FIG. 7.15. Relationship between aggregate abrasion value, polished stone value and aggregate impact value (AIV) for arenaceous roadstones (Hawkes & Hosking 1972).

Inadequate resistance to abrasion of road surfacing aggregates causes an early loss of the texture depth that is necessary to maintain high-speed skid resistance (Hawkes & Hosking 1972).

(b) Aggregate attrition value (BS 812: 1943). This test, sometimes referred to as the 'Deval' test, is little used in the UK except for railway ballast and is no longer in BS 812. Reproducibility is poorer than other aggregate tests including the Los Angeles test, which is more widely favoured (ASTM C131).

Samples are rotated in a closed, inclined cylinder resulting in mutual attrition of the aggregate. The percentage of material removed from the sample during the test is the Aggregate Attrition Value. The test is performed both dry and wet.

(c) Los Angeles abrasion value (ASTM Designation C131 and C535). A sample charge with 6 to 12 steel balls is rotated in a steel cylinder (Fig. 7.16a) for 500 or 1000 revolutions at 33 rpm for material less and greater than 19 mm respectively. This causes attrition through mutual tumbling and impact of the particles and the steel balls. After the test the sample is screened on a 1.68 mm aperture sieve. The coarser fraction, washed and oven dried, is weighed and the loss in weight, as a percentage of the original weight, is the Los Angeles abrasion value. Values for this test are numerically similar to the ACV of similar sized charges for values up to about 30, i.e. for all aggregates that would normally be used in bituminous surfacing (Shergold 1960). Aggregate in the Los Angeles Test suffers a combination of attrition and impact, with the latter probably more significant. In consequence, Los Angeles abrasion values

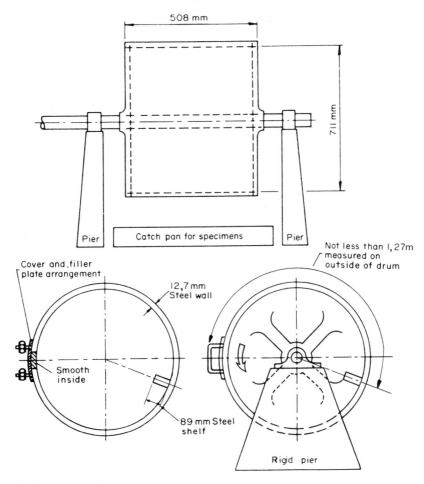

FIG. 7.16a. Los Angeles abrasion machine.

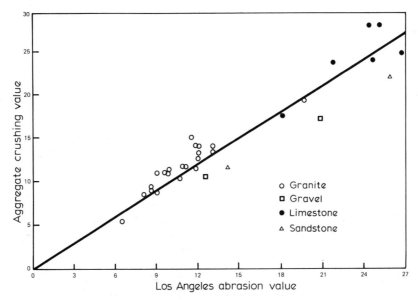

FIG. 7.16b. Correlation between results of aggregate crushing test and Los Angeles test.

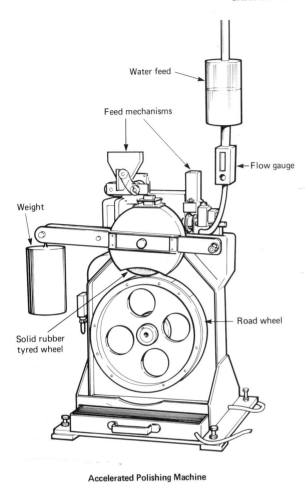

Accelerated Polishing Machine

Fig. 7.16c. Accelerated polishing machine.

are influenced by the same geological and clast features which affect ACV and AIV. Tests at the Road Research Laboratory in 1940 showed that there is a very good (1:1) correlation between Los Angeles abrasion values and the ACV as shown in Fig. 7.16b.

(d) Polished stone value (PSV). The polished stone value was designed as a predictive measure of the susceptibility of a stone to polishing, when used in the wearing surface of a road (BS 812: Part 114: 1989). An accelerated polishing apparatus simulates the action of dust-laden tyres on samples of aggregate set in a polyester resin backing mounted in standard moulds on a rotating 'road wheel'. A 200 mm diameter × 38 mm broad tyre bears on the aggregate with a total force of 725N. Corn emery and water are continuously fed to the surface of the tyre. This is repeated using emery flour as abrasive. Fig. 7.16c shows the apparatus.

The polish of the specimens is then measured using a standard pendulum arc friction tester. The deflection of

a pointer on a calibrated scale yields the coefficient of friction expressed as a percentage, and this is the polished stone value. A higher value signifies greater resistance to polishing.

Cox (1973) provided a perceptive review of this test, highlighting the procedural problems and providing a perspective on numerical reproducibility.

(e) Discussion. Skid resistance is provided by the roughness of a road surface and a suitable aggregate should retain a high degree of roughness in service. In the PSV test hard and tough rocks do not necessarily yield the best results as such rocks, because of their dense texture and hardness, can take on a good polish. Igneous rocks with a small proportion of soft minerals have a high polish resistance. Foliation in basalt also increases resistance to polish while fresh, fine-grained igneous rocks accept a high polish. Secondary minerals, if their hardness differs from the bulk mineral content, increase resistance. Gritstones tend to be resistant as a result of grain plucking continually renewing the rough surface. Limestone, especially with a small volume of insoluble residue, has a low resistance to polishing although this increases with the volume of the residue. Monomineralic, well-bonded quartzite, hornfels and flint take a high polish (Fig. 7.17) (Hartley 1970, 1971).

Values over 65 indicate a highly polish-resistant rock especially suitable for road wearing courses in high-risk areas. The number of sources of material of this quality in the UK is limited (Chapter 11).

For a suite of greywackes, meta-greywackes and arkoses of Precambrian to Upper Carboniferous age, Hawkes & Hosking (1972) demonstrated a broad correlation between the values obtained from the mechanical tests concerned with aggregate strength properties, e.g. crushing and impact strength and abrasion resistance, but an inverse relationship between abrasion resistance and polishing resistance (Fig. 7.15).

(f) Micro-Deval value. In other European countries the micro-Deval test is often used as the method of determining the resistance of an aggregate to abrasion. The procedure used in this research is that given in French Standard NF P 18-572 (AFNOR 1978). The abrasion of the aggregate is produced by a charge of stainless steel balls in a rotating cylinder. The test may be carried out either wet or dry: 2.5 litres of water are added to the test cylinder prior to testing in the wet state.

The micro-Deval value is calculated as $100\,m/M$, where M is the weight of the aggregate tested and m is the weight of the material which passes through the 1.6 mm sieve after the test. The result obtained is identified as either:

micro-Deval value (dry) (or MDS : S representing 'sec' or dry), or micro-Deval value (wet) (or MDE : E representing 'eau' or water).

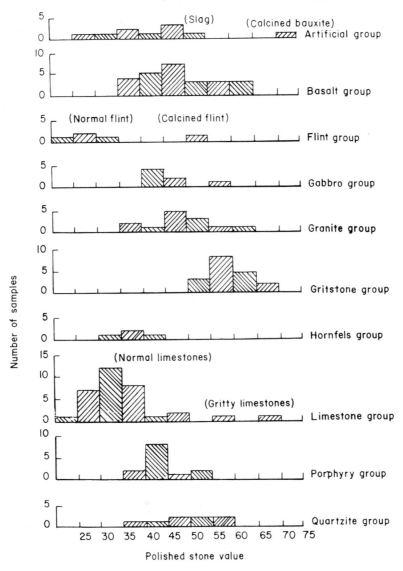

Fig. 7.17. Distribution of polished stone value in different groups of rock (Road Research Laboratory Report LR 84, 1968).

Very rough rules-of-thumb for indicating approximate values of MDS and MDE from aggregate abrasion values are:

(1) for crushed rock aggregates excluding blast furnace slag MDS = 0.5 AAV;
(2) for crushed rock aggregates excluding blast furnace slag and limestone MDE = 2.6 AAV.

7.5.4.2. Physico-chemical tests. (a) Soundness. This is the term used for the ability of an aggregate to resist excessive volume changes as a result of changes in the physical environment, e.g. freeze–thaw, thermal changes at temperatures above freezing, slaking, i.e. alternate wetting and drying. The rocks most susceptible to such volume changes are dolerite, porous chert, shales and any rocks with a significant content of clay minerals, e.g. montmorillonite or illite. Used in concrete, such material could lead to deterioration through scaling or more extensive cracking.

The soundness of a rock may be decreased through weathering or alteration. Weathering is a phenomenon most commonly developed on a geological time scale, but in some situations can occur in service over a period of months or years in some freshly exposed rock surfaces. The weathering is manifested by an increase in porosity and water absorption and this in turn can affect the response of the rock to the physical environment.

(b) Slake durability index (Franklin 1970). This is a measure of the resistance of a rock to slaking and was developed as an index test for mud rocks. A number of small samples of known weight are placed in a wire-mesh drum and immersed in water. The drum is rotated at a fixed speed for 10 minutes, causing the specimens to rub and abrade. After 10 minutes, the specimens are dried and weighed and any loss in weight is expressed as a percentage of initial weight, the slake durability index.

For some rocks, e.g. compacted shales, weathered rocks etc., slaking causes internal swelling pressures or softening. The resultant weakening is accentuated by the rotation and mutual collisons. In aggregates this test is only relevant to the lowest grade materials whose weakness is self-evident and which might be employed in road sub-base material.

An alternative to the slake durability value is the Washington Degradation test. The degradation factor is a measure of the quantity of fines produced by rock particles when they are abraded in the wet condition. A sample is sieved into size fractions 13.20 to 9.50 mm; 9.50 to 6.70 mm; 6.70 to 4.75 mm and 4.75 to 2.00 mm, which are washed and oven-dried. Equal proportions of each fraction are combined into a representative test sample which is placed in the test canister with water. This is agitated for 20 min in a sieve shaker. After shaking, the sample is washed over 2.00 mm and 75 μm sieves into a measuring cylinder. The solids in the wash water are brought into suspension by 10 rapid inversions of the cylinder and transferred to a 380.0 mm tall graduated tube. After further agitation the fines are allowed to settle for 20 min. The height of the sediment column (H) is measured and the degradation factor given by

$$D = \frac{(380 - H)}{(380 + 1.75H)} \times 100 \; .$$

(c) Modal analysis. Determination of the secondary minerals created by weathering or alteration is achieved by means of point-count or modal analysis of thin sections (Chayes 1949). Weinert (1964) established a link between the soundness of dolerite and the proportion of these secondary minerals. He found that in satisfactory dolerites less than 30% of the ferro-magnesian minerals were identifiably altered. This proved reliable for prediciton of performance, save in the borderline range of 30% to 33%. This was considered adequate as a first indication of the degree of weathering.

Irfan & Dearman (1978) characterized weathering of a granite by a microcpetrographic index, similar to that of Mendes *et al.* (1966), calculated from the ratio of sound to unsound constituents determined from modal analysis. This index is correlatable with the widely-used weathering grade scheme (Geol. Soc. Rep. 1977).

(d) Sulphate Soundness Test. The sulphate soundness test has a long history. It is reported that it first appeared in France around 1818 as a test for classifying the resistance of building stone to deterioration under freeze-thaw conditions. In North America it has been incorporated in the ASTM book of Standards under designation C88 since 1931. In the United Kingdom it did not come into widespread use until the late 1970s and it has now been standardized (BS 812: Part 121: 1989).

In the test, as described in BS 812, a sample of aggregate in the size range 10 mm to 14 mm is subjected to five cycles comprising immersion in a saturated solution of magnesium sulphate followed by oven-drying at 105°C to 110°C. This subjects the sample of aggregate to the disruptive effects of the repeated crystallization and rehydration of magnesium sulphate within the pores of the aggregate. The extent of the disruption is dependent upon the soundness of the aggregate. The degree of degradation arising from the disruptive effects is measured by the extent to which material finer than 10 mm in particle size is produced. The test is carried out in duplicate and the mean result to the nearest whole number is taken as the magnesium sulphate soundness value (MSSV).

Crystallization tests in general, and the magnesium sulphate test in particular, are severe tests. Such tests are known to give different results depending on the nature of the crystallization medium and the number of cycles involved. Also, the shape, size, porosity and permeability of the aggregate particles have significant effects. Commonly in practice these tests may measure the number of friable particles among otherwise sound aggregate rather than the general performance of a uniform aggregate. Thus these tests are only applicable in special circumstances where an exceptional minimum of particle deterioration is being sought. The normal applications involve aggregates used in the surface of airfield runways, taxiways and hardstandings, as well as motorways and trunk roads.

In reporting the performance of a series of low grade roadstone aggregates from UK, South Africa and Mauritius, Hosking & Tubey (1969) employed sulphate soundness in conjunction with other standard and modified mechanical tests. An arbitrary limit of 20% loss was suggested for the sulphate test for the boundary between the 'doubtful' and 'unacceptable' categories.

For the poorer material the sulphate test may be a valid means of differentiating them into sound and unsound, but how far this is applicable is uncertain. Weinert (1964) cautioned that absolute meanings should not be attached to test values.

In the ASTM test the magnesium sulphate soundness value is expressed in terms of the percentage loss during the test whereas in the BS test the magnesium sulphate soundness value is defined in terms of the percentage retained during the test. The reader should bear this in mind when considering test results.

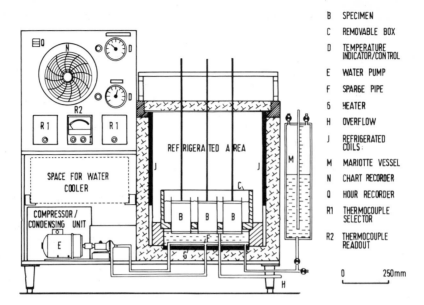

B   SPECIMEN

C   REMOVABLE BOX

D   TEMPERATURE
     INDICATOR/CONTROL

E   WATER PUMP

F   SPARGE PIPE

G   HEATER

H   OVERFLOW

J   REFRIGERATED
     COILS

M   MARIOTTE VESSEL

N   CHART RECORDER

Q   HOUR RECORDER

R1   THERMOCOUPLE
     SELECTOR

R2   THERMOCOUPLE
     READOUT

0   250mm

FIG. 7.18. Self-refrigerated unit for frost heave test.

(e) Frost susceptibility. Frost-heave can occur during prolonged periods of freezing when the temperature of the road pavement at depth falls below 0°C. If other conditions allow, water will be drawn from the water-table into the freezing zone where it will form ice-lenses. As these form, further water may be drawn into the freezing zone and more ice produced which can result in considerable expansion. It is the freezing of this transported water, rather than the 9 per cent volume increase of water on freezing, which is the prime cause of frost-heave. The formation of ice-lenses in the lower layers of the road pavement may cause considerable heaving at the surface. After thawing, the foundations of the road are weakened by the excess moisture and, unless traffic is kept off throughout the period of thaw, the whole pavement structure may fail.

The test for frost susceptibility is a simulative test which was developed at TRRL and has since been standardized (BS 812: Part 124: 1989). In the test cylindrical specimens of aggregate compacted at a pre-determined moisture content and density are placed in a self-refrigerated unit (SRU) (Fig. 7.18). This unit is designed so that the upper surfaces of the specimens are subjected to freezing air at −17°C whilst their lower ends are allowed access to water maintained at +4°C. This temperature gradient created through the specimens causes water to be drawn into the freezing zone and may lead to the formation of ice lenses. These lead to an increase in height of the specimens which is measured at intervals over a period of 96 hours. The maximum increase in height recorded is defined as the frost-heave of the aggregate.

The SRU can accommodate nine specimens and usually a test run will consist of three specimens of three different materials. Currently (Roe & Webster 1984) a material is classified as non-susceptible if the mean heave after 96 hours of a valid test is less than 9.0 mm and as susceptible if the mean heave is more than 15.0 mm. Because of the poor precision of the test, if the mean heave is between 9.1 mm and 14.9 mm, further tests are required at two other laboratories. The material is then classified as non-frost susceptible if the grand average heave is less than 12 mm.

The original test had very poor precision and, although work at TRRL has brought about a marked improvement, the reproducibility of the test result is still high in relation to the criteria set for acceptance. Recent work (Pike et al. 1990) has shown that the reproducibility of the test can be improved by the incorporation in each test run of control specimens of a material of known heave. An amendment to BS 812: Part 124 to allow for the use of control specimens of known heave has been accepted in principle. A draft amendment to the British Standard has therefore been prepared which is currently (1991) being circulated for public comment.

If this is adopted, it should be possible to set a single limit of 15 mm to distinguish between non-susceptible and susceptible materials.

(f) Freezing and thawing test. A freezing and thawing test for concrete aggregates is described in the German Standard DIN 4226 (1971). Two procedures are given: total immersion freezing and thawing, and air freezing followed by thawing in water. In the former procedure the temperature of the immersed sample in the freezing cabinet is reduced over a period of 7–10 hours and then held at a temperature of −15 to −20°C for at least 4 hours. Afterwards the test portion is thawed in water at 20°C for five hours. This cycle is applied ten times. Each fraction is dried and sieved on the next smaller sieve size, and the percentage loss in mass is determined. For the air freezing procedure aggregate soaked for two hours is drained and placed in a freezing cabinet at a temperature of −15 to −20°C for six hours and then thawed in water at 20°C for 1 hour. The cycle is applied 20 times and the subsequent treatment of the test sample is the same as that for the total immersion test.

(g) Methylene blue absorption test. Methylene blue is an organic dyestuff that dissolves in water to give a blue solution, and which can be absorbed from the solution by swelling clay minerals of the smectite type. The purpose of the methylene blue test is to obtain an assessment of the quantity of these clays in a sample of rock or aggregate by measuring the amount of methylene blue absorbed. A detailed test method is described by Hills & Pettifer (1985). It is carried out on a representative powdered sample passing the 75 µm test sieve. A test portion of 1 g taken from this sample is dispersed in 30 ml of water and then titrated by successively adding 0.5 ml increments of methylene blue solution that has been prepared by dissolving 0.1 g of methylene blue in 100 ml of distilled or de-ionized water. After each addition, the suspension is agitated for one minute and a drop removed with a glass rod and spotted on to a filter paper. This procedure is repeated at intervals until a pale blue halo is seen to have formed when the filter paper is held up to daylight. This is the end-point, and it indicates that the particles are no longer capable of further absorption. The methylene blue value (MBV), expressed as the percentage mass of methylene blue absorbed by the test portion, is:

$$\text{MBV} = \frac{0.1\, V}{M}$$

where V (ml) is the total volume of methylene blue solution added to the suspension to reach the end-point and M (g) is the mass of the test portion.

The methylene blue test is used as a standard test in France, but experience is limited. The Department of the Environment of Northern Ireland specifies a limit of 1.0% for basalt and 0.7% for gritstone aggregates. Although the test requires only simple chemical apparatus, it does require a laboratory rock grinder to produce the powdered samples for analysis.

7.5.5. Chemical tests

7.5.5.1. Organic content. The presence of organic mat-

ter in aggregates can have two separate and unrelated effects.

If present in significant amounts in fine aggregate to be used for mortar renderings or concrete it may cause disfigurement without necessarily affecting durability. The inorganic minerals which comprise commercially available fine aggregates for concrete or mortar almost without exception have a particle density greater than 2.0. By immersing a suitable sample of the fine aggregate in a liquid of density just below 2.0, lower density materials, such as organic contaminators, can be caused to float on the liquid, facilitating their removal for examination and quantification.

More serious is the possible presence of organic compounds which may retard, or completely inhibit, the hydration of Portland cement. Simple measurement of the total amount of organic matter present is of little value as it is the type of organic compound, rather than the total amount present, which is the controlling factor. Many of the organic retarders which occur in aggregates can be detected by their ability to discolour an aqueous solution of sodium hydroxide. In some circumstances, the degree of discoloration in a standard test can provide a rough guide to the degree of contamination of the aggregate. The weakness of the test is that it assumes that all retarders will give a brown coloration and that if a brown coloration is obtained retarders must be present. Neither of these assumptions is necessarily true but as the test is so easy to carry out it has some value as a rapid indication of whether or not a problem is likely to arise.

7.5.5.2. Chloride content. A test method for measuring the amount of water soluble chloride present in aggregate is given in BS 812: Part 117: 1988. The method is based on that of Volhard where an excess of standard silver nitrate solution is added to the chloride solution acidified with nitric acid, and the excess silver nitrate is back-titrated with potassium thiocyanate using ferric ammonium sulphate as an indicator.

Other methods are the Mohr direct titration method in neutral solution, using potassium chromate as an indicator; measurement of chloride concentration by specific ion electrode or, for field work and production control work of saline aggregates, the use of test strips (Figg & Lees 1975).

The method given in BS 812, and that of Figg & Lees is designed particularly for testing those aggregates, such as marine-dredged flint, where the chloride is a surface contamination only. With porous aggregates, or those of sedimentary or evaporite origin, where the chloride can be disseminated throughout the particles, complete water extraction may not be achieved unless the aggregates are finely ground before test.

The presence of chlorides in concrete can present potential hazards with some cements, e.g. by reducing sulphate resistance, and can considerably increase the risk of corrosion of embedded metal. Chlorides can also contribute to the alkaki–silica reaction.

7.5.5.3. *Sulphate content.* The sulphate content usually refers to the total acid soluble sulphate content expressed as a percentage of SO_3 and methods for carrying this out are included in several British Standards for testing aggregates and related materials (e.g. BS 812: Part 118; BS 1047, BS 1377: Part 3). All the methods involve the extraction of the sulphates with hydrochloric acid and the gravimetric determination of the sulphate ions by precipitation with barium chloride.

The determination of the total sulphate content can give a false impression of the potential damage to concrete since if all the sulphate is present as the sparingly soluble calcium sulphate the risk of sulphate attack is much reduced because of its low solubility. For this reason several of the Standards include a method that involves the extraction of the sulphate ions with a limited amount of water (usually two parts by mass of water to 1 part of aggregate) because this limits the importance attached to calcium sulphate. If calcium sulphate is the only sulphate present then water extraction can only give a value for sulphate content up to 1.2 g SO_3/litre as this is the solubility of calcium sulphate. Values in excess of 1.2 g/litre must indicate the presence of soluble and potentially more harmful sulphates.

The sulphate salt most likely to be found in mineral aggregates is calcium sulphate (gypsum). Other sulphates are infrequent in mineral aggregates but often occur in waste materials and by-products such as colliery spoil and PFA. These may also contain sulphides which given the right conditions can oxidize to sulphates.

The presence of large amounts of soluble sulphate in concrete made with ordinary Portland cement may result in cracking and expansion (see Chapter 8). This is because of their ability in the presence of excess water to react with the calcium aluminates in the cement to form calcium sulphoaluminate (ettringite). The accompanying increase in volume creates forces within the hardened concrete which can lead to its complete disintegration. BS 5328: 1976 requires that the total amount of sulphate in Portand cement concrete, including that contributed by the cement, should generally not exceed 4 per cent of cement. No limits for the sulphate content of naturally occurring aggregates are given in BS 812: Part 118 but BS 1047 for blast furnace slag used in concrete sets limits of 2.0 per cent of total sulphur and 0.7 per cent acid soluble sulphate.

The possible effects of sulphates in aggregates on the durability of concrete made from aggregates which contain them is the major worry. However, there is also a potential problem of soluble sulphates in unbound aggregates leaching out and contaminating any concrete in close proximity. In this case it is clearly the water soluble sulphates which are the main concern. For this reason, in the United Kingdom, the Department of Transport in its *Specification for Highway Works* (Department of Transport 1986) requires that, 'any material

placed within 500 mm of cement-bound materials, concrete pavements, concrete structures or concrete products shall have a sulphate content (expressed as SO_3) not exceeding 1.9 g/litre' when tested by the water extraction method given in the Standards to which reference has already been made.

A standard method for the determination of sulphate in artificial aggregates (clinker, foamed slag, pulverized-fuel ash) is given in BS 3681 'Methods for the sampling and testing of lightweight aggregates for concrete'. This method can also be used for testing mineral aggregates. Methods for determining sulphate and total sulphur contents are given in BS 1047: Part 2: 1974 'Air-cooled blast furnace slag aggregate for concrete'. Methods for the determination of sulphate generally require that the test sample is finely ground. An exception could be made in the case of impervious, insoluble aggregates, such as flint gravel and silica sands. In these cases, the procedure given in BS 812: Part 4: 1975 for extracting chlorides can be used, substituting a measured volume of 10% hydrochloric acid for the water, and determining the sulphate present in an aliquot. Artificial aggregates, in particular blast furnace slag, can also contain sulphides. In slag, these are mainly calcium sulphide, although iron and manganese sulphides may be present in smaller amounts.

7.5.5.4. *Potential alkali reactivity.* Disruptive expansion of concrete can result from reactions between certain minerals in aggregates and alkali metals (sodium and potassium) present in cement. The most widely known is the alkali–silica reaction which can occur when the aggregates contain silica as tridymite, cristobalite, opal, chalcedony or in a glassy form. Less common are alkali–carbonate reactions involving certain dolomitic carbonate rocks.

The assessment of potential alkali-reactivity is presently done in three basically different ways. The first of these is the identification of potentially reactive forms of silica in the coarse and fine aggregate; the method of doing this is petrographical analysis. The second is the direct measurement of expansion, as carried out in the mortar bar test and the concrete prism test. The third are the various chemical tests (such as the gel pat test) using treatment with sodium hydroxide to reveal any reactivity in the aggregate.

In the United Kingdom, the Concrete Society's *Technical Report No 30*, the Department of Transport's *Specification for Highway Works* and British Standard BS 8110 all provide lists of rock types considered unlikely to be reactive with some guidance on reactive minerals. The use of these lists, of course, requires petrographical examination of the aggregate. Another approach would be to specify potentially reactive minerals and give guidance on their identification, and to define suitable limits for them. This approach is being considered for inclusion in British Standard BS 882. The

Department of Transport require quarry inspection if the aggregate source is to be classified as non-reactive (see Chapter 6).

In the United States petrographical examination, mortar bar tests and the gel pat test are all used (see below). In Canada a concrete prism test is used using large prisms (350 mm long). In France petrographical examination is required, while in Germany a special test for dissolution in sodium hydroxide is used. In South Africa an accelerated concrete prism test is used. Further details are given by Hobbs (1988).

Test methods used to assess potential alkali–silica reactivity are petrographic examination (ASTM Designation C295 and BS 812: Part 104, see Chapter 6), measurement of length changes of mortar bars (ASTM Designation C227), chemical tests (ASTM Designation C289) and gel pat tests (Jones & Tarleton 1958). The Conrow test for potential volume change of mortar bars (ASTM Designation C342) is applicable particularly to certain aggregate–cement combinations widely used in the United States, and is not generally adopted elsewhere.

The mortar bar test gives a direct measurement of expansive reactivity, but is time consuming. Except with a few highly expansive aggregates it is necessary to continue length measurements for at least six months. For siliceous aggregates, an increase of 0.10 per cent at six months, or not less than 0.05 per cent at three months, is said to indicate deleterious expansion. However, minerals other than reactive silica (gypsum for example) can cause expansion of the specimens, and where length increases greater than those given above are recorded, it is recommended that a petrographic examination is made of the aggregate.

In the chemical test the sample is crushed to between 300 and 150 microns, then digested for 24 hours with a known volume and concentration of hot sodium hydroxide solution. After digestion the solution is analysed to determine the amount of alkali which has entered into reaction and the amount of silica dissolved from the aggregate during the reaction. Potential reactivity is assessed from the analytical results by reference to a graph given in the method which correlates test results with the known field performance of a number of aggregates. The chemical test does not give reliable indications when the aggregates contain carbonates or certain silicates and, where marginal reactivity is indicated, confirmatory petrographic examination is recommended. Mortar bar measurements are recommended to confirm chemical test results which indicate 'deleterious' or 'potentially deleterious' degrees of activity.

In the gel pat test pieces of aggregate are cast into cement paste pats, which after curing are ground to expose the aggregate surfaces. The pats are stored in sealed containers in an alkaline solution and arranged so that the aggregate faces are uppermost. The presence of reactive silica is shown by formations of white siliceous liquid or gel on the exposed surfaces. These may be apparent within seven days, but the tests should be extended to four weeks, and can be usefully continued for longer. Some laboratories have claimed success for accelerated indicative testing by storage of gel pats at elevated temperatures (Sims & Poole 1980). The test gives a fairly rapid positive indication of the presence of reactive silica and does not require the analytical precision of the chemical method. However, it does not necessarily follow that an aggregate showing reactivity in the test will be expansively reactive in concrete and it is recommended that positive results are confirmed by petrographic examination or mortar bar tests.

The potential alkali reactivity of carbonate rock aggregates may be assessed by ASTM Designation C586 in which the length change of rock specimens immersed in sodium hydroxide solution is measured. It is emphasized that the test is intended as a fairly rapid screening method, rather than a specification, and that acceptance or rejection of aggregate sources should not be based solely on the results. Aggregates which show expansion in the test should be tested in concrete.

Examination of the mineralogical composition and testing by an experienced petrographer remains the most reliable method for evaluating the potential reactivity of carbonate aggregates.

It should be noted that certain unusual reactive rock types do not always respond to the normal alkali-reactivity tests and other more sophisticated procedures have sometimes been adopted (Gillott 1975). He emphasizes the important role of initial petrographic examination.

Although the mechanisms of the various types of alkali–aggregate reactivity differ they all require a relatively high content of alkalis in the concrete and the presence of moisture. The alkali–silica reaction is attributed to the swelling of a gel, resulting in pressures which can exceed the tensile strength of the concrete and result in expansion and cracking. The expansion of concrete containing alkali-reactive carbonate rock aggregates is believed, at least in some cases, to be due to moisture absorption by clay or clay-like constituents following a dedolomitization reaction. Where susceptible minerals are present in an aggregate, disruptive expansion of concrete generally will not occur if the total alkali content of the cement used does not exceed 0.6 per cent (as equivalent Na_2O): exceptions to this have been reported, especially when alkalis are available from external sources such as sea water.

7.5.5.5. Draft British Standard procedures. A British Standard method for petrographic examination of aggregates is currently in draft form (BS 812: Part 104); this is fully described in Chapter 6. A British Standard method for assessing alkali–silica reactivity of aggregates by the concrete prism method is currently in draft

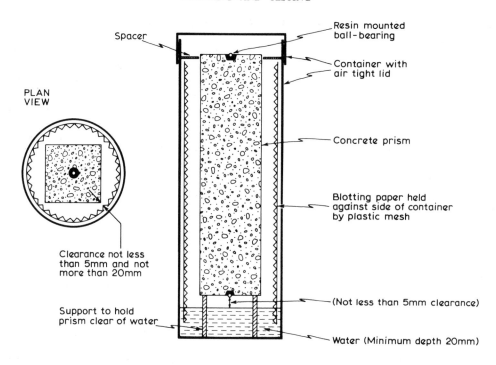

FIG. 7.19. Container to provide humid environment for concrete prism test.

form (BS 812: Part 123). In the draft procedure, concrete prisms (250 × 75 × 75 mm) are made from the combination of aggregates under test, and are stored for a period of twelve months in a humid environment (see Fig. 7.19) to promote any potential alkali–silica reaction. During this time precise measurements of the length of the prisms are made at periodic intervals to determine any expansion that occurs. The prisms are stored at a temperature of 38°C to accelerate the chemical reaction. If the expansion of the prisms exceeds 0.05% after six months some degree of alkali–silica reaction is considered to have taken place, and if the expansion exceeds 0.10% after 12 months the aggregate combination is considered reactive, according to the criteria of the Building Research Establishment. The method is designed as an accelerated laboratory test for a particular aggregate combination and should not be considered to be a performance test for any actual concrete.

7.5.6. Adhesion tests

Adhesion tests are not confined to aggregates but are interface tests between aggregates and the bituminous binder and influenced by the properties of both. For discussion of these tests refer to Chapter 11.

7.5.6.1. Static immersion tests. Coated aggregate particles are immersed in jars of distilled water and the degree of stripping is assessed as the visually estimated percentage of uncoated surface area after periods of 1, 3, 24 and 48 hours at 25°C and 40° respectively. This test has only low reproducibility due to the human factor. A variety of static immersion tests appears in Queensland Standards Q16-1966 where the aggregate is not completely coated before immersion. In this test 50 representative pieces of the aggregate sample are pressed into a thin layer of the bituminous binder, left therein in an oven at 60°C for 24 hours and then immersed for four days in a water bath at 50°C. The particles are then plucked by hand from the tray and the degree of retention of binder assessed visually. In this test and the immersion tray test described below (§7.5.6.6) there is a strong risk of influencing the result by the handling process i.e. dust coatings are removed to varying degrees by handling and varying amounts of oil/perspiration are deposited from the fingers of the handler. These factors contribute to the low reproducibility mentioned above.

The Texas Boiling Test is a more recent modification of the static immersion test in which boiling water is used (Kennedy *et al.* 1984). However, it is subject to all the limitations of the other forms of the test.

7.5.6.2. Chemical immersion tests. As for static immersion tests but a chemical solution is used in place of distilled water, generally Na_2CO_3 in varying concentrations.

7.5.6.3. Dynamic immersion tests. Similar to the static test but agitation or stirring is involved.

7.5.6.4. Immersion mechanical tests. These follow a variety of types of tests on graded and compacted coated material. After soaking for a specified number of hours at a specified temperature the materials are subjected to tests for say compressive strength, flexural strength, tensile strength, cone penetration, abrasion resistance (e.g. modified Deval, modified Los Angeles). It has been commented (Road Research Laboratory 1962) that little is known about correlation between the tests and performance in service and that with many comparatively dense and strong mixes which have been assessed by these means it is doubtful whether an important practical problem really exists.

7.5.6.5. Immersion trafficking test. An attempt to introduce the known significant factor of trafficking into adhesion testing came with the development of circular track machines and reciprocating loaded wheels (the immersion wheel tracking test 1962). The time to failure of the specimens (continuously 'trafficked' under water at 40°C) is taken as a measure of resistance to stripping. Fairly good correlation with service behaviour has been established and examples are given in the reference to show the effect of different fillers on laboratory and field resistance to stripping.

7.5.6.6. Coating tests. These differ from those above in that the aggregate is not coated initially and its resistance to stripping subsequently assessed or measured. In coating tests the ability of the aggregate to attain a coating through the medium of water is assessed. The immersion tray test (Lee 1936) involves the placing of a layer of binder in a tray which is then covered with water. The aggregate particles are then applied by hand to the binder film, left therein for ten minutes, then removed and the percentage of binder adhering to the face of the stone which has been pressed on the binder surface assessed visually. The test, while low in reproducibility, has been found useful to assess the degree of effectiveness of adding certain types and proportions of adhesion agent to standard bituminous binders.

Adhesion can also be assessed by more fundamental tests including measurement of contact angle (θ) and interfacial tension between binder and water (γ_{BW}) (Lees 1963; Hallberg 1950) and by direct measurement of adhesion tension ($\gamma_{BW} \cos \theta$) (Hallberg 1950).

7.5.6.7. Discussion. In spite of all the work that has been done on adhesion testing and all the variations of test method that exist, no completely satisfactory method appears to have been developed.

Many of the tests involve handling the aggregate particles and it has been observed that the quality of adhesion varies with both the amount of dust removed and human skin oils deposited in the handling process. The dustiness of the aggregate has a considerable adverse effect on adhesion. The relative dustiness and angularity of aggregates from different sources may cause them to appear in reverse order of merit in regard to adhesion compared with the order in which they would have been placed if those factors could have been held constant. In spite of these comments some indication can be obtained of the relative order of merit of aggregates and of the effectiveness of adhesion agents by several of the tests described.

7.6. Quality assurance

Aggregate testing laboratories, in common with much of the construction industry, are moving towards the adoption of quality assurance schemes. Quality assurance is defined in BS 5750: 1987 as 'All those planned and systematic actions necessary to provide adequate confidence that a product or service will satisfy given requirements for quality'. The advantages of implementing quality assurance are seen as increasing confidence in the fitness for purpose of products and services, reducing the client's need for and desire to check the product for compliance, and increasing overall efficiency and competitiveness. The European countries are also developing quality assurance systems in accordance with International Standard ISO9000, which is identical to BS 5750.

There are three basic elements in a quality assurance scheme. Firstly, for any test there must be a written specification of how the test is carried out. This is usually a British Standard, but it can be a foreign standard (e.g. ASTM), an international standard (e.g. ISO), or if a standard does not exist for the test, the laboratory can write its own specification or the client can prepare one. Secondly, the staff carrying out the test must be properly trained and registered. Thirdly, all apparatus used in the test must be traceable in their calibration to national standards; in Great Britain these are National Physical Laboratory standards.

In principle, there are three methods by which a quality assurance scheme may be implemented. In first-party quality assurance the laboratory itself monitors the operation of the scheme as well as setting it up and running it. In second-party quality assurance the client for the testing monitors the scheme, and in third-party quality assurance an independent authority monitors the scheme. In practice in Great Britain the third-party method has been the one mainly followed and the

TABLE 7.7. *BS 812: 100 Series status as at October 1990*

Part	Title	Status
100	General requirements for apparatus and calibration	Published 1990
101	Guide to sampling and testing aggregates	Published 1984
102	Methods for sampling	Published 1984
103	Methods for determination of particle size distribution	Published 1985
	103.2 Sedimentation test	Published 1989
104	Procedure for qualitative and quantitative petrographic examination of aggregates	Standstill 1990
105	Methods for determination of particle shape:	Published 1989
	105.1 Flakiness index	Published 1989
	105.2 Elongation index of coarse aggregate	Published 1990
106	Method for determination of shell content in coarse aggregate	Published 1985
107	Methods for determination of particle density and water absorption	Standstill 1990
108	Methods for determination of bulk density, optimum moisture content, voids and bulking	Standstill 1990
109	Methods for determination of moisture content	Published 1990
110	Methods for determination of aggregate crushing value (ACV)	Published 1990
111	Methods for determination of ten per cent fines value (TFV)	Published 1990
112	Method for determination of aggregate impact value (AIV)	Published 1990
113	Method for determination of aggregate abrasion value (AAV)	Published 1990
114	Method for determination of polished stone value	Published 1989
115	Method for determination of polished mortar value	Standstill 1990
117	Method for determination of water-soluble chloride salts	Published 1988
118	Methods for determination of sulphate content	Published 1988
119	Method for determination of acid-soluble material in fine aggregate	Published 1985
120	Method for testing and classifying drying shrinkage of aggregates in concrete	Published 1989
121	Method for determination of soundness	Published 1989
122	Method for determination of the content of deleterious materials in fine aggregate	Standstill 1990
123	Determination of alkali–silica reactivity—concrete prism method	Standstill 1990
124	Method for determination of frost-heave	Published 1989

independent authority that monitors it is the National Measurement Accreditation Service (NAMAS) operated by the National Physical Laboratory. NAMAS assesses, accredits and monitors laboratories which, if they come up to the required standard, are authorized to issue formal reports and certificates for specific measurements and tests. Note that NAMAS accreditation is not applied blanket-fashion to a laboratory, but specifically for individual tests.

Impetus for quality assurance is now coming from the clients for materials testing; the Department of Transport currently requires NAMAS accreditation for the following tests:

Analysis of bituminous materials BS598
Particle size analysis BS812
Aggregate Crushing Value BS812
10% fines value BS812
Flakiness Index BS812
Moisture Content BS1377
Liquid Limit BS1377
Plastic Limit BS1377
Plasticity Index BS1377
Compressive strength of concrete BS1881

7.7. European Standards

The revision of this report coincides both with the revision of BS 812, which is currently incomplete, and with the introduction of pan-European standards. These European standards are being introduced by the European Committee for Standardization (CEN) as part of the new approach to harmonization of standards in Europe. Work on the testing of aggregates is part of this programme and, because of this, national work on standards, including the revision of national standards, will become subject to 'standstill'. The standstill is an obligation on the part of members of CEN not to publish a new or revised national standard which is not completely in line with a European Standard (EN) or a Harmonized Document (HD) in existence or in preparation. This may well mean that the standstill will prevent the full revision of BS 812 by preventing the publication of parts of BS 812 that are in preparation. The status at October 1990 is shown in Table 7.7.

The first of the new CEN standards relating to aggregate testing has been circulated in draft form. It is the draft CEN Standard for Aggregates for Concrete. In general the standard refers to ISO Standards, or methods that are in national standards, or refers to European Standards that do not yet exist. Until the European Standards for test methods have been published the presumption must be that methods of test in ISO Standards or national standards will be acceptable to specify aggregates for concrete. Further details of International and European Standards applicable to aggregate testing are given by Pike (1990), but the situation with respect to European Standards is changing so rapidly that any statement quickly becomes out of date. A useful source of information on the testing of aggregates used in road construction is the Permanent International Association of Road Congresses (PIARC). PIARC's technical committee on the Testing of Road Materials publishes details of international test methods in its reports to the PIARC World Congressses, and in its special publications such as *Recommendations on methods to be used for testing aggregates (1987)* and *Marginal Materials: state of the Art* (1989). These are available from PIARC, 27 Rue Gueneguad, 75006, Paris.

References

AMERICAN SOCIETY FOR TESTING AND MATERIALS 1989. Potential volume change of cement-aggregate combinations. ASTM Designation C342-79.

—— 1989. Water-soluble chlorides present as admixes in graded aggregate road mixes. ASTM Designation C1411-82.

—— 1989. Specific gravity and absorption of coarse aggregate. ASTM Designation C127-88.

—— 1989. Specific gravity and absorption of the aggregate. ASTM Designation C128-88.

—— 1989. Unit weight and voids in aggregate. ASTM Designation C29-89.

—— 1989. Sieve analysis of fine and coarse aggregates. ASTM Designation C136-84.

—— 1989. Soundness of aggregates by use of sodium sulphate or magnesium sulphate. ASTM Designation C88-83.

—— 1989. Resistance to abrasion of small-size coarse aggregate by use of the Los Angeles machine. ASTM Designation C131-89.

—— 1989. Standard specifications for concrete aggregates. ASTM Designation C33-86.

—— 1989. Resistance to abrasion of large-size coarse aggregate by use of the Los Angeles machine. ASTM Designation C535-89.

—— 1989. Standard test method for potential reactivity of aggregates (chemical method). ASTM C28-8.

—— 1989. Standard test method for potential alkali reactivity of cement-aggregate combinations (mortar-bar method). ASTM C227-87.

—— 1989. Standard test method for potential alkali reactivity of carbonate rocks for concrete aggregate (rock cylinder method). ASTM C586-69.

AFNOR (L'ASSOCIATION FRANCAISE DE NORMALISATION) 1978. Norm Francaise Enregistrée NF P 18-572. Essai d'usure micro-Deval. Paris.

BRITISH GRANITE AND WHINSTONE FEDERATION 1966a. Sampling. Pamphlet INF/9.

BRITISH STANDARDS INSTITUTION BS 812: 1975. Methods for sampling and testing of mineral aggregates and fillers.

—— BS 812: 100 Series, Testing aggregates. (For list of parts and dates of publication see Table 7.7)

—— BS 882: 1983:1201. Aggregates from natural sources for concrete.

—— BS 1377: 1975. Methods of test for soil for civil engineering purposes.

—— BS 1377: 1983: Part 3: 1990, Chemical tests.

—— BS 5328: 1976. Methods for specifying concrete.

—— BS 5835: 1980. Recommendations for testing of aggregates. Part 1 Compactability test for graded aggregates.

—— BS 1047: 1983, Specification for air-cooled blastfurnace slag aggregate for use in construction.

BROCK, E. & FRANKLIN, J. A. 1972. The point-load strength test. *International Journal of Rock Mechanics and Mining Science* **9**, 669–97.

CHAYES, F. 1949. A simple point counter for thin-section analysis. *American Mineralogist* **34**, 1–11.

COX, E. A. 1973. Roadstone assessment—an art or a science? *Quarry Managers Journal, London* **57**, 169–77.

DEPARTMENT OF TRANSPORT 1986. *Specification for Highway Works*, Part 3, HMSO, London.

DHIR, R. K., RAMSAY, D. M. & BALFOUR, N. 1971. A study of the Aggregate Impact and Crushing Value Tests. *Journal of the Institution of Highway Engineers* **18**, 17–27.

DIN (Deutshes Institut für Normung) 1971. *Zuschlag für Beton. Prüfung von Zuschlag mit dichtem oder porigem Gefüge.* DIN 4226, Blatt 3 (1971). Deutschen Normenausschusses, Berlin.

DUNCAN, N. 1969. Engineering geology and rock mechanics. Vol. 1 and 2. International Textbook Co.

EDWARDS, A. G. 1963. Shrinkage of natural aggregates in concrete. *Building Research Station Digest* **35**.

—— 1967. Properties of concrete made with Scottish crushed rock aggregates. *UK Building Research Station* Garston, *England, Pap.* **42**.

—— 1970a. Scottish aggregates: rock constituents and suitability for concrete. *Building Research Station CP* **28/70**.

—— 1970b. Shrinkable aggregates. *Building Research Station Scottish Laboratory*, East Kilbride. *SL* **1** (1) 70.

FIGG, J. W. & LEES, T. P. 1975. Field testing the chloride content of sea-dredged aggregates. *Concrete* September 1975.

FOOKES, P. G., DEARMAN, W. R. & FRANKLIN, J. A. 1971. Some engineering aspects of rock weathering with field examples from Dartmoor and elsewhere. *Quarterly Journal of Engineering Geology*, **4**, 139–85.

FRANKLIN, J. A. 1970. Observations and tests for engineering description and mapping of rocks. *Proceedings of the Second Congress of the International Society for Rock Mechanics. Belgrade*, Vol **1**, paper 1–3.

GEOLOGICAL SOCIETY ENGINEERING GROUP WORKING PARTY REPORT 1970. The logging of rock cores for engineering purposes. *Quarterly Journal of Engineering Geology*, **3**, 1–24.

—— 1977. The description of rock masses for engineering purposes. *Quarterly Journal of Engineering Geology*, **10**, 355–388.

GILLOTT, J. E. 1975. Alkali–aggregate reactions in concrete, Review, *Engineering Geology* **9**, 303–326.

GOODSALL, G. D. & MATHEWS, D. H. 1970. Sampling of road surfacing materials, *Journal of Applied Chemistry* 361–6.

GRANT, E. L. 1952. Statistical quality control. McGraw-Hill,

New York, 557 pp.

GRIFFITHS, J. C. 1967. Scientific method in analysis of sediments. McGraw-Hill, New York.

HALLBERG, S. 1950. The adhesion of bituminous binders and aggregates in the presence of water. *Meddelande 78*, Statens Vaginstitut, Stockholm.

HARR, M. E. 1977. *Mechanics of particulate media*. McGraw-Hill, New York.

HARTLEY, A. 1970. The influence of geological factors upon the mechanical properties of road surfacing aggregates (with particular reference to British conditions and practice). Proceedings of the 21st Symposium Highway Geological University of Kansas.

—— 1971. The development and testing of artificial gritty aggregate. Proceedings of a symposium on the influence of the road surface on skidding. University of Salford.

HAWKES, J. R. & HOSKING, J. R. 1972. British arenaceous rocks for skid-resistant road surfacings. Report LR 488, Road Research Laboratory, Crowthorne.

HILLS, J. F. & PETTIFER, G. S. 1985 The clay mineral content of various rock types compared with the methylene blue value. *Journal of Chemical Technology and Biotechnology*, **35A**, 4, 168–180.

HOBBS, D. W. 1988 *Alkali–Silica Reaction in Concrete*, Thomas Telford, London.

HOSKING, J. R. & TUBEY, L. W. 1969. Research on low grade and unsound aggregates. Report LR 293, Road Research Laboratory, Crowthorne.

HURLBUT, C. S. & KLEIN, C. 1977. *Manual of mineralogy*. Wiley, New York.

IRFAN, T. Y. & DEARMAN, W. R. 1978. The engineering petrography of a weathered granite in Cornwall, England. *Quarterly Journal of Engineering Geology*, **11**, 233–44.

JONES, F. E. & TARLETON, R. D. 1958. National Building Studies Research Paper No. 25. Reactions between aggregates and cement. H.M.S.O., London.

KENNEDY, T. W., ROBERTS, F. L. & LEE, K. W. 1984, Evaluating moisture susceptibility of asphalt mixtures using the Texas Boiling Test, Transport Research Record 986, p 45–54.

KRUMBEIN, W. C. 1941. Measurement and geological significance of shape and roundness of sedimentary articles. *Journal of Sedimentary Petrology*, **11**, 64–72.

—— & PETTIJOHN, E. J. 1938. *Manual of sedimentary petrography*. Appleton-Century Crofts Inc. New York.

LEE, A. R. 1936. Adhesion in relation to bituminous road materials. *Journal of Society Chemical Industry, London*, **55**, 23T–29T.

LEES, G. 1963. A new method for determining the angularity of particles. *Sedimentology* **3**, 2–21.

—— 1964. The measurement of particle shape and its influence in engineering materials. *Journal of British Granite and Whinstone Federation* **4**, 1–22.

MENDES, F., AIRIES-BARROS, L. & PERES RODRIGUEZ, F. 1966. The use of modal analysis in the mechanical character of rock masses. Procedings of the 1st Congress of the International Society of Rock Mechanics, Lisbon, **1**, 217–23

NORTHEN MINERAL PRESS LTD. 1955. Mining explained in simple terms. Toronto.

PIKE, D. C. 1978. Variability in grading results caused by standard sample-reduction techniques for aggregates. Supplementary Report SR 489. Transport and Road Reseach Laboratory, Crowthorne.

—— 1990. *Standards for Aggregates*. Ellis Horwood, London.

——, SHERWOOD, P. T. & SYM R. 1990. The BS Frost-Heave Test—Development of the standard and suggestions for

further improvement, *Quarry Management*, February.

PROPERTY SERVICES AGENCY 1979a. Standard specification clauses for airfield pavement and works, Pt. 4 Bituminous surfacing Appendix 4B. Soundness of aggregate. Property Services Agency, Department of the Environment.

—— 1979b. Standard specification clauses for airfield pavement and works. Pt. 3, Concrete. Appendix 3A. Property Services Agency, Department of the Environment.

RAMSAY, D. M. 1965. Factors influencing Aggregate Impact Value in rock aggregate. *Quarry Managers Journal, London* **49**, 129–34.

——, DHIR, R. K. & SPENCE, J. M. 1973. Non-geological factors influencing the reproducibility of results in the Aggregate Impact Test. *Quarry Managers Journal, London* **57**, 179–81.

——, —— & —— 1974. The role of rock and clast fabric in the physical performance of crushed-rock aggregate. *Engineering Geology* **8**, 267–85.

——, —— & —— 1977. The practical and theoretical merits of the Aggregate Impact Value in the study of crushed-rock aggregate. *Proceedings of the Conference on Rock Engineering, Newcastle upon Tyne, England*.

ROAD RESEARCH LABORATORY, 1959. Roadstone tests data presented in tabular form. Road Note 24. HMSO, London.

—— 1962. *Bituminous Materials in Road Construction*. HMSO, London.

ROE, P. G. & WEBSTER, D. C. 1984. Specification for the TRRL frost-heave test. Supplementary Report SR829. Transport and Road Research Laboratory, Crowthorne.

ROSSLEIN, D. 1941. Steinbrecheruntersuchungen unter besonderer Berucksichtigung der kornform. Forsch a.d. Strassenwesen Band 32, Berlin.

SHERGOLD, F. A. 1950. The classification and mechanical testing of road making aggregates. *Quarry Managers Journal, London* **34**, 27–35.

—— 1959. A study of the granulators used in the production of road making aggregates. Road Research Tech. Paper No. 44.

—— 1960. The classification, production and testing of road making aggregates. *Quarry Managers Journal, London* **44**, 47–54.

—— 1963. A study of the variability of roadstones in relation to sampling procedures. *Quarry Managers Journal, London* **47**, 3–8.

—— & HOSKING, J. R. 1963. Investigations of test procedures for argillaceous and gritty rocks in relation to breakdown under traffic source. *Roads and Road Construction*, **41**, 376–8.

—— & GREYSMITH, M. G. 1947. Factors governing the grading and shape of crushed rocks—a survey of the literature. *Quarry Managers Journal, London* **30**, 703–12.

SIMS, I. & POOLE, A. B. 1980. Potentially alkali-reactive aggregates for the Middle East. *Concrete* **14** (5) 27–30.

TUBEY, L. W. & SZAFRAN, W. 1970. Aggregate Abrasion Test: an improved technique for preparing test specimens. *Quarry Managers Journal, London* **54**, 185–7.

WADELL, H. 1933. Sphericity and roundness of rock particles. *Journal of Geology*, **41**, 310–31.

WEINERT, H. H. 1964. Basic igneous rocks in road foundations. *C.S.I.R. Research Report* **218**, 1–47.

WOODRUFF, S. D. 1966. Methods of working coal and metal mines Vol. 1. Pergamon, Oxford.

WRIGHT, P. J. F. 1955. A method of measuring the surface texture of aggregate. *Mag. Concrete Research*, **7**, 151–60.

ZINGG, T. 1935. Beitrag zur schotteranalyse. *Schweiz. mineral. Petrog. Mitt.*, **15**, 39–140.

General references

CONCRETE SOCIETY 1987 *Technical report* No. 30, Concrete Society, London.

LAWSON, J. E. & DELTON, J. P. 1978. Sampling and evaluating potential aggregate deposits. Annual Convention of National Sand and Gravel Association, Las Vegas, Nevada. 1–8.

LEES, G. 1969. The influence of binder and aggregate in bituminous mixes. *Journal of the Institution of Highway Engineers* **16**, 7–19.

—— & KENNEDY, C. K. 1975. Quality, shape and degradation of aggregates. *Quarterly Journal of Engineering Geology*, **8**, 193–209.

PERONIUS, A. N. 1979. Statistical applications for road soil surveys, *Journal of the Institution of Highway Engineers*, **26**, 15–18.

PRENTICE, J. E., 1990, *Geology of Construction Materials*, Chapman & Hall, London.

RILEM TECHNICAL COMMITTEE 17BM, 1979. Problem of the bond between bituminous binders and aggregates, Paris.

RITTENHOUSE, G. 1943. The relation of shape to the passage of grains through sieves. *Ind. Eng. Chem. Anal. Ed.* **15**, 153–5.

SHERGOLD, F. A. 1953. The percentage voids in compacted gravel as a measure of its angularity. *Mag. Concrete Research* **5**, 3–11.

—— 1955. Results of tests on single-sized road-making aggregates. *Quarry Managers Journal, London* **39**, 2–8.

SHERWOOD, P. T. & RYLEY, M. D. 1970. Sulphates in colliery shale: effect on cemented materials. *Surveyor* 1–7.

SPENCE, J. M., RAMSAY, D. M. & DHIR, K. R. 1974. A conspectus of aggregate strength and the relevance of this factor as the basis for a physical classification of crushed rock aggregate. *International Congress on Rock Mechanics.* **2A**, 79–84.

TUBEY, L. W. & JORDAN, P. G. 1973. The reproducibility and repeatability of the PSV determination. TRRL Report LR 552.

WEST, G. & SIBBICK, R. G. 1988, Petrographical comparison of old and new control stones for the accelerated polishing test. *Quarterly Journal of Engineering Geology*, **21**, 375–378.

8. Aggregates for concrete

8.1. Introduction

Concrete may be defined as a mixture of water, cement or binder, and aggregate, where the water and cement or binder form the paste and the aggregate forms the inert filler. In absolute volume terms the aggregate amounts to 60–80% of the volume of concrete and is, therefore, the major constituent. The aggregate type and volume influences the properties of concrete, its mix proportions and its economy.

The desirable and undesirable properties of aggregates for concrete have been thoroughly reviewed in a number of texts on concrete technology (Orchard 1976; American Society for Testing and Materials 1978; Murdock & Brook 1979; Fookes 1980; Neville 1981). In practice, difficulties are frequently encountered in translating these properties into specification requirements for aggregates, or in assessing aggregate test results to determine compliance or otherwise with already specified parameters. This chapter considers the principal properties of concrete aggregates with the aim of assisting in the selection of appropriate specification requirements.

The essential requirement of an aggregate for concrete is that it remains stable within the concrete and in the particular environment throughout the design life of the concrete. The characteristics of the aggregate must not affect adversely the performance or cost of the concrete in either the fresh or hardened state.

For both technical and contractual reasons, these requirements have to be defined quantitatively. This involves the selection of relevant tests and assessment procedures and the specification of appropriate acceptance criteria. However, despite the guidance given in Chapter 7, it can be difficult to assure the long-term satisfactory performance of an aggregate combination solely by means of a number of British or other standard tests and limits. In such cases there is a need for experienced judgement, but the specifier's aim should always be to minimize this need. For example, contract specifications often include the generalized requirements derived from previous editions of BS 882 that aggregates ... be hard, durable and clean and of approved quality. These are qualitative requirements without specific acceptance limits which, therefore, necessitate subjective judgements sometimes leading, in turn, to contractual

disputes. This phrase was deleted from BS 882: 1983.

It is important to avoid specifying aggregate qualities which are contradictory, thus creating a potential for dispute. Specifications which are not relevant or which are unnecessarily superior to the needs of the particular works, thereby restricting use to unduly expensive materials should also be avoided. Thus, the specifier bears considerable responsibilities in these respects under a contract. Hence the need for continued vigilance despite the rare incidence of arbitrations and litigations resulting from disputes about aggregate quality.

In the United Kingdom, the assessment of aggregate quality in both new and established deposits is not generally justified in view of the well established characteristics for most UK aggregate sources and the long-standing of the UK aggregate production industry. Quality should, nevertheless, be confirmed by independent testing and periodic rechecks. The ready mixed concrete industry carries out inspection and testing as part of a quality assurance precheck.

However, in many locations overseas this situation does not exist and extensive aggregate source and product investigations may be appropriate, even essential. Another important factor overseas, but often less well recognized, is that National Standards and Codes of Practice inevitably relate to the climatic regimes and other influences which prevail in the country of origin. For this reason Standards and Codes should be studied with some care before their recommendations are specified for works in climatic regimes appreciably different from those of the country in which they were published.

This chapter is almost entirely concerned with the use of normal dense aggregates producing a concrete with a density of about 2400 kg/m^3. Sometimes, however, concrete is required to have either a lower or a higher density. By the use of a lightweight aggregate the concrete density can be less than 2000 kg/m^3 and when a heavyweight aggregate is used the density can be greater than 3000 kg/m^3.

Lightweight aggregate may be simply classified into natural or artificial aggregates. Pumice is an example of a natural lightweight aggregate and is used mostly in the production of concrete blocks. Artificial lightweight aggregates may be formed by expanding clay, shale or slate, by sintering pulverized fuel ash and by foaming

molten blast-furnace slag. They are all capable of producing concrete strengths in excess of 25 N/mm^2 with
densities ranging from 1500–2000 kg/m^3. The composition of the aggregates and their properties, for example
bulk density, has an influence on the resulting concrete
properties (Short & Kinniburgh 1978).

Heavyweight aggregates may also be classified as
natural or artificial materials. The most widely used
natural materials are barytes and the iron ores such as
haematite and magnetite, whereas the artificial materials
are based on iron shot or lead shot. The resulting
concrete strength is not of paramount importance but is
usually in excess of 30 N/mm^2. The densities will vary
from 3500 kg/m^3 to 8000 kg/m^3 depending on the type
of aggregate used (Miller 1983).

8.2. Specification

In British practice, specifications commonly only require
compliance with the requirements of BS 882 for aggregates from natural sources for concrete and BS 3797
for lightweight aggregates. BS 882: 1992 contains quantitative compliance requirements for particle shape (flakiness), shell, grading, cleanliness (fines) and mechanical
properties.

The widespread use of this long-established British
Standard presupposes a substantial weight of experience
to justify the view that this limited number of requirements has proved adequate for most concrete construction work in the United Kingdom. However, experience
in recent years has shown that problems can arise on
overseas contracts when specifications are based solely
upon BS 882 (Fookes & Collis 1975a,b). For example,
an unsound aggregate which is mechanically strong in
the dry state may comply with this specification, but
could be unsound and impair the durability of concrete
in certain environments.

In contrast with the limited number of quantitative
requirements given in BS 882, the related British Standard covering the testing of aggregates, BS 812, provides
test methods for a wide, though not exhaustive, range of
properties. However, BS 812 does not provide any guidance for interpretation of the test results. Hence there is
a need to appreciate the relevance of the various tests
and to select appropriate tests and limits on the basis of
experience of use in particular contract locations and
environments; for example, aggregate shrinkage testing
and Scottish aggregates (Building Research Establishment 1968; Edwards 1970).

The specification of concrete aggregates for overseas
projects, especially where there are no local Standards or
Codes, necessitates considerable care in order to impose
appropriate requirements to minimize the risk of ambi-
guities of under or over-specification with the resultant
risk of claims and cost difficulties. When preparing

specifications for such works it is essential to acquire
detailed and up-to-date knowledge about current aggregate resources and their mineralogical, physical and
chemical characteristics. This should enable the majority
of undesirable features of the local aggregates to be
identified. If it is considered that such features can be
eliminated or reduced, by measures which are both
practical and economic, then appropriate qualitative
requirements, test methods and quantitative limits must
be selected and specified. In this way the tenderer is
afforded the opportunity to make any necessary allowances for the cost of implementing such measures and,
thereby, meeting the specified requirements.

A good aggregate specification must be relevant to the
available resources and to the characteristics required
of the concrete in which the aggregates will be used.
Although aggregate quality can be improved if the job
so demands, sufficient flexibility for judgement should be
provided in order to prevent the unintended exclusion of
either superior or lower quality aggregates which, for
transport reasons, may be expensive (see Table 8.4).

A Committee (CEN TC 154), began the preparation
and development of European standards for aggregates
(CEN TC 154) in 1988 and a working draft standard for
"Aggregates for concrete", including those for use in
roads and pavements (Cen TC 154 SC2), has been
produced. It covers natural and artificial aggregates with
a particle density exceeding 2000 kg/m^3 for use in concrete. The requirements include size distribution, particle
shape, shell content, fines and clay minerals, physical
requirements (strength, abrasion) chemical requirements
(chlorides, sulphates, alkali–aggregate reaction, other
harmful components), quality control, designation and
description and marking and labelling. A similar standard for lightweight aggregates (CEN TC 154 SC5) has
also been prepared. Limits for the various requirements
are being considered.

8.3. Classification and composition

The provisions in BS 882 do not require a supplier to
furnish a petrological classification unless it is requested
by the specifier or purchaser. In the past this information
has rarely been requested but with the concern over
alkali reactive aggregates there has been an increase in
this type of testing. However, even though provided, the
brevity of the BS 812: Part 102: 1984 classification provides little information of real value, either for engineering or materials control purposes. This aspect is discussed more fully in Chapter 6.

Detailed information on the petrography of an aggregate involving field inspection can be of considerable
value when assessing its potential suitability in terms of
rock type and the state of geological alteration or subaerial weathering (Hammersley 1989). Also, simple

petrographic examination is particularly useful for monitoring the variability of aggregates during the course of construction. Petrographic examinations can identify, fairly rapidly and relatively inexpensively, the presence of detrimental features or potentially alkali reactive or deleterious materials, which may be present either naturally or as contaminants (Mielenz 1955). These examinations should ideally be carried out during the feasibility study but certainly no later than the Tender stage. Although the results are normally only semi-quantitative, they can indicate whether further investigations and quantitative tests are desirable.

A further benefit of petrographic analysis is that, in conjunction with other physical and chemical tests, they can help to 'fingerprint' an aggregate or parent rock (Fookes & Collis 1975b). This can be of value as a means of defining an approved material and can also be helpful subsequently should any disputes arise as to the nature of the originally approved material. It can, however, be dangerous to infer engineering properties from a petrographic analysis.

The complete chemical analysis of an aggregate is not usually considered necessary for the appraisal for suitability for use in concrete. The effects of certain specific constituents, such as sulphates, chlorides, organic materials and selected metals, will be discussed later. A thorough petrographic analysis together with some specific chemical testing may be necessary in assessing a concrete aggregate.

An analytical aspect of special relevance to aggregates for concrete concerns the aggregate correction factors involved in the analysis of hardened concrete to determine the original cement content and aggregate/cement ratio. These determinations are very common in building and civil engineering work, usually for dispute purposes, and the results are relevant to the assessment of compliance with specifications and any liability issues. The aggregate correction factors can have a significant influence but representative samples of the aggregates originally used are often not available at the time of analysis. Thus, it could be of value to specify that the correction factors are determined for reference purposes at the time the materials are approved, using the procedures given in BS 1881: Part 124: 1988.

8.4. Aggregate properties: introduction

The properties of aggregates discussed in the following sections are those which are of prime concern to the concrete producer. The aggregate properties which affect the properties of the fresh concrete are those which are under the control of the aggregate producer. Properties such as the particle size and shape, which are influenced by selective crushing and the use of the appropriate type of crusher for the particular rock type, as well as the cleanliness in terms of fines and clay content have a great influence on the water requirement of the concrete. Figures 8.1 and 8.2 show the influence of particle size and shape on water demand for different levels of workability. The strength and durability properties of the hardened concrete may also be affected by any change in the water demand. The aggregate producer, however, usually has little control over aggregate properties such as strength, particle density and water absorption although these on occasions may be of some importance and be limited in concrete specifications. Processing may have some effect but, in general, these properties remain essentially the same as the parent rock. Improvements can sometimes be made by the use of a jig for the removal of low density particles which

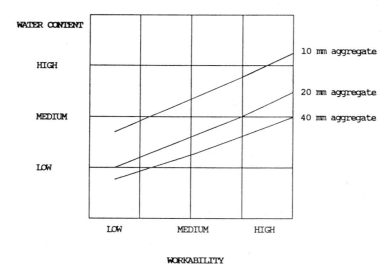

FIG. 8.1 Typical relation between water content, maximum aggregate size and workability.

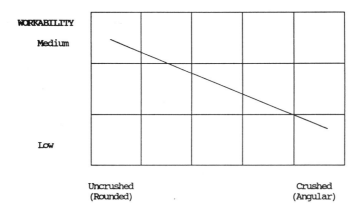

FIG. 8.2 Relation between the particle shape of aggregate and the workability of concrete using a constant water content.

may influence the overall strength, density and water absorption of the end product or the use of special screens to extract exceptionally flaky particles. These forms of processing are considered in Chapter 5.

The form of production quality control applied to any aggregate will generally depend on the end use of the aggregate.

If Quality Assurance (QA) certification of the aggregates is required, this should be achieved by the use of a quality system available in UK and Europe complying with BS 5750 Quality Systems or the equivalent EN29000 Quality management and quality assurance standards. Although products such as portland cement, reinforcing steel and admixtures are covered by QA schemes only a few individual pits and quarries have a QA scheme for aggregates. Precast concrete is covered by a scheme operated by the BSI and most ready mixed concrete companies supply to the requirements of the quality scheme for ready mixed concrete (QSRMC). The levels of the QA schemes in operation are different.

8.5. Maximum size and grading

The European aggregate standard will allow aggregate product sizes (mm) to be selected from the Basic Set plus Set 1 or Set 2.

Basic Set: 0.5; 1; 2; 4; 8; 16; 31.5; 63; 125

Set 1:   5.6; 11.2; 22.4; 45; 90

Set 2:   6.3; 10; 12.5; 14; 20; 40

Product sizes shall also be separated by a ratio of not less than 1.4.

The European preferred term for 'fine aggregate' as used in the UK is 'sand', the maximum size of which may be reduced from 5 to 4 mm.

In general the overall grading of combined coarse aggregates and sand should provide a material having the lowest possible surface area and void content per unit volume, thus requiring the lowest possible water and cement contents to achieve the desired workability, strength and other concrete properties. The extent to which these aims can be achieved is dependent *inter alia*, upon the actual grading of the available coarse aggregate and sand and, most importantly, upon their uniformity within and between deliveries to site. The use of appropriately proportioned coarse aggregate and sand gradings, each within the relevant envelopes given for example in BS 882, normally provides concretes having at least adequate properties in the fresh and hardened states.

Although infrequently appreciated by aggregate users, the four fine aggregate grading 'zones' given in earlier editions of BS 882 (1954, 1965 & 1973) simply represented a classification of fine aggregate gradings readily available in the UK, not envelopes based on experience or research (Foreword to BS 882: 1954). The DoE method of concrete mix design (Design of normal concrete mixes, 1988) refers to the fine aggregate and the percentage passing the 600 µm sieve which is related to the zone classification. Some specifiers for airfield pavements also prefer the use of Zone 1 or Zone 2 sand. In the 1983 edition of BS 882, the overall fine aggregate grading limits were widened, on the evidence of an exhaustive survey (BSI News, 1983), to permit use of a finer material and three overlapping sets of additional grading limits (termed C, M and F) replaced the previous four 'Zones'. The BS 882: 1992 sand (fine aggregate) grading limits are given in Table 8.1.

TABLE 8.1. *BS 882: 1992 Sand grading limits (% by mass passing BS sieve)*

Sieve size	Overall limits	Additional limits for grading		
		C	M	F
10.00 mm	100	—	—	—
5.00 mm	89–100	—	—	—
2.36 mm	60–100	60–100	65–100	80–100
1.18 mm	30–100	30–90	45–100	70–100
600 μm	15–100	15–54	25–80	55–100
300 μm	5–70	5–40	5–48	5–70
150 μm	0–15*	—	—	—

* Increased to 20% for crushed rock sand, except when used for heavy duty floors.

The overlapping character of the grading limits allows a sand to comply with two of the three categories (C and M, or M and F), which may be found to be confusing. However, satisfactory materials are less likely to be needlessly excluded for failing to comply with an artificially rigid grading envelope than was sometimes the case previously with the four zone system. Moreover, BS 882 also permits the use of sands which do not comply with the grading limits provided that 'the supplier can satisfy the purchaser that such materials can produce concrete of the required quality'.

However, it should be understood that more care is generally necessary when designing concrete mixes using either very coarse or very fine sands. The important consideration is that the grading of an exceptionally fine sand is suitable for the aggregate blend in a particular concrete and that repeated gradings for the same source do not vary excessively. In respect of the latter, BS 882 requires that not more than one in ten consecutive samples should fall outside the specified grading limits.

Where very coarse sands are used, the concrete mixes can be 'harsh' and suffer 'bleeding' (for concrete terminology, see Barker 1983), especially at lower cement contents. Exceptionally fine sands present a conflict between the amounts required to ensure that the concrete is sufficiently cohesive and the need to minimize the effect on water demand of the high aggregate surface area (Gaynor 1964). However, these problems can be reduced or even eliminated by careful design of the concrete mixes, also by the judicious selection and use of air entrainment for coarse sands and water-reducing admixtures for exceptionally fine sands (Concrete Society 1980; Higgins 1984).

In certain areas of the United Kingdom, for example South Wales and the South East English Channel Coast, the gradings of the locally available natural sands may not lie within specified 'zones' or grading limits. However, they are acceptable in all other relevant aspects and on the basis of their long-term use in the area. In such situations it is usually possible to design concrete mixes

to obtain adequate strength and durability potentials.

Improved overall gradings of sand are often achieved by blending. This is particularly true when a coarse crushed rock sand can only be considered for use in concrete when blended with a fine natural sand.

Where concrete of particularly high strength, uniformity or aesthetic quality is required, it is usually beneficial to specify that single-sized coarse aggregates are used; further that they are separately batched to provide continuous or non-continuous overall gradings as appropriate. This may present problems of storage for the ready mixed concrete supplier and becomes an expensive option. In general, continuously graded aggregates tend to provide relatively straightforward and easy-to-place concretes, whereas gap-graded concretes usually require appreciably more expertise in mix design, production, handling and placing (Shacklock 1959; Schaffler 1979). For these reasons the labour costs of placing gap-graded concretes may sometimes be greater, but this may be justified where their special properties can be used to advantage; for example, where high mechanical stability is required immediately after compaction, or where increased resistance to scour is required in inter-tidal work.

The maximum size of aggregate permitted by BS 882 for use in concrete in the UK is 40 mm. However, the size most frequently used is 20 mm since consideration has to be given to the cover and bar spacing in reinforced concrete. For some situations 10 mm maximum size aggregate may be used, especially when the structure size is limited or the preference is for a very cohesive concrete for use in a slipform operation. Although 40 mm maximum size is permitted in pavement quality concrete it is normally only used in the bottom of the two layer construction with 20 mm aggregate used in the top layer. The handling of the concrete also plays a very important part in the decision as to which maximum size to use. Of prime importance is the consistency of the maximum size within the limits of BS 882 since a change can influence the water demand of

TABLE 8.2. *BS 882: 1992. Coarse aggregate grading limits*

Sieve size (mm)	Percentage by mass passing BS sieves for nominal sizes							
	Graded aggregate			Single-sized aggregate				
	40 mm to 5 mm	20 mm to 5 mm	14 mm to 5 mm	40 mm	20 mm	14 mm	10 mm	5 mm*
50.0	100	—	—	100	—	—	—	—
37.5	90–100	100	—	85–100	100	—	—	—
20.0	35–70	90–100	100	0–25	85–100	100	—	—
14.0	25–55	40–80	90–100	—	0–70	85–100	100	—
10.0	10–40	30–60	50–85	0–5	0–25	0–50	85–100	100
5.0	0–5	0–10	0–10	—	0–5	0–10	0–25	45–100
2.36	—	—	—	—	—	—	0–5	0–30

* Used mainly in precast concrete production.

the concrete and hence affect both the strength and the durability. The inclusion of limits for the 14 mm material in the 40–5 mm and 20–5 mm graded coarse aggregate and 20 mm single sized aggregate will help the situation. The BS 882 grading limits for coarse aggregate are given in Table 8.2.

Coarse aggregates of nominal maximum size greater than 40 mm are sometimes specified for massive placements, the aims usually being to minimize the cement content and, thereby reduce heat generation. To specify, for example a 75 mm or 150 mm maximum size, presumes that the physical characteristics of the larger size fractions are not inferior to those of the 40 m and smaller sizes, in which case small but possibly significant reductions in cement content and cost may be achieved. This presumption is not always correct, especially in weathered rocks.

The possibility of increased risks of segregation should not be overlooked, however. Certain rock types may produce crushed aggregates whose shape characteristics may be dependent on particle size and this could negate the technical and cost benefits that might otherwise be obtained. Such an effect will occur with rock materials that normally benefit from an improvement in particle shape during secondary and tertiary crushing to produce smaller aggregate sizes or with some thickly bedded or coarsely cleaved rock sources. Thus, some investigation into the likely shape characteristics should be undertaken before specifying exceptionally large nominal maximum sized aggregates for mass concrete placements (Bloem 1959).

In the United Kingdom, attention is rarely given to the question of gradings, probably because of the abundant supplies of materials whose gradings have not given cause for any general concern. However, this situation does not always apply overseas, and the specifier should investigate the grading characteristics of potential aggregate resources, in order to minimize the risk of imposing impracticable and uneconomic specification requirements.

The selection of aggregate types and gradings for architectural concrete involves special considerations in view of the aesthetic requirements involved, also those of aggregate and concrete durability, and reference should be made to specialist literature on this subject (Monks 1981, 1985a,b, 1986, 1988a,b; Blake 1967).

8.6. Particle shape

The shape characteristics of aggregate particles are classified in qualitative terms in BS 812, but this Standard only provides test methods for quantifying the proportions of 'flaky' or 'elongated' particles in coarse aggregates, and these vary according to the crushed or uncrushed nature of the aggregate. The requirements in BS 882 are that the flakiness index of the combined coarse aggregate shall not exceed 50 for uncrushed gravel and 40 for crushed rock or crushed gravel.

No limits are provided in BS 882 for the percentage of 'elongated' particles and, indeed, limits are rarely specified for the 'elongation index'. Flakiness and elongation are not usually specified for sands, although these characteristics are easily determined qualitatively by visual examination under low-power microscope.

Experience suggests that the absence, until recently, of quantitative limits on the shape characteristics of concrete aggregates generally has not resulted in any undue difficulties with structural concretes in the UK. The probable reasons for this include the natural adequacy in this respect of the majority of UK gravels, and also the success with which aggregate producers have been able to control the shape characteristics of those materials which have greater tendencies on crushing to produce flaky and or elongated particles. However, the industry is now having to consider the more marginal deposits and the difficulties that arise from producing flaky aggregates are becoming more common.

The shape characteristics of coarse aggregates and sand can have marked effects on the properties of both fresh and hardened concrete (Lees 1964), these effects tending to be beneficial where the predominant particle shape is generally equidimensional, and detrimental where it is flaky and/or elongated (Kaplan 1958, 1959; Neville 1981). Figure 8.2 shows the relationship between the particle shape of the aggregate and the workability of the concrete.

Flakiness of coarse aggregate can have an adverse influence on the workability and mobility of concrete and may cause blockages in pump pipelines due to particle interference. Experiments have shown that the workability of concrete as measured by the compacting factor is reduced by 10% when changing from a rounded to an angular shaped particle (Kaplan 1958). The strength of concrete also tends to be reduced by increasing aggregate flakiness, with flexural strength being more affected than compressive strength (Kaplan 1959). Flakiness in fine aggregate also affects the properties of the fresh concrete by increasing the water demand of the concrete mix. This can lead to problems of 'bleeding' (Barker 1983) and segregation in the fresh mix leading to reduced strength and durability of the resultant hardened concrete. Finishing of the concrete can also be affected adversely (Richards 1982).

Particle shape limits for concrete aggregates can be a major consideration when developing and designing aggregate production plant for new sources and aggregates at the limiting values can present difficulties. In the case of overseas works, the producer or the specifiers should seek to select target maxima for flaky and elongated particles in coarse aggregates. The cost-benefit of complying with relatively low target maxima is largely a matter for investigation by the aggregate producer and, for overseas work particularly, by the consulting engineer at the earliest possible time.

Improvement of aggregate particle shape usually increases production costs, but may result in an enhancement of the strength and durability potential of the concrete.

8.7. Particle surface texture

The main influence of particle surface texture is the effect on the bond between the aggregate and the cement paste in hardened concrete. The classification in BS 812 is generalized; it is based on subjective assessment and does not therefore lend itself to specified limitations. Indeed, the specific exclusion of material of any particular surface texture is virtually unknown.

Surface texture is generally only considered in relation to concrete flexural strengths, which are frequently found to reduce with increasing particle smoothness. However, inadequate surface texture can similarly adversely affect compressive strength in high-strength concretes (say $> 60 \text{N/mm}^2$), when the bond with the cement matrix may not be sufficiently strong to enable the maximum strength of the concrete to be realized (Kaplan 1959; Neville 1981). Recent advances in concrete technology have made it possible to produce very high strength concrete (100N/mm^2) with aggregate having a relatively smooth surface texture.

8.8. Bulk density

The bulk density of an aggregate, or its unit mass, reflects in part its void content at a given degree of compaction and is, therefore, an indirect measure of the grading and shape characteristics. The bulk density of aggregates ranges from $1200-1800 \text{ kg/m}^3$ for normal aggregates and $500-1000 \text{ kg/m}^3$ for lightweight aggregates. The bulk density is most commonly used to enable concrete mixes specified by volume to be converted into gravimetric proportions, and thus enable batch masses to be determined. The use of bulk density measurements has, therefore, declined with the increasing application of designed, prescribed and standard gravimetric concrete mixes (BS 5328: 1991). However, bulk density is still used for lightweight aggregates because of the difficulty in measuring the particle density.

More generally, the value of bulk density and void content determinations lies in providing another reference property for a material, although it is little used for this purpose. A particular use could be as a comparative measure of variations in the particle shape characteristics of fine aggregates since no British Standard tests are available to measure these directly. However, these are not properties which should be limited in contract specifications, although they may be used by concrete producers to assist in the comparison of mix designs using alternative materials.

8.9. Particle density

The particle density (relative density) of dense aggregates is a property of particular value in concrete mix design, concrete yield checks, and in the assessment of compaction and void content of hardened concrete. This is an aggregate property which is not usually subject to limits in contract specifications, except where, for design reasons, there is a need to ensure a minimum concrete density; for example in gravity structures such as dams or marine armouring, or for radiation shielding.

In such cases, contract specifications often impose a minimum limit on the 'specific gravity', but it is often

TABLE 8.3. *Particle density comparisons for various aggregates*

Aggregate ref:	A	B	C	D	E
Water absorption (%)*	9.5	3.7	1.6	0.6	0.2
Particle density (kg/m³)*					
Oven dry	2030	2360	2670	2680	2730
Saturated surface dried	2230	2450	2720	2700	2740
Apparent	2520	2590	2790	2730	2750
Numerical difference (Oven dry-apparent):	490	230	120	50	20

* As determined in accordance with BS812: Part 2: 1975.

not made clear whether this refers to particle density calculated on the oven dried basis, the saturated surface dry basis, or the apparent basis. The differences between these values can sometimes be substantial and contractual disputes can arise where the appropriate particle density is not specified, or is mis-stated. Some examples to illustrate this aspect are shown in Table 8.3.

8.10. Water absorption

Water absorption is an indirect measure of the permeability of an aggregate which, in turn, can relate to other physical characteristics such as mechanical strength, shrinkage, soundness and to its general durability potential. These relationships are imprecise, although in general less absorptive aggregates often tend to be more resistant to mechanical forces and to weathering. A reliable classification of water absorption values for UK natural dense aggregates is not available, but a 'low' absorption value might reasonably be considered as less than 1%, with an acceptable range for UK aggregates being from less than 1% to about 5% (Newman 1959). The effect that the water absorption of an aggregate has on the properties of concrete will depend on the value and the type of concrete. Lightweight aggregates generally have higher water absorption values ranging from 5–20%. However, the size and the characteristics of the pores are different from natural dense aggregates and it is possible to make durable concrete from these materials.

Absorption limits are rare in British standards, although BS 8007: 1987 does include a recommendation that the aggregate absorption should not 'generally' be greater than 3% with a maximum value of 2.5% often specified for overseas works. Limits are also specified by national bodies such as the PSA for airfield pavements and the Department of Transport for concrete carriageways.

Contract specifications do not normally include a maximum limit on the water absorption of an aggregate. Indeed, limits should not be imposed unless it has been established, for a particular material, that water absorp-

tion relates closely to some other undesirable property, such as poor resistance to frost or other weathering agencies. Although an aggregate may satisfy a water absorption limit there is no guarantee that problems with the concrete will not occur. In such cases it may be more expedient to adopt absorption limits for control and compliance purposes, rather than specify other more time consuming and costly test procedures which cannot be carried out readily in a site laboratory.

In Germany an aggregate with a water absorption of less than 0.5% is considered non-frost-susceptible. If the value is between 0.5% and 1.0% the water absorption test is repeated under pressure and if there is no increase then the aggregate is accepted as non-frost-susceptible. Aggregates with water absorptions in excess of 1.0% are assumed to be frost susceptible. Frost susceptibility is also considered in §8.12.3.

8.11. Mechanical properties

BS 882 includes quantitative requirements for the mechanical properties of aggregates based upon the ten per cent fines value test or, as an alternative, the aggregate impact value test. The various criteria, which differ according to the intended application of the concrete, are given in Table 8.4. BS 812 provides several other mechanical test procedures for the determination of the aggregate crushing value, aggregate abrasion value and polished stone value. Different American test procedures are also available, including the Los Angeles test for resistance to impact (ASTM C131). Adoption of these tests, and others, which are not specified in BS 882 is a matter for judgement by individual specifiers.

Some selected mechanical tests are summarized in Table 8.5 and fully discussed in Chapter 7.

The mechanical properties of coarse aggregates should be such that the material does not disintegrate or degrade (which could occur during handling, transportation, concrete mixing or compaction) and that the compressive strength and subsequent performance of the concrete is not impaired. For structural concretes, except concrete road pavements and abrasion resistant floors,

TABLE 8.4. *BS 882: 1992 mechanical property requirements for coarse aggregate*

Type of concrete	Ten per cent fines value (kN) (not less than)	Alternatively, aggregate impact value (%) (not exceeding)
Heavy duty concrete floor finishes	150	25
Pavement wearing surfaces	100	30
Others	50	45

TABLE 8.5. *Selected mechanical property tests for aggregates*

Test	Standard or country of origin	Measurement principle
Aggregate impact value	BS 812	Fines produced by specified shock or impact loading.
Aggregate crushing value	BS 812	Fines produced by slowly increasing load to a specified maximum.
Ten per cent fines value	BS 812	Slowly increasing maximum load required to produce a specified amount of fines.
Aggregate abrasion value	BS 812	Loss produced by specified amounts of abrasion.
Dory hardness	USA	Loss produced by specified amounts of abrasion.
Polished stone value	BS 812	A measurement of friction after a specified amount of polishing.
Los Angeles abrasion	(ASTM C131) (ASTM C535)	Fines produced by attrition on tumbling of rock pieces with steel spheres for specified number of revolutions.
	CEN TC 154 SC6 Draft	Modified ASTM procedure.
Aggregate crushing strength	(BS 812)	Uniaxial compressive strength of rock cores (now deleted from BS 812).
Franklin point load index	UK	Splitting strength (of cores or irregular lumps of rock) and indirect measure of compressive strength.
Micro Deval	France AFNOR	
Schlagversuch	Germany DIN	

the extent to which it is generally necessary to specify mechanical property requirements in addition to those given in BS 882 is limited. Any significant degradation of an aggregate prior to the concrete mixing phase should be detected more directly by routine acceptance tests for grading and fines content. During mixing, degradation of the aggregate could be detected by the analysis of the fresh concrete. Furthermore, the more stringent of the BS 882 limits (for pavement wearing surfaces and heavy duty concrete floor finishes) in respect of the ten per cent fines value should ensure that the characteristic strength of other than high strength concrete is not limited on this account (Orchard 1976).

Relationships between the mechanical properties of aggregates and their subsequent effects on the performance of concretes are generally uncertain (Bloem & Gaynor 1963). However, the selection of a suitably high characteristic concrete strength alone is normally taken to assure a sufficient potential resistance to impact, abrasion and attrition, provided that sufficient attention is paid to the concrete mix design, placement and curing. The mechanical strength of the aggregate is usually not considered apart from routine compliance with BS 882 or an equivalent specification.

Where the performance requirements for concrete surfaces are exceptionally rigorous and beyond what might be reasonably expected of a normal structural concrete, special finishing operations (such as the use of vacuum mats, power floating, metallic surface dressings, or other treatments) may have to be employed in addition to the careful selection of both coarse and fine aggregates (Fookes & Poole 1981).

For concrete carriageways the aggregate plays an important part in determining the abrasion and polishing of the surface which influence the skidding resistance. Extensive research has shown that the carbonate content of the sand has the greatest effect on these properties. For this reason the sand must not contain more than 25% of acid soluble material in either the fraction retained or passing the 600 μm sieve (Dept of Transport 1986; Stock 1988).

8.12. Aggregate durability

The overall stability of concrete aggregates may be defined as the ability of individual particles to retain their integrity and not to suffer physical, mechanical or chemical changes to an extent which could adversely affect the properties or performance of concrete in either engineering or aesthetic respects. Aggregate stability cannot, therefore, be divorced from concrete durability which, in recent years, has become of increasing concern to the construction industry (Russell 1976) and its clients. However, the importance of the quality of the cement paste system (type of cement, minimum cement content, maximum water/cement ratio) must be recognized).

Furthermore, the consideration of aggregate stability also may be dependent upon the performance requirements for a concrete in the particular environmental conditions involved. For example, a low-strength, high-absorption aggregate may be acceptable for low- to medium-grade concrete in a non-aggressive internal environment. The same aggregate might also be considered acceptable for concretes exposed to severe climatic or industrial conditions, subject to the concrete satisfying the specified durability requirements. Additionally, both climate and industrial environments can vary greatly even within a single project or structure and may necessitate using a superior quality aggregate in particular locations.

The responsibility for determining the concrete durability criteria and, thereby, any aggregate performance requirements in a project, normally rests with the engineer or consultant. Published reports of concrete durability failures in recent years have highlighted this responsibility (Ryell & Smith 1968; Fookes & Collis 1975a), which can be especially onerous in the field of industrial construction, where the long-term and sometimes even immediate in-service performance requirements may not reasonably be foreseeable, even by the client. Post-construction investigations of concrete durability problems occasionally reveal that the likely in-service conditions, and the appropriate aggregate requirements, were not adequately investigated or even appreciated (Fookes et al. 1982), in which cases both contractual issues and professional liabilities may arise.

The factors which govern aggregate stability are manifold and may merit detailed consideration in specific construction situations. The principal characteristics influencing durability normally stem from the geological nature and origin of the parent rock, an understanding of which is important, especially when investigating the potential of new deposits. It is also necessary to appreciate that the apparent in situ stability of a source rock is not necessarily a certain indication of its stability as a processed aggregate in the totally different environment of concrete.

Aggregates can sometimes be impaired by the effects of seasonal climatic, diurnal and other influences acting upon the concrete. These may include temperature, tides, evaporation, rainfall, dewfall, humidity, ultraviolet radiation, ice, snow and frost. Any combinations of these influences and their degrees of aggression may vary widely depending upon local conditions. In turn these can include significant variations in microclimate; for example, in leeward, windward, splash zone or shaded locations (Fookes et al. 1983; Leeming 1983). In addition to these natural influences, considerations of operating conditions may be necessary in certain situations; for example, industrial waste and effluent treatment plants, cooling water outfalls, high temperature, potential fire hazard, cryogenic conditions and chemical plants (American Concrete Institute 1979).

8.12.1. Soundness

In the United Kingdom, soundness has rarely been a specified requirement for concrete aggregates except, in the non-specific sense, where qualitative specification clauses include the requirement that the aggregate should be 'sound'. Although 'soundness' tests were not included in previous editions of BS 812 they have now been included. There is a need, in some circumstances, for a test to identify certain aggregates which are apparently suitable for use on the basis of strength tests but which fail in service. Precision tests were carried out on four possible 'soundness' tests; modified aggregate impact value, modified ten per cent fines, methylene blue test for clays and magnesium sulphate soundness. The last test was selected as the most appropriate and the full details are given in BS 812 Part 121: 1989. No limits for soundness are given in BS 882. The only national specification for aggregate soundness is given by the Property Services Agency (PSA) and concerns airfield pavement concretes (Department of the Environment, 1979) in which aggregate soundness limits are given together with a soundness test procedure. The American specifications for aggregate soundness and test method are given in ASTM C33 and ASTM C88 respectively. Although the PSA and the ASTM soundness test procedures are quite similar, experience has shown that small procedural variations can sometimes produce significantly different results.

Soundness tests measure the resistance of aggregates to degradation or disintegration resulting from the crystallization of salts within the pores and interstitial structures of the aggregate particles, also to the wetting–drying and heating–cooling cycles which are involved in the test procedure (Bloem 1966). The test subjects aggregate samples, both coarse and fine, to forces and influences which are in some ways similar to the effects of natural freeze–thaw cycles or salt weathering. Correlation between soundness test results for an aggregate and its actual performance in concrete is largely subjective (Bloem 1966). Consequently, careful consideration should be given to the appropriateness of the test for particular situations and, similarly, to the specification of acceptance limits.

The soundness limits given in ASTM C33 vary according to aggregate particle size, either coarse or fine, and the type of sulphate salt being used in the test, either magnesium or sodium. Additionally, the coarse aggregate limits apply only to certain categories of construction or exposure conditions. These various limits are presented in simplified form in Table 8.6.

TABLE 8.6. *ASTM C33-81 Soundness limits for coarse and fine aggregates*

	Maximum weighted overall loss after 5 cycles, %	
	Coarse aggregate	Fine aggregate
Magnesium sulphate soundness	18	15
Sodium sulphate soundness	12	10

For airfield pavement works, the PSA specifies a maximum loss value in the magnesium sulphate soundness test of 18% for either coarse or fine aggregates with no individual size tested to have a loss greater than 30% (Department of the Environment 1979).

Although the limits in these specifications have remained unchanged for many years, compliance with them does not necessarily guarantee satisfactory performance of the aggregates in concretes subjected to freeze-thaw and salt weathering, or to other aggressive environments. However, only test results which are substantially lower than these limits are frequently considered to be indicative of 'sound' material.

Non-compliance does not inevitably lead to perform-ance failures, but should cause more detailed assessments to be made of possible consequences. These should include consideration of the observations made during the course of the tests, which may indicate that certain particles suffered total disintegration whereas others remained wholly unimpaired.

In such cases, which are not exceptional, simple petrographic examinations of the samples, both before and after testing, possibly coupled with geological and extraction studies at the quarry or pit, should enable the potentially less sound constituents in the aggregate to be identified. It may then be possible to reduce the proportion of unsound material in the aggregate products by selective quarrying and processing. This has been the case, for example, with certain North African quarries, in which sound limestones are sometimes interbedded with smaller quantities of highly unsound argillaceous limestone or gypsum material, and selective quarrying has optimized the content of 'sound' limestone in the resultant aggregate. However, some specifiers stipulate that apparently sound particles are required to be tested separately. If they fail the test the source is deemed to be unacceptable even if these particles represent a small percentage.

Considerable work on 'soundness' test is being carried out by a Task Group (CEN TC 154) involved with the preparation of European Standards for aggregates. It is anticipated that the new test will comprise a combined water absorption and freeze–thaw test not the magnesium sulphate soundness test.

8.12.2. Alkali reactivity

Field investigations and research findings over many years have demonstrated that various forms of reaction can occur in concrete between certain aggregates and alkali hydroxides derived from the concrete mix (Gillott 1975; Building Research Establishment 1988; Hobbs 1988, 1990). The physico-chemical mechanisms involved are complex and research continues to extend understanding and to reveal new features. The reader is, therefore, recommended to study the published work for a more detailed understanding of a complicated subject and the various options for minimizing the risk of the reaction.

The principal effects of alkali–aggregate reactivity are that affected concrete suffers expansion and cracking. The expansion causes misalignment of structures and can threaten structural integrity. Cracking can lead to reinforcement corrosion and other durability problems (Institution of Structural Engineers 1988).

The main types of alkali-reactivity identified may be categorized as follows:

(i) Alkali–silica reaction. This is the most common form of alkali–aggregate reaction. It involves a reaction between alkali hydroxides in the pore solution of the concrete and certain forms of silica in the aggregate, producing an alkali silicate gel. This gel may imbibe water and swell, sometimes causing disruption of the concrete.

For damaging alkali–silica reaction to occur there must be all three of the following:

(a) a critical amount of reactive silica in the aggregate;
(b) a sufficiently alkaline pore solution in the concrete;
(c) a sufficient supply of moisture.

The reactivity of silica minerals depends principally on the amount of order in the crystal structure. Opal has a highly disordered structure and is the most reactive form of silica. At the other end of the scale, well ordered unstrained quartz is normally unreactive. Other varieties of silica may exhibit intermediate reactivity (see Table 8.7).

The proportion of reactive silica has a major influence on the resulting expansion. As the proportion of reactive silica is increased, expansion due to alkali–silica reaction increases up to a maximum. As the reactive silica content is further increased the expansion then reduces. The silica content at which the greatest expansion occurs is called the pessimum. For the most reactive forms of opal the pessimum may be as low as 2 to 4% (BRE 1988 Digest 330). For less reactive varieties of silica the pessimum occurs at higher proportions. The explanation of the observed pessimum effect appears to depend on the nature of the reactive silica and the characteristics of the aggregate combination, and has been discussed by Hobbs (1988).

(ii) Alkali–silicate reaction. The term alkali–silicate reaction has been used to refer to reactions involving phyllosilicates such as vermiculite, chlorite and mica, present in rock such as phyllites, argillites and greywackes. The reactions are complicated and difficult to characterize but may be expansive (Gillott et al. 1973). In some cases the principal cause of the expansion may be the formation and swelling of an alkali–silicate gel, possibly associated with the presence of finely divided silica in the rocks. The reaction should, therefore, strictly be referred to as alkali–silica reaction.

(iii) Alkali–carbonate reaction. Reactions involving carbonate rocks may be either expansive or non-expansive (French & Poole 1974; Poole & Sotiropoulos 1981; Sims & Sotiropoulos 1983; Gillott & Swenson 1969). The potentially deleterious carbonates appear to contain appreciable quantities of dolomite and usually also clay minerals; micro-textures may also be important. Mechanisms vary in detail, but one of the best known involves dedolomitization by alkalis, followed by swelling

due to moisture-activation of the interstitial clay. Damaging alkali–carbonate reaction is rare.

TABLE 8.7. *Varieties of potentially reactive silica and their geological occurrence*

Variety of silica	Common geological occurrence
Opal	Vein material and vugh filling in a variety of rock types, a constituent of some types of chert, a replacement for siliceous fossil material and a cementing material in some sedimentary rocks.
Volcanic glass	A constituent of some igneous volcanic rocks ranging from acid to basic composition. Volcanic glass devitrifies over geological time and devitrified glass may also be potentially reactive.
Tridymite and cristobalite	High temperature metastable polymorphs of silica found as a minor constituent in some acid and intermediate volcanic rocks.
Microcrystalline and cryptocrystalline quartz	The principal constituent of most cherts and flint. Vein material and vugh fillings in a variety of rock types, groundmass mineral in some igneous and metamorphic rocks, cementing material in some sedimentary rocks.
Chalcedony	A fibrous variety of micro-crystalline quartz found as a constituent of some cherts and flint. Vein material and vugh fillings in a variety of rock types, cementing material in some sedimentary rocks.
Strained quartz	Found especially in metamorphic rocks, but also in some igneous rocks, subjected to high stresses. Also occurs as a detrital mineral in clastic sediments. Current opinion is that strained quartz itself is probably not reactive and reactivity may be associated with poorly ordered silica at the highly sutured grain boundaries commonly associated with strained quartz.

Note: Opal is the most reactive variety of silica. The relative reactivity of the other varieties shown on Table 8.7 will be controlled by many petrographic factors and the order of the minerals is not intended to rank them in terms of reactivity.

As certain types of potentially reactive silica occur as veins or other localized features within a quarry, a geological site inspection is considered essential (§6.5.6). Confirmation usually includes petrographic examination but these tests can only indicate whether an aggregate has a reactivity potential. Engineers usually need to decide whether any reactivity is likely to be detrimental · in a particular concrete structure in a specific environ-

TABLE 8.8. *Selected testing procedures frequently used in assessments of potential alkali–aggregate reactivity*

BS Draft	Procedure for qualitative and quantitative petrographic examination of aggregates
BS Draft	Guidance on the interpretation of petrographical examinations for alkali–silica reactivity
BS Draft	Alkali–silica reactivity—concrete prism method
ASTM C294	Standard Descriptive Nomenclature of constituents of natural mineral aggregates
ASTM C295	Standard Recommended Practice for petrographic examination of aggregates for concrete
ASTM C289	Standard Test Method for potential reactivity of aggregates (chemical method)
ASTM C227	Standard Test Method for potential alkali reactivity of cement-aggregate combinations (mortar bar method)
ASTM C586	Standard Test Method for potential alkali reactivity of carbonate rock for concrete aggregates (rock cylinder method)
Building Research Station (BRS)	National Building Studies Research Paper No. 25, 1958
BRS	Reactions between aggregates and cement, Part VI
BRS	Alkali–aggregate interaction: Test procedures. HMSO, London

ment, since not all potentially reactive aggregates are necessarily deleterious in service.

A number of test procedures is available to assist in the investigation of alkali-reactivity potential and some of the more common ones are listed in Table 8.8 and considered in Chapter 7. The first stage of such an investigation should involve the petrographic examination of the materials in question, since this should enable known potentially reactive constituents to be identified. On the basis of the findings it is then necessary to exercise judgement concerning the need for various supplementary tests. Knowledge of the potentially reactive components, identified by petrographic means, largely dictates the choice of subsequent test procedures, and will assist in the interpretation of the results (Sims 1981; Grattan-Bellew 1983). Long-term physical expansion tests, such as the mortar-bar method (ASTM C227) and the rock cylinder method (ASTM C586), sometimes may be considered necessary.

Thus, various laboratory procedures are available for evaluating the alkali-reactivity of aggregate materials, but it should be appreciated that the results are not necessarily conclusive and that considerable reliance sometimes has to be placed on experience and expert opinion, especially when reliable and appropriate evidence of local concrete performance is not available.

Little guidance is given in BS 882 on the subject of alkali reactivity other than referring to the requirements of BS 8110. These recommendations, together with those in BS 5328, are essentially similar to the guidance provided by the Concrete Society Working Party (Hawkins *et al.* 1983) for minimizing the risk of alkali–silica reaction in the UK but are not necessarily reliable where opal is included in the aggregate (Concrete Society Technical Report No. 30, BRE Digest 330). ENV 206 also lays down the precautions to be taken but the main requirements rest with the standards or regulations valid in the place of use followed by previous history and experience with the particular combination of cement and aggregate.

8.12.3. Frost susceptibility

Certain aggregates may contain fragments of friable sandstone, porous limestone, chalk or white flint cortex particles. These materials are microporous, and hence potentially frost susceptible (Roeder 1977). A few weak or absorbent particles within a body of a concrete will not affect its strength or water absorption to any significant extent. But should these particles be close to the surface exposed to weather and, in particular, frost then unsightly 'pop outs' may occur.

The frost susceptibility of an aggregate depends on the size and continuity of the pores together with the degree of water saturation. To avoid exceeding the tensile strength of the aggregate the water in the pores must flow into unfilled pores or escape from the particle. It has been estimated that pores less than 4 µm in size can be emptied effectively only at pressures high enough to cause damage and failure to both the aggregate and the concrete (Verbeck & Landgren 1960; Cordon 1966).

Some aggregate particles are able to withstand these high stresses by elastic accommodation without failing but expand sufficiently to cause damage to the surrounding mortar by a pop-out. The volume of pores in aggregate particles varies widely from nearly 0 to over 20% of the gross volume depending on the type of aggregate. According to Neville (1981) granites have low porosities ranging from 0.4 to 3.8%. White flint cortex particles analysed by an Image Analysing Computer gave results ranging from 7 to 46% with about 75% of the pores smaller than 4 µm.

The behaviour of aggregate may vary in different solutions of de-icing salts (Sommer 1980) and the use of urea, which reduces the surface tension of the water, can lead to penetration of water into finer pores causing damage (Rauen 1980).

Work on the development of suitable test methods for European standards continues within the CEN TC 154 SC6 Task Group.

TABLE 8.9. *BS 882: 1992 limits upon fines content*

Aggregate type	Quantity of clay, silt and dust (max. % by mass)
Uncrushed, partially crushed or crushed gravel	2
Crushed rock	4
Uncrushed or partially crushed sand or crushed gravel sand	4
Crushed rock sand	16 (9 for use in heavy duty floor finishes)
Gravel all-in aggregate	3
Crushed rock all-in aggregate	11

8.13. Impurities

8.13.1. Clay, silt and dust

Clay, silt and dust in aggregates was defined by BS 882: 1983 as being all the material passing a 75 μm sieve. In practice, however, the nature of the minus 75 μm material, if any, can have a considerable influence upon the properties of concrete. The relative proportions of clay-sized (minus 2 μm) and silt-sized (2–75 μm) particles are important. There will also be a significant difference between the influence of clay-sized material comprising 'rock flour' and that of clay-sized material actually comprising water-active clay minerals which swell in the presence of water. BS 882 currently defines fines as any solid material passing the 75 μm sieve and the limits are given in Table 8.9.

Limits for fine materials (such as clay) figure in most European aggregate standards and differ from BS 882. It is probable that the European aggregate standard will define fines as material passing a 63 μm sieve.

Coarse aggregates and natural sands produced in the UK only rarely fail to meet the BS 882 limits, whereas compliance with the crushed rock fines limit was less well assured in the past. Nowadays, the 75 μm material in crushed rock sand is often recovered as a separate filler product or to reduce environmental dust problems. Clay or silt sized material tends to predominate in the fines of natural (uncrushed) coarse and fine aggregates, whilst relatively coarser 'dust of fracture' is usually predominant in crushed rock aggregates.

The principal detrimental effects which these fine materials have on concrete are to increase the water demand of a concrete to achieve a given workability and, where present as coatings which are not removed during mixing, to impair the aggregate-matrix bond (Neville 1981). The higher limit given for crushed rock sand in BS 882 reflects the typically coarser character of these fines. The American Specification for concrete aggregates

(ASTM C33), also imposes a limit of 7% (or 5% if the concrete is subject to abrasion), provided the fine material consists of the 'dust of fracture' with clay or shale being essentially absent. The French permit up to 10% passing the 80 μm sieve for sand subject to the fines satisfying other quality requirements. This further illustrates the assumed difference between dust and clay.

The presence of substantial amounts of material passing the 75 μm sieve can result in misleading overall gradings when the sample is subject to routine sieve analysis in the dry condition only. This is particularly so for crushed rock sand, as is illustrated by the data given in Table 8.10. This example demonstrates that a routine dry sieve analysis can underestimate the amount of material passing the 75 μm sieve, and also indicates a markedly coarser grading than is actually the case. Where such an effect is not appreciated, errors can be made when assessing the nature and yield of both natural and crushed resources, also in preliminary mix designs, decisions regarding admixtures, in estimates of material demands, and in fines disposal.

TABLE 8.10. *Grading comparisons for crushed rock sand*

Sieve size	% by weight passing	
	A	B
10.00 mm	100	100
5.00 mm	99	100
2.36 mm	88	89
1.18 mm	59	64
600 μm	39	45
300 μm	26	32
150 μm	17	23
75 μm	11	17

A, grading determined by dry sieving; B, grading determined by dry sieving after the removal of the 75 μm material by washing.

Sometimes, higher amounts of fine material can be less harmful or even beneficial, for example, where the concrete strength and durability requirements are less critical and a particularly cohesive concrete is required, or perhaps when the cement used is coarsely ground. A high fines content in coarse aggregate may sometimes help to improve workability when the local natural sand and/or crusher-run sand are coarse and 'sharp'. In the case of some fine dune sands, the roundness and smoothness of the particles may help to compensate, in terms of workability, for the fineness (Fookes & Higginbottom 1980). These examples illustrate the general importance of flexibility in approach when considering limits for particular situations.

Occasionally and particularly overseas, it is necessary to consider whether British Standard or other limits could be relaxed for practical or economic reasons. In these circumstances comparative concrete trial mixes are essential but, as explained earlier, it is also helpful to identify the composition of the fine material involved. This identification is desirable because BS 882 defines 'fines' as being all material finer than 75 μm, whereas in soils terminology (BS 1377) 'clay' and 'silt' materials are separated on the basis of particle size (clay being less than 2 μm and silt less than 63 μm) and also these materials can be characterized and defined mineralogically. Thus, the minus 75 μm component of a sand may be found to be entirely clay-grade material consisting of clay minerals, when the BS 882 maximum limit of 3% (for crushed rock coarse aggregate or natural sand) might be considered too high. Conversely the minus 75 μm component might be entirely silt-grade material, when a higher maximum limit might be tolerated.

Some European countries, for example, France, adopt a three-stage approach to the testing of fines: sizing, sand equivalent and methylene blue test (AFNOR NF P18-301). If the material fails the first test (limit of %wt passing 80 μm) it is subjected to the second and then third tests until finally accepted or rejected.

Where 'clay, silt and dust' are present, they may occur partially as particle coatings and this can have an adverse effect on aggregate-matrix bond, especially when present as clay-grade material. Clay may also occur in the form of discrete particles or 'clay lumps' which, due to normal dust coatings, may be visually indistinguishable in the field from the aggregate particles themselves. However, their presence normally becomes apparent if the aggregate is wetted or washed, when partial or total disintegration may occur, although some clay lumps may be hard enough to survive the concrete mixing process. The presence of clay lumps in an aggregate could, for example, affect adversely the soundness test results, the local effectiveness of cover to reinforcement, and also the durability or aesthetic appearance of a concrete surface. Certain forms of clay minerals, such as montmorillonites, exhibit unusual degrees of swelling when wetted and contraction when dried. The presence of these clay minerals in large quantities may exacerbate concrete drying shrinkage and moisture movement characteristics.

Overall, it is generally more prudent to assume that the presence in aggregates of excessive amounts of 'clay' size and 'silt' size particles is potentially detrimental to strength, durability and cost, unless or until it can be established otherwise.

A recent project (Smith 1987) showed that limestone dust on the coarse aggregate had some benefit to the strength of the concrete when the cement content did not exceed 360–380 kg/m³. Above this value strength and other properties were affected detrimentally.

In a report to BSI by Pike (DCP313, 1989) concerning the regulation of fines in sands for concrete and mortar, it states that a controlled amount of mineral flour other than clay minerals may be tolerable (and occasionally useful) but clays are to be avoided: smectites are particularly harmful and their content should be severely restricted. Reference to these harmful materials is made in Chapter 7.

8.13.2. Chlorides

Chlorides, usually sodium chloride or common salt, occur naturally in marine and some coastal sources of aggregates and also occur at significant levels in some inland sedimentary deposits. Severe chloride contamination of aggregate sources is a particular problem in the Arabian Gulf and some other parts of the Middle East (Fookes & Collis 1976; Fookes & Higginbottom 1980; Kay *et al.* 1982).

Chloride has little significant influence on the properties of plain concrete, except that the sulphate resistance of sulphate-resisting portland cement may be impaired by the presence of chlorides. However, the presence of chlorides in reinforced concrete introduces corrosion risks for the embedded steel (Building Research Establishment, 1980, 1982). These risks have been increasingly recognized since the mid-1970s (Simm & Fookes 1989) and have been associated with the amount of chloride present in relation to the cement content. However, it was not until 1977 that the maximum amounts of chloride in concrete permitted by British Standards Codes of Practice and Specifications were substantially reduced. The current requirement in BS 5328 is given in Table 8.11. BS 8110 requirements are essentially the same except that they do not refer to other concrete. The European Standard ENV 206 requirements are given in Table 8.12. ISO and European aggregate standards also have requirements for chlorides.

BS 882 does not specify limits for the content of chlorides in aggregates, neither for plain concrete nor for concrete containing embedded material. However, guidance values are provided in Appendix C of BS 882 for 'when it is required to limit the chloride ion content'. These values are based upon the levels of the chloride ion permitted for concrete in BS 5328 but do not necessarily assure compliance with the latter, particularly for

TABLE 8.11. *Chloride content of concrete BS 5328*

Type or use of concrete	Maximum total chloride content expressed as % of chloride ion by mass of cement
Prestressed concrete. Heat cured concrete containing embedded metal	0.10
Concrete containing embedded metal and made with cement complying with BS 4027	0.20
Concrete containing embedded metal and made with cement complying with BS 12, BS 146, BS 4246, BS 6588 or combinations with with ggbs or pfa	0.40
Other concrete	No limit

TABLE 8.12. *Chloride contents ENV 206*

Concrete	% chloride ion per mass of cement
Plain	1.0
Reinforced	0.4
Prestressed	0.2

prestressed concrete. These guidance values are given in Table 8.13.

Where chlorides are present in solution, as is the case for marine aggregates, the introduction of simple but thorough washing techniques coupled with adequate dewatering normally enables the amounts present to be reduced to comply with the guidance values given in BS 882. Where the washing water is recirculated it is most important to monitor the chloride content. However, when present in rock deposits, more extensive efforts are usually necessary to obtain adequate chloride reductions in coarse aggregates and crushed rock sands.

In the United Kingdom, the chloride content of aggregates is normally determined by the water extraction method described in BS 812: Part 117.

Reference to alkali reactivity was made in §8.12.1 and the alkalis contributed by 'salt' in aggregates has also to be considered. This is dealt with in §8.13.5.

8.13.3. Shell

Calcareous shell debris is present in aggregates from marine and coastal land deposits, occurring as broken, whole flat or whole hollow shells. The primary effect of plate shell fragments in aggregate is to increase the water demand to maintain a given concrete workability (Sand and Gravel Association 1968), whilst complete hollow shells may render concrete frost susceptible when occurring near to an exposed concrete surface (Shirley 1981).

BS 882 provides limits for the shell content of coarse aggregates but has no requirement in respect of aggregate finer than 5 mm. The GLC Specification (Greater London Council 1979) for Marine Aggregates for Concrete had included limitations on shell content for many

TABLE 8.13. *BS 882: 1992 (Appendix C): limits for chloride content of aggregates*

Type or use of concrete	Chloride ion content expressed as % by mass of combined aggregate
Prestressed concrete and heat-cured concrete containing embedded metal	0.01
Concrete made with cement complying with BS 4027 with or without embedded metal	0.03
Concrete containing embedded metal and made with cement complying with BS 12, BS 146, BS 1370, BS 4246, BS 6588, BS 6610 or combinations with ggbs or pfa	0.05
Concrete with no embedded metal except concrete made with BS 4027 cement	No limit

TABLE 8.14. *BS 882: 1992 Shell content limits for aggregates*

Size	Limits on shell content (%)
Fractions of 10 mm single size, or of graded or all-in aggregate that are finer than 10 mm and coarser than 5 mm	20
Fractions of single sizes or of graded or all-in aggregate that are coarser than 10 mm	8
Aggregates finer than 5 mm	no requirements

years, although these had been criticized for being unduly restrictive for most applications (Chapman & Roeder 1979). The GLC Specification also provided separate limits for total shell content and 'hollow shell' content. These various limits are summarized in Tables 8.14 and 8.15.

TABLE 8.15. *Greater London Council (1979) Shell content limits for marine aggregates for concrete*

Nominal size of aggregate (mm)	Maximum shell content, % by weight of dry aggregate	
	Total shell	Hollow shell
40 graded	6	1
20 graded	10	1
10 single size	15	2
Fine	No limit	No limit

BS 8110 does not include limits for the shell content in concrete but does warn that hollow or flat shells, if present in sufficient quantities, may adversely affect the properties of fresh and hardened concrete.

ENV 206 does not refer to shell in concrete, although some European countries do impose limits.

Although not strictly a shell, coral is related material that is occasionally the sole source of both coarse aggregates and sand for concrete, for example in some parts of the Pacific (Vines 1982; Rollings 1988). The successful use of coral aggregates over many years demonstrates the extent to which limits are often related to the best material available rather than to absolute criteria (American Society for Testing and Materials 1976).

8.13.4. Organic matter

Organic matter is usually considered to represent a potentially deleterious impurity in aggregates intended for use in concrete. Some types of organic material, including humus, fuel oil and sugars, can retard or even prevent the hydration of cement and the consequent hardening of concrete, even when present in only trace concentrations (Sherwood & Roeder 1965; Lees 1987).

Other forms of organic material, such as coal and lignite, are frequently regarded as undesirable, mainly because they tend to occur as mechanically weak and physically unsound particles, but also because of the unsightly stains they can cause on the surface of the concrete.

Specifications commonly call for aggregates to be 'free' from organic impurities. In practice such a requirement must refer to the exclusion of detectable organic contamination, so that much depends upon the reliability and usefulness of tests for organic impurities. A chemical analysis procedure for organic matter is given for soils in BS 1377: 1990, but interpretation may be difficult if used for aggregates, except that any values found above 'trace' level could be considered potentially undesirable and merit further investigation.

A simple qualitative colour test is given in ASTM C40 and BS 812 Part 122.1 Appendix. A more complex test measuring the pH of mortar mixes was, until recently, given for sands in BS 812 (BS 812: 1967), but neither of these procedures is capable of identifying all varieties of deleterious organic material (Roeder 1963; Lea 1970; Foreword to BS 812: 1975). A test to determine fulvo-acid, a component of humic acid, claimed to retard the setting and detailed in the Netherlands Standard (NEN 5920) will be included in European Standards for aggregates.

Indirect indications of harmful organic impurities are obtained by comparative strength and setting time tests, using either concrete or mortar mixes. However, such procedures are rarely included in routine aggregates assessment programmes unless the simple colour test has already indicated a possible organic impurity. The apparently low incidence of concrete failure due to undetected organic contamination of aggregates may justify the absence of such performance tests from most materials evaluations and contract specifications. However, these difficulties in providing conclusive test results should be understood by the specifier who requires aggregates to be 'free' from organic impurities.

ASTM C33 provides maximum limits for coal and lignite, in coarse or fine aggregates, of 0.5% or 1.0% respectively, depending upon the importance of the concrete appearance. However, in testing samples of aggregate for either coal and lignite or other types of lightweight contamination (BS 812 Part 122.2), it must be recognized that the concentration of such materials within aggregate sources is likely to exhibit very considerable variability.

ISO and some European Standards for natural aggregates for concrete limit organic matter and coal or lignite. For example, in Belgium any sand failing the sodium hydroxide colorimetric test is subjected to a quantitative test with the maximum limit of 0.5% organic matter. The limits for coal or lignite in Spain are the same as the ASTM requirements.

8.13.5. Alkalis

Salt-contaminated aggregates can liberate alkali metal ions (sodium and potassium) in concrete. Specifications such as the Department of Transport Specification for Highway Works (1991), in relation to the prevention of alkali–silica reaction, require that alkalis contributed by salt from the aggregates should be included in the calculation of the reactive alkali content of the concrete mix. For UK marine aggregates both specifications take the chloride content of the aggregate and multiply this by a factor of 0.76 to obtain the contribution of equivalent Na_2O. (The figure of 0.76 is based on a consideration of the composition of UK sea water.) For other salt contaminated aggregates the factor of 0.76 may not be valid, requiring a determination of the water soluble Na_2O and K_2O content.

A number of common rock forming minerals such as feldspars and phyllosilicates contain appreciable Na_2O and K_2O. Rocks containing these minerals are, therefore, characterized by high total alkali contents, for example whole rock analyses on granite give equivalent Na_2O contents commonly between 6% and 8%. Work by Van Aardt & Visser (1977) suggested that calcium hydroxide attack on feldspars and clay minerals could release alkalis and that this process could possibly occur in concrete. It was also suggested that the release of alkalis may be greater from more highly altered feldspars. Their experiments were, however, conducted on powdered samples under more severe conditions than would be encountered in practice.

There has, however, been little published evidence to support alkali release from feldspar or phyllosilicate minerals in aggregates contributing to alkali–silica reaction. Recent joint research undertaken by the Building Research Establishment and Aston University (pers. comm.) revealed no significant release of alkalis from relatively unweathered granite aggregate in concrete.

On the basis of the current state of knowledge it would appear that for most relatively unweathered igneous and metamorphic rocks, including types commonly used as aggregate such as granite, a significant release of alkalis in concrete is unlikely. The possibility of alkali release from highly weathered igneous and metamorphic rocks remains uncertain but such materials

would, in any event, probably be unsuitable for use as concrete aggregate for other reasons.

With certain alkali-reactive sedimentary rocks such as greywackes and shales it is possible that alkalis derived from within the aggregate may have contributed to the reaction.

8.13.6. Sulphates

When present in sufficient quantity, sulphates in aggregates can result in excessive expansion and, ultimately, the disruption of hardened concrete in wet or damp conditions, owing to reaction with cement compounds (Lea 1970). Although sulphates occur in the ground and ground waters in various parts of the United Kingdom, their occurrence to any significant extent as contaminants in aggregate sources is rare. However, in areas of the Middle East and in tropical coastal plains, sulphates commonly occur in rock, sand and gravel sources (Fookes & Collis 1975b).

The form of the sulphate is important in determining the likelihood of reaction with concrete, with solubility in water being the critical consideration (Lea 1970). Magnesium and sodium sulphates are easily soluble and, thereby, potentially more aggressive to concrete, whereas calcium sulphate is only slightly soluble and thereby capable of only a slow, albeit progressive, attack. Barium sulphate is hardly soluble at all and indeed (as barytes) is used as heavy aggregate for concrete (Miller 1983). Research over many decades has examined the effects of external sulphates (e.g. from adjacent ground, groundwater and sea water) on concrete (Lea 1970; Neville 1981). However, research into the effects of excess sulphate within concrete has been limited to date (Fookes & Collis 1975a; Samarai 1976), but in some locations 'internal sulphate attack' may be of some significance (Crammond 1984).

BS 882 gives no limits for sulphates in natural aggregates although it does require compliance with BS 8110 Part 1 (1985). This states that the total acid soluble sulphate content of the concrete mix, expressed as SO_3, should not exceed 4% SO_3 by mass of the cement in the mix, the sulphate content being calculated as the total from the various constituents of the concrete. BS 5328 states that within the UK sulphate problems caused by natural aggregates are rare but worldwide the sulphate levels in aggregates may be sufficient to cause disruption of the concrete. BS 5328 recommends that when the source of an aggregate is new or suspected of containing sulphate then sulphate content tests are advised.

Sulphate limits are laid down for slag aggregates and lightweight aggregates complying with BS 3797. ISO and many European countries impose a requirement for sulphates in aggregates for concrete and reference to these Standards is advisable.

Whilst it is relatively easy to advocate stringent limits

on the sulphate content of aggregates, it is, in the present state of knowledge, extremely difficult to specify the maximum amounts that can be tolerated in any particular concrete.

8.13.7. Chalk

Chalk is a distinctive form of limestone that outcrops extensively, including the South and East of England, and is a fairly common constituent of natural gravels and sands that may be considered for use as concrete aggregates. Chalk-like material also occurs elsewhere, such as some of the soft young limestones of the Arabian Gulf area, in North Africa and northern Europe. Typical chalk particles are mechanically weak, soft and unusually absorbent, although the particles surviving in some coarser gravels could represent the relatively harder and more durable varieties of chalk. In small proportions, weak absorbent chalk particles are probably not detrimental in concrete, except that they may give rise to occasional 'pop-outs' when occurring close to concrete surfaces exposed to freeze–thaw action (Lees 1987).

BS 882 does not specify a limit for the content of chalk particles. Chalk contamination of aggregates has sometimes been subjected to local controls in geographical areas such as Hertfordshire and Essex where experience has revealed such impurities, but the acceptance criteria have usually been somewhat arbitrary and then based upon the calcium carbonate content determined by chemical analysis, rather than chalk determined by petrographical techniques (Russell 1976). Such a localized approach can lead to the unfortunate application of inappropriate limitations in other parts of the country, where controls of calcium carbonate content could exclude completely acceptable limestone aggregates (Lees 1987).

8.13.8. Mica

Micas, most commonly in the forms of muscovite or biotite, are relatively common components of various rocks commonly used for aggregate production, including granites, gneisses and some sandstones. Discrete mica particles can occur in natural sands, also in crushed rock sands as the result of being released from the parent rock. The main effect of their presence is to increase the water demand of concrete usually with adverse effects on related concrete properties such as abrasion resistance, strength and durability (Dewar 1963; Forder 1972; Fookes & Revie 1982). Mica within the coarse aggregate particle does not, normally, present any problems.

There have been few authoritative research programmes to quantify the effect of discrete mica in concrete aggregates. In one series of tests, using granitic sands from Southwest England, it was demonstrated that the strength of a concrete mix may be reduced by as much as 5% by the presence of 1% of muscovite mica by weight in the total aggregate (Dewar 1963). Neither BS 882: 1992 nor ASTM C33 specifies limits for discrete mica in aggregates, but a maximum content of 1% mica has been suggested by some authors for sand (Lees 1987). However, in some circumstances, where the decorative appearance of concrete is considered more important than strength and durability, the presence of mica in the aggregates may be advantageous.

The presence of mica in aggregates is readily seen with the naked eye or with a hand lens and identified by petrographic examination. It is possible to obtain quantitative determinations of mica contents by physical separation, counting and weighing procedures. These methods are not easily adaptable for general use on site, but this has been achieved in locations where mica in aggregates was found to be a serious and continuous problem (Fookes & Revie 1982). Production control and specification compliance difficulties have then to be resolved in advance of construction. It is a particularly troublesome contaminant, since it is virtually impossible to remove it completely from an aggregate and, although washing helps to some extent, it is difficult even to reduce the amount present using the normal aggregate production plant found in the construction industry. The removal of mica is considered in Chapter 5.

It is important to identify whether new sources of aggregate may be mica bearing, especially overseas where alternative sources may not be available or economic. The scale of the problem must then be assessed before specifications are finalized, also before processing plant design is completed so that consideration can be given to the cost-benefit of employing potentially costly mineral processing techniques. Geological assessment of the source deposits may enable mica-free material to be obtained by selective quarrying.

8.13.9 Pyrites and other metallic impurities

Certain metal compounds can seriously affect the setting rate of concrete, even when present in only trace amounts (Lea 1970). Examples are lead or zinc oxides (Midgley 1970), which can occur in mine tailings used as aggregates, and in some natural sources. Thus knowledge of the source geology could be of value in assessing the likelihood of retardation problems on this account, also whether the cause of any difficulties is likely to be general throughout a deposit or restricted to local concentrations.

Iron pyrites (pyrite or iron sulphide) is another naturally occurring contaminant in some aggregate deposits; for example, in some of the flint gravels of Southern England (Midgley 1958). Some forms of iron pyrites are able to oxidize, with the resultant expansion, when situated at or near concrete surfaces. This activity thus leads to the development of surface defects with considerable attendant staining of the surface by iron oxide. The surface deterioration is usually of no structural or durability significance, but the unsightly appearance may be considered excessive in comparison to the small size and incidence of the causative pyrite particles and can be very expensive and significant in contractual terms.

Not all pyrite particles are 'reactive' in this way, and a simple lime-water test has been devised which may differentiate 'reactive' and 'non-reactive' types of pyrite (Midgley 1958). However, this test is only applicable to individual particles separated from an aggregate sample and is, therefore, not usually helpful for overall suitability assessments. Also, pyrite concentrations, whether 'reactive', 'non-reactive' or both, usually show very considerable variability within an aggregate source, so that it would be difficult to control the pyrite content by specification without actually disallowing certain general types of aggregate for concrete works in which surface appearance was paramount.

Deterioration of building blocks and some other concrete made using mine waste known as 'mundic' has occurred in SW England. This is apparently caused by the instability of some pyritic and slatey rock constituents (DoE 1991).

8.14. Aggregate drying shrinkage

A limited number of United Kingdom aggregates suffer higher than normal volume changes on wetting and drying which, in turn, can affect adversely the drying shrinkage and wetting expansion characteristics of concretes. This finding resulted from investigations of failure and subsequent research by the Scottish Building Research Station (Snowdon & Edwards 1962; Edwards 1966; Building Research Establishment 1968) which revealed that, with certain aggregates, concrete could suffer as much as a fourfold increase in drying shrinkage. Weathered rock (either tropically or temperately) aggregate must be considered to be potentially highly shrinkable unless proved otherwise.

The rock types that exhibit excessive shrinkage characteristics are found to contain clay or mica minerals. Hence, altered dolerites and basalts ('whinstones') can be affected, also some greywacke sandstones, mudstones, shales and mica-schists. For some sources, it has been possible to derive a predictive relationship between water absorption of the aggregate and the aggregate drying shrinkage (Snowdon & Edwards 1962). In South Africa, work with heavily-altered dolerites has shown a good relationship between the content of secondary minerals and the shrinkage potential (Winert 1968).

Shrinkage of aggregate in concrete, particularly the coarse aggregate, may lead to cracking or crazing of the concrete, thereby increasing the vulnerability of that concrete to deterioration by other agencies, such as frost action. In the case of reinforced concrete, apart from the increased risk of corrosion as a result of cracking of the concrete cover, excessive deflections of beams and other structural units can be caused by excessive drying shrinkage of the aggregates within the concrete. An aggregate shrinkage test procedure has been developed by the Building Research Establishment (Digest 35, 1968) comprising a concrete drying shrinkage test employing a standardized concrete mix in which only the aggregate source varies. The results are classified to provide the designer and specifier with a basis for assessing whether or not particular aggregate combinations require the adoption of special design or concrete production measures.

It is therefore essential for the test to be carried out at an early stage of a project, when consideration is being given to the potential suitability of local sources of aggregates, and subsequently for approval and monitoring purposes. The classifications given in BRE Digest 35 are reproduced in Table 8.16.

The shrinkage test method and implementation of the appropriate recommendations can only provide assurance against the likelihood of concrete shrinkage problems due to the composition of the aggregates. However, cracking and other problems resulting from excessive concrete shrinkage can occur due to a variety of factors which are wholly or largely independent of the nature of the aggregate employed (Concrete Society 1982).

BS 812 Part 120 provides a method for testing and classifying the shrinkage of aggregates in concrete. Although the test has its origins in the BRE Digest 35 test, it has a simpler procedure and classification into two categories. These are reproduced in Table 8.17. It should be noted that the values are specific to parts of the UK.

BRE Digest 35 has now been replaced by BRE Digest 357 which takes into account the BS 812 Part 120 test but provides a method for aggregates outside the scope of the standard.

8.15. Thermal movement

The heating and cooling of concrete can cause expansion and contraction. When heated, concrete expands uniformly with temperature rise over the range 0–60°C. Therefore, for most structural applications the thermal coefficient of linear expansion may be assumed to be constant between these temperatures with values of 5–15 microstrain/°C.

One of the main factors affecting the value of the coefficient for concrete is the type of aggregate. Since

TABLE 8.16. *Aggregate shrinkage categories and recommendations given in Building Research Establishment Digest 35 (1968)*

Drying, shrinkage of concrete (in BRE test) (%)	Remarks	Use
Not exceeding 0.045	Possible with several types of very low shrinkage such as granite, unaltered felsite, blast-furnace slag and a few dolerites and gabbros. Quartz, flint gravel and marble which are very hard and non-shrinking will produce concrete with a shrinkage less than 0.025%.	Suitable for all concreting purposes. If very low values of drying shrinkage for pre-cast products are required it may be necessary to cure with high-pressure steam but this would not apply to concrete made with quartz, flint, gravel and marble.
0.046–0.065	Possible with hard dense aggregates having low shrinkage and with softer non-shrinkable aggregates. Most of the aggregates in Central Scotland are in this range.	Suitable for most applications. Special care should be taken in the design of such units as cladding panels and cast in situ floors, particularly if heated. Span/depth ratios should be reduced below their values given in CP114 or CP116 or alternatively, additional reinforcements should be provided in the compression zone of the section. For prestressed concrete an extra allowance should be made for loss of prestress.
0.066–0.085	Possible with aggregates covering a wide geological range. At this and higher levels of drying shrinkage the durability of the concrete is likely to become affected.	Suitable for all general purposes but for unreinforced or thin reinforced members exposed to the weather air-entrained concrete should be used.
Exceeding 0.085	These are gravels consisting mainly of sedimentary rocks such as greywacke, shale and mudstone. They have produced concrete which has resulted in severe warping and widespread deterioration.	Suitable only in positions where complete drying out never occurs, for mass concrete surfaced with air-entrained concrete and for members that are not exposed to the weather.

Notes:
1. Different batches of ordinary portland cement may be expected to give rise to variations of the order of 0.005% in the drying shrinkage of the concrete.
2. In general, although the coarse aggregate plays the major part in determining the shrinkage of the concrete, the type and grading of the fine aggregate also affect the result. When a low-shrinkage fine aggregate is used with a high-shrinkage coarse aggregate (in place of the fine aggregate from the same source) the shrinkage of the resulting concrete may be reduced by as much as 0.03%. Also, changing the grading of the fine aggregate from Zone 4 to Zone 1, BS 882: 1973, may in extreme cases decrease the shrinkage by as much as 0.02%.
3. It is assumed that the normal recommendations for quality control given by the appropriate Code of Practice for the particular job will be observed.

TABLE 8.17. *Classification of aggregate shrinkage BS 812 Part 120: 1989*

Category	Range of values	Use
A	0 to 0.075%	All concreting purposes.
B	Greater than 0.075%	Positions where complete drying out never occurs. Mass concrete surfaced with air entrained concrete. Members symmetrically and heavily reinforced not exposed to the weather.

concrete is predominantly aggregate, the aggregate or rock expansion dominates in determining the expansion of the composite, concrete.

The thermal coefficient of expansion of rocks ranges from 1 to 16 microstrain/°C due to their differing mineralogical composition. The expansion coefficient for siliceous minerals such as quartz (12 microstrain/°C) is much higher than for most other minerals such as calcite (1–5 microstrain/°C), calcite being present in limestones. Therefore, the thermal expansion coefficients of rocks generally increase with an increase in the silica content but wide variations can occur within a rock group (Browne 1972).

Table 8.18 shows that rocks containing nearly 100% silica have the highest coefficients and limestone has the lowest value. Rocks with lower proportions of silica

TABLE 8.18. *The thermal expansion of rocks and the related concretes*

Rock	Silica content (%)	Thermal expansion coefficient $1 \times 10^{-6}/°C$	
		Rock (average value)	Concrete (average value)
Chert	94	11.8	13.2
Quartzite	94	10.3	12.1
Sandstone	84	9.3	11.4
Granite	66	6.8	9.6
Basalt	51	6.4	9.3
Limestone	Trace	5.5	8.6

occupy intermediate values. Concretes made from these rock types follow a similar pattern of thermal movement (Browne 1972).

The thermal expansion of a neat cement paste depends on its moisture condition and ranges from 20 microstrain/°C in the partially saturated condition to 14 microstrain/°C in the dry state. It is likely that differential expansion between cement paste and aggregate may contribute to the deterioration of concrete and influence the spacing of expansion joints in pavement quality concrete (Baluch *et al.* 1989; Venecanin 1989; Al-Tayyib *et al.* 1989).

8.16.   Fire resistance

Concrete has a high degree of fire resistance which makes it a very desirable structural material. This property of concrete is allied to the low coefficient of thermal expansion and, as with thermal movement, the resistance to fire is affected by the type of aggregate. A highly siliceous material such as flint has relatively poor resistance due to inversion of the quartz present which causes disruptive expansion in the aggregate. Limestone is not subjected to this particular weakness and is thus a more satisfactory aggregate for fire resistance. It has been reported that the calcination of dolomitic gravel is an endothermic reaction which absorbs heat and delays a further temperature rise. The calcined material has a lower density and therefore provides some surface insulation (Abrams & Gustaferro 1986). Abrams (1971) confirmed that at temperatures around 430°C siliceous aggregate concrete loses a greater proportion of its strength than concretes made with limestone but once the temperature has reached 800°C the difference is small. Concretes made with siliceous or limestone aggregate show a change in colour with temperature. This is dependent on the presence of iron compounds. The colour change is permanent and an estimate of the maximum temperature reached during a fire can be made depending on the depth of colour. The colour ranges from pink, red, grey and buff for temperatures between 300° and 1000°C (Zoldners 1960). Lightweight

aggregates and hence lightweight aggregate concrete show excellent thermal properties.

References

ABRAMS, M. S. 1971. *Comprehensive strength of concrete at temperatures to 1600°F*, Temperature and Concrete ACI Special Publication, **25**, 33–58.

—— & GUSTAFERRO, A. H. 1986. Fire endurance of concrete slabs influenced by thickness, aggregate type and moisture. Portland Cement Association, Research and Development Lab. 10. No. 2 pp 9.24.

AL-TAYYIB, A. J., BALUCH, M. H., AL-FARABI, SHARIF, M. & MAHAMUD, M. M. 1989. The effect of thermal cycling on the durability of concrete made from local materials in the Arabian Gulf Countries. *Cement & Concrete Research*, **19**, 131–142.

AMERICAN CONCRETE INSTITUTE (ACI). 1979. Committee 515. A guide to the use of waterproofing damp-proofing, protective, and decorating barrier systems for concrete. *Concrete International*, **1** (11), 41–81.

AMERICAN SOCIETY FOR TESTING AND MATERIALS. 1976. *Living with Marginal Aggregates*. ASTM STP 597.

—— 1978. *Significance of Tests and Properties of Concrete-making Materials*. ASTM STP 169B.

BALUCH, M. H., AL-NOUR, L. A. R., AZAD, A. K., AL-MANDIL, M. Y., SHARIF, A. M. & PEARSON-KIRK, D. 1989. Damage characterisation of thermally degraded concrete. *Proceedings of 3rd International Conference on Deterioration and Repair of Reinforced Concrete in the Arabian Gulf*. **1**, 543–560.

BARKER, J. A. 1983. *Dictionary of Concrete*. Construction Press, London.

BLAKE, L. 1967. *Recommendations for the production of high-quality concrete surfaces*. C. & C.A. Tech. Advisory Series.

BLOEM, D. L. 1959. Effect of maximum aggregate size on strength of concrete. *Cement, Lime and Gravel*, **34**, 170–174.

—— 1966. Soundness and deleterious substances. ASTM STP 169A, 497–512.

—— & GAYNOR, R. D. 1963. Effects of aggregate properties on strength concrete. *Journal of the American Concrete Institute*, **60** (10), 1429–1455.

BRITISH STANDARDS INSTITUTE NEWS, July 1983.

BROWNE, R. D. 1972. Thermal movement of concrete. *Concrete*, November 1972, 51–53.

BUILDING RESEARCH ESTABLISHMENT (BRE). 1968. Shrinkage of natural aggregates in concrete. BRE Digest 35.

—— 1980. Deterioration due to corrosion in reinforced concrete. Information Paper IP12/80.

—— 1982. The durability of steel in concrete: Part 1, Mechanism of protection and corrosion. BRE Digest 263.

—— 1988. Alkali aggregate reactions in concrete. BRE Digest 330.

—— 1991. Shrinkage of natural aggregates in concrete. BRE Digest 357.

BUILDING RESEARCH STATION 1958. Reactions between aggregates and cement. Part VI. Alkali–aggregate interaction: Test procedures. National Building Studies Research Paper No. 25, HMSO, London.

CHAPMAN, G. P. & ROEDER, A. R. 1970. The effects of sea shells in concrete aggregates. *Concrete*, 4, 2, Feb. 1970, 71–79.

CONCRETE SOCIETY, THE 1980. Guide to chemical admixtures for concrete, Technical Report 18.

—— 1982. Non-structural cracks in concrete, Technical Report 22.

—— 1988. Alkali–silica reaction: minimising the risk of damage to concrete, Technical Report 30.

CORDON, W. A. 1966. Freezing and thawing of concrete—Mechanisms and control. ACI Monograph No. 3.

CRAMMOND, N. J. 1984. Examination of mortar bars containing varying percentages of coarsely crystalline gypsum and aggregates. *Cement and Concrete Research*, 14, 225–230.

DEPARTMENT OF THE ENVIRONMENT 1979. Standard specification clauses for airfield pavement works. Part 3, Concrete. Property Services Agency.

—— 1991. Advice on certain unsound rock aggregates in Cornwall and Devon.

DEPARTMENT OF TRANSPORT 1991. Specification for highway works, 7th Edition. HMSO, London.

DEWAR, J. D. 1963. Effect of mica in the fine aggregate on the water requirement and strength of concrete. C & CA Technical Report TRA/370.

EDWARDS, A. G. 1966. Shrinkage and other properties of concrete made with crushed rock aggregates from Scottish sources. *BGWF Journal*, Autumn 1966, 23–41.

—— 1970. Scottish aggregates: rock constituents and suitability for concrete. BRE Current Paper CP28/70.

FOOKES, P. G. 1980. An introduction to the influence of natural aggregates on the performance and durability of concrete. *Quarterly Journal of Engineering Geology*, 13, 207–229.

—— & COLLIS, L. 1975a. Problems in the Middle East. *Concrete*, 9 (7), 12–17.

—— & —— 1975b. Aggregates and the Middle East. *Concrete*, 9 (11), 14–19.

—— & —— 1976. Cracking and the Middle East. *Concrete*, 10 (2), 14–19.

——, COMBERBACH, C. D. & CANN, J. 1983. Field investigation of concrete structures in South West England. Parts 1 & 2. *Concrete*, 17 (3) & (4), 54–56 & 60–65.

—— & HIGGINBOTTOM, I. E. 1980. Some problems of construction aggregates in desert areas, with particular reference to the Arabian Peninsula. 1. Occurrence and special characteristics. 2. Investigation, production and quality control. *Proceedings of the Institution of Civil Engineers*. Part 1, 68, February 39–67 and 69–90.

——, POLLOCK, D. J. & KAY, E. A. 1982. Concrete in the Middle East, Part 2, Rates of Deterioration, 12–22. Viewpoint Publication by Eyre & Spottiswoode Publications Ltd.

—— & POOLE, A. B. 1981. Some preliminary considerations on the selection and durability of rock and concrete materials for breakwaters and coastal protection works. *Quarterly Journal of Engineering Geology*, 14, 97–128.

—— & REVIE, W. A. 1982. Mica in concrete—a case history from Eastern Nepal. *Concrete*, 16 (3), 12–16.

FORDER, I. 1972. ACT Project. Some observations on the use of: beach sand, micaceous sand in concrete. Institute of Concrete Technology.

—— & POOLE, A. B. 1974. Deleterious reactions between dolomites from Bahrain and cement paste. *Cement and Concrete Research*, 4, 925–937.

GAYNOR, R. D. 1964. Effect of fine aggregate on concrete mixing water requirement. *Cement, Lime & Gravel*, January 1964.

GILLOTT, J. E. 1975. Alkali–aggregate reactions in concrete. *Engineering Geology* 9, 303–326.

——, DUNCAN, M. A. G. & SWENSON, E. G. 1973. Alkali–aggregate reaction in Nova Scotia. Part IV. Character of the reaction. *Cement and Concrete Research* 3, 521–535.

—— & SWENSON, E. G. 1969. Mechanism of the alkali–carbonate rock reaction. *Quarterly Journal of Engineering Geology* 2, 1969, 7–23.

GRATTAN-BELLEW, P. E. 1983. Re-evaluation of standard mortar bar and concrete prism tests for alkali–aggregate reactivity. *Materiaux et Constructions*, 16 (94), 243–250.

GREATER LONDON COUNCIL (GLC). 1979. Marine aggregates for concrete—a revised GLC specification. GLC Bulletin No. 121 (2nd series), March 1979, 2/1–2/2.

HAMMERSLEY, G. P. 1989. The use of petrography in the evaluation of aggregates. *Concrete*, 23 (10).

HAWKINS, M. R. et al. 1983. *Alkali–aggregate reaction—Minimising the risk of alkali–silica reaction—Guidance Notes—Report of a Working Party*. Published for the Working Party by the C & CA, ref. 97–304.

HIGGINS, D. D. 1984. Admixtures for concrete. *Cement and Concrete Association*, ref. 45.041.

HOBBS, D. W. 1988. *Alkali–Silica Reaction in Concrete*. Thomas Telford, London.

—— 1990. Cracking and expansion due to the alkali–silica reaction: its effect on concrete. *Structural Engineering Review*, 2, 65–79.

INSTITUTION OF STRUCTURAL ENGINEERS. 1988. Structural effects of alkali–silica reaction. Interim technical guidance on appraisal of existing structures. ISE 1988.

KAPLAN, M. F. 1958. The effects of the properties of coarse aggregates on the workability of concrete. *Magazine of Concrete Research*, 10 (29), 63–74.

—— 1959. Flexural and compressive strength of concrete as affected by the properties of coarse aggregates. *Journal of the American Concrete Institute*, 55, 1193–1208.

KAY, E. A., FOOKES, P. G. & POLLOCK, D. J. 1982. Concrete in the Middle East, Part 2. Deterioration related to chloride ingress, 23–32. Viewpoint Publication by Eyre & Spottiswoode Publications Ltd.

LEA, F. M. 1970. *The Chemistry of Cement and Concrete*. 3rd edition, Edward Arnold, London.

LEEMING, M. B. 1983. Corrosion of steel reinforcement in offshore concrete—Experience from the Concrete-in-the-Oceans Programme. Chapter 4, Corrosion of reinforcment in concrete construction, Society of Chemical Industry, London.

LEES, G. 1964. The measurement of particle shape and its influence in engineering materials. *Journal of the British Granite and Whinstone Federation*, 4 (2).

LEES, T. P. 1987. Impurities in concreting aggregates. British Cement Association, Ref. 45.016.

MIDGLEY, H. G. 1958. The staining of concrete by pyrite. *Mag. Concr. Res.* 10, (29), 75–78.

—— 1970. The effect of lead compounds in aggregate upon the

setting of Portland Cement. *Mag. Concr. Res.* **22** (70), 42–44.

MIELENZ, R. C. 1955. *Petrographic examination.* ASTM STP 169, 253–273.

MILLER, E. W. 1983. High density concrete: Part 1. (Concrete Society Current Practice Sheet No. 90). *Concrete*, **17**, (12), 33–34.

MONKS, W. 1981. Appearance Matters 3, Control of blemishes in concrete. British Cement Association Ref. 47.103.

—— 1985a. Appearance Matters 8. Exposed aggregate concrete finishes. British Cement Association Ref. 47.108.

—— 1985b. Appearance Matters 9, Tooled concrete finishes. British Cement Association Ref. 47.109.

—— 1986. Appearance Matters 7, Textured and profiled concrete finishes. British Cement Association Ref. 47.107.

—— 1988a. Appearance Matters 1, Visual concrete: Design and production. British Cement Association Ref. 47.101.

—— 1988b. Appearance Matters 2, External rendering. British Cement Association Ref. 47.102.

MURDOCK, L. J. & BROOK, K. M. 1979. *Concrete Materials and Practice.* 5th Edn, Edward Arnold, London.

NEVILLE, A. M. 1981. *Properties of Concrete.* 3rd Edn, Pitman, London.

NEWMAN, K. 1959. The effect of water absorption by aggregates on the water–cement ratio of concrete. *Mag. Concr. Res.* **11** (33), 135–142.

ORCHARD, D. F. 1976. *Concrete Technology.* Volume 3, Properties and testing of aggregates. Applied Science, London.

POOLE, A. B. & SOTIROPOULOS, P. 1980. Reactions between dolomite aggregate and alkali pore fluids in concrete. *Quarterly Journal of Engineering Geology*, **13** (4), 281–287.

OSRMC Quality scheme for ready mixed concrete. Technical Regulations 1989. QDRMC, Walton on Thames.

RAUEN, A. 1980. *Frost Resistance of Concrete.* Vienna, June 1980.

RICHARDS, R. I. 1982. ACT Project. An investigation into the influence of crushed flint fine aggregate on the properties of fresh concrete. ICT.

ROEDER, A. R. 1963. The detection and determination of organic impurities. *Cement, Lime and Gravel*, 283–286.

—— 1977. Some properties of flint particles and their behaviour in concrete. *Mag. Concr. Res.*, **29** (99), 92–99.

ROLLINGS, R. S. 1988. Substantial materials for pavement construction. 14th Australian Road Research Board Conference, 28 August–2 September 1988, Canberra Materials and Testing. Vol. 14. Proceedings, Part 7. Vermont South, ARRB, 1988 pp 148–161.

RUSSELL, P. 1976. Effect of aggregates on the durability of concrete. C & CA Advisory Note, Publication ref. 45.021, 2nd Edition.

RYELL, J. & SMITH, P. 1968. Case histories of poor concrete durability in Ontario highway structures. *Performance of Concrete*, University of Toronto Press, Chapter 11, 181–204.

SAMARAI, M. A. 1976. The disintegration of concrete containing sulphate-contaminated aggregates. *Mag. Concr. Res.*, **28** (96), 130–142. (Corrigenda, 29 (100), 155).

SAND AND GRAVEL ASSOCIATION. 1968. Sea-dredged aggregates for concrete. *Proceedings of a symposium held at Fulmer Grange, Slough, 9th December 1968.*

SCHAFFLER, H. 1979. Concrete with gap-graded aggregates. Betonwerk + Fertigteil-Technik, Part 1, **45** (6), 341–345.

SHACKLOCK, B. W. 1959. Comparison of gap- and continuously graded concrete mixes. C & CA Technical Report TRA/240.

SHERWOOD, P. T. & ROEDER, A. R. 1965. Organic impurities in sand that interfere with the hydration of Portland cement. *The Surveyor and Municipal Engineer*, July 1965.

SHIRLEY, D. E. 1981. Impurities in concreting aggregates. C. & C. A. Construction Guide ref 45.016, 2nd edition.

SHORT, A. & KINNIBURGH, W. 1978. *Lightweight concrete.* 3rd edition, Applied Science, London.

SIMM, J. D. & FOOKES, P. G. 1989. Improving reinforced concrete durability in the Middle East during the period 1960–1985: an analytical review. *Proceedings of the Institution of Civil Engineers*, Part 1, 1989. 86 Apr. 333–358.

SIMS, I. 1981. Application of standard testing procedures for alkali-resistivity, Parts 1 and 2. *Concrete*, **15** (10), 27–29 and 15 (11), 29–32.

—— & SOTIROPOULOS, P. 1983. Standard alkali-reactivity testing of carbonate rocks from the Middle East and North Africa. *Proceedings of the 6th International Conference, Alkalis in Concrete, Research and Practice.* Copenhagen, June 1983.

SMITH, I. M. 1987. The passing 75 µm content of a crushed carboniferous limestone coarse aggregate and its effect on certain concrete properties. ACT Project.

SNOWDEN, L. C. & EDWARDS, A. G. 1962. The moisture movement of natural aggregate and its effect on concrete. *Mag. Concr. Res.* **14** (41).

SOMMER, H. 1980. Frost resistance of concrete. Vienna, June 1980.

STOCK, A. F. 1988. *Concrete Pavements.* Elsevier, New York.

VAN AARDT, J. H. P. & VISSER, S. 1977. Formation of hydrogarnets: Calcium hydroxide attack on clays and feldspars. *Cement and Concrete Research*, 7, 39–44.

—— & —— 1977. Calcium hydroxide attack on feldspar and clays. Possible relevance to cement aggregate reactions. *Cement and Concrete Research*, 7, 643–648.

VENECANIN, S. D. 1989. Thermal properties of limestones affecting phenomenon of thermal incompatibility of concrete components and durability of concrete. *Proceedings of 3rd International Conference on Deterioration and Repair of Reinforced Concrete in the Arabian Gulf*, **1**, 561–751.

VERBECK, G. & LANDGREN, R. 1960. Influence of physical characteristics of aggregates on frost resistance of concrete. PCA Research Development Bulletin 126.

VINES, F. R. 1982. Experience with use of coral detritus as concrete aggregate in Western Samoa. *Australian Road Research*, **12** (1), 17–28.

WEINERT, H. H. 1968. Engineering petrology for roads in South Africa. *Engineering Geology*, **2** (5), 359–362.

ZOLDNERS, N. G. 1960. Effect of high temperatures on concretes incorporating different aggregates. Mines Branch Report R64 (Dept. of Mines & Technical Surveys, Ottawa 1960.

British, European and American Standards

AMERICAN SOCIETY FOR TESTING MATERIALS ASTM C33-86 (1986). *Specification for Concrete Aggregates.*

—— ASTM C40-79 (1979). *Testing for organic impurities in fine aggregates for concrete.*

—— ASTM C88-83 (1983). *Test for soundness of aggregates by use of sodium sulphate or magnesium sulphate.*

—— ASTM C131-81 (1987). *Test for resistance to abrasion of small size coarse aggregate by use of the Los Angeles machine.*

—— ASTM C227-87 (1987). *Test for potential alkali-reactivity of cement: aggregate combinations (mortar-bar method).*

—— ASTM C289-87 (1987). *Test for potential reactivity of aggregates (chemical method).*

—— ASTM C294-86 (1986). *Descriptive nomenclature of constituents of natural mineral aggregates.*

—— ASTM C295-85 (1985). *Recommended practice for petrographic examination of aggregates for concrete.*

—— ASTM C535-87 (1981). *Test for resistance to degradation of large-size coarse aggregate by abrasion and impact in the Los Angeles machine.*

—— ASTM C586-69 (1986). *Test for potential alkali-reactivity of carbonate rocks for concrete aggregates (rock cylinder method).*

BRITISH STANDARDS INSTITUTION BS 12: 1989. *Portland Cements.*

—— BS 812: Parts 1 to 3:1975. *Methods for Sampling and Testing of Mineral Aggregates, Sands and Fillers.*

—— BS 812: Parts 101–124. *Testing Aggregates.*

—— BS 882: 1992. *Specification for Aggregates from Natural Sources for Concrete.*

—— BS 1377: Parts 1 and 2: 1990. *Soil Stabilisation.*

—— BS 1881: Part 124: 1988. *Testing Concrete. Part 124: Analysis of Hardened Concrete.*

—— BS 3797:— *Specification for Lightweight Aggregates for Concrete.*

—— BS 4027: 1980. *Specification for Sulphate-Resisting Portland Cement.*

—— BS 4248: 1974. *Supersulphated Cement.*

—— BS 5328: 1990. *Concrete.*

—— BS 5750: 1988. *Quality Systems Part 1 Specifications for Design/Development, Production, Installation and Servicing.*

—— BS 8007: 1987. *Code of Practice for Design of Concrete Structures for Retaining Aqueous Liquids.*

—— BS 8110: 1985. *Code of Practice for Design and Construction.*

EUROPEAN STANDARD EN 29000: 1987. *Quality Management and Quality Assurance Standards—Guidelines for Selection and Use.*

General references

The Use of Crushed Rock Aggregates in Concrete. BRE 1978, RR18.

Porous Aggregates in Concrete: Jurassic Limestones. BRE Information Paper IP 2/86.

Porous Aggregates in Concrete: Sandstones from N.W. England. BRE Information Paper IP 16/89.

Sea Dredged Aggregates in Concrete. BRE Information Paper IP 7/87.

Marine Aggregates—Off-shore Dredging for Sand and Gravel. RMC 1986.

Marine Dredged Aggregates—an Established Contribution to UK Concreting Resources. RMC 1989.

Expansion of Concrete due to Alkali–Silica Reaction. C & CA Reprint 1/84.

The Diagnosis of Alkali–Silica Reaction. BCA 1992. Ref. 45.042.

Standard Specification Clauses for Airfield Pavement Works. Part 3 Croydon, Property Services Agency. 1979.

9. Aggregates for mortar

9.1. Introduction

This chapter, which is concerned with aggregates for mortars, necessarily introduces some degree of overlap with Chapter 8. However, there are major differences between mortars and concretes, arising mainly from the manner of their use.

The term 'mortar' is used in the building industry to denote a mixture of natural sand or other fine aggregate and some binding agent, used as a jointing or a surface plastering and rendering material (Fig. 9.1). In the United Kingdom the demand for building sand grew steadily up to 1973 to reach a peak of 23.6 Mt, representing some 18% of the total sand and gravel production (HMSO 1989) for the country. Since then it has fluctuated considerably, falling to 15.7 Mt in 1981 but rising again to 21.89 Mt in 1988 (Fig. 9.2). It should be noted that the output figures for building sands are far in excess of figures for mortar production.

Until about 30 years ago the choice of binders in the UK was limited to lime or cement or cement–lime mixes. Mortars made with lime alone as binder are no longer used for building except for some specialist applications in the repair of historic buildings. The choice of cement binders has been widened to include masonry cements

(specially blended mixtures of Portland cement with finely divided mineral plasticizers and air-entraining agent).

Increasingly, air-entrainment in mortars, not only to confer frost resistant properties but also to aid workability, is being used even with cement/lime/sand mortars. The use of factory produced ready-mixed mortars has grown enormously in recent years.

Mortars are commonly used for the bedding and jointing of building units such as bricks and blocks (masonry) and also for surface finishes (rendering, plastering and screeding). Rendering is a term usually applied to external finishes, plastering being used for internal finishes, whilst floor screed refers to types of regularized floor surfaces to which a finishing coat may be applied. Historically, the bricklayer and plasterer made mortar mixes from the materials at hand, giving what skill taught to be the most suitable properties for the job. Consequently, older specifications were based largely on the average sands used in practice (Bessey 1966).

Natural sand is defined in BS 882: 1983 (i.e. fine aggregates resulting from the natural disintegration of rock, or a mixture of uncrushed gravel fines). However, the greater proportion of the fine aggregates used for

FIG 9.1. Typical brick and mortar construction for jointing.

FIG 9.2. Production of building sand for construction purposes (land-use and marine-dredged totals) (BACMI 1991).

mortars have size gradings generally finer than BS 882 and their sources in the UK range in age from the Permian to Recent. They are excavated from sand and gravel pits in unconsolidated clastic deposits derived from the weathering of existing rock types, the sands being predominantly quartzose in composition. They are often used in their natural form or processed by screening and/or washing and classifying (see Chapter 5). In some areas crushed rock fines, having broadly similar gradings to natural sands, are used. Building mortars are composed principally of sand (or crushed stone), lime, cement, air and water together with special additives as appropriate. The accepted British Standard terminology is for 'admixtures' to describe chemicals or other materials added at the mixer whilst 'additives' refers to materials added at the cement plant. Sand is the major constituent and so any variations in its quality will have a considerable effect on the properties of the resulting mortar. Bessey (1966) has indicated that the main factors affecting sand quality are:

(i) average particle size;

(ii) the range of the particle size;

(iii) the particle shape;

(iv) impurities, particularly the clay content.

It should be noted that the British Standards for building sands published in 1976 (BS 1198, 1199 and 1200) were often ignored by both producers and users because they did not fully describe the materials that were commercially available and the sands that provided satisfactory performance in the UK. As a result of recent research, amendments to those Standards have been published which provide more acceptable grading limits to meet current usage (see §9.5).

The design of mortar mixes is normally based on the premise that the voids in the bulk volume of sand, which generally amount to 25 to 40% (typically about 33%), should be filled with binder. Inability to fill the voids completely does not necessarily result in failure, however, but an increasing proportion of unfilled voids in a mix can increase the probability of trouble arising (Beningfield 1980).

9.2. Types of mortars

As stated above, the various common types of mix depend on the fact that a quantity of binder (lime and cement), equal to about 1/3 of the bulk volume of an average sand, is required to fill the voids between the sand grains and thus give the wet mix sufficient workability. The ratio of cement to lime is varied to give the required range of strength properties. With mixes containing only cement and no lime, air-entrainment is used to extend the volume of binders (cement and air) so that good workability is maintained but without excessive strength development. Masonry cement contains an integral air-entraining agent, as well as a finely divided mineral plasticizer, to accomplish the same effect.

In recent years there has been a rapid growth in the ready-mixed mortar sector of the building industry where considerable advantages are achieved as a result of the greater degree of control over the production processes as compared with that generally obtainable on site.

It should be appreciated that ready-mixed mortar is the general name given to factory made mortars, but there are a number of varieties of these factory types. In particular, there are retarded ready-to-use mortars; pre-mixed lime: sand mortars (these are not complete because they still require the addition of cement); and dry packed mortars. Current good practice is set out in BS 4721 (1981).

In addition, there are locally produced mixtures of cement dried-sand and optional lime in large silos of about 15 tonnes capacity.

Although no official statistics are available on the ratio of site mixed to ready-mixed mortar it is generally considered that in the UK some 25–35% of the market is supplied by ready-mixed mortars. Approximately 40% of this is produced as coloured mortars.

More recently a new concept is that of supplying a silo with two compartments, one containing damp sand and the other cement. These silos are delivered to the site and the materials mixed on demand using a smaller mixer incorporated at the bottom of the silo.

Thus, to call all these materials 'ready-mixed mortars' can be misleading. There may be a case for the wet mixes to be termed 'retarded ready-to-use mortars', the lime-sand mixes termed 'ready-mixed lime-sand for mortar', the dry bagged or dry siloed mortar 'ready-mixed dry mortars', and those in the divided silo, 'twin silo mortars'. There is no standardized terminology and the European Committee for Standardization (CEN) is attempting to reconcile different ideas within Europe.

9.2.1. Masonry (brickwork or general purpose) mortars

To function as a bonding material for bricks or other masonry units some strength is necessary but the mortar must also be able to yield sufficiently to accommodate the various differential moisture or thermal movements which occur in a structure. If these movements are small, the stresses set up are usually within the elastic limits of the materials used. Beyond these limits the stresses are relieved by yielding along lines of relative weakness in the structure. In a composite construction of bricks and mortar the cracking will penetrate the bricks themselves if the mortar is stronger than the bricks; an unsatisfactory state of affairs. Where the mortar is weaker than the bricks the relief of stresses results in a series of fine cracks distributed inconspicuously among the vertical joints in the brickwork, there being only small relative movement between the bricks and the mortar in the horizontal joints. (McIntosh 1970; BRE Digest 160 1973).

However, caution must be exercised in following this precept since weak mortars lack durability, especially to frost. In general, mortar quality, of which strength is a part, is selected to provide durability for the expected exposure condition.

9.2.2. Rendering and plastering

External rendering (Fig. 9.3) has been practised for many hundreds of years, the applications known as wattle and daub, used on primitive buildings as a weather resistant coating can still be seen in use in some Mediterranean countries. Mixtures of lime and pozzolan with hydraulic properties (i.e. which hardened under water) were used extensively by the Romans. Calcined argillaceous limestones mixed with sand were misleadingly termed Roman cement from about AD 1800 onward and were in common use as an external rendering up to the beginning of the 20th Century. The 'Roman' variety was subsequently replaced by Portland cement, a material which when mixed with lime produces rendering mixes having good application properties together with adequate strength and resistance to weathering. Portland cement : sand rendering mortars, usually with an air-entraining plasticizer, are also widely used.

Internal plastering mortars provide a continuous, smooth, plane surface to the walls and ceilings suitable for receiving a decorative finish. Plasters can vary considerably in strength and porosity but, in practice, those with the ability to absorb and release moisture and moisture vapour have certain advantages over the relatively impervious finishes. The greater majority of internal plastering (final coats) is based on gypsum lime (or sand) blends with some cement sand and cement lime sand plaster mixes in use today.

Some misunderstanding has arisen in the past due to the term 'plaster' being used as synonomous with gypsum-based plasters. Furthermore, some guidelines for plastering (BRS Digest, 1971) distinguish between

FIG 9.3. Typical rendered outside wall on upper part of a house.

FIG 9.4. Typical floor screed.

cement-based and gypsum-based mixes. The latter have some advantage in that they are capable of hardening more quickly than the former and drying shrinkage is much less than with cement-based mixes.

However, gypsum has some solubility in water and, therefore, in all except arid climates is generally restricted to interior use.

9.2.3. Floor screeds

Cement–sand screeds are generally used for levelling a concrete sub-floor to provide both a level and a smooth surface, usually to receive a decorative floor finish. (Fig. 9.4). It has been suggested that floor screed mixes bonded directly to a concrete sub-floor and subsequently covered with a decorative finish should have a mix ratio of 1:3 to 1:4½ by weight of Portland cement to sands (BRE Digest 160, 1973). Mixes richer than 1:3 are not recommended because of the higher risk of drying shrinkage which can result in cracking and curling of the screeds. Mixes weaker than 1:5 may tend to be damaged either by abrasion or impact, but these problems can be reduced if the mixes are designed correctly to cover service conditions. Floor screeds should not be used as a wearing surface except as a temporary expedient during construction. Sands for floor screeds are now selected by reference to BS 882.

9.3. Description, classification and testing of mortar sands and fillers

9.3.1. Description and classification

The present British Standard BS 812, Part 102: 1989 includes provision for a simple petrological classification. Whilst most British natural sands are quartzose, Ragsdale & Birt (1976) have recommended that a petrological examination be carried out so that the constituents of the sand and, in particular, the presence of any deleterious material can be identified. Chapter 6 should be referred to for the recommended method for petrographic examination.

Particle shape and surface texture, whilst easily ascertained for coarse aggregates, are more difficult to determine for finer grained particles. Microscopic study will show particle shape (such as rounded and angular (Fig. 9.5(a)) but the surface texture (i.e. glassy, smooth etc.) as defined in BS 812 (1989) may not be so easy to describe.

A classical geological approach to shape classification is reported in Fookes & Poole (1981) where measurements of the particles are made on the dimensional axis of each fragment. To achieve the shape classes, a ratio is made between these dimensions which, when plotted in four areas shown in Fig. 9.5(b), allow the establishment of the four classes. In the figure shown (based on Zingg 1935) only prismatic shapes have been selected to illustrate the classification; rounded shapes could have been chosen.

The names for each class are those given by Zingg and the names following in brackets are those in common usage in the British Standard or from other classifications. Fookes and Poole state that the names only approximately equate. For example, the British Standard departs from equi-dimensional indices in flakiness and elongation.

The geological occurrence of the deposits in which the sands are found will usually give an indication of the petrology of the fine aggregate to be expected. Natural sands have rounder, smoother particles than manufactured sands. The latter material, with its characteristic sharp and angular particle shape, is likely to produce mortars with workability properties quite different from those made with naturally occurring sands.

In considering the quality of sands, BS 1198, 1199 and 1200 (1976) indicate that 'sands shall consist of natural sand, crushed stone sand or crushed gravel sand, or a combination of any of these. They shall be hard, durable, clean and free from adherent coatings, such as clay, and from any appreciable amount of clay in pellet form'. However, all three standards allow for a proportion of clay, silt and dust, defined as material passing 75 μm. The limits for these fine fractions are greater for crushed stone sources than for sand or crushed gravel sources, it being established that the fine powder resulting from the artificial crushing of rocks is more acceptable than clay. A controversy currently exists about the suggestion that the powder resulting from crushed rock is always of a different type. Very often, for example, clay seams or larger deposits of clay are found in limestone with the result that sometimes the fines fraction in the processed limestone is not dissimilar to that in conventional sands.

As mentioned below (§9.3.5), washing and decantation followed by dry sieving is required for the determination of clay, silt and fine dust in aggregates. Sedimentation is used to further characterize the separated fines especially for crushed rock sands. Results obtained by dry sieve testing may be quite different from those obtained by the specified procedure.

9.3.2. Sampling and testing of fine aggregates

In the UK sampling and testing of sands are carried out in accordance with the requirements of the appropriate sections of BS 812 (1975), a standard which is currently under revision. Gradings of sands for particular use (according to British Standards) are determined by sieve analyses, the sizes used being as follows: 5.00 mm, 2.36 mm, 1.18 mm, 600 μm, 150 μm, 75 μm. Changes to these sizes are expected when European Standards are in place.

As the sand portion of mortar generally forms a large part of the total volume of a mix, its characteristics will influence the performance and properties of the fresh or hardened mortars in many ways. The inherent properties of the sand, such as chemical inertness, thermal coefficient of expansion and durability, are important but, in particular, the shape and grading of the fine aggregate particles are likely to have a major influence on the properties of the mortar mix.

9.3.3. Grading of sands

Early work by Connor (1948) on the performance of sands concentrated on the grain size and the range of sieve fractions, detailed investigations giving strong indications that the graded quality of the sand in the mortar was very important. Further investigation by Connor (1953) on sieve analyses of sands which produced good mortars confirmed that the standard grading requirements recommended in the USA were not entirely reliable and should only be considered as tentative.

A well known method of representing the results of sieve analyses is to plot the data cumulatively on log-probability paper to give a particle size distribution chart. By this method the line or grading curve obtained can be described in terms of its median size and slope, the former being the grain size in micrometres corresponding to the 50 per cent passing size. The slope is a

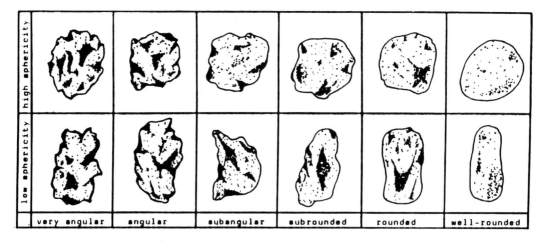

FIG 9.5 (a). Degree of particle roundness for sediment grains with each category showing low and high sphericity (after Tucker 1982).

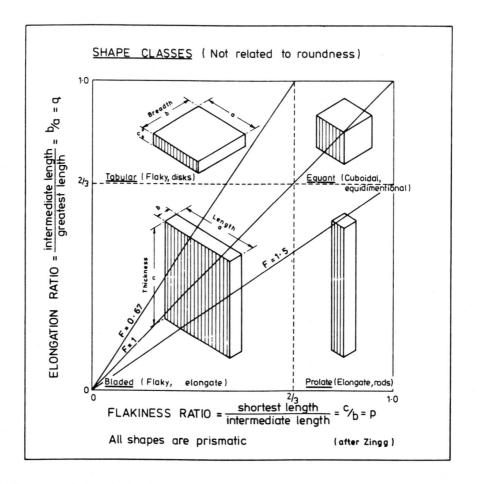

FIG 9.5 (b). Shape categories bounded by arbitrary limits based on the measurement of dimensional axial ratios (Fookes & Poole 1981, after Zingg).

TABLE 9.1. *Grade size variations for mortars referred to BS 1200 gradings for sands for general purpose and reinforced mortars (Swallow 1964)*

	Low limits for both types	High limits for reinforced mortars	High limits for general purpose mortar
Median particle size	900 μm	340 μm	230 μm
Standard deviation	470 μm	160 μm	80 μm

measure of the standard deviation of the log-normal distribution. Swallow (1964) investigated several sands by this method and concluded that 'good' sands have a median value of 440 μm to 570 μm and standard deviation of the log-normal distribution between 220 μm and 275 μm. By determining these particle size characteristics for a mortar sand and comparing them with Swallow's 'good' sand values, it is possible to indicate whether a sand is too fine or coarse and whether the particle size distribution is too wide or too narrow. By plotting particle size limits for sand recommended for general purpose mortars and for reinforced brickwork as given in BS 1200 (1955), the results shown in Table 9.1 were obtained. Swallow (1964) noted that the limits set for grading sands in BS 1200 (1955) were far too wide when compared with this scheme of median particle size and standard deviation. This indicated that, although a sand may comply with the specifications, it may not be satisfactory when used to produce masonry mortars.

However, the slope of the log-probability plot is usually calculated over a restricted portion of the line and ignores the 'tails' at the coarse and fine end. These 'tails' may have a pronounced effect on the properties of mortar and omission of their contribution restricts the usefulness of this method of assessing sand gradings.

The debate on the revision of British Standards for building sands continues and an attempt was made in 1984 (Pike 1990) by the BSI to bridge the gap between what is specified and what is used by bringing in amendments to BS 1199 and BS 1200 (see §9.5.1. below).

The new British Standard BS 1200 (1984) is widely used and it is generally considered to be an effective document. Previously the 1976 British Standards were known not to cover the full range of fine aggregate types that were used for masonry, plasters and floor screeds in the UK. Currently BS 1200 provides for two sand gradings, general purpose masonry (G Type), and special mortars (S Type). However, these are only accepted by some research bodies as temporary solutions pending further investigations.

In §9.5, reference is made to the proposed concept of 'ideal' sands. This has been suggested as a useful alternative to the BS grading limits specification which could be used with confidence by Industry.

9.3.4. Impurities

There has long been concern with impurities in building sands. British Standard 1200 (1984) refers to the possible occurrence of 'harmful materials such as iron pyrites, salts, coal or other organic impurities, mica, shale and similar laminated materials, and flaky or elongated particles'.

Prior to the revision of BS 812 (1975) the presence of organic impurities was assessed using caustic soda, a method which was quick, simple and widely used. This method is still current in ASTM Standard C144 (1989). It was, however, subject to some defects such as, for example, the failure to detect a serious contaminant like coal, where a single particle would not produce a colour change sufficient to detect the impurity. 'Loss on ignition determination' has similar limitations in that the presence of calcium carbonate could also obscure the presence of coal (Westbrook 1960). There is a particular need for a test for identifying lignite, coal and similar organic impurities likely to cause blemishes in the mortar.

ASTM C123 specifies a method for determining the lightweight particles (those that float in a solution of relative density 2.0) and a British Standard method based on this is currently in draft form. The separated lightweight particles can be subjectively characterized by, for example, visual examination under a microscope.

Organic contamination that significantly retards the hydration of Portland cement is not often observed in commercial mortar sands in the UK. However, organic impurities such as coal and lignite are likely to be found in some areas such as northern England, the Midlands, parts of Wales and the central area of Scotland.

Research carried out by A. J. Shirvill (1982) on the effects of lignite on concrete quality and durability could be applied to mortar application. The more friable, soft, peaty lignite matter is most commonly found in the fine aggregate and produces characteristic brown staining on the hardened mortar surface. Thus, lignite contamination is more critical for rendered surfaces and floor screeds and Shirvill reported that lignite, with a relative density just exceeding unity, will tend to segregate from the mix and migrate in a vertical direction giving concentration in the upper and surface layers where it is least desirable.

He found that migration patterns are generally related to workability, increased migration into the surface layer coinciding with an increase in workability, with any air entrainment modification to the mix possibly providing beneficial effects by marginally decreasing migration.

Furthermore, Shirvill's investigations suggested that, where surface appearance or durability is important, lignite contamination should be negligible and this was particularly important for flat horizontal areas where the deleterious effects of small quantities of lignite may be enhanced by migration during casting. For surface appearances he suggested that 0.5% maximum limit given in ASTM C33 for aggregate lignite limit may be too conservative and should preferably be zero.

According to Pike (1990), mortar sands with organic contaminants that fail the sodium hydroxide-discolouration test can then be used to prepare a standard mortar which may then be compared with an identical mortar made with the same sand freed of organic contamination by ignition in air at 600°C. Comparisons of the setting times and rates of strength development of the two mortars can then give a basis for evaluation.

Although iron compounds which generally provide the colouration are present in most sands, pyrites can occur as discrete particles which can then be considered as an impurity. The identification of pyrites is carried out by visual inspection. At the present time there is a need for a more satisfactory means of determining the quantitative effects of pyrites in sands used for building mortars.

Mica is considered as a deleterious material according to BS 812 and yet, when used in renderings, it can provide a very acceptable sparkle. In the construction where it has been used in the past, the mica quantities (% not known) present in such mixes are suggested as causing problems (Westbrook 1960). However, in a detailed investigation (Lattey 1981 pers. comm.) on micaceous mortars, the mica particles are known to change the aggregate properties with increasing mica contents. The decreased bulk density of a micaceous aggregate will mean a lower weight of aggregate will be required to make up a certain volume of water but more cement paste will be required to fill the voids and coat the particles.

The increased water absorption of the mica will mean that the water requirement of the mix will increase.

Furthermore, the increase in water requirement of the mix with mica as a result of water being used to spread the cement paste further over the increased surface area of the particles and into the increased void space, will produce a diluted cement paste and a weakened mortar.

Mica also has a potential to flake and, if this flaking occurs during mixing, then a whole new surface will be presented which may not become coated with cement paste. It follows that in order to achieve full coating of the particles and fill the voids of a micaceous aggregate, the cement paste has to be increased, thereby making the resulting mortar more expensive.

In southwest England, micaceous sands occur as a by-product of china clay production and they have a mica content varying from 0.5% to 15%. This apparently has no noticeable effect on the durability of the finished work where they have been used as mortar sands and may be due to the type of mica mineral in the mix. Being a by-product, the sands were not specifically processed to conform to British Standards. However, problems have been known to occur with surface finishes related to 'shelling out' (particles popping out). It should, however, be noted that renderings to pre-World War II houses in Middlesex, where 2–3% mica grains were incorporated in the mix for decorative effect, showed no noticeable problems (Ragsdale & Birt 1976).

In some overseas countries natural micaceous sands used in the production of mortar for masonry work are known to have given rise to a number of problems such as poor strength, poor bond and porosity of mortars as, for example, that reported by Fookes & Revie (1982) in Eastern Nepal. Tests carried out to determine optimum mixes for a series of mica contents in sands conforming to a fine BS 882 Zone 3/Zone 4 grading, gave the following limits:

Mica content	Mix ratios
1 to 2%	$3:1$
2 to 6%	$2\frac{1}{2}:1$
6 to 8%	$2:1$
Above 8%	Not suitable

These mixes gave the desired initial strength and bonding properties for low grade mortar but strict control of the water, sand and mica contents was needed to ensure success.

Mica can be detected in sands because it is distinguished in hand specimens by its flat cleavage. Muscovite mica can be recognized by its white, silvery (glistening) appearance, whilst biotite, being a dark mica, may not be so easy to detect.

Testing for mica depends on a process of separation of the mineral from the sand grains and this can be achieved by (a) the flotation or density separation method, (b) the wind blowing method, or (c) the rocking platform method (Hoon & Venkateswarlu 1962). The flotation method is reputed to give the maximum results of mica elimination, and use is made of an inert liquid medium consisting of a solution of potassium iodide in mercuric iodide having a density range of 2.8 to 3.0. Thus a micaceous sand immersed in this solution will allow the lighter siliceous particles to float whilst the higher density mica settles at the base of the solution.

Removal of the floating sand particles then allows the micaceous fraction to be assessed.

In plastering, rendering or similar work the presence of soluble salts in excessive quantities is likely to influence the movement of water within the materials. Thus, since sea salts are deliquescent, dampness can occur as a result of their presence and danger can then arise from the corrosion of metal work, conduits etc. The movement of salts to the surface as a result of the water present at the time of construction, or from exposure or condensation, can cause efflorescence and damage to finishes. Sea water contains 2 per cent of chloride ion and Chapman & Roeder (1969) have stated that for sands having up to 10% moisture an acceptable limit for chloride content would appear to be 0.2%. The chloride content of sands is determined by the method described in BS 812: Part 117.

Excessive amounts of soluble sulphate in sand can cause deleterious expansions in cement-based mortars. It is generally accepted that sulphate (expressed as SO_3) levels in excess of 5% by mass of cement in the mortar can cause sulphation. Because of the difficulty of writing an analytical test method for total water soluble sulphate when gypsum, with a limited water solubility, is present, it has been suggested that limits be based on dilute-acid soluble sulphate. Taking into account the sulphate already present in cement (up to 3.5% SO_3) in the UK and conventional mortar mix proportions, a limit of 0.15% SO_3 for sand has been proposed. The test method used is described in BS 812: Part 118.

Mortars made from sands derived from some river and glacial sources have long been known to suffer from brown staining due to the mineral pyrites, FeS_2 (iron sulphide). Normally the staining is not obvious when used for brick mortar but with rendering and plastering, isolated particles of pyrites might affect the finished appearance and, therefore, sand sources high in pyrites may need to be avoided in those circumstances.

Pyrite may be physically hard but is chemically unstable and sulphide particles present near the finished mortar surface will oxidize slowly on weathering, eventually forming brown stains which may be impossible to remove. These reactive sulphides may be detected by immersing a representative sample of the fine aggregate in saturated lime water. If they are present the lime water will slowly become tinged with green as the sulphide particles react to form ferrous hydroxide.

9.3.5. Testing for fines

It is often assumed that all very fine particles in a mortar sand are clay, possibly because of a convention used in soil mechanics and geology that clay is material having a settling velocity equivalent to, or less than, spherical particles having a diameter of 2 µm (Pike 1990). This can be misleading in two ways: (1) because clay minerals are plate-shaped they settle more slowly than spheres of the same mass (the plates can reach sizes of 40 µm and some can be extremely small i.e. sub-micron size; (2) some material finer than 2 µm consists of material other than clay minerals.

Clay minerals can also vary widely in their properties with some having much greater effects on mortars than others.

In the size testing of building sands, BS 812 accepts that dry sieving will not give the same result as wet sieving, the differences in the results occurring because of possible aggregation of particles. The standard now requires pre-treatment of the sample by decantation through a 75 µm sieve prior to dry sieving as the standard method unless it can be demonstrated that dry sieving alone gives the same results.

As the material finer than 75 µm increases so does the difference between the wet and dry test results and the amendment to BS 1199, 1200 requires the wet pretreatment for all mortar sands.

Research by Pike & Limbrick (1981) reported that the proposal to use a 38 µm test sieve for decantation was questionable because of the inability of the flimsy 38 µm sieve meshes to withstand the normal wear and tear of laboratory use. They also found a strong correlation between the fraction finer than 75 µm and that finer than 38 µm. Thus, they opposed the introduction of the 38 µm sieve and its use in a wet sieving test for building sand.

The methylene blue adsorption test by titration has been considered as a simple, meaningful and reliable method for testing for fines and is based on the fact that clay minerals adsorb basic dyes from aqueous solutions, whereas mica, quartz and other non-clay minerals are virtually non-staining. The methylene blue test is considered simple to use and has been adopted as a way of measuring clay contents of aggregates in France, Italy, USA and Australasia.

Although the methylene blue test is not in general use in the UK for assessing clay, its potential is recognized. However, various research workers have reported conflicting results of the reliability of the test because the different types of clays (i.e. kaolinite, illite, montmorillonite etc) can have unpredictable effects on mortar sands. The French, nevertheless, have developed a method using a turbidometer (basically a spectrophotometer) which is now standardized as AFNOR P 18-595 (1981) and is reputed to be a reliable test. The methylene blue titration test is currently considered the most promising method for application for control of harmful fines in sand in mortar (Pike, pers. comm.).

BS 812 provides for a sedimentation test for measuring particle sizes below 75 µm and, although the older standards measured the content of material finer than 20 µm, this has now been modified so that the content of fines to 2 µm can be established. The method was the principle of 'Stokes' Law', although in theory the latter may not be applied indiscriminately to all particles settling in a fluid. This is because clay particles are not always spherical and thus may appear to be smaller than their real largest dimensions where tested by sedimentation. In practice their particle size distribution measured in this way is often expressed in terms of 'equivalent spherical diameter', this measurement relating to their settling velocity rather than their geometry.

The sedimentation technique applied in the UK according to BS 812 (pt 103.2) to measure the particle distribution of fines from aggregates, requires a test portion to be shaken up with distilled water and a deflocculating agent (sodium hexametaphosphate with sodium carbonate). The suspension is then allowed to stand. After prescribed times have elapsed, a special pipette is carefully lowered into the suspension and a small test portion of the suspension taken. This is then evaporated and weighed and the solids content of the test portion when scaled up to the size of the sample is taken as the content of material finer than the size that is appropriate to the selected settling time.

Thus, the time taken for particles having an equivalent spherical diameter of 2 μm to settle through 100 mm is 6 hours and 42 minutes when the particle density is 2.70.

As a way forward, Pike (1990, pers. comm.) has suggested a three-step system for identifying harmful fines: (a) washing and sieving on a 75 μm sieve and checking against the limits of BS 1200; (b) carrying out a methylene blue test and, if the limit is not met, (c) making standard mortar mixes to demonstrate that the sand is suitable compared to a mortar made from the same sand with the fines removed by preliminary washing. A service history of good performance in practice of similar sands in similar mixes used in similar conditions should also be taken into account.

9.4. Influence of sand and fines characteristics on mortar properties

The distribution of particle sizes has a major influence on the main properties of mortars, such as workability, water retentivity, strength and durability.

9.4.1. Workability

The working properties of mortar have two essential aspects: (a) the consistence, which is the characteristic affected by the amount of water added to the solid and active constituents and (b) the plastic characteristics referred to simply as 'cohesiveness' at a given consistence. Although cohesiveness is improved by the presence of increased fine material including cement, lime and air-entraining additives, the presence of some silt and clay has the effect of making the mix more workable and also provides the 'fattiness' so typically required by the artisan (McIntosh 1970). However, too much silt and clay can reduce the consistency and thus the workability.

The shape and grading of the sand and silt particle also has a marked effect on the workability, or handling properties, of a mortar mix in the same way that aggregate shape and grading is known to influence concrete workability.

Apart from hydrating the cement, water also lubricates the cement, lime and sand in a mortar mix and so makes the mix workable. The lubricating water subsequently evaporates leaving voids in the set mortars. Thus the ideal mix is that which has an optimum water content providing both good workability together with the minimum number and volume of voids.

Two main characteristics of the aggregates which affect the water content of a mix are the total surface area and the particle interference. Both are functions of grading according to McIntosh (1970) who states that the greater the surface area of the mix constituents, the larger will be the amount of water required to lubricate the surface of the particles. A large surface area can be either the result of a fine grading or the presence of a large proportion of sharp, angular particles or any combination of both.

In trying to achieve consistent workability of mortars the shape of the particles must influence the grading to be employed if a particular surface area is to be maintained. It follows that aggregates having a wide variety of shapes and gradings can possess the same total surface area and so result in the same water content requirement or workability. However, the surface area concept is apparently less reliable with very fine particles because these appear to provide their own lubricating mechanism which requires less water than that needed for the relatively larger particles.

Since high workability and cohesiveness are the principal requirements of masonry mortar, the grading of building sands is finer than that of concrete sands. Within the grading envelopes of BS 1200 (1984), coarser sands are commonly known in the building industry as 'sharp', whilst finer grained and rounded sands are referred to as 'soft'. The same terms have been used to differentiate concrete sands (sharp) from mortar sands (soft).

The factors of size and shape of fine aggregates could benefit from further investigation and research to provide more information on the influence that they have on mortar properties. Figure 9.5(a) shows some of the more common shapes that can occur in fine grained particles.

9.4.2. Water retentivity

The water retention characteristic of a mortar is an important property closely related to workability. It is indicated by the mortar's ability to retain the mix water and still remain workable when brought into contact with an absorptive brick. The water retentivity of a mortar can be increased by the use of air-entraining agents or finely ground particles and the presence of clay has also been shown to influence retentivity. The use of a well graded sand helps reduce the void content and also the separation of materials in a mortar mix which, in turn, reduces bleeding and improves water retentivity.

The water requirement and, therefore, the strength of a mortar is influenced by the shape and texture of the aggregate particles and these factors are expressed indirectly by the packing of the aggregate, i.e. the percentage of voids when the sand is in a loose condition (Currie & Sinha 1981).

9.4.3. Strength

The effect of sand grain size on mortar strength has been the subject of some research, the characteristics of the sand, together with the proportion of cement to sand, being found to be a significant factor (McIntosh 1970). In some instances mortar strength is improved by the presence of a few voids indicating that a completely dense mortar is not always suitable. A well graded mix improves compressive strength more than transverse strength.

Mortar strength, as related to brickwork strength, has been considered by many investigators, the common conclusion being that excessive mortar strength is to be avoided. It is generally considered that the adhesion between bricks and mortar basically depends upon the flow of moisture from the body of the mortar carrying cementitious particles to the brick–mortar interface. However, the mechanism of adhesion involved at this interface is not fully understood.

Tests have shown that compressive strengths of mortars made with two different sands can differ more than would be expected from the effects of grading alone (McIntosh 1970). The particle shape, together with the presence of chemical impurities, are all possible causes of this strength difference.

Fookes & Marsh (1981) noted a significant reduction in workability and strength due to the presence of discrete white mica particles in mortars in East Nepal. Though the longer-term effects of free mica in cement mixes are not well understood it is generally thought to be related to the mineralogy of the micas present.

9.4.4. Durability

The structural integrity and visual acceptability of masonry is strongly related to the performance of mortar (Harrison & Bowler 1990). However, when mortar failures do occur they are difficult to remedy and expensive rebuilding is often the only solution.

Mortar specifications normally take into account the

need for adequate durability and the protection of any embedded reinforcement. The grading of the sand is important when considering frost resistance, although normal protection from frost can be achieved by sufficient minimum cement content being used in relation to the grading. With well graded sands, a lower cement content is needed than for a poorly graded material which has an increased water demand (Beningfield 1980). Thus, the grading of fine aggregates is important in the production of a mix in which the packing of the particles is such as to make it possible for the cement paste to fill the voids.

Particle shape will affect the particle interference whereby the distance between the larger particles is such that it is not possible to allow free passage of the smaller ones and the voids ratio is affected. Particle interference usually occurs as a result of the fine aggregate containing an excess of larger sizes.

Although some general observations are available on fine aggregate shapes, their packing and association in mortar mixes to produce acceptable strengths and durability requires more detailed information. This area of knowledge, therefore, offers considerable scope for research, and recently Harrison (1986) has shown differences in durability for different sands which cannot be explained by 'fineness' alone.

9.5. UK specifications and practice

Following a revision of the specifications for building sands and changes to BS 812 and BS 410 a more acceptable understanding of the grading characteristics for building sands is now available.

Reference to these standards is made below, but it should be noted that it is common practice in the UK to use sands which differ considerably in their properties and characteristics from those specified in British Standards, simply because local sources in many parts of the country provide the cheapest available form of fine aggregate.

9.5.1. Masonry mortars

Sand gradings are an important factor in determining the strength of a mix (Bessey 1966; Lee & Pyle 1969; Lee 1975). Early cement based mortars were commonly produced, probably unknowingly, by filling the sand voids with cement, in the proportion of approximately 1:3 cement to sand. This could vary, however, from about 1:4 if a coarse well graded sand were used, to about 1:2.5, or less, with a poorly graded sand containing excessive fines (Beningfield pers. comm.).

In some cases, however, sands may not give the expected strengths, even though they comply with the wide limits set by BS 1200 (1984) because they need a high water content to obtain the necessary workability. Water in the mix has been referred to as a 'necessary evil' (Pyle 1967). The 'evil' results from the fact that the water required to hydrate the cement is only about 20–25% by weight of cement, the remainder is necessary to provide a mix of workable consistency and subsequently evaporates during the early life of the building with a consequent lowering of strength.

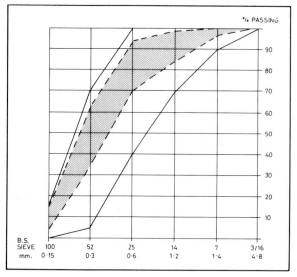

FIG 9.6. BS grading limits of sand for use in general purpose mortars (BS 1200: 1976) 'ideal' sand limits shown hatched (see Table 9.2 and Table 9.4).

Sands having gradings which comply with BS 1200 (1976) have been widely accepted in the past for general purpose mortars. These grading limits are shown in Fig. 9.6 and the tabulated values are given in Table 9.2.

TABLE 9.2. *Sands for general purpose mortars (BS 1200: 1976)*

BS sieve size	% by weight passing BS sieves
5 mm	100
2.36 mm	90–100
1.18 mm	70–100
600 μm	40–100
300 μm	5–70
150 μm	0–15

However, in 1984 amendments to BS 1200 (see Table 9.3 and Fig. 9.7) included changes in grading limits to take account of a change in test method, from dry sieving to washing and sieving.

TABLE 9.3. *Revisions to BS 1200 (1984)*

BS sieve	% by weight passing BS sieve	
	Type S	Type G
5.00 mm	98–100	98–100
2.36 mm	90–100	90–100
1.18 mm	70–100	70–100
600 μm	40–100	40–100
300 μm	5–70	20–90
150 μm	0–15	0–25
75 μm	0–5	0–8

Previously BS 1200 had made no allowance for fines less than 75 μm except that lumps and coatings of clay were specifically excluded by name (Pike 1990). The 1984 amendment attempted to provide for suitable limits in fines within the types S and G.

Where reinforced brickwork mortars are required, sands complying with BS 1200 can be used and it has been found that even sand at the fine end of BS 1200 is capable of producing satisfactory results.

Historically, common practice showed that the BS limits were too wide for some mortar applications and early research proposed moderations of the limits of the fraction from the 1.18 mm size downwards (Smith & Plowman 1972) which would provide higher strengths generally. Some producers, however, are still of the opinion that British Standard grading limits are so wide as to require considerable manipulation in order to produce the 'ideal' sand (Table 9.4).

TABLE 9.4. *Grading limits of a suggested "ideal" sand for general purpose mortars (Beningfield, pers. comm.)*

BS sieve	% by weight passing BS sieves
5.00 mm	100
2.36 mm	97–100
1.18 mm	85–99
600 μm	70–95
300 μm	25–65
150 μm	5–15

In the UK the grading limits agreed in 1984 greatly increase the number of buidling sands that comply with the grading limits of the Standard when they are tested by washing and sieving but, even so, there are still sands in use that are finer than Type G (Pike 1990).

BS 1200 (1984) states that sands containing deleterious materials such as pyrite, salt, coal, mica, shale or similar laminated materials or flaky or elongated particles which may adversely affect the hardening, strength and durability of the mortar, are not acceptable.

Durability may be taken to refer not only to structural integrity, but also to maintenance of appearance. Thus

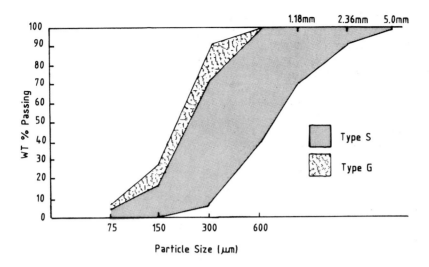

FIG 9.7. Revised grading limits for sands for general purpose brick mortars (BS 1200: 1984).

the deleterious effects of materials which can cause staining of mortar surfaces e.g. pyrites, lignite, etc., have also to be considered.

In practice, however, it is usually very difficult to assess the degree to which these materials are really deleterious and several sources are known in the UK producing 'contaminated' sands which are being used to produce mortar (§9.7).

9.5.2. External renderings

The materials used for external rendering mixes are frequently the same as those used for brickwork mortars but sand grading becomes more critical where the finished appearance and durability is important (Ragsdale & Birt 1976). A relatively weak rendering made with an acceptably graded sand is likely to perform much better than one which is rich in cement but made from poorly graded sand.

Nevertheless, sands used in renders give better performance if a significant proportion of the sand consists of coarser particles in the range 1.18 mm to 5.0 mm so as to reduce shrinkage (Pike 1990). Therefore, in practice, many craftsmen mix a medium (Grade M) concreting sand with a building sand to provide a suitable grading.

In some cases, unwashed dry-screened sands have been used and although sometimes complying with BS 1199 they require high water contents and so produce mortars which are relatively weaker and more prone to shrinkage than those made with well-washed sands. These defects may be due to particles of agglomerated clay passing as coarse sand grains which in normal wet processing would be removed.

In 1986 BS 1199 was amended to take better account

of the materials that are used in practice; the grading limits being set out in Table 9.5 with wider limits on the sieve sizes to give greater flexibility.

TABLE 9.5. *Grading requirements for mortar sands for plastering and rendering (BS 1199: 1986)*

BS sieve	% by weight passing BS sieve	
	Type A	Type B2
5.00 mm	95–100	95–100
2.36 mm	60–100	80–100
1.18 mm	30–100	70–100
600 μm	15–100	55–100
300 μm	5–50	5–75
150 μm	0–15	0–20
75 μm	0–15	0–5

9.5.3. Internal plastering

Plastering is intended to conceal unevennness in the background and to provide a finish that is smooth, crack-free, hygienic, resistant to damage and easily decorated.

Historically, sands used for cement–sand and cement–lime–sand plasters have been shown by experience to be acceptable when complying with BS 1198 (1976) as set out in Table 9.6. In the more usual case where gypsum is used as the cementing agent the more fine grai ɔd sands within the limits of BS 1198 (1976) were also generally acceptable.

If the surface to which the plaster is applied has a very high suction (e.g. aerated concrete or insulating bricks)

TABLE 9.6. *Sands for gypsum plastering (BS 1198: 1976)*

| | % by weight passing BS sieves | | |
BS sieve	Under Coats Type 1	Under Coats Type 2	Finishing Coats Type 3
5.00 mm	100	100	100
2.36 mm	90–100	90–100	100
1.18 mm	70–100	70–100	90–100
600 μm	40–80	40–100	55–100
300 μm	5–40	5–50	5–50
150 μm	0–10	0–10	0–10

the water may be absorbed from the plaster mix so rapidly that its adhesion to the background is weakened. To deal with this problem by excessive wetting of the surface before plastering is to invite risk of trouble from drying shrinkage, efflorescence or spoiled decorations. It is better to use mixes such as plasters with cellulose additives which retain their water in contact with high suction surfaces.

In the past in the UK it was not uncommon for sands to be used for rendering and plastering which did not comply with British Standards (Ragsdale & Birt 1976).

The quality of the sand is known to have an appreciable effect on the strength of the plaster/sand mixes, poorly graded sands not normally being recommended. When poorly graded sands (i.e. those with a higher proportion passing 600 μm and 300 μm) only are available, gypsum mixes are sometimes preferred.

9.5.4. Floor screeds

Until recently, little published guidance was available for floor screeds. The development of special mixes and of ready-mixed materials, together with the widening range of special applications such as insulated and heated floors, has resulted in more attention being given to the technical requirements of such mortars.

The BRE Digest 104 (1973) proposed that the most suitable sands for mixes for floor screeds are those complying with BS 882, but that the finer sands conforming with BS 1199 can also be used. According to Bessey (1966) the decision to include floor screeds in BS 1199 was taken on the basis that the application of such screeds is similar to that of a cement/sand rendering on a wall and that, furthermore, the specification was considered to be unduly restrictive at the coarser end, since a few per cent of material between 10 mm and 5 mm can be tolerated and may indeed be beneficial. In BS 882 (1973) Zone 3 sand (Table 9.7) was considered to be the nearest in grading to BS 1199 requirements. Furthermore, in recent years, the mortar industry has shown a tendency towards sands coarser than those required by BS 1199 (1976), one suggested 'ideal' grading being that shown in Table 9.9.

TABLE 9.7. *Specifications for sands complying with BS 882 Zone 3 (1973)*

BS sieve size	Percentage by weight passing BS sieve
10.00 mm	100
5.00 mm	90–100
2.36 mm	85–100
1.18 mm	75–100
600 μm	60–79
300 μm	12–40
150 μm	0–10

TABLE 9.8. *Specifications for sands complying with BS 1199 Table 1 (1976) for external renderings, internal cement plastering, internal lime undercoats and floor screeds*

BS sieve size	Percentage by weight passing BS sieve
5.00 mm	100
2.36 mm	90–100
1.18 mm	70–100
600 μm	40–80
300 μm	5–40
150 μm	0–10

TABLE 9.9. *An ideal sand grading for floor screeds (Beningfield pers. comm.)*

BS sieve size	Ideal	Ideal range
5.00 mm	100	96–100
2.36 mm	90	85–95
1.18 mm	70	60–80
600 μm	55	45–60
300 μm	20	15–25
150 μm	3	0–5

Historically, sands used for sand screeds, nevertheless, could be related to BS 1199 (1976) Table 1 (see Table 9.8) but, in the revised standards of 1986, floor screeds

TABLE 9.10. *Some relevant overseas Standards (after Ragsdale & Birt 1976) with additions*

Country	Reference	Use for which Standard applies
USA	ASTM C114-70	Masonry mortar
USA	ASTM C35-70	Gypsum plaster
Canada	A82.56	Masonry mortar
Canada	A82.57	Interior plaster
Belgium	NBN 589-101	General requirements for building sand
Belgium	NBN 589-106	Sands for masonry mortar
Belgium	NBN 589-108	Sands for facings (rendering)
Bulgaria	2271-67	Building
Denmark	DS 405.9	Masonry mortar
Finland	SFS 5516	Masonry mortars
W Germany	DIN 1053	Masonry mortars
W Germany	DIN 18550	Plastering mortars

The year of issue has been excluded because of the considerable changes taking place with various Standards in recent years.

have been excluded, it being more appropriate to treat mortars used as floor screeds as concrete without coarse aggregates. The revised system of classification of fine aggregates for concrete in BS 882 (1984) using three overlapping grades greatly increases the number of sources of satisfactory sands that are described by the new grading classification (Pike & Harrison 1984).

However, two major differences can be established between mortars and concretes. Firstly, the water content of concrete does not usually change much from time of placing over the succeeding few hours if good practice is followed. Mortars, on the other hand, can suffer substantial water losses. Secondly, it is generally accepted that the structural contribution of concrete can be characterized by means of compressive strength but, for mortars, compressive strength is of limited significance.

9.6. Specifications and practice outside the UK

European Standards for mortar sands are being drafted by the European Committee for Standardization (CEN) and in 1993/94 the new standards will supersede all current European National Standards. The discussion in this clause, therefore, applies only to the existing situation.

A review of standards applicable in other countries has been carried out by Ragsdale & Birt (1976) in which comparisons were made of specifications in Belgium, Bulgaria, Canada and the USA (Table 9.10). Particular note was made of the wide range of grading requirements used to meet these various specifications. Thus, in the USA and Belgium, a limitation on the fineness modulus is included (i.e. the sum of the total percentage retained on the $150\,\mu m$, $300\,\mu m$, 1.18 mm, 2.36 mm and 5 mm sieves divided by 100), and acceptable limits are

suggested which range from 1.88 for fine to 3.30 for coarse mixes. This criterion is not incorporated into British Standards because this method of describing the sand grading relationships causes problems in that there appears to be limited correlation between fineness modulus and the performance properties of the sand in mortars.

The grading limits for plastering sand in the USA and Canada are identical and allow less fine material than the corresponding UK standards for sands when used with gypsum plaster. However, there is no standard in either of these countries for sands to be used in external rendering. They also noted that whilst Belgium has established standards for building for various purposes, the Netherlands has only one standard for sand which is applicable solely to reinforced and pre-stressed concrete. In contrast, Bulgaria has two categories of sand 'for building purposes' which are termed (a) coarse and (b) fine. Whilst the finer limits of category (b) are close to those of BS 1200, the coarse limits of category (a) are much higher than those permitted by the corresponding British Standards.

Ragsdale & Birt (1976) also provided comparative graphs applicable to the standards used in Canada, USA, Belgium and the UK (Fig. 9.8) which again shows the wide difference in standards from country to country. In view of this divergence of specifications, the suggestion has been put forward by the UK industry that the only real criteria are price and the ability of the material to perform satisfactorily in a variety of mixes. Thus, in Hong Kong, crushed rock sands are used together with supplies from marine dredged material as fine aggregates in mortar, the blending of the two sources producing a sand which is acceptable and complies with BS 1200.

Investigation of the particle size distribution of the building sands used in West Germany (Albrecht & Wisotzky 1968) confirmed that the variations in grading observed within the mortar industry could be attributed

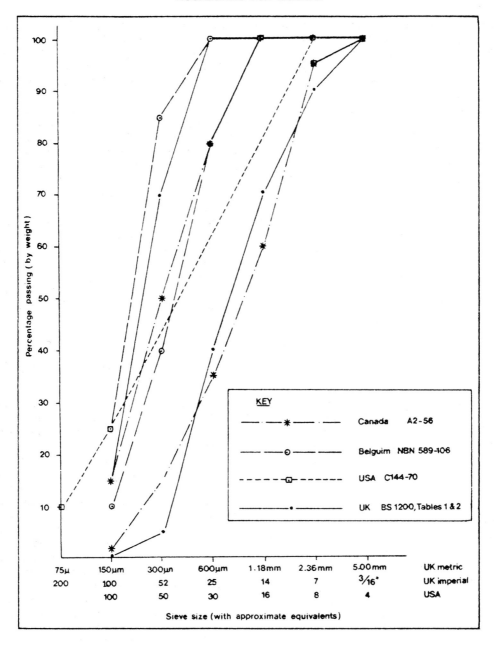

FIG 9.8. Some selected grading limits for masonry sands (after Ragsdale & Birt 1976).

to the differences in their geological and geographical distribution. The sands are derived from river and glacial deposits as washed and unwashed pit products, some sources being dredged materials from rivers and lakes. Where better quality sources are not available, crushed rock sand, or even sands washed out of pumice gravel are used (e.g. as in the Coblenz region). This accounts for the fact that the specification and recommendation of the West German Standards are only met by some of the sands used.

Aggregates for mortar in Denmark are specified on the basis of their standard DS 405.9 and with the proviso that the materials should not contain impurities of such kind and quality that they may affect adversely the setting and hardening or damage the materials that are in contact with the mortar. The sand for standard mortar should comply with the specified limits. The use of sand with other grading limits is permissible if its suitability is proven by type testing.

In France it is reported that there does not seem to be

a distinction between sands for concrete and mortar (Pike 1990). It is also stated that the limits on fines content in France are more liberal than those in the UK, with up to 10% of fines allowed in natural sands and crushed sands for mortar and concrete in that country. For the UK the limits on fines in mortar sand range up to 8% for natural sands and 12% for crushed rock sands.

Sands used in West Germany for mortar are required to comply with DIN 1053 (1974) and research carried out by Schneider (1977) indicates that a fines content (i.e. material less than 63 μm) up to 8% by weight can be an acceptable quantity without affecting the performances of the mortar mixes.

In Finland standards for sands used for mortar are specified in SFS 5516 (1989) for masonry mortars and the grain size distribution is recommended to remain within specified limits. The grain size distribution of the sands may deviate if they can be shown by preliminary tests to be reliable as aggregates for mortar. High mica content is specially mentioned as being a possible problem in that it may decrease the usability of the mix especially if crushed rock sources are used. The silt content of the sand is restricted to 10% in volumetric terms and any impurities that have a detrimental effect on the hardening and appearance of the mortar are excluded.

Both Japan and the USA have general grading specifications for sands for mortar which give wide limits on the sieve sizes (see Table 9.11) whilst in South Africa six grades are recognized according to the different types of sand and for the different types of application (Pike 1990).

TABLE 9.11. *Sand gradings for laying bricks and blocks in Japan and USA (after Pike 1990)*

Sieve sizes	% by weight passing indicated sieve	
	Japan	USA
5.00 mm	100	100
2.36 mm	90–100	95–100
1.18 mm	70–100	70–100
600 μm	40–100	40–75
300 μm	5–75	10–35
150 μm	0–25	2–35
75 μm	0–10	—

Although most sands used as sources of aggregates for mortars are silica rich or quartz sands, carbonate sediments (containing more than 50% carbonate minerals) are sometimes the only local available source to supply the market. These carbonate sands may form in a semi-arid climate or very slowly in an arid climate, and dunes composed of carbonate sands are abundant along tropical and hot arid coasts (Fookes 1988). In these cases

beaches may consist of skeletal fragments, oolites and other carbonate grains. Many famous islands such as Bermuda and the greater part of the Bahamas consist entirely of carbonate dune deposits and, necessarily, must provide the only available fine-grained sources of aggregate for mortar.

The initial composition of a carbonate sediment clearly depends on the local marine environment and its life forms (Semple 1988). Some carbonate sands are non-skeletal, for example, ooliths formed by direct chemical precipitation of calcite coating particles of foreign matter.

The carbonate minerals are relatively weak compared to quartz (having a Moh's hardness of 2–3 compared to 7), and may produce variable cementation of the 'sands'. Nevertheless, as Holocene or Tertiary age deposits they will probably be loose and easily quarried, depending on the geological history of the region in which they occur.

However, one of the problems with beach sands is that they are usually somewhat single sized and their use as a building sand may result in bleeding because of their inability to retain moisture between the grains.

9.7. Occurrence of mortar sands in the UK

The current use of local sands for all building purposes is a matter of their commercial availability and the fact that they often perform satisfactorily, although they may not comply with existing standards.

In Scotland particularly, sands conforming to the 1974 British Standards were difficult to obtain (Ragsdale & Birt 1976) and many non-standard sands from glacial and fluvial sources were accepted provided they were washed and had an acceptable performance history. Sands used for mortars in Scotland were shown to exhibit a wide range of lithology in a study by Currie & Sinha (1981), the grains including basalts, limestones and mudstones but with quartzite predominating. An exception to the glacial or fluvio-glacial source materials is a soft white friable sandstone near Kilwinning in Strathclyde which has been worked as a source of foundry sand in the past but is now often used for plastering and external rendering mortar mixes (BGS, 1977 pers. comm.). Lignite is a common impurity in some Scottish sands and the occurrence of shrinkage problems is thought to be related to the presence of high percentages of greywacke in some sources.

The major sources of building sands for mortars in Northern Ireland are the fluvio-glacial deposits which are well distributed in the south-east part of the country. In addition some sands are dredged from Loch Neagh to meet the needs of the Belfast area, the source deposits probably being pre-glacial in origin.

In England and Wales, mortar sands are obtained from a wide variety of strata. Thus in Durham, non-

Fig 9.9. Typical dry screening operation in UK sand quarry.

standard Permian sands have commonly been used, the coarse washed varieties being applied for rendering work to avoid possible shrinkage problems. More recently, these sands have been used in their dry-screen form and in consequence the mixes have been found to be subject to shrinkage problems.

The building industry in the English Midlands utilizes a high proportion of the fine sand derived from gravel processing, which fell outside the limits for BS 1199 Table 1 (1976). One local authority has insisted on the use of a non-local, non-standard sand of this type, because it has an established reputation as a good rendering sand (Ragsdale & Birt 1976), presumably when used by local labour experienced in its properties.

Sea-dredged sands are used extensively in the Merseyside area (the local name of 'Mersey grit' or 'Mersey sand' covering a wide variety of marine sands taken from the Mersey estuary) and one such fine washed gravel sand has been successfully used for rough cast and stucco work without any apparent defects. The finer graded Mersey sands are used mainly for brickwork mortars and rendering. They tend to be single sized, between 300 µm and 150 µm, and so fall outside the grading requirements for BS 1200 and BS 1199. Although the shell content is fairly high in these sands, with up to 8% of fragmented shell present, no apparent defects have been reported and neither does the combined salts content of up to 0.1% appear to have caused any damage.

In the past in West Cheshire, where most of the sands used are of glacial origin, only one sand pit produced material within the limits of BS 1200 (1976). Blending of sands from one local source with another outside the producer areas is a common practice and typical examples can be seen in North Wales where glacial sands

are notoriously variable and fine-grained sands need upgrading to comply with specifications to meet standards from general purpose mortars and floor screeds.

Mortar sand sources throughout Wales are usually in the extensive deposits of glacial sands and gravels which occur well distributed over North and South Wales. In addition, very fine grained beach sands from Porthcawl near Swansea have found local uses as general mortar aggregates.

In recent years it has been accepted that sea-dredged sands can be used successfully to produce mortar mixes. However, it is sometimes necessary to add a plasticizer, such as limestone dust filler, to increase the workability due to the single sized nature of these fine grained aggregates. In the Bristol and Cardiff areas, marine sands taken from the Bristol Channel are commonly utilized as building sands as well as sources from the English Channel and the North Sea where licences are granted by the Crown for dredging to take place on the sea bed.

The extensive outcrops of sand in the Folkestone Beds within the Lower Greensand Series in SE England provide some well graded mortar sands, particularly after washing. Considerable lateral and vertical variation in lithology is common and many quarries excavate up to 40 metres depth of sand from these deposits, some from below the water table (Humphries 1964). Other horizons within the Lower Greensand of the Weald which yield building sands are the sandy facies of the Hythe Beds and the Sandgate Beds in the Redhill area although the latter are usually very fine-grained and limited in their use because of the high clay fraction. Although economic factors still dictate the use of local sands which are outside specifications, the building industry is usually able to obtain the sand it needs from indigenous sources without blending. For example, the local 'Runfold' sands, taken from the Folkestone beds near Farnham in Surrey, can produce sand material complying with BS 1200, 1198 and 1199, in addition to BS 882 concreting sands after some processing such as dry-screening (Fig. 9.9).

In the western part of the Hampshire Basin, the sands in the Reading Beds and Bagshot Beds are common sources of building sands. The popular 'Sherfield English' pits located in the Reading beds near Romsey have been noted for many years as the classical general mortar sand supplied to local markets.

9.8. Engineering performance and problems of mortars with particular reference to UK case histories

It is commonly known that when the proportioning of cement to sand for a mix is by volume, the weight of sand in a given volume can vary by as much as 30% between the dry and damp condition and hence the true proportions used will not be known (Bessey 1966). This, together with the fact that the bulk density of cement is known to alter, can lead to disputes between contractor and client should defects occur. It follows then, that the use of the BS 812 (1975) methods for assessing relative density and water absorption are of particular importance, especially with crushed rock sands where the water absorption can vary considerably in hot conditions. In recent years, a better understanding of the materials used for mortars has enabled more reliable guidance to be given as to the type of mix suitable for various uses and conditions.

The main ingredients of mortars in the UK are Portland cement, sand and water and thus there is a tendency to consider that the principles developed in concrete technology should also apply to mortar (Harrison & Bowler 1990). However, whereas the function of concrete is to represent the main structural element, that of mortar is to provide an adjustable, quick, effective and durable jointing material between structural units always much larger in volume than itself.

9.8.1. Effect of grading

Early research (Furnas 1931) applied to mortars considered the close packing of solid particles and concluded that the best workability and results were obtained from using continuously graded aggregates.

Later research (Bloem 1962) on 1 : 3 cement/sand mortars suggested the employment of air-entrainment so that coarser sands than those permitted by ASTM specifications could be used.

Sand gradings are critical to the rheological properties of fresh mortars and the structure of the hardened

product (Harrison & Bowler 1990). Thus the most recent revisions of BS 1200, 1199 have been an attempt to reconcile current usage of sands with performance.

Historically, investigations by Bessey (1966) proposed rationalized methods for specifying natural sands for mortars, using the median diameter and a sorting coefficient, but these have generally lacked the definition that can be achieved by the traditional gradings. Lee & Pyle (1968) and Lee (1975) then went on to show that for some sands used in mortars the strength of a mortar can be related to the grading of the aggregate. On the assumption that the aggregate complies with the requirements of BS 1200 and assuming that the cement content and water–cement ratio remain constant, Lee (1975) proposed that proportions of material retained on a $600\,\mu m$ sieve, those passing the $600\,\mu m$ but retained on the $150\,\mu m$ sieve, and those passing a $150\,\mu m$ sieve could be plotted on triangular graph as shown in Fig. 9.10. The results can provide a possible prediction of mortar strength. It can be seen that, as the central region is approached, so the particle packing characteristics improve until an ideal packing is obtained at the centre point. This would have a blend of 1/3 of each fraction (sand, cement, lime and filler, if present), which would be expected to produce maximum packing and, therefore, optimum strength for the mortar. In theory the ideal mortar sand with 66.7% passing a $600\,\mu m$ sieve and 33.3% passing a $150\,\mu m$ sieve, when plotted on log normal paper, would show the grain size distribution given in Fig. 9.11.

In practice, it was suggested that the ideal sand is generally finer grained than that shown in Fig. 9.11, the reason being that this is necessary to obtain good workability. Again, the Lee method cannot differentiate sands by the nature of the $150\,\mu m$ fraction which can have a very large effect on mortar properties.

The ideal gradings are seldom available. Some of the more common gradings of sands used by the Industry are shown diagrammatically in Fig. 9.12. Sands in the regions B and C can be used without further treatment to produce satisfactory cement–lime–sand and gypsum–lime–sand mortar. Sands in region A will require blending and, in this case, the experience of the bricklayers and plasterers is usually necessary to establish the mix required.

The packing of sand influences its void content (Lee 1975) and the dry compacted bulk density may be considered as a true indication of the voids present. Silica has a relative density of $2635\,kg\,m^{-3}$ (Table 9.12). However, in practice it is found that dry natural sands have compacted dry bulk densities of between 1400 and $1800\,kg\,m^3$ and thus the void content represents 47 and 32% respectively

A poorly graded sand, i.e. having a low dry compacted density, requires a high proportion of material to fill the voids (Lee 1975). If this material is cement or water, then high drying shrinkage will result. Poorly

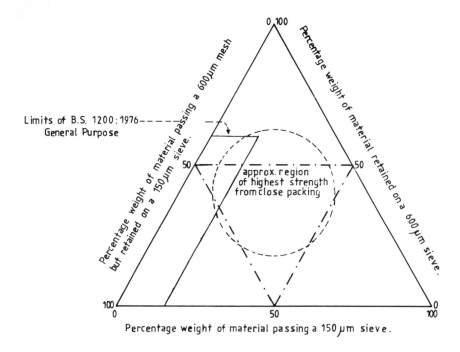

FIG 9.10. Use of triangular graph paper for showing sand gradings (after Lee 1975).

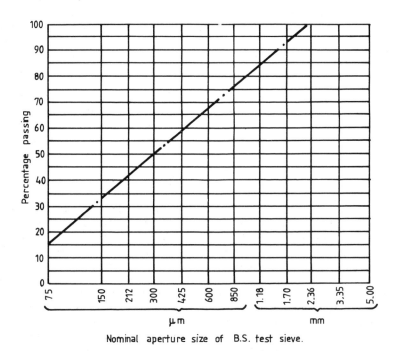

FIG 9.11. Ideal grading curve of a building mortar if no voids (after Lee 1975).

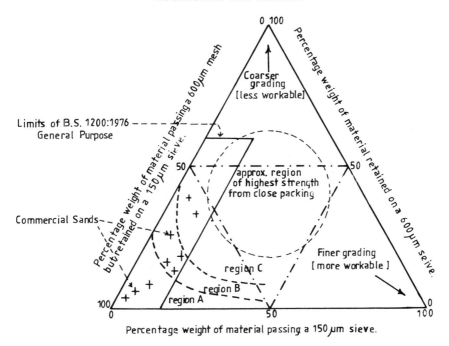

FIG 9.12. Gradings of some commercial sands (after Lee 1975).

graded sands can be improved by blending with other sands but when this is not possible, the upgrading can be achieved by adjusting the lime content or adding an air-entraining agent so that discrete air pockets are formed.

TABLE 9.12. *Void contents of sands (Lee 1975)*

Sand dry bulk density (kg/m³)	Void (%)
2635	0
1800	32
1700	35
1600	39
1500	43
1400	47

A study of the factors affecting the packing and porosity of particles has been made by Lees (1970) on aggregate gradings for dense asphaltic compositions which may have similar applications for the mortar mix design. Although a general association between strength properties and density can be assessed, Lees' studies indicated that there is no unique ideal maximum grading curve. The correct proportions for minimum voids are inevitably affected by changes in aggregate particle shape both from source to source and from size to size. Later investigations on the structural arrangements of aggregate particles in concrete were used by Lees (1970)

to develop a method by which the packing properties can be designed such that maximum-density gradings can be derived which take into account the changes in aggregate packing properties that may occur at any size level. In addition, the method recognizes the importance of any lubricating or adhesive coatings present, the surface static effects on small particles and the degree or type of compactive effect as well as the effect of external boundaries. These findings may have a use in the design of mortar mixes and further research into the relationship between density and the engineering properties of mortars could prove worthwhile.

9.8.2. Current experience

Mortar has in the past been mainly a site product, dependent for its properties upon the mixing skill of the bricklayer and plasterer, rather than a material which could be precisely specified and manufactured. However, with the much greater use of factory made ready-mixed mortars this position has changed and the emphasis is now on the use of known sources of sand and close control of the mix proportions with a consequent reduction in the site labour. The move from site mixing towards the ready-mixed product means that the use of local sands will become less common, and there will be a greater input of technical expertise from the ready-mixed industry.

Nevertheless, workmanship is a very important aspect of masonry construction and good brick laying technique in particular results in improved bond between brick and mortar minimizing rain penetration problems.

In a case study analysis of some 63 sands in the UK by Ragsdale & Birt (1976), it was found that only 8% complied in all respects with the British Standards against which they were supplied. Even so, the customers were generally prepared to accept these sands without complaint. The sands involved were mostly supplied for external rendering and brickwork mortar. The grading tests showed that only 2 (4.5%) of the sands for rendering complied with BS 1199 Table 1 (1976) whilst some 26 (59%) of the sands for mortar complied with BS 1200 (1976).

All modern UK mortars use Portland cement as the principal binder, but in rich 1 : 3 mixes the rigidity that this introduces can lead to cracking in some structures (Harrison & Bowler 1990). The replacement of different proportions of the cement with lime, which reduces the overall cement content and acts as a plasticizer, will also reduce the rigidity of the mortar, allowing it to accommodate small movements without cracking. However, the ability for cement–lime–sand mortar to withstand severe weathering is progressively reduced as the cement is replaced by lime (Harrison & Bowler 1990).

Furthermore, the volume of cement binder can be conventionally extended by air-entrainment in non-lime mixes and such mixes have good frost resistance.

9.8.3. Future trends in the use of sands

It has long been recognized that sands containing appreciable amounts of material passing the 150 µm sieve are needed to achieve adequate workability of the freshly-mixed mortar, although this material is unnecessary in terms of performance. In the past it has been suggested that for external rendering and dubbing out as much as 20% to 25% of the material should pass the 150 µm sieve, while still maintaining a good continuous grading for the coarse fraction. This would have the effect of flattening the present grading envelope of BS 1199 Table 1 (1976), thereby reducing the maximum amount passing the 2.36 mm, 1.18 mm, and 600 µm sieves by about 10%, 15% and 35% respectively. Recent experience suggests that 20–25% of the material passing the 150 µm sieve would be much too high (Beningfield, pers. comm.). As a better understanding of the technology of sands in mortars is developed, the trend towards blending of sands from different sources will become more practical and economical to ensure consistency of product.

It is intended that the new European Standards being progressed by CEN will be performance related as far as possible, as this will lead to the greater use of designed mixes for mortars where the properties are defined

rather than the mix proportions. Recently there has been considerable interest in the concept of a 'universal mortar mix' (Harrison & Bowler 1990) which would be suitable for inner and outer leaf masonary in external walls of all low-rise buildings. Its use for both internal and external walls would involve a compromise between the need for a robust mortar to resist external weather and a weaker mortar to accommodate small thermal and moisture movements without causing excessive plaster cracking.

9.8.4. Artificial aggregates used in mortars

Lightweight aggregate has been used as a total or partial replacement for sand in some mortars for many years.

Indeed, some of the earliest mortars known, dated from the Roman era contain lightweight and or semi-lightweight aggregates based on volcanic trass, pumice and similar exfoliated materials.

The use of these naturally occurring lightweight aggregates appears to have fairly continuous history up until the present date.

It is current practice to use perlite, mined in Greece, USA and other countries which is exported to the UK in dense form and then expanded. Vermiculite is also used in the expanded form for specialist lightweight mortars in the fields of refractories and special roof screeding mortars.

Expanded polystyrene is also used as an alternative to polystyrene in applications for lightweight block laying mortars and also for plastering and rendering mortars.

The requirements of lightweight aggregates for use in mortar are that they shall have an appropriate density but, in addition, fire resistance, durability and strength are also important.

The market for these materials is larger in Continental Europe than in the UK where market growth has probably been below the predictions of some of the producers.

9.9. Discussion

Much of the sand used for the production of mortar in the UK, particularly that used for external rendering, does not conform to the appropriate limits prescribed by the current British Standards. Nor is reference made to the quantitative limits on 'impurities' in the existing UK standards, there being a considerable difference of opinion by both producers and users on the acceptability of sands continuing impurities such as mica, lignite or high salts content.

The amendments to BS 1199 and 1200 have done much to improve the acceptable limits for good performance, and there is increasing awareness in the UK and elsewhere in Europe of the need to ensure quality products.

Although the use of non-compliant sands is a common practice, both in the UK and elsewhere in the world, the most important criterion for performance appears to be the quality of cleanliness. Unwashed dry-screened sands, including crushed rock sands, whilst sometimes complying with British Standard requirements, tend to produce mortars having a high water demand. As a result they are relatively weaker and more prone to shrinkage than mortars made with well-washed sand, where the clay content has been considerably reduced. Standards differ from country to country, largely due to the fact that they are based on the availability of natural resources and the manner of their use. Hence sands which are acceptable in one place may well be rejected elsewhere. The use of different cements and construction techniques will also influence whether particular sands can be accepted as suitable for construction mortars.

The recent years have seen no dramatic breakthroughs and although it is difficult to try to predict future trends, there is likely to be an increasing emphasis on energy conservation in the future to which the industry will need to apply itself.

Although much technical data is available for concrete aggregates, it is clearly apparent that the accumulation of comparable information relating to the fine-grained aggregates used in the production of mortars continues to be much neglected.

It is also important that future research should consider how wisespread is the potential threat from clay minerals to mortar and there is a need to assess the mineralogy of the fines in representative samples of sands from various regions in the UK and mainland Europe. Such a survey would need to take account of variations in the natural deposit, and the variations conferred on the products by the extraction and processing methods.

References

ALBRECHT, W. & WISOTZKY, I. T. 1968. Survey of the particle size composition of sand for masonry and plastering mortars. *Bau und Bauindustrie*, **11**, 692–697.

AMERICAN SOCIETY FOR TESTING AND MATERIALS 1989. Standard specification for aggregate for masonry mortar C144-89.

—— 1989. C123 Test method for lightweight pieces in aggregate.

BACMI 1990. *British Aggregate Construction Material Industries*, London Statistical Year Book.

BENINGFIELD, N. 1980. Aspects of cement-based mortars for brickwork and blockwork. *Concrete* (Jan.) 27–30.

BESSEY, G. E. 1966. Current developments affecting the design and use of mortars for building purposes. *Journal of Applied Chemistry*, **16**, 313.

BLOEM, D. L. 1962. Effects of aggregate grading on properties of masonry mortar. Symp. on Testing. ASTM. Spec. Tech. Publ. No. 320. 67–92.

BUILDING RESEARCH STATION DIGEST 1971. Choosing specification for plastering, **49**, 1–7.

BUILDING RESEARCH ESTABLISHMENT DIGEST 104. 1973. Floor screeds.

—— 160. 1973. Mortars for Bricklaying. 1–4.

BRITISH STANDARDS INSTITUTION 1973. Specification for aggregates from natural sources for concrete (including granolithic): BS 882.

—— 1975. *Methods for sampling and testing of mineral aggregate sands and filters*. BS 812: Part 1.

—— 1976. *Sands for mortar for plain and reinforced brickwork, blockwalling and masonry*: BS 1200.

—— 1976. *Sands for internal plasters with gypsum plasters*. BS 1198.

—— 1976. *Sands for external renderings, internal plastering with lime and Portland cement, and floor screeds*: BS 1199.

—— 1981. *Ready mixed building mortars*: BS 4721.

—— 1984. *Specifications for building sands from natural sources—sands for mortars for bricklaying*: BS 1200.

—— 1986. *Specifications for building sands from natural sources—sands for mortars for plastering and rendering*: BS 1199.

CHAPMAN, G. P. & ROEDER, A. R. 1969. Sea dredged sands and gravels. *Quarry Managers Journal*, 251–263.

CONNOR, C. C. 1948. Factors in the resistance of brick masonry walls to moisture penetration. *Proceedings of the American Society for Testing Materials*, **48**.

—— 1953. Some effects of the grading of sand on masonry mortar. *Proceedings of the American Society for Testing Materials*, **52**, 933–948.

CURRIE, D. & SINHA, B. 1981. Survey of Scottish sands and their characteristics which affect mortar strength. *Chemistry and Industry* 639–645.

DENMARKS STANDARD 1978—DS405.9 *Masonry Mortars*.

FINLANDS STANDARDISERINGSFORBUND 1989—SFS.5516 *Masonry Mortars*.

FOOKES, P. G. 1988. The geology of carbonate soils and rocks and their engineering characterisation and description. *In*: JEWELL, R. J. & KHORSCHID, M. S. (eds) *Engineering for calcareous sediments*. Balkema, Rotterdam, 787–806.

—— & MARSH, A. H. 1981. Some characteristics of construction material in the low to moderate metaphoric grade rocks of the Lower Himalayas of East Nepal, 2: Engineering Characteristics. *Proceedings of the Institution of Civil Engineers*, Pt 1, **70**, Feb. 139–162.

—— & POOLE, A. B. 1981. Some preliminary considerations on the selection and durability of rock and concrete materials for breakwaters and coastal protection works. *Quarterly Journal of Engineering Geology*, **14**, 97–128.

—— & REVIE, W. A. 1982. Mica in Concrete—a case history from Eastern Nepal. *Concrete*, **16**, 3, 12–16.

FURNAS, C. C. 1931. *Industrial Engineering Chemistry* **23**.

HARRISON, W. H. 1986. *Magazine of Construction Research*, **38**, June, 95–110.

—— & BOWLER, G. K. 1990. Aspects of mortar durability. *British Ceramic Transactions Journal*, **89**, 93–101.

HOON, R. C. & VENKATESWARLU, V. 1962. Beneficiation of micaceous sands for use as fine aggregates. *Indian Concrete Journal*, July.

HMSO 1979. *Production of Aggregates in Great Britain. 1977 and 1978*.

HUMPHRIES, D. W. 1964. The stratigraphy of the Lower Greensand of the South West Weald. *Proceedings of the Geologists Association*, **75**, 39–59.

INSTITUTION OF GEOLOGICAL SCIENCES 1977. *Mineral Resources Consultative Committee. Mineral Dossier No. 18. Silica.* HMSO London.

LEE, H. N. 1975. The technology of mortar design. *Chemistry and Industry* 114–117.

—— & PYLE, M. A. 1968. The design of mortars for calculated load bearing brickwork. *Proceedings of the British Ceramic Society*, **11**, 143–161.

LEES, G. 1970. The rational design of aggregate gradings for dense asphaltic compositions. *Proceedings of the Association of Asphalt Paving Technology*, 39–97.

MCINTOSH, J. D. 1970. Specifying the quality of bedding mortars. *Proceedings of the British Ceramic Society*, **17**, 65–82.

PETTIJOHN, F. J. 1949. *Sedimentary Rocks.* Harper & Row.

PIKE, D. C. 1990. *Standards for Aggregates.* Ellis Horwood, London.

—— & HARRISON, R. 1984. Revision of BS 882 background and changes. *Cement & Industry.* Feb. 139–143.

—— & LIMBRICK, A. 1981. A study of sieve tests for building sands. *Chemistry & Industry*, **19**, 626–630.

PYLE, M. 1967. Modern mortars for brick and brickwork. *Building Materials.*

RAGSDALE, L. A. & BIRT, J. C. 1976. Building sands availability, usage and compliance with specification requirements. *Ciria Report* **39**, 1–30.

SCHNEIDER, H. 1977. Effect of the fineness of the masonry sand on mortar strength using mid ratios according to German Standard Specification DIN 1053. Z1 International. May, 223–237.

SEMPLE, R. M. 1988. The mechanical properties of carbonate soils. *In*: JEWELL, R. J. and KHORSHID, M. S. (eds). *Engineering for Calcareous Sediments*, Balkema, Rotterdam.

SHIRVILL, A. J. 1982. *The effects of lignite on some aspects of concrete quality and durability.* RMC Technical Services Limited internal publication.

SMITH & PLOWMAN, 1972. *Bricks and Mortars.* Ibstock Building Products Ltd. Publication No. 1.

SWALLOW, H. T. S. 1964. *Mortars and Bricks.* British Ceramic Research Association Technical Note 57.

TUCKER, M. E. 1982. *The Field Description of Sedimentary Rocks.* Open University, Milton Keynes.

WESTBROOK, E. L. E. 1960. *Sands for plastering, rendering and mortar work.* Sand and Gravel Association of Great Britain.

ZINGG, T. 1935. Beitrag zur Schotteranalyse. *Schweiz-mineral. Petrog. Mitt.*, **15**, 39–140.

10. Aggregates in unbound pavement construction

10.1. Introduction

In highway and airfield pavements, aggregates are used in various types of unbound or bound materials (standard nomenclature for pavements as used in the United Kingdom is illustrated in Fig. 10.1). This chapter is concerned with both primary (naturally occurring) and secondary (artificial or recycled) aggregates which are not bound by cementitious or bituminous binders. Unbound layers are used in the UK mainly for sub-bases or capping, but elsewhere may be used for bases or, in the case of low volume roads, the whole structure. Cement bound aggregates are discussed in Chapter 8 and bitumen and tar bound aggregates are discussed in Chapter 11. Figure 10.2 shows bitumen macadam being laid over unbound sub-base.

Unbound layers in pavement construction may fulfil some or all of the following functions:

(a) a working platform for construction;
(b) a structural layer (load spreading and resistance to rutting);
(c) a replacement for frost-susceptible subgrade (if necessary);
(d) a drainage layer.

The main use in the UK is as sub-base for which (a) is probably the most important function. Guidance is given in Powell *et al.* (1984).

The ability to spread load (high stiffness) and to resist rutting (low permanent deformation) is usually associated with closely graded materials whereas open gradings are thought necessary for good drainage. The apparent conflict between these requirements has received considerable attention over recent years (Roy 1981; Jones & Jones 1989). These and other aspects of the states of the art and practice relating to unbound aggregates in roads in the UK and beyond have been discussed at the series of Symposia 'Unbound Aggregates in Roads' (UNBAR).

Unbound aggregates perform less well than bound aggregates as a structural layer in the final pavement as evidenced by full-scale trials (Croney & Croney 1991) and evaluation of existing pavements (Brunton *et al.* 1992). Nevertheless their other advantages and comparatively low cost* mean that very large quantities of unbound aggregate materials have been and are still being used in pavement construction. While this is true for construction in the United Kingdom and other

---

*This lower cost applies to the straight comparison of price per tonne. It has, however, frequently been pointed out that the better load distributing properties of the bound materials would enable them to be laid at a lesser thickness than the unbound. While this is the case in certain circumstances, for example where the requirement for frost protection of the subgrade does not apply, the overall economic advantage in terms of price per square metre is still generally with the unbound materials.

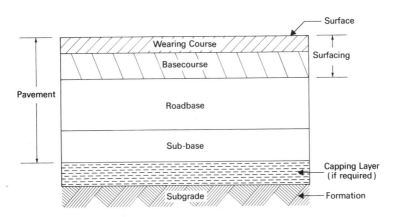

Fig. 10.1. Typical flexible pavement construction layers.

Fig. 10.2. Bitumen macadam being laid over unbound sub-base.

developed countries, it is even more so in the developing countries where unbound aggregate materials may comprise the whole of the structural component of the road construction, with or without a thin application of single or multiple coat surface dressing.

Furthermore, aggregates can be used in conjunction with geosynthetics which can provide reinforcement, bulk separation or assist in filtration (Brown *et al.* 1987; DTp 1987b).

The performance of an aggregate layer depends on (a) its intrinsic properties (b) the particle shape and grading (which may be influenced by processing) and (c) the method of placing. As with other uses of aggregates for construction materals it should not be supposed that an aggregate's suitability can be defined by its petrographic type alone.

The main characteristics which define whether a material will be suitable as an unbound aggregate are:

(a) hardness, i.e. resistance to abrasion and attrition during mixing, handling and transporting.
(b) toughness, i.e. resistance to crushing and impact loads during compaction and under traffic.
(c) soundness, i.e. resistance to breakdown from weathering by chemical and physical processes.

(d) pore size distribution which, if unfavourable can increase frost susceptibility.

In this chapter the main types of available aggregates, both natural (primary) and artificial or recycled (secondary) are reviewed briefly. This is followed by a detailed discussion of factors affecting the resistance to wear and decay, and the effect of water migration. Finally, current specifications in the UK, Europe and elsewhere are reviewed.

10.2. Primary aggregates

10.2.1. Igneous rocks

In the unweathered state igneous rocks as a class are usually hard, due to the nature of the silicate minerals from which they are formed, and strong, due to the interlocking nature of the constituent minerals. Plutonic varieties are in general less tough than their hypabyssal and volcanic counterparts (Knight & Knight 1948). In addition the plutonic varieties rich in mica tend to show less resistance to abrasion than those containing appreciable quantities of hornblende and augite. (See also §11.4

for further discussion on strength properties of igneous, sedimentary and metamorphic rock aggregate.)

10.2.2. Sedimentary rocks and unconsolidated sediments

Sedimentary rocks to be used as aggregates fall generally into the two categories of sandstones and limestones. Of the former the quartzites tend to show the greatest strength due to the near complete cementation with secondary silica. As is well known, the lower strengths of calcium carbonate and iron oxide cements combined with a tendency to less complete cementation leads to generally lower strength for calcareous and ferruginous sandstones.

Post-Carboniferous limestones also tend to be lower in strength due to incomplete cementation but limestones of the Carboniferous and earlier periods frequently possess aggregate crushing values equal to many igneous rocks.

Excessive amounts of clay mineral in argillaceous Silurian limestones have been known to lead to base failure in road sites in Staffordshire. In one case plastic fines from the decomposed base intruded the open textured bitumen macadam base course and resulted in disintegration of this layer under traffic.

The component particles of the unconsolidated sediments classified as gravels and sands possess the intrinsic strength and durability properties of the constituent rock and mineral types. In the mass, as in the case of all other rock types, the properties are governed by the shape (including ratio of crushed to uncrushed particles) and grading characteristics and degree of compaction.

10.2.3. Metamorphic rocks

Metamorphic rocks of the foliated varieties, owing to the preferential orientation of flaky minerals (slaty, schistose and gneissose textures), are comparatively low in toughness and wearing resistance. Non-foliated varieties (e.g. hornfels and some gneisses) in which more or less complete recrystallization of quartz and other minerals has occurred and which are often rich in hornblende, augite and garnet, are extremely hard and tough.

10.3. Secondary aggregates

10.3.1. Overview

Secondary aggregates include artificial aggregates, industrial by-products and waste materials. Reviews of sources and uses have been undertaken by OECD (1977)

BSI 6543 (1985), Giannattasio & Marchionna (1987) and Whitbread et al. (1991). There is considerable pressure, particularly in mainland Europe, to use secondary aggregates because of both the scarcity of primary aggregates and the environmental benefits.

The following selected extracts from the conclusions of the PIARC report by Giannattasio & Marchionna (1987) are especially relevant: 'Highway engineers are making increasing use of non-traditional materials in pavement construction for reasons concerned with both economics and protection of the environment. . . . Spread of the use of these materials is very uneven. For some of them operational use is already possible in a large number of countries. Enough is known about their behaviour and when necessary special technical specifications have been drawn up. Because of this it can be said of these materials that they have almost entirely lost their 'marginal' quality. This is the case with blast furnace slags and steel wastes. A similar situation exists for some other materials but only in a few countries . . .'.

Allowance must be made for the fact that even in the case of widely used non traditional materials it is never possible to rely solely on the experience of other countries. . . . This is because their properties may vary from one country to another. It is, therefore, necessary to exert caution and undertake the required laboratory and field experiments'.

Whitbread et al. of Arup Economics and Planning, in their report for the UK Department of Environment suggest that the main reason that secondary aggregates are not used is price. Transport costs tend to be high, since wastes are often located at considerable distances from the market (particularly SE England). They suggest a tax on primary aggregates to reduce the price differential and to encourage the use of secondary sources. BACMI (1991) refute these conclusions and point out that much of the waste available is not suitable as aggregates but only bulk fill.

The principal secondary aggregates available for use as unbound aggregates in roads are reviewed below.

10.3.2. Colliery spoil

Most colliery spoil now available is unburnt and is not used as unbound aggregate. Well burnt colliery shale, if available, is potentially suitable, provided that it meets the specification. Frost susceptibility can be a problem (see §10.6.2)

10.3.3. Spent oil shale

Oil shale waste has been used successfully in Scotland as sub-base and as capping on the M9. This material has also been used with success in Western Canada.

10.3.4. Power station ashes

Neither pulverized fuel ash (PFA), nor furnace bottom ash (FBA) is normally considered as unbound aggregate. However, although not fulfilling the DTp requirements (§10.7.1), Dawson & Bullen (1991) concluded that the use of FBA should be encouraged on low trafficked roads.

10.3.5. Wastes from quarries

Slate waste from North Wales is a potential Type 1 sub-base (§10.7.1). The economics of its transport to South East England are discussed in detail by Whitbread et al. (1991).

Care should be taken in the use of wastes from the quarrying or mining of metal ores, since they may have high concentrations of hazardous metallic components.

10.3.6. Incinerated refuse

Incineration of solid urban wastes yields materials which when cooled in water and screened may be used in capping and sub-bases. France and Switzerland are quoted as examples of countries where this approach to the disposal of municipal wastes has been successful, but warning is given that, in some localities, danger of polluting groundwaters by this type of refuse may inhibit its use (Hirt 1976).

10.3.7. Demolition wastes

Crushed concrete from airfields has been used in unbound sub-bases for many years. Demolition rubble needs to be processed to reduce contaminants (wood, glass, plastics etc.) to a minimal level. Even so, variability of the source material is inevitably reflected in the final product. UK experience discussed by Mulheron et al. (1990) lags behind other European countries such as Holland (Sweere 1991) and Germany (Suss 1989).

10.3.8. Metallurgical slags

By-products from the metallurgical industry which have been used in the construction of the unbound layers of flexible pavements include blast furnace slag and the much less common non ferrous slags of copper, nickel, zinc, tungsten etc. Slags of various types may be imported, for example, into SE England from Northern Europe. British blast furnace slags are usually air cooled rather than granulated slags (formed by rapid cooling in water jets). The ratio of calcium to other elements in blast furnace slag to be used as aggregate is restricted by

BS 1047: 1983 to avoid 'falling' (lime) unsoundness. Iron unsoundness, due to the presence of ferrous sulphide, is a rare phenomenon which is shown up if the slag disintegrates on soaking.

Good results have been obtained from the use of blast furnace slags in road bases and sub-bases in many countries (Belgium, Finland, France, Germany, The Netherlands, Spain, UK and USA). Remarkable binding qualities may be achieved with granulated blast furnace slags in the presence of lime, gypsum-lime and soda. French highway authorities have been especially active in the field of development of gravel-slag and sand-slag road base materials (LCPC 1973). Proportions of slag in these mixes vary between 10 and 25%, together with about 1 per cent of a basic activator (generally hydrated lime) which in the presence of added water (say 10%) reacts slowly to produce a gradual but significant gain in strength. Luxembourg, Italy, Hungary, Algeria and Tunisia have had success in following the French experience.

Steel slags differ fundamentally from blast furnace slags. In particular they contain calcium or magnesium oxides which may subsequently hydrate. Some countries specify that the free lime content must not exceed 4.5 to 5.0%. Verhasselt and Choquet (1989) recommended that steel slags produced by the Linz–Donawitz (LD) process and intended for use as road aggregates should have an initial lime content not exceeding 4.5% at the time of production. The British Specification (DTp 1991a) requires that steel slags be well weathered.

Potential harmful leachates pose a problem for non-ferrous slags.

10.4. Resistance to wear

10.4.1. The degradation process

Whether occurring in the pavement or in laboratory testing, the degradation of particles proceeds in the following manner (Lees & Kennedy 1975). Initially, as a crushing load is applied, the load is transmitted to the solid through its protruding points, if any, leading to the crushing of these points and the formation of larger contact areas. As the load is increased, either the crushing or flexural strength is exceeded and a crack is formed, leading to particle breakage.

10.4.2. Types of degradation

In respect of all the above the degradation process may be considered as:

(1) the breakage of particles into approximately equal parts;

(2) the breakage or crushing of angular projections which may exist on the exterior surface of the particles;

(3) the grinding of small-scale asperities off the major faces or planes of the particles.

The distinction between these processes is mainly in the different ratios of size of the broken product to the size of the original particle. Their relative importance differs with shape and petrology of the aggregate. For example, non-crushed high sphericity rounded gravels will only experience type-1 degradation as will parallel sided slabby particles. Angular cubical particles and tapering rod, disc and blade-like particles will often experience type-2 degradation before any type-1 breakage occurs. Weakly cemented sedimentary rock particles and surface weathered rock particles will be susceptible mainly to type-3 degradation. Repeated stressing at small strains, a fatigue process, will also tend to produce this kind of surface degradation. Attrition of this nature may eventually degrade the particles to their individual crystal or grain sizes.

Discussion of the mathematical solutions to the theory of degradation are contained in Rittinger (1867), Kick (1885), Gaudin (1926), Shelburne (1940), Bond (1952) and Yashima *et al.* (1970).

10.4.3. Influence of particle shape and size

The strength of a particular rock type (as distinct from aggregate strength) is an intrinsic property of the rock itself but both shape and size of particle affect the strength of an aggregate as measured in laboratory tests and as encountered in service. Examples are the effect of flakiness index upon aggregate impact value of a variety of petrological types (Ramsay 1965) and the effect of size of particle upon aggregate crushing value (Markwick & Shergold 1945).

In the former case, the greater degradation of flaky (and of elongate) particles of a given size (i.e. volume) is associated with the greater bending moments that can be applied to given cross sectional areas. The latter case concerning the effect of size, demonstrates that the theory of statistical distribution of flaws, which states that the probability of a critical flaw occurring increases as the size of the member increases, applies to irregular rock particles in a similar way as it applies to concrete cubes and beams, metal test specimens etc.

10.4.4. Influence of moisture content

The British test Specifications for the ten per cent fines value (TFV) (BS 812 Pt 111, 1990) and for aggregate impact value (AIV) (BS 812 Pt 112), but not ACV

(BS 812 Pt 110), include procedures for both a soaked condition and an oven dry condition. The specification for Highway Works (DTp 1991a,b) demands testing, for TFV only, in the soaked condition (in which the material is surface dried after soaking).

Testing aggregates only in the dry state would conceal the extent to which aggregate strength falls with increasing moisture content, e.g. the loss in strength was found by Markwick & Shergold (1946) to be up to 40% for some igneous rocks. Work to investigate this tendency further has continued at the Transport and Road Research Laboratory in more recent studies. Irwin (1959) as reported by Hosking & Tubey (1969) showed that some low grade aggregate types from East and West Africa gave significantly poorer results when tested in a saturated state, with lateritic gravels losing nearly 20% of strength, some limestone losing nearly 80% of its strength and murram gravels losing over 20%. Coral limestone from the Bahamas showed a strength loss of some 38%.

Shergold & Hosking (1963) compared results of tests on dried and water saturated samples of various low grade argillaceous and gritty rocks from the UK. For aggregate judged on engineering experience to be acceptable, modified aggregate impact tests showed about 17% loss in strength while the modified 10% fines value fell by 24%. Aggregates which had been judged unacceptable from practical experience showed much greater loss in strength in the saturated condition, namely 35% loss in the modified aggregate impact test and 63% loss in the modified 10% fines test. Shergold & Hosking concluded that, in respect of aggregates for unsurfaced roads, bases on lightly trafficked roads and sub-bases, useful tentative limits would be a maximum of 40 for a soaked AIV and a minimum of 5 tonnes (50kN) for a soaked TFV.

10.4.5. Influence of grading on aggregate degradation

Where aggregate of low crushing strength is considered for use it should be borne in mind that the amount of crushing to be expected is a function not only of the intrinsic strength for a given size and shape, but also of the aggregate grading. Clearly the standard aggregate crushing and aggregate impact tests cannot assess this factor since they are carried out upon 'single-size' materials. Even the Los Angeles test which permits the test to be carried out on a limited variety of gradings does not set out specifically to measure this effect since the resistance to degradation is tested only in a loose 'tumbling' state rather than in a compacted state where the effect of grading would most clearly be seen.

The importance of grading on crushing is seen in Table 10.1 (after Ghani 1969) which demonstrates that the denser gradings experience much less degradation

TABLE 10.1. *Degradation of a Millstone Grit aggregate from Ambergate, Derbyshire, combined to five different gradings (after Ghani 1969)*

	Grading	Initial porosity (after vibration)	Aggregate Grading Impact Value AGIV	Marshall hammer compaction on dry aggregate 50 blows each 'face'	
			% increase in fines (passing BS 2.36 mm sieve)	% increase in fines (passing BS 2.36 mm sieve)	% increase in surface area
BS 594	Base course 79% stone content			25.0	
BS 594	Base course 59% stone content			14.0	
BS 594	Wearing course 48% stone content			8.3	
Fuller (1907)	Grading curve	22.9	20.0	13.4	33.3
Lees (1970)	Grading method	18.7	13.5	7.5	14.3

than the more open gradings. The results encountered by Ghani in this series of tests prompted him to propose that modifications to the aggregate crushing test and aggregate impact test might be helpful in assessing aggregates susceptible to degradation. In these tests an AGIV (aggregate grading impact value) and an AGCV (aggregate grading crushing value) are determined by substituting the combined aggregate grading for the standard single size aggregate of BS 812. The values calculated are the increase in per cent fines, passing the 2.36 mm sieve, and the per cent increase in total surface area. In these tests the main advantage is that the extent of crushing of the aggregate is studied on the basis of the actual grading to be used in service, from which it also follows that the grading to produce least degradation can be chosen. The aggregate considered in this study was a Millstone Grit and the tests were carried out without a binder. Other work performed both at the University of Birmingham (same series of tests) and in the USA (Shelburne 1940; Moavenzadeh & Goetz 1963) has shown that employing the aggregates within the context of a bituminous mix, while generally reducing the degree of crushing, did not appear to affect the order of merit of the gradings or rock types used. It thus appears that an increasing use of low crushing strength aggregates and of flaky and/or elongate aggregrates is possible provided dense gradings are designed to suit their special characterstics (Lees 1970; Lees & Zakaria 1987).

As in all such cases where lower strength aggregates, either primary or secondary, with no track record are considered for use, a careful programme of field trials should be carried out.

10.4.6. Engineering effects of degradation

The initial effect of degradation of a dry granular material, in service, is therefore likely to be a reduction in the two principal original components of stability, namely rock particle interlock and interparticle surface friction between the original particles. However, densification, due to the smaller fragments produced filling the spaces within the aggregate structure is likely to occur, thus producing additional points of interparticle contact within the structure at which surface friction may be mobilized. In summary, the physical significance of disintegration of an aggregate structure is dependent upon the relative importance of these two changes. Stability will decrease if the effect of the additional number of contact points formed by degradation is less than the effect of reduced interlock and surface friction between the major particles but will increase if the reverse is true.

For example, it is by now generally accepted that in single size unbound or water bound aggregates of large maximum size intended for road bases and sub-bases, some crushing of the aggregate under the roller is desirable because of the greater density and further frictional contacts which result. It is emphasized that in order to be beneficial this process must take place under the roller i.e. during initial compaction. Post-rolling degradation under traffic inevitably leads to a certain degree of rutting due to the further compaction which takes place, independently of whether the final aggregate product has a higher or lower shearing resistance than the original.

The importance of designing dense gradings to reduce particle degradation, particularly where low crushing strength aggregate is employed, has been stressed. However, Thom & Brown (1988) have shown that open gradings at least of a dry material can be stiffer than denser gradings. Dense gradings also tend to become saturated or near-saturated more easily. Transient pore pressures due to traffic loadings can then reduce both stiffness and stability (Brown & Selig 1991). Where aggregates of low initial strength or of suspect long-term strength (because of evident weathering) are required to be used for economic reasons the importance of considering the pavement structure as a whole is also stressed. In such cases it is highly desirable to employ strong, dense and impermeable surfacing materials to distribute the traffic stresses, to protect the unbound aggregate from surface water, and to provide drainage systems which will remain adequate throughout the lifetime of the road.

10.4.7. Correlation between tests and service behaviour

It has been shown (Turner & Wilson 1956; Scott 1955; Collett *et al.* 1962) from investigations of failures of a number of American highways that aggregates which perform adequately under tests with the Deval abrasion machine, will not necessarily prove suitable in pavement construction. The failure of such tests to predict performance lies in their inability to reproduce the degradation pattern that occurs in the pavement, the fines produced in the road tending to be far more plastic and hence more harmful than those produced in conventional laboratory tests.

It appears improbable that the increased plasticity of fines produced in the pavement over those produced in laboratory tests is due to any significant production of clay minerals by chemical weathering during service. The more likely explanation is that softening and solution condition the aggregate in use to further mechanical breakdown and hence to translocation and concentration of already formed clay and associated minerals.

By contrast, normal mechanical tests on aggregates carried out in the laboratory are so accelerated (and usually, though not always, carried out on dry aggregate) that the fines produced are merely ground down particles of the same average chemical composition as the parent aggregate and so show lower plasticity than the predominantly clay fines produced in the field by a softening, mechanical breakdown, solution and concentration process.

Sweet (1948) commented as follows on work performed by Goldbeck (1935). The results from the Los Angeles, Deval and toughness tests were compared with those of a laboratory roller test (simulating the action of a roller in the field). Goldbeck concluded 'In view of the fact that the roller test is really a service test, it is clear that neither the toughness test nor the Deval abrasion test can be relied upon to indicate service behaviour, but on the other hand, the Los Angeles rattler test does agree exceptionally well with the service behaviour'. A further direct comparison of aggregate crushing resistance to the Los Angeles test results was obtained by Shelburne (1940). He determined the amount of degradation produced by 5 and 10 ton rollers on different aggregates and found good agreement between the change in surface area caused by fourteen passes of a 10 ton roller and 100 revolutions in the Los Angeles machine. Although there was considerably more degradation from 500 revolutions in the machine (the standard number in ASTM 131), the relative resistance of the aggregates in the abrasion test remained in accord with their resistance to the roller.

Notwithstanding the good agreement shown in these cases, none of the results relates to the kind of long-term degradation occurring in the field results referred to above. Thus, although it has been shown that good agreement exists between the Los Angeles test and short-term crushing under the roller, somewhat lower correlation may occur between these laboratory tests and longer-term degradation under traffic in wet climates where partially weathered rocks are concerned.

Earland & Pike (1986) have related trafficking trials to the performance of aggregates in a 300 mm shear box (see §10.7.2).

Bullas & West (1991) have related the actual performance of aggregates, albeit in relation to bitumen coating, to TFV and soundness tests. The threshold value of 75 for soundness (BS 812 Pt 121) has been included in the 1991 DTp specification in relation to unbound aggregates (§10.7.2.).

10.5. Resistance to decay

10.5.1. Mechanisms and assessment

A considerable degree of resistance to weathering during the service lifetime is required, including resistance to disintegration with cycles of wetting and drying or freezing and thawing.

Hosking & Tubey (1969) report examples of unsound aggregates from Australia, Basutoland, Fiji, Great Britain, Kenya, Mauritius, South Africa and the USA. All rocks subject to this decomposition in stock piling and/or in use are of basic composition, and all gave satisfactory results in initial routine laboratory strength testing.

Some of the severest cases of failure of roadstone in unbound bases have been associated with physical breakdown of rock already suffering from varying degrees of chemical weathering, e.g. Washington State

(Turner & Wilson 1956; Minor 1959), Virginia (Melville 1948), Oregon (Scott 1955) and Idaho (Day 1962).

The rock types identified in the majority of these studies were black basalts and gravels of Eocene age, although a number of other rock types including other Tertiary sandstones and shales and gravels of Mesozoic age have also been involved. In the failed areas a layer of saturated, high plasticity fines has practically always been found between the surface layers and the underlying base. This slurry, which may be as much as 10 mm deep in severe cases, is formed when aggregate containing secondary minerals degrades into plastic fines under the combined action of water plus movement of rock against rock (attrition) as the pavement is flexed under moving loads. The plastic fines quickly permeate the entire base course. When this happens the stability of the base course is reduced sharply and failure of the pavement structure is inevitable.

Scott (1955), Day (1962), Weinert (1968) and Wylde (1976) all showed that, rather than the primary minerals, it is the secondary minerals formed from the primary minerals under the action of weathering and disintegration on a geological time scale that are the principal causes of distress and failure of granular layers in pavements.

For South African rocks, Weinert (1964) established reasonable agreement between degree of alteration (determined by point count analysis) of mainly ferromagnesian minerals and risk of decomposition. Suspect materials in general showed a greater than 30% degree of alteration.

Irfan & Dearman (1978a), following Mendes et al. (1966), calculated a micropetrographical index I_p from the modal analysis as:

$$I_p = \frac{\% \text{ sound constituents}}{\% \text{ unsound constituents}}$$

for a weathered granite from Cornwall. Sound constituents were the primary minerals such as quartz, plagioclase, potash feldspar, biotite, muscovite and accessory minerals such as zircon and magnetite; unsound constituents were secondary minerals such as sericite, gibbsite, kaolinite (altered feldspars), chlorite, secondary muscovite, iron oxides, together with microcracks and voids resulting chiefly from weathering. The inclusion of microcracks and voids as 'unsound constituents' is novel and may be justifiable here. However, it might lead to a false conclusion of a highly weathered state if applied outside the context of this study e.g. to porous sandstones or vesicular unweathered basalts.

In a companion paper Irfan & Dearman (1978b) have carried out 'laboratory and field determinations of a range of physical and mechanical properties of the various stages of weathering in granite materials. The results correlate with both micropetrographic and microfracture indices, often as a simple linear relationship with a high correlation coefficient'.

Sedimentary rocks employed as aggregates, chiefly the sandstones and limestones, being themselves the product of weathering processes suffer comparatively little from mineral alteration. (Exceptions occur where feldspathic sandstones or arkoses formed in desert type climates are later exposed to wet temperate or tropical conditions.) Sedimentary rocks do, however, suffer to varying degrees from softening and disintegration due to wetting and drying and freezing and thawing. Porosity, pore size distribution and water absorption are the main factors influencing susceptibility to these mechanical weathering effects.

A comprehensive study of the phenomenon of physical and chemical weathering of rock aggregates (and rock used in other forms in civil engineering) during service lifetime has been produced by Fookes et al. (1988).

Under the heading of physical weathering, particular emphasis is laid on crystallization processes such as freeze–thaw and salt weathering and on the volume changes associated with temperature and moisture content variation. Chemical weathering is summarized in Fig. 10.3 (Fookes et al. after Mellon 1985) with emphasis on rock disintegration by solution of some minerals and by the formation of weak secondary minerals which also typically have lower density and hence occupy greater volume than the primary minerals from which they were formed.

A table has been produced by these authors summarizing a large number of reported failures where in-service deterioration has occurred within an engineering time scale. These failures have occurred in countries as far apart as USA, Ethiopia, Australia, New Zealand, Mauritius, South Africa and Great Britain and confirm the observations made earlier in this chapter that the prime factors associated with the failures are (1) the use of igneous (usually basic igneous) rock, and (2) the presence of secondary minerals in such rocks.

Fookes et al. stress, by restatement of the opinion of 'numerous authors (e.g. Weinert 1964, 1968; Wylde 1976, 1977; Fookes 1980; Minty et al. 1980), that it is weathering in geological time which dictates the durability of crushed and uncrushed rock material in engineering time'. To this must be added the significant effects of processing methods (Hosking & Tubey 1969), engineering usage and climatic conditions. With reference to processing, Fookes et al. state 'Shockwave propagation through the rock, generated by blasting, may lead to the development and/or enhancement of microfractures within the material. Though these microfractures can aid later crushing processes, within the larger aggregate size ranges and within riprap, for example, these flaws can be carried into the service life of the material. Crushing processes also have the potential to induce or enhance the development of intragranular, transgranular and grain contact flaws and weaknesses. Screening and washing processes are often set up to maximize removal of dust and soft materials from the good aggregate; these can add to degradation of the good aggregate by wetting and drying, abrasion and impact.'

An example of the effect of deleterious exploitation of these microfractures combined with the effect of moisture on secondary minerals is quoted from the study by Balch (1972) in New Zealand where overrolling and overwatering of chlorite-rich and smectite-rich basalt aggregate resulted in highly mobile slurries in an unbound road pavement.

Both Fookes *et al.* and Sampson (1991) conclude that no single test has proved adequate for assessing durability. Sampson recommends the use of the Durability Mill (Sampson & Roux 1986) and the modified AIV. Fookes *et al.* propose a rock durability indicator, RDI, which is a function of water absorption, saturated surface dry specific gravity together with either magnesium sulphate soundness and point load index (for static conditions) or modified AIV for dynamic conditions.

As stated in Chapter 8, specifications do not normally limit the water absorption value of an aggregate. However, a value below 1% would be considered low and generally associated with a more resistant aggregate, while 1% to 3% would be a typical range. If durability is suspect, petrological examination should be carried out together with tests for water absorption, related where necessary to standard freeze–thaw tests or soundness tests (Chapters 7 and 8).

10.5.2. Discussion

If laboratory tests are correctly to predict behaviour of certain types of already partially weathered rock in wet climates it is necessary that the solution and softening actions are correctly simulated and combined with the mechanical action normal in such tests.

Weinert (1968) has already stressed the importance of climate in assessing the potential risk of weathering of rocks used in road construction in South Africa. Amongst the several meteorological factors which comprise climate, Weinert regards availability of moisture as the most important, and has produced a map of climatic zones based on an analysis of precipitation and evaporation records. Further, Weinert has produced a classification of rock types based upon the percentage of secondary minerals present which is then related to the climatic factor. Thus by comparison of present degree of weathering and the climatic factor Weinert suggested that it would be possible to predict which rocks would be sound and which unsound in practice.

This approach has much to commend it. The importance, however, of recognizing the precise climatic factors which would apply to regions different from South Africa is stressed. Also even for South African

conditions a further factor relating to the potential stress environment and exposure environment of the aggregate would further improve the method. In other words it would appear that many rocks which would be unsuitable if used as unbound aggregates, because of the risk of softening and further weathering, would suffer little or not at all if used in a dense bituminous (or concrete) mix which would provide both an impermeable coating and structural support to the aggregate in question. Further discussion on the engineering properties of aggregates and the relation between tests and service behaviour is contained in Meininger (1978).

Finally, the importance of local, as opposed to regional, climatic conditions is emphasized together with the location of the unbound aggregate in relation to existing hydrological zones e.g. as the latter may vary in cut, fill or level ground in a given locality.

10.6. Effects of water migration

10.6.1. Permeability

The need for good pavement drainage is now well established (Roy 1981; Biczysko 1985; Brown & Selig 1991). Jones & Jones (1989) analysed the permeability required for adequate drainage of different widths and thickness of sub-bases and concluded that a value of around 10^{-3} m/s was needed. Gradings specified to achieve this are shown in Table 10.2. The measurement of permeability is discussed in Appendix A10.1.

10.6.2. Frost heave and thaw weakening

Frost heave and associated thaw weakening is a function of the pavement system so that consideration needs to be given to subgrade properties and to the water table position as well as to the unbound aggregate. Within a given system, frost heave of the aggregate is controlled by both the between particle pores (the size distribution of which is governed by the initial grading, the compaction and the degradation on laying) and the within particle pores which are a function of the parent rock. Thus, knowledge of the grading, saturation moisture content and suction characteristics is a valuable aid in the preliminary assessment of frost susceptibility.

The influence of these and related factors, background to the test and its relation to tests used in other countries have been reviewed by Jones (1987).

10.6.3. Moisture movements and salt damage in road foundations

While it will be generally true that an impermeable

TABLE 10.2. *Specification requirements for sub-bases*

(a) British gradings

Sieve size	Type 1 (1)	Type 2 (1)	Type 1X (2)	803A Somerset (3)
75 mm	100	100	100	100
50 mm	—	—	80–100	
37.5 mm	85–100	85–100	—	85–100
20 mm			40–75	
10 mm	40–70	40–100		40–70
5 mm	25–45	25–85	20–35	25–45
600 μm	8–22	8–45	0–10	5–15
75 μm	0–10	0–10	0–5	0–5

Notes: Gap-graded materials not permitted. (1) DTp 1991a; (2) Biczysko 1985; (3) Roy 1981.

(b) Other requirements in Britain and overseas

	Max Liquid Limit (LL)	Plasticity Index (PI)	Max % Wear (LAA)	Min TFV/kN	Soundness	CBR%	Other requirements (see Key)
Sub-base							
Type 1	—	NP		50	75 (b)	—	A, C, D
Type 2	—	<6	45	50	75 (b)	20–30	B, C, D
Overseas (a)	25	<6(Wet) <12 (Dry)		35	20(c)	40	E

Key
A   Materials shall be crushed (rock, slag or concrete) or well burnt colliery shale.
B   Materials shall be as A above or natural sands and gravels.
C   If within 500 mm of elements containing OPC, sulphate content of 2:1 water aggregate extract BS 1377 Part 3 <1.9 g/litre.
D   If within 450 mm (or 350 if freezing index less than 50 deg C (days) of surface, frost heave in amended BS 812 Pt 124 test (SHW Clause 705) > 15 mm.
E   May be limit on water soluble salt content (e.g. 2%).

Notes
(a) TRRL 1987. Gradings usually within DTp Type 1/2 but grading after compaction may be specified if LAA > 40. Rounded gravels may have to be crushed to give at least one fractured face.
(b) Min MSSV (BS812: Pt 121: 1990) at source (Retest on site if water absorption > 2%. Not applicable to known durable aggregates). (c) Maximum Na_2SO_4 loss.

surfacing is desirable (§10.4.6), an exception occurs in drier climates where evaporation from capillaries has hitherto kept the water table at a low level (Brakey 1970). In such circumstances the provision of an impermeable cover may prevent the normal evaporation and cause a rise in the water table into the higher subgrade and even into the road foundations with possible disastrous consequences. A surfacing of adequate vapour permeability is called for in such cases.

The contrary case of soluble salt damage to surfaced roads has been discussed by Fookes & French (1977). In this case it is the continuous rise of capillary moisture and the precipitation of soluble salts carried to the surface thereby that causes the distress to the pavement structure. To alleviate this situation one of the recommendations made by these authors is to provide an impermeable surfacing layer. It is clearly of great im-

portance to distinguish between these two types of potential failure due to capillary moisture movement since one requires a permeable surfacing and the other an impermeable surfacing. It is also of course possible for the risk of both processes to exist at the same site i.e. for crystallization of salts to occur if capillary rise is allowed to occur and for the water table to rise if capillary rise and evaporation are prevented. In this case, very careful analysis of the conditions is required. One solution may be to risk the latter event i.e. the rise in water table and as recommended by Fookes and French to design the road on the basis of a low CBR value. Attention to roadside drainage conditions will very materially assist in reducing both risks.

A further study by Obika *et al.* (1989) critically examines the recommended limits of salt concentration that have been placed by various authors for materials

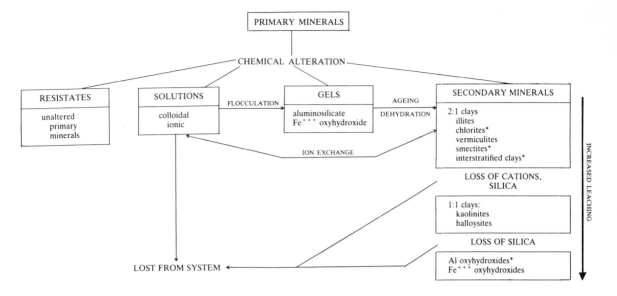

FIG. 10.3. Processes and products of chemical alteration (from Mellon 1985). An asterisk indicates those processes considered to be most applicable to an engineering timescale.

in highway construction. In quoting a case study in Australia (Cole & Lewis 1960), the authors refer to the observed deterioration of compacted base course aggregates in the presence of high salt content (NaCl) ground water. Subsequent investigations by Cole & Lewis showed that materials with less than 0.5 per cent salt were free from salt damage while materials above this salt content showed evidence of degradation. Cole and Lewis recommended a maximum salt limit of 0.2 per cent in order to provide a reasonable safety factor.

Weinert & Clauss (1967) reported an investigation in southern Africa where the problematic salts were present not in the natural groundwater but were a constituent of the aggregate construction material. From these investigations Weinert & Clauss accepted the 0.2 per cent limit for chloride and added a maximum limit of 0.05 per cent for sulphate (with special reference to quartzite wastes from industrial mine processes which have involved the addition of sulphuric acid).

Obika *et al.* also refer to the study by Netterberg (1970) which noted that both Cole & Lewis (salts naturally present in the ground water) and Weinert & Clauss (salts derived from highway construction materials) had based their proposed limits on analyses carried out on materials obtained from the top few centimetres of the base, after upward migration of the salts had occurred, and which were therefore not necessarily related to the initial salt concentration of the bulk material. New limits based solely on South African experience with crusher run materials were proposed by Netterberg (1979) as follows.

Sulphate as SO_3: 0.25% for lime and cement treated materials if cohesive
Total soluble salt: 1.0% non-cohesive materials
Total soluble salt: 0.2% untreated materials
Total soluble salt: 0.25% untreated materials: fines

It is clear from these studies that this is a controversial and complex subject and while the above mentioned limits give a guide as to probable risks and their limitation, it is important that anyone directly involved in dealing with problems in this area should pay special attention to the published literature in order to judge the applicability to the particular local case and should consider the advisability of carrying out further tests to establish the vulnerability of relevant local materials. In particular attention would need to be given to the influence of climatic factors on the risk of salt damage to aggregates, i.e. the relative risk of damage due to a given salt concentration in contrasting climatic environments increases as the ratio of water loss by evaporation to precipitation increases.

10.7. Specifications

National, state and local specifications exist in all continents. They reflect the materials, climate, traffic conditions and economic constraints of the locality. Within the terms of reference of this book, the main emphasis is on UK specifications with a brief mention of specifications in Europe and elsewhere.

10.7.1. Department of Transport (United Kingdom) specification

The Department of Transport Specification for Highway Works 1991 Clause 801 refers to unbound materials for sub-base and road base. However, the only unbound granular materials specified are sub-bases Types 1 and 2 since wet mix bases are not permitted in current designs. Type-1 materials can be crushed rocks, crushed concrete, crushed slag or well burnt non-plastic colliery shale (Table 10.2.). Type 2 includes sands and gravels. Both Type-1 and Type-2 aggregate must have a minimum soaked TFV of 50 kN.

Blast furnace slag must comply to BS 1047: 1983. Steel slag must be weathered and conform to BS 4987: Part 1. Essentially a compacted density of 1700–1900 kg/m^3 is required. (In the previous Department of Transport specification all slags had to conform to BS 1047).

Aggregates other than slag which may be placed within 500 mm of concrete structures or concrete pavements or cement bound paving materials shall have a soluble sulphate content (SO_3) not exceeding 1.9 g/l when tested in accordance with BS 1377: Part 3.

All materials intended for use within 450 mm of the surface shall be non-frost susceptible on the basis of the modified BS 812 Part 124 Test (DTp 1991a Clause 705). However, if the frost index of the site is less than 50 degC days, the required depth is reduced to 350 mm (see Chapter 7).

Some guidance on freezing indices to be expected in the UK is given in Sherwood & Roe (1986).

10.7.2. Discussion of the DTp specification

Type-1 materials are intended to withstand substantial trafficking both during construction and in the permanent structure. Department of Transport (1987a,b) restrict the use of Type-2 materials to roads initially carrying less than 400 commerical vehicles/day although if local experience has shown that Type-2 materials can be used satisfactorily they can be substituted (NG 894, DTp 1991b). Earland & Pike 1986 showed that some Type-2 sand and gravel aggregates could perform at least as well as Type-1 aggregates. Although shear box tests provide some guidance as to the in-service performance, trafficking trials may well be needed to establish the satisfactory performance of proposed sand and gravel sub-bases.

Type-2 sub-grades should be laid at about their optimum moisture content (BS 5835, 1980). It is preferred that road-base is applied before the sub-base is wetted after laying (DTp 1991b).

Restrictions on the fines content and the plasticity of the fines have appeared in several editions of the Department of Transport Specification. The 1963 edition restricted the fines passing 75 μm to a maximum of 2%, this percentage being permitted to rise to 10% if the fines of *this* size were non-plastic. Since 1976 specifications have permitted the 10% maximum of passing 75 μm material to operate provided that the fraction passing the 425 μm sieve is non-plastic for Type-1 materials and with a PI less than 6 for Type-2 materials. This relaxation, recommended by Dunn (1966) and others restored to full compliance, many satisfactory aggregates which had become outside the specification limits.

Dunn showed that the inclusion of a test for plasticity on material passing the 75 μm sieve was unjustified not merely because it had led to the exclusion of many materials but because it could be shown that maximum soaked and unsoaked CBR values often occurred with fines contents of 4 to 9% even when the fines (< 425 μm) were plastic.

The requirement for a minimum ten per cent fines value was introduced in the 1976 specification. Type-2 aggregates may have an additional requirement for a minimum CBR (BS 1377: Pt 4 1990) at equilibrium moisture content. The value required is normally 30% (DTp 1991b) but this may be reduced to 20% if the traffic loading is less than 2msa. If more than 10% of the material is retained on a 20 mm sieve, the whole of the material can be assumed to have a CBR of 20% without test.

Both Type-1 and Type-2 aggregate sources may be required to have a magnesium sulphate soundness value (MSSV) greater than 75 (BS 812 Pt 121) although routine testing at site would only be required if the water absorption was more than 2%. The soundness test is not intended to be mandatory for known durable aggregates.

Note that MSSV is based on the percentage *retained* on the control sieve whereas earlier 'soundness' values were based on the percentage *lost*.

10.7.3. European specifications

In Europe, a CEN Committee has been set up to cover the requirements for aggregates in construction.

Increases in transport costs, shortage of primary aggregates and environmental pressure to use secondary aggregates will be important factors in shaping future specifications.

Papers discussing specifications for unbound aggregates in roads in many European Countries are summarized by Dawson (1989). Most countries specify grading limits, an aggregate crushing test of some sort and an attrition test (usually the Los Angeles Abrasion Test). Limits on fines are given in terms of grading, plasticity index or the sand equivalent test (see Chapter 7). Site testing, for in situ density, CBR or a plate bearing value is common. As in the UK the client, who is usually the specifier, can call on appropriate National Standards.

10.7.4. Non-European specifications

Specifications in use in tropical and sub-tropical countries (TRRL 1977) are briefly summarized in Table 10.2. In the USA, specifications vary widely from state to state (Barksdale 1989). Many states incorporate some of the specifications of the American Association of State Highway and Transportation Officials (AASHTO, 1986) or the ASTM Annual Book of Standards into their own specifications.

References

AMERICAN ASSOCIATION OF STATE HIGHWAY AND TRANSPORTATION OFFICIALS 1986. *Standard Specifications for Transportation Materials and Methods of Sampling.* Washington D.C.

AMERICAN SOCIETY FOR TESTING AND MATERIALS, ASTM C131-89. *Test for resistance to abrasion of coarse aggregate particles by use of the Los Angeles machine.* Section 04.03.

BALCH, I. W. 1972. Supervision and quality control of aggregates and asphaltic concrete construction. *Proceedings New Zealand Road Symposium* 2, 549–561.

BARKSDALE, R. D. 1989. A summary of selected US base course specifications. *In:* JONES, R. H. & DAWSON, A. R. (eds) *Unbound Aggregates for Roads.* Butterworths, London, 298–303.

BICZYSKO, S. J. 1985. Permeable sub-bases in highway construction. *Proceedings of the 2nd Symposium on Unbound Aggregates in Roads* (JONES, R. H. ed.). University of Nottingham, 81–92.

BOND, F. C. 1952. The third theory of communication. *Transactions of the American Institute of Mining Engineering,* 193, 484–494.

BRAKEY, B. 1970. Colorado Division of Highways Denver Colo. Personal communication.

BRITISH AGGREGATE CONSTRUCTION MATERIALS INDUSTRIES (BACMI) 1991. The occurrence and utilisation of mineral and construction wastes. A BACMI response to the report by Arup Economics commissioned by DoE.

BRITISH STANDARDS INSTITUTION *Specification for constituent materials and asphalt mixes. BS 594.*

—— *Testing aggregates: BS 812*
   Pt 110, 1990 *Method for the determination of aggregate crushing value.*
   Pt 111, 1990 *Method for the determination of ten per cent fines value.*
   Pt 112, 1990 *Method for the determination of aggregate impact value.*
   Pt 121, 1989 *Method for the determination of soundness.*
   Pt 124, 1989 *Method for determination of frost heave.*

—— *Air-cooled blast-furnace slag aggregate for use in construction: BS 1047.*

—— *Methods of testing soils for engineering purposes: BS 1377.*
   Part 3 1990 *Chemical and electro-chemical tests*
   Part 4, 1990, *Compaction related tests*

—— Part 1: 1988 *Coated Macadam for roads and other paved areas. Part 1: Specification for constituent materials and mixes: BS 4987.*

—— Part 1: 1980 *Recommendations for testing of aggregates: Part 1: Compactability of graded aggregates: BS 5835.*

—— 1985 (confirmed 1990) *BS Guide to the use of industrial by-products and waste materials in building and civil engineering: BS 6543.*

BROWN, S. E., DAWSON, A. R & BARKSDALE, R. D. 1987. Innovations for pavement foundations. National Workshop on Design and Construction of pavement foundations. Inst of Highways and transportation, 121–141.

BROWN, S. F. & SELIG, E. T. 1991. The design of pavement and track foundations *In* O'REILLY, M. P. & BROWN, S. F. (eds) *Cyclic Loading of Soil.* Blackie, Glasgow, 249–305.

BRUNTON, J. M., ARMITAGE, R. J. & BROWN, S. F. 1992. Seven years experience of pavement evaluation. *7th International Conference on Asphalt Pavements,* Nottingham Vol. 3, p 17–30.

BULLAS, J. C. & WEST, G. 1991. *Specifying Clean Hard and Durable Aggregate for Bitumen Macadam Roadbase.* Res Rep 284 TRRL Crowthorne.

COLE, D. C. H. & LEWIS, J. C. 1960. Progress report on the effect of soluble salts on stability of compacted soils. *Proceedings of the 3rd Australia-New Zealand Conference on Soil Mechanics and Foundation Engineering,* Sydney, August, 29–31.

COLLETT, F. R., WARNOCK, C. C. & HOFFMAN, D. S. 1962. Prevention of degradation of basalt aggregates used in highway base construction. *Highway Res. Board Bull.* 334, 1–7.

CRONEY, D. & CRONEY, P. 1991. *The design and performance of road pavements.* McGraw-Hill.

DAWSON, A. R. 1989. General report: the specification of granular materials for unbound pavement layers. *In:* JONES, R. H. & DAWSON, A. R. (eds) *Unbound Aggregates for Roads.* Butterworths, London, 17–26.

—— & BULLEN, F. 1991. Furnace bottom ash: its engineering properties and its use as sub-base material. *Proceedings of the Institution of Civil Engineers,* 90, 993–1009.

DAY, H. L. 1962. A progress report on studies of degrading basalt aggregate bases. *Highway Research Board Bulletin,* 334, 8–16.

DEPARTMENT OF TRANSPORT 1987a. Departmental Standard HD 14/87 Structural design of new road pavements.

—— 1987b. Advice Note HA35/87. Structural design of new road pavements.

—— 1991a. Specification for highway works (7th Edition), HMSO, London.

—— 1991b. Notes for guidance on the specification for highway works, 7th Edition, HMSO, London.

DUNN, C. S. 1966. The stability of aggregates used in road sub-bases. *Roads and Road Construction,* 44, 77–81.

EARLAND, M. G. & PIKE, D. C. 1986. *Stability of gravel sub-bases.* Research Report 64, TRRL Crowthorne.

FOOKES, P. G. 1980. An introduction to the influence of natural aggregates on the performance and durability of concrete. *Quarterly Journal of Engineering Geology,* 13, 207–29.

—— & FRENCH, W. J. 1977. Soluble salt damage to surfaced roads in the Middle East. *Highway Engineering,* 24, 10–20.

——, GOURLEY, C. S. & OHIKERE, C. 1988. Rock weathering in engineering time. *Quarterly Journal of Engineering Geology,* 21, 33–57.

GAUDIN, A. M. 1926. An investigation of crushing phenomena. *Trans. Am. Inst. Ming Eng.* 73, 253–316.

GHANI, I. 1969. *The Design and Properties of Dense Asphaltic Mixes with Low Crushing Strength Aggregates.* PhD Thesis, University of Birmingham.

GIANNATTASIO, P. & MARCHIONNA, A. 1987. Non-traditional materials—residuary products. Technical Committee Report No. 8 (Flexible Roads), Permanent International Association of Road Congresses, XVIII World Road Congress, Brussels, 73–88.

GOLDBECK, A. T. 1935. Discussion on the Los Angeles Abrasion Machine. *Proceedings of the ASTM*, **35** (2) 530.

HIRT, R. 1976. *L'utilisation de matériaux non normalisés dans la construction routière*. Bau Selection, 5–11.

HOSKING, J. R. & TUBEY, L. W. 1969. *Research on Low-grade and Unsound Aggregates*. Road Research Laboratory Report LR 293. Crowthorne.

IRFAN, T. Y. & DEARMAN, W. R. 1978a. Engineering petrography of a weathered granite. *Quarterly Journal of Engineering Geology*, **11**, 233–244.

—— & —— 1978b. Engineering classification and index properties of a weathered granite. *Bulletin of the International Association of Engineering Geologists*, **17**.

JONES, R. H. 1987. Developments in the British Approach to prevention of frost heave in pavements. *Transportation Research Record 1146*, Transportation Research Board, Washington, 33–40.

—— & JONES, H. A. 1989. Keynote paper:- Granular drainage layers in pavement foundations *In*: JONES, R. H. & DAWSON, A. R. (eds) *Unbound Aggregates in Roads*. Butterworths, London, 55–69.

KICK, F. 1885. *Das Gesetz der proportionalen Widerstande und seine Anwedung*. Leipzig.

KNIGHT, B. H. & KNIGHT, R. G. 1948. *Road Aggregates, their Uses and Testing*. Edward Arnold, London.

LABORATOIRE CENTRAL DES PONTS ET CHAUSSEES, 1973. *Directives pour la realisation des assises de chaussees en graves-laitiers et sable-laitiers*, Paris.

LEES, G. 1970. The rational design of aggregate gradings for dense asphaltic compositions. *Proceedings of the Association of Asphalt Paving Technology*, **39**, 60–97.

—— & KENNEDY, C. K. 1975. Quality, shape and degradation of aggregates. *Quarterly Journal of Engineering Geology*, **8**, 193–209.

—— & ZAKARIA, M. 1987. Degradation and load bearing characteristics of unbound aggregates, *Highways and Transportation*, **7** (34), 32–36.

MARKWICK, A. H. D. & SHERGOLD, F. A. 1945. The aggregate crushing test. *Journal of the Institution of Civil Engineers*, **24** (6), 125–133.

MEININGER, R. C. 1978. *Aggregate Abrasion Resistance, Strength, Toughness and Related Properties*. ASTM Spec. Tech. Publ. 169B.

MELLON, P. 1985. *An Investigation of Altered Basalts used for Road Aggregate in Ethiopia*. PhD Thesis, Hatfield Polytechnic.

MELVILLE, P. L. 1948. Weathering study of some aggregates. *Proc. Highway Res. Board*, **28**.

MENDES, F., AIRE-BARROS, L. & PERE RODRIGUES, F. 1966. The use of modal analysis in the mechanical characterisation of rock masses. *Proceedings of the 1st Congress of the International Society of Rock Mechanics, Lisbon*, **1**, 217–23.

MINOR, C. E. 1959. *Degradation of Mineral Aggregates*. ASTM Special Technical Publication, 277.

MINTY, E. J., PRATT, D. N. & BRETT, A. J. 1980. Predicting the durability of rock. *Proceedings Australian Road Research Board*, **10**, 10–20.

MOAVENZADEH, F. & GOETZ, W. H. 1963. Aggregate degradation in bituminous mixtures. *Highway Research Record*. **24**.

MULHERON, M. & O'MAHONY, M. M. 1990. Properties and performance of recycled aggregates. *Highways & Transportation*, **2** (37), 35–37.

NETTERBERG, F. 1970. Occurrence and testing for deleterious salts in road construction materials with particular refer-

ence to calcretes. *Symposium on Soil and Earth Structures in Arid Climates*, Adelaide, May, 87–92.

—— 1979. Salt damage to roads—interim guide to its diagnosis, prevention and repair. *Proceedings of the 8th Regional Conference for Africa on Soil Mechanics and Foundation Engineering*, Harare, 311–318.

OBIKA, B., FREER-HEWISH, R. J. & FOOKES, P. J. 1989. Soluble salt damage to thin bituminous road and runway surfaces. *Quarterly Journal of Engineering Geology*, **22**, 59–73.

ORGANISATION FOR ECONOMIC CO-OPERATION AND DEVELOPMENT, 1977. *Use of waste materials and by-products in road construction*, Paris, 1–66.

POWELL, W. D., POTTER, J. F., MAYHEW, H. C. & NUNN, M. E. 1984. *The Structural Design of Bituminous Roads*. Transport and Road Research Laboratory Report 1132.

RAMSAY, D. M. 1965. Factors influencing Aggregate Impact Value in rock aggregate. *Quarry Managers Journal*.

RITTINGER, P. 1967. Lehrbuch der Aufbereitingskunde. Berlin.

ROY, M. 1981. The sub-surface drainage of road pavements. *Proceedings of a Symposium on Unbound Aggregates in Roads*. Department of Civil Engineering, University of Nottingham, 79–90.

SAMPSON, L. R. 1991. Aggregate durability: recommended tests and specification for road base course. *In*: BLIGHT *et al.* (eds) *Geotechnics in the African Environment*. Balkema, Rotterdam, 197–204.

—— & ROUX, P. L. 1986. *The Durability mill test for the assessment of unstabilised aggregates*. Res. Rep. RP31 DRTT CSIR Pretoria.

SCOTT, L. E. 1955. Secondary minerals in rock as a cause of pavement and base failure. *Proceedings of the Highway Research Board*, **34**, 412–17.

SHELBURNE, T. E. 1940. Crushing resistance of surface treatment aggregates. *Purdue University Engineering Exp. Stn.*, **24** (5), 7–67.

SHERGOLD, F. A. & HOSKING, J. R. 1963. Investigation of test procedures for argillaceous and gritting rocks in relation to breakdown under traffic. *Roads and Road Construction*, **41** (492) 376–378.

SHERWOOD, P. T. & ROE, P. G. 1986. *Winter Air Temperatures in Relation to Frost Damage on Roads*. Res. Rep. 45, TRRL, Crowthorne, 15 pp.

SUSS, G. H. 1989. Natural and waste material—a chance for competition? *In*: JONES, R. H. & DAWSON, A. R. (eds) *Unbound Aggregates in Roads*. Butterworths, London, 219–227.

SWEERE, G. T. H. 1991. Re-use of waste in road construction. *IRF Reg. Conf. for Europe*. Roads between East and West Europe after 1992.

SWEET, H. S. 1948. Physical and chemical tests of mineral aggregates and their significance. *ASTM Special Technical Publication 83*, 49–73.

THOM, N. H. & BROWN, S. F. 1988. The effect of grading and density on the mechanical properties of a crushed dolomitic limestone. *Proceedings of the Australian Road Research Board*, **14** (7), 94–100.

TRANSPORT AND ROAD RESEARCH LABORATORY 1977. *Guide to the Structural Design of Bitumen Surfaced Roads in Tropical and Sub-tropical Countries*. Rd Note 31 HMSO, London.

TURNER, R. S. & WILSON, J. D. 1956. Degradation study of some Washington aggregates. *Washington State Institute of Technology Bulletin*, **232**.

VERHASSELT, A. & CHOQUET, F. 1989. Steel slags as unbound aggregate in road construction: problems and recommendations *In*: JONES, R. H. & DAWSON, A. R. (eds) *Unbound*

Aggregates for Roads. Butterworths, London, 204–211.
WEINERT, H. H. 1964. Basic igneous rocks in road foundations, NIRR. South Africa Report 218 (681), 1–47.
—— 1968. Engineering petrology for roads in South Africa. *Engineering Geology*, **2(b)**, 363–395.
—— & CLAUSS, M. A. 1967. Soluble salts in road foundations. *Proceedings of the 4th Regional Conference for Africa on Soil Mechanics and Foundation Engineering*, Capetown, 213–218.
WHITBREAD, M., MARSAY, A. & TUNNELL, C. (Arup Economics) 1991. *Occurrence and utilisation of mineral and construction wastes.* HMSO, London.
WYLDE, L. J. 1976. *Degradation of road aggregates.* Australian Road Research, **6** (1), 22–29.
—— 1977. An investigation of the basic crushed rock materials used for the Sydney University Test Track experiments of 1976. *Australian Road Research Board, Internal Report AIR*, 172–174.
YASHIMA, S., MOROHASHI, S., AWANO, O. & KAUDA, Y. 1970. (Chem. Eng. Japan). 34. English Abst. Particulate Matter.

General references

JONES, R. H. & DAWSON, A. R. (eds) *Unbound Aggregates in Roads* (Proc. UNBAR3) Butterworths, London.
ORGANISATION FOR ECONOMIC CO-OPERATION AND DEVELOPMENT, 1981. *Utilisation des granulats marginaux en construction routière, Paris.*

Appendix A10.1.
Horizontal permeability of drainage layers

A10.1.1.   Direct measurement

The horizontal permeability test recently introduced by the Department of Transport (DTp 1990) incorporates modifications and the method of interpretation developed by Jones & Jones (1989). Essentially the apparatus consists of a galvanized steel box which can accommodate a specimen 300 mm square and 900 mm long (Fig. A10.1). The box is designed to accommodate Type-1 sub-base gradings of top size less than 37.5 m. Specimens are compacted by vibrating hammer. After compaction, a layer of non-intercellular neoprene is placed on top of the specimen before the lid is tightened down to seal the upper boundary of the specimen. Every effort is made to flush the remaining air from the specimen.

Hydraulic gradients are established by adjustment of the weirs in the constant head devices. Smaller hydraulic gradients are achieved by jacking up one end of the box. The head loss is recorded by manometer tubes at each end. If a quantity of water Q is collected in a time t the coefficient of horizontal permeability, k_h, is calculated from

$$k_h = Q/Ai$$

where i is the hydraulic gradient (i.e. head loss/distance) and A is the cross sectional area. Typical results are shown in Fig. A10.2. It should be noted that Darcy's law is only valid at very low hydraulic gradients with this type of material.

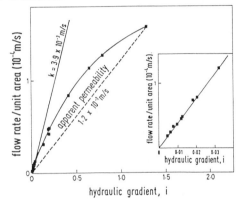

FIG. A10.2. Typical results from the horizontal permeameter on Type-1 granular material sized less than 37.5 mm (after Jones & Jones 1989).

A10.1.2.   Empirical estimates

Many empirical methods exist for the estimation of permeability, some also taking into account void ratio (see, for example, Loudon 1952; Cedegren 1974; Moulton 1980; Powers 1981; NAVFAC 1982).

The most popular is the Hazen formula

$$k = 0.01 \, d^2_{10} \text{ m/s}$$

where d_{10} is the effective size (mm).

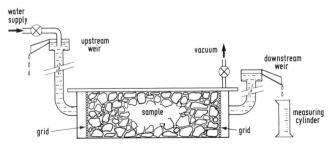

FIG. A10.1. The horizontal permeameter (after Jones & Jones 1989).

This formula was originally devised for sands with $0.1 < d_{10} < 3$.

A recent study (Abbott 1990) showed that a better estimate for Type-1 materials was obtained with the equation proposed by Sherard *et al.* (1984), namely

$$k = 0.0035d_{15}{}^2.$$

Not the least of the problems with these formulae is estimating d_{10} or d_{15} accurately, since grading curves tend to be nearly horizontal in this range.

References

ABBOTT, H. A. 1990. *Permeability and Suction Characteristics of Compacted Unbounded Aggregates*. PhD Thesis, University of Nottingham.

CEDEGREN, H. 1974. *Drainage of Highway and Airfield Pavements*. Wiley, Chichester.

DEPARTMENT OF TRANSPORT 1990. *A Permeameter for Road Drainage Layers*. Advice Note HA 41/90.

JONES, H. A. & JONES, R. H. 1989. Horizontal permeability of compacted aggregates. *In*: JONES, R. H. & DAWSON, A. R. (eds) *Unbound Aggregates in Roads*. Butterworths, London, 70–77.

LOUDON, A. G. 1952. The composition of permeability from simple soil tests. *Géotechnique*, **3**, 165–183.

MOULTON, L. K. 1980. *Highway Sub Drainage Design*. US Dept of Transport Report FHWA-TS-80-224.

NAVFAC (Naval Facilities Engineering Command) 1982. DM-7.1, *Design Manual, Soil Mechanics*, US Department of Navy.

POWERS, J. P. 1981. *Construction Dewatering—a Guide to Theory and Practice*. Wiley, New York.

SHERARD, J. L., DUNNIGAN, L. P. & TALBOT, J. A. 1984. Basic properties of sand and gravel filters. *Journal of the Geotechnical Division* ASCE 110, GT6, 684–700 & GT12, 1467–1472.

11. Aggregates in bituminous bound construction materials

11.1. Introduction

Both natural and artificial aggregates of coarse and fine sizes are employed in bituminous mixtures for highway and airfield pavements (Fig. 10.1) and in hydraulic and building applications (The Shell Bitumen Handbook 1990).

The emphasis in this chapter is upon the use of bituminous materials in pavement construction. The same factors affecting mix density, strength, stiffness and adhesion, apply in hydraulic applications as in pavement construction. However, in the former, greater attention is paid to such properties as permeability (which may be required to be high or low depending on the particular application), resistance to flow on steep slopes and, where relevant, to wave impact (Hills & McAughtry, 1986). Polishing resistance characteristics of aggregates clearly have no importance in hydraulic applications but, in building construction, mastic asphalts used in bridge decks and in decks and ramps of multi-storey car parks retain a high skid resistance requirement. Chief among the requirements of mastic asphalt for bridge decks, roofing and car parks is impermeability in order to protect the underlying concrete construction from water and frost attack and from the effect of de-icing salts and other chemicals (Mastic Asphalt Conferences 1989). The major factor in these applications is the mix design, involving use of a high bitumen content in accord with the high content of fine aggregate and filler in the aggregate grading.

It should be noted that, at the time of going to press, several relevant developments were taking place with respect to the specification of aggregates for bituminous mixes but none was concluded. European standards (EN) were under discussion by CEN Committees namely: CEN TC 154 SC3 'Aggregates for Bituminous Mixtures', CEN TC 227 WG1 'Bituminous Mixtures' and CEN TC 227 WG2 'Surface dressing etc.' The Department of Transport was also due to revise Technical Memorandum H16/76 but no publication date was available.

11.2. Petrological types of aggregate used in bituminous compositions

A wide range of rocks of igneous, sedimentary and metamorphic origins and a number of artificial aggregates are used in bituminous mixes. The general requirement is for rocks which will be durable (i.e. resistant to abrasive wear), strong (i.e. resistant to slow crushing loads and to rapid impact loads) and where appropriate, i.e. in wearing course and surface dressing applications, resistant to the polishing action of traffic.

A further property required especially for aggregates for surface dressing and for macadam and asphalt-type mixes in pavement and hydraulic applications is that they should show good adhesion with bituminous binders.

Some early works on the subject of roadstone aggregates such as that by B. H. and R. G. Knight (1935) carefully described the desirable qualities of rocks and proceeded to relate mineralogical and textural details to strength (and to a slight extent to polishing characteristics). Considerable emphasis was laid in such works on defining the best type of rock for a particular purpose. While such search for exactness is normally to be commended in engineering, the requirement for the best economic use to be made of available raw materials has in current practice proved to be of far greater significance. Both the high costs of haulage of aggregates and the depletion of some natural resources are of importance in this respect. In other words, the present problem is not so much how to identify the best type of rock for a certain usage but to decide what is the boundary between acceptable and non-acceptable (a boundary which must be recognized as a shifting boundary as technology changes) and how best to use what is acceptable. The latter will involve the evolution and application of improved design and control methods for bituminous mixes in order to enable satisfactory use of the most economically available suitable aggregates.

11.3. Desirable properties of aggregates for bituminous mixes

It is generally recognized (Hosking 1970; Hartley 1974; Lees & Kennedy 1975) that the main qualities required from a roadstone to be used in pavement surfacing materials are:

(i) Toughness (a) resistance to slow crushing, assessed by the aggregate crushing test and ten per cent fines

: Chapter 7 for discussion and detailed refer-
1 all tests in this section, except for tests on
on (Appendix A11)).

istance to rapid loading, assessed by the aggregate impact test, modified aggregate impact test and
the Los Angeles test.

(ii) Hardness: resistance to abrasion/attrition—
assessed by the Deval test, aggregate abrasion test
and, to a limited extent, by the Los Angeles test.

(iii) Resistance to polishing (for wearing course materials and surface dressings)—assessed by the accelerated polishing test.

(iv) Resistance to stripping (ability to maintain adhesion
to any bituminous binder with which the aggregate is
used)—assessed by various tests described by Mathews (1958), TRRL (1962), the Property Services
Agency (1979) and in the standards of various other
national and regional authorities. (See Chapter 7 for
descriptions of these tests.)

(v) Resistance to weathering effects in the pavement
(e.g. resistance to frost action, swelling and softening by water)—assessed by determination of water
absorption, sodium sulphate/magnesium sulphate
soundness tests.

(vi) Ability to contribute to strength and stiffness of
total mix by intrinsic aggregate strength and shape
properties.

11.4. Influence of aggregate petrography on engineering properties

11.4.1. Crushing strength

Hartley (1974) provided a useful summary of the main
petrographical factors affecting the toughness or crushing
strength of aggregates. Referring to the engineering classification for intact rock material devised by Deere & Miller
(1966) he states:

"Of the rocks tested few have strengths in excess of
$225 \, MN/m^2$ and those which do are almost entirely non-
porous rocks possessing an interlocking texture, i.e.
quartzites, dolerites and dense basalts. The rocks classified as of high strength ($110-210 \, MN/m^2$) include the majority of the igneous rocks, the stronger metamorphic
rocks, well cemented sandstones and indurated shales and
about 40 per cent of the limestones and dolomites tested.
The medium strength range includes poorly bonded porous rocks and foliated rocks. Rocks in the low and very
low strength ranges are generally very porous, weakly
bonded sedimentary rocks, highly foliated igneous and
metamorphic rocks or chemically altered rocks of any
origin".

11.4.1.1.   Igneous rocks. The main factors causing a
reduction in the strength of igneous rocks are thus an
increase in porosity, grain size and the proportion of soft
minerals, and the development of flow structure. Chemical alteration in general increases the proportion of soft
minerals e.g. clays and allied minerals (with the exception
of epidotization) and peripheral alteration may result in
weakening of the intergranular bonding. Vesicular texture decreases the strength, while the effect of amygdales
depends upon the nature of the infilling material.

11.4.1.2.   Sedimentary rocks. With sedimentary rocks,
the interlocking fabric and mineralogy of limestones and
dolomites appear to be responsible for their relatively
high strength and Young's modulus. The main factors
influencing the strength of sandstones are the intergranular bonding and porosity.

In both calcareous and arenaceous rocks the tendency
is for cementation to occur with time and hence for
strength to increase with age. In the arenaceous rocks the
nature of the cementing agent is important, with calcareous and ferruginous sandstones and gritstones being
typically of lower strength than quartzites. Chemical
alteration effects, though much less common due to the
secondary nature of the sedimentary rocks are, when they
occur e.g. in the weathering of the feldspars of a feldspathic sandstone or arkose, similar to the effects encountered in igneous and metamorphic rocks. Anisotropy
related to the fabric of the sediment results in variation of
the modulus ratio according to whether the load axis is
placed perpendicular or parallel to the plane of the laminations.

11.4.1.3.   Metamorphic rocks. The principal factors
causing a reduction in the strength of metamorphic rocks
are increase in grain size, porosity, proportion of soft
minerals and, in particular, an increase in schistosity or
foliation. The extent of the intergranular bond is also
highly important. The effect of chemical alteration is similar to that noted for igneous and sedimentary rocks.

Fundamental strength tests such as that described
above are not generally used in the UK as a method of
assessing the potential of roadstone aggregates due to
their poor reproducibility (Shergold 1948). The effects of
variability of individually prepared specimens have been
reduced by the introduction of aggregate tests using specimens composed of a number of pieces of the aggregate.
Even so the petrographical characteristics listed above
together with the particle shape do influence the behaviour of the individual aggregate particles (Dhir *et al.*
1971).

11.4.1.4.   Artificial aggregates. Industrial by-products
(blastfurnace slags, steel slags, lead–zinc slags) and industrial and municipal wastes (fly ash, ash, clinker, demolition wastes) are all reported in use as aggregates for
bituminous courses in pavement construction. Where
used, the angularity of crushed coarse and fine aggregates
ensure good pavement stability (OECD 1977).

For quality control, slags are generally required to meet the same specification requirements as traditional materials with, in addition, special requirements for steel slag (mostly LD [oxygen converter] slag). In the latter case it is necessary to ensure that any free lime and magnesia are slaked, otherwise disruption can occur. In order to avoid this disruption and the risk of swelling and/or 'sweating' (i.e. the throwing off of the bitumen coating) when steel slags are used in bituminous mixes, various countries advise using the slags only after a period of open-air ageing, which may last from a few months to about a year. For example, Belgium specifies a period of nine months, Japan specifies three months (Giannattasio & Marchionna 1987).

Blastfurnace slag is rejected for use in Sweden, Finland and Austria because of reported low strength. In Hungary it is permitted in road bases only, while in the United Kingdom and Germany it is in use in wearing course compositions even on heavily trafficked roads. Variations in density and binder absorption are catered for by increase in binder content as appropriate and by volumetric approach to mix design (Herbst *et al.* 1983).

Steel slag is in general of higher density, higher strength and higher abrasion resistance than blastfurnace slag but with a lower (though for some use categories still adequate) polishing resistance (§11.4.2.4 and §11.4.3.3). Typical AIV for steel slags would be between 12 and 17 while for blastfurnace slags typical values would be in the region of 23 to 30.

11.4.2. Resistance to abrasion

Abrasion of road surfacing aggregate takes place by the action of tyres carrying detritus. This detritus is in part material worn off the road surface and in part naturally derived sand and clay materials and artificial debris carried or blown onto the road (Maclean & Shergold 1958).

Hartley (1974) considers the important petrographical characteristics are: the degree of hardness and proportion of hard minerals, the proportion, orientation and distribution of cleaved minerals, the grain size, the nature of the intergranular bond and the degree of liability to chemical alteration of the mineral content.

11.4.2.1. Igneous rocks. Of the fresh igneous rocks, those containing a high free silica content tend to resist abrasion better than the basic rocks which have a high ferromagnesian content. This is due to the hardness and lack of cleavage of the quartz in the former. Chemical decomposition generally results in increased abrasion, particularly if a high degree of peripheral alteration exists since this can destroy the intergranular bond and allow the harder cores to be plucked from the rock surface. Vesicular texture generally reduces the resistance to abrasion while the nature of the mineral infilling determines the effect of amygdales.

11.4.2.2. Sedimentary rocks. Among the sedimentary rocks, the low hardness and cleavage facility of the minerals contained in the younger and more porous limestones and dolomites renders them liable to rapid wear while the abrasion resistance of siliceous rocks is almost entirely dependent upon the nature of the intergranular bond. Thus flint and quartzite are highly resistant whilst poorly cemented ferruginous and calcareous sandstones are soon abraded due to plucking of the grains. Mixed mineral sedimentary rocks such as greywacke tend to have poor abrasion resistance although this is not always the case, especially with Palaeozoic examples.

11.4.2.3. Metamorphic rocks. Of the metamorphic rock used in road surfacing, gneisses tend to behave similarly to igneous rocks of the same mineralogy while hornfels and quartzites have a high abrasion resistance due to their hard mineral content and dense interlocking texture.

11.4.2.4. Artificial aggregates. As stated above, steel slags in general exhibit a higher abrasion resistance than blastfurnace slags (typically with AAV in the region of 2 to 5, compared with AAV in the region of 9 to 15 for blastfurnace slags).

11.4.3. Resistance to polishing

The importance of aggregate microtexture in tyre/road friction has been recognized since research by Knill (1960) drew attention to the significance of detailed aggregate petrology in promoting or opposing development of a state of polish on particle surfaces. Rocks which contained minerals of sufficiently different hardness or which were friable, i.e. consisted of grains rather insecurely cemented together, were found to give high polishing resistance.

In highway or airfield pavements the state of polish attained results from the opposing effects of traffic (tending to increase the state of polish) and of weathering where frost action, wetting and drying and temperature changes all tend to remove or reduce the polished state (Lees 1978). While most clearly demonstrated in the case of carbonate rocks, Szatkowski & Hosking (1972) have shown that weathering effects are still significant with other rock types. Figure 11.1 for example shows the increase in skid resistance on the Colnbrook by-pass Middlesex, which accompanied a reduction in traffic intensity (and hence a relative increase in the weathering effect) following the diversion of traffic to a newly constructed alternative route.

11.4.3.1. Igneous and metamorphic rocks. Rocks of these categories which show a moderate degree of decomposition by weathering effects give higher PSV than fresh unweathered rocks, due to the lower hardness of the secondary minerals (kaolinite, chlorite, serpentine, seri-

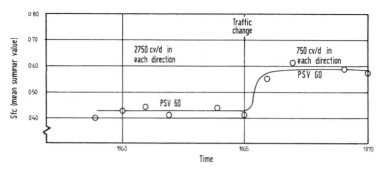

FIG. 11.1. The increase in the level of skidding resistance recorded on Trunk Road A4, Colnbrook by-pass, when traffic decreased due to the opening of a motorway (Szatkowski & Hosking 1972).

cite etc.) compared with the primary minerals (quartz and unaltered feldspar, augite, hornblende etc.). Alteration to epidote is observed to be an exception to the above since the hardness of epidote is of the same order as that of the primary minerals. Again, because of their differential hardness, metallic ore inclusions disseminated through the rock have been found to lead to an increase in polish resistance, as is also the case with fractured grains of medium to large size. Grain size in general appears to have only a slight effect on polish resistance, a coarser grain size leading to a small increase in PSV. Further, as reported by Hartley (1974) a well dispersed system of vesicles generally increases the resistance to polishing. The effect of amygdales depends upon their size and distribution throughout the stone and the relative hardness of the secondary infilling and the enclosing original minerals.

Of the metamorphic rocks only gneisses, hornfels and metaquartzites are generally considered as likely aggregates for road surfacing. Hartley observed that orthogneisses behave in a similar manner to the equivalent igneous rock whilst the hornfels and quartzites tend to take a high polish since they generally have a fine-grained interlocking texture and are either monomineralic or composed of uniformly relatively hard minerals (>5 on Moh's scale).

11.4.3.2. Sedimentary rocks. (i) Sandstones. Among the sedimentary rocks, clastic sandstones of variable mineral content and certain sedimentary quartzites tend to be polish resistant. In describing the properties of gritstones, Hawkes & Hosking (1972) demonstrated the relationships between petrography, polishing resistance and abrasion resistance, amplifying the explanations of Knill (1960) and others that the retension of a rough nonpolished texture in this category of rocks is due primarily to the dislodgement of weakly cemented grains before they can attain a high state of polish. It follows that there is in general an inverse relationship between polishing resistance and abrasion resistance.

In contrast to the somewhat more friable clastic sedimentary rocks mentioned above, some of the well cemented quartzites have lower PSV. The crypto-crystalline flints and cherts and opaline gravels typically assume a high degree of polish, due to their low porosity and uniform hardness.

(ii) Limestones. In a study of the carbonate rocks Shupe & Lounsbury (1959) and Gray & Renninger (1963, 1965) demonstrated that a degree of impurity, as measured by the insoluble residue, significantly improves the polishing resistance. While this improvement correlated well with an increase in insoluble residue (consisting chiefly of quartz sand grains, mica and clay mineral matter) Gray and Renninger found that an even better correlation existed if the insolubles measured were restricted to those of sand size, i.e. coarser than 0.5 mm. This restriction eliminates from consideration the clay and silt size mineral matter whose hardness would differ little from the carbonate matrix. Thus, attention is concentrated on the difference in hardness between quartz (7 on Moh's scale) and calcite and dolomite (3 and 3.5–4 respectively on Moh's scale). These authors found in addition that sand-size mica flakes (with lower hardness than the carbonate minerals) also led to high skid resistance i.e. the difference in mineral hardness operated to aid resistance to polishing whether the insoluble residue was harder or softer than the carbonate matrix.

Hosking (1970) confirmed these findings with respect to UK carbonate rocks (Fig. 11.2). Differential solubility (e.g. of fossil inclusions, patches of coarsely crystalline calcite) has been shown to have considerable effect on the pendulum skid resistance value (SRV) of carbonate rocks subjected (a) to cycles of alternate wetting and drying and (b) to natural weathering cycles (Williams & Lees 1970). These treatments converted (in the absence of any trafficking effect) a highly polished state to a roughened state (Fig. 11.3) increasing the skid resistance value (SRV) from 45 (the value obtained at the conclusion of the accelerated polishing test) to 75 (after weathering).

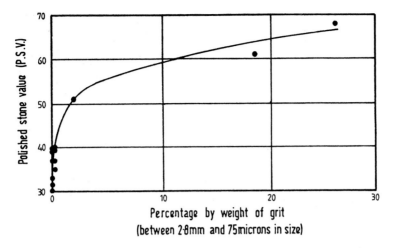

FIG. 11.2. The relation between the polished-stone value and percentage grit in samples from 19 limestone quarries (Hosking 1970).

11.4.3.3. Artificial aggregates. In addition to those artificial materials described above which are industrial by-products or wastes there is, in the field of bituminous bound aggregates, a group of products specifically manufactured to meet the particular engineering needs of skid resistance and/or light reflection. These include calcined bauxite, calcined flint, ballotini and Synopal amongst others.

(a) Industrial by-products. It has been noted above that in general steel slags have a lower polishing resistance than blastfurnace slags. The superiority of the latter is principally due to their higher vesicularity which leads to higher angularity on crushing and to the possession of pressure-relieving internal drainage channels (Hosking 1973).

Blastfurnace slags typically yield polished stone values in the region of 59 to 64, while values in the region of 48 to 54 are typical for steel slags (although it is recorded that in-service skid resistance is frequently higher than would be predicted from laboratory values). These lower values for steel slags may in any event be considered adequate for certain 'less difficult' site categories with lower risk rating and traffic intensity.

A road trial of a bituminous wearing course including lead–zinc slag aggregate carried out in Bristol, England, revealed good wearing properties but only moderate skid resistance (Gutt *et al.* 1974).

(b) Special products. The principal reasons for the development of special artificial aggregates have been to provide either (i) superior polishing resistance in the context of high skidding risk sites (e.g. calcined bauxite in the extremely successful bitumen extended epoxy resin surface treatments such as Shellgrip and similar proprietary products) (Hatherly & Young 1977), or (ii) enhanced light reflecting properties for specialized use, e.g. motor-

way hard shoulders (calcined flint), road marking materials (ballotini) or for general use (e.g. Synopal which has been especially favoured in Denmark to increase the light reflecting properties of bituminous surfacings, in spite of its established poor polishing resistance (Hosking & Tubey 1972)). The use of Synopal for its light reflecting properties may be compared with the experimental use of arclyt, a natural monomineralic anorthosite plagioclase rock from Norway, for similar purposes in Northern Ireland and elsewhere.

In addition to the above materials which have reached various levels of commercial application, Tubey & Hosking (1972) have described a variety of other types of synthetic aggregates some of which, although not currently commercially produced, might have potential in favourable economic circumstances.

11.4.4. Resistance to stripping

Adhesion failure implies a breakdown of the bonding forces between a stone aggregate and its coating of bituminous binder, leading to a physical separation. It is not, however, invariably followed by mechanical failure of the road in which the adhesion failure occurs (Cawsey & Raymond-Williams 1990).

Mechanical failure by fretting and subsequent ravelling of the surface is one possible consequence of adhesion failure, but mechanical failure does not invariably follow adhesion failure if the stripping, though permanent, occurs at a low level in the construction and the degree of mechanical interlock of the stone particles is sufficient to resist traffic stresses. In other words stripping which occurs in surface dressings and coated macadam wearing course is very likely to result in failure of that course, but with stripping or detachment occurring in coated maca-

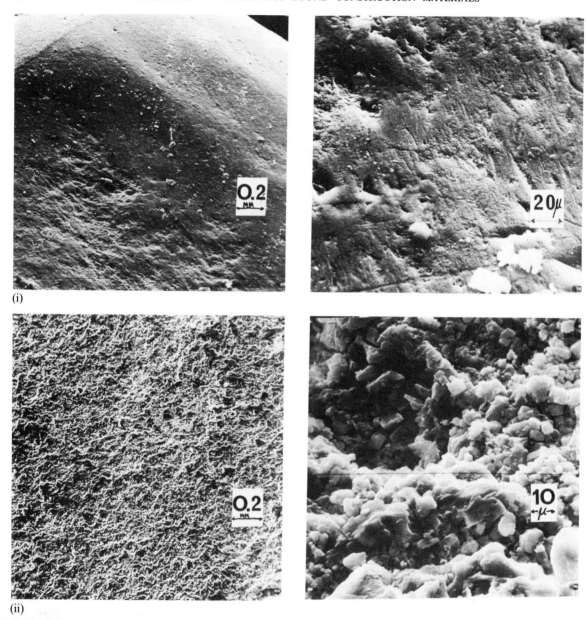

(i)

(ii)

FIG. 11.3. Scanning electron micrographs to show effect on microtexture of differential solubility of mineral components of carbonate rock (Carboniferous Limestone). (i) After 6 hours standard polishing on the accelerated polishing machine (BS 812): wet skid resistance value = 47. (ii) After subsequence natural weathering for 1 year (without traffic): wet skid resistance value = 75.

dam base course, there may be no failure where the mechanical strength remains high enough to resist the stresses imposed. Since stripping is a phenomenon associated with the presence of water it follows that dense asphalts of low void content are practically immune and that the performance of aggregates in stripping tests becomes largely irrelevant in such usage.

11.4.4.1. Influence of aggregate petrography. Hallberg (1950, 1958) observed that, although statistically basic rocks have shown up better in adhesion quality than acid rocks, some pure quartzites had exhibited good adhesion in his experiments using the Swedish Road Research Institute Adhesion Meter. He concluded that silica percentage did not appear to be the sole criterion. Two samples of pure feldspar (one microline, the other orthoclase) gave low values of adhesion tension and Hallberg suggested this might be due to the release of sodium (Na) and potassium (K) and possibly aluminium (Al) ions from the mineral surface and the consequent formation of hydrox-

TABLE 11.1. *Influence of mineral composition on detachment (Hughes et al. 1960)*

Classification (BS 812)	Composition of mineral	State of adhesion after immersion in water for 1 week
Type 1 Granite group	Mainly quartz and feldspar with some biotite, mica and hornblende inclusions. Traces of chlorite.	Bitumen films readily detached from quartz and feldspar inclusions, but less readily from the isolated dark brown and green components.
Type 6 Gritstone Group	Large, well-defined feldspar inclusions in a heterogeneous mixture of iron-magnesium silicates.	Bitumen film could be detached from the large feldspar inclusions but not from the green ferro-magnesium base.
Type 2 Basalt Group	Fairly fine grained igneous rock containing feldspar, hornblende, augite, olivine, and analcite.	Bitumen film could be detached from feldspar inclusions but not from the darker green regions.
Type 3 Gabbro Group	Hornblende picrite: an ultrabasic rock containing a high proportion of olivine.	No detachment could be detected from any part of the section.

TABLE 11.2. *Grading limits, specified size and maximum flakiness index for surface dressing aggregates*

BS test sieve	Nominal size of aggregates			
	20 mm	14 mm	10 mm	6 mm
(a) Grading limits. Percentage by mass passing BS test sieve				
28 mm	100	—	—	—
20 mm	85–100	100	—	—
14 mm	0–35	85–100	100	—
10 mm	0–7	0–35	85–100	100
6.3 mm	—	0–7	0–35	85–100
5 mm	—	—	0–10	—
3.35 mm	—	—	—	0–35
2.36 mm	0–2	0–2	0–2	0–10
600 μm	—	—	—	0–2
75 μm	0–1	0–1	0–1	0–1
(b) Specified size. Minimum percentage by mass retained on BS test sieve (see clause 3)				
	65	65	65	65
(c) Maximum flakiness index				
	25	25	25	—

ides adjacent to that surface. These molecules in the water would have the effect of lowering the interfacial tension and hence also the adhesion tension. It is suggested, therefore, that the comparatively poor performance of acid rocks may be not only related to the high silica content but also to the formation of hydroxides of sodium, potassium and aluminium in the aqueous medium adjacent to the mineral surface. Hallberg further noted in a comprehensive series of tests that adhesion to the basic rock (marble) was in most cases better than to the acid rock (pegmatite).

A convincing example of the general superiority in adhesion of the more basic types of rock and of the influence of detailed mineralogy has been presented by Hughes *et al.* (1960) who showed (Table 11.1) that a detached state existed frequently on quartzo-feldspathic minerals but rarely or not at all on ferro-magnesian minerals.

In regard to the adhesion characteristics of slags the vesicular nature of blastfurnace slags leads to a mechanical key with the bituminous binder. In addition, in both blastfurnace and steel slags, the prevailing chemical/mineralogical composition of calcium and magnesium silicates and alumino-silicates and the occasional presence of iron oxide inclusions, all lead to a favourable tendency towards good adhesion qualities, as in the case of basic igneous and metamorphic rocks and limestones. However, some steel slags are produced which are glassy in composition and smooth in texture. Such slags tend to show poor adhesion to bitumen, similar to that exhibited by glassy igneous rocks and quartz.

Apart from the petrological nature of the aggregate, its cleanliness is also an important factor. Dust inhibits adhesion and, in the case of aggregate used for surface dressing, the current standard (BS 63: 1987) limits the amount

TABLE 11.3 (a). *Concentrations of a surfactant required with various aggregates to reduce stripping to an acceptable level in a full-scale experiment with bitumen macadam (Lee 1958)*

| Aggregate | Concentration of agent required to give satisfactory results (i.e. not > 2% stripping) | | | | Results with 10 per cent of road tar in bitumen* |
	Agent A (amine)	Agent B (amine)	Agent C (amine)	Agent D (Quaternary ammonium comp)	
Group 1 Flint gravel	No satisfactory results obtained				
Quartzite					
Group 2 Granite A	0.5	1.0	1.0	0.56	NS
Porphyry A	0.5	1.0	0.75	0.56	NS
Porphyry B	0.5	1.0	0.75	0.56	
Porphyry C	0.25	1.0	0.5	0.42	NS
Basalt A	0.5	1.0	0.5	0.56	S
Basalt B	0.75	1.0	0.75	0.56	S
Group 3 Gritstone A	0.25	1.0	0.5	0.28	
Gritstone B	0.25	1.0	0.5	0.28	
Hornfels A	0.25	0.5	0.5	0.28	S
Granite B	0.25	0.5	0.5	0.28	S
Basalt C	0.25	1.0	0.5	0.28	S
Group 4 Slag A	Performed satisfactorily without agents				
Slag B					
Basalt D					
Limestone A					
Limestone B					

* NS = Not Satisfactory, S = Satisfactory

TABLE 11.3 (b). *Percentage of agent required for good adhesion at 20°C*

Surface active agent	Granite A	Porphyry A	Flint gravel A	Basalt A	Basalt B
A	1.0	2.5	2.0	0.5	2.0
B	1.0	2.5	2.0	1.5	2.5
C	2.0	2.5	2.0	2.0	2.0

of material sized less than 75 micrometre to 1%, see Table 11.2. This limit is difficult to obtain by dry screening and may require washing of the single size aggregate. The importance of aggregate cleanliness is also recognized by the TRL Report RR284 (Bullas & West 1991) which proposes appropriate limits (see Surface Dressing Association 1990).

11.4.4.2. Influence of binder and adhesion agents. Since adhesion is known to be a property specific to type of binder and type of stone it follows that bituminous binders (which are slightly negatively charged) adhere better to positively charged rocks such as basic igneous and metamorphics, limestones, dolomites, bauxites etc. Binders to which cationic agents (such as the amines) have been added are accordingly much improved over unmodi-

fied binders in promoting adhesion to the negatively charged acid rocks. It has, however, been noted that cationic agents appear also to improve the adhesion with positively charged aggregates such as limestones. While not explained with any certainty this may be due to the acid nature of the medium carrying the cationic agent which, in slightly dissolving the limestone, may expose relatively more of any negatively charged clay mineral impurities at the surface.

In further studies, Lee (1958) investigated the effect of adding 10% tar or small percentages of certain tertiary amine or quaternary ammonium compounds to bitumen as adhesion agents. He noted that different percentages of given agents were required to achieve satisfactory results even with rocks of the same BS Trade Group. For example (Table 11.3(a)) Granite A required double the quantity of all agents tried compared with Granite B to achieve a satisfactory field performance. Also Granite B could achieve satisfactory resistance to stripping with 10% tar added to the bitumen whereas Granite A was not satisfactory with this treatment. (Tar is known to possess improved adhesion properties over bitumen by reason of its higher content of phenolic and naphthenic constituents.)

Further it was noted that while a satisfactory performance could be achieved at some percentage of additive for most rocks studied (Groups 2, 3 and 4 of Table 11.3(a)) others, namely a flint gravel and a quartzite, could not provide a satisfactory adhesion at any percentage (up to 1.0% maximum) of any agent or with 10% tar.

In an associated laboratory study using the Immersion Tray Test, Lee showed (Table 11.3(b)) that for a given agent A, Porphyry A required five times as much of the agent to produce the same degree of satisfactory coating as Basalt A. A simple relationship with Trade Group classification is, however, clearly not established since Basalt B required four times as much of the agent as Basalt A.

These results, while confirming a general superiority in adhesion with the basic rocks, demonstrate convincingly that, as noted in respect of other engineering properties, a Trade Group classification has no merit in grouping natural rocks into categories of similar engineering behaviour.

11.4.5. Resistance to weathering effects in service

Resistance to weathering is not an engineering property in itself but a measure of the reaction to weathering agencies which result in greater or less change in the engineering properties of strength, resistance to abrasion, polishing and adhesion described above.

The majority of roadstones that are utilized in the UK and other developed countries for bituminous surfacing materials are sufficiently strong and durable to undergo little or no weathering during the life of the pavement material of which they form a part. However, some examples of weathering by frost action, by softening and by solution have been mentioned above and instances have been reported in the United Kingdom where dolerites and teschenites used in road surfacing have failed prematurely as a result of deterioration whilst stockpiled and while in service (Hosking 1967; Hosking & Tubey 1969).

The effects of clay and other secondary minerals in basalt aggregates is also reported by Woodside & Woodward (1989) who suggest a testing regime in order to quantify the degree of weathering.

The Department of Transport specification (1991) specifies that aggregate used in bitumen bound materials shall have a magnesium sulphate soundness value of greater than 75% (BS 812) as a method of specifying

durability. In all the cases of potential aggregate weathering, the risks are of course much less where the coating of binder is adequate and the mix is designed to be virtually impermeable.

11.4.6. Ability to contribute to strength and stiffness of the total mix

This property applies to both coarse and fine aggregates and to fillers and, assuming that the criterion of adequate intrinsic strength and durability of the aggregate particles is satisfied, refers to the mass aggregate properties of interlock and internal friction. In these respects both angularity and roughness of surface texture are important contributors to the strength and deformation resistance properties of the bituminous mixture. It has been shown (Lottman & Goetz 1956; Lees 1964; Heukelom 1965; Szatkowski 1980; Kavussi & Lees 1990) that both the strength and stiffness properties and the binder requirement are very considerably affected (for given aggregate grading and binder type) by the shape and absorption properties of coarse and fine aggregates and of fillers.

11.5. Detailed requirements and conflicting requirements for aggregates for bituminous pavement materials

Certain aggregate properties have greater significance in some contexts than others. For example, high crushing strength is required of aggregates for surface dressing and heavily trafficked open texture macadams. Good adhesion is similarly required in these situations but is less important as a factor in dense impermeable asphalts. High resistance to polishing is required for wearing course materials, surface dressings and coated chippings in difficult sites of high traffic intensity and high risk rating (Salt & Szatkowski 1973) but is of less significance in easier sites and regions of lower traffic intensity and clearly irrelevant in the selection of base and base course aggregates except where, during stage construction, traffic may run on the base or base course for some significant time before being overlaid by wearing course or surface dressing treatment.

Apart from the need to recognize the different significance of the various properties in different engineering contexts, several of these traditionally designated 'desirable' qualities are partially or completely conflicting, e.g. hard minerals are frequently brittle, hence high resistance to abrasion may be accompanied by low resistance to crushing or impact e.g. quartz, flint, chert. Further these silica minerals, while highly abrasion resistant, are also known to have poor adhesion to bituminous binders in the presence of water (Lee 1936; Mathews 1961).

TABLE 11.4. *Summary of tentative limits that have been suggested for the mechanical properties of roadstone (Shergold 1948)*

Type of construction	Dry attrition loss (%) (max) DEVAL	Impact (no. of blows) (min) PAGE	Crushing strength (lb./sq. in) (min)	Los Angeles test (% fines) (max)	Aggregate crushing test (% fines) (max)
(a) Light or medium traffic					
Waterbound					
Light traffic	8.0	5	15 000	35	30
Medium traffic	5.0	10	25 000	25	23
Concrete					
Body of road	–	–	10 000	50	40
Surface of road	–	–	12 000	40	35
Bituminous					
Body of road	8.0	5	15 000	35	30
Surface of road	5.0	10	25 000	25	23
(b) Heavy traffic					
Waterbound	2.7	18	40 000	13	13
Concrete					
Body of road	–	–	12 000	40	35
Surface of road	–	–	15 000	35	30
Bituminous					
Body of road	5.7	10	15 000	35	30
Surface of road	4.0	13	30 000	17	17

Note: This table has been drawn up from figures given in a number of the papers that have been studied.

It is important to remember that in every case the figures are intended for use as an approximate guide to the properties required in aggregates for use in different forms of construction. They are not intended to be applied as rigid specification limits.

This conflict in desirable properties extends also into the province of particle shape since it can be shown that highly rounded particles would have the best anti-stripping tendencies (Mathews 1958) while being inferior to angular particles in terms of shearing resistance (Herrin & Goetz 1954; Lottman & Goetz 1956). In practice the latter property would be considered by far the more important since poor adhesion can be attended to by the use of adhesion agents or restriction to use in dense mixes.

Another familiar example of conflicting properties in roadstone concerns the qualities of skid resistance and resistance to abrasion as mentioned above. Although abrasion resistance is generally considered a desirable quality in a roadstone, since in general it will be associated with durability of the pavement, a rock which is uniformly hard will also wear uniformly, albeit slowly. Hence a polished and slippery surface will result. Conversely, a rock which exhibits some wear, presents by so doing fresh and unpolished surfaces to the tyre.

11.5.1. Detailed requirements: strength

The basic requirement for crushing strength remains in the case of coated materials as in the case of uncoated stone (Chapter 10) and concrete aggregate (Chapter 8).

Certain categories of use, however, will be less demanding than others. Still others, such as for example surface dressings compacted by steel wheeled rollers on hard surfaces, will be very demanding and require aggregates of the highest strength (see below). Also the strength generally expected for an aggregate situated higher up in the construction layers is greater than for one situated at lower levels because of the diminution of the traffic stresses with depth.

An example of the different suggested minimum strength values required from aggregate intended for different uses is seen in Table 11.4 (Shergold 1948). The strength values are stated in terms of one current BS 812 test (the aggregate crushing test), one current ASTM test (the Los Angeles test) and some older tests not in current British use (the 'Deval' dry attrition test, the 'Page' impact test and the crushing strength test). Shergold reported a good correlation between Los Angeles results, aggregate crushing value and field performance in New South Wales, Australia. These results according to Shergold showed that an upper limit of 25 for the aggregate crushing test and 35 for the Los Angeles test would eliminate nearly all of the unsatisfactory aggregates for this particular form of construction.

The table illustrates the principle that aggregates of different performance can be suitable for different lo-

TABLE 11.5. *Summary of tentative limits suggested for the mechanical properties of roadstones*

Type of construction	Traffic cv/1/day H = heavy M = medium L = light	Los Angeles (max)	ACV (max) [AIV] (max)	10 per cent fines (dry) (min) [Modified AIV: dry] (max)	10 per cent fines (wet) (min) [Modified AIV: wet] (max)	10 per cent fines: wet/dry variation [Modified AIV: wet/dry variation] (max)	Mg sulphate soundness (max) [Na sulphate soundness] – to be phased out
Unbound	Heavy (>6000)	25	23 [23]	130 [23]	80 [30]	<35 [<35]	coarse aggregate 18 [12]
	Medium (1500–6000)	30	27 [27]	115 [27]	65 [35]	<35 [<35]	
	Light (<1500)	35	30 [30]	100 [34]	50 [40]	<60* [<60]*	fine aggregate 15 [10]

* For values in this column between 35 and 60 the aggregate should only be used with approximately 2% hydrated lime as a stabilizing agent

Bitumen bound Surface dressing & pervious macadam	H(>6000)	16	16 [16]	— —	—	—	coarse 18 [12]
	M/L(0–6000)	25	23 [23]	130 [23]	80 [30]	<35 [<35]	fine 15 [10]
Dense wearing course	H(>6000)	25	23 [23]	130 [23]	80 [30]	<35 [<35]	—
	M/L(0–6000)	30	27 [27]	115 [27]	65 [35]	<35 [<35]	—
Base course & base	H/M/L (0–>6000)	35	30 [30]	100 [34]	50 [40]	<35 [<35]	—
Cement bound Concrete wearing course	H(>6000)	30	27 [27]	115 [27]	65 [35]	<35 [<35]	—
	M/L(0–6000)	35	30 [30]	100 [34]	50 [40]	<60 [<60]	—
Base course & base	H/M/L (0–>6000)	35	35 [35]	50 [40]	40 [50]	<60 [<60]	—

Note: (with acknowledgement to Shergold 1948). This Table has been drawn up from a number of specifications and other publications listed in the references. It is important to remember that in every case the figures are intended for use as an approximate guide to the properties required in aggregates for use in different forms of construction. They are not intended to be applied as rigid specification limits. However, specification limits may be drawn up from these guidelines in the light of local experience.

cations in the pavement construction, for different types of material composition and under different traffic stresses. For example, it is suggested that an aggregate of ACV not greater than 13 would be required for a waterbound madadam (or unbound material, Chapter 10) to be used under heavy traffic while at the other extreme, aggregate for concrete (Chapter 8) to be used in the body of the road in light to medium traffic conditions might be permitted to have an ACV up to 40. These differences emphasize the point that aggregates receive different degrees of support in the context of different engineering compositions, as well as experiencing differ-

ent stresses according to position in the construction and traffic loadings. Even within the bituminous materials (which are not in this Table identified as of any particular composition) it is suggested that for the least exacting condition (body of road under light or medium traffic) the maximum ACV would be 30 and for the most exacting (surface of road under heavy traffic) the maximum ACV would be 17.

Following the same principles and with several decades of experience since Shergold's work, a revision of Table 11.4 is included in the present text. This table (Table 11.5) is based upon international published work

(Bartholomeusz 1987; Bartley 1987; Brennan 1987; Cyprus 1986; Department of Transport 1991). As in the note to Shergold's table, it is again strongly emphasized that such a table is for guidance only and should not be used as a blanket specification covering all cases. For example, local experience may show that certain aggregates in practice perform better (or worse) than would be indicated by their laboratory test values. However, provided that this local experience is taken into account, the revised table may become a useful basis for local national and regional specifications.

Furthermore, no matter how accurate a relationship is established between laboratory tests and service behaviour there can never be any justification for absolute prohibition of an aggregate until the economic factors of long-term durability for high initial cost versus shorter life for low initial cost have been assessed. These factors will vary from year to year and with geographical location. For example, in countries or localities where sources of high-quality stone are scarce, higher values of

ACV, AIV and AAV may well be tolerated in aggregates for road construction.

Current British Standards for bituminous mixes (BS 594: 1985 and BS 4987: 1988) state only that natural aggregate shall belong to one of the following groups (BS 812: 1975) (Note these groups are not reproduced in BS 812: 1989): basalt, gabbro, granite, gritstone, hornfels, limestone, porphyry or quartzite, but add that certain aggregates not belonging to the above groups may be permitted by agreement with the purchaser. Thus the only 'group' excluded is the Schist group comprising phyllites, schists, slates and all severely sheared rocks. Gravels are permitted provided they are from one or more of the approved groups listed above or are of flint.

The Department of Transport Specification for Highway Works (1991) prefaces the above by specifying a minimum 10% fines value of 140 kN. For surface dressing BS 63: Part 2, 1987 requires a minimum 10% fines value of 160 kN.

FIG. 11.4. Sideway force coefficient routine investigation machine (SCRIM) used to monitor the skidding resistance of in-service roads (Transport and Road Research Laboratory).

11.5.2. Detailed requirements—polishing resistance and abrasion resistance: Department of Transport (UK)

For several years the Department of Transport Specification for Road and Bridge Works gave the only further guidance as to desirable quality and then only in the following terms for aggregates for wearing course materials: 'the minimum polished stone value and the maximum aggregate abrasion value shall be as described in the contract'. In 1976, however, the Department's Technical Memoradum H16/76 laid down specific requirements for aggregate properties (and texture depth) for bituminous surfacings for new motorway and trunk road construction. This memorandum based upon work of the Transport and Road Research Laboratory (Hosking & Tubey 1972; Szatkowski & Hosking 1972; Salt & Szatkowski 1973) had the objective of matching the desired skidding resistance with different highway conditions and with anticipated traffic flows. Skidding resistance is measured as the sideway force coefficient (SFC) as obtained with the sideway force coefficient routine investigation machine (SCRIM), see Fig 11.4 (Hosking & Woodford 1976), and traffic flows are computed as commercial vehicles/lane/day calculated to be using the lane at the end of the anticipated life of the surfacing (Table 11.6.). For this purpose, commercial vehicles are defined as those exceeding 15 kN unladen vehicle weight.

TABLE 11.6. *Categories of sites and minimum polished stone value for flexible roads*

Site	Approximate percentage of all roads in England	Definition	Minimum Polished Stone Value	Remarks
A1 (difficult)	Less than 0.1%	(i) Approaches to traffic signals on roads with 85%ile speed of traffic greater than 40 mile/h (64 km/h) (ii) Approaches to traffic signals, pedestrian crossings and similar hazards on main urban roads	Less than 250 cv/lane/day: 60 250 to 1000 cv/lane/day: 65 1000 to 1750 cv/lane/day: 70 More than 1750 cv/lane/day: 75	Risk rating 6 Values include +5 units for braking/ turning
A2 (difficult)	Less than 4%	(i) Approaches to and across major priority junctions on roads carrying more than 250 commercial vehicles per lane per day* (ii) Roundabouts and their approaches (iii) Bends with radius less than 150 m on roads with 85%ile speed of traffic greater than 40 mile/h (64 km/h) (iv) Gradients of 5% or steeper, longer than 100 m	Less than 1750 cv/lane/day: 60 1750 to 2500 cv/lane/day: 65 2500 to 3250 cv/lane/day: 70 More than 3250 cv/lane/day: 75	Risk rating 4 Values include +5 units for braking/ turning * In (i), the 250 cv/ lane/day applies to each approach
B (average)	Less than 15%	Generally straight sections of and large radius curves on: (i) Motorways (ii) Trunk and principal roads (iii) Other roads carrying more than 250 commercial vehicles per lane per day	Less than 1750 cv/lane/day: 55 1750 to 4000 cv/lane/day: 60 More than 4000 cv/lane/day: 65	Risk rating 2
C (easy)	Less than 81%	(i) Generally straight sections of lightly trafficked roads i.e. less than 250 cv/day (ii) Other roads where wet skidding accidents are unlikely to be a problem	45	No risk rating applied Many local aggregates have a PSV well above 45 and normally these should be used

Note: Values should be amended in accordance with paragraph 4.1.4 of this Memorandum where abnormal risks occur. (Tech. Memo. H16/76).

TABLE 11.7. *PSV of aggregate necessary to achieve the required skidding resistance in bituminous surfacings under different traffic conditions (Salt & Szatkowski 1973)*

Required mean summer SFC at 50 km h^{-1}	PSV of aggregate necessary Traffic in commercial vehicles per lane per day					
	250 or under	1000	1750	2500	3250	4000
0.30	30	35	40	45	50	55
0.35	35	40	45	50	55	60
0.40	40	45	50	55	60	65
0.45	45	50	55	60	65	70
0.50	50	55	60	65	70	75
0.55	55	60	65	70	75	—
0.60	60	65	70	75	—	—
0.65	65	70	75	—	—	—
0.70	70	75	—	—	—	—
0.75	75	—	—	—	—	—

TABLE 11.8. *Minimum values of skidding resistance for different sites (Salt & Szatkowski 1973)*

Site	Definition	SFC (at 50 km h^{-1}) Risk rating									
		1	2	3	4	5	6	7	8	9	10
A1 (v. difficult)	(i) Approaches to traffic signals on roads with a speed limit greater than 40 mile h^{-1} (64 km h^{-1}) (ii) Approaches to traffic signals, pedestrian crossings and similar hazards on main urban roads*						0.55	0.60	0.65	0.70	0.75
A2 (difficult)	(i) Approaches to major junctions on roads carrying more than 250 commercial vehicles per lane per day (ii) Roundabouts and their approaches (iii) Bends with radius less than 150 m on roads with a speed limit greater than 40 mile h^{-1} (64 km h^{-1}) (iv) Gradients of 5% or steeper, longer than 100 m				0.45	0.50	0.55	0.60	0.65		
B (average)	(i) Generally straight sections of and large radius curves on: (i) Motorways (ii) Trunk and principal roads (iii) Other roads carrying more than 250 commercial vehicles per lane per day	0.30	0.35	0.40	0.45	0.50	0.55				
C (easy)	(i) Generally straight sections of lightly trafficked roads (ii) Other roads where wet accidents are unlikely to be a problem	0.30	0.35	0.40	0.45						

* Main urban roads would generally be included in Marshall road categories, 1, 2 and 3

Tables 11.7 and 11.8 are reproduced from the Laboratory Report by Salt & Szatkowski referred to above and give more fully the information upon which Technical Memorandum H16/76 is based. Table 11.7 gives the value of PSV required to achieve a given sideway force coefficient at 50 km/h under given traffic densities.

Table 11.8 gives guidance on the minimum SFC$_{50}$ values required for certain highway situations and risk ratings.

In 1987 the Department of Transport issued Technical Memorandum HD15/87 in which are stated investigatory levels of skid resistance at or below which investigation of the surface condition should take place with a

TABLE 11.9. *Investigatory skidding resistance levels for different categories of site (based on average sites but see Departmental Advice Note HA 36/87, Section 6; additional advice).*

Site category	Site definition	(i) Investigatory Levels $MSSC_{50}$ (at 50 km/h) or equivalent (ii) Corresponding risk rating							
		0.30	0.35	0.40	0.45	0.50	0.55	0.60	0.65
		1	2	3	4	5	6	7	8
A	Motorway (mainline)		*						
B	Dual carriageway (all purpose) – non-event sections		*						
C	Single carriageway – non-event sections			*					
D	Dual carriageway (all purpose) – minor junctions			*					
E	Single carriageway – minor junctions				*				
F	Approaches to and across major junctions (all limbs)				*				
G1	Gradient 5% to 10%, longer than 50 m dual (downhill only) single (uphill and downhill)				*				
G2	Gradient steeper than 10%, longer than 50 m dual (downhill only) single (uphill and downhill)						*		
H1	Bend (not subject to 40 mph or lower speed limit) radius ≤ 250m				*				
J	Approach to roundabout						*		
K	Approach to traffic signals, pedestrian crossings, railway level crossings or similar						*		

Site category	Site definition	(i) Investigatory Levels $MSSC_{20}$ (at 20 km/h) or equivalent (ii) Corresponding risk rating							
		0.40	0.45	0.50	0.55	0.60	0.65	0.70	0.75
		1	2	3	4	5	6	7	8
H2	Bend (not subject to 40 mph or lower speed limit) Radius ≤ 100m					*			
L	Roundabout				*				

* Investigatory Levels

Notes

(a) Investigatory levels are for the mean skidding resistance within the appropriate section length.
(b) investigatory levels for site categories A, B and C are based on 100 metre section lengths.
(c) Investigatory levels for site categories D, E, F, J and K are based on the 50 metre approach to the feature.
(d) Investigatory levels for site categories G and H are based on 50 metre section lengths, or for H the length of the curve if shorter.
(e) The investigatory level for site category L is based on 10 metre section lengths.
(f) Residual section lengths less than 50% of a complete section should be attached to the penultimate section.
(g) Individual values within each section should be examined and the significance of any values which are substantially lower than the mean value assessed.
(h) No precise definitions of Major/Minor Junctions have been included as judgement will have an important input.

Technical Paper MC/TP/33/89
(with acknowledgement to TRRL)

TABLE 11.10. *Traffic loadings and maximum aggregate abrasion values for flexible surfacings*

Commercial vehicles per lane per day	Under 250*	Up to 1000	Up to 1750	Up to 2500	Up to 3250	Over 3250
Maximum AAV for chippings	14	12	12	10	10	10
Maximum AAV for aggregate in coated macadam wearing courses	16	16	14	14	12	12

* For lightly trafficked roads carrying less than 250 commerical vehicles per lane per day aggregate of higher AAV may be used where experience has shown that a satisfactory performance is achieved by aggregate from a particular source. (Technical Memorandum H16/76 Dept. of Transport.)

view to the possible need for remedial work (Table 11.9).

In the Departmental Standard which will replace Technical Memorandum H16/76 it is probable that recognition of this work will be made and that revised polished stone values will be specified for new bituminous surfacings including resurfacing and surface dressing of motorways and trunk roads (see also Hosking 1992).

Further recommendations on desired strength for aggregates are contained in Road Note 39, Third Edition (TRRL 1992) which recommends that, when very hard surfaces are being dressed, aggregates having a 10% fines value greater than that specified by BS 63 i.e. 140 kN, should be used (see also TRRL Report LR908, 1979).

11.5.3. General comments

With the exceptions noted above, which all concern wearing course or surface dressing materials, current practice in the UK (and those countries following UK practice) has been not to specify or even recommend tentative limits in terms of strength or chemical properties. However, the Department of Transport Specification, 1991, as previously mentioned, now identifies criteria of strength, durability and cleanliness but the values quoted still place the responsibility with the Engineer to assess the local requirement and to judge the potential quality and life of the materials available for purchase. This implies the need for a high standard of relevant education and experience. For conventional premixed bituminous materials the absolute lower limit of aggregate strength that may be tolerated will be that for which the aggregate can be screened, mixed, transported and laid without undue degradation (as confirmed by analysis methods of BS 598 and similar overseas specifications). This will tend to exclude all aggregates with an AIV greater than 35 (Hawkes & Hosking 1972) and AAV greater than 16 (Technical

memorandum H16/76), but it may be noted that the footnote to Table 11.10 suggests that aggregates of AAV > 16 may be used for lightly trafficked roads where experience has shown satisfactory performance.

11.5.4. Detailed requirements—
Property Services Agency UK
(Airfields Branch)

For airfield pavements in the United Kingdom (and certain overseas territories), the Property Services Agency (Airfields Branch) of the Department of the Environment summarizes (Table 11.11) the aggregate types permitted for various types of bituminous surfacing.

11.5.5. Relationship between mix
composition and desirable
aggregate properties

As implied in Table 11.11 and elsewhere in this chapter, lower crushing strength aggregates can be included in dense bituminous mixes than would be acceptable in open texture mixes, because of the support afforded in the former case by the bituminous mortar and by the increased impermeability to water and air. This applies not only to the intrinsic strength of the rock but also the influence of particle shape on strength. For example, the traditional aversion to low crushing strength aggregates and for flaky and elongate particles in aggregates for bituminous construction materials arises chiefly out of the greater degradation they exhibit both in conventional aggregate tests and in service behaviour as open texture macadam aggregates such as friction course and as surface dressings. In the two uses quoted, the breaking of aggregate particles is at once evident and harmful (by reason of producing uncoated cohesionless surfaces). The breakage occurs readily in these high void

TABLE 11.11. *Properties of aggregates for various categories of bituminous surfacing (Property Services Agency)*

Surfacing material	Flakiness index (% MAX) [All aggregates]		Aggregate crushing value (% MAX)		Absorption (% MAX) [Crushed rock and gravel (BS 812)]	Aggregate soundness (% MAX)	Stability	Sulphur content (% MAX) [Slag (BS 1047)]	Bulk density (Kg/m³) (MIN)	Absorption (% MAX)	Stripping test (in accordance with Appendix 4(A)) [All aggregates]
	Crushed Rock or Slag	Gravel	Crushed Rock or Slag	Gravel							
Marshall asphalt	30	30	30	25	2	18 (3)	—	—	—	—	Not greater than 6 particles from a 150 particle test sample shall indicate evidence of stripping
Marshall DTS	30	30	30	25	2	18 (3)	—	—	—	—	Not greater than 6 particles from a 150 particle test sample shall indicate evidence of stripping
Rolled asphalt wearing course	30	30	30	25	2	18 (3)	Requirements to Appx (A) of BS 1047	2%	1120 (2)	4	Not greater than 6 particles from a 150 particle test sample shall indicate evidence of stripping
Macadam base course	30	30	30	25	2	—	Requirements to Appx (A) of BS 1047	2%	1120 (2)	4	Not greater than 6 particles from a 150 particle test sample shall indicate evidence of stripping
Dense tar surfacing	30	30	30	25	2	18 (3)	Requirements to Appx (A) of BS 1047	2%	1120 (2)	4	Not greater than 6 particles from a 150 particle test sample shall indicate evidence of stripping
Friction course	25 (1)	—	16 (1)	—	1.5	18 (3)	—	—	—	—	Not greater than 3 particles from a 150 particle test sample shall show evidence of stripping

Notes: (1) Crushed rock only of specified groups.
(2) Min when aggregate sample used in test complies with Table I of BS 63 for 20 mm nominal single-sized aggregate.
(3) Overall percentage mass loss based on the mass losses of the various nominal sizes tested from any one supply source.

content or single layer mixes because the aggregate particles are in especially vulnerable situations, with little or no protection from the development of high stresses. It is for these reasons that a maximum permissible limit on Flakiness Index was first incorporated in BS 63 (1951) and re-stated in BS 63 (1987) *Specification for single size aggregates for general use* (Table 11.2).

On the other hand it has been shown (Lees 1964; Salehi 1968) that the risk of deleterious crushing of flaky aggregate decreases, in some cases to negligible proportions, when the so-called 'suspect' aggregate is used in dense bituminous mixes where support from the bituminous mortar is mobilized.

A method for designing aggregate gradings for dense bituminous compositions which takes into account variations in aggregate shape and other relevant factors has been described by Lees (1970).

Considerations of structural requirement (deformation resistance and fatigue resistance) and skid resistance requirements have subsequently been incorporated into a design method for dense asphaltic mixes for different thicknesses of bituminous pavement construction and for different traffic levels (Lees 1987).

11.6. Conclusions

In specifications concerning aggregates for bituminous materials the following factors are considered relevant:

(a) the type of usage e.g. highway or airfield pavement, hydraulic engineering;
(b) the type of bituminous material, e.g. surface dressing, friction course, rolled asphalt, asphaltic concrete;
(c) the intensity of traffic;
(d) the location in the pavement e.g. wearing course or base course;
(e) the site category and risk rating for skid resistance purposes;
(f) the reputation and reliability of traditional sources of aggregate supply.

Degrees of guidance varying from vague advice to precise specification limits have been given by various authorities in the United Kingdom and overseas in accordance not only with variation in usage, but also in accordance with history.

The wide variation in availability of suitable types of aggregate and in economic circumstance throughout the world makes impractical any attempt to establish a single uniform range of specifications applicable to all countries.

Emphasis is therefore placed on the following as aids to good engineering practice:

(i) good education and experience in the field of the components and the design of bituminous materials;
(ii) the use of stage construction especially where economics dictates that known lower quality materials have to be used;
(iii) a move towards end product specification for bituminous mixes based upon defined strengths, stiffness, and durability criteria (and skid resistance where appropriate) allowing the designer/manufacturer the freedom to design mixes in the most effective way to maximize the qualities of good aggregates and minimize the risks where aggregates of inferior quality need to be used (ASTM 1989).

References

AMERICAN SOCIETY FOR TESTING AND MATERIALS 1989. ASTM Standards Designation Part 15 D1075.

BARTHOLEMEUSZ, W. G. 1987. Laboratory testing of basecourse aggregates. New Zealand Roading Symposium, National Roads Board, Wellington.

BARTLEY, F. G. 1987. Basecourse specification. New Zealand Roading Symposium, National Roads Board, Wellington.

BRENNAN, G. H. 1987. Selection of marginal aggregates for sealed road construction. New Zealand Roading Symposium, National Roads Board, Wellington.

BRITISH STANDARDS INSTITUTION, 1987. *Specification for single size aggregates: BS 63.*

—— 1985. *Hot rolled asphalt for roads and other paved areas: BS 594.*

—— 1975, 1989. *Sampling and testing of mineral aggregates, sands and fillers: BS 812.*

—— 1988. *Coated macadam for roads and other paved areas: BS 4987.*

BULLAS, J. C. & WEST, G. 1991. *Specifying Clean, Hard and Durable Aggregate for Bitumen Macadam Roadbase.* TRRL Research Report RR 284, Transport and Road Research Laboratory, Crowthorne.

CAWSEY, D. C. & RAYMOND-WILLIAMS, R. K. 1990. Stripping of macadams: performance tests with different aggregates. *Highways and Transportation* 7 (37), 16–21.

CYPRUS (Republic of), MINISTRY OF COMMUNICATIONS & WORKS. 1986. Cyprus specification—Cys 99.

DEERE, D. U. & MILLER, R. P. 1966. *Engineering Classification and Index Properties for Intact Rock.* Technical Report AFWL-TR-65-116 Air Force Weapons Laboratory, Kirtland.

DEPARTMENT OF TRANSPORT. 1976. Technical Memorandum H16/76. *Specification Requirements for Aggregate Properties and Texture Depth for Bituminous Surfacings to New Roads.*

—— 1991. *Specification for Highway Works.* Part 3. HMSO, London.

—— 1987. Technical Memorandum HD15/87, and Advice Note HA36/87. *Skidding Resistance of In-service Trunk-Roads.*

DHIR, R. K., RAMSAY, D. M. & BALFOUR, N. 1971. A study of the aggregate impact and crushing value tests. *Journal of the Institution of Highway Engineering,* **18**, 1, 17–27.

GIANNATTASIO, P. & MARCHIONNA, A. 1987. Non-traditional materials—residuary products. Technical Committee Report No 8 (Flexible Roads), Permanent International Association of Road Congresses, XVIII World Road Congress, Brussels, 73–88.

GRAY, J. E. & RENNINGER, F. A. 1963. Limestone and dolomite sands in skid resistant Portland cement mortar surfaces. Res. Report of National Crushed Stone Assoc., Washington.

—— & —— 1965. Skid resistant properties of carbonate aggregates. Res. Report of National Crushed Stone Assoc., Washington.

GUTT, W., NIXON, P. J., SMITH, M. A., HARRISON, W. H. & RUSSELL, A. D. 1974. A survey of the Locations, Disposal and Prospective Uses of the Major Industrial By-products and Waste Materials. CP19/74, Building Research Establishment, Watford.

HALLBERG, S. 1950. The adhesion of bituminous binders and aggregates in the presence of water. *Meddelande 78*. Statens Vaginstitut, Stockholm.

—— 1958. Tests with oiled gravel roads. *Meddelande 90*. Statens Vaginstitut, Stockholm.

HARTLEY, A. 1968. Petrographic aspects of the polishing of roadstones. *Proceedings of the Symposium on the Influence of the Road Surface on Skidding, University of Salford,* 2.1–2.34.

—— 1974. Mechanical properties of road surface aggregates. *Quarterly Journal of Engineering Geology,* 7, 69–100.

HATHERLY, L. W. & YOUNG, A. E. 1977. The location and treatment of urban skidding hazard sites. *Transportation Research Record 623*, Transportation Research Board, Washington, 21–28.

HAWKES, J. R. & HOSKING, J. R. 1972. British arenaceous rocks for skid-resistant road surfacings. Transport and Road Research Laboratory Report LR 488. Crowthorne.

HERBST, C., GORDON, R. G., NEMESDY, E., SOMMERSALO, A. & VANDERKIMPEN, N. 1983. Chapter 5 'Aggregate', in Technical Committee Report on Flexible Roads, XVII World Road Congress, Permanent International Association of Road Congresses, Sydney, Australia, 55–66.

HERRIN, M. & GOETZ, W. H. 1954. Effect of aggregate shape on stability of bituminous mixes. *Proc. Highway Research Board,* 33, 293–308.

HEUKELOM, W. 1965. The role of filler in bituminous mixes. *Proceedings of the Association of Asphalt Paving Technologists* 34, 396–429.

HILLS, J. F. & McAUGHTRY, D. 1986. Deformation of asphalt concrete linings on slopes. *Journal of Engineering Mechanics,* American Society of Civil Engineers, 12 (10) Paper 20989, 1076–89.

HOSKING, J. R. 1967. *An experiment comparing the performance of roadstones.* Road Research Laboratory Report LR 81. Crowthorne.

—— 1970. *Synthetic aggregates of high resistance to polishing: Part 1—gritty aggregates.* Road Research Laboratory Report LR 350. Crowthorne.

—— 1973. *The effect of aggregate on the skidding resistance of bituminous surfacings: factors other than resistance to polishing.* Transport & Road Research Laboratory Report LR 553. Crowthorne.

—— & TUBEY, L. W. 1969. Research on low-grade and unsound aggregates. Road Research Laboratory Report LR 293. Crowthorne.

—— & —— 1972. *Aggregates for resin-bound skid resistant surfacings.* Transport & Road Research Laboratory Report LR 466. Crowthorne.

—— & WOODFORD, G. C. 1976. Measurement of skidding resistance: Part 1. Guide to the use of SCRIM. Transport & Road Research Laboratory LR 737. Crowthorne.

—— 1992. *Road aggregates and skidding,* State of the Art Review 4, TRL, HMSO, London.

HUGHES, R. I., LAMB, D. R. & PORDES, O. 1960. Adhesion in bitumen macadam. *Journal of Applied Chemistry,* 10, 433.

KAVUSSI, A. & LEES, G. 1990. An accelerated weathering technique to assess the hardening of bitumen and filler-bitumen mixes. *Journal of the Institute of Asphalt Technology,* 42, 22–29.

KNIGHT, B. H. & KNIGHT, R. G. 1935. *Road Aggregates, their Uses and Testing.* Edward Arnold, London.

KNILL, D. C. 1960. Petrographic aspects of the polishing of natural roadstones. *Journal of Applied Chemistry,* 10, 28–35.

LEE, A. R. 1936. Adhesion in relation to bituminous road materials. *Journal of the Society of Chemical Industry,* 55, 23T–29T.

—— 1958. *Roads and Road Construction.*

LEES, G. 1964. The measurement of particle shape and its influence in engineering materials. *Journal of British Granite & Whinstone Federation* 4(2), 17–38.

—— 1969. The influence of binder and aggregate in bituminous mixtures. *J. Inst. highway Eng.* 16 (1) 7–19.

—— 1970. The rational design of aggregate gradings for dense asphaltic compositions. *Proceedings of the Association of Asphalt Paving Technologists* 39, 60–97.

—— 1978. in 'Developments in Highway Pavement Engineering' Ed. P. S. Pell, Applied Science Publishers.

—— 1987. Asphalt mix design for optimum structural and tyre interaction purposes. Sixth International Conference on the Structural Design of Asphalt Pavements. Ann Arbor, Michigan, 404–17.

—— & KENNEDY, C. K. 1975. Quality, shape and degradation of aggregates. *Quarterly Journal of Engineering Geology,* 8, 193–209.

LOTTMAN, R. P. & GOETZ, W. H. 1956. Effect of crushed gravel fine aggregate on the strength of asphaltic surfacing mixtures. *National Sand and Gravel Association Wash. Circular 63,* 3–22.

MACLEAN, D. J. & SHERGOLD, F. A. 1958. *The polishing of roadstone in relation to the resistance to skidding of bituminous road surfacing.* DSIR Road Research Technical Paper 43, HMSO, London.

MASTIC ASPHALT CONFERENCES (6th–9th), 1989. *Journal of the Institute of Asphalt Technology,* 41, 12–60.

MATHEWS, D. H. 1958. Adhesion in bituminous road materials: a survey of present knowledge. *J. Inst. Pet. London* 44 (420), 423–32.

—— 1961. *Surface-active Agents in Bituminous Road Materials.* Dept of Scientific and Industrial Research. RRL Research Note 3926/DHM.

ORGANISATION FOR ECONOMIC CO-OPERATION AND DEVELOPMENT, 1977. *Use of waste materials and by-products in road construction,* Paris, 1–166.

PROPERTY SERVICES AGENCY. 1979. *Standard specification clauses for airfield pavement works. Part 4 Bituminous Surfacing.*

SALEHI, M. 1968. *A study of the internal structure and flexural strength properties of bituminous paving materials.* PhD Thesis, University of Birmingham.

SALT, G. F. & SZATKOWSKI, W. S. 1973. *A guide to levels of skidding resistance for roads.* Dept of the Environment, TRRL Report LR 510.

SHELL BITUMEN HANDBOOK. 1990. compiled by D. Whiteoak. Shell Bitumen UK, Chertsey, Surrey.

SHERGOLD, F. A. 1948. *A review of available information on the significance of roadstone tests.* Road Research Technical Paper 10. DSIR, HMSO, London.

SHUPE, J. W. & LOUNSBURY, R. W. 1959. Polishing characteristics of mineral aggregates, *Proceedings of the First International Skid Prevention Conference,* 509–37.

SURFACE DRESSING ASSOCIATION, 1990. *Code of Practice for surface dressing.*

SZATKOWSKI, W. S. 1980. Rolled asphalt wearing courses with high resistance to deformation. *In: The Performance of Rolled Asphalt Road Surfacings.* Institution of Civil Engineers, London.

—— & HOSKING, J. R. 1972. *The effect of traffic and aggregate on the resistance to skidding of bituminous surfacings.* Department of the Environment. TRRL Report LR 504.

TRANSPORT AND ROAD RESEARCH LABORATORY, 1962. Bituminous materials in road construction. HMSO, London.

—— 1979. *Surface dressing: proposed amendments to Road Note 39.* N Wright LR 908.

—— 1992. *Road Note 39. Recommendations for road surface dressing.*

TUBEY, L. W. & HOSKING, J. R. 1972. *Synthetic aggregates of high resistance to polishing. Part 2 Corundum-rich aggregates.* Transport and Road Research Laboratory LR 467. Crowthorne.

WILLIAMS, A. R. & LEES, G. 1970. Topographical and petrographical variation of road aggregates and the wet skidding resistance of tyres. *Quarterly Journal of Engineering Geology,* **2,** 217–236.

WOODSIDE, A. R. & WOODWARD, W. D. H. 1989. *Assessing Basalt Durability: Rapid Alternative Techniques,* TRL, Crowthorne.

Appendix A11.1. Adhesion tests

Static immersion tests. Coated aggregate particles are immersed in jars of distilled water and the degree of stripping is assessed as the visually estimated percentage of uncoated surface area after periods of 1, 3, 24 and 48 hours at 25°C and 40°C respectively. This test has only low reproducibility due to the human factor. A variety of static immersion test appears in Queensland standards Q16-1966 where the aggregate is not completely coated before immersion. In this test 50 representative pieces of the aggregate sample are pressed into a thin layer of the bituminous binder, left therein in an oven at 60°C for 24 hours and then immersed for 4 days in a water bath at 50°C. The particles are then plucked by hand from the tray and the degree of retention of binder assessed visually. In this test and the immersion tray test described below there is a strong risk of influencing the result (as the present author has found in his own laboratory) by the handling process, i.e. dust coatings are removed to varying degrees by handling and varying amounts of oil/perspiration are deposited from the

fingers of the handler. These factors contribute to the low reproducibility mentioned above.

Chemical immersion tests. As for static immersion tests but a chemical solution is used in place of distilled water, generally Na_2CO_3 in varying concentrations.

Dynamic immersion tests. Similar to the static test but agitation or stirring is involved.

Immersion mechanical tests. These follow a variety of types of tests on graded and compacted coated material. After soaking for a specified number of hours at a specified temperature the materials are subjected to tests for say compressive strength, flexural strength, tensile strength, cone penetration, abrasion resistance (e.g. modified Deval, modified Los Angeles). It has been commented (HMSO 1962) that little is known about correlation between the tests and performance in service and that with many comparatively dense and strong mixes which have been assessed by these means it is doubtful whether an important practical problem really exists.

Immersion trafficking test. An attempt to introduce the known significant factor of trafficking into adhesion testing came with the development of circular track machines and reciprocating loaded wheels (the Immersion Wheel Tracking Test, HMSO 1962). The time to failure of the specimens (continuously 'trafficked' under water at 40°C) is taken as a measure of resistance to stripping. Fairly good correlation with service behaviour has been established and examples are given in the reference to show the effect of different fillers on laboratory and field resistance to stripping.

Coating tests. These differ from those above in that the aggregate is not coated initially and its resistance to stripping subsequently assessed or measured. In coating tests the ability of the aggregate to attain a coating through the medium of water is assessed. The immersion tray test (Lee 1936) involves the placing of a layer of binder in a tray which is then covered with water. The aggregate particles are then applied by hand to the binder film, left therein for 10 minutes, then removed and the percentage of binder adhering to the face of the stone which has been pressed on the binder surface assessed visually (HMSO 1962). The test, while low in reproducibility has been found useful to assess the degree of effectiveness of adding certain types and proportions of adhesion agent to standard bituminous binders.

Adhesion can also be assessed by more fundamental tests including measurement of contact angle (θ) and interfacial tension between binder and water (γ_{bw}) (Lee 1936; Hallberg 1950) and by direct measurement of adhesion tension ($\gamma_{bw} \cos \theta$) (Hallberg 1950).

12. Railway track ballast

12.1. Introduction

Railway track formations generally consist essentially of a layer of coarse aggregate, or ballast, in which the sleepers are embedded (see Fig. 12.1). The ballast may rest directly on the subgrade or, depending on the bearing capacity, on a layer of blanketing sand. The layer of ballast is intended to provide a free draining base which is stable enough to maintain the track alignment with the minimum of maintenance. The function of the blanketing sand is primarily to provide a filter to prevent contamination of the ballast by fine particles derived from ascending waters (see Fig. 12.2).

FIG. 12.1. Track ballast being delivered by self-discharging train (courtesy Balfour Beatty Railway Engineering Ltd).

FIG. 12.2. Blanketing sand being laid (courtesy K. Rowlands, British Rail Civil Engineering).

The fundamental engineering is reasonably well understood. It concerns the transmission of the load from the base of the sleeper onto an area of closely packed ballast beneath. The sleeper bears onto the points of the angular ballast which are, in consequence, liable to fracture or abrade under load, a problem more severe with concrete than with wooden sleepers. If the layer of ballast is not close-packed and of sufficient depth there is a tendency for the sleepers to move up and down as the wheels of the traffic pass in succession, eventually causing the sub-grade to be disturbed.

Consequently the ballast layer must be thick enough to hold the track in position and prevent traffic loads from distorting the subgrade, while the aggregate under the sleepers must be tough enough to resist the abrasion and degradation caused by the intermittent traffic loads. The main requirement, confirmed by practice on many railway systems, seems to be for a strong angular aggregate with a very good resistance to abrasion. Many tough, dense, siliceous rocks seem to be suitable but limestones, as a general rule, are distrusted because of their low resistance to abrasion.

Specifications for ballast normally involve size, shape and rock quality requirements, the aim being to obtain a coarse angular material, the particles of which will interlock to form a layer of good dimensional stability. In addition, individual particles are required to be strong enough to resist surface attrition and degradation caused by the hammering action of rail traffic. It is important to exclude very fine material as its presence tends to reduce the bulk stability and creep resistance of the ballast.

The thickness of the ballast layer can be as low as 150 mm on lightly trafficked lines increasing to 400 mm on lines with high speed trains or heavy traffic. When concrete sleepers are used the ballast thickness may be increased by at least 50 mm. The blanketing sand layer normally has a minimum thickness of 150 mm.

It will be clear from the descriptions of requirements in various countries that the selection of suitable materials for railway ballast involves similar considerations throughout the world. There is, however, a widespread lack of data linking in-service performance with various types of ballast. Hence specifications are more often based on experience and judgement than on experimental evidence. This situation is not unusual with aggregate specifications but, in the case of railway ballast especially, there appears to be a dearth of reliable information.

TABLE 12.1. *Great Britain production of crushed rock for railway ballast, 1975–1988 (thousand tonnes)*

	Sandstone	Igneous rock	Limestone/dolomite	Total
1975	508	2307	1448	4263
1976	552	2418	1413	4383
1977	557	2291	1321	4169
1978	546	2144	1281	3971
1979	552	2029	1006	3587
1980	630	2311	703	3644
1981	—	2385	983	—
1982	—	—	729	—
1983	—	—	784	—
1984	532	3099	798	4429
1985	—	2809	—	—
1986	174	2953	406	3533
1987	78	2831	314	3223
1988	103	3102	368	3573

Source: Business Statistics Office

12.2. Rock types suitable for track ballast in Great Britain

Application of the Wet Attrition Test (BS 812: 1951, Clause 27) to various aggregates in the UK, mainly by British Rail, suggests that rocks which give the best values are likely to have high crushing strength, high resistance to abrasion and often relatively low resistance to polishing. Such rocks, which fall mainly in the igneous and metamorphic category, might be of little value in other markets if low resistance to polishing makes them unattractive as wearing coarse aggregate in roads. Hence, the provision of optimum material for railway ballast might well justify the operation of a special quarry.

Materials currently produced in Great Britain which appear to have outstanding properties as railway ballast, in terms of the Wet Attrition Test, include rock which has been subjected to thermal metamorphism (e.g. hornfels) and certain fine-grained acidic rocks (e.g. rhyolites or microgranites). Coarser grained igneous rock together with dolerites and basalts often produce good quality ballast, but sedimentary rocks are not widely used although some quartzites and dolomites are considered adequate.

The quantities of materials used for railway ballast in recent years are given in Table 12.1. It will be noticed that the total amount of ballast produced has decreased and there has been an even more significant decrease in the proportion of rock derived from other than the igneous rock category. In the case of the limestone/dolomite category the decrease is attributed to a greater insistence on the 4% limit in the Wet Attrition Test, a value which few carbonate rocks can match. At present the only significant amounts of aggregate produced in this category are from some tough Carboniferous dolomites from South Wales. No conventional non-dolomitic limestones are currently used for track ballast in the UK.

The only significant amount of track ballast currently produced in the sandstone category is from the Cambrian quartzite from Nuneaton although very small amounts of greywacke are used in southern Scotland and even smaller amount of Caithness Flags in the Highland Region.

Otherwise track ballast in 1988/1989 was supplied from 18 quarries in igneous and metamorphic rock, but mostly from five large producers which include the microdiorite at Pemaenmawr, the hornfels at Meldon, and three quarries in the granites and diorites of Leicestershire. Most of the remainder comes from minor intrusions of dolerite and from smaller granite or fine grained acidic rock quarries in Scotland. Very little metamorphic rock, other than hornfels, is used except for minor quantities of Moine rocks in Scotland.

12.3. British practice

British Rail currently require aggregates for ballast to be finer than 63 mm and not more than 0.8% finer than 1.18 mm with most of the material lying between 50 and 28 mm, according to the following specification:

Square mesh sieve size (mm)	wt % passing
63	100
50	100–97
28	20–0
14	2–0
1.18	0.8–0

The material is otherwise required to be hard, durable stone, angular in shape with all dimensions nearly equal and free from dust.

The major quality requirement is specified in terms of a Wet Attrition Value, defined in BS 812: 1951, but now only applied to track ballast although it is related to abrasion resistance. The Wet Attrition Value should not exceed 4% unless by previous written agreement with the Regional Chief Civil Engineer British Rail, when values up to 6% may be allowed.

In addition, neither the flakiness index nor the elongation index should exceed 50%; not more than 2% of the particles by weight should have a dimension exceeding 100 mm and not more than 25% by weight should have a dimension exceeding 75 mm.

Quarries supplying rail ballast are expected to notify British Rail when they open a new face or when there is an apparent change in the mineral quality in an existing face and submit new samples for testing.

Sand used in the blanketing layer is specified in terms of the following size distribution:

Sieve size (mm)	% passing by weight
14	100
2.36	80–100
1.18	70–90
0.60	48–76
0.30	24–60
0.15	5–42
0.075	0–10

If more than 4% of the material is finer than 75 µm it should not show any plasticity (i.e. the plasticity index should be zero (BS 1377).

12.4. European practice

12.4.1. Germany

Track ballast for use on the Deutsche Bundersbakes in Germany is required to consist of a quarried rock that is judged to be resistant to weathering, on the basis of the appropriate DIN Standard, and to have an apparent density within specified limits depending on the rock type. It must also have a compressive strength of at least 180 N/mm² and have a specified resistance to impact.

The material is expected to lie within the size range 70–20 mm, contain less than 1% of material finer than 0.063 mm and otherwise correspond to the following grading envelope based on round hole test screens:

Particle size (mm)	% by weight
25/30	0–10
30/40	15–25
40/50	25–35
50/60	30–40
60/65	5–15

In terms of shape, the ballast is to consist of irregular, sharp edged grains, which are not excessively flaky and otherwise be free of organic impurities, marl, clay and any other deleterious substances.

To effect the necessary quality control a suitability certificate issued by the purchaser following inspection of the deposit, the method of extraction, processing, storage and locality is required. The certificate also contains a scientific report containing details of the geological, petrographic and tectonic character of the deposit. In addition, the contractor is expected to make routine tests of the material during production and keep records for three years during which time they are to be made available for inspection.

12.4.2. France

In France, ballast used by the SNCF is subject to extensive and detailed specifications. The aggregate is expected to consist of freshly worked igneous rock, other than pumice or pozzolanic material; sediments are excluded. Each quarry must be approved by the railway organization and suppliers must submit a geological report and petrographic analysis.

The main physical requirements are specified in terms of strength and resistance to abrasion as defined by the Los Angeles test and the Micro-Deval test respectively. The values recorded by either of these tests are correlated with a coefficient of harness (DRI) which is used in the actual specification. In any one quarry DRI values from a number of samples are incorporated in a statistical analysis from which a global value (DRG) for the whole quarry is calculated.

The DRG at an approved quarry must not be less than 16 if it is to be considered as a source of rail ballast. In addition, for high-speed lines a minimum DRG of 20 is required. On ordinary lines there is a minimum DRG requirement of 17 for major works which is lowered to 16 for ordinary maintenance. For purposes of correlation a coefficient of hardness (DRI) of 16 is equivalent to a Los Angeles value of 23 or a Micro-Deval value of 14. A DRI value of 17 is equivalent to Los Angeles and Micro-Deval values of 22 and 15 respectively. A DRI value of 20 is equivalent to Los Angeles and Micro-Deval values of 19.5 and 18.5 respectively.

The ballast is expected to have a size distribution (square mesh) in which 100% is finer than 63 mm, at least 85% is finer than 50 mm, not more than 5% is finer than 25 mm and not more than 1% finer than 16 mm. Intermediate sizes are also specified. Otherwise the ballast particles are expected to be polyhedral in shape and have sharp edges. There are also limits on the presence of elongate and flat fragments. The ballast must, in addition, be free from sand, dust, earth and other deleterious matter.

12.4.3. Italy

In Italy, ballast used by the State Railways is required to consist of newly quarried crushed stone particles, mainly 60–30 mm in size, which are frost resistant, of low porosity and not weathered. They must be free of dust, vegetable or other foreign matter and devoid of materials that are harmful to the health of the operatives. The main quality requirement is specified in terms of the Los Angeles Test in which three categories are defined. In the first category, igneous and metamorphic rock is required which has a Los Angeles value of less than 16. The second category additionally allows sedimentary rocks with a Los Angeles value in the range 16–22. The third category allows only sedimentary rock with a Los Angeles value in the range 22–28.

The size range of the ballast is tested using perforated steel plates with round holes of 20, 30, 60 and 80 mm diameter and is expected to conform to the following limits:

100–98% will pass 80 mm
100–92% will pass 60 mm
  0–6% will pass 30 mm
  0–1% will pass 20 mm.

Particle shape is controlled by a requirement that not more than 25% of the ballast by weight should be composed of particles with a minimum dimension less than one third of the maximum.

Ballast within a given contract that falls slightly outside the limits specified with respect to size, shape or Los Angeles value, may still be acceptable subject to a price discount depending on the variation. For example, departures from the Los Angeles value limit of 1, 2 or 3 units are subject to price discounts of 1%, 5% or 15% respectively. Greater variations render the contract void as do major changes in the lithology of the rock. However, no increase in the price is payable if the ballast is found to have properties superior to those in the original specification. Quality control is effected by making at least one test for every 10 000 m³ of ballast used.

12.4.4. Spain

Specifications for track ballast used in Spain by the state railway organization (RENFE) are very comprehensive. New quarries proposing to supply railway ballast, or existing suppliers where the product quality is suspect, are required to provide a geotechnical report together with appropriate geological maps at scales 1:5000 and 1:25 000 covering the quarry and the surrounding area. The report is to include comment on the history of the quarry, the results of a petrographic study and classification of the rock assisted by point counting or by quantitative X-ray diffractometry, the results of specified physical tests for strength, wear and frost resistance on at least four samples and an estimate of the quarriable reserve.

Track ballast is classified into two types: A and B. Type A consists of siliceous rock, usually igneous although sedimentary and metamorphic rocks are also included. It is used on heavily trafficked lines carrying an average of over 4000 tonnes per day. Type B ballast consists of limestone and is used where the average traffic loading is less than 4000 tonnes per day. Mixing of the two types of ballast is prohibited.

Physical requirements of the two types of ballast are specified in the following terms.

(i) A simple crushing test involving an axial load on a cylindrical specimen or a Franklin point load test. Type A and Type B ballasts are expected to withstand point loads of 1200 kg/cm² and 1000 kg/cm² respectively.
(ii) Wear resistance determined by the Los Angeles test. Type A and Type B ballasts are expected to have values of 19 and 22 respectively. In addition, a value of 26 is specified for Type B fine ballast.
(iii) Frost resistance determined by five cycles of the magnesium sulphate test. The maximum allowable weight loss for both types of ballast is 8%.

The particle size of the ballast is expected to be less than 80 mm and to lie mostly between 63 and 31.5 mm, with less than 1% finer than 20 mm. Grading curves are specified, based on plate screens with round holes; somewhat more latitude is allowed over the grading of Type B ballast in the middle size ranges, but otherwise the requirements are very similar. A fine ballast in both Type A and Type B is specified which lies mainly in the range 25–16 mm.

Otherwise the ballast is expected to be free from dust or soil and there is a restriction on the proportion of acicular or platy particles.

12.5. US practice

Materials allowed for use as railway ballast in the USA include crushed stone, crushed air-cooled blast-furnace slag, crushed open hearth slag and crushed or uncrushed gravel. The materials are to be composed of hard, strong durable particles, free from injurious amounts of deleterious substances.

The main quality requirement is that the wear coefficient, when tested by the Los Angeles method, should not be greater than 40 unless specified by the engineer. The soundness of the ballast, when used in regions where frost occurs, should be such that the sodium sulphate soundness test does not cause a weight loss in excess of 10% after five cycles. Otherwise the proportion of weak, friable pieces in the ballast should not exceed 5%, the proportion of material passing a 200 mesh sieve should not exceed 1% and the proportion of clay lumps should not exceed 0.5%. All tests are carried out by ASTM methods.

For crushed stone and slag ballast five separate size distributions are allowed, the coarsest being not more than 10% coarser than 60 mm, while the finest is not more than 5% coarser than 25 mm. The proportion at intermediate sizes and the fines content are also specified.

For gravel, three size distributions are permitted: 80–100%, 65–100% and 60–95% respectively finer than 25 mm. The percentage passing through finer sieves is also specified.

In the case of blanketing layer or sub-ballast a wide range of materials is allowed depending on local economics and availability, providing they correspond to the current ASTM specification (D 1241). The thickness of the sub-ballast layer can vary but the American Railway Engineering Association notes that excellent results have been obtained with a depth of 300 mm. Where practical, sub-ballast is to be placed in layers and thoroughly compacted in accordance with standard practice to form a stable foundation for the ballast.

General references

AMERICAN RAILWAY ENGINEERING ASSOCIATION (AREA) 1976. Report on Committee 22, Bulletin 656, Chicago, 312–317.
—— 1976. Manual Recommendations, Special Committee on Concrete Ties, Bulletin 660, Chicago, 133–138.
AMERICAN RAILWAY RECOMMENDATIONS, COMMITTEE 1, 1976. Report on Assignment 2, Ballast, Bulletin 660, AREA, Chicago, 110–115.
DALTON, C. J. 1973. *Field Durability Tests on Ballast Samples as a Guide to Specification Requirements.* Canadian National Railways Technical Research Centre, St. Laurent, Quebec.
GASKIN, P. N. & RAYMOND, G. P. 1976. Contribution to Selections of Railroad Ballast. *Proceedings of the American Society of Civil Engineers,* **102** (TE 2), 377–394.
HAY, W. W., BAUGHER, R. & REINSCHMIDT, A. J. 1977. *A Study of Railroad Ballast Economics.* U.S. Department of Transportation Report No. FRA/ORD-77-64, Federal Railroad Administration, PB 275102.
KNUTSON, R. M. & THOMPSON, M. R. *et al.* 1977. *Materials Evaluation Study.* U.S. Department of Transportation Report No. FRA/ORD-77-02, PB 264215.
MAJIDZADEH, K. 1976. *An Evaluation of Engineering and Physical Properties, and Use-Specifications for Locally Available Ballast Materials.* Report of Development Project 6017, Engineering Experiment Station, Ohio State University, Civil Engineering Materials Laboratory.
RAIL INTERNATIONAL 1978. No. 9 Sept.
THE PERMANENT WAY INSTITUTION 1971. *British Rail Track, Design, Construction and Maintenance.*

13. Aggregates for use in filter media

13.1. Introduction

Although the total volume of aggregate used for filters is relatively small, filters nevertheless play important and diverse roles in many projects. Table 13.1 shows some of the main uses of filter aggregates and the first four parts of this chapter discuss some of the requirements and properties of these materials. The final three parts of the chapter describe the functions and specification of filter aggregates in their three main applications, namely water filtration, effluent treatment and as drainage filters for earthworks and other civil engineering structures. These will normally be subject to different design criteria and may also call for filter materials with distinct sets of physical and mechanical properties.

Filter aggregates generally consist of sand, gravel or crushed rock. Manufactured aggregates are also occasionally used and these often include blast-furnace slags.

Although filter materials for water and effluent treatment works are often used in relatively small quantities, the high quality of aggregate normally required is not always readily available from commercial production processing, which may be designed to yield a satisfactory general purpose aggregate at least cost. On the other hand, drainage layers in major civil engineering works, such as embankment dams, are usually designed to make the best use of the available natural materials with the minimum of processing.

TABLE 13.1. *Uses of filter aggregates*

Category of works	Filter application	Principal function		
		Drainage	Pressure relief	Filtration
Land drainage	Surface blanket drainage	*		
	Ditch/trench fill	*		
	Drain/soakaway fill	*		
	Pipe filters			*
	Pipe envelopes	*		
Structure drainage	Foundation drainage	*	*	
	Roadbed drainage	*		
	Runway drainage	*		
	Retaining structure drainage	*	*	
	Embankment dam drains	*	*	*
	Slope drainage	*		
Remedial and stabilization works	Uplift pressure relief		*	
	Seepage force prevention		*	
	Saturation control	*	*	
	Piping prevention		*	*
Water supply	Well filters			*
	Well envelopes	*		
Filtration and purification works	Fine & coarse filter beds			*
	Gravel underdrain envelope	*		*
Marine works	Bedding layers		*	
	Transition layers			*
	Pressure relief		*	

13.2. Key properties of filter aggregates

13.2.1. General

Particle size, grading, strength and durability are the key properties, as these determine permeability, ease of construction, stability and longevity.

Particle sizes in filter aggregates can range from fine sands to boulder-sized material. The aggregates are usually placed and compacted in an unbound condition.

The completed filter layer or bed will usually need to have the following properties: structural stability (especially if placed in an unconfined situation); durability; high permeability combined with resistance to internal erosion of fines; low frost susceptibility; low susceptibility to salt aggression, chemical attack and solution loss. Physical and chemical breakdown in service may seriously impair the design grading of a filter, adversely affecting its performance.

The strength, shape, surface texture and composition of the individual particles will have an important influence on the above properties as will the abrasion resistance and crushing strength of the aggregate since, if these are deficient, it may degrade during placing and compaction.

13.2.2. Grading

This is fundamental to the design of a filter, detailed consideration of which is beyond the scope of this report. Filters in contact with natural soils or controlled fill material may be designed in accordance with criteria originally given by Terzaghi & Peck (1964), but current practice favours the design criteria developed by Sherard & Dunnigan (1985, 1989) and issued as guidelines by the U.S. Department of Agriculture (1986).

Multi-layered construction will tend to be used for the thicker filter layers. A very wide range of particle sizes, from fine sand up to boulders, might, therefore, be used in different parts of a filter zone. An important requirement is freedom from silt and clay and it is commonly specified that any material passing the 425 µm BS sieve shall be non-plastic when tested in accordance with BS 1377. It would also normally have a fines content below 10%.

13.2.3. Aggregate strength

Since in the absence of a cementitious binder, the stability and load-bearing properties of a filter depend on the aggregate particles alone, these must be strong enough to prevent breakdown during construction and when in use. Fine-grained materials normally used for filters are generally those which nature has selected as the most durable. Thus, many sands and gravels, and particularly

the finer gravels, are composed mainly of the hard and stable mineral quartz. However, aggregate particles coarser than fine gravel are not usually monomineralic but are composed of rock fragments in which the strength is derived from the interlocking or cementation of individual mineral grains. Serious consideration must then be given to the assessment of the strength and abrasion resistance of these aggregates.

13.2.4. Particle durability

Durability can be defined as the resistance of the aggregate under its working conditions to cyclic variations in temperature, load, moisture content, freezing and thawing, and chemical environment. It is essential that filter aggregates are durable in the long term and this is particularly important where high strength is not a characteristic of the aggregate. Any breakdown of the constituent particles would increase the fines content of the filter and alter its design grading and efficiency.

13.2.5. Particle shape

This property is, after grading, as important as strength in a filter aggregate and can be discussed under two main headings. The first relates to whether a particular particle is basically equidimensional in shape or whether it is flaky or elongated. In general, it is desirable for filter aggregates to be essentially equidimensional as this aids the flow distribution through the medium and also facilitates packing of the coarser and fine constituents and improves the effectiveness of the filter. The second important shape characteristic is roundness and again it is better for the filter aggregate to have rounded, as opposed to angular, edges to most particles.

However, rather different considerations apply to biological percolating filters, where the aggregate acts mainly as a supporting medium to a microbial film and its specific surface is, therefore, important. This is discussed in §13.5.

13.2.6. Particle texture

Surface texture affects to a lesser extent both the flow of liquid through the filter and the filtration characteristics of the material. A smooth glassy surface is useful from a drainage aspect but not so efficient from a filtration or fines ingress viewpoint, where a rougher surface texture is considered more advantageous.

13.2.7. Surface coatings

Some aggregates have a coating that may, or may not,

TABLE 13.2. *Suggested tests for evaluation of aggregates for general filter applications*

Category of test	Test	Proposed guideline acceptance criteria*
Physical properties	Grading	Design test only
	Shape } flakiness index elongation index	Not more than 30
	Relative density (oven dried)	No less than 2.5
	Water absorption	Not more than 3% by weight
Mechanical properties	10% fines value	Not less than 100 kN
	Aggregate crushing value	Not more than 30
	Aggregate impact value	Not more than 30
	Aggregate abrasion value	Not more than 20
	Los Angeles abrasion value	Not more than 40
Durability properties	Soundness (MgSO₄)	Not more than 12% loss†
	Deleterious substances }	To be assessed after
	Petrographic analysis	examination

*Dependent on conditions of use and to be evaluated collectively, not in isolation.
†See special requirement for biological filters in §13.5

be easily removed during initial processing. Coatings are commonly composed of clay, silt, calcium carbonate, iron oxides, silica or gypsum, but other coatings can occur. Such coatings may vary in thickness and hardness and are, on the whole, undesirable in filter aggregates. They should either be removed by scrubbing or be as strong and durable as the particle itself.

13.2.8. Particle porosity

The functions of drainage and filtration are not significantly affected by particle porosity which can, however, be expected to have a negative correlation with strength and durability. Therefore, the aggregate porosity, or a related property such as water absorption, should be measured in order to assess its possible effects on, for example, durability, chemical reaction, freeze/thaw or other breakdown mechanisms.

13.2.9. Chemical reactivity

There are generally no specified requirements for chemical inertness or solubility but these should nevertheless be taken into account in relation to the use of the filter media. It is important that the aggregate is not affected by the chemical properties of the liquid to be treated and also that constituents are not leached from the filter medium into the filtrate. The latter is more likely to occur with artificial aggregates, such as slag, than with naturally occurring aggregates. Slag may also be aggressive to concrete and, if used, is generally required to

comply with the stability and sulphur content requirements of BS 1047.

13.3. Testing of aggregates

Tests relevant to filter aggregates are essentially those used for general aggregate testing and are listed in Table 13.2 which also proposes some guideline acceptance criteria.

Additional criteria applicable to some special purposes are considered in the following sections which describe the main engineering applications of filters.

13.4. Water treatment: filtration through sand

13.4.1. General

There are basically two types of sand filter:

(i) filters characterized by slow filtration rates, using a fine sand and requiring infrequent cleaning;

(ii) rapid filters, which are coarser, operating at higher filtration rates and requiring frequent cleaning.

The action of a filter bed in removing fine suspended matter is complex and not yet fully understood, being a combination of (i) straining, (ii) physical forces, which

(a)

(b)

Fig. 13.1. (a) Gravel filter media for water treatment (courtesy Thames Water plc). (b) Sand filter (courtesy Thames Water plc).

determine the conveyance of particles towards and onto the sand grains, and (iii) surface forces which hold the suspended particles to the grains. In slow sand filters the bed usually comprises from 0.6 m to 1.2 m of fine sand supported by layers of graded gravel 0.2 m to 0.3 m thick, see Figs 13.1(a) and 13.1(b). Rapid filters usually comprise from 0.6 m to 0.8 m of coarse sand supported

on several layers of fine to coarse gravel to give a total bed thickness of 1.0 m to 1.3 m.

13.4.2. Filter bed sand

The sand should be hard, abrasion resistant and free

from contaminants. It should not lose more than 2% by weight after immersion for 24 hours in 20% hydrochloric acid at 20°C. Both rounded and angular grains may be used, but they should not be flaky. Filter sand is normally obtained from natural sand deposits by sieving, although crushed fines produced from rocks composed predominantly of quartz are sometimes used.

13.4.3. Filter gravel

The gravel or coarse layer in a filter system has several functions. It supports the sand, permits the filtered water to move freely towards the underdrain and, in the case of a rapid filter, facilitates a uniform flow distribution. The coarse material should be clean, hard, durable, and free from flat, flaky or elongated particles.

13.5. Aggregates for biological percolating filters

The term 'filter' is a misnomer as the process involved is not truly filtering but a biological contact process. The filter medium is primarily required to support colonies of organisms, including bacteria and fungi, which exist in microbial layers on the surface of the media and over which sewage or other pollutant liquids are trickled so that the colonies may feed, in an aerobic environment, upon the organic matter present, see Fig. 13.2.

The degree of treatment attained is largely dependent upon the area of microbial film to which the liquid is exposed and it, therefore, follows that the surface area per unit volume of the media should be as large as possible, consistent with adequate aeration and permeability.

This is best achieved with single-sized filter media. Percolating filters of optimum surface area and void ratio can either be manufactured, usually of plastic, or alternatively, filter beds may be constructed from natural aggregates which may not possess optimum characteristics but have the advantage of low unit cost.

Biological percolating filters formed with natural aggregates typically consist of between 1.5 m and 3.0 m thickness of single-sized coarse aggregate over which the liquid to be treated is distributed. BS 1438 recommends that the aggregate should be selected from the range 14 mm to 63 mm, the actual size specified depending on the operating conditions of a system. Undersized material should not exceed 2% if the filter is to operate efficiently. A layer of 100 mm size aggregate is often used to support the filter.

The aggregates may be naturally occurring or crushed and should preferably be angular and of rough surface texture so as to maximize the surface area. For example, a 25 mm single-size slag was found to have a specific surface area of $206 \, \text{m}^2/\text{m}^3$ whereas the corresponding figure for crushed gravel was $176 \, \text{m}^2/\text{m}^3$ (Bruce 1968).

The aggregates must be strong enough to sustain their own weight and, in particular, must be durable and resistant to cyclic wetting over periods of many years. It is found in practice that most strong rocks are suitable for filter media, as are certain artificial materials such as clinker and slag. Softer or potentially soluble aggregates, such as some types of limestone, have to be selected with care and are frequently found to give unacceptable results in the sodium sulphate soundness test.

BS 1438 sets out the particular requirements for aggregates for biological percolating media in respect of size, shape, flakiness, cleanness and durability. Durability is tested according to this standard by 20 cycles of the sodium (not magnesium) sulphate soundness test, samples showing more than 3% loss by this method being considered unsound.

FIG. 13.2. Biological percolating filter (courtesy Thames Water plc).

13.6. Filters for civil engineering structures

13.6.1. General

Protective or pressure relief filters for civil engineering structures usually consist of one or more layers of free-draining sand and/or gravel material placed on or within

FIG. 13.3. Filter media placed behind sea-wall.

FIG. 13.4. Filter media in dam construction (courtesy P. G. Fookes).

a less pervious soil to remove seepage water and prevent erosion of the soil or damage to the overlying structures from uplift pressure. The soil which is to be protected by the filter is commonly referred to as the base or the base material. A given base material can be protected by a filter layer having a grading related to that of the base material, according to the Terzaghi criteria for filter design (Lambe & Whitman 1969).

Sherard & Dunnigan (1985, 1989) have modified these design criteria using field and laboratory studies and design guidelines based on their findings have been issued by the U.S. Department of Agriculture (1986). Current practice favours the use of the Sherard and Dunnigan criteria.

Filters may consist either of a single layer, or of several layers each with a different grading, in which case they are known as zoned filters. The filter or filter layers may be classed as uniform (i.e. having a narrow range of major particle sizes), or well graded (i.e. having a broad range of particle sizes). In large structures, such as embankment dams, it is more usual to design the filter layers to make the best use of locally available natural materials, rather than to process large quantities of material to suit a pre-conceived design. Deficiencies in grading may be compensated by varying the thickness of the filter.

A full account of the criteria and methods used in the design of civil engineering filters is outside the scope of this work but selected references are given. Uses of filter media are illustrated in Figs 13.3 and 13.4.

13.6.2. Specification of aggregates

The specification of filters, drains, etc. and their related aggregates is often rather loose and occasionally gives rise to serious contractual or technical difficulties. The following suggestions may prove useful to those formulating specifications.

The specifications of aggregates for filters and drains should avoid the use of general terms such as pervious and free-draining, unless used in conjunction with specific quantitative requirements for grading, soundness and permeability that assure the necessary physical properties. When grading requirements are part of a specification, the time and place of the sampling during project construction should be clearly stated, otherwise confusion arises, and enforcement of the designers' requirements is difficult. Aggregates which break down and develop a greater proportion of fines during handling, placement, and compaction may meet a grading specification at the plant or when they arrive at the works but could fail when tested after compaction. The important criteria are the grading and permeability of the material as it will be in the finished work. Hence, additional samples for testing should be taken after the filter materials have been placed and compacted to determine whether there has been any degradation during handling and placement. However, this identifies a potential contractual difficulty because specifications, unfortunately, are rarely explicit as to the stage at which the compliance criteria are deemed to apply. In the absence of any requirement to the contrary, it is more normal practice for compliance to be assessed on samples prior to placement in the works, post placement sampling and testing being for engineering rather than contractual purposes.

With regard to the acceptance criteria which can be applied to a potential filter aggregate, very little is published. However, the following guidelines might prove useful. The aggregates should be hard, durable, clean and should not contain deleterious materials of such a form or in sufficient quantity to adversely affect the efficient operation or longevity of the filter. Durability should include resistance to frost, corrosion and dissolution. Examples of deleterious materials are: clay, flaky and/or elongate particles, excessively porous and/or laminated materials, and chemically unsound or readily soluble materials.

A typical specification might thus combine some or all of the following particular requirements:

(i) oven dried relative density not less than 2.5;
(ii) water absorption not greater than 3% by weight;
(iii) aggregate impact value not more than 30
   or
   aggregate crushing value not more than 30
   or
   10% fines value not less than 100 kN;
(iv) maximum flakiness and elongation indices not greater than 30;
(v) aggregate abrasion value not greater than 20
   or
   Los Angeles abrasion value not greater than 40;
(vi) magnesium sulphate soundness value not more than 12% loss.

These requirements should be regarded as the minimum acceptable. In some situations, where the proper functioning of the filter is critical to the safety of a structure, more stringent acceptance criteria may be required and a specification applicable to high-quality concrete aggregate may be more appropriate (see Chapter 8).

13.7. Concluding remarks

It is hoped that this short account will have made it clear that the properties required of filter aggregates are dominated by the highly diverse purposes for which they may be intended. Indeed in some cases, such as sewage treatment, their main role is not truly filtration at all, but to support microbial colonies active in a biological process. In other cases, the shape and size of the filter, its operating conditions (including the chemical environment), and both the character and quantity of available natural materials can each affect design, making a general specification impossible. The over-riding needs are for durability and dimensional stability, which will usually have to be assessed from a wide range of physical and chemical properties. This may call for a considerable degree of judgement and experience on the part of the designer.

References

BRITISH STANDARDS INSTITUTION 1971. *Specification for Media for Biological Percolating Filters*: BS 1438 (amended Aug. 1972, Dec 1980).
—— 1983. *Specification for air-cooled blast furnace slag coarse aggregate for concrete*: BS 1047.
LAMBE, T. W. & WHITMAN, R. V. 1969. *Soil Mechanics* (see esp. pp 292–4). Wiley, New York.
SHERARD, J. L. & DUNNIGAN, L. P. 1985. Filters and leakage control in embankment dams. Seepage and leakage from dams and impoundments. *ASCE*, New York, NY, 1–29.
—— & —— 1989. Critical filters for impervious soils. *ASCE Journal of Geotechnical Engineering*, **115**, 7, 927–947.
TERZAGHI, K. & PECK, R. B. 1964. *Soil Mechanics in Engineering Practice*. Wiley, New York.

US DEPARTMENT OF AGRICULTURE, Soil Conservation Service, 1986. Soil Mechanics Note No. 1. Guide for determining the gradation of sand and gravel filters. Lincoln, NE, USA.

General references

AMERICAN WATER WORKS ASSOCIATION 1971. Water quality and treatment. 3rd edn. New York, McGraw-Hill.
BRUCE, A. M. 1968. The significance of particle shape in relation to percolating filter media. *Journal of British Granite and Whinstone Federation* **8** (2), 1–15.
DEGREMONT COMPANY (eds). 1973. *Water Treatment Handbook* New York, Taylor-Carlisle.
DEPARTMENT OF TRANSPORT. 1986. *Specification of highway works* 6th edn. HMSO, London.
FAIR, G. M. *et al.* 1968. *Water and wastewater engineering*. Vol. 2: Water purification and wastewater treatment and disposal. New York, Wiley.
HOLDEN, W. S. (ed.) 1970. *Water treatment and examination*. Churchill Livingstone, Edinburgh.
HUISMAN, L. & WOOD, W. E. 1974. *Slow Sand Filtration*. Geneva, World Health Organisation.
IVES, K. J. 1975. Specifications for granular filter media. *Effluent and Water Treatment Journal*, **15** (6), 296, 298–299, 301–305.
TWORT, A. C., HOATHER, R. C. & LAW, F. M. 1974. *Water Supply*. 2nd edn. Edward Arnold, London.
US CORPS OF ENGINEERS 1952. *Seepage Control, Soil Mechanics Design*. Department of Army, Washington DC.
US DEPARTMENT OF THE INTERIOR. *Earth Manual* 2nd edn. 1974 (see esp. pp 305–9).
US DEPARTMENT OF THE NAVY. 1971. *Design Manual*, NAVFAC DM-7. Alexandria, USA.

Appendix: Aggregate properties

In this appendix some information on aggregate properties is given. First some properties of currently produced British aggregates, second some more generalized data on aggregate properties worldwide, and third some information on how weathering affects the properties of aggregates. It is strongly emphasized that all the information given in this Appendix must be regarded as providing only a general appreciation of aggregate properties and should not be relied upon for specific test values for particular rocks or sources.

Properties of some British aggregates

Table A1 gives some test results for 96 aggregates from quarries in Great Britain. The information is not exhaustive but comes solely from fact-sheets issued by the suppliers or from information provided to members of the Working Party by the suppliers. None of the data has been confirmed independently. Where the quarry is not named in the Table this omission is at the request of the supplier. Because aggregate properties are liable to vary, the test results in the Table should not be taken as an indication of present production for particular quarries; instead prospective users should seek up-to-date information from the suppliers. It should be borne in mind that suppliers will not usually work poor quality sources of aggregate, nor provide data on them.

The rock descriptions are those of the suppliers, supplemented in some cases by reference to entries in directories of quarries (BGS 1984 and BACMI 1986).

The classification in Table A1 is by the broad rock groups used in the aggregates industry, including many of the suppliers of the data. Tables A1.1 and A1.2 describe crushed rock aggregates and Table A1.3 gravel aggregates.

The Table reflects the fact that a common aggregate in England and Wales is limestone (see Chapter 4), this rock being supplied by 36 quarries. The dominance of limestone as an aggregate is undoubtedly because of the widespread outcrop of the Carboniferous Limestone in northern England, Derbyshire, Wales and the Mendips. Limestone is an aggregate suitable for many purposes except for the surfacing of roads, for which its polished stone value is often too low (see Chapter 11), and railway track ballast (see Chapter 12).

Following limestones in the Table are gritstones (nine quarries), basalts (eight quarries) and granites (five quar-

ries). These rocks have higher polished stone values and the gritstones, in particular with very high PSVs (all above 60), are probably quarried predominantly for road surfacing aggregates as well as other purposes.

All the samples are of reasonably high strength (all except two have 10% fines values of 150 kN or more) illustrating the abundance of strong aggregates in Great Britain. For those few samples for which Los Angeles abrasion values have been reported, a good correlation with aggregate crushing value is seen (see Chapter 7).

For the 21 samples for which magnesium sulphate soundness values have been reported, all save one have values of 90 or more, again indicating the ready availability of high-quality aggregates. In Table A1 the magnesium sulphate soundness values quoted are the percentages *retained* after the test, as specified in the British Standard test specification (see Chapter 7).

Although only four in number, the flint gravels show little variation in the properties reported. It is certain that flint gravels are under-represented in Table A1, because this aggregate is widely won in southeast England.

The means and standard deviations given in Table A1 should only be used to obtain a general comparison of overall properties and their ranges for the different groups and should not be used for any other purpose. See also the caveat at the foot of the Table regarding the data in general.

For further information on British aggregates, it can be noted that some properties of 78 British aggregates currently used for bitumen macadam roadbase are given by Bullas & West (1991). The properties tabulated are adherent silt and clay content, magnesium sulphate soundness, aggregate impact value and 10% fines value, but neither the quarries nor their locations are identified.

Properties of some aggregates from worldwide sources

Table A2 gives some property data based primarily upon a synthesis of the test results for 285 samples of materials used as aggregate from sources around the world including the United Kingdom. These test results were obtained over a ten-year period in the London laboratories of Sandberg. Samples were included in the survey only when it was considered that the aggregate type has been established reliably, either because a petrographical

TABLE A1.1 *Examples of properties of some British aggregates*

Quarry	Location	Rock description	Geology	Aggregate impact value	Aggregate crushing value	Aggregate abrasion value	10% fines value kN	Polished stone value	Water absorption %	MgSO$_4$ soundness value	Los Angeles abrasion value
Belford	Belford, Northumberland	Quartz-dolerite basalt	Intruded into Carboniferous	8	11	3.2–3.6	380	50–56	0.4–0.5	99	
Cragmill	Belford, Northumberland	Medium grey basalt	Intruded into Carboniferous	14	15	4.6	270	56	1.1		
Divethill	Hexham, Northumberland	Medium grey dolerite	Intruded into Carboniferous	10	11	3.1	375	57	0.8		
Greystone	Launceston, Cornwall	Dolerite	Intruded into Carboniferous	13	13	5.5	295	57	0.6		12
Langside	Kennoway, Fife	Dolerite	Permo-Carboniferous	9	13	2.4	330	48	1.2		
Moons Hill	Bath, Avon	Pyroxene-andesite		14	17	5.6	260	59	0.9	98	
New England	Plymouth, Devon	Dolerite	Intruded into Devonian	13	14	5.9	298	57	0.6	—	16
—	Strathclyde	Quartz-dolerite	Intruded into Carboniferous	14	14	5.9	310	63	1.1	—	—
			Mean	11.9	13.4	4.7	314.9	56.7	0.9		
			Standard deviation	2.3	1.8	1.3	41.5	4.2	0.2		
Dean	Helston, Cornwall	Gabbro	Lizard Gabbro	17	17	4.1	240	54	0.5		
Croft	Croft, Leics	Quartz-diorite		20	20	5.4	190	54	1.2		22
Glensanda	Glensanda, Argyll	Pink medium granite	Strontian Granite	20	20	3.0	190	52		99–97	27
—	Warwicks	Quartz-diorite		13	15	5.5	190	63	1.1		
Mountsorrel	Loughborough, Leics	Granite		20	20	2.6	190		0.1	—	—
Shap Pink	Penrith, Cumbria	Pink granite	Intruded into Lower Palaeozoic	23	25	3.4	150	54	0.6	—	—
			Mean	19.2	19.9	4.0	182.0	55.8	0.7		
			Standard deviation	3.3	3.2	1.2	16.0	4.3	0.4		
Brindister	Lerwick, Shetland	Sandstone/Gritstone	Devonian	8	10	9.4	400	64	0.8		
Dry Rigg	Settle, N. Yorks	Sandstone/Gritstone	Silurian (Horton Formation)	9	11	7.0	320	62	0.5	98	
Gilfach	Neath, W. Glamorgan	Medium grey gritstone	Carboniferous (Pennant Sandstone)	20	18	7.1	215	67	1.0		
Hafod	Mid Glamorgan	Sandstone	Carboniferous	16	16	8.3	260	70	1.1		
	Newbridge, Gwent	Sandstone/Gritstone	Carboniferous (Pennant Sandstone)			8.0	280	70			
Haughmond	Shrewsbury, Shrops	Greywacke		11		5.7	400	64	0.2		
Ingleton	Ingleton, N. Yorks	Sandstone/Gritstone	Cambrian (Ingleton Series)	12	11	4.8	380	60–63	1.5		
—	Dyfed	Gritstone		15	15	8.2	280	68	1.0	—	18
Venn	Barnstaple, Devon	Gritstone	Carboniferous	16	15	5.4	259	63	0.7	—	—
			Mean	13.4	13.7	7.1	310.4	66.3			
			Standard deviation	3.8	2.8	1.4	64.2	3.1			
Balmullo	Leuchars, Fife	Dacite	Intruded into Devonian	10	11	3.3	350	59	2.0	99	
Harden	Morpeth, Northumberland	Albite biotite porphyry	Intruded into Carboniferous	12	27	1.2–2.0	220	50–55	1.0–1.5	98	
Quartzite	Wotton-under-edge, Avon	Pink quartzitic sandstone	Carboniferous (Cromhall Sandstone)	18	18	6.0	230	60	0.6		
Rockbeare Hill	Exeter, Devon	Quartzite	Triassic (Bunter Pebble Beds)	17	14	1.8	293	53	0.7		

N.B. The data in this table should not be used for contractual or other purposes

TABLE A1.2 *Examples of properties of some British aggregates*

Quarry	Location	Rock description	Geology	Aggregate impact value	Aggregate crushing value	Aggregate abrasion value	10% fines value kN	Polished stone value	Water absorption %	MgSO₄ soundness value	Los Angeles abrasion value
Shap Blue	Penrith, Cumbria	Grey/black hornfels	Metamorphosed Palaeozoic	9	10	1.4	380	55	0.5		
—	Clwyd	Limestone	Carboniferous	16	20	5.6	200	46	0.3		
Backwell	Bristol, Avon	Light grey limestone	Carboniferous	20	22	9.0	200	34	0.7		
Blaenyfan	Kidwelly, Dyfed	Grey limestone	Carboniferous	22	20	10.0	170	39	0.6		
—	N. Yorkshire	Limestone	Carboniferous	19	22	9.0	174	48	0.9		
Doves Holes	Buxton, Derby	Light grey limestone	Carboniferous (Bee Low Limestone)	22	23	10.0	180	37–39	0.4		
—	Avon	Limestone	Carboniferous	20	21	9.9	190	47	0.3		
Eldon Hill	Buxton, Derby	Grey/white limestone	Carboniferous (Bee Low Limestone)	14	23	12.0	180	40	0.3		
Eskett	Frizington, Cumbria	Limestone	Carboniferous	17	24		155		0.6		
Forcett	Richmond, N. Yorks	Limestone	Carboniferous	19	25	8.1–9.0	190	45–50	0.8–1.3	94	
—	Mid Glamorgan	Limestone	Carboniferous	20	20	7.9	210	44	0.4		
Giggleswick	Settle, N. Yorks	Limestone	Carboniferous (Great Scar Limestone)	15	23	7.2	180	40	0.5	99	
Goddards	Sheffield, S. Yorks	Grey limestone	Carboniferous (Monsal Dale Limestone)	17	22	8.5	180	46	0.6	98	
Graig	Mold, Clwyd	Biosparite limestone	Carboniferous	19	20	9.7	240	44	4.8		
—	Mid Glamorgan	Limestone	Carboniferous	23	23	10.0	190	41	0.4		
Halkyn	Holywell, Clwyd	Grey/black limestone	Carboniferous	28	25		180	50	0.9		
Lea	Much Wenlock, Shrops	Limestone	Silurian (Wenlock Limestone)		26		180		1.8		30
Trimm rock	Mold, Clwyd	Limestone	Carboniferous (Loggerheads Limestone)		26				1.6		
Trimm rock	Mold, Clwyd	Limestone	Carboniferous (Cefn Mawr Limestone)		26				1.2		
Marsden	Whitburn, Tyne & Wear	Limestone	Permian	25	32	15.7	90	46–47	1.0–1.5	93	
Minera	Wrexham, Clwyd	Limestone	Carboniferous	18	25	14.3	167	46	0.6		
Moorcroft	Plymouth, Devon	Limestone	Devonian	26	28	10.0	132	38	0.7		27
Raisby	Coxhoe, Durham	Dolomitic limestone	Permian	26	24–26	10.0	160–180	43	1.1	>90	
—	Colwyn Bay, Clwyd	Medium grey limestone	Carboniferous	21	23		180	40–45	0.7		
Shining Bank	Bakewell, Derby	Grey/black limestone	Carboniferous (Monsal Dale Limestone)	18	25	11.8	180	47	1.6	95	
Stainton	Stainton, Cumbria	Limestone	Carboniferous	17	22	12.6	157	37	1.0		
Stoneycombe	Newton Abbot, Devon	Limestone	Devonian	17	24	7.4	150	33	0.8		
Stoneycombe	Newton Abbot, Devon	Limestone	Devonian	24	27	12.0	150		0.3		26
Swinden	Skipton, N. Yorks	Limestone	Carboniferous (Reef Limestone)	23	25	13.0	150		0.5	98	
Taffs Well	Cardiff, S. Glamorgan	Dolomitic limestone	Carboniferous	15	18	10.0	290		0.3	97	
Threshfield	Skipton, N. Yorks	Limestone	Carboniferous (Great Scar Limestone)	19	20	8.5	180		0.7	99	
Torr Works	East Cranmore, Somerset	Hard grey limestone	Carboniferous	21	23	7.1	184	41	0.5		
Wardlow	Waterhouses, Staffs	Limestone	Carboniferous (Milldale Limestone)	14	22	9.0	190	40	0.6		
Wenvoe	Cardiff, S. Glamorgan	Light grey limestone	Carboniferous	26	21	9.0	170	45	0.5		
Westleigh	Tiverton, Devon	Limestone	Carboniferous	19	21		187	47	0.7		22
Wick	Bristol, Avon	Light grey limestone	Carboniferous	20	22	9.0	200	40	0.6		
Wickwar	Wotton-under-edge, Avon	Light grey limestone	Carboniferous	21	21	9.0	210	40	1		
Mean				20.0	22.3	9.6	181.8	40.5	0.8	96.6	26.3
Standard deviation				3.6	4.7	2.9	32.0	4.4	0.8	2.2	2.9

N.B. The data in this table should not be used for contractual or other purposes.

TABLE A1.3 *Examples of properties of some British aggregates*

Quarry	Location	Rock description	Geology	Aggregate impact value	Aggregate crushing value	Aggregate abrasion value	10% fines value kN	Polished stone value	Water absorption %	MgSO₄ soundness value	Los Angeles abrasion value
Chard Junction	Chard, Somerset	Flint gravel	Cretaceous (River Axe Valley Gravel)	22	18	1.7	223	43	3.6		
Kilmington	Axminster, Devon	Flint gravel	Cretaceous (River Axe Gravel)	21	17	1.2	239	43	3.0		
Little Paxton	St Neots, Cambridgeshire	Flint gravel	Cretaceous (River Ouse Gravel)	21	19	1.1	227	36	2.7		22
Warmwell	Dorchester, Dorset	Flint gravel	Cretaceous (Plateau Gravel)	21	17	0.9	239	43	3.7	—	—
			Mean	21.3	17.8	1.2	232.0	41.3	3.2	—	—
			Standard deviation	0.4	0.8	0.3	7.1	3.0	0.4	—	—
Blackhill	Exeter, Devon	Quartzite gravel		15	13	1.9	327	53	0.7		19
Brampton	Carlisle, Cumbria			20	17	7.5	270		1.8		
Branston	Branston, Staffs	Quartzite gravel	River Trent Gravel	16		1.6	350	50	1.4		
Cardewmires	Carlisle, Cumbria		River Cardew Gravel	18	16	4.4	220	49	1.0–2.0	98	
Cheadle	Cheadle, Staffs	Quartz/Quartzite gravel	Triassic (Sherwood Sandstone Group)	16		2.4	340	50			
Cleasby	Darlington, N. Yorks		Glacial (Vale of York Gravels)	25	27		180		1.3–1.7	88	
Cochranes Wharf	Middlesbrough, Cleveland	Quartz/Limestone gravel	Marine	19	31	3.3	320	46	0.5–0.7	100	
Coundarbour	Cound, Shrops		Glacial	18		3.5	310	59			
Dockacres	Carnforth, Lancs	Limestone gravel	Glacial	13			290		0.9	96	
Elford	Lichfield, Staffs	Quartzite gravel	River Tame Gravel	18	17	2.0	330	47			
Farnham	Knaresborough, N. Yorks	Quartz/Limestone gravel	Glacial (Vale of York Gravels)	23	21		180		2.3	93	
Gonsall	Gonsall, Shrops		Glacial	17		4.4	350	57			
Hemington Fields	Shardlow, Derby	Quartzitic gravel		17		2.0	370	50			
Hereford	Stretton Sugwas, Hereford	Quartz/Quartzite gravel	Glacial	25		6.1	250	55			
Hillhead	Uffculme, Devon	Quartzite gravel		20	17	2.4	265	53	0.9		
Howdon Jetty	Newcastle, Tyne & Wear	Quartz/Limestone gravel	Marine	17	16	3.3	280	46	0.4–0.6	100	22
Huntington	Cannock, Staffs			18		2.1	360	49			
Huntley Wood	Cheadle, Staffs	Quartz gravel	Triassic (Sherwood Sandstone Group)	17		2.2	320	49			
Kingsbury	Sutton Coldfield, W. Midlands	Quartz/Quartzite gravel	Triassic (Sherwood Sandstone Group)	15		2.4	320	50			
Manor Park	Kings Bromley, Staffs	Quartz/Sandstone gravel	River Trent Gravel	17		1.8	330	52			
Marfield	Ripon, N. Yorks	Quartz/Limestone gravel	Glacial (Vale of York Gravels)	20	21		200		1.5		
Mercaston	Brailsford, Derby	Quartz/Sandstone gravel	Triassic (Sherwood Sandstone Group)	16		2.1	350	52			
Packington	Meriden, Warwicks	Quartz/Gritstone gravel		19		1.9	320	48			
Perry Barr	Great Barr, Warwicks	Quartz gravel		18		2.0	330	49			
Repton	Willington, Derby		River Trent Gravel	22		2.0	350	50			
Ryton	Ryton-on-Dunsmore, Warwicks	Quartz/Quartzite gravel	River Avon Gravel	19		1.7	340	44			
Weeford	Canwell, Staffs			17		2.1	350	48			
Willington	Cople, Beds	Quartzitic gravel		17		2.1	320				
			Mean	18.4	20.3	2.8	303.5	50.1	1.3	95.8	
			Standard deviation	2.7	5.1	1.5	54.1	3.5	0.7	4.3	

N.B. The data in this table should not be used for contractual or other purposes

TABLE A2 *Comparison of some property data for various materials used as aggregate from worldwide sources including the UK. Each entry shows the range of values found and the median value in bold print (Sims, in preparation)*

Aggregate type* (alphabetical order)	Water absorption (%)	Unconfined compressive strength[†] (N/mm²)	Aggregate impact value (%)	Aggregate crushing value (%)	10% fines value (kN)	MgSO₄ soundness[‡] (% loss)
Andesite/Trachyte	1.4–7.9	210–280	12–31	11–12	170–190	0–96
(16)	**3.0**	—	**18**	—	**180**	**4**
Basalt	0.4–5.4	160–310	10–22	11–58	160–350	0–16
(18)	**1.8**	—	**18**	**19**	**220**	**2**
Blastfurnace slag	2.0–4.8	90	15–33	33–42	55–210	—
(8)	—	—	**28**	**34**	**85**	—
Flint/Chert gravel	0.4–7.6	200	16–24	14–31	160–320	0–6
(96)	**1.6**	—	**20**	**16**	**2360**	**3**
Gabbro/Dolerite	0.2–5.7	180–190	9–40	11–36	50–380	0–1
(10)	**0.6**	—	**18**	**19**	**190**	—
Gneiss/Granulite	0.4–0.7	—	24–28	—	230	1–2
(5)	**0.6**	—	—	—	—	**1**
Granite	0.2–1.9	150–250	11–35	13–32	75–280	1–31
(27)	**0.6**	—	**21**	**24**	**155**	**2**
Hornfels	—	340–370	16–17	11–15	—	—
(—)	—	—	—	—	—	—
Limestone/Dolomite	0.2–7.5	130–190	14–43	19–31	110–250	0–71
(58)	**1.6**	—	**24**	**24**	**170**	**6**
Quartzite gravel	0.7–1.2	280–390	13–22	16	140–250	—
(4)	**0.7**	—	—	—	**195**	—
Sandstone	0.3–31.0	190–260	10–58	12–31	100–350	0–100
(20)	**1.0**	—	**18**	**15**	**200**	**4**
Serpentinite gravel	0.5–6.6	—	17–23	—	150–260	3–17
(21)	**1.4**	—	**21**	—	**240**	**8**
Slate	1.8–3.0	—	20–22	19–22	140–170	—
(2)	—	—	—	—	—	—

* Number of samples in the survey shown in parentheses for each aggregate type. Not all of the samples were tested for all of the properties shown.
[†] Tests carried out on 25 mm diameter × 25 mm length cylinder specimens.
[‡] After five cycles of the ASTM C88 test.

examination had been carried out on the sample itself or occasionally because the source was well known. Data were also taken into account from other published sources (Phemister *et al.* 1946; Chapman 1967; Orchard 1976; Neville 1981).

Ranges of values are given for water absorption, unconfined compressive (or crushing) strength, aggregate impact value (AIV), aggregate crushing value (ACV), 10% fines value and magnesium sulphate soundness. In all cases, except soundness, the testing was carried out in accordance with the methods given in BS 812 (see Chapter 7).

The soundness testing was carried out in accordance with the ASTM C88 method and the results represent percentage *loss* values after five test cycles, higher values thus suggesting poorer soundness. The soundness values given in Table A2 are broadly comparable with the results likely to be obtained in the recently published BS 812 method for soundness, except that the BS 812 method records the percentage *retained* after 5 test cycles, where higher values would suggest better soundness.

It is apparent that a wide range of values can be expected for any property and any aggregate type, so that the ranges given in Table A2 are presented for indicative purposes only. Moreover, the nature of commercial materials assessment frequently means that, in practice, only aggregate sources pre-established as likely to be suitable for use are subjected to laboratory testing.

In Table A2, where the number of data is deemed sufficient, a median value is given (in bold print) in addition to the range. Although the median values might be regarded as being sensibly 'typical' for each aggregate type, it is very important to recognize the magnitude of the potential deviations from that value which are exemplified by the wide ranges found in the survey.

The data in Table A2 show clearly that prospective suitability cannot be judged on aggregate type alone. The median values are broadly acceptable for all properties and all natural aggregate types, but the ranges found illustrate that, for many properties, either extremely good or extremely poor results can be obtained for any aggregate type.

In the case of granite aggregate, for one example, the median 10% fines value is 155 kN, but samples give results variously as poor as 75 kN and as good as 280 kN

TABLE A3 *Effect of weathering on the properties of a granite from southwest England (Irfan 1977 and Dearman 1979 pers. comm., reported in Fookes 1980)*

Mass weathering grade		Uniaxial compressive strength saturated (MN/m²)	Bulk density saturated (g/cm³)	Saturation mositure content (%)	Aggregate impact value (%)	Aggregate impact value modified (%)	Aggregate abrasion value (%)	MgSO₄ soundness value (%) retained	Secondary minerals (%)
I	Fresh	262	2.61	0.11	6	7	3.5	100	6
	Stained rim of block	232	2.62	0.35					
II	Whole sample II 90% stained	163	2.58	1.09	8	10	4.7	99.9	10
II	Completely stained II block	105	2.56	1.52	14	16	8.0	99.8	12
	Rock core of III block	46	2.55	1.97					
III–IV	Rock core of IV block	26	2.44	4.13	24	49	17.1	66.6	17
V	Weakly cemented soil (coreable)	5	2.24	10.0	nd.	nd.	nd.	nd.	

nd: not determinable

TABLE A4 *Effect of weathering on the properties of a granite from southwest England (Gourley 1986)*

Weathering grade	Micro-petrographic index (I_p)	Relative density oven dry (tonne/m^3)	Water absorption (%)	Aggregate impact value (saturated) (%)	MgSO$_4$ soundness value (% retained)
IB	6.7	2.62	0.4	6	99
II	2.8	2.52	2.1	13	93
III	1.2	2.42	4.8	17	83
III–IV	1.1	2.14	9.2	38	44

TABLE A5 *Effect of weathering on the properties of a dolerite from southwest England (Gourley 1986)*

Weathering grade	Micro-petrographic index (I_p)	Relative density oven dry (tonne/m^3)	Water absorption (%)	Aggregate impact value (saturated) (%)	MgSO$_4$ soundness value (% retained)
IB	10.0	2.84	0.6	4	99
II	2.3	2.60	1.9	9	93
III	1.5	2.35	6.6	22	10
IV–V	0.6	2.11	11.9	26	0

TABLE A6 *Effect of weathering on the properties of a dolerite from southwest England (Motswagole 1990)*

Weathering grade	Secondary mineral (%)	Relative density oven dry (tonne/m^3)	Water absorption (%)	10% fines value (kN)		
				Dry	Saturated	$\dfrac{\text{Sat'd}}{\text{Dry}} \times 100$
IB	12	2.84	0.5	290	260	90
II	17	2.64	1.4	200	180	90
III	32	2.62	1.8	170	120	71
IV	52	2.49	4.2	120	50	42

(i.e. -50% and $+80\%$ approximately). As another example, sandstone aggregate exhibited a median magnesium sulphate soundness loss of just 4%, but some samples produced no loss at all, whilst others experienced a total (i.e. 100%) loss in the test.

The effect of weathering on aggregate properties

The effects of weathering on the properties of aggregates have been referred to in §2.7 and §6.2.3. Weathering can have a significant effect on the properties of aggregates especially in the case of igneous and metamorphic rocks, where rock material from different levels within a quarry can have significantly different physical and mechanical properties and durability.

To illustrate the effects of weathering, Tables A3 to A6 show data obtained from quarries in two rock types commonly used as aggregate, namely granite and dolerite. The data presented are merely examples of the changes which can occur in aggregate properties due to weathering and should not be taken as implying the range in properties which can be expected for the two rock types. The effects of weathering must be assessed for every quarry taking account of the petrological composition of the rock and the climatic environment under which the weathering occurred.

The micropetrographic index (I_p) listed in Tables A4 and A5 is

$$I_p = \frac{\% \text{ sound constituents}}{\% \text{ unsound constituents}}$$

determined by point count analysis of petrographic thin section.

References

BACMI 1986. *BACMI Guide 1986*. British Aggregate Construction Materials Industries, London.

BGS 1984. *Directory of Mines and Quarries*. British Geological Survey, London.

BULLAS, J. C. & WEST, G. 1991. Specifying clean, hard and durable aggregate for bitumen macadam roadbase. *TRRL Research Report RR 284*, Transport and Road Research Laboratory, Crowthorne.

CHAPMAN, G. P. 1967. *Cylinder splitting tests on concretes made with different natural aggregates*. Sand and Gravel Association of Great Britain, Research Note SR 6701.

FOOKES, P. G. 1980. An introduction to the influence of natural aggregates on the performance and durability of concrete. *Quarterly Journal of Engineering Geology*, **13**, 207–229.

GOURLEY, C. S. 1986. *Rock Weathering in Engineering Time*. MSc Dissertation, Queen Mary College, University of London.

IRFAN, T. Y. 1977. *Engineering Properties of Weathered Granite*. PhD Thesis, Univesity of Newcastle Upon Tyne.

MOTSWAGOLE, K. J. 1989. *Implications of the proportion of secondary minerals on the durability of a crystalline rock*. Laing Technology Group Construction Materials Course Project Report (unpublished).

NEVILLE, A. M. 1981. *Properties of Concrete*. 3rd edn, Pitman, London.

ORCHARD, D. F. 1976. *Concrete Technology, Vol. 3, Properties and Testing of Aggregates*, 3rd edn. Applied Science, London.

PHEMISTER, I., GUPPY, E. M., MARKWICK, A. H. D. & SHERGOLD, F. A. 1946. *Roadstone: Geological Aspects and Physical Tests*. Road Research Special Report No. 3, DSIR, HMSO, London, UK.

SIMS, I. (in preparation). *Concrete Aggregates. In*: FOOKES, P. G. & HAWKINS, A. B. (eds), *Handbook of Engineering Geomaterials*, Blackie, Glasgow.

Glossary

To save space, many definitions in this glossary have been simplified and abbreviated as far as was judged possible for comprehension of the main text of the report. For more detailed definitions, readers are referred to existing technical dictionaries, such as the *Penguin Dictionary of Civil Engineering* (3rd edition, 1980) and the *Penguin Dictionary of Geology* (2nd edition, 1979), both published by Penguin Books Limited, Harmondsworth, Middlesex, England, the *Concise Oxford Dictionary of Earth Sciences*, Oxford University Press, 1990; also to *BS 6100: 1984, Glossary of Building and Civil Engineering Terms*, and Barker (1983) *Dictionary of Concrete* (see refs Chapter 8).

accessory minerals	Minerals which are only minor constituents of a rock and are not essential to its broad classification, though they may be used to distinguish varieties of rock.
accretion	The gradual addition of sediment by natural agencies, such as the spreading of silt and clay on a flood-plain by streams or the deposition of sand on a beach by waves.
aeolian	Deposits whose constituents were transported and dropped by the wind, such as dune sand and some volcanic debris.
agglomerate	A volcanic breccia, i.e. a chaotic assemblage of mainly coarse angular to rounded pyroclastic materials.
aggregate	Particles of rock which, when brought together in a bound or unbound condition, form part or whole of a building or civil engineering structure.
——, 'all in'	A well graded mixture of fine aggregate and coarse aggregate.
——, coarse	Aggregate which is mainly retained on a 5 mm BS 410 test sieve and containing only so much finer material as is permitted for the various sizes described in BS 882.
——, fine	Aggregate mainly passing a 5 mm BS 410 test sieve and retained on the 75 µm sieve, and containing only so much coarser material as is permitted for the various grading zones described in BS 882.
——, natural	Aggregate produced from naturally occurring sands and gravels.
aggregate abrasion value (AAV)	Resistance of an aggregate to abrasion as measured in the aggregate abrasion test. The smaller the value, the more resistant to abrasion is the rock.
aggregate crushing value (ACV)	Resistance of an aggregate to crushing as measured in the aggregate crushing test. The smaller the value, the more resistant to crushing is the rock.
aggregate impact value (AIV)	Resistance of an aggregate to impact as measured in the aggregate impact test. The smaller the value, the more resistant to impact is the rock.
alkali–silica reaction (ASR)	Expansive reaction that can take place in concrete when an alkaline solution reacts with a siliceous aggregate to form alkali–silica gel.
alluvium	A general term for unconsolidated detrital material such as clay, silt, sand and gravel, deposited by rivers and streams as sorted or semi-sorted sediment in the stream-bed or on the flood plain.
alteration	Chemical changes in the rock as a result of weathering or hydrothermal action (q.v.). Usually accompanied by loss of strength and/or soundness.
amphibole	A group of rock-forming silicate minerals typically containing calcium, iron, magnesium and sometimes aluminium. Hydroxyl ion (OH) is always present. Hornblende (q.v.) is the best-known example.

amphibolite	Metamorphic rock composed primarily of amphibole with some plagioclase feldspar. The texture may be schistose or linear, i.e. parallel alignment of amphibole needles.
amygdale	Ellipsoidal to irregularly-shaped cavity in volcanic and some hypabyssal rocks formed during the evolution of gas. These cavities are generally infilled by minerals not present in the rock body e.g. zeolites, calcite, different forms of silica, chlorite.
amygdaloidal	Amygdale-bearing.
analcite	A variety of zeolite (q.v.); a hydrous sodium aluminium silicate, nearly always a secondary mineral (q.v.) infilling veins or amygdales (q.v.).
andesite	A dark or medium-dark coloured, fine-grained extrusive rock of intermediate compositon (52–66% silica), commonly containing scattered conspicuous crystals of pale-coloured feldspars; the extrusive equivalent of diorite.
ANFO	Ammonium nitrate–fuel oil mixture used as a blasting agent in many quarries.
Anglian	The first major cold phase of the Quaternary in Great Britain, resulting in the most southerly advance of glaciation (to the latitude of London), beginning about 480,000 years ago. The so-called 'Great Ice Age'.
anisotropy	Variation in physical or textural properties with direction.
anticline	A convex-upward fold, such that older strata occupy its core (antiform: a similar fold in which the stratigraphic sequence is not known).
aquifer	A permeable geological formation which is capable of storing and yielding groundwater.
arenaceous	Sandy; said of a sediment consisting wholly or partly of sand-size fragments.
argillite	A generic term for rocks formed from indurated (q.v.) silt and clay, e.g. mudstone, siltstone, shale. Often restricted to slightly metamorphosed argillaceous sediments.
argillaceous	Clayey or silty; term applied to sediments consisting wholly or partly of clay or silt-sized particles.
arkose	Sandstone with feldspar content in excess of 25%.
asphalt	A natural or artificial mixture in which bitumen is associated with a substantial proportion of mineral matter.
asphaltic cement	Bitumen, a mixture of lake asphalt and bitumen, or lake asphalt and flux oils or pitch or bitumen, having cementing qualities suitable for the manufacture of asphalt pavements.
augite	The most abundant of the pyroxene (q.v.) family of rock-forming minerals.
back breakage	Separation of fragments behind the quarry face.
backfilling	The tipping of material (normally waste material) into a former mineral working in order to recreate a usable land surface.
ball-deck	Design of screen employing trapped balls to prevent pegging.
ball mill	A grinding machine consisting of a short, horizontal, rotating cylinder charged with steel balls and mineral fragments. Breakage is produced by the tumbling action of the balls during rotation.
banana screen	Screen in which the angle of inclination of the deck decreases progressively from feed point to discharge.
barite (or barytes)	Natural barium sulphate ($BaSO_4$); a dense (S.G. 4.5) mineral used, for example, as an aggregate in radiation shielding.
basalt	A dark or medium-dark, commonly extrusive (lava), locally intrusive (as in a dyke

or sill), glassy to fine-grained igneous rock; the extrusive equivalent of gabbro. SiO_2 content 45–62%. Rich in ferromagnesian minerals (>60% by volume) and labradorite feldspar.

base course	In a road pavement, the layer below the wearing course (q.v.) and above the road base; it serves to protect the less durable base materials from damage and provides a flat surface on which the wearing course is laid.
bauxite	A natural mixture of hydrated aluminium oxides formed by the in situ breakdown by tropical weathering, usually of basic igneous rocks. The ore of aluminium. Used as calcined bauxite (q.v.) in friction courses.
bedding	The arrangement of distinct sedimentary rock layers or beds one upon another; the flat (planar) surface that separates successive beds is a bedding plane.
belt-weigher	Continuous weighing device included in a belt conveyor.
benches, benching	Horizontal levels to which successive quarry faces are taken.
beneficiation	The processing of rocks and minerals to remove unwanted constituents.
bin	Storage vessel or silo.
binder	Any soil or aggregate cementing agent, e.g. water, clay, cement, lime, bitumen, synthetic resins.
bioherm	A mound or dome shaped reef composed almost entirely of the remains of sedentary organisms, such as corals, algae, molluscs and gastropods and surrounded or enclosed by rock of a different kind.
biotite	A dark-coloured iron-bearing member of the mica group of rock forming minerals. Biotite occurs as an original constituent of many igneous and metamorphic rocks.
bitumen	A viscous liquid, or a solid consisting essentially of hydrocarbons and their derivatives; it is substantially non-volatile and softens gradually when heated. It is black or brown in colour and possesses waterproofing and adhesive properties. It is obtained by refinery processes from petroleum, and is also found as a natural deposit or as a component of naturally occurring asphalt, in which it is associated with mineral matter.
bitumen emulsion	An emulsion in which, with the aid of suitable emulsifying agents, bitumen is dispersed in water, or in an aqueous solution.
bitumen macadam	(see macadam).
bituminous	Containing road tar, bitumen, pitch or mixtures thereof.
Blake crusher	A jaw crusher with the moving jaw pivoted near the top to allow maximum leverage to be exerted on the coarsest material.
blast (shot) hole	A hole drilled into a rock formation into which explosive is placed, the detonation of which shatters or fragments the rock mass.
bleeding	The release of water from a concrete or mortar mix after placing.
blinding	The obstruction of a screen surface which occurs when the apertures become blocked by an accumulation of very fine material. Also a layer of mortar or concrete used to protect or regulate a surface prior to construction.
blow-bar	Component of impact crusher.
boss	An igneous intrusion usually a few square kilometres in surface extent that is roughly circular in plan and is thought to extend to considerable depth.
boudin	elongated barrel-shaped inclusion formed by the more or less regular thinning and breakage of a more rigid rock layer sandwiched between more deformable rocks, to resemble a string of sausages (boudins).

boulder clay	A glacial deposit consisting of sub-angular pebbles and boulders of all sizes embedded in stiff or hard reworked clay or rock flour. The term 'till' is preferable because it covers the wide range of lithologies included here and does not imply the presence of either boulders or true clay.
bound aggregate	Aggregates which are bound or coated with cementitious or bituminous binders, i.e. as in concrete or bituminous macadam.
brachiopod	The lamp-shell; a solitary marine invertebrate with two bilaterally symmetrical, commonly calcareous, shells usually unequal in size and shape. A frequent fossil in limestones.
braided deposit	Sediment deposited from a tangled network of several small, branching and reuniting shallow stream channels (braided stream) resembling the strands of a complex braid. Such sediments are thought to indicate the inability of the stream to carry all of its sediment load.
breccia	A rubble-rock: a coarse-grained clastic (q.v.) rock composed of large, angular broken rock-fragments held together in a finer-grained matrix. Breccia is similar to conglomerate (q.v.) except that most of the fragments have sharp edges and unworn corners; it can be of any origin, mode of accumulation or composition. Hence brecciated: a rock converted into, characterized by or resembling a breccia.
bucket capacity	The volume able to be retained in an excavator bucket.
building sands	Sand with a grading suitable for use in mortars.
bund	Bank of soil or waste used to obscure a quarry visually.
bunker	Bin or silo for storage.
calcined bauxite	Bauxite (q.v.) which has been heated to produce corundum (Al_2O_3) as one of the main mineral phases, giving the material very good polish-resisting properties when used as a roadstone wearing course.
Cambrian	The earliest period of the Palaeozoic era between about 590 and 505 Ma B.P., and the corresponding system of rocks. Named after Cambria, the Roman name for Wales.
carbonate rocks	A generic term for rocks formed predominantly from the carbonates of calcium, magnesium, iron etc., occurring either singly or in combination. Limestone (calcium carbonate) is the most familiar example.
Carboniferous	The geological period of time (360 to 286 Ma B.P.) and the corresponding system of rocks, which in Britain contains the Carboniferous Limestone, an important source of crushed rock aggregate.
cement	Natural or synthetic material which binds rock particles together. In sedimentary rocks this may be silica, calcium carbonate, clay or iron oxide etc.
chalcedony	Cryptocrystalline (q.v.) variety of silica.
chert	Microcrystalline or cryptocrystalline rock comprising quartz and, sometimes, chalcedony.
chlorite	Family of greenish platy clay minerals frequently occurring as alteration products of ferromagnesian minerals and as a prograde constituent in low grade metamorphic rocks. Hydrous silicates of aluminium, ferrous iron and magnesium.
choke-feed	Means of feeding a crushing so that the crushing chamber remains full at all times.
classification	In mineral processing, a method of sizing fine particles by exploiting differences in settling velocity in water, or occasionally in air. A 'classifier' is a device which effects this type of separation.
classified tip	An accumulation of material (tip) which, by virtue of its volume, area, height or

other measure exceeding certain minimum values, is subject to the provisions of the Mines and Quarries (Tips) Act, 1969 and subsequent Regulations, 1971.

classifier	Particle sizing device based upon the relative motions of particles in a viscous fluid, air or water.
clast	A rock fragment; commonly applied to a fragment of pre-existing rock included in a younger sediment.
clastic	A term relating to a rock or sediment composed principally of broken fragments of pre-existing rocks or minerals that have been transported individually from their place of origin.
clay minerals	A complex group of finely crystalline to amorphous hydrous silicates essentially of aluminium, formed chiefly by alteration or weathering of primary silicate minerals such as the feldspars, pyroxenes and amphiboles. The three most common clay minerals are kaolinite, illite and montmorillonite (smectite).
cleavage	An ease-of-splitting direction in minerals, controlled by the atomic lattice. In deformed rocks such as slates etc. it is an ease-of-splitting direction induced by the deformation.
coagulant	A simple soluble salt that causes particles dispersed in water to agglomerate and settle more rapidly.
coated chippings	Aggregate chippings which have been coated thinly with bituminous material for scattering over a wearing course or use in surface dressing.
coated macadam	A road material consisting of graded aggregate that has been coated with a tar or bitumen, or a mixture of the two, and in which the intimate interlocking of the aggregate particles is a major factor in the strength of the compacted roadbase or surfacing.
cold asphalt	A close-textured type of coated macadam wearing course material, consisting of aggregate wholly passing 6 mm BS sieve for the fine grade, and wholly or substantially passing 10 mm BS sieve for the coarse grade, coated with a binder solely or substantially of bitumen, the composition of the mixture being so adjusted that the material can be spread and compacted while cold or warm, and if required, after storage.
comminution	Reduction of particle size.
compaction	The process of causing soil or aggregate particles (bound or unbound) to pack more closely together, thereby causing an increase in the density.
competent	Describes a bed or rock body that is able to withstand folding without flowage or change in original thickness.
compression jointing	Fractures in a rock produced by compressive forces.
concave	The upper lining of the crushing chamber of a cone crusher.
cone crusher	A crushing machine consisting essentially of two upward pointing, concentric, conical crushing surfaces. The crushing action is produced by the eccentric rotation of the inner conical surface within the outer.
conglomerate	A coarse-grained, clastic sedimentary rock composed predominantly of rounded fragments (generally larger than 5 mm in diameter) set in a fine-grained matrix of sand, silt or natural cementing material.
contact metamorphism	See metamorphism, contact.
country rock	The rock intruded by and surrounding an igneous rock body; rock enclosing or traversed by a mineral deposit.
Cretaceous	The last period of the Mesozoic era (between 144 and 65 Ma B.P.) and the corresponding system of rocks.

crinoid	Popularly referred to as a (fossil) sea-lily, this echinoderm consists of a five-rayed globular body enclosed by calcareous plates and supported by a stem or column comprising numerous circular disc-like calcareous elements. The skeletal plates and discs disaggregate and represent the major constituents of crinoidal limestones.
cristobalite	A high temperature polymorph of the mineral quartz (SiO_2) i.e. possessing a different atomic structure but identical chemical composition.
cross bedding	Describes the inclination of minor beds or laminae in a stratum at various angles to the original depositional surface or principal bedding plane. Formed by swift, local, changing currents (of water or air) and characteristic of granular sedimentary rocks (e.g. sandstones) laid in channels, dunes, deltas etc.
crusher	A device for breaking rock in which the components contacting the rock follow a strictly controlled path.
crusher-run aggregate	Unsized material produced by a simple crushing procedure without screening.
crust	The outermost layer or shell of the Earth, above the Moho discontinuity and consisting overwhelmingly of alumino-silicate rocks.
cryptocrystalline	Very finely crystalline material in which the crystals are so small as to be indistinguishable except under powerful magnification.
cut-back bitumen	Petroleum bitumen whose viscosity has been reduced by the addition of a suitable volatile diluent.
cycle time	The time elapsed during the completion of a single cycle of an operation. Common examples are (i) the cycle of a dump truck travelling from loader to discharge and return including the time of loading and dumping and (ii) the excavation (digging), raising, swinging (slewing), discharge (dumping) and return components of the cycle of an excavator bucket.
cyclone	A classifying (q.v.) device which utilizes a vortex to effect a size separation.
decibel (dB)	Unit of measurement of sound intensity
deck	Screening surface.
decomposition	In geology, the predominantly chemical changes in a rock, usually accompanied by physical deterioration, which result from weathering or hydrothermal alteration (q.v.).
decoupling	In blasting, applied when the explosive charge is not in proper physical contact with the rock, thereby reducing the effect of the explosion.
deep-cone	Type of thickener designed to consolidate flocculated clays.
delayed action blasting	The firing of multiple charges in a timed sequence by the use of delay detonators. Advantages are improved fragmentation, reduced ground vibration, better control of rock pile, etc.
deliquescence (ent)	The property possessed by materials which can absorb so much water from the atmosphere that they may eventually dissolve in it.
dense medium separation	Separation of particles on the basis of density employing a suspension of a dense powder (media) in water to produce a fluid of density intermediate between those of the minerals it is desired to separate.
dense tar surfacing	A hot process wearing course material consisting of aggregate, filler and road tar, in such gradings and proportions that when spread and compacted it provides a close textured impervious mixture.
detonation impedance	The resistance of the rock to blasting, which has the effect of retarding the action of the blast.
detonator	A sealed device containing a very small charge of explosive that can be discharged

(fired) safely, remotely and reliably by several means including electric current (electric detonators), heat (safety fuse) and shock (detonating cord). The discharge of the detonator initiates the detonation of a larger mass of explosive.

detrital	Relating to or formed from detritus, which is a collective term for loose rock and mineral fragmental material, such as sand, silt and clay, derived from older rocks by mechanical means, mainly abrasion and disintegration by erosion and weathering.
Devensian	The most recent glacial stage of the Quaternary period in Britain, beginning about 20,000 years ago.
Devonian	A period of the Palaeozoic era, preceded by the Silurian and succeeded by the Carboniferous and spanning the time between 395 and 360 Ma B.P.; named after the county of Devon, where rocks of this age were first studied.
diabase	A basic crystalline (granular) rock of doleritic composition but altered to the extent that few if any of the original minerals survive.
diamict	An unsorted or poorly sorted terrigenous sediment containing a wide range of particle sizes, for example a glacial till or a pebbly mudstone.
diapir	A dome or anticlinal fold above which the overlying rocks have been ruptured by upward squeezing and mobilization of the plastic core material, which in sedimentary strata is commonly salt or shale. Igneous rocks may also show diapiric structure.
diggability	A general expression of the excavation characteristics of the mineral or rock to be dug.
diorite	A range of dark-coloured plutonic (q.v.) igneous rocks intermediate in composition (SiO_2 content 52–66%) and characterized by the common presence of the amphibole hornblende, plagioclase feldspar and sometimes a small amount of free quartz.
discontinuity	As used in this report, the term denotes any interruption in the mechanical integrity of the rock, such as by a joint, fissure or cavity.
disc crusher	Form of gyratory crusher designed to produce sand sized material.
disintegration	The breaking down of a rock into smaller particles by physical processes, without significant chemical alteration.
Dodge crusher	A jaw crusher in which the moving jaw is pivoted near the base of the unit to give a fixed discharge area.
dolerite	A dark coloured, fine to medium grained igneous rock of basic composition (that is, without free quartz), found in intrusions of moderate size (especially dykes and sills), so allowing moderately rapid cooling of the magma.
dolomite	A double carbonate mineral of calcium and magnesium, $CaMg(CO_3)_2$; also a carbonate rock containing a significant proportion (usually over 50 per cent) of mineral dolomite.
dolostone	A carbonate rock consisting entirely of the mineral dolomite (q.v.).
double-handling	Stocking and reclaiming of product rather than direct outloading.
double-toggle jaw crusher	A jaw crusher in which the moving jaw is hung from a non-eccentric pivot and has a simple lateral motion.
drainage	In the special geotechnical sense, means the removal of water (usually by gravity) from a foundation, embankment or other parts of a structure where the development of excessive water pressures could endanger stability.
drop balling	Rock breakage by dropping a heavy weight on a cable suspended from a crane or excavator jib.

dropstones	Pebbles and boulders which have sunk from floating ice masses into the soft usually fine-grained sediments being deposited from a body of water; the weight and impact of the dropstones commonly give rise to deformation of the soft unconsolidated sediments.
drumlin	A low, rounded ovoid ridge, mound or hill of compacted glacia! till, shaped and elongated by the movement of an overlying ice sheet, sometimes around a rocky prominence.
dry-bound macadam	Crushed aggregates laid in two separate sizes, coarse and fine, compacted dry by rolling and/or vibration to a dense layer.
dry-screened sand	Building sand which has been passed dry through an appropriate sieve to remove over-sized materials.
dyke	A tabular igneous intrusion that cuts across the planar structure of the adjacent host rocks (q.v.): a discordant usually wall-like rock mass which may extend many miles across country, following usually vertical or near-vertical discontinuities in the host rocks.
dynamic metamorphism	See metamorphism, dynamic.
eccentric	The mechanism of a gyratory or jaw crusher in which the shaft connected to the crushing member is located eccentrically in a rotating sleeve.
effective size	The effective size is D_{10}. In other words, 10% of the particles are finer and 90% coarser than the effective size; often used in soil classifications.
elastic limit	The stress level above which a material remains permanently deformed when the stress is removed.
Eocene	An epoch of the Tertiary (q.v.) period between 54 and 38 million years ago.
epidote	A group of minerals comprising the basic silicates of calcium, aluminium, iron and manganese. They commonly occur in regionally metamorphosed rocks.
epidotization	The process whereby epidote is formed as the product of hydrothermal alteration of plagioclase feldspar.
esker	A long, narrow, sinuous, steep-sided ridge or mound of irregularly stratified sand and gravel representing the course of a stream below or within a melting and retreating glacier. Typically up to 20 m high and possibly tens of kilometres long, though usually much less in Britain.
fabric	The physical arrangement and orientation of particles or minerals in a rock which characterizes its texture and structure either on a visible or microscopic scale.
facies	The particular lithological and palaeontological characteristics of a sedimentary rock, from which its origin and conditions of formation may be deduced.
fault	A surface, or closely spaced surfaces, of rock fracture along which there has been displacement, which may range from a few millimetres to many kilometres. A fault plane is a fault surface, normally more or less planar.
feldspar, felspar	The most important single group of rock-forming silicate minerals. They are aluminosilicates of potassium, sodium or calcium, depending for example on whether orthoclase (q.v.) or plagioclase (q.v.) feldspars are present.
felsite	A light-coloured, fine-grained extrusive or hypabyssal rock composed mainly of quartz and feldspar.
filler	In asphaltic technology, is inert material (e.g. cement, limestone dust or fly ash) finer than 75 μm. Its function is to fill in voids and modify the viscosity and the temperature-viscosity relationship of the bitumen binder. Also a possible aid to binder/aggregate adhesion.

filtration	A solid–liquid separation process employing a permeable membrane or medium.
fine cold asphalt	A wearing course of bitumen and fine aggregate which is spread and compacted while cold or warm.
fines	Material finer than 60 µm, i.e. the silt and clay-sized fraction, but in connection with aggregates it usually refers to material finer than 75 µm.
flint	Variety of chert occurring in Cretaceous chalk of northern Europe.
flocculant	A polymeric chemical used to promote the sedimentation of solids suspended in water.
flotation (froth)	A mineral separation process for fine particles suspensed in water in which selected particles are attached to air bubbles and rise to form a froth.
flowsheet	A diagrammatic representation of the flow of material through a processing plant, showing the sequence of operations and their interrelationships.
flow structure	The parallel alignment of particles (usually crystals) in the direction of movement of a fluid medium, such as lava.
fluvial	Relating to a river; a deposit produced by the action of a river. Geologists tend to use fluviatile for the product of river action, for example, fluviatile sand.
fluvioglacial (or glaciofluvial)	May be applied to sediment transported and deposited by running water discharged from an ice mass.
foliation	The planar arrangement of textural or structural features in any type of rock, for example, the schistosity in a metamorphic rock.
fossil weathering	Ancient weathered rock preserved below more recent material.
fracture-cleavage	A type of cleavage developed in mechanically deformed but only slightly metamorphosed rocks by incipient shearing and slipping along individually recognizable, often closely-spaced, parallel fractures.
fragmentation	A term associated with hard rock quarrying to describe the degree of mechanical breakdown produced by blasting.
free silica	In igneous rocks, silica (q.v.) which is present as quartz or one of its polymorphs, as opposed to silica present in the combined state as one of the many silicate minerals.
friction course	A uniformly graded asphalt material, with a high voids content and coarse texture, giving good drainage and skid resistance properties, used primarily on airfields.
gabbro	A coarse-grained basic plutonic rock containing plagioclase, a pyroxene and very commonly olivine. SiO_2 content 45–52%, dark minerals over 60% by volume.
gabion	A stone-filled rectangular wire mesh box. Gabions may be laid to form self-standing structures or as mattresses to form flexible linings for coastal and river bank protection.
gap-graded	Absence or near-absence in the proportions of particular size fractions in a grading; also known rarely as 'skip' or 'intermittent' grading.
garnet	A group of complex silicates of aluminium, iron, manganese, chromium, calcium and magnesium. Usually found in metamorphic rocks but also in some granites (q.v.) and pegmatites (q.v.).
geomaterial	Processed or unprocessed soils, rocks or minerals used in construction, including man-made construction materials manufactured from soils, rocks or minerals.
geomorphology	The classification, description, nature, origin and development of landforms, their relation to underlying geological structure, and the history of geological changes recorded by these surface features.
geophysics	The study of the physical characteristics of the Earth by means of instruments, and

methods to determine subsurface conditions by analysis of such physical properties as specific gravity, electrical conductivity, magnetic susceptibility, radio-activity, seismic wave propagation, heat flow, etc.

gibbsite A hydrous aluminium oxide commonly occurring in deposits of bauxite (q.v.) and as an alteration product of aluminium silicates.

glacial deposits, glacial debris or glacial drift heterogeneous material transported by glaciers or icebergs and deposited directly on land or in the sea without sorting of the constituents.

glacial till See till.

gneiss A foliated rock formed by regional metamorphism in which bands or lenticles of granular minerals alternate with bands or lenticles in which minerals of flaky or elongate prismatic habit predominate.

grade, graded size sorting category in which all the particles fall within specified size limits (see sorted). Also used in geology to denote degrees of alteration, e.g. by metamorphism or weathering, usually with reference to an agreed scale.

graded bedding Bedding in which successive layers show gradual, progressive change in particle size, usually from coarse at the base to fine at the top of a sequence.

grading The proportions of different sizes present in an aggregate, established by sieve analysis; particle size distribution.

granophyre An extrusive porphyritic rock of acid composition chacterized by a crystalline-granular groundmass.

granite Generally, any completely crystalline quartz-bearing plutonic rock with light-coloured feldspars and micas as essential constituents (over 60% by volume). There may be a speckling of dark minerals. SiO_2 content over 66%.

granodiorite A coarse-grained plutonic (q.v.) rock intermediate in composition between granite (q.v.) and diorite (q.v.). Light-coloured minerals over 60% by volume, SiO_2 content over 66%.

granulite A metamorphic rock characterized by granular texture. Originated under conditions of high grade regional metamorphism.

gravel In the British Standard particle size classification (BS 1377: 1975 and BS 5930: 1981) the term denotes granular material in the size range 2 mm to 60 mm.

greywacke A dark-coloured sandstone comprising mineral and rock fragments, poorly-sorted and bound together with clay cement.

grinding A process for breaking rock in which the motion of the machine components (media) that contact the rock is not strictly controlled and the components may touch.

gritstone The BS 812: 1975 trade group which includes all clastic rocks with sand-sized particles, such as arkose, greywacke and sandstone. The term grit(stone) is generally used in geology for a sand(stone) with coarse angular particles.

grizzly A coarse screening device in which the screen surface consists essentially of massive parallel bars.

ground-bunker Storage comprising a stockpile at ground level under which is a tunnel containing a reclaim conveyor.

ground moraine Rock debris generally fairly evenly though thinly spread beneath a glacier or ice sheet to give a gently rolling till surface when the ice has wasted away.

gypsum Hydrous calcium sulphate: $CaSO_4.2H_2O$, associated with other evaporite minerals in extensive beds interstratified with limestone, shales and clays. Used, for example, as a soil additive, as a retarder in portland cement and in making plaster-board.

gypsum plaster	A plaster consisting of calcium sulphate, either partially hydrated or anhydrous, made by the controlled heating of gypsum.
gyratory crusher	A crushing machine consisting of an upward pointing eccentrically rotating cone set inside an inverted cone.
haematite or hematite	A natural oxide of iron (Fe_2O_3) with a high specific gravity (4.9 to 5.3), sometimes used as an aggregate for special-purpose dense concretes.
hammer mill	An impact crusher consisting of a fast moving rotor with fixed hammers. If the hammers are hinged the crusher may be called a 'swing hammer mill'.
hang-up	Material interlocked in a bunker preventing free flow.
harp screen	A form of woven wire screening medium designed to overcome pegging and blinding.
heavy-media separation	A mineral processing operation in which rock fragments can be separated on the basis of density differences by being allowed to float or sink in a heavy medium. The medium consists of finely divided particles of a high density solid, such as magnetite, dispersed in water (see dense medium separation).
high energy sedimentary environment	Turbulent action, such as that created by waves and currents, which prevents the settling and accumulation and abrasion of pebbles and sand grains.
Holocene	See Recent.
hopper	Small bunker.
horizontal screen	A vibrating screen which utilizes directed impulses to transport particles across its surface.
hornblende	One of the most abundant rock-forming minerals of the amphibole (q.v.) family.
hornfels	A fine-grained rock made of a mosaic of mutually interfering silicate minerals without preferred orientation and typically formed by contact metamorphism. Commonly yields strong aggregate when homogeneous and uniformly granular.
hydrocyclone	A classifier and dewatering device employing centripetal forces generated within a vortex of water (see cyclone).
hydrosphere	A collective name for all the water on the Earth's surface, in the atmosphere and underground.
hydrothermal alteration	Process of alteration to secondary minerals (q.v.) through the action of hot groundwater, i.e. late stage igneous activity.
hypabyssal	A term applied to intrusive igneous rocks, commonly dykes and sills, intermediate between plutonic (q.v.) and volcanic, generally medium grained.
ice contact deposit	Normally stratified glacial drift deposited in contact with melting glacier ice; the deposit may exhibit an ice-contact slope marking the position of the ice mass at the time it was laid down.
ice front	The usually cliff-like limit of a mass of glacier ice where the supply of ice is balanced by wasting through thawing (on land) or erosion (by the sea).
igneous	Describes a rock or mineral that solidified from molten or partly molten material.
illite	A broad term for one of the commonest groups of clay minerals, formed by the alteration of micas, alkali feldspars etc. under alkaline conditions.
impactor	A crusher employing impact.
indurated	Rock or soil hardened and compacted by the action of pressure, heat and cementation after deposition. Induration is a progressive, natural process.
industrial screening	The separation of particles by sieving (screening) on an industrial, as distinct from a laboratory, scale.

initiation	In blasting, the method used to fire the charge, or the instant at which the explosion begins.
in-pit	Description of a process conducted within the quarry itself.
intermontaine	Located between mountains or mountain ranges.
intrusion	The process of emplacement of molten rock (magma) in pre-existing rock, also the igneous rock body so formed within the surrounding rock (the country rock). The term may also be applied to mobilized sediments, which may be injected along discontinuities or form plug-like masses under the influence of gravity.
iron pyrites	(see pyrite).
ironstone	Imprecise term, but usually denoting an impure iron carbonate occurring as nodules in some clays, e.g. London Clay, or a ferruginous sandstone.
isopach, isopachyte	A line drawn on a map through points of equal thickness of a specified rock unit.
jaw crusher	A crushing device consisting of one near-vertical fixed crushing face and an inclined mobile face which moves so as alternately to increase and decrease the gap between the two faces.
jig, jigging	A mineral processing machine/operation in which particles are separated on a density basis by water pulsation.
joint	A plane of discontinuity, fracture or parting in a rock, normally involving no displacement. Joints commonly occur as parallel sets, cutting the rock mass into joint blocks.
Jurassic	A period of the Mesozoic era between 213 and 144 Ma B.P., and the corresponding system of rocks. Named from the Jura mountains of France.
kame	A low, steep-sided mound, hummock or short irregular ridge of poorly-sorted glaciofluvial sand and gravel deposited by a sub-glacial stream as an alluvial fan or delta against or on the margin of a melting glacier.
kaolinite	A common white or greyish white clay mineral, formed by hydrothermal alteration (and to some extent, the chemical weathering) of feldspars and other alumino-silicate minerals through the process known as kaolinization. The process adversely affects the usefulness of rocks for concrete or road aggregate.
kettlehole	Commonly basin or bowl-shaped depression in glacial drift (q.v.), without surface drainage, but often containing a lake or bog; formed by the melting of masses of stagnant (or 'dead') ice left behind by a retreating glacier within or upon the glacial drift. Kettles may be a few metres to a few tens of metres across.
lacustrine	Relating to materials formed in or by lakes, for example lacustrine beach deposits.
lagoon (silt)	A contained volume of water providing time for the sedimentation of silt and, perhaps, clays, to permit the re-use or discharge of clean water.
laterite	Highly weathered residual soil material rich in oxides or iron and aluminium, traditionally useful for brickmaking and exceptionally for low quality aggregate where hard iron-pan (ferricrete) layers have developed.
leaching	Selective removal of soluble constituents from a soil or rock mass by the action of percolating water.
lean mix concrete	Generally a concrete with a cement:aggregate ratio of 1:10 or greater, i.e. a low cement content which often incorporates an all-in aggregate (q.v.).
ledge rock	In situ rock.
lignite	A brownish-black coal in which the alteration of vegetable matter has proceeded further than in peat but not so far as in bituminous coal.
lime	Quick lime is calcium oxide made by heating limestone above 900°C. Slaked lime (calcium hydroxide) is the product of the reaction between quick lime and water.

limestone	A sedimentary rock composed mainly of calcium carbonate occurring as the mineral calcite or occasionally as aragonite in recent deposits.
lithified	Made into rock: lithification is the process of consolidating a loose sediment into a solid rock.
lithology	The description of the physical nature of a rock: including its grain size, mineralogical composition, structure, colour.
live-storage	That portion of a stockpile in a ground bunker that can be reclaimed without the use of mobile equipment.
log-normal distribution	Graphical presentation of data on log paper which provides a clearer picture of normal distribution curves.
log-washer	A mineral processing device usually used for scrubbing or washing adhering clay from solid particles.
Los Angeles abrasion value	Resistance of an aggregate to a combination of impact and abrasion as measured in the Los Angeles abrasion test. The smaller the value, the more resistant the rock.
low-grade metamorphism	see metamorphism, low grade.
Lower Palaeozoic	Early part of the Palaeozoic (q.v.) era, ranging in time from 590 to 395 million years ago and comprising the Cambrian, Ordovician and Silurian (q.v.) Systems.
macadam	Crushed stone mechanically locked by rolling and cemented together by application of stone screenings and water. Bituminous macadam is crushed material in which the fragments are bound together by bituminous materials.
magma	Naturally occurring deep molten rock material from which igneous rocks are formed.
magnesium sulphate soundness value (MSSV)	Soundness of an aggregate as measured in the magnesium sulphate soundness test. In the British Standard method, the larger the value, the sounder the rock. In the ASTM method, the smaller the value, the sounder the rock.
magnetite	An iron ore mineral, Fe_3O_4. It occurs as a primary constituent of most igneous rocks.
mantle	Lining of a gyrating crushing member.
marble	Metamorphic rock produced from limestone through recrystallization.
marine aggregate	Sand and gravel which is excavated by dredger from the sea bed and taken ashore for processing and distribution.
mass-flow	Design of bunker to prevent hang-up and material segregation.
massive	In geology, without stratification, cleavage or schistosity; particularly applied to igneous rock-bodies but can be used to describe thick or obscured bedding in stratified rocks.
mastic asphalt	A type of asphalt composed of suitably graded mineral matter and asphaltic cement in such proportions as to form a coherent, voidless, impermeable mass, solid or semi-solid under normal temperature conditions, but sufficiently fluid when brought to a suitable temperature to be spread by means of a float.
mat	Element of a screening surface usually replaceable.
mesh	The apertures in a screen surface, or the size of the apertures.
Mesozoic	The era following the Palaeozoic (q.v.), ranging in time from 230 to 70 million years ago. It comprises the Triassic, Jurassic and Cretaceous systems (q.v.).
meta	Prefix implying instability or change, e.g. as in metamorphism (q.v.).
metamorphism	Mineralogical and structural changes of rocks in their solid state in response to altered physical and chemical conditions.

——, contact	The process of localized thermal metamorphism brought about by the intrusion (and to a lesser extent, extrusion) of magma into rocks; changes are effected at or near the contact by heat and materials emanating from the magma and by some deformation arising from the emplacement of the igneous mass.
——, dynamic	Changes in rock structure and mineralogy brought about commonly on a regional scale by crushing and shearing in the Earth's crust; high temperatures may be involved, leading to extensive recrystallization of rocks.
——, low grade	Metamorphic grade is measured by the amount of change that the original (parent) rock has undergone. Thus the conversion of shale to slate (q.v.) would indicate low grade metamorphism whilst its continued metamorphism to schist would be regarded as high-grade.
——, regional	Metamorphism affecting an extensive region usually brought about by deep burial of material in the Earth's crust.
——, thermal	Essentially the chemical reconstitution of rocks brought about by elevated temperature influenced, to some extent, by the confining pressure of deep burial in the earth's crust (though this is not essential).
mica	The group of layered-lattice silicates (including muscovite and biotite) characterized by very strong cleavage.
micaceous	Mica-bearing.
microcline	A member of the feldspar group of minerals ($KAlSi_3O_8$) found generally in acid igneous rocks, pegmatites and metamorphic rocks.
Micro-Deval value	(MDS dry, MDE wet) Resistance of an aggregate to abrasion as measured (either dry or wet) in the Micro-Deval test. The smaller the value, the more resistant to abrasion is the rock.
microdiorite	A range of hypabyssal igneous rocks of intermediate composition. Microdiorites are the hypabyssal equivalent of andesites and consist usually of intermediate plagioclase feldspar, hornblende or biotite (q.v.) and occasionally a small amount of quartz.
microganite	A granite in which a majority of the crystalline matter requires microscopic examination to differentiate individual crystals.
migmatite	A composite rock formed by solid-state reconstruction of igneous and/or metamorphic materials by injection of magma and/or in situ melting.
mill	A grinding device.
mineral	(i) A naturally formed chemical element or compound and normally having a characteristic crystal form and a definite composition. (ii) A mass of naturally occurring mineral material (such as metallic ores and aggregate minerals) which is judged, against arbitrary physical, chemical and economic criteria, to have foreseeable use.
mineral reserve	That part of a mineral resource considered producible at a profit at the time of classification.
mineral resource	A concentration of naturally occurring materials in such form that economic extraction is currently or potentially feasible.
mineralogy	The science concerned with the study of minerals, including their occurrence, composition, forms, properties and structure.
Mohs' scale of hardness	A scale of scratch resistance graduated in terms of the relative hardness of ten common minerals which, in order of increasing hardness, are: 1, talc; 2, gypsum; 3, calcite; 4, fluorite; 5, apatite; 6, orthoclase; 7, quartz; 8, topaz; 9, corundum; 10, diamond.

monominerallic	Rock composed essentially of one mineral species.
montmorillonite	Member of smectite clay mineral group characterized by marked swelling properties when contacted with water.
moraine	A mound or ridge of unsorted, unstratified glacial drift, commonly till (q.v.), deposited directly by glacier ice.
mortar	A mixture consisting essentially of cement, sand and water, and the hardened product of such a mixture.
mudstone	An indurated mud (or mud-rock), commonly massive, blocky, non-fissile and comprising about equal proportions of clay and silt.
mundic	A Cornish word for iron pyrites which is commonly found in mineralized zones in the Cornish granites and the surrounding rocks of Devonian geological age.
muscovite	A light coloured member of the mica (q.v.) group of rock forming minerals.
nearsize	Particles of a size between 1 and 1.5 times the aperture size of a screen.
norite	A coarse-grained plutonic rock of basic composition, related to gabbro.
normal frequency distribution	Bell-shaped frequency distribution curve symmetrical with respect to the mean value.
nuisance	An undesirable but non-hazardous environmental impact of quarrying.
olivine	Common rock-forming mineral in basic, ultrabasic and low-silica igneous rocks; typically dark olive-green to brown magnesium iron silicate: $(MgFe_2)SiO_4$. Alters to serpentine.
oolite	A sedimentary rock commonly a limestone (hence oolitic limestone), made chiefly of ooliths cemented together. Ooliths are spherical or ovoid accretionary bodies resembling the egg-roe of a fish, made of concentric layers typically deposited around a nucleus (such as a shell fragment or sand grain) in shallow moving water. Ooliths range in size from 0.25 to 2.00 mm, but are typically between 0.5 mm and 1.0 mm in diameter.
opal	Amorphous and hydrous variety of silica.
open-area	Proportion (%) of total screen area represented by the apertures.
ophiolite	An assemblage of ultrabasic to basic rocks, frequently layered, with an upward succession from plutonic to hypabyssal and volcanic (q.v.). These represent sections of oceanic crust and the upper part of the underlying mantle incorporated into a sedimentary sequence during strong disturbances caused by plate underthrusting.
Ordovician	A period of the Palaeozoic era between 505 and 435 million years ago, and the corresponding system of rocks. Named from the Ordovices, an ancient Celtic tribe of Central Wales.
orthoclase	A potassium feldspar (q.v.) $KAlSi_3O_8$ occurring as an essential constituent of the more acid igneous rocks and also found in some metamorphic rocks.
orthoquartzite	A very hard sandstone in which the constituent quartz grains have been cemented by secondary silica so that the rock breaks across individual grains rather than around them. Often loosely termed 'quartzite' (q.v.).
outcrop	The total area over which a particular rock unit or structure occurs at the ground surface or immediately below the superficial deposits (q.v.), whether visibly exposed or not.
outwash	Stratified deposits, mainly sand and gravel, washed from a glacier by melt-water streams and deposited as an outwash cone or outwash plain, the coarser materials being deposited nearer to the ice. An outwash plain mainly of sand is called a sandur (plural: sandar).

Palaeozoic	The era ranging in time from 590 to 213 Ma B.P. It comprises the Cambrian, Ordovician, Silurian, Devonian, Carboniferous and Permian Systems (q.v.).
patterned ground	General term embracing more or less symmetrical arrangements of pebbles, stones and boulders which in plan assume polygonal, circular, reticulate or striped forms, through the action of intensive frost action, usually in superficial deposits in cold, typically periglacial, climates.
pavement	The whole constructed thickness of a road or similar slab whether of concrete, asphalt, macadam, stabilized soil, etc.
payrock	The rock or mineral extracted from a mine or quarry which has a value and for which payment is expected.
pegging	The obstruction of a screen surface by single fragments which become wedged in the apertures.
pegmatite	A very coarse grained igneous rock, conventionally refers to a rock of granite (q.v.) composition. Also used for other plutonic rocks whose names are used as a prefix, e.g. gabbro-pegmatite.
pelite	A sediment (or sedimentary rock) composed of the finest (i.e. clay or mud sized) detrital particles.
periglacial	A term describing the influence of the cold temperature around an ice mass on the climate, topography, and natural processes, in which frost action is a primary factor.
Permian	The final period of the Palaeozoic (q.v.) era between 286 and 248 Ma B.P., and the corresponding system of rocks. Named from the province of Perm in Russia.
petrography	The branch of geology dealing with the description and systematic classification of rocks especially by the microscopic study of thin sections.
phenocryst	A relatively large, conspicuous crystal set in a finer-grained or glassy ground-mass.
phyllite	A cleaved metamorphic rock, coarser grained and less perfectly cleaved than slate (q.v.), but finer grained and better cleaved than schist. Formed by low temperature regional metamorphism (q.v.).
piano-wire	Form of woven wire mesh employing high tensile steel wires and elongated apertures to overcome pegging and blinding.
pillow-lava	A lava displaying *pillow-structure* and considered to have been formed under water, usually from a basaltic or andesitic magma.
pitch	The residue, liquid when hot and almost solid when cold, obtained from the distillation of tars, etc. When no source is specified, it is implied that it is obtained from coal tar.
pitch-bitumen binder	Penetration grade binder (q.v.) containing pitch and predominance of bitumen suitable for use in rolled asphalt or dense bitumen macadam.
plagioclase	The group of soda-lime feldspars (q.v.). They are one of the most common rock forming mineral groups, having a continuous gradation in chemical composition between albite $NaAlSi_3O_8$ and anorthite $CaAl_2Si_2O_8$.
plaster shooting	Small-scale blasting of boulders, using a surface charge.
plasticizer	An additive to mortar or concrete which has the ability to entrain air in the mix and improve its working qualities.
plasticity index	The numerical difference between the liquid and plastic limits, representing the range of moisture content at which the soil is plastic. Together with the liquid limit it gives an indication of the sensitivity of the soil to changes in moisture condition.

Pleistocene	The earliest epoch of the Quaternary Period and during which the Ice ages occurred. Spans the period between 2 million and 10 thousand years ago.
plutonic	Applies to igneous rocks formed at great depth, which are characteristically medium or coarse-grained and of granite-like texture.
pneumatic impact breaker	A tool for breaking rock, concrete etc. consisting of a chisel driven by a pneumatic vibrator, either hand held or machine controlled.
point load strength	Rock material strength determined by loading a rock specimen to failure between two conical points. The result is expressed as a point-load index (I_s) which is the force at failure divided by the square of the length of the loaded axis.
polished stone value (PSV)	Resistance of an aggregate to polishing as measured in the accelerated polishing test. The larger the value, the more resistant to polishing is the rock.
poorly graded	In engineering terms this implies the absence or a low proportion of essential grade sizes. In geological terms it implies the presence of a proportion of all essential grade sizes.
pop drilling	The breaking up of large boulders by drilling holes for small explosive charges.
porosity	The ratio between the volume of voids in a material and its total volume.
porphyry	An igneous rock that contains conspicuous large crystals (phenocrysts) in a fine-grained groundmass. Hence porphyritic, the texture of a porphyry.
pozzolana	Naturally occurring deposits which, when finely ground, combine chemically with hydrated limes at normal temperatures and so can be used in mortars.
Precambrian	That period of time (about 4000 million years) from the consolidation of the earth's crust to the beginning of the Palaeozoic era, and the corresponding system of rocks.
primary blasting	Describes the initial blast, where more than one stage of blasting is needed to obtain the required fragmentation.
primer	A relatively small mass (often 0.5 kg) of high explosive, into which the detonator is inserted. It is necessary to initiate the detonation of insensitive explosives such as the blasting agent, ANFO.
probability screen	Screen employing the relationship between duration of screening, aperture size, inclination and particle size to effect a size separation.
psammite	Metamorphic rock derived from an impure sandstone.
pulp	A suspension of mineral particles in water; i.e. a slurry.
pumice	A light-coloured highly vesicular glassy volcanic rock commonly of rhyolitic composition.
pyrite	Iron sulphide (FeS_2), the most abundant of the sulphide minerals; it occurs most commonly as cubes and nodules in sedimentary rocks and as veins associated with other minerals such as copper with which it may be mined. Undesirable in aggregates because it decomposes giving rise to iron-oxide in mass concrete, and may oxidize to ferrous sulphate, which causes sulphate attack.
pyroclastic	Descriptive of broken rock material formed by volcanic explosion or by being thrown from a volcanic vent. A pyroclastic rock may be made of rock fragments of a wide size range and largely unsorted.
pyroxene	A group of rock-forming silicates, somewhat similar in general composition to amphibole (q.v.) but without hydroxyl (OH). Augite is the best-known example.
QA	Quality assurance.
quartering	Reduction of a sample to a desired volume by dividing a cone of material into four quarters and combining alternate quadrants. This is repeated until the desired sample quantity is obtained.

quartz	Crystalline silica, SiO_2; an important durable rock-forming mineral (see also silica).
quartzite	Metamorphic rock consisting mainly of quartz and formed by recrystallization of sandstone or chert by thermal or regional metamorphism. Also loosely used synonymously with 'orthoquartzite' (q.v.).
quartzo-feldspathic minerals	Minerals of the quartz and feldspar groups, generally imparting a light colour and relatively low specific gravity to the rock.
Quaternary	The latest era of geological time, from 2 Ma B.P. to the present, largely represented in Britain by superficial deposits such as glacial drift (q.v.).
Recent	The current epoch in the earth's history, comprising the 10 000 years or so since the end of the last glaciation. Also called Holocene.
reduction ratio	A term used in crushing to indicate the ratio between the maximum particle sizes in the feed and the product.
reef limestone	A limestone consisting of the fossilized remains of reef-building organisms, such as corals, bryozoans, algae and sponges.
refined lake asphalt	Lake asphalt from which unwanted materials, such as water and vegetable matter, have been removed.
regional metamorphism	See metamorphism, regional.
regression	The retreat of the sea from a land area and the consequent evidence preserved in the strata; for example beach deposits may overlie offshore deposits in a geological sequence.
remote sensing	The measurement and recording (often in image form) of information about an object or group of objects that is not in physical contact with the recording device, for example airborne photography. Other techniques used are television cameras, ultra-violet and infra-red detectors, radio frequency and microwave receivers, radar systems and so on.
residual soil	A soil developed in situ from residual materials, originally consisting of fresh rock.
resonance	Type of horizontal vibrating screen.
respirable dust	Dust not filtered from inhaled air by the body's defences, essentially finer than 5 µm.
rhyolite	A fine-grained to glassy acid volcanic rock, mineralogically similar to granite. The more glassy members of the group are termed obsidian.
riffling	Sample reduction using riffle box. This is a box comprising a number of internal chutes directing alternatively towards the two receiving trays. By this means each sample pass is halved and the material of one tray is rejected.
rippability	The facility with which a rock can be excavated by ripping.
ripper	A tractor or bulldozer with a hooked tine or array of tines which can be forced into the ground hydraulically to break it up as the tractor moves forward.
ripping	The process of excavating rock with a ripper.
riprap	A material used to protect slopes against the action of water, consisting of broken stone placed on the slope surface.
road base	The main structural element in a road pavement. Its function is to spread the concentrated loads from traffic over an area of subgrade large enough to sustain them.
roche moutonnée	A small elongated hillock of bedrock, rounded and scratched by debris-laden ice at the bottom of a glacier; usually no more than a few metres in height, length, breadth.

rock-box	A design by which broken rock accumulates to protect an underlying surface from impact and abrasion.
rock-forming minerals	Those minerals which are widespread in nature and which contribute significantly to the common rock groups, serving to define and classify the common rocks.
rock pile	The mass of broken rock resulting from a primary blast.
rod-deck	A screening surface made from loosely located parallel rods.
rod mill	A horizontal cylindrical mill charged with steel rods and mineral fragments (c.f. ball mill).
rolled asphalt	A material used as a dense wearing course, base or roadbase material. It consists of a mixture of aggregate and asphaltic cement.
rotary-pick	A crusher comprising one or two rotating shafts fitted with hardened steel teeth or picks.
sabkha	A salt flat (usually coastal) which is inundated only occasionally.
sand	In the British Standard particle size classification (BS 1377: 1975 and BS 5930: 1981) sand is a granular material in the size range 0.06 mm to 2 mm. In the sense of 'concreting sand', however, the nominal upper size limit is 5 mm and there are constraints on the particle size distribution (see BS 882: 1983).
sandur (pl. sandar)	An Icelandic term (for 'sand') commonly used for outwash plain.
sandstone	A sedimentary rock made of abundant fragments of sand size set in a fine-grained matrix or cementing material. The sand particles are usually of quartz. The term sandstone may be used to describe any clastic (q.v.) rock containing individual grains visible to the unaided eye.
sand waves	Large, linear, subaqueous sand dunes or sand ripples formed by currents on the bed of the sea or in a river; the smallest sand waves in sedimentary rocks are ripple marks, larger ones are megaripples. May be applied to wind-blown ripples—that is sand dunes.
scalping	Removal of finer fraction of feed to process plant with the objective of rejecting deleterious material.
schist	Metamorphic rock characterized by a parallel arrangement of the bulk of the constituent minerals. The common minerals which give rise to the layered structure are the micas (q.v.).
Schmidt rebound number	Value obtained from test with the Schmidt concrete test hammer. The larger the value, the greater is the 'elasticity' of the rock. May be empirically correlated with rock strength.
screen	A particle sizing device like a sieve, consisting of a surface (usually flat) which is perforated by apertures of characteristic size and shape. Screening is a sizing operation effected by means of a screen.
scrubber/scrubbing	A mineral processing machine/operation in which adherent fine fragments or clay coatings are washed from the surface of larger particles.
secondary minerals	Minerals formed by alteration or replacement of the original rock minerals e.g. serpentine after olivine (q.v.).
sedimentary rock	A rock resulting from the consolidation of loose sediment that has accumulated in layers, or a chemical rock formed by precipitation or an organic rock consisting largely of the remains of plants and animals.
sericite	A secondary mica usually resulting from the alteration of other rock-forming minerals. Chemically similar to muscovite (q.v.).
settling pond	A reservoir of still water in which very fine material is allowed to settle (see lagoon).

shaking table	A device for separating mineral grains on the basis of differences in their density. It consists of a slightly inclined vibrated deck over which a stream of water moves at right angles to the direction of the vibration. Low density material is carried along the deck into an area where it can be recovered.
shale	Fine-grained sedimentary rock composed of clay minerals and other finely divided material. These rocks are characterized by a well-marked bedding-plane fissility.
shelling-out	Particles or fragments breaking off rock as a result of frost action or other physical or chemical changes.
shield area	A large area, usually of low relief, exposing ancient basement rocks. Typically at the heart of a continental land-mass and surrounded by sediment-covered platforms (e.g. Canadian Shield, Baltic Shield).
sieve-bend	A fixed wet screening device containing a steeply inclined, curved screening surface.
silica	The chemically and physically resistant dioxide of silicon, SiO_2, which occurs naturally as quartz, flint, chert, opal or chalcedony and combines in silicates as an essential constituent of many rock-forming minerals.
sill	A tabular or sheet-like minor igneous intrusion that conforms with the bedding or other layered structure of the host (or country) rock.
silt	A deposit which has the average grain size between that of sand and clay (q.v.).
siltstone	An indurated fine grained rock in which the amount of silt grade material exceeds that of clay; it tends to be flaggy, hard and durable.
Silurian	A period of the Palaeozoic era between 435 and 395 million years ago, and the corresponding system of rocks. Named from the Silures, an ancient Celtic tribe of the Welsh Borderland.
single-toggle jaw crusher	A jaw crusher in which one jaw is suspended from an eccentric pivot and moves both vertically and laterally.
slate	A low grade regionally metamorphosed argillaceous (q.v.) rock which has developed a well marked cleavage (q.v.) but has undergone little recrystallization, so that the rock is still very fine grained.
slickenside	A polished and smoothly striated rock surface formed by friction along a fault plane.
slime	Very fine material, often clay particles, in suspension which usually presents a processing and dewatering problem. 'Desliming' is an operation which involves removing very fine material from a pulp or slurry.
slurry	A suspension of mineral particles in water.
slurry seal	A mixture of binder, fine aggregate and mineral filler with water added to produce a material of slurry consistency used as a barrier in construction.
smectites	A group of clay minerals including montmorillonite. They are 'swelling' clay minerals and can take up water or organic liquids between their layers, and they show cation exchange properties.
soil	In engineering geology: all unlithified material overlying the bedrock. In Britain it comprises most material of Tertiary and Quaternary age. In soil science: the natural medium for the growth of land plants and classifiable into soil types and soil horizons on characteristic physical properties such as structure, texture, colour and chemical composition including organic content, acidity, alkalinity etc.
soil creep	Slow downhill movement of soil and rock debris under the influence of gravity.
solifluction	Slow, viscous, downslope flow of waterlogged soil and superficial materials, especially in cold climate conditions.

sorted	Referring to the size distribution of unconsolidated sediments e.g. sands, gravels etc., size separation having taken place naturally.
sorted, well	Having a relatively narrow size distribution free of coarse particles and fine clays.
sorted, poorly	Having a relatively wide size distribution.
spheroidal weathering	The progressive splitting away, from a central core, of usually fine-grained rock of concentric or spherical shells ('onion-skins') of chemically weathered material. Also brought about by mechanical weathering through the freezing of water which has penetrated progressively into blocks, boulders or pebbles, or by differential expansion and contraction by alternating heating and cooling, usually on a daily cycle in response to insolation (i.e. heating by the sun).
spilite	A chemically altered basalt characterized by presence of secondary minerals giving a greenish colour ('greenstone').
spotting	Mechanical ability of extraction equipment to pick up individual rock fragments.
stratified	Sedimentary material laid down in layers or beds; bedded.
stratum	A distinct layer or bed of sedimentary material. Commonly used in the plural form: strata.
strip mining	Opencast excavation of minerals by the method of removal in defined sections or strips.
stucco work	Plaster used for coating walls.
subaerial	Said of natural processes taking place in the atmosphere usually near to the surface of the land, such as aeolian deposition (sand dunes) and erosion of all kinds.
sub-base	In a road pavement, a layer of usually granular material below the road base. Its functions include insulating the pavement from the subgrade (q.v.), increasing the pavement thickness to protect against frost and to provide an adequate surface for construction plant.
subgrade	Rock or soil horizon immediately beneath a pavement (q.v.).
subsoil	The weathered soil or rock immediately below the topsoil.
superficial, or surficial (Am.), deposits	Deposits formed on or close to the present land surface by processes (e.g. glaciation) usually of Quaternary age. Their distribution and thickness are related essentially to the surface relief and not to the structure of the underlying bedrock.
surface dressing	One or two coats of single-sized aggregate rolled into the wearing-course to provide a non-skid, abrasion-resistant surface.
syenite	A coarse-grained plutonic igneous rock, characteristically with pink feldspar and dark minerals (especially hornblende) but little quartz.
syncline	A concave-upward fold containing stratigraphically younger rocks in the core. The converse of 'anticline' (q.v.). Where age-relationships of rocks are unknown such a fold is termed a synform.
tar	A viscous liquid, black in colour, having adhesive properties, obtained by the destructive distillation of coal, wood, shale etc. Where no specific source is stated it is implied that the tar is obtained from coal.
tar emulsion	An emulsion in which, with the aid of suitable emulsifying agents, tar is dispersed in water, or in an aqueous solution.
tarmacadam	A road material consisting of stone coated in tar or a tar bitumen mixture. It has very little fine aggregate and a high proportion of voids.
ten per cent fines value (TFV)	Resistance of an aggregate to crushing as measured by the force in kN applied in the ten per cent fines test. The larger the value, the more resistant to crushing is the rock.

tension jointing	Fractures in a rock resulting from tensile stresses.
Tertiary	The era following the Mesozoic (q.v.), ranging in time from 65 to 2 million years ago, and the corresponding series of rocks.
teschenite	An alkali-rich variety of gabbro generally containing soda rich amphiboles or pyroxenes (q.v.), calcic plagioclase and analcite.
texture depth	A measure of the macrotexture of a paving surface; it determines the rate at which the skidding resistance of the surface changes with change in vehicle speed.
thermal metamorphism	See metamorphism, thermal.
thickener	A continuous solid–liquid separation device in which suspended solids are allowed to sediment producing a clarified water overflow and concentrated underflow slurry.
throw	The direction of the principal axis of the elliptical motion of a vibrating screen.
throw distance	The distance to which blasted materials are thrown by the explosion.
till	Unstratified, unsorted drift deposited directly by a glacier without reworking by water from the glacier; comprises a heterogeneous mixture of clay, sand, gravel and boulders. Includes boulder clay.
tillite	An indurated, lithified glacial till, especially a pre-Quaternary till, e.g. the late Carboniferous tillite of India and South Africa.
toast-rack	Colloquial name given to compartmentalized ground bunkers.
toe	The base of a quarry face or the base of a slope of an accumulation or tip of material. A remnant 'toe', comprising a mass of solid, unbroken rock at the base of the face projecting into the quarry, may result from poor blast design. Also sometimes used to refer to the base of natural slopes where an abrupt change of gradient occurs.
toe breakage	Separation of fragments from the base of the quarry face.
toggle	Component of the actuating mechanism of a jaw crusher.
transgression	Invasion of land areas by extension of the sea (brought about by a rise in sea level or subsidence of the land) and the evidence of this that is demonstrated by the strata. New marine deposits may spread over a former land surface in unconformable (q.v.) relationship to it, or deep-water environments may occupy areas formerly occupied by shallow-water conditions.
Triassic	The earliest period of the Mesozoic (q.v.) era between 248 and 213 Ma B.P., and the corresponding series of rocks. Named from the three-fold division of the period which can be made at the type locality in Germany.
tridymite	High temperature polymorph of quartz.
trommel	A rotating, cylindrical, screening device.
tuff	A compacted, commonly stratified, pyroclastic deposit having up to half of its bulk composed of clay to sand-sized particles.
unbound aggregate	Aggregate which is not bound or coated with cementitious or bituminous binders (i.e. various forms of wet or dry mix macadam as used in bases and sub-bases for road pavements).
unconformity	An interruption in a geological sequence representing an interval of geological time during which no sediments or other rocks were formed. The underlying older rocks may have been deeply eroded, tilted, folded or even metamorphosed (q.v.) before sedimentation was resumed, resulting in non-parallelism of the structure above and below the unconformity.

unconsolidated	A broad term describing sediments which have not been hardened by deep burial and/or cementation and correspond to the engineering meaning of 'soil', i.e. clays, silts, sands and gravels.
uniformity coefficient	The ratio between the D_{60} size on a grading curve and the D_{10} size, the D_{60} size being that at which 60% of the material is finer, the D_{10} size being that with 10% of finer material. The ratio D_{60}/D_{10} gives a measure of the soil grading, with a well graded (q.v.) soil having a coefficient of five or more.
unsoundness	The inadequate resistance of a material to chemical attack or to repeated physical changes such as temperature, moisture content, stress etc.
vein quartz	A coarsely crystalline variety of quartz characteristic of hydrothermal (q.v.) veins.
vermiculite	A layered silicate mineral of the chlorite (q.v.) family which on heating expands greatly to give a light cellular material much used for thermal insulation.
vesicular, vesiculate	Describes the texture of a rock, especially a lava, containing abundant bubbles or vesicles formed by expanding gases when the lava was fluid; the vesicles may subsequently become filled with secondary minerals (such as calcite or quartz) to form amygdales.
volcaniclastic	Clastic material of volcanic origin.
VSI	Vertical shaft impactor, impact crusher in which the rotor revolves around a vertical axis.
washing	See scrubbing.
water absorption	Percentage of water by mass that can be absorbed by an aggregate when in a saturated surface-dried condition.
water-bound aggregate, or water-bound macadam	Usually a road base or sub base in which a layer of aggregate has sand watered in to fill the voids.
wearing course	In a road pavement, the uppermost layer. It contains the highest quality materials in the pavement and its function is to provide the desired riding and non-skid properties to the road.
weathering	A comprehensive term for all the processes by which rock and soil are altered under the direct influence of the hydrosphere and atmosphere.
well-graded	In civil engineering, natural or artificial aggregate with a wide range of particle sizes distributed in a continuous sequence. In geology, in contrast, denotes a single sized grading, e.g. aeolian dune sand.
wet-mix	Pre-mixed water-bound macadam (q.v.) consisting of crushed aggregate, usually 50 mm down to filler, with a carefully controlled amount of water, usually 2–5% by weight.
wet screening:	Screening employing water sprays directed onto the deck.
wet-mix bituminous macadam	A method of road surfacing in which wet aggregate is mixed with a small quantity of hydrated lime or Portland cement. This is then mixed with an acidified cut back bitumen binder to coat the particles. It has the advantage that expensive aggregate drying plant is not required.
whinstone	A colloquial term which includes any dark fine-grained igneous rock, e.g. andesite, basalt, dolerite. Derived from Whin Sill in northern England.
winning	Extraction of minerals by stripping of overburden and open excavation of underlying mineral matter.
workability	For practical purposes, the ease with which a concrete or mortar mix can be handled and placed in its final form.

xenolith

An inclusion in an igneous rock of an unrelated rock-type, derived from the country-rock (q.v.) or carried up from depth.

zeolite

A group of hydrated silicates of calcium and aluminium, sometimes with sodium and potassium. They are secondary minerals resulting, in general, from the alteration of feldspars and other aluminous minerals in igneous rocks.

zircon

Zirconium silicate, $ZrSiO_4$. The mineral occurs as a primary constituent of igneous rocks, especially the more acid, e.g. granite.

Index

abrasion, in comminution, 108
abrasion resistance, 285
  road surfacing, 267
accelerated polish test, 266
acoustic impedance, 82
acoustic prospecting, 60
adamellite, 157
adhesion, bituminous mixes, 269–73
adhesion tests, 192–3, 284
adits, 99
Admiralty Charts, 60
Advisory Committee on Aggregates, 46
agglomerate, 7
aggregate abrasion test, 266
aggregate abrasion value, 108, 183, 276, 280
aggregate colour, 158
aggregate crushing test, 265, 274
aggregate crushing value, 108, 178–80, 253, 260, 275–6
aggregate crushing value residue, 181
aggregate drying shrinkage, 218–19
aggregate grading crushing value, 254
aggregate grading impact value, 254
aggregate grading tests, 172–3
aggregate impact test, 266
aggregate impact value, 108, 177–80, 208, 253–4, 257, 276, 280
aggregate impact value residue, 181
aggregate properties, for concrete, 201
aggregate resource maps, 42–4
aggregate shape tests, 173–4
aggregate shrinkage, 177, 200, 219
aggregate sizes, for concrete, 202–3
aggregate testing, unbound pavements, 253
aggregate types, 150
aggregate/cement ratios, 201
aggregates, sampling, 168
air blast, 82, 84, 96
air cyclones, 124
air photographs, 44, 49
airfield pavements, 206, 208–9, 280
alkali content, in concrete, 216
alkali reactivity, 190–2, 200, 209–11
alkali-carbonate reaction, 210
alkali-silica reaction, 145, 189, 209
alkali-silicate reaction, 210
alluvial deposits, 16–17
alluvial fans, 14, 19
alluvial plains, 17–19
alteration, 32, 55
alucrete, 30
anchor dredging, 92
andesite, 7, 9
ANFO, 82
Anglian Glaciation, 16, 24
angularity, 175, 285
anthracite, 129

Antrim Basalts, 9, 33
arclyt, 269
arenite, 13
argillite, 14, 210
arkose, 13
artificial aggregates
  in mortars, 246
  road surfacing, 266–7, 269
ASTM 2419, 173
ASTM C33, 155, 209, 212, 215, 217, 232
ASTM C40, 215
ASTM C88, 187, 209
STM C123, 231
ASTM C131, 183, 206, 255
ASTM C144, 231
ASTM C227, 191, 211
ASTM C289, 191
ASTM C294, 155–6
ASTM C295, 155–6, 159–60, 191
ASTM C342, 191
ASTM C535, 183
ASTM C586, 191, 211
ASTM D692, 155
ASTM D693, 155
ASTM D1241, 289
attrition, in comminution, 108
augers, 56, 58
augite, 250–1, 268

back-hoes, 76
  hydraulic, 86, 87
Bagshot Beds, 243
ball-deck screens, 121
ballotini, 269
banana screens, 119
barge transport, 134
barrel washers, 125
barytes, 200, 216
basalt, 5, 7, 9
  crushing, 112
  polish resistance, 185
bathymetric surveys, 60
bauxite, 129, 272
bauxitic soils, 30
beach gravels, 26
Beauly, 26
bedding, 34
belt weighers, 134
bench heights, 83
benches, 64
beneficiation, 124–30
biotite, 217, 232
bitumen, 192
bituminous mixes, 281

Blackheath Beds, 27
blast furnace slag, 190, 252, 260, 267, 269, 271, 291
blast holes, 79
blasting, 81–4
  agents, 82
  environmental effects, 96
  ratio, 84
  regulations, 82–3
  specification, 83
  vibration, 82
blinding, 117, 120–1
block-fields, 24
blow-bars, 112
boles, 33
Bond Work Index, 108
boomers, 60
boudins, 36
boulder clay, 19
Bovey Beds, 27
braided stream deposits, 17
'breeze' blocks, 14
brickearth, 24
Bristol Channel, 242
British Geological Survey, 42, 44, 46–7, 63, 69
British Standards, 153, 155
BS 63, 151–2, 271, 276, 280, 282
BS 410, 235
BS 594, 152, 276
BS 598, 280
BS 812, 55–6, 151–3, 155, 157–60, 158–9, 160–2, 164, 167–8, 170–1, 173, 175–7, 176–7, 181, 183, 185, 187–91, 194, 204–6, 214–15, 218–19, 229, 231, 233–5, 243, 253, 274, 276, 287
BS 882, 146, 172, 190, 199–200, 202–4, 203–4, 206–7, 211–14, 216–17, 225, 228, 238
BS 1047, 190, 252, 293
BS 1198, 226, 229, 237, 243
BS 1199, 226, 229, 231, 237–8, 242–3, 246
BS 1200, 226, 229, 231, 234, 236–7, 242–3, 246
BS 1377, 167, 213, 215, 292
BS 1438, 295
BS 1881, 181, 201
BS 3681, 190
BS 3797, 200, 216
BS 4029, 56
BS 4721, 227
BS 4987, 276
BS 5328, 190, 205, 211, 213–14, 216
BS 5750, 137, 193, 202
BS 5835, 260
BS 5930, 7, 15, 55–6, 58, 146, 148, 158, 160
BS 6349, 60
BS 8007, 206
BS 8110, 190, 211, 213, 215–16
Budleigh Salterton Beds, 28
building sand, 225–6, 233
building stone, 13
bulk density, 176, 205
bulldozers, 77, 92
Bunter Pebble Beds, 19, 28, 56

cable percussion boring, 58–9
CADAM, 153–5, 157
Caithness Flags, 286
calcareous mudstone, 12
calcined bauxite, 269

calcined flint, 269
calcined limestone, 227
calcium sulphate, 216
calcrete, 28, 31, 84
caliche, 31
carbonate sands, 29, 241
carbonate sediments, classification, 147
Carboniferous Limestone, 9, 13
cationic agents, 272
cement, 225
CEN standards, 158, 194
  CEN TC 154, 200, 209
  CEN TC 154 SC2, 200
  CEN TC 154 SC3, 265
  CEN TC 154 SC5, 200
  CEN TC 154 SC6, 211
  CEN TC 227 WG1, 265
  CEN TC 227 WG2, 265
centrifugal classifiers, 123–4
chalk, 14, 217
chemical reactivity, filters, 293
chemical tests, 189–92
chemical weathering, 33, 256
chert, 14, 268
Chesil Beach, 26
china clay, 10, 129
chloride content, 189, 259
chlorides, in concrete mixes, 213–14
chlorite, 210, 257, 268
choke feed, 114
civil engineering filters, 297
classification
  aggregates, 150–9
  by properties, 149
  for engineering, 145–6
  geological, 145
  weathering, 146–9
classification schemes, 151–9
classifiers, 122–6, 131
clay lumps, 213
clay minerals, 233
claystone, 14
coagulation, 131–2
coal, 12
Coal Measures, 9, 13–14
coastal deposits, 24–6
coating tests, 193
coefficient of hardness, 287
colliery waste, 14, 190, 251
columnar jointing, 35, 37
combe deposits, 24
comminution, 107–16
competence, bedding, 36
compression, in comminution, 108
concealed resources, 13
concrete, 109
concrete bleeding, 203, 205
concrete density, 199–200
concrete mixes, 203
conductivity mapping, 49, 51–2
cone crushers, 113–14
conglomerate, 5, 14–15, 27–8
conglomerates
  cemented, 89
  drilling, 56
contraction joints, 37

Control of Substances Hazardous to Health, 95
conveyors, 89, 92, 94, 99
coral, 215
core logging, 56
coring, 55
corrosion, reinforced concrete, 213
Cotswolds, 19
Crag formations, 27–8
crawler loaders, 103
crawler tractors, 77, 78, 84, 101
Criggion Quarry, 99
cross-bedding, 34
cross-sections, 61
crushed rock
    output, 74
    production, 1
    sampling, 169
crushing equipment, 109–15
crushing plant, 79
crushing strength, 266, 273–4, 280
cryoturbation, 23
cup and ball jointing, 35
current-bedding, 34
Danbury Hill, 24
Danish standards, 240
Dartmoor, 33
decking, 82
dedolomitization, 210
deflaking screens, 128
degradation
    engineering effects, 254
    unbound pavements, 252
delay detonation, 82
demolition wastes, 252
density separation, 127
Department of Transport specifications, 260
depositional terrains, 15–16
Derbyshire Dome, 13
desert deposits, 28
detonators, 82
Deval test, 183, 193, 255, 266, 274, 287
Devensian Glaciation, 15, 24
Devon, basic igneous rocks, 9
dewatering, 89, 130
DIN 1053, 241
DIN 4226, 188
diorite, 7, 9
dip–joints, 37
Dogger Bank, 26
dolerite, 7, 9–10, 218, 273, 286
dolocrete, 28
dolomite, 12, 210, 272, 286
    crushing, 112
dolomitic limestone, 12
dolostone, 12
Douglas Muir Quartz-conglomerate, 27
down-the-hole drilling, 80, 81
Downwash Gravels, 24
drag scrapers, 92
dragline excavators, 89, 91
draglines, 102
dredging, 16–17, 74, 92
    for sampling, 60
drift deposits, 15
drift mining, 99
drifter drills, 80

drill equipment selection, 94
drill hole patterns, 79
drill rigs, 102
drilling
    in quarrying, 79–80
    for sample collection, 55–6
drop balling, 85
dropstones, 26
drumlins, 20
dry pit working, 91
dump trucks, 77, 88, 104, 109
dune deposits, 24
dune sands, 29
Dungeness, 26
durability
    concrete, 208
    filters, 292
    mortars, 235
Durability Mill, 257
duricrusts, 28, 31
dust hazards, 95–6
dust pollution, 107
dust problems, process plant, 136
dykes, 9

echo sounding, 60
edge-runner mills, 116
efflorescence, 233
elongation index, 173–4, 204
EN 29000, 202
end tipping, 77
English Channel, 26
ENV206, 211, 213–15
environmental factors, process plant, 136
Environmental Protection Act, 95, 136
eskers, 20, 26
estimating methods, reserves, 62
ettringite, 190
European Standards, 156, 194–5, 200, 209, 239
    mortar sands, 239
excavation techniques, sand and gravel, 89
excavator, back-hoe, 77
explosives, 82
extraction planning, 92
extrusive igneous rocks, 7

face shovels, 76, 85, 103
false-bedding, 34
fan-deltas, 21
faults, 36
feldspar, 216, 268, 270
felsite, 9–10
Fenland, 26
ferricrete, 30–1, 84
field relations, rocks, 54
'fill' uses, 13
filter aggregate uses, 291
filter aggregates, 291–8
filter bed sand, 294
filter gravel, 295
filtration, dewatering, 133
fine aggregate, 203
fines, in concrete mixes, 212-13

fines tests, for mortars, 233
finishing operations, for concrete, 208
Finnish standards, 241
fire resistance, concrete, 220
Firth of Forth, 26
fixed plant, 107
flakiness index, 173–4, 204–5, 282
Flandrian, 26
flint, 14, 16
    polish resistance, 185
flint gravels, 19
float-sink separation, 127
floating grab dredgers, 104
flocculants, 132
flood-plain deposits, 17
floor screed mortars, 228, 238
flow layering, 35
flowsheets, process plants, 137–41
fluvial deposits, 16–19
foamed slag, 200
folds, 36
foliation, 10, 35
Folkestone Beds, 242–3
fossils, 12–13
foundry sand, 241
fracture cleavage, 36
fracture spacing, 85
Franklin point load tests, 181, 288
free silica content, 108, 112
freeze–thaw cycles, 256
freeze–thaw tests, 188
French standards, 156, 185, 213, 233
frost heave, 257
frost resistance, 206, 288
frost susceptibility, 14, 211
    tests, 188
froth flotation, 130
furnace bottom ash, 252

garnet, 251
gel pat tests, 191
geological appraisal, 53
geological classification, 53
geological maps, 41–2, 69, 71
geological profile maps, 42
geological structure, 33
geological time–scales, 5–6
geomorphological terrains, 16
geophysical methods, 49
geostatistics, 63–4
geosynthetics, 250
German standards, 188, 241
Giants Causeway, 35
glacial deposits, 19–24, 20
glacial sand and gravel, 23
glacio-deltaic deposits, 21
glaciofluvial deposits, 7, 21
glaciofluvial terraces, 21
glass sand, 129
GLC Specifications, 214–15
Glensanda quarry, 10, 99
gneiss, 5, 10, 35, 251
goethite, 129
grab dredgers, 90
grab sampling, 60

graded bedding, 34
gradients, on haul roads, 94
grading
    and aggregate degradation, 253
    filters, 292
    sands, 229–31
grading characteristics, for concrete, 204
grading effects, mortar sands, 243–5
grading limits
    masonry mortars, 235–7
    mortar sand, 239–40
grain-size classification, 44
granite, 5, 7, 9–10
    weathering, 33
granodiorite, 10
granulated slags, 252
gravitational classifiers, 122–3
gravity surveys, 53
Great Glen Fault, 36
Great Limestone, 13
greywacke, 13, 210, 286
    polish resistance, 185
grinding, 115–16
gritstone, crushing, 112
grizzly screens, 121, 125
ground bunkers, 133–4
ground radar surveys, 52
ground vibration, 96
Group Classification, 152, 157
gypcrete, 28
gypsum, 14, 190, 228
gypsum plaster, 227
gyratory crushers, 110, 111
gyratory disc crushers, 114

Hampshire Basin, 243
hard rock, output, 73
hard rock quarries, 74–89
haulage roads, 77, 88, 93
hauling equipment selection, 94
haystack hills, 31
head deposits, 24
Health and Safety at Work Act, 83, 95, 136
Health and Safety Executive, 95
heavy concrete, 216
heavyweight aggregates, 200
hematite, 129, 200
high explosives, 82
Hill Gravel, 24
hill-side quarries, 74, 75
hoggin, 24
Hong Kong
    granite, 10
    weathering, 76
horizontal screens, 120
hornblende, 250–1, 268
hornfels, 5, 10–11, 32, 156, 251, 286
    polish resistance, 185
hydraulic back-hoes, 91, 103
hydraulic drilling, 80
hydraulic excavators, 86, 89, 103
hydraulic hammers, 85
hydrocyclones, 123–4, 131
Hythe Beds, 242

igneous layering, 35
igneous rock bodies, 8
igneous rocks, 5
    acid, 9, 286
    basic, 9
    classification, 7
    distribution, 10
    intermediate, 9
    road surfacing, 266–8
    unbound aggregates, 250
immersion tests, 192–3
immersion tray test, 273
impact, in comminution, 108
impactors, 111–13
impurities
    in concrete mixes, 212
    in mortars, 231–2
in-pit crushing, 87, 89, 98, 109, 110
in-stream mining, 16
incinerated refuse, 252
infra-red imagery, 49
iron shot, 200
ironstone gravel, 30
Irvine, River, 21
ISO 9000, 193
isopachytes, 62

Japan, offshore deposits, 26
jaw crushers, 110–11
jigging, 127
jointing, 35, 82
joints, 37

kame terraces, 20–1
kames, 20
kaolinite, 30, 32, 268
kaolinization, 10, 32
Kent coalfield, 13
Kentish Ragstone, 14
Kesgrave Formation, 17, 24, 28
kettle-holes, 21
Kilwinning, 241
Kyleakin, 26

ladder dredgers, 105
landfill, 97
Landsat, 47, 49
lateritic soils, 30
lavas, 7, 10
layer tipping, 77
leachate, 97
leaching, desert deposits, 28–9
lead oxides, 217
lead shot, 200
libraries, 47
lightweight aggregate, 199
lightweight mortars, 246
lignite, 231, 241
limestone, 5, 12–13, 272
    crushing, 112
    polish resistance, 185
limestone resources, Peak District, 44
limewater test, 218
load equipment selection, 94

loading equipment, 85
load-haul-dump, 99–100
loess, 24
log washers, 125
lorry movements, 136
Los Angeles abrasion value, 183
Los Angeles test, 183, 185, 193, 206, 253, 255, 260, 266, 274, 287, 289
Lough Neagh, 241
Lower Greensand, 242

macadam, 269–70
McKelvey diagrams, 61
magnesian limestone, 12–13
magnesium sulphate, 216
magnesium sulphate soundness value, 187, 208–9, 260, 273, 295
magnetic separation, 129
magnetite, 200
Main Limestone, 13
marble, 149, 271
March, 26
marine aggregates, 26–7, 91–2
    washing, 126
marine exploration, 58–61
marine geophysical surveys, 53
marine-dredged sands, 242
Market Deeping, 26
masonry mortar, 227, 235–7
mechanical properties, for concrete, 206–7
mechanical property tests, 177, 207
mechanical weathering, 32
Mendip Hills, 13
Mersey grit, 241
metallic impurities, 217–18, 252
metamorphic rocks, 5, 10–11, 286
    classification, 11
    road surfacing, 266–8
    unbound aggregates, 251
metamorphic shield areas, 11
methane control, 97
methylene blue test, 189, 208, 213, 233
mica, 210, 217, 232, 235, 250
micro-Deval test, 185, 287
microdiorite, 286
microfractures, 256
microgranite, 7, 9–10
migmatite, 11
Millstone Grit, 14
    degradation, 254
mine waste, 217–18
Mineral Assessment Reports, 44, 62–3, 70
mineral extraction, 73
Mineral Planning Authorities, 136
Mines and Quarries (Tips) Act, 77, 93
mining, 73
mobile crusher, 140
mobile plant, 107
modified aggregate impact value, 181
Mogensen sizer, 122
moisture content, unbound pavements, 253
moisture movement, unbound pavements, 258
monitors, 105
montmorillonite, 213
moraines, 19
mortar bar tests, 191
mortar sands, 229

UK, 241
mortar strength, 243
mortar types, 227
mortars, uses, 225
Mount Sorrel, 10
mudrock, 5
    classification, 148
mudstone, 17
multi-bucket excavators, 105
mundic, 218
Munsell colour scheme, 159
muscovite, 217, 232

NAMAS accreditation, 194
NEN 5920, 215
Netherlands standards, 215
'Newer Drift', 15
Newer Granites, 10
NF P18–101, 156
NF P18–301, 156, 213
NF P18–556, 156
NF P18–557, 156
NF P18–572, 185
NF P18–595, 233
NF P85–592, 156
Nigeria, granites, 33
noise hazards, 95
noise levels, process plant, 136
noise pollution, 107
normal faults, 36
North Sea, mortar sands from, 242
Northern Ireland, mortar sands, 241
nuisance, 96–7
    process plant, 136

oblique shear joints, 37
Ochil Hills, 10
offshore areas, 46–7
offshore sampling, 60
oil shale waste, 14, 251
Old Red Sandstone, igneous rocks in, 9
opaline silica, 14, 268
open pit quarries, 74, 75
Ordovician, igneous rocks in, 10
ore passes, 99
organic content
    in concrete, 215
    in mortar, 232
organic content tests, 189
outloading, 134
outwash deposits, 21, 26
outwash gravels, 46
over-pressure, 96
overburden, 64
    disposal, 77
overburden removal, 74, 76–7, 89
overburden/payrock ratios, 93
overpressure, 82

Page impact test, 274
palisades, 35
particle classification, 107
particle density, 205–6

particle shape, 109, 158
    for concrete mixes, 204–5
    filters, 292
    unbound pavements, 253
particle size classification, 122
particle size distribution, 108–9
particle sizes, 107–8
    filters, 292
particle sizing, 116–17
particle texture
    for concrete, 205
    for filters, 292
Peak District, 44
peat, 12
pebble beds, 27–8
pegging, 117, 119, 121
pegmatite, 271
Pennant Sandstone, 14
Pennines, 9
Pennsylvania Abrasion Index, 108
percolating filters, 292
percussion boring, 58
periglacial deposits, 24
perlite, 246
permeability
    horizontal, 263–4
    unbound pavements, 257
Peterhead, 33
petrographic description, 159, 164
petrographic examination, 160
petrological classification, 151, 200
petrological group classification, 152
petrological names, 150
petrology
    bituminous mixes, 265
    effects on adhesion, 270–1
phyllite, 10, 210
phyllosilicates, 216
physical characteristics, 150
physical weathering, 256
PIARC, 195, 251
piedmont fans, 29
pillow lavas, 34
pingers, 60
pipeline bedding, 33
placer deposits, 64, 127
plaster blasting, 85
plastering mortars, 227, 237
plastic fines, 256
plasticizers, in mortar sands, 242
Plateau Gravel, 24
platy jointing, 35
plutonic rocks, 7
pneumatic drills, 80
point load strength, 85
point load test, 288
polished stone value, 10, 168, 185, 268, 277–8
polishing resistance, 273–4
    road surfacing, 267
polystyrene, in mortars, 246
pop shooting, 85
pore pressures, 255
porosity, 7
    filters, 293
porphyry, 7, 9
Portland Beds, 14

Portland cement, 190, 227, 243, 246
primary crushing, 109–10
primary fragmentation, 79
primary sampling, 167
primary structures, 34
process control, 137
production, for ballast, 286
production blast drilling, 83
production units, 73
psammite, 10
pulverized fuel ash, 14, 190, 199, 252
pulverizers, 116
pumice, 7, 199
pumping, of concrete, 205
pyrite, 129, 217–18, 232–3
pyroclastic rocks, 5, 7

quality assurance, 137, 193–4, 202
quarries, hard rock, 74–89
Quarries (Explosives) Regulations, 79, 82
quarry face profiles, 79
quarry haulage, 88
quarry output, 73–4
quarry plans, 93
quarry sampling, 168
quarrying, 73
quartz-dolerite, 9
quartzite, 10, 14, 16, 32, 156, 286
    crushing, 112
    polish resistance, 185
Queensland Standard Q16-1966, 192

raised beaches, 26
random sampling, 167
Reading Beds, 243
ready-mixed mortar, 227, 245
recrystallization, 10
reduction ratio, 108, 110–12, 115
regolith, 15
relative density, 176
reliability, estimates, 62
remote sensing, 41–2, 47, 49
rendering mixes, 237
rendering mortars, 227
rendering sands, 242
repeatability, testing, 170
reports, aggregate resource, 46
reproducibility, testing, 171
reserves and resources, terminology, 61
residual soils, 30
resistivity mapping, 49, 51–2
resistivity surveys, 49–51
resource classification, 61–2
resource maps, 44
    derivative, 44–6
resource surveys, offshore, 47
resources and reserves, 41
restoration, 77, 89, 93, 97
reverse faults, 36
reversed circulation drilling, 58
reworked deposits, 58
rhyolite, 35
rinsing, 127
rippability, 55, 84

rippers, 101
ripping, 77, 78, 84
ripple-bedding, 34
river channel deposits, 16–17
river gravels, Thames Valley, 44
river terrace deposits, 17–19
river terrace gravels, 24
road pavement, 6
road transport, 135
roadstone, 151
    classification, 151–3
    flowsheets, 139–41
    mechanical properties, 275
    weathering, 33
rock colour, 33
rock durability indicator, 257
rock porosity, 7
rock properties, estimation, 6
rock samples, 160
rocks, definitions, 5
rod decks, 118
rod mills, 115–16
rolls crushers, 115
Roman cement, 227
rotary drilling, 80
rotary pick, 115
roundness tests, 176
Rowley Regis, 9

sabkhas, 28–9
salcrete, 28
salinas, 28
sample collection, 55
sample reduction, 167
sample sizes, 169
sampling, 167
    for mortars, 229
sampling procedures, 168–9
San Andreas Fault, 36
sand equivalent value, 173
sand filters, 293–4
sand and gravel, 14–15
    distribution, 15–16
    flowsheets, 138–9
    occurrence, 14–15
    production, 1, 73
    quarrying, 89–91
    sampling, 168
Sandgate Beds, 242
sandstone, 5, 13–14
sandurs, 20
satellite imagery, 47, 49
scalping, 125
schist, 5, 10, 35
Schlumberger arrays, 49
Schmidt rebound number, 181
Scotland
    Midland Valley, 9
    mortar sands, 241
scour-hollows, 17
scrapers, 77, 78, 89, 92, 101
screen mats, 118
screening, 117–22
screening efficiency, 117
screens, for dewatering, 130–1

screes, 24
sea-level changes, 26
secondary aggregates, unbound pavements, 251
secondary breaking, 85
secondary structures, 34, 36
sedimentary rocks, 5
    classification, 12, 147
    road surfacing, 266–8
    unbound aggregates, 251
sedimentation tests, 233–4
seismic surveys, 48, 52
    offshore, 60
seismic velocities, 84
self-discharging trains, 134
semi-variograms, 63
sericite, 268
serpentine, 268
SFS 5516, 241
shale, 32
Shap quarries, 11
shape sorting, 127–8
sheared rocks, 10
sheet joints, 37
shell
    in concrete mixes, 214–15
    in mortar sands, 242
shell and auger sampling, 58
Shellgrip, 269
Sherwood Sandstone Group, 28, 56
shingle ridges, 26
ship transport, 134
shock waves, in blasting, 81–2
shot-firing, 83
shrinkage, 218–19
shrinkage joints, 37
side-scan sonar, 60
sideway force coefficient, 276–8
Sidlaw Hills, 10
sieve bends, 127
sieving, 172, 229
silcrete, 30–1
silica, reactive, 210
silica dusts, 95
sills, 9
siltstone, 14, 17
Site Investigations, Code of Practice, see BS 5930
sizing, 125
skid resistance, 185, 267–8, 277–9
Skylab, 47
slack line excavators, 90, 104
slag, for ballast, 288–9
slags, unbound pavements, 252
slake durability index, 187
slate, 10, 14, 32
slate waste, 14, 252
sleepers, concrete, 285
slickensides, 36
small-scale mapping, 46
smectite, 257
sodium sulphate, 216
sodium sulphate soundness value, 295
soil survey maps, 42
solifluction deposits, 24
soluble salt damage, 258–9
soluble salts, in mortars, 233
sonic drills, 58

sorting, 129
soundness, for concrete, 208–9
soundness tests, 186
South Africa, 7, 33
    volcanic rocks, 7
Southern African standards, 156
Specification for Highway Works, 162, 190, 216, 260, 276
Specification for Road and Bridge Works, 277
Spey, River, 17
sphericity tests, 176
SPOT satellite, 49
Staffa, 35
static immersion tests, 192
statistics, 169–70
steel slag, 252, 260, 267, 271
stemming, 83–4
stockpiles, 108, 133, 168
storage, 133
storage bunds, 89
storm beaches, 26
Strathmore, 28, 33
stratigraphic column, 6
strength, mortars, 235
strength tests, 177
strike-joints, 37
strike-slip faults, 36
stripping, 269–70, 274
stripping tests, 266
Strontian Granite, 10
structural concrete, 6
sub-base specifications, 258
subgrade drilling, 84
suction dredging, 90, 92
sulphate content, 259–60
sulphate content tests, 190
sulphate resistance, 213
sulphate soundness test, 187
sulphate test, 208–9
sulphates, in concrete, 216
super-quarries, 73–4, 98
superficial deposits, 5
surface coating, filters, 292–3
surface dressing, 276
surface texture, 158
surface texture tests, 176
surfactants, 272
surficial deposits, 15
swelling, clay minerals, 213
swing hammers, 112
Synopal, 269

Taele Gravel, 24
talus, 24
tar, as bitumen additive, 272–3
Tayside, 9
ten per cent fines tests, 180, 208, 253, 265, 280
tension gashes, 36
tension joints, 37
terminology, 149
terra rossa, 29
terrace gravels, 16
teschenite, 273
testing, 171–2
    standards, 172
Texas Boiling Test, 192

Thames, River, 17–19
Thames Estuary, 26
Thames gravels, 19
thaw weakening, 257
thermal expansion, 220
thermal imagery, 49
thermal movement, 218, 220
thickeners, 131
thickness, deposits, 54
Threlkeld, 10
till, 19–21, 23
top-hammer drilling, 80, 81
topographic maps, 41
Town and Country Planning Acts, 136
Trade Group Classification, 151, 273
traditional names, 150
trail dredging, 92
tramp metal, 129
trench sampling, 168
trenching, 56
Trent, River, 19
trial pits, 56
trommel screens, 120–1
tropical aggregates, 30–1
tuff, 7

unbound pavements, 249
unconfined compressive stress, 108
underground quarrying, 99
unsound aggregates, 255

vapour permeability, 258
vein-quartz, 16
vermiculite, 210, 246
vertical shaft impactors, 113
vibrating screens, 118, 120
vibrocorers, 58, 60
visual impact, 41, 97
void contents, mortar sands, 245
volcanic necks, 9

wadi deposits, 29

Wales
  basic igneous rocks, 9
  mortar sands, 242
washing, 125
Washington Degradation Test, 187
washouts, 17
waste tips, 77
waste transport, 76
water absorption, 7, 13, 206
  concrete, 206
water absorption tests, 176
water retention, mortars, 234
water tables, 89
Weald, 17
wear coefficient, 289
weathering, 30, 32–3, 55, 146–9
  bituminous mixes, 273
  granite, 10
weathering grade, 31, 33, 76, 148
  classification, 76
weathering resistance, 255–6, 266, 273
weigh-bridges, 134
weighing methods, 134
wells, for dewatering, 89
Wenner arrays, 49
Western Approaches, 26
Westleton Beds, 27
wet attrition test, 286–7
wet screening, 120
wet working, 90
wheeled loaders, 86, 88, 104
Whin Sill, 9
whinstone, 149
wireline drilling, 55
workability, mortars, 234, 246
working faces, 64

xenoliths, 35

yield, constraints on, 64
Ystwyth, River, 16

zinc oxide, 217